Maternity and parent.. ..g

a guide to parents' legal rights at work

Camilla Palmer and **Joanna Wade** are partners at Palmer Wade, a firm of solicitors specialising in employment discrimination and particularly maternity and parental rights. Both have been solicitors for twenty years and have worked exclusively in employment discrimination law for many years. Camilla Palmer is co-author of *Discrimination Law Handbook* (2nd edn, forthcoming 2006, Legal Action Group) and they are co-authors of the maternity and flexible working sections of the Equal Opportunities Commission's website for legal advisers. Both are part-time employment tribunal chairs.

Alexandra Heron has worked as a lawyer on British and Australian labour law issues, including sex discrimination. She is currently based in France and her work includes comparative sex discrimination law. She has recently worked as a consultant for the Organisation for Economic Co-operation and Development (OECD) on employment issues, and for the UK Equal Opportunities Commission on pregnancy discrimination. Prior to this she has worked for trade unions, NGOs and Governments in Britain and Australia.

Katie Wood is a barrister specialising in employment and sex discrimination law. She has worked as director of advice services at the Equal Opportunities Commission and as legal officer at the Maternity Alliance. She is author of *Maternity and Parental Rights: a practical guide for employers* (Stationery Office, 2001).

NASUWT

This book is published in association with Working Families (WF). WF would like to thank NASUWT for their support.

The Legal Action Group is a national, independent charity which campaigns for equal access to justice for all members of society. Legal Action Group:

- provides support to the practice of lawyers and advisers
- inspires developments in that practice
- campaigns for improvements in the law and the administration of justice
- stimulates debate on how services should be delivered.

Maternity and parental rights

a guide to parents' legal rights at work

Camilla Palmer, Joanna Wade,
Alexandra Heron and Katie Wood

 Legal Action Group
2006

Third edition published in Great Britain 2006
by LAG Education and Service Trust Limited
242 Pentonville Road, London N1 9UN
www.lag.org.uk

© Camilla Palmer, Joanna Wade and Katie Wood 2006

First edition published in 1996 as *Maternity Rights*. © Camilla Palmer

Second edition 2001. © Camilla Palmer and Joanna Wade

While every effort has been made to ensure that the details in this text and correct, readers must be aware that the law changes and that the accuracy of the material cannot be guaranteed and the author and the publisher accept no responsibility for any losses or damage sustained.

The rights of the author to be identified as the author of this work has been asserted in accordance with the Copyright, Designs and Patents Act 1988.

British Library Cataloguing in Publication Data
a CIP catalogue record for this book is available from the British Library.

Crown copyright material is reproduced with the permission of the Controller of HMSO and the Queen's Printer for Scotland.

ISBN 10: 1 903307 40 6
ISBN 13: 978 1 903307 40 6

Typeset by Refinecatch, Bungay, Suffolk
Printed by Biddles Ltd, King's Lynn, Norfolk

Foreword

by The Hon Mrs Justice Cox DBE

The idea that employers should so organise their workplaces as to ensure that they are more friendly to families, and enable a better balance to be struck between the work and the family lives of those who provide their services, has gradually been gaining acceptance in the national psyche since the first edition of this book was published almost exactly ten years ago. Since its arrival in 1997 the 'New Labour' Government has deployed a whole range of approaches, including education, general awareness-raising campaigns and, significantly, legislation, all with the expressed aim of changing the culture of relations in and at work, and of reflecting a new relationship between work and family life.

The promotion of such policies has been viewed, by some, with suspicion. In comparison with many other EU countries the British workplace has generally been regarded as characterised by long hours and poor maternity provision. Public childcare provision has been viewed as inadequate, in contrast with that available in other European states. In that context, with the added factor of gender job segregation, in which low pay and sex discrimination persist, the promotion of 'flexible' working arrangements has been seen as associated more with job insecurity and exploitation than with securing a better balance between work and family life. Others, however, have welcomed the Government's initiatives, praising the obvious benefits they bring to the physical and emotional well-being of hard-working employees with family commitments, in particular working mothers.

The need to combat poverty and social exclusion, to improve the lot of women in the workplace and to avoid all the unfortunate consequences, and costs, of exhausted workers struggling to balance work commitments and family life, undoubtedly forms part of the motivation behind the Government's policies, not least because of our EU obligations, the health and dignity of workers and sex equality at work being the driving factors in European social policy. The EU legislators have, in turn, often been informed and influenced by relevant international instruments, in particular the Conventions of the International Labour Organisation, the specialist industrial limb of the UN, whose concern since its inception has been social justice, the eradication of exploitation and discrimination, and the dignity and welfare of workers worldwide.

Primarily, however, family friendly policies have been viewed, domestically, as a necessary response to the dramatic changes taking place, internationally, in the world of work – the global shift in the economic, technological and social tectonic plates. Classic employment law traditionally contemplated a fixed, social model in which the male breadwinner remained in full-time paid work until retirement, whilst women assumed primary responsibility for the home, caring for children or other dependants, and, on occasions, carrying out unpaid work in the local community. A variety of factors over the intervening years have now almost completely eradicated such a model, including the entry of women into paid employment in ever increasing numbers; their efforts to secure economic equality; the growth in dual career or single parent households and in alternative family structures; and the changing attitudes of men and women to work and to careers generally.

Simultaneously, enormous technological advances in communication, information and transportation, and global economic integration have transformed the organisation of production and of employment; and have changed, fundamentally, the nature of the employment relationship. Traditional job descriptions are now, in many instances, being replaced by more flexible, open-ended responsibilities. More and more paid work is now being carried out under 'flexible' contractual arrangements, rather than standardised terms and conditions; with variable, performance-based pay schemes replacing fixed wage rates. Globalisation has banished, forever, the notion of a job for life.

In this brave new world of rapid change, family-friendly policies seek to ensure that everyone has access to the workplace and to economic independence; and that unemployment, state dependency and expenditure are thereby reduced. The workplace must therefore adapt to the needs of parents, which will bring advantages not only to employees but also to employers, who will have a wider, more skilled and more flexible pool of productive and contented workers. Family friendly policies, in this scenario, are good for everybody.

So much, then, for the thinking behind all these laws and the laws still to come in April 2007 and beyond. Whilst acceptance of such policies in principle is steadily growing, however, the effective implementation in practice of all the laws in this area still has a long way to go. This is well demonstrated by research recently carried out by the Equal Opportunities Commission showing that, each year, half of all pregnant working women still suffer some form of disadvantage at work on grounds of their pregnancy or maternity leave, or following requests for flexible working upon their return to work. It is a striking fact that almost half of all the sex discrimination claims brought in Employment Tribunals in recent years involve complaints by working women of discrimination against them by their employers on one or more of these pregnancy or maternity related grounds. Whilst family friendly laws and flexible working arrangements benefit both fathers and mothers, it is undoubtedly still the case that more women than men suffer the consequences of employers' unwillingness to take steps which would help working parents to balance their work and their family commitments more easily.

The reasons for such unwillingness are various and are still underpinned, in some instances, by hostility towards pregnancy and maternity or, at any rate, towards their effects in terms of additional cost and administration. Primarily, however, many employers are, in my view, simply unaware of, or do not properly understand, the wide range of laws relating to maternity and parental rights at work and how they should be applied in practice. This is not surprising given the present, patchwork provision of relevant rights in employment, discrimination and social security legislation, some of which are inconsistent with each other and all of which are accurately described by the authors of this book as 'a hotchpotch' of European and UK law. Mastering these statutory provisions, and the vast library of domestic and European case law interpreting and applying them, is not for the faint-hearted. It remains a matter of serious concern that important laws governing the working lives of so many, addressing employment status, maternity, paternity and parental leave, maternity pay and benefits, adoption and dependants' leave, part-time workers' rights, rights to flexible working and sex discrimination, are still so confusing and inaccessible.

Herein lies the real and substantial benefit of this book, now in its third edition, which sets out clearly, intelligibly and in logical sequence, the current and anticipated legislative provisions and the relevant principles established in the case law. The fact that this edition has almost doubled in size shows the scale of the changes to the law which it has had to address. Yet it has retained its attractive and user-friendly style and presentation.

The authors, whose encyclopaedic knowledge of the complex laws in this area is already well recognised, have succeeded in providing comprehensive and readily accessible coverage of all the laws governing the rights of working parents and the employment status of those whom they benefit. Of particular value, in my view, are the boxes of 'key points' at the start of each chapter, summarising the main principles; the occasional tables, boxes and flow charts which show, at a glance, the relevant rights, qualification and notice requirements in each case; and the appendices, containing helpful information, precedents and checklists. There is also useful guidance on applicable procedure, before and after claims are made to Employment Tribunals, and to available remedies including the calculation of compensation in successful cases.

This book is essential reading for everyone who has to advise upon, implement or think about these laws and the issues which they raise. Published once again by the Legal Action Group, it remains the essential text in this area for lawyers, students, trade unionists, advice workers, human resources personnel and, indeed, for everyone who needs or wants to understand more about the laws which govern the working lives of so many people.

Laura Cox
Justice of the High Court
September 2006

Contents

Table of cases

Table of statutes

Table of statutory instruments

Table of European legislation

Table of Abbreviations

AAL	Additional adoption leave
ACAS	Advisory, Conciliation and Arbitration Service
All ER	All England Law Reports
AML	Additional maternity leave
APL	Additional paternity leave
Article 141	Article 141 of the Treaty of Rome (the Treaty Establishing the European Community)
ASPP	Additional statutory paternity pay
BPD	Burden of Proof Directive (97/80/EC)
CA	Court of Appeal
CDA 1976	Congenital Disabilities (Civil Liability) Act 1976
CPR	Civil Procedure Rules
CTC	Child Tax Credit
CS	Court of Session
DCLD	Discrimination Case Law Digest
CEHR	Commission for Equality and Human Rights
DDP	Statutory Disciplinary and Dismissal Procedure
DR Regs	Employment Act 2002 (Dispute Resolution) Regulations 2004
DTI	Department of Trade and Industry
DWP	Department of Work and Pensions
EA	Employment Act 2002
EAT	Employment Appeal Tribunal
EC	European Community (see also EU)
ECJ	European Court of Justice
ECtHR	European Court of Human Rights

EDT	effective date of termination of contract of employment
EEA	European Economic Area
EOC	Equal Opportunities Commission
EOR	Equal Opportunities Review
EPD	Equal Pay Directive (75/117/EEC)
EPA 1970	Equal Pay Act 1970
Eligibility Regs 2002	Flexible Working (Eligibility, Complaints and Remedies) Regulations 2002 SI No 3236
Eligibility Amendment Regs	Flexible Working (Eligibility, Complaints and Remedies) (Regulations) Regulations 200[ ] SI No [ ] (draft)
ERA 1996	Employment Rights Act 1996
ERelA 1999	Employment Relations Act 1999
ET	Employment tribunal
ETAD	Equal Treatment Amendment Directive (2002/73/EC)
ETD	Equal Treatment Directive (76/207/EEC)
ET Regs 2004	Employment Tribunals (Constitution and Rules etc) Regulations 2004 SI No 1861
ET1	Application to employment tribunal
ET3	Response to a claim to employment tribunal
EU	European Union (see also EC)
EWC	Expected week of childbirth
EWCA Civ	England and Wales Court of Appeal Civil Division
EWHC (Admin)	England and Wales High Court (Administrative Division)
FTE Regs 2002	Fixed-term Employees (Prevention of Less Favourable Treatment) Regulations 2002 SI No 2034
GMF	Genuine material factor
GP	Statutory Grievance Procedure
HC	High Court
HL	House of Lords
HRA 1998	Human Rights Act 1998

HSE	Health and Safety Executive
HSWA 1974	Health and Safety at Work Act 1974
IB	Incapacity benefit
ICR	Industrial Cases Reports
IDS	Incomes Data Services
IE	Independent expert
IRLR	Industrial Relations Law Reports
IS	Income support
JSA	Jobseekers allowance
LAG	Legal Action Group
LEL	Lower earnings limit for National Insurance
LSC	Legal Services Commission
MA	Maternity Allowance
MAP	Maternity allowance period
MA Regs 1987	Social Security (Maternity Allowance) Regulations 1987 SI No 416
MA (Earnings) Regs 2000	Social Security (Maternity Allowance) (Earnings) Regulations 2000 SI No 688
MAT B1	Certificate showing EWC/date of birth
MHSW Regs 1999	Management of Health and Safety at Work Regulations 1999 SI No 3242
MoD	Ministry of Defence
MPL Regs 1999	Maternity and Parental Leave etc Regulations 1999 SI No 3312
MPL (Amend) Regs 2002	Maternity and Parental Leave (Amendment) Regulations 2002 SI 2789
MPL & PAL amendment Regs 2006	Maternity and Parental Leave etc. and the Paternity and Adoption Leave (Amendment) Regulations 2006 SI No 2014
MPP	Maternity pay period
MPL Regs	Maternity and Parental Leave Regulations 1999
NI	National insurance
OAL	Ordinary adoption leave
OML	Ordinary maternity leave
PAL Regs 2002	Paternity and Adoption Leave Regs 2002 SI 2788

PCP	Provision, criteria or practice (in respect of indirect discrimination)
PLD	Parental Leave Directive (96/34)
Procedural Regs 2002	Flexible Working (Procedural Requirements) Regs 2002 SI No 3207
PTWD	Part-time Workers Directive (97/81/EC and 98/23/EC)
PTW Regs 2000	Part-time Workers (Prevention of Less Favourable Treatment) Regulations 2000 SI No 1551
PWD	Pregnant Workers Directive (92/85/EEC)
QW	Qualifying week
SAP	Statutory Adoption Pay
SDA 1975	Sex Discrimination Act 1975
SMP	Statutory maternity pay
SMP Regs 1986	Statutory Maternity Pay (General Regulations1986 SI No 1960
SMP(MA) Regs 2000	Statutory Maternity Pay (General Modification and Amendment) Regulations 2000 SI No 2883
SMP and MA (Amend) Regs 2006	The Statutory Maternity, Social Security (Maternity Allowance) and Social Security (Overlapping Benefits) (Amendment) Regulations 2006 SI No 2379
SPP	Statutory paternity pay
SPP and SAP Regs	Statutory Paternity Pay and Statutory Adoption Pay (General) Regulations 2002
SPP and SAP (Amendment) Regs 2006	The Statutory Paternity Pay and Statutory Adoption Pay (General) and the Statutory Paternity Pay and Statutory Adoption Pay (Weekly Rates) (Amendment) Regulations 2006 SI No [tba when final regs published end Aug]
SSA 1989	Social Security Act 1989
SSCBA 1992	Social Security Contributions and Benefits Act 1992
SSP	Statutory sick pay

ToD	Time off for Dependants
TULRCA	Trade Union and Labour Relations (Consolidation) Act 1992
TUPE	Transfer of Undertakings (Protection of Employment) Regulations 2006
WFA 2006	Work and Families Act 2006
WTC	Working Tax Credit
WTD	Working Time Directive
WT Regs 1998	Working Time Regulations 1998 SI No 1833

Overview of maternity and parental rights

Key points

- Equal Opportunities Commission (EOC) research shows that half of the 444,000 women who become pregnant each year suffer some sort of discrimination and 30,000 lose their jobs.
- Research shows huge pay decreases for women after childbirth, which is particularly acute for part-timers.
- There is a statutory regime which sets out employees' rights to health and safety protection, family leave and pay; this will change, in some respects, where the expected birth or placement is on or after 1 April 2007.
- Only employees are entitled to family rights under the Employment Rights Act (ERA) 1996 and there are a few exceptions, such as the armed forces and share fishermen.
- Any less favourable treatment of a woman on grounds of her pregnancy or absence on maternity leave will be sex discrimination – except she is not entitled to pay during her leave.
- European law, such as the Pregnant Workers Directive (PWD), Equal Treatment Directive (ETD) and article 141 of the Treaty of Rome 1957 (which provides for equal pay), may provide greater protection than UK law.
- Employees still have other employment rights, such as protection from ordinary unfair dismissal and statutory holiday entitlement during leave.
- Employers and employees must follow the statutory disciplinary and dismissal procedures (DDP) and grievance procedure (GP) where they apply or risk either being barred from making a claim or an adjustment in compensation for failure to do so.
- Workers are protected under the Sex Discrimination Act (SDA) 1975 and may be entitled to maternity allowance and other benefits.

Introduction: some facts and figures

1.1   Women's employment has increased from a rate of 56% in 1971 to 70% in 2005, which is 4 million more women in work, an increase partly caused by an increase in working mothers.[1] A survey of employees in 2005 showed that eight out of ten working mothers

1   Office for National Statistics *Labour Market Review 2006* (www.statistics.gov.uk/labourmarketreview).

return to work before their babies were 18 months old. The proportion changing their employer on return to work was only 20%, as opposed to 41% in 2002.

1.2   Research carried out by the EOC in 2004–2005 found that around 440,000 women are pregnant in Great Britain each year and half experience some form of disadvantage at work, simply for being pregnant or taking maternity leave.[2] More than 30,000 women are forced out of their jobs and left without work. Thus pregnant women and new mothers remain very vulnerable despite the increasing rights and protection against discrimination. The causes, according to the research, are a lack of knowledge and understanding of maternity rights, lack of dialogue and planning, costs associated with pregnancy and negative attitudes towards pregnancy and maternity. Nearly 50% of sex discrimination claims brought in employment tribunals (ETs) involve discrimination on the basis of the claimant's pregnancy or maternity leave or a refusal of flexible working.

1.3   A report by the Institute for Fiscal Studies (IFS) for the Department for Work and Pensions (DWP)[3] found that mothers are returning to employment more quickly following childbirth, are more likely to return between births and are more likely to be in employment subsequent to childbirth than older generations. However, important changes occur at the time of first births and school entry, which include a sharp movement by women into part-time work following birth and the general transition towards non-permanent positions and non-supervisory roles.

1.4   The IFS report's findings support the theory that gender differences in the formal labour market stem from the division of parental duties between mothers and fathers in the home. There is a divergence between men's and women's work behaviour when children are born, in that men's hours increase and women's decrease and the pay gap widens substantially. There is also very clear persistence of gender discrepancies even after children have grown up or left home. The gender wage gap for all workers (full-time and part-time) before children is 91.3%. With children it is 66.6% and it is still 71.5% after children have left home.[4] Thus, the gap between female

2   *Greater expectations: Final report of the EOC's investigation into discrimination against new and expectant mothers in the workplace,* June 2005.

3   *Newborns and new schools: critical times in women's employment* by Mike Brewer and Gillian Paul, carried out by the Institute for Fiscal Studies.

4   For full-time workers it is 93.7% before children, 73.9% with children and 78.6% after children have left home.

and male average wages is more than 20% following children and this does not close even after children have left home.

1.5   Research set out in the IFS report (above) shows that 80% of women return to work within 18 months of childbirth. 60% return to their original employer. Between the early 1970s and 2005 the proportion of mothers with children under five who were economically active rose from 25% to 55%. However, most of the growth in women's labour has been in part-time work, where pay is lower and terms and conditions worse. In 1997, 42.9% of working women and 63.9% of women whose child was aged less than four worked part-time. In 2005 the percentage of working women who worked part-time or flexibly was 57%.[5]

1.6   There are 6.9 million part-time workers in Great Britain, making up a quarter of all those in employment, and more than three-quarters of them are women.[6] This country has the second highest proportion of part-time workers in the European Union.[7] Women working part-time are earning 40% less per hour on average than men working full-time, about the same as 30 years ago.[8] The EOC report into part-time work found that:

- part-time working is mostly only available in low-level, low-paid jobs, concentrated in certain sectors;
- working part-time has a detrimental and long-term impact on women's earnings, even for short periods;
- many part-time workers are working below their potential, though full-time workers are overworked and stressed;
- forward-looking businesses that use flexible working have found they resulted in vital recruitment advantage, higher levels of staff retention, lower absence rates, better employee relations and morale, and hence increased productivity;[9]
- many employers have found that it works best to open up flexibility to all employees, not just parents and carers.

---

5   See 'Facts about women and men in Great Britain 2006', a survey published annually by the EOC Maternity and Paternity Rights and Benefits – survey of employees 2005, Policy Studies Institute 2006.
6   *Labour Force Survey Historical Supplement*, London: Office of National Statistics.
7   Romans and Hardarson, *2005 Labour market latest trends – 4th quarter 2004 data. Statistics in focus*, Luxembourg: Eurostat, June 2005.
8   *Britain's hidden brain drain; The EOC's investigation into flexible and part-time working* September 2005.
9   *2005 Flexible working: impact and implementation – an employer survey*, London: Chartered Institute of Personnel and Development.

Development of the law on maternity rights

1.7 Prior to 1994, only women with two years' service (five years' service for part-timers) were entitled to return to work after maternity absence. Many women with less than two years' continuous employment were dismissed when pregnant. In October 1994 the government was obliged to implement the EU Pregnant Workers Directive (PWD). The PWD sets minimum standards for health and safety protection and maternity leave and pay, and prohibits dismissal on grounds of pregnancy. Only the minimum requirements were implemented at the time and little was done to achieve a coherent and accessible set of maternity rights and benefits.

1.8 In 1999, whilst implementing the Parental Leave Directive, the Labour government took steps to simplify maternity rights. It amended the ERA 1996 and introduced the Maternity and Parental Leave etc Regulations (MPL Regs) 1999.[10] Maternity leave was extended and unpaid parental leave and time off for dependants were introduced. Parallel changes were introduced in Northern Ireland.[11]

1.9 In April 2003 further changes came into effect which included 26 weeks' ordinary maternity leave (OML), a further 26 weeks' additional maternity leave (AML) for those with 26 weeks' service, the introduction of 52 weeks' adoption leave, two weeks' paternity leave and the right to request flexible working patterns.

Changes where EWC/Placement is on or after 1 April 2007

1.10 Where the expected birth or placement for adoption is on or after 1 April 2007 there will be further changes which are contained in the Maternity and Parental Leave etc and the Paternity and Adoption Leave Regulations 2006 SI No 2014 which amend the MPL Regs 1999 and the Paternity and Adoption Leave Regulations 2002. They are set out in chapters 4–9. They include:

10 SI No 3312.
11 See Employment Rights (Northern Ireland) Order 1996 SI No 1919 as amended by Employment Relations (NI) Order 1999 SI No 2790) and Employment (NI) Order 2002 SI No 2836 and Maternity and Parental Leave etc (NI) Regulations 1999 SI No 471 as amended by various amendment regulations in 2002 which came into effect on 6 April 2003. The Work and Families (Northern Ireland) Order 2006 SI No 1947 (NI16) replicates the measures set out in the Work and Families Act 2006.

- entitlement to AML for all employees irrespective of length of service;
- the extension of statutory maternity and adoption pay from 26 to 39 weeks;
- an increase in the notice period which the employee must give of their intention to return to work before the planned date of return from maternity or adoption leave from 28 days to eight weeks;
- provision for contact to be maintained between employer and employee during maternity and adoption leave;
- the ability for mothers and adopters to work 10 days during their maternity/adoption leave, without losing their statutory maternity or adoption pay (SMP/SAP);
- the removal of the small employers' exemption in relation to the right to return after AML or AAL.

More changes to come

1.11   There are further proposals to:

- extend the right to request flexible working arrangements to employees caring for sick or disabled adults; these regulations are expected in late 2006;
- extend SMP, maternity allowance and SAP to one year;
- introduce six months' additional paternity leave (some of which may be paid) where the mother or adopter returns to work before their entitlement to pay has expired;
- the amalgamation of the Commissions under the Equality Act 2006 to create the Commission for Equality and Human Rights;
- introduce a duty on public authorities to promote equality of opportunity between men and women and to prohibit sex discrimination in the exercise of public functions.

The present statutory framework

1.12   The statutory framework is a hotchpotch of European and UK employment, discrimination and social security legislation providing a patchwork of rights, some of which conflict. It is set out below.

UK law

1.13   There are eight main strands under UK law, which should be considered in relation to each individual:

1) protection from sex discrimination under the SDA 1975;
2) the right to equal pay and terms and conditions under the Equal Pay Act (EPA) 1970;
3) statutory maternity and parental rights under the ERA 1996, MPL Regs 1999 and Paternity and Adoption Leave Regulations 2002 as amended;
4) contractual rights;
5) protection under heath and safety legislation including the Management of Health and Safety at Work Regulations (MHSW Regs) 1999;
6) linked rights and protection such as the right to request flexible working, protection from less favourable treatment for part-time workers;
7) ordinary employment protection rights, generally under the ERA 1996, such as from ordinary unfair dismissal and minimum holiday under the Working Time Regulations;
8) rights to pay and benefits during leave.

Protection from discrimination under SDA 1975 and EPA 1970

1.14   Although there are extensive statutory provisions setting out maternity and other family rights (such as leave, pay, time off) the vast majority of disputes arise and cases are brought under the SDA 1975. There is a different definition for direct discrimination based on pregnancy and maternity leave to the definition based on sex alone. See chapter 2 for a comprehensive overview of discrimination law.

1.15   Direct discrimination on grounds of sex occurs where there is less favourable treatment of a woman (or man) on the ground of her (or his) sex. It is necessary to show that a person of a different sex was or would have been treated more favourably. Thus, proof of discrimination involves a comparison between the claimant and an actual or hypothetical comparator. No male comparator is required in pregnancy or maternity cases. The new statutory definition of discrimination on grounds of pregnancy and maternity leave is set out at para 2.40.

1.16   The SDA 1975 provides that, in relation to non-contractual matters, it is unlawful discrimination to treat a woman less favourably, where the treatment is on the ground of her pregnancy or maternity leave.[12] This includes less favourable treatment on grounds of pregnancy-related sickness.[13]

1.17 The EAT have said that 'The law is skewed, and deliberately so as a result of both Parliamentary intention, and European directives, in favour of protection of employees more so than is ordinarily the case in the commercial field'.[14] This recognises that, in relation to women who are pregnant and/or on maternity leave, they are protected from unfavourable treatment irrespective of the inconvenience and cost to their employer.

1.18 Pay and contractual terms are covered by the EPA 1970. The EPA 1970 requires an actual male comparator, though this may not be necessary where the difference in pay is related to pregnancy or maternity leave (see para 2.103 and chapter 5). A woman cannot usually make an equal pay claim under EPA 1970 while on maternity leave (see para 2.106 and chapter 5).

1.19 The detailed provisions of the SDA 1975 are set out in chapter 2, as are the relevant provisions of the EPA 1970 as they apply in pregnancy and maternity cases.

1.20 Apart from maternity and parental rights – such as paid time off for antenatal care, maternity and adoption leave and pay, other family leave and adoption and health and safety provisions – there is also protection from detriment and dismissal for any reason related to pregnancy, family leave or flexible working. The protection from detriment and dismissal comes under the maternity and parental regime in the ERA 1996 and regulations but also under the SDA 1975. It is important to consider all the various statutory provisions. These are shown in the table below and covered in more detail in later chapters.

European law

1.21 In addition to UK statutory rights and protection, it is important to consider whether European law provides greater rights than UK law (see also para 17.12 onwards). European Communities Act 1972 s2(1) provides that rights and obligations under EC law which are sufficiently clear and precise, must be recognised and article 141 of the Treaty establishing the European Community (known as the Treaty of Rome or EC Treaty) can be directly enforced in the UK.[15]

---

12 SDA 1975 s3A(1).
13 SDA 1975 s3A(3)(b).
14 *Ursell v Manor Bakeries Ltd* [UKEAT/0759] 21 February 2005.
15 European Communities Act 1972 s2(1) provides that all 'rights, powers, liabilities, obligations and restrictions from time to time created or arising by or

1.22   The main relevant EC provisions are:

- *Article 141* which provides that 'men and women should receive equal pay for equal work'. The *Equal Pay Directive*[16] (EPD) further provides that: 'The principle of equal pay for men and women outlined in Artice 141 of the Treaty . . . means, for the same work or for work to which equal value is attributed, the work to which equal value is attributed, the elimination of all discrimination on grounds of sex with regard to all aspects and conditions of remuneration'.
- The *Pregnant Workers Directive* (PWD), the details of which are set out in each chapter where relevant. In brief it makes provision for health and safety protection of pregnant workers and new mothers, for a minimum period of maternity leave and pay, for maintenance of rights during leave and protection from dismissal.
- The *Equal Treatment Directive* (ETD) as amended by Directive 2002/73/EC (see para 2.2), which provides that there shall be 'no discrimination whatsoever on grounds of sex, either directly or indirectly, in particular by reference to marital or family status'. It covers all aspects of employment (access to employment, promotion, vocational guidance and training, working conditions, dismissal and pay). It also provides that 'less favourable treatment of a woman related to pregnancy or maternity leave within the meaning of the PWD shall constitute discrimination within the meaning of the ETD'.
- The *Parental Leave Directive* (PLD) which was adopted in June 1996 and implemented in the UK on 15 December 1999 provides for parental leave and time off for dependants (see chapters 10 and 11).

under the Treaties, and all such remedies and procedures from time to time provided for by or under the Treaties, as in accordance with the Treaties are without further enactment to be given legal effect or used in the UK shall be recognised and available in law, and be enforced, allowed and followed accordingly; and the expression "enforceable Community right" and similar expressions shall be read as referring to one to which this subsection applies'. Section 2(4) provides that 'any enactment passed or to be passed . . . shall be construed and have effect subject to the foregoing'. The Recast Directive 2006/54/EC consolidates the gender Directives (but not the PWD) and will come into effect in August 2008. Although the PWD is not repealed, the Recast Directive does cover less favourable treatment relating to pregnancy and maternity leave (Article 2(2)(c)).

16   Council Directive No 75/117/EEC.

- The *Burden of Proof Directive* (BPD), which puts a greater onus on the employer to explain any less favourable treatment on a prohibited ground (see chapter 17).
- The *Part-time Workers Directive* (PTWD) which prohibits discrimination against part-time workers unless justified on objective grounds (see chapter 14).

1.23   Key points to note about the applicability of EC law are that:

- In all cases, UK tribunals and courts must interpret UK law in accordance with EC law. For example, in *Webb v EMO Air Cargo (UK) Ltd*[17] the House of Lords held that:

  . . . it is for a United Kingdom court to construe domestic legislation in any field covered by a Community directive so as to accord with the interpretation of the directive as laid down by the European Court, if that can be done without distorting the meaning of the domestic legislation . . . This is so whether the domestic legislation came after or, as in this case, preceded the directive . . .[18]

- Article 141, which provides for equal pay for equal work, takes precedence over any conflicting UK law, provided its terms are sufficiently clear and precise, unconditional and unqualified and not subject to further implementing measures.
- Directives are binding on emanations of the state, such as public bodies or employers carrying out public functions. An employee working for a private individual or company cannot directly rely on the provisions of a directive against her employer, though tribunals and courts must interpret UK law consistently with EC law, where possible.
- The ECJ have held that once the period for the transposition of a Directive has expired, national courts must interpret domestic law in the light of the wording and purpose of the Directive (see *Adeneler & Others v Ellinikos Organismos Galaktos* C-212/04, 4 July 2006).
- EC law often offers more protection to workers than UK law; this is particularly true in the area of pregnancy and maternity discrimination.
- Directive 2006/54/EC (5 July 2006) on the implementation of the principle of equal opportunities and equal treatment of men and women comes into force in August 2008. It does not affect the

17   [1992] 4 All ER 929 at 939; [1993] IRLR 27, HL.
18   See also *Von Colson and Kammann v Land Nordrhein-Westfalen* [1984] ECR 1891.

EU provision	What it says	Effect on UK law	Parallel UK right
Article 141	Equal pay for equal work, including pro rata rights for part-time workers	Binding on UK courts and tribunals	EPA 1970, SDA 1975, ERA 1996 (deduction of wages)
Equal Pay Directive (EPD)	As above	It does not add to article 141 so its effect is persuasive	As above
Equal Treatment Directive (ETD) as amended	Prohibits direct and indirect sex discrimination, harassment and victimisation	Aid to interpretation in all cases. Binding on emanations of state	SDA 1975 but should consider EPA 1970 and ERA 1996
Pregnant Workers Directive (PWD)	Provides for leave and protection for pregnant workers and women on leave	As ETD	ERA 1996, MPL Regs 1999, SDA 1975 (but see para 8.47)
Parental Leave Directive (PLD)	Provides for parental and dependant leave for employees	As ETD	ERA 1996, MPL Regs 1999
Part-time Workers Directive (PTWD)	Equal treatment for part-timers	As ETD	Part-time Workers Regulations (PTW Regs) 2000, SDA 1975, EPA 1970
European Council Recommendation on Childcare	Recommends initiatives for working parents	Persuasive but not binding	Flexible Working Regulations
Working Time Directive (WTD)	Minimum health and safety requirements relating to working hours and holidays	As ETD	Working Time Regulations (WT Regs) 1998
Burden of Proof Directive (BPD)	Shifts burden of proof	As ETD	SDA 1975, EPA 1970 but not yet implemented

For more details on European law see *Discrimination Law Handbook* (2nd edn, forthcoming, 2006, Legal Action Group).

PWD. This recast Directive must not lead to any reduction in the level of protection for workers than they previously enjoyed. Its purpose is to simplify and consolidate gender discrimination and it is not intended to create any new rights.

- Any EC claim must be linked to the parallel UK statutory provision, such as the SDA 1975, the EPA 1970 and the ERA 1996.
- Domestic procedures, such as time limits, apply in EC claims.
- A tribunal or court can refer a question of interpretation to the European Court of Justice (ECJ) and must do so in certain circumstances.

Human Rights Act 1998 and the European Convention on Human Rights

1.24   Rights under the Human Rights Act (HRA) 1998 are only enforceable against public bodies or, in some circumstances, private bodies with public functions. Tribunals must interpret the law in accordance with rights under the European Convention on Human Rights (ECHR) where relevant. However, tribunals can only hear a direct claim under the HRA 1998 if it has before it another legal question within its jurisdiction, such as discrimination. The details are outside the scope of this book as it will be unusual for a claim under the HRA 1998 to add more protection in areas covered by this book than exists under UK or EU law.[19]

1.25   The only explicit prohibition on discrimination is contained in article 14 and this only applies in relation to the exercise of other rights; there is no freestanding protection from discrimination. Under the HRA 1998 there is a defence of reasonable and objective justification to direct discrimination, unlike the SDA 1975.

1.26   The main area where the HRA 1998 is likely to be significant in the areas covered by this book is the prohibition of discrimination in relation to the right to family life, though the rights and protection provided by UK and EC law are generally greater than those under the HRA 1998. However, it is arguable, for example, that a man should be entitled to more than two weeks' paternity leave and pay, as

---

19 See, for example, Starmer, *European Human Rights Law* (2000, Legal Action Group) and Palmer et al *Discrimination Law Handbook* (2nd edn, forthcoming, 2006, Legal Action Group).

to deny him more leave would be discrimination in relation to his right to family life. Although it is likely to be objectively justified to give women at least six months' maternity leave and pay even though this is not available to men, arguably a man should be entitled to more than two weeks where women are entitled to a year. This has yet to be tested.[20] See also para 18.89 where the EAT referred to the HRA when considering if there was a breach of the Article 6 right to a fair trial.

How does a worker's employment status affect her/his maternity and parental rights?

1.27 Parents' and adopters rights will depend on their employment status. Many maternity and parental rights are available to 'employees' only. Certain very limited classes of employee are also specifically excluded from the protection of the ERA 1996. However, workers who are not 'employees' under ERA 1996 do have protection under the SDA 1975 and EPA 1970.

Who is an 'employee' under the ERA 1996?

1.28 The ERA 1996 s230 defines an 'employee' as 'an individual who has entered into or works under (or, where the employment has ceased, worked under) a contract of employment'. A contract of employment means 'a contract of service or apprenticeship, whether express or implied, and (if it is express) whether it is oral or in writing'.[21] The definition of employee under the SDA 1975 and EPA 1970 is set out in chapter 2.

1.29 There is no definitive test for deciding whether someone is an employee. The 'label' attached to the employment relationship is not conclusive. The courts have increasingly scrutinised agreements which state that the relationship is not one of employer and employee

---

20 Though see *Petrovic v Austria* 20458/92 [1998] ECHR 21, 27 March 1998 where a father argued that the refusal to allow him to claim parental leave payments so that he could care for his child while his wife worked, was a breach of article 8 in conjunction with article 14 of the European Convention on Human Rights. He was unsuccessful, though it was only a majority decision. At the time of the decision there was no common standard in this field across the contracting states and Austria had not exceeded the margin of appreciation allowed to them. The position may be different now.

21 ERA 1996 s230(2). A worker is defined by s230(3).

where the reality of the working arrangement is in fact one of employment. This may include implying a contract of employment between two parties even if there is a written (or oral) contract stating the opposite. For example, where an employment business or agency supplies a person to an end-user business, who continues to work for that same end-user for a substantial period of time, there may be an employment relationship between that person and the end-user. The fact that the claimant has a contract for services with an employment agency, which included a clause stating this comprised the entire agreement between the parties, did not preclude the existence of an implied contract of employment with the end-user.[22] The relationship may change over time. The details are outside the scope of this book but the main indicators of an employment relationship are:

- mutuality of obligation, so that the employer is obliged to provide work and the worker is obliged to carry it out;
- an obligation for the worker to carry out the work personally; if there is a power to subcontract work, it is unlikely to be an employment relationship;
- the exercise of day-to-day control by the employer of the worker; this may include control over work carried out and hours of work (though some flexibility will not negate an employment relationship);
- indicators which are not essential but will be relevant are whether the employer provides equipment for the worker, including for example, a mobile phone, whether the worker has tax and national insurance deducted at source, whether s/he is covered by the employer's disciplinary and grievance procedure, whether s/he can take holiday when s/he chooses and length of period the worker has worked for the employer.

22 *Dacas v Brook Street Bureau (UK) Ltd* [2004] ICR 1437, *Bunce v Postworth Ltd t/a Skyblue* [2005] IRLR 557, *Royal National Lifeboat Institution v Bushaway* [2005] IRLR 674. In *Cable and Wireless v Muscat* [2006] IRLR 354, CA the Court of Appeal approved the decision in *Dacas* saying that whether the existence of an implied contract will be inferred will depend on the circumstances. The irreducible requirements of mutuality will have to be present, as will control by the 'employer' and it will have to be necessary to infer the existence of the implied contract in order to give business reality to what is happening. Bank nurses and carers were held to be employed by an employment business (that engaged them) there being close management and disciplinary control by the business (*N Cube and Others v (1) 24/7 Support Services, (2) Secretary of State for Trade and Industry and (3) Trust Healthcare Management Ltd*, ET/2602005/05).

1.30 Only employees have full maternity and parental rights. It is arguable that the UK did not adequately give effect to the PWD when its provisions were implemented in ERA 1996. Arguably the right to maternity leave and parental leave should extend to all workers and not just to 'employees', as the PWD and PLD refer to workers throughout.

Who is excluded from ERA 1996 rights and protection?

1.31 Employees who ordinarily work (but not exclusively) outside Great Britain are now protected by ERA 1996 as ERA 1996 s196 has been repealed by section 32(3) of the Employment Relations Act 1999. Employees not entitled to family leave and associated time off (such as time off for antenatal care, maternity, adoption, paternity, parental leave, time off for dependants, health and safety rights) or protection from detriment and dismissal are:

- *Members of the armed forces.* ERA 1996 s192 has yet to be implemented. When it is, a complainant will be obliged to go through an internal complaints procedure first before bringing proceedings in an employment tribunal.[23]
- *Police officers* employed in the police service, although they have similar protection under the Police Regulations 2003.[24] Prison officers, however, are not excluded.
- *Share fishermen and women* who are either the master or crew of a fishing vessel and are paid by a share in the profits or gross earnings of the vessel.[25]

Who is an 'employee' under social security legislation?

1.32 To qualify for SMP a woman must be an employee, but the social security legislation has developed a different definition of 'employee' from that in ERA 1996 and there are different exceptions (see chapter 6).

---

23 EC law may, however assist. A member of the armed forces can rely directly on the ETD. SDA 1975 and EPA 1970 do apply, see paras 2.9 and 2.101.
24 SI No 527 which gives the Secretary of State discretion to give leave etc.
25 ERA 1996 s199(2) but see also s199(7) which provides that employment on board a Great Britain registered ship is protected provided the employee does not work wholly outside Great Britain and is ordinarily resident in Great Britain.

Summary of statutory maternity and parental rights

A summary of entitlement to maternity and parental rights by length of service is as follows:

Length of service	Entitlement
No service qualification	OML, time off for dependants
26 weeks by the 15th week before the EWC (ie, 40 weeks by the EWC)	AML, SMP, paternity leave and SPP (birth) (after 1 April 2007 there will be no service qualification for AML)
26 weeks by the week the parent is notified of having been matched with a child for adoption	OAL, AAL, SAP, paternity leave and SPP (adoption)
One year	Parental leave

1.33   A summary of rights to family leave, time off and protection from detriment and dismissal are set on the following page.

Contractual rights

1.34   Some contracts provide for more favourable rights, such as higher pay, longer leave. To the extent that the contract provides for more favourable rights this takes precedence. However, where there is a more favourable statutory right, this takes precedence (see chapters 4 and 9 on maternity and adoption leave).

Other employment rights

1.35   Apart from the specific family rights, account should be taken of other employment rights, such as protection from ordinary unfair dismissal (for employees with one year's service) and entitlement to the statutory four weeks' holiday entitlement per annum which also applies during maternity leave.

Workers' rights at work

1.36   Even if a woman is not an 'employee' she may qualify for 20 days' annual leave under the Working Time Regulations (WTR) 1998 and protection from less favourable treatment under the Part-Time Workers (Less Favourable Treatment) Regulations 2000 (PTW) (see

The right	Length of service with same employer	Employment Status	Notice requirements	Evidence
Paid time off for antenatal care during working hours (see chapter 3)	None	Employee (see para 3.100)	After first appointment, employer may require written proof of appointments	If requested by employer, medical certificate showing woman is pregnant
Health and safety protection (see chapter 3)	None	Workers have basic protection, employees have rights to alternative work and paid suspension	Must notify employer in writing of pregnancy, birth or that she is breastfeeding	A doctor's letter may help the employer with the risk assessment
26 weeks of ordinary maternity leave; can start from 11th week before EWC (see chapter 4)	None	Employee including those on fixed-term contracts	15 weeks before EWC or as soon as reasonably practicable	If requested by employer, doctor's or midwife's certificate giving EWC
26 weeks' AML immediately after OML (see chapter 4)	26 weeks' continuous employment by the 15th week before EWC *(from 1 April 2007 no qualifying period)**	Employee	As above	As above
Rights during maternity leave (see chapter 5)	None, but rights during OML are more extensive than rights during AML	Employee, as above	Only entitled if she has given the correct notice for maternity leave	None
Right to return to same job after OML (chapter 5)	None	Employee, as above	Notice is only required for early return: 28 days' notice *(eight weeks from 1 April 2007)*	N/A

* The new rights apply when the EWC or the expected date of placement for adoption is on or after 1 April 2007.

The right	Length of service with same employer	Employment Status	Notice requirements	Evidence
Right to return to same or similar job after AML (chapter 5)	26 weeks' continuous employment by the 15th week before EWC	Employee, as above	Notice is only required for early return: 28 days' notice (*eight weeks from 1 April 2007*)	N/A
SMP: six weeks on 90% of pay and then 20 weeks (*from 1 April 2007, 33 weeks*) on £108.85 (see chapter 6)	26 weeks' service by the 15th week before the EWC (ie nine months' service at the EWC)	Employed earners (all those liable to class 1 NI) with average earnings of at least £84 pw	28 days before start of SMP	Medical evidence of EWC (eg MAT B1)
Maternity allowance: 26 weeks' pay of up to £108.85 per week or 90% of average earnings (*from 1 April 2007, 39 weeks*) (see chapter 7)	26 weeks' work in the year and three months before the EWC and weekly earnings of £30 or more	Employed and self-employed earners	Claim may be backdated three months	Medical evidence of EWC (eg MAT B1) plus, if working, SMP1
Paternity leave (birth) one or two consecutive weeks (see chapter 8)	26 weeks' continuous employment by 15th week before EWC	Employee	15 weeks before EWC or as soon as reasonably practicable	Declaration of purpose for leave and of entitlement (if requested by employer)
Paternity leave (adoption) one or two consecutive weeks (see chapter 8)	26 weeks' continuous employment by the week notified matched with a child	Employee	Within seven days of notification of match with a child or as soon as reasonably practicable	Declaration of purpose for leave and of entitlement (if requested by employer)
Statutory paternity pay £108.85 per week for up to two weeks	26 weeks' continuous employment	Employed earners (all those liable for class 1 NI) with average earnings of at least £84 pw	See chapter 8	See chapter 8

The right	Length of service with same employer	Employment Status	Notice requirements	Evidence
Statutory adoption leave: 26 weeks' OAL and 26 weeks AAL (see chapter 9)	26 weeks' continuous employment by the week in which notified matched with a child	Employee	Within seven days of notification of match with a child	Matching documents from adoption agency (if requested by employer)
Statutory adoption pay – 26 weeks at £108.85 per week (from 1 April 2007, 39 weeks)	26 weeks' continuous employment by the week in which notified matched with a child	Employed earners (all those liable for Class 1 NI) with average earnings of at least £84 pw	See chapter 9	See chapter 9
Parental leave of 13 weeks (see chapter 10) unpaid leave, taken by the week, usually 4 weeks a year	One year's service by start of parental leave	Employee taking leave to care for a child under 5	Default scheme provides that 21 days' notice of leave must be given	Proof of birth or placement for adoption within the last five years etc may be required
Time off for dependants (see chapter 11) reasonable unpaid time off	No qualifying period	Employee with responsibility for a dependant	No minimum notice, but notice must be given as soon as reasonably practicable	
Right to request flexible working (see chapter 12)	26 weeks by the time of the request	Employee	Reasonable notice	Child must be under 6
'Right' to flexible working: indirect sex discrimination (see chapter 13)	None	Worker, including employee, self-employed, contract workers, trainees	N/A	See chapter 13
Pro rata rights for part-time workers (see chapter 14)	No qualifying period	Worker	N/A	N/A

The right	Length of service with same employer	Employment Status	Notice requirements	Evidence
Protection from discrimination (including rights to child-friendly working hours) (see chapters 2, 13 and 15)	No qualifying period	Worker, including employee, self-employed, contract workers, trainees	N/A	N/A
Protection from automatically unfair dismissal on family leave grounds (see chapter 15)	No qualifying period	Employees	N/A BUT loses protection in limited circumstances	N/A
Protection from 'ordinary' unfair dismissal (see chapter 15)	One year's continuous employment	Employee	N/A	N/A

chapter 14). These regulations apply to 'workers' who are those who 'work under a contract of employment or any other contract . . . to do or perform personally any work or services' (see WT Regs, reg 2 and PTW Regs, reg 1). In addition, although only 'employees' as defined by ERA 1996 enjoy full health and safety rights, employers do have general duties towards all the people working in their workplace (see chapter 3). The right not to suffer an unlawful deduction from wages under ERA 1996 applies to 'workers' as well as to 'employees'.

1.37   Subject to a few exceptions, not only employees but also workers including prospective and former workers, agency temporary workers and self-employed contractors are protected by SDA 1975 and EPA 1970 (see para 2.9).

Benefits and protection for unemployed workers

1.38   Unemployed workers may also be entitled to claim maternity allowance or incapacity benefit based on what they were earning while still at work. If their family income is low, they will also be entitled to claim means-tested benefits (see chapter 9). Job applicants are protected from discrimination under the SDA 1975, so it is discriminatory not to employ a woman because she is pregnant.

Statutory dispute resolution provisions: a summary

1.39   The statutory dispute provisions of the Employment Act 2002 and associated regulations came into force on 1 October 2004. The aim of this procedure is to encourage the parties to resolve their disputes before resorting to the employment tribunal (ET). The regulations set out:

a)   the procedure employers must follow in dismissal cases, ie, the disciplinary and dismissal procedure (DDP);

b)   the procedure employees must follow (before lodging a claim with the ET) where they have a grievance, ie the grievance procedure (GP);

c)   the circumstances in which time for lodging a claim with the ET will be extended – by three months;

d)   the effect that the failure to comply with the procedure has on the employee's ability to bring a claim in the tribunal and on the amount of compensation the tribunal can award.

1.40   The general rule is that in all discrimination cases including constructive dismissal (as well as many others), an *employee* (not a worker) must, within three months (or a maximum of four) of the discrimination, or other complaint, put in a *written* grievance *and* wait 28 days before lodging a claim with the ET. The main exception is when the employee is dismissed by the employer or the employer is contemplating dismissal.

1.41   Similarly, an employer who is contemplating dismissing an employee must go through the statutory disciplinary procedure if the employee has one year's service, otherwise the dismissal will be automatically unfair.

1.42   Where the grievance procedure applies – and there are exceptions – the time limit for lodging a claim with the tribunal will usually be extended by three months from the date of the discrimination or act complained of.

1.43   Where a claim for discriminatory dismissal is successful and the employer has not followed the DDP then, even if the employee has less than one year's service, compensation is likely to be increased as a result. Employers who fail to follow the procedures in relation to employees with one year's service will face a finding of automatically unfair dismissal and/or increased compensation (see para 16.2 for an overview).[26]

1.44   Failure to follow the procedures may lead, for the employee, to a claim being barred from proceeding or compensation being reduced.[27] Chapter 15 deals with the relationship between unfair dismissal and the DDP. Chapter 16 covers the procedures in details and the relationship with time limits.

---

26   Employment Act 2002; Employment Act 2002 (Dispute Resolution) Regulations 2004 SI No 752.
27   Employment Act 2002 ss29–33 and Schs 2–4; Employment Act 2002 (Dispute Resolution) Regulations 2004 SI No 752.

Overview of sex discrimination

2.108   Provisions relating to pay rises and bonuses in the EPA
         1970

Key points

- The Sex Discrimination Act (SDA) 1975 covers recruitment, transfer, training, promotion, benefits, dismissal and any other detriment. It does not generally cover contractual terms.
- The Equal Pay Act (EPA) 1970 covers contractual terms. An employee cannot generally bring a claim under the EPA 1970, in relation to pay attributable to the maternity leave period, because she is in a 'special protected' position.
- The category of workers protected from discrimination is much wider than under the Employment Rights Act (ERA) 1996 and includes the self-employed, contract workers, partners, agency workers etc. Job applicants are protected and there is no qualifying service (unlike the ERA 1996).
- An employer is liable for discrimination carried out by a worker in the course of his/her employment. The worker is also liable.
- Discrimination by other bodies, such as trade unions, vocational training bodies and employment agencies, is also unlawful.
- There are some exclusions from the SDA 1975.
- Less favourable treatment of a woman on the ground of her pregnancy or maternity leave will automatically be unlawful direct sex discrimination without the need to compare her with a man, except that a woman on maternity leave is not entitled to her full pay; this is often referred to as automatic sex discrimination.
- Protection from automatic sex discrimination lasts from the beginning of pregnancy until the end of maternity leave, ie the protected period.
- Pregnancy and/or maternity leave does not have to be the only reason for the treatment, but to be unlawful it must be a substantial or effective reason.
- There is no defence to direct discrimination.
- Refusal to allow a woman to work child-friendly working hours may be indirectly discriminatory on grounds of sex and marital status.
- Less favourable treatment of a woman who takes parental or dependants' leave may be indirect discrimination.
- Workers who are victimised for bringing a claim or making allegations of discrimination can also make a claim for victimisation.

- In sex discrimination and equal pay claims, EC law should always be considered.
- Men taking family leave are not as well protected and cannot claim automatic sex discrimination but can claim direct discrimination if treated less favourably than a woman taking similar leave in the same circumstances.

Background and relevant legislation

2.1 This chapter summarises the key principles relating to direct discrimination as it relates to pregnancy, maternity leave and other family leave. The principles are applied and illustrated in subsequent chapters. From 1 April 2007 there will be a duty on public authorities to promote equality of opportunity between men and women and to prohibit sex discrimination in the exercise of public functions (see para 18.167).

2.2 For women who are pregnant or on maternity leave, discrimination law generally provides more extensive protection than the ERA 1996 and the Maternity and Parental Leave etc Regulations (MPL Regs) 1999[1] which provide a basic range of family leave rights for employees. It is always important to consider discrimination law, which provides protection from less favourable treatment on grounds of pregnancy and maternity leave. The vast majority of tribunal claims are brought under the discrimination legislation.[2] The relevant UK provisions are the SDA 1975 and EPA 1970. The parallel provisions for Northern Ireland are the Equal Pay Act (Northern Ireland) 1970 and the Sex Discrimination (Northern Ireland) Order 1976.[2a] The SDA must be interpreted consistently with the Equal Treatment Directive[3] (ETD) and the EPA consistently with article 141 of the Treaty of Rome 1957 (which provides for equal pay). However, as the ETD now covers pay as well as discrimination relating to

---

1 SI No 3312 as amended by the Maternity and Parental Leave (Amendment) Regulations 2002 SI No 2789 from 24 November 2002 and most recently by the Maternity and Parental Leave (Amendment) Regulations 2006 which came into force on 1 October 2006.

2 Nearly 50% of sex discrimination claims related to pregnancy, maternity leave or flexible working sought by returning mothers.

2a SI No 1042 (NI 15) as amended.

3 76/207/EEC as amended by Directive 2002/73 the implementation of which was required by 5 October 2005. This is sometimes referred to as ETAD and will be replaced by the Recast Directive (2006/54/EC) by August 2008.

pregnancy and maternity leave,[4] the EPA must also be interpreted consistently with the ETD (see paras 1.22–1.23).[5] Account must also be taken of the Pregnant Workers Directive (PWD) (see paras 1.22, 3.1–3.2, 5.42). These EC provisions are summarised at para 1.23. Case-law, and especially European Court of Justice case-law, has had a profound influence on how the legislation is interpreted and it must always be considered when applying discrimination law.

2.3   The main advantages of a discrimination claim (under UK law) are:

- the SDA 1975 and EPA 1970 protect a wider category of workers than the ERA 1996 and MPL Regs 1999, which only apply to employees (see para 1.28); job applicants and ex-employees are also protected;
- there is no qualifying period for a discrimination claim unlike ordinary unfair dismissal, so protection starts from day one (note there is no qualifying period for automatically unfair dismissal);
- once the claimant has shown a 'prima facie' case (or facts raising a presumption of discrimination) the burden of proof shifts to the employer to show an absence of discrimination; unlike unfair dismissal it is not a question of what is fair and reasonable;
- the questionnaire procedure can be used (see paras 17.28–17.37);
- there is no cap on the amount of compensation (see para 18.43);
- compensation can include injury to feelings, interest, personal injury and aggravated damages (see para 18.41 onwards);
- there is a broader test for extending time limits under the SDA 1975, ie, where it is just and equitable, though under the EPA 1970 there is a fixed six-month time limit which cannot be extended, but see chapter 16 for effect of dispute resolution procedure.

Difference between SDA 1975 and EPA 1970

2.4   Broadly speaking, the EPA 1970 covers pay and other contractual terms and conditions and the SDA 1975 covers non-contractual matters.[6] The two Acts are intended to cover different situations.

---

4   Article 2(7).
5   See Article 3(1)(c).
6   There are complex provisions regulating the relationship between the SDA 1975 and the EPA 1970 which depend on whether there is a comparator, whether the complaint concerns contractual or non contractual matters and whether the complaint concerns the offer of a contractual term or the terms of existing employees, see SDA 1975 s6(5) and (6), s8(3) and (5).

However, the Court of Appeal has said that they should be construed and applied as a harmonious whole.[7] They should also be interpreted consistently with EC law (see para 1.23) and the Human Rights Act (HRA) 1998 (see para 1.24). We look first at the SDA 1975, which will apply in most situations, then the EPA 1970 but only as it relates to pregnancy and maternity claims.

Sex Discrimination Act 1975

2.5 The SDA 1975 provides protection, in defined circumstances, against

- direct discrimination on the ground of pregnancy and maternity leave (SDA 1975 s3A); the exceptions are set out in section 6A;
- direct and indirect discrimination on the ground of sex (SDA 1975 s1); section 2 provides that men are similarly protected;
- direct and indirect discrimination on ground of marital status and civil partnership (SDA 1975 s3);
- harassment (SDA 1975 s4A);
- victimisation (SDA 1975 s4).

2.6 Generally, the SDA 1975 applies only to non-contractual terms, such as recruitment, promotion, access to benefits (including discretionary bonuses), transfer, training, dismissal and any other detriment (see below).[8] Provided the employer is aware of the woman's pregnancy, it will usually be unlawful direct discrimination under the SDA 1975 to treat a woman less favourably for a reason related to her pregnancy (including pregnancy related sickness, childbirth) or maternity leave (see para 2.34 onwards). This may involve treating a pregnant woman more favourably than another worker in order to achieve substantive equality. For example, it is direct discrimination to disadvantage a pregnant worker for any pregnancy related sickness absence (prior to her maternity leave), however long. This applies even if another worker would be disadvantaged, for example disciplined, for a similar length of absence (see para 2.46 onwards and para 3.118 onwards). This is necessary to remove the disadvantages that would otherwise be experienced by pregnant women as a result of

---

7 *Shields v E Coomes (Holdings) Ltd* [1978] ICR 1159 at 1178.
8 The SDA 1975 applies in relation to the offer of a contractual term where there is an appropriate comparator for EPA 1970 purposes, or if there is no comparator and the claim does not relate to a provision for the payment of money, see SDA 1975 s8(3).

their pregnancy. The employer has no defence to direct discrimination irrespective of any inconvenience to its business. The exceptions are set out below at paras 2.22–2.23 and see also para 5.28. Note that the SDA 1975 applies equally to men, apart from the exception relating to pregnancy and maternity leave.

Equal Pay Act 1970

2.7   The EPA 1970 covers pay and other contractual benefits. It will be a breach of the EPA 1970 to pay a woman less, or give her less benefits, if she is pregnant. Thus, a pregnant woman who is off sick must be paid the same sick pay as a non-pregnant employee who is sick for a similar period. A claim under the EPA 1970 cannot usually be made for equal pay and benefits during maternity leave (see chapter 5).

2.8   It is not always clear whether a provision is contractual or non-contractual, for example bonuses (see para 5.83 onwards). If in doubt, a claimant should argue the SDA 1975 and EPA 1970 in the alternative as well as citing EC law in cases where it appears to provide greater protection than the UK law (see para 2.101 onwards for coverage of the EPA).

Sex Discrimination Act 1975

Who is protected?

2.9   The definition of employee under the SDA 1975 is much wider than ERA 1996. It includes those working under a contract of service or of apprenticeship or a contract personally to execute any work or labour.[9] The dominant purpose of the contract must be for the worker to perform the work personally,[10] and the contracting parties must be the person doing the work and the person for whom the work is done.[11] There are no maximum or minimum age limits or minimum

---

9   SDA 1975 s82(1) which covers 'employment under a contract of service or of apprenticeship or a contract personally to execute any work or labour'. EPA 1970, s1(6) also has this definition.
10   SDA 1975 ss6 and 82 see *Quinnen v Hovells* [1984] IRLR 227 EAT where the EAT said the definition of employment was a 'wide and flexible concept' see *Mirror Group Newspapers v Gunning* [1986] IRLR CA; *BP Chemicals Ltd v Gillick* [1995] IRLR 128.
11   *BP Chemicals Ltd v Gillick* [1995] IRLR 128.

length of service requirements. The following can make a claim of discrimination:

- *job applicants;*[12]
- *employees;*[13]
- *ex-employees* in relation to detriment or harassment which arises out of and is closely connected to the previous relevant relationship – relevant relationship is one during which there has been unlawful discrimination;[14]
- *the self-employed;*[15]
- *partners*[16] (partners are protected in respect of recruitment and the terms of partnership offered, access to benefits, facilities or services, expulsion or being subject to any other detriment);
- *barristers and advocates;*[17]
- *trainees,* who are protected whether working under a contract of employment or apprenticeship;[18] those seeking or undergoing training are protected;
- *vocational trainees;*[19]
- *civil servants;*[20]
- *staff of the House of Commons and House of Lords;*[21]
- *office holders;*[22]

---

12 SDA 1975 ss6 and 82.
13 Cases on the meaning of employment include *Loughran and Kelly v Northern Ireland Housing Executive* [1998] IRLR 594, *Patterson v Legal Services Commission* [2004] ICR 312 (both involving solicitors' firms though in *Patterson* the claim came under SDA 1975 s13 (see para 2.21), *Mingeley v Pennock v Ivory* [2004] IRLR 373 (taxi driver), *Percy v Church of Scotland Board of National Mission* [2006] IRLR 195 HL (priest).
14 SDA 1975 s20A.
15 SDA 1975 ss6 and 82; ERA 1996 only protects and provides rights for employees, not the self-employed. Thus, only employees are entitled to redundancy pay, protection from unfair dismissal, maternity rights.
16 SDA 1975 s11.
17 SDA 1975 ss35A–35B.
18 SDA 1975 s82.
19 SDA 1975 s14 amended from 1 October 2005 which covers access to training, terms and facilities concerned with such training, refusal or termination of training, detriment or harassment, for discrimination by educational establishments and local education authorities carrying out their functions as schools (see SDA 1975 ss22 and 23, claims are made in the county court).
20 EPA 1970 s1(8), SDA 1975 s85(2).
21 SDA 1975 ss85A–85B.
22 SDA 1975 ss10A–10B as from 1 October 2005; an office holder is someone whose appointment is made, recommended or approved by a minister, or someone who is appointed to discharge functions personally, is paid and is

- *the police;*[23] a police officer is treated as employed by the chief officer of police who should be named in proceedings;
- *the armed forces;*[24] though a member of the armed forces must first bring a complaint under the relevant service redress procedure;[25]
- *ministers of religion;*[26]
- *contract workers;*[27] these are individuals employed by one organisation (the employer) but supplied to do work for another (the principal) under a contract made between the employer and the principal. They are not employed by the principal but by a third party such as an employment agency;[28] the contract worker is protected from discrimination by both the employer and principal. The principal must not discriminate between one contract worker and another nor between a contract worker and its own employees.[29]

Contract workers

2.10 Contract workers include, for example:

- temporary workers, such as secretaries, who are employed (as defined by the SDA 1975, not the ERA 1996) by the agency but sent to work for different companies.[30] The secretary may be an employee of the agency, so is protected as an employee under the SDA 1975 and possibly the ERA 1996. S/he will also be protected from discrimination by her principal, ie, the person for whom she does the work. This covers not only contract workers who are working but where the principal refuses to employ a worker

subject to the direction of another person as to when and where s/he performs his functions. It does not cover political office or post holders or elected office holders. There are a number of exceptions set out in ss10A(3), 10B(5–7)

23 SDA 1975 s85(2)(b) and s17, EPA 1970 s1(8)(b); there are detailed provisions about liability which need to be considered in police cases.

24 SDA 1975 s85(2)(c); EPA 1970 s7A(1). There is an exception for the purpose of ensuring combat effectiveness.

25 EPA 1970 s7A(5)–(7); the Equal Pay (Complaints to Employment Tribunals) (Armed Forces) Regulations 1997; SDA 1975 s85(9A)–(9E); and the Sex Discrimination (Complaints to Employment Tribunals) (Armed Forces) Regulations 1997.

26 SDA 1975 s19. There are exceptions to comply with religious doctrines.

27 SDA 1975 s9. There are some exceptions which are set out in s9.

28 See, for example, *Harrods Ltd v Remick* [1997] IRLR 583, CA and *MHC Consulting Services Ltd v Tansell and others* [1999] IRLR 677.

29 *Allonby v Accrington & Rossendale College* [2001] IRLR 364, CA.

30 SDA 1975 s9.

because, for example, she is returning to work after having a baby;[31]

• workers supplied by concessionaires to stores[32] (this is where there is an agreement between a store (the principal) and the concessionaires to supply goods (and workers to sell the goods) to a store. The worker is protected from discrimination against both the employer and principal (the store);

• workers employed by a company which supplied them to an agency which in turn supplied them to an end-user (provided there is an unbroken chain of contracts between an individual and the end-user, the end-user is the principal);[33]

• workers employed in contracted-out services;

There is always a question as to whether workers are in fact employees. If they are, they are protected in the same way as other employees.[34]

2.11   Contract workers are protected in relation to the terms on which they are allowed to work, not being allowed to work, in access to benefits, facilities or services and by subjecting them to a detriment. In *BP Chemicals v Gillick and Roevin Management Services Ltd*[35] the Employment Appeal Tribunal (EAT) held that a contract worker could bring a complaint against her principal that he had discriminated against her by not allowing her to return to work after time off having a baby.[36]

31 *BP v Chemicals v Gillick* [1995] IRLR 128, EAT. Some temporary workers have been found to be employees under the ERA 1996 and so enjoy both ERA 1996 and SDA 1975 protection (see paras 1.28–1.29).

32 See *Harrods Ltd v Remick and others* [1997] IRLR 583; [1998] ICR 156, CA, which was a race case whereby a contract between Harrods and concessionaires required any person employed by a concessionaire within the store to comply with Harrods' dress and conduct code. The Court of Appeal held that the workers in the concessions did work for Harrods which was their principal and so was liable for any discrimination.

33 See *Abbey Life Assurance Co Ltd v Tansell* [2000] IRLR 387 where the EAT held that a contract worker can bring a discrimination complaint directly against an end-user as a principal, even where there is no direct contractual relationship between the contract worker's employer and the end-user.

34 See *Dacas v Brook Street Bureau (UK) Ltd* [2004] ICR 1437 and see further paras 1.28–1.29.

35 [1995] IRLR 128, EAT.

36 See also *Patefield v Belfast City Council* [2000] IRLR 664 where the Court of Appeal (NI) held that the council discriminated against the claimant worker when it replaced her with a permanent employee when she went on maternity leave. It would not have done this if she had not been absent having a baby. See also *Johnson v Queen Elizabeth Hospital NHS Trust* [2003] UKEAT 1331/01 where the

Employment agencies

2.12   In addition, it is unlawful for an employment agency to discriminate:

- in the terms on which the agency offers its services;
- by refusing, or deliberately omitting, to provide its services;
- in the way it provides its services; and
- harassment.[37]

2.13   For example, if an agency refused to provide services to a woman because she only wanted part-time work, this may be indirectly discriminatory. A failure by an employment agency to carry out a risk assessment in relation to a pregnant woman (when it was obliged to do so under an arrangement with the employing company) which resulted in her losing her employment was held to be sex discrimination in *Brocklebank v Silveira*.[38]

Examples

2.14   The following could make a claim of sex discrimination:

- a job applicant who is not considered for a job because she is pregnant or wants to work part-time;
- an employee who is not allowed to return to work part-time after maternity leave (see chapters 13 and 15) or who is given different work because her replacement is doing her job;
- a self-employed person who is not considered for work because she has just had a baby;
- a woman seeking work from an employment agency who is told not to return until after she has had her baby as the agency will not be able to find her work while she is pregnant;
- a contract worker who is told she will not be allocated to a business because she is pregnant; she will have a claim against the principal and/or agency;[39]
- an employed solicitor who is told that if she works part-time she will never be made a partner;

EAT held that removal of the claimant from a list of bank midwives, because of a rule that those who had not worked for one year would automatically be removed was discrimination if her absence was caused by her pregnancy. The rule meant that no consideration was given to the fact that an individual woman may not be available for a period because of her pregnancy.

37   SDA 1975 s15.
38   UKEAT/0571 11 January 2006.
39   *Lana v Positive Action Training in Housing (London) Ltd* [2001] IRLR 501.

- a man refused part-time or other flexible working in circumstances where a woman would be offered it.

Liability of employers and individuals

2.15 An employer is liable for discrimination carried out by a worker in the course of his/her employment whether or not it was done with the employer's knowledge or approval, unless the employer can prove that s/he took such steps as were reasonably practicable to prevent it.[40] The worker is also liable.[41] This covers all workers, including managers.[42] 'In the course of employment' has been interpreted widely so it covers any discrimination occurring in the workplace and sometimes outside it, for example at an office party or during a business trip.[43] The employer has a defence if 'he took such steps as were reasonably practicable to prevent the employee from doing that act, or from doing in the course of his employment acts of that description'.[44]

2.16 Principals are liable for the discriminatory acts of their agents.[45] Where an agent has authority to act for the principal, both principal and agent will be liable for the discriminatory acts of the agent. In *Lana v Positive Action Training in Housing (London) Ltd*[46] the respondent placed the claimant with a company (WM) who terminated the arrangement soon after the claimant said she was pregnant. The respondent then terminated its training contract with the claimant as it did not have any work for her. The EAT held that the claimant could

---

40 SDA 1975 s41 provides that anything done by a person in the course of his employment shall be treated as done by his employer as well as by him, whether or not it was done with the employer's knowledge.
41 SDA 1975 s42(2) provides that an employee (or agent) for whose act the employer (or principal) is liable under section 41 is deemed to aid the act of the employer. Section 42(1) says that 'a person who knowingly aids another person to do an act made unlawful by this Act shall be treated . . . as himself doing an unlawful act . . .'.
42 SDA 1975 s41(1).
43 See *Jones v Tower Boot* [1997] ICR 254, CA a case under the Race Relations Act 1976 but which would also apply to sex discrimination cases. However, in *Sidhu v Aerospace Composite Technology* [2000] IRLR 81 the Court of Appeal held that harassment during a family day out at a theme park was not within the course of employment, but see also *Chief Constable of the Lincolnshire Police v Stubbs* [1999] IRLR 81 where harassment during a drink in a pub after the shift was held to be in the course of employment.
44 SDA 1975 s41(3).
45 SDA 1975 s42(1).
46 [2001] IRLR 501.

claim against the respondent as WM was its agent and the respondent was liable for any discriminatory acts done by the agent. There was liability where authority had been given to do an act which was capable of being done in a discriminatory manner even if the principal was not aware of the discrimination.

2.17   The worker who discriminates in the course of his or her employment is also liable and can be named as a respondent and the tribunal can award compensation against that individual as well as the employer. In *Miles v Gilbank*[47] Sedley LJ pointed out that while the employer may be able to escape liability by showing that it had done what it could to prevent discrimination, the employee who nevertheless discriminates against other staff in the course of his or her employment becomes and remains personally liable for it.

2.18   In *Miles v Gilbank* the first respondent, Quality Hairdressing Limited (known as 'QH') was dissolved before the tribunal hearing and an award was made personally against the second respondent, Ms Miles, a director who was also the main shareholder. Ms Miles did not dispute liability for her own acts of discrimination but disputed her liability to compensate the claimant for the discriminatory conduct of other employees. The members of the Court of Appeal gave slightly different reasons for upholding the ET and EAT decision regarding the liability of Ms Miles but the end result was that she was personally liable for discrimination by other employees as she had encouraged the discriminatory treatment of the claimant by other staff, thus subjecting the claimant to a detriment.

2.19   Sedley LJ summarised the legal position:[48]

> A worker who discriminates 'in the course of his employment' such that his employer is liable for it (or would be but for the statutory defence. . . .) is personally liable under the SDA 1975, RRA [Race Relations Act] 1976 or DDA [Disability Discrimination Act] 1995 for that discrimination. . . . This is because the perpetrator is deemed to 'aid' his or her employer's vicarious liability for his or her actions. This applies even where the employer makes out the statutory defence. . ., in which case the guilty employee will find himself solely liable. . . .

2.20   Sedley LJ said that Ms Miles' acts were attributed to the company so the company had subjected the claimant to a detriment by reason both of Ms Miles' own behaviour and her encouragement of the behaviour of other staff. In any event, Ms Miles was deemed to have

47   [2006] IRLR 538, CA.
48   Quoting from the Discrimination Law Handbook, see para 48.

aided the company to discriminate so was deemed to have acted unlawfully herself.

Discrimination by bodies other than employers

2.21   In addition, it is unlawful for the following bodies to discriminate:

- *trade unions and professional and employers' organisations* must not discriminate in relation to access to membership nor against members;[49] refusal to allow a person to join because s/he works part-time may be discriminatory;
- *vocational training bodies* must not discriminate. In *Fletcher*[50] the EAT held that this includes the provision of facilities such as a bursary.[51] Limiting training to those who can attend residential courses or evening sessions may be indirectly discriminatory if not justified, as it is a requirement that is likely to have an adverse effect on women with childcare responsibilities (see chapter 13);
- *employment agencies*[52] (see para 2.12);
- *business partners*[53] (see para 2.9);
- *qualifying bodies*, ie an authority or body that can confer an authorisation or qualification which is needed for or facilitates, engagement in a profession or trade,[54] such as the Law Society; such bodies must not discriminate in the terms on which an authorisation or qualification is conferred, in relation to refusing to grant it or withdrawing or varying the terms on which it is held.

Exclusions from the SDA 1975

2.22   There are some exceptions under the SDA 1975. The main exceptions relating to pregnancy and maternity leave are set out in:

- section 2(2) which provides that it is not discrimination against

---

49   SDA 1975 s12.
50   *Fletcher and others v Blackpool Fylde & Wyre Hospitals NHS Trust and others* [2005] IRLR 689.
51   SDA 1975 s14 was extended on 1 October 2005 to cover the prohibition of discrimination in selection arrangements for access to vocational training in the terms offered by refusing training, terminating training or subjecting a trainee to a detriment. Vocational training is defined by SDA 1975 s82.
52   SDA 1975 s15.
53   SDA 1975 s11.
54   SDA 1975 s13. See *Patterson v Legal Services Commission* [2004] ICR 132, CA.

men to provide special treatment of women in connection with pregnancy or childbirth;

- section 6A which excludes claims in relation to access to certain terms and conditions during maternity leave. This covers remuneration during ordinary maternity leave, except maternity-related remuneration, and the benefit of any terms and conditions during additional maternity leave, apart from those set out in section 6A(3).[55] This is covered in more detail in chapter 5.

2.23   Other exceptions include:

- health and safety provisions (see chapter 3); this exception is, in practice, of little or no effect because of the positive duties employers have towards pregnant and breastfeeding women and the protection from discrimination made clear by European Court of Justice (ECJ) decisions (see para 3.88);
- genuine occupational qualification;[56]
- employment for the purposes of an organised religion to comply with the doctrines of the religion;[57]
- illegal contracts in some cases; though this will depend on the nature of the illegality. An employee may still complain of discrimination where the contract is tainted by illegality as the claim is not based on the contract of employment; however, the position may be different if the employee is actively involved in the illegality so that the claim is inextricably bound up with the illegality;[58]
- acts done under statutory authority, but this is very limited;[59]
- employment outside Great Britain. Employment is covered if the employee works 'wholly or partly in Great Britain' or where the employee works wholly outside Great Britain but (a) the employer has a place of business at an establishment in Great Britain and (b) the work is for the purposes of the business at that establishment and (c) the employee is ordinarily resident in Great Britain either when s/he applies for or is offered employment or any time during her or his employment.[60] Employment (as above) includes:

---

55   The exceptions are maternity-related remuneration, the implied duty of trust and confidence, notice, redundancy compensation, disciplinary or grievance procedures or membership of a pension scheme.
56   SDA 1975 s7; this is very unlikely to be relevant in family rights cases.
57   SDA 1975 s19 as amended from 1 October 2005.
58   *Hall v Wooston Leisure Ltd* [2000] IRLR 578, CA; *Vakante v Addey & Stanhope School* [2004] All ER 1056.
59   SDA 1975 s51.
60   SDA 1975 s10(1) as amended from 1 October 2005.

- employment on board a ship if the ship is registered at a port in Great Britain; and
- employment on aircraft or hovercraft registered in the UK and operated by a person who has his or her principal place of business, or is ordinarily resident, in Great Britain.

Prohibited types of discrimination

2.24 Where a claim for discrimination is made under the SDA 1975, a woman must show that:

- there has been either direct or indirect sex or marital and civil partnership discrimination, harassment or victimisation (see paras 2.5–2.6); and
- the employer or other liable body has done a prohibited act.

Prohibited acts

2.25 Discrimination alone is not unlawful. What is prohibited is discrimination, in relation to certain areas of employment is set out below:

- the arrangements made by an employer for deciding who should be offered employment, for example, selection procedures;
- the terms and conditions on which a woman or man is offered employment;
- by refusing or deliberately omitting to offer a person employment, for example, because she is pregnant, might become pregnant or because she has asked to work reduced hours (the latter may be indirect discrimination);[61]
- in the way the person affords access to opportunities for promotion, transfer or training;
- in the way the person affords her/him access (or refusal of) benefits, facilities or services;[62]
- dismissal (including constructive dismissal),[63] for example, where a woman resigns because the employer will not allow her to work child-friendly hours;
- any other detriment (this means treating a woman or man less favourably in any other way and includes not allowing a woman to work child-friendly hours).[64]

61 SDA 1975 s6(1)(a)–(c).
62 SDA 1975 s6(2)(a).
63 SDA 1975 s82(1A)(b) and s6(2)(b).
64 SDA 1975 s6(2)(b).

The Equal Opportunities Commission code of practice

2.26   The Equal Opportunities Commission (EOC) has produced two codes of practice, one under the SDA 1975 and one under the EPA 1970.[65] The code provides guidance for employers about practices that they recommend should be adopted to promote equality. The codes do not have the same effect as legislation, but failure by an employer to observe any provision of a code may be taken into account by a tribunal or court.[66] A tribunal must take the code into account and failure to do so may result in a successful appeal.[67]

2.27   The EOC code under the SDA 1975 recommends that employers should consider whether certain jobs can be carried out on a part-time or flexi-time basis (see para 43 of the code). It also states that questions about marriage plans or family intentions should not be asked at interview, as they could be construed as showing bias against women (para 23 of the code).

Direct sex discrimination; not on grounds of pregnancy/ maternity leave

2.28   Direct sex discrimination (other than on grounds of pregnancy or maternity leave where no comparator is needed) occurs where a woman has been treated less favourably than a man has been or would be treated and the reason for the less favourable treatment is on grounds of her sex.[68] Men are protected in the same way. There are three questions:

a)   whether the woman was treated less favourably than a man was or would have been treated in similar circumstances;
b)   whether that treatment was on the grounds of the individual's sex;
c)   whether the discrimination is prohibited by the SDA 1975.

2.29   In most cases, tribunals will adopt a two-stage approach in relation to (a) and (b), asking first whether there was less favourable treatment; and second whether this was on a proscribed ground. However, in *Shamoon v Chief Constable of the Royal Ulster Constabulary*[69] the House

65   The purpose of which is to eliminate discrimination in employment and to promote equality of opportunity: SDA 1975 s56A.
66   SDA 1975 s56A(10). The power to issue codes will be transferred to the Commission for Equality and Human Rights (CEHR): SDA 1975 s76E.
67   *Berry v Bethlem and Maudsley NHS Trust and Hinks v Riva Systems* [1997] DCLD No 31.1.
68   SDA 1975 s1(1).
69   [2003] IRLR 285.

of Lords suggested that in many cases, particularly where the identity of the relevant comparator is in dispute, the tribunal could simply ask why the complainant was treated as s/he was: was it on the proscribed ground or was it for some other reason – the 'reason-why issue'.

2.30 However, slightly different tests have been adopted by the courts in different cases. In many of the more straightforward cases of less favourable treatment the question asked is whether, 'but for' her sex, would she have been treated in that way? If the answer is 'yes', it will be direct discrimination.[70] The advantage of this is that it is simple and avoids analysing the motive or intention of the discriminator. It will often provide the answer as it did in *James v Eastleigh BC* when the question was whether it was sex discrimination to deny a man aged between 60 and 65 free swimming as he has not reached retirement age when his wife (also aged between 60 and 65) had reached retirement age so was given free swimming. However, in *Nagarajan v London Regional Transport* (a victimisation case) the House of Lords indicated that the 'but for' test was not the only test and the question was whether sex was a 'cause, the activating cause, a substantial and effective cause, a substantial reason, an important factor.[71]

2.31 When comparing the treatment of a woman and man, for non-pregnancy/maternity cases, the SDA 1975 provides that the relevant circumstances of the woman and man must be the same or similar.[72] Thus, the comparison is between a man and a woman (actual or hypothetical) in a similar situation; like must be compared with like.

2.32 The SDA 1975 provides that the burden of proof passes to the respondent once the claimant has established a prima facie case (ie facts showing a presumption of less favourable treatment related to sex). It is important to bear this in mind when considering how sex discrimination is established. See para 17.124.

2.33 The main principles that apply in direct discrimination cases (including those on grounds of pregnancy/maternity leave) are as follows:

70 *James v Eastleigh BC* [1990] IRLR 288; *Fletcher v Blackpool Fylde and Wyre Hospitals NHS Trust* [2005] IRLR 689.
71 *Nagarajan v London Regional Transport* HL [1999] IRLR 572 at para 19 although this was a race discrimination case the same principles apply. Another way of describing the effect is that the grounds had 'a significant influence on the outcome, discrimination is made out'. See also *O'Neill* at para 2.73 onwards.
72 SDA 1975 s5(3).

- protection applies to women irrespective of length of service, hours worked, whether they are on a permanent or fixed-term contract, the size of the employer or the extent of the pregnancy (ie one month or eight weeks);
- the sex of the worker, or pregnancy, need not be the only reason for the less favourable treatment, but it must be a substantial reason or an effective reason;
- direct discrimination may not be conscious; it is well acknowledged by the courts that people hold prejudices that they are not aware of or do not admit, even to themselves;
- negative stereotypical assumptions about a woman or pregnant worker, such as assuming that women with young children will no longer be committed to work, will be discriminatory if acted upon;
- there is no defence to direct discrimination so that the employer cannot avoid liability by saying that it was acting out of good motives or to protect the woman;
- it is not a defence for an employer to say that there was no intention to discriminate. Although the existence of intention or a discriminatory motive will help a claimant prove discrimination, it is not necessary to show that there was such a motive;
- it is not discriminatory to treat a woman less favourably where the treatment has nothing to do with her sex or pregnancy.

Automatic direct discrimination on pregnancy/ maternity grounds

2.34   In pregnancy/maternity cases the definition of direct discrimination is significantly different from the definition which applies in other situations such as where the claimant is not pregnant or on maternity leave, or where men taking or seeking to take family leave are treated less favourably. However the main principles set out above also apply in pregnancy/maternity related cases, except that with pregnancy/ maternity there is no need to show that a man was or would have been treated more favourably.

2.35   In relation to pregnancy/maternity leave cases, tribunals initially said there is no male equivalent of a pregnant woman, and without this comparison, there could be no discrimination. Subsequently, tribunals compared a pregnant woman with a sick man. It has now been established, mainly through European cases, that there is no appropriate comparator and less favourable treatment of a woman relating to her pregnancy (or childbirth or maternity leave) is automatic discrimination without the need to compare the position of a woman with a man (see para 2.42 onwards) The first issue, however, is whether the employer was aware of the employee's pregnancy.

Knowledge of pregnancy

2.36   Clearly, there will be no discrimination (or unfair dismissal) on grounds of pregnancy if the employer was not aware of the woman's pregnancy. This will be a question of fact. For example, the provision of a sick note that refers to the woman's pregnancy (even in Latin) should be sufficient (see *Day v Pickles*[73]). However, in *Del Monte Foods Ltd v Mundon*[74] the employee was dismissed for continued absence caused by gastro-enteritis. The day after the dismissal the company discovered she was pregnant and the EAT held that the dismissal was not automatically unfair because the employers were unaware that the absence was connected to her pregnancy. Similarly, in *Denton Directories Ltd v Hobbs*[75] the EAT held that a reason for dismissal can only be connected with pregnancy if the employers 'knew or believed that the woman was pregnant'. In *Ramdoolar v Bycity Ltd*[76] the EAT reiterated the decision in *Mundon* saying that an employer was not obliged to undertake enquiries about whether a woman was pregnant as this itself may be regarded as a detriment under MPR Regs 1999 reg 19. However, the EAT also added one qualification saying:

> It is conceivable that circumstances will arise in which an employer, detecting the symptoms of pregnancy and fearing the consequences, if the employee is in fact pregnant, but neither knowing nor believing that she is, simply suspecting that she might, dismisses her before his suspicion can be proved right. In such circumstances it may well be that a dismissal would be automatically unfair.

2.37   The other question that arises is where an employer becomes aware of the worker's pregnancy after raising concerns about her performance but before taking any disciplinary action. For example, if the employer holds an initial meeting to discuss a woman's poor

73 [1999] IRLR 217 EAT.
74 [1980] IRLR 224 EAT.
75 DCLD 34.
76 UKEAT/0236/04/DM 30 July 2004, unreported, para 24.

performance, not knowing prior to the meeting about her pregnancy and at the meeting she says that her performance has been affected by pregnancy-related sickness. In these circumstances, once her pregnancy is known, any detrimental action taken will be unlawful discrimination if it arguably is indeed related to her pregnancy or the consequences of it.

The definition of discrimination on grounds of pregnancy/maternity leave in the SDA 1975

2.38   As from 1 October 2005 the SDA 1975 was amended to include an explicit prohibition of discrimination on the ground of pregnancy or maternity leave. Prior to October 2005, the SDA1975 had to be read so as to give effect to the ETD and ECJ decisions.[77] However, it is not clear that the SDA 1975 amendments provide the full degree of protection required by European law. As UK law must be interpreted consistently with European law, including the judgments of the ECJ, the new definition under the SDA 1975 must be interpreted at least as favourably to employees as the old law. The new law is set out first and then analysed in the context of pre-existing case-law.

2.39   The ETD, which prohibits discrimination in access to employment, working conditions, pay and dismissal provides:

> Less favourable treatment of a woman related to pregnancy or maternity leave within the meaning of Directive 92/85/EEC [Pregnant Workers Directive] shall constitute discrimination.

A similar definition is included in the Recast Directive 2006/54/EC, article 2, para 2(c).

---

77 The amendments arguably give effect to the EC PWD and amended ETD but not to ECJ decisions (since 1991) because the ETD now bases its definition of discrimination on the provisions in the PWD which implemented in the ERA 1996. However, although the ECJ case-law makes it clear that any less favourable treatment related to pregnancy or maternity leave is automatically sex discrimination, the PWD imposes a protective code rather than setting out principles of anti-discrimination.

Statutory definition under the SDA 1975

2.40 Section 3A of the SDA 1975 states:

(1) A person discriminates against a woman if–
   (a) at a time in a protected period, and on the ground of the woman's pregnancy, the person treats her less favourably than he would treat her had she not become pregnant; or
   (b) on the ground that the woman is exercising or seeking to exercise, or has exercised or sought to exercise, a statutory right to maternity leave, the person treats her less favourably than he would treat her if she were neither exercising nor seeking to exercise, and had neither exercised nor sought to exercise that right.

(2) In any circumstances relevant for the purposes of a provision to which this subsection applies, a person discriminates against a woman if, on the ground that section 72(1) of the Employment Rights Act 1996 (compulsory maternity leave) has to be complied with in respect of the woman, he treats her less favourably than he would treat her if that provision did not have to be complied with in respect of her.

(3) For the purposes of subsection (1)–
   (a) in relation to a woman, a protected period begins each time she becomes pregnant, and the protected period associated with any particular pregnancy of hers ends in accordance with the following rules–
      (i) if she is entitled to ordinary but not additional maternity leave in connection with the pregnancy, the protected period ends at the end of her period of ordinary maternity leave connected with the pregnancy or, if earlier, when she returns to work after the end of her pregnancy;
      (ii) if she is entitled to ordinary and additional maternity leave in connection with the pregnancy, the protected period ends at the end of her period of additional maternity leave connected with the pregnancy or, if earlier, when she returns to work after the end of her pregnancy;
      (iii)if she is not entitled to ordinary maternity leave in respect of the pregnancy, the protected period ends at the end of the 2 weeks beginning with the end of the pregnancy;
   (b) where a person's treatment of a woman is on grounds of illness suffered by a woman as a consequence of a pregnancy of hers, that treatment is to be taken to be on the ground of the pregnancy.

2.41   Note that any reference to discrimination or sex discrimination in the SDA 1975 includes both direct discrimination and discrimination on grounds of pregnancy and maternity leave within section 3A.[78]

Summary of principles

2.42   Before considering the detail of the statutory provisions and where they may fall short of EC provisions and case-law, we summarise below the principles that are clear from the amended SDA 1975:

- Less favourable treatment of a worker or employee on the ground of her pregnancy or consequences of pregnancy is automatically sex discrimination.
- A woman does not need to compare her treatment to that of a male colleague, because there can be no comparison between a pregnant woman or woman on maternity leave and a man. The comparison is with how the employer would treat the woman had she not become pregnant. This is similar to the 'but for' test.
- Any less favourable treatment of a woman on the ground of pregnancy-related sickness will be automatically sex discrimination. Thus, if she is absent with such sickness, irrespective of the length of absence, she must not be treated less favourably.
- Employees are protected from automatic discrimination on the ground of pregnancy from the beginning of their pregnancy but only until the end of statutory maternity leave or their return to work, whichever is the sooner.
- Less favourable treatment on the ground of an employee's maternity leave is also sex discrimination. Maternity leave is the period of leave that only an employee is entitled to under the ERA 1996. Again, a male comparator is not required. After maternity leave, it is possible to argue that there has been less favourable treatment on the ground that the woman *has* exercised a right to maternity leave. Any less favourable treatment, whenever it occurs, on the grounds that the woman has been on maternity leave will be discrimination.
- For non-employees (not entitled to leave), protection from automatic discrimination on the ground of pregnancy extends only to the end of the two weeks beginning with the end of the pregnancy and no further.

---

78   SDA 1975 s5(1). This provision applies to employment, barristers and advocates and vocational training under SDA 1975 Part 3 (SDA 1975 s3A(5)).

- Under SDA 1975 s3A it is not discrimination to deprive a woman on statutory maternity leave of her normal pay ('remuneration') or to allow her to benefit only from the terms and conditions to which she is entitled under the ERA 1996 (SDA 1975 s6A) (see paras 2.53 and 5.28).

2.43 An employee or a worker can always argue that there has been less favourable treatment of a comparable man in similar circumstances in order to prove that there has been less favourable treatment but it is not necessary to do so in order to show automatic sex discrimination on grounds of pregnancy/maternity leave.

2.44 Examples of what is unlawful discrimination under the amended SDA 1975 include the following (see also chapters 3, 5 and 15):

- dismissing or disciplining a woman who is (or has been) absent with a pregnancy-related illness;
- failing to promote a woman because she is pregnant (or on maternity leave);
- abbreviating a woman's probationary period on grounds of pregnancy, or by reason of her absence on maternity leave;[79]
- demoting or dismissing an employee because she is absent with pregnancy-related illness or on maternity leave.[80] This would include dismissal of a woman following her inability to attend a disciplinary hearing because her doctor considered she was emotionally unfit to attend and was likely to remain so until after her pregnancy was over;[81]
- denying a woman training on grounds of her pregnancy or impending maternity leave;[82]
- giving a woman inferior or different work because she is pregnant, or is about to go on or has just returned from maternity leave;
- dismissing a woman on grounds of her pregnancy or maternity leave. This would include choosing her for redundancy and/or failing to offer her alternative work because she is pregnant or about to go on maternity leave;
- treating an employee on statutory maternity leave less favourably in relation to her working conditions on the ground that she is

---

79 *Lee v Relate Berkshire* [2003] UKEAT 1458, 27 March 2003.
80 Women's Equality Unit (WEU) guidance p12.
81 *Abbey National plc v Formoso* [1999] IRLR 222.
82 *Visa International Service v Paul* [2004] IRLR 42, EAT.

exercising or seeking to exercise or has exercised or sought to exercise a statutory right to maternity leave. Thus it will be discrimination:

- to fail to consult a woman on maternity leave about a redundancy situation or a reorganisation;
- not to give a woman on maternity leave an appraisal;
- to dismiss a woman on grounds of her absence on maternity leave;

- an employee who is absent with pregnancy-related sickness is entitled to be paid the same as any other employee with comparable sickness absence. She is not entitled to full pay during the whole period of her absence where other employees would not be entitled to such pay.[83]

Interpretation of SDA 1975 consistent with EC law

2.45   What is not clear from the amended SDA 1975 is whether it can be interpreted consistently with EC law which appears to offer greater protection in relation to the following:

- the wider definition of direct discrimination in that the ETD prohibits discrimination 'relating to' pregnancy whereas the SDA 1975 prohibits discrimination 'on grounds of' pregnancy and maternity leave;
- the interpretation of 'less favourable treatment' and the nature of the comparison to be made between the pregnant woman and the same woman not pregnant; previously courts accepted that no comparison was necessary;
- the extent of the protection of workers, not employees, taking time off to have a baby;
- the rights and benefits to which employees are entitled during maternity leave (see chapter 5);
- the nature of the right to return after maternity leave (see chapters 4 and 15);
- whether and when there will be automatic discrimination after maternity leave where the treatment is on grounds of or related to the pregnancy and/or absence on maternity leave.

---

83   *North Western Health Board v McKenna* [2005] IRLR 895, ECJ.

Less favourable treatment 'on the ground of' pregnancy/maternity

2.46   The wider definition in the ETD,[84] the definition of less favourable treatment and the nature of the comparison to be made need to be considered together as they are an integral part of proving direct discrimination.

2.47   First, it is important to reiterate that in pregnancy/maternity leave cases, the concept of less favourable treatment (unlike other sex discrimination claims) does not mean that the claimant has to compare herself with another worker who is being treated more favourably. EC law has established that a woman should not be disadvantaged in her working conditions for a reason related to her pregnancy. This may sometimes involve apparently more favourable treatment to protect her from the disadvantages suffered because of pregnancy, such as absence on account of pregnancy-related illness, morning sickness, tiredness or health and safety requirements. It is only by providing extra protection that there can be substantive equality (see *Fletcher*, para 2.58). It is notable that the ECJ often refers not to 'less favourable treatment' but 'unfavourable treatment'. This is a more accurate description as it makes it clear that no comparison is necessary. It is not about 'different treatment' and it is substantive equality that is required, ie the removal of disadvantages associated with pregnancy and maternity leave.[85]

2.48   'Less favourable treatment' has always been broadly defined by the courts and should be interpreted in the same way as in other sex discrimination cases. For example, in *Herbert Smith Solicitors & George Kalorkoti v Langton*[86] the claimant asked what Mr Kalorkoti's plans were for her and he replied 'That really depends on what your long-term plans are . . . Are you planning on having any more children?'. The EAT upheld the tribunal's finding that an act taking the form of a single comment which would not be made to a man, and which has an adverse effect on a female claimant, is both less favourable treatment of her and constitutes a detriment. In addition, the EAT upheld the tribunal's finding that the claimant had been treated less favourably when reporting childcare commitments as a male senior manager would have been treated differently.

2.49   Under SDA 1975 s3A the treatment must be 'on the ground of' the woman's pregnancy/maternity leave and the comparison is with the

---

84 'Related to' instead of 'ground of', see para 2.39.
85 See *Sarkatzis Herrero v Institute Madrileño de la Salud* [2006] IRLR 296, ECJ, paras 41 and 46.
86 UKEAT/0242/05 10 October 2005.

woman's position had she not become pregnant. This appears to be narrower than the test under the ETD, which refers to the treatment being 'related to' the pregnancy, thus removing any need for any comparative exercise and covering any treatment linked to pregnancy, for example sickness, tiredness due to pregnancy, miscarriage or health and safety considerations. The ETD definition is consistent with a long line of ECJ decisions on pregnancy discrimination, which have made it clear that any treatment related to pregnancy and its consequences is unlawful, irrespective of whether a person who is not pregnant would be treated the same way. To interpret it more narrowly would be a breach of EC law.

What is the nature of the comparison to be made?

2.50   The SDA 1975 provides for a comparison between the position of the pregnant woman with how she would have been treated had she not been pregnant. The comparison should be with a woman who has none of the problems or issues associated with pregnancy that led her to be treated unfavourably, ie the woman as she was before she became pregnant.[87] Thus if her complaint is that her performance appraisal has been adversely affected because of pregnancy-related tiredness or the need to work shorter hours for reasons relating to her pregnancy, the relevant comparison is how she would have been treated if she did not have pregnancy related tiredness and/or did not have to work shorter hours. It would be wrong to compare her, for example, with an employee with non-pregnancy related tiredness which impacted on her performance. If she is marked down because her performance has been affected by her pregnancy-related tiredness or shorter hours, this will be less favourable treatment on grounds of her pregnancy and therefore discrimination.[88] This is consistent with the interpretation given by the DTI's Women and Equality Unit which states that the SDA 1975 now makes it 'explicit that women are protected from discrimination on the ground that they are pregnant or exercising their statutory maternity rights'.

2.51   Discrimination on grounds of pregnancy and maternity leave is different from other forms of direct discrimination as there is no need to show the woman was, or would have been, treated less

---

87   This is similar to the interpretation adopted by the Court of Appeal in the disability case of *Clark v Novacold* [1999] IRLR 318.

88   A parallel interpretation was given to a similar question under the Disability Discrimination Act 1995, see *Clark v Novacold*.

favourably than a man or other worker. The test in most cases is whether 'but for' her pregnancy – or factors related to her pregnancy – she would have been treated the way she was. This is often referred to as 'automatic sex discrimination' as a result of the woman's 'protected status' which for employees at least applies from the time the employer was aware she was pregnant until the end of her maternity leave. See also *Establishing a pregnancy-related reason for discrimination* at para 2.72 onwards, below.

The protection of workers who are not employees

2.52 Under the amended SDA 1975 it is only employees who are entitled to statutory maternity leave who are protected from automatic sex discrimination during leave. Non-emloyees are protected during their pregnancy and for the two weeks following the birth. This means that if a woman, who is not an employee, is told that she cannot return to the job she was doing before her absence having a baby, she is not protected under SDA 1975 s3A. However, it has already been established that it was discrimination against a contract worker (who was not an employee) to replace her with a permanent employee when she left to have a baby.[89] In these circumstances the worker would have to rely on SDA 1975 s1(1) and the 'old' law and there would still be no need for her to rely on a comparator.

Rights and benefits to which employees are entitled during maternity leave

2.53 The ERA 1996 and MPL Regs 1999 lay down employees' rights during maternity and other family leave. The aim of the amendments to the SDA 1975 is to prevent a discrimination claim being brought to challenge the fairly restrictive rights available to women on maternity leave, particularly AML. This issue is discussed in detail in chapter 5.

Length of protection on grounds of pregnancy

2.54 Although section 3A(1)(a) does not extend protection on the ground of pregnancy to the period after maternity leave, the ECJ in *Brown v Rentokil* (see para 2.65) made it clear that it is automatic discrimination to treat a woman less favourably by taking into account (to the worker's detriment) pregnancy or maternity leave at any time. For

---

89 See *Patefield v Belfast City Council* [2000] IRLR 664 NICA and *BP Chemicals Ltd v Gillick* [1995] IRLR 128 EAT (see para 2.11).

example, it would be discrimination if a redundancy selection process took into account pregnancy-related absence or the employer refused to consider a woman for promotion because she had missed training courses due to her pregnancy. Section 3A(1)(a) should therefore be interpreted in accordance with existing case-law to protect women who are treated less favourably on their return from maternity leave where the reason for the treatment relates back to their pregnancy (such as pregnancy-related sickness) or maternity leave. See para 2.65.

2.55   An employee would not be protected, however, under SDA 1975 or EC case-law if she became ill, following her return, for a reason relating to her pregnancy provided any period of pregnancy related sickness prior to the end of maternity leave was *not* taken into account (see para 2.64).

Length of protection on grounds of maternity leave

2.56   Section 3A(1)(b) prohibits less favourable treatment on the ground that the woman:

- is exercising or seeking to exercise a statutory right to maternity leave; or
- has exercised or sought to exercise a statutory right to maternity leave.

2.57   Unlike section 3A(1)(a), subsection 3A(1)(b) is not specifically limited to the protected period. Any less favourable treatment of a women on the ground that she is about to go on maternity leave, is on maternity leave or because she has been on maternity leave, will be discrimination. Thus, if after her return to work she is treated less favourably for a reason related to her maternity leave this will be automatic sex discrimination. This would cover the situation:

- where an employee's job has been changed for the worse because the maternity locum or another employee has taken over some or all of her work;
- where, under the ERA 1996 provisions, an employee was given another job on return from maternity leave because it was not considered reasonably practicable to allow her to return to her original job and the reason was related to her absence on leave, see chapter 15.[90]

90   There is a conflict between SDA 1975 and ERA 1996 as the latter enables an employer to offer a suitable alternative job in some circumstances.

The main principles of ECJ case-law on direct pregnancy/maternity discrimination

2.58   The EAT, in *Fletcher v Blackpool Fylde & Wyre Hospitals NHS Trust*,[91] helpfully summarised key principles relating to pregnancy/maternity discrimination including important ECJ decisions. This case was decided before SDA 1975 s3A was introduced but remains good law. In *Fletcher* trainee midwives (classed as vocational trainees) had their bursaries facility withdrawn when they became pregnant and complained this was a breach of SDA 1975 s14 which prohibits discrimination against such trainees. It is important to note that although the facility which was withdrawn in this case was a bursary, this case was about discrimination against trainees. It was not about the rights of employees who are entitled to maternity leave and pay and who are covered by the protective code during maternity leave so that they are prevented from claiming equal pay (see para 2.106). The decision does not therefore apply directly to employees on maternity leave claiming equal pay as they are covered by the special protective regime (see chapter 5).

2.59   The EAT in *Fletcher* made the following points:

a)   'Discrimination in EU law, when considered in the context of sex equality, is defined as meaning either that different rules are applied to men and women in comparable situations, or that the same rule is applied to men and women who are in different situations. . . . As applied to pregnancy and maternity cases, the second limb of this definition means that treating pregnant workers or women on maternity leave in the same way as other employees during the "protected period" (that is the start of pregnancy through to the end of maternity leave), in circumstances in which they are disadvantaged because of their pregnancy or maternity, is applying the same treatment to different situations and is therefore discrimination. In this way, the law aims to ensure substantive equality for working women, who would otherwise be disadvantaged by their pregnancy.'[92] Referring to the decisions in *Webb v EMO Air Cargo (UK) Ltd, Brown v Rentokil, CNAVTS v Thibault* and *Hoj Pedersen* the EAT said that: 'These cases establish that no male comparator is required in

91   [2005] IRLR 689, EAT.
92   Para 64.

order to demonstrate sex discrimination. If the reason for the treatment is pregnancy then the detriment resulting, whatever it is, is unlawful sex discrimination even though other employees in the same circumstances are or would be treated in the same way. The same rule is being applied to different situations and is therefore discriminatory.'

b)   Although women on maternity leave are in a special, protected position and cannot compare themselves to men and women at work, this does not rule out a comparison in all circumstances. The EAT held that women should not be prevented from comparing their treatment with more favourable treatment given to sick men or women, where appropriate, in order to demonstrate that a different rule is being applied in comparable circumstances and that discrimination has occurred. Thus, in *Fletcher* student midwives' bursary installments ceased during their absence from midwifery training by reason of pregnancy and childbirth and they were not entitled to maternity leave. They could rely, in the alternative, upon the more favourable treatment of sick trainee midwives, who would receive bursary payments for 60 days of absence, to show that they were treated less favourably.

c)   'In deciding whether less favourable treatment is on grounds of pregnancy, it is not permissible to say that the treatment is on grounds of absence from the course, rather than on grounds of pregnancy, and that other absent employees are treated equally so that there is no sex discrimination.' When deciding the question of causation, namely whether her dismissal was on the grounds of pregnancy, the basic question is what is the 'effective and predominant cause' or the 'real and efficient cause' of the act complained of.[93]

d)   The 'but for' test is the established test for determining direct discrimination as a matter of law. Absent the protective maternity code, the established test for determining direct discrimination must apply.[94]

2.60   The key principles, which still apply, are set out in the ECJ and House of Lords cases of *Webb, Tele Danmark, Dekker, Hertz, Brown v Rentokil, Busch, Sass* and *Herrero* (see below). The principles apply to all areas

---

93   *Fletcher* para 77 following *O'Neill v Governors of St Thomas More RCVA Upper School* [1996] IRLR 372.
94   Para 91.

of prohibited discrimination, ie recruitment, training, transfer, promotion, detriment and dismissal.

2.61 In *Webb*[94a] the ECJ held:

- 'there can be no question of comparing the situation of a woman who finds herself incapable, by reason of pregnancy discovered very shortly after the conclusion of the employment contract, of performing the task for which she was recruited with that of a man similarly incapable for medical or other reasons'. This would apply in all pregnancy cases, whether concerning recruitment, promotion, detriment or dismissal;
- dismissal of a pregnant woman recruited for an indefinite period cannot be justified because she is unable to work for a temporary period because of her pregnancy; note that this has subsequently been applied to all fixed term contracts even if the woman is unavailable for the whole contract (see also chapter 15);
- 'the protection afforded by Community law to a woman during pregnancy and after childbirth cannot be dependent on whether her presence at work during maternity is essential to the proper functioning of the undertaking in which she is employed';
- discrimination cannot be justified by the financial loss which an employer who appointed a pregnant woman would suffer for the duration of her pregnancy;[95]
- any less favourable treatment of a woman because she is pregnant or because of the consequences of pregnancy is discrimination.

2.62 In *Tele Danmark*,[96] where the fixed-term contract of a pregnant woman was terminated when she told her employer that she was pregnant, the ECJ held that:

- dismissal will be sex discrimination if it is on the ground of pregnancy, notwithstanding that the woman was recruited for a fixed period, failed to inform the employer that she was pregnant even though she was aware of this when she was employed, and because of her pregnancy was unable to work during a substantial part of the term of that contact; it makes no difference if the contract was indefinite or for a fixed term;
- dismissal of a worker on account of pregnancy constitutes direct

---

94a *Webb v EMO Air Cargo (UK) Ltd* [1994] IRLR 482, ECJ; [1995] IRLR 645, HL.

95 Advocate General in *Webb* approved in *Fletcher*, see para 67.

96 *Tele Danmark A/S v Handels-og Kontorfunktionaerernes Forbund I Danmark (HK) acting on behalf of Brandt-Nielsen* [2001] IRLR 853.

discrimination on grounds of sex, whatever the nature and extent of the economic loss incurred by the employer as a result of her absence;[97]

- there is no exception to the prohibition of dismissing pregnant workers, save in exceptional cases not connected with their condition (see also *Tele Danmark* at para 15.45).

2.63   In *Dekker*[98] the ECJ held that it was a breach of the ETD for an employer to refuse to appoint a suitable female applicant because of the possible adverse consequences of her pregnancy (see para 3.141), which includes her inability to work on health and safety grounds[99] (see para 3.88). The ECJ said:

- as employment can only be refused to women because of pregnancy, such a refusal is direct discrimination on grounds of sex;
- it is discrimination to refuse to recruit a woman on health and safety grounds.

2.64   In *Hertz*[100] the ECJ held that:

- The dismissal of a female worker because of her pregnancy constitutes direct discrimination on grounds of sex, in the same way as does the refusal to recruit a pregnant woman. Therefore, a woman is protected from dismissal because of her absence during the maternity leave from which she benefits under national law. However, the ETD does not prohibit the dismissal of a woman as a result of absence due to pregnancy-related illness where this occurs after the end of maternity leave though it may still be discriminatory if related to her sex (see para 2.28) or unfair (see chapter 15).

2.65   In *Brown v Rentokil*[101] the ECJ held:

- 'dismissal of a female worker during pregnancy for absences due to incapacity for work resulting from her pregnancy is linked to

---

97 Nor is it a defence that the employer did not intend to discriminate or acting in that way to protect the woman.
98 *Dekker v Stichting Vormingscentrum voor Jonge Volwassenen (VJV-Centrum) Plus* [1991] IRLR 27, ECJ.
99 See also *Mahlburg v land Mecklenburg-Vorpommern* [2000] IRLR 276 ECJ.
100 *Handels-og Kontorfunktionaerernes Forbund I Danmark (acting for Hertz) v Dansk Arbejdgiverforening (acting for Aldi Marked K/S)* [1991] IRLR 31, ECJ.
101 [1998] IRLR 445, ECJ.

the occurrence of risks inherent in pregnancy and must therefore be regarded as essentially based on the fact of pregnancy. Such a dismissal can affect only women and so constitutes direct discrimination on grounds of sex'.[102] In *Fletcher* the EAT said that there was nothing in the judgment to suggest that there was any distinction between dismissal and other working conditions.

- Any absence owing to illness resulting from pregnancy or childbirth cannot be taken into account for computation of the period justifying her dismissal under national law. In *Fletcher* the EAT said that it was impermissible for an employer to defend a complaint of sex discrimination by a pregnant woman by saying that all employees are treated in the same way, thereby applying the same rule to different situations.[103]

2.66   In *CNAVTS v Thibault*[104] the ECJ held that it was contrary to the ETD for a woman to be treated unfavourably in relation to her working conditions by being deprived of the right to an annual assessment of her performance because she was on maternity leave (see para 5.76). The ECJ said:

> The principle of non-discrimination requires that a woman who continues to be bound to her employer by her contract of employment during maternity leave should not be deprived of the benefit of working conditions which apply to both men and women and are the result of that employment relationship. In circumstances such as those of this case, to deny a female employee the right to have her performance assessed annually would discriminate against her merely in her capacity as a worker because, if she had not been pregnant and had not taken the maternity leave to which she was entitled, she would have been assessed for the year in question and could therefore have qualified for promotion.

Failure to disclose pregnancy prior to discrimination not relevant

2.67   The employer cannot justify treating a woman less favourably on the basis that she did not disclose her pregnancy prior to the discrimination, for example when she was appointed. As the Advocate General said in *Webb*:

> It is of no significance whatever . . . that the employer would not have

---

102   Para 24, see also para 68 of *Fletcher*.
103   Para 69.
104   [1998] IRLR 399, ECJ, para 29.

recruited the person in question if he had been aware of her pregnancy. [105]

2.68   However, at the time of the less favourable treatment the employer must be aware that she is pregnant, otherwise the treatment will not be on grounds of her pregnancy (see paras 2.36–2.37). In *Busch*[106] the claimant took parental leave intending to be away for three years. She became pregnant and asked to return early and this was agreed. She then told her employer she was pregnant and the employer rescinded its consent to her returning to work on grounds of fraudulent misrepresentation as she only wanted to return to work to get the benefit of maternity allowance. The ECJ held that:

- since the employers may not take the employee's pregnancy into consideration for the purpose of her working conditions, she is not obliged to inform her employer that she is pregnant;
- discrimination on grounds of sex cannot be justified by the fact that a woman is temporarily prevented from performing all of her duties;
- an employee canot be refused the right to return to work before the end of parental leave due to temporary prohibitions on performing certain work duties;
- discrimination on grounds of sex cannot be justified on grounds relating to the financial loss for an employer;
- the fact that Ms Busch returned to work in order to receive a maternity allowance higher than parental leave allowance, could not legally justify sex discrimination in relation to working conditions.

Sass *and* Herrero: *protection during maternity leave*

2.69   In *Herrero*[106a] and *Brandenburg v Sass* [2005] IRLR 147, ECJ the ECJ reiterated the wide protection given to women on maternity leave. In *Sass* the ECJ said:

> . . . a female worker is protected in her employment relationship against any unfavourable treatment on the ground that she is or has been on maternity leave [para 35];

> . . . a woman who is treated unfavourably because of absence on

---

105   See Advocate General at para 9 cited with approval in *Fletcher*.
106   *Busch v Klinikum Neustadt GmbH & Co Betriebs-KG*, C-320/01 [2003] IRLR 625, ECJ.
106a   *Sarkatzis Herrero v Instituto Madrileño de la Salud* [2006] IRLR 296, ECJ.

maternity leave suffers discrimination on the ground of her pregnancy and of that leave. Such conduct constitutes discrimination on the grounds of sex within the meaning of Directive 76/207.[107]

2.70   In *Herrero* the ECJ held that:

> . . . since the aim of Directive 76/207 is substantive, not formal equality, Articles 2(1) and (3) and 3 of that Directive must be interpreted as precluding any unfavourable treatment of a female working on account of maternity leave or in connection with such leave, which aims to protect pregnant women, and that is so without it being necessary to have regard to whether such treatment affects an existing employment relationship or a new employment relationship [para 41].

The fact that other people, in particular men, may, on other grounds, be treated in the same way as Ms Herrero has no bearing on an assessment of her position since the deferment of the date on which her career is deemed to have started stemmed exclusively from the maternity leave to which she was entitled.

2.71   These decisions are discussed in more detail at para 5.57 onwards.

Establishing a pregnancy/maternity-related reason for direct discrimination

2.72   It is unlikely that an employer will admit to treating a woman less favourably because she is pregnant or on maternity leave. Usually, there will be allegations relating to poor performance, a reorganisation or redundancy. It is for the woman to raise a presumption that the less favourable treatment is related to pregnancy, childbirth or maternity leave. Thus, for example, where a woman has had a good performance record, or been told that her future is secure and these messages change following the announcement of her pregnancy, this is likely to raise an inference that any less favourable treatment is for a reason related to her pregnancy. Similarly, questions about whether she is likely to have children or comments that it is not possible to combine a career with childcare may imply, depending on the circumstances, that different treatment following pregnancy is related to the pregnancy and impending maternity leave. In these circumstances the burden of proof is likely to shift to the employer to show

---

107 Equal Treatment Directive, see para 2.39.

that the treatment was not in any way related to her pregnancy (see para 17.124 onwards). Important tools are the questionnaire procedure (see para 17.28 onwards) and discovery (see para 19.94 onwards).

2.73   In *O'Neill v Governors of St Thomas More RCVA Upper School*,[108] the claimant was an unmarried pregnant teacher, working in a Catholic school, who was dismissed when the school discovered that the father was a Catholic priest. The EAT said that the relevant principles in determining whether treatment is directly discriminatory on the ground of sex is not one of subjective mental processes of the respondents ie, as to their intentions, motives, beliefs or subjective purposes. A condition of liability in the expression 'on the ground of her sex' is an objective test of causal connection. The relevant question is 'Would the applicant have received the same treatment but for her sex? (see *James v Eastleigh Borough Council*).[109] The principles are set out below:

i) The tribunal's approach to the question of causation should be 'simple, pragmatic and commonsensical'.

ii) The question of causation has to be answered in the context of a decision to attribute liability for the acts complained of. It is not simply a matter of a factual, scientific or historical explanation of a sequence of events, let alone a matter for philosophical speculation. The basic question is: what, out of the whole complex of facts before the tribunal, is the 'effective and predominant cause' or the 'real and efficient cause' of the act complained of? As a matter of common sense, not all the factors present in a situation are equally entitled to be treated as a cause of the crucial event for the purpose of attributing legal liability for consequences.

The approach to causation is further qualified by the principle that the event or factor alleged to be causative of the matter complained of need not be the only or even the main cause of the result complained of (though it must provide more than just the occasion for the result complained of). It is enough if it is *an effective cause.*

2.74   In *O'Neill v Governors of St Thomas More RCVA Upper School* the EAT makes the following important points:

• 'Pregnancy is unique to the female sex. The concept of "pregnancy per se" is misleading, because it suggests pregnancy as the sole

108   [1997] ICR 33; [1996] IRLR 372, EAT.
109   [1990] IRLR 288, HL, citing with approval the decision in *Banque Bruxelles v Eagle Star Insurance Co Ltd* [1995] 2 WLR 607 at 620H–621E.

ground of dismissal. Pregnancy always has surrounding circumstances, some arising prior to the state of pregnancy, some
accompanying it, some consequential on it.'

- 'The critical question is whether, on an objective consideration of
  all the surrounding circumstances, the dismissal or other treatment complained of by the [claimant] is on the ground of
  pregnancy.'
- 'It need not be only on that ground. It need not even be mainly on
  that ground. Thus, the fact that the employer's ground for dismissal is that the pregnant woman will become unavailable for
  work because of her pregnancy does not make it any the less a
  dismissal on the ground of pregnancy ... she is not available
  because she is pregnant.'
- 'In the present case, the other factors in the circumstances surrounding the pregnancy relied upon as the "dominant motive" are
  all causally related to the fact that the [claimant] was pregnant –
  the paternity of the child, the publicity of that fact and the consequent untenability of the [claimant's] position as a religious
  education teacher are all pregnancy bases or pregnancy related
  grounds. Her pregnancy precipitated and permeated the decision
  to dismiss her. It is not possible, in our view, to say on the facts
  found by the Industiral Tribunal, that the ground for the [claim-
  ant's] dismissal was anything other than her pregnancy.'

2.75   The difficulty is in distinguishing the causal link between the pregnancy, including its consequences, and the less favourable treatment
from the surrounding circumstances which are only peripheral to the
pregnancy or maternity leave. Thus, if a woman is dismissed on
maternity leave because it is only then that the employer discovers
she has behaved fraudulently, the 'but for' test may lead to a finding
of less favourable treatment linked to maternity leave even though
the 'reason why' or the 'effective reason' for the dismissal is clearly
the fraud, not the maternity leave absence.

2.76   Thus, although a useful question to ask is: 'Would the woman
have been treated in the same way *but for* the fact that she was pregnant, had given birth or was on or had taken maternity leave?', this
will not always be sufficient, particularly where the predominant
cause is not pregnancy.[110] An alternative question is to ask the 'reason

---

110   This test was established in the House of Lords cases of *R v Birmingham City
Council ex p EOC* [1989] IRLR 173, and *James v Eastleigh BC* [1990] ICR 554. It
was followed by the EAT in *O'Neill*.

why' she was treated as she was, or what was the effective cause.[111] In *Barbara Wilson t/a Wilson's Greengrocers v Knight*[112] the employer argued that the reason for the claimant's dismissal was the fact that the claimant's husband had threatened the respondent, Mrs Wilson, and that any employee would be dismissed in these circumstances whether or not they were pregnant. The tribunal found that because Mr Wilson said that if Mrs Knight had not been pregnant he would have sought an explanation or apology from her (and if received she would have been able to return to work) she had been dismissed for a reason connected with her pregnancy, so her dismissal was automatically unfair. The EAT said that it was not enough simply to show that 'but for' being pregnant a dismissal or other detriment would not have occurred. The correct approach is to ask, as the EAT did in *O'Neill v Governors of St Thomas More RCVA Upper School*, whether pregnancy was the effective and predominant, though not necessarily the only or main, cause of the dismissal or other detriment.

2.77   In practice, the shifting burden of proof is often the key to whether direct discrimination is established, as once the claimant has provided a presumption (or prima facie case) that there has been less favourable treatment on grounds of pregnancy it is for the employer to show that the treatment was not related to her pregnancy (see chapter 17).

Pregnancy need not be the only reason

2.78   In *O'Neill v Governors of St Thomas More RCVA Upper School*, the EAT held that the crucial question was whether the dismissal was on the ground of pregnancy, motive being irrelevant. The EAT said that the event or fact which is said to have caused the discrimination 'need not be the only or even the main cause of the result complained of' but 'it is enough if it is an effective cause'. Thus, where pregnancy is a factor without which the less favourable treatment would not have happened this should be enough to establish discrimination (see para 2.74).

---

111 *Shamoon v Chief Constable of the Royal Ulster Constabulary* [2003] IRLR 285, HL where Lord Nicholls said that it was sometimes more appropriate to concentrate on the reason why the claimant was treated as she was. 'Was it on the proscribed ground or was it for some other reason?'

112 [2003] UKEAT 1022 30 April 2003.

Stereotyping

2.79　Stereotyping is likely to be discriminatory. An assumption that, for example, a woman's work will become less important after childbirth so that she can be given less responsible work will, if acted upon, be discriminatory.[113] It is not uncommon for a pregnant woman to be told that once she has children her priorities will be different and this will affect her work. If she is treated less favourably as a result this will be discrimination.

Motive or purpose is irrelevant

2.80　Once it has been shown that the less favourable treatment was related to the woman's pregnancy, it is irrelevant that the employer may have a benign motive, such as a desire to protect the woman.[114]

Evidence

2.81　If there is evidence that other pregnant workers have been treated in a discriminatory way in that, for example, they have not been allowed to return to the same job and work, this may give rise to an inference that the complainant, who has been treated in a similar way, has been treated less favourably on grounds of her pregnancy or maternity leave.[115] Evidence of a glass ceiling for women, and particularly mothers, may give rise, in some circumstances, to an inference that there is discrimination in the workplace (see chapter 17).

113　*Hurley v Mustoe* [1981] IRLR 208, EAT where the EAT said that an employer must not simply apply a rule of convenience, or a prejudice, to exclude a whole class of women or married persons because some members of that class are not suitable employees.

114　See *James v Eastleigh BC* [1990] IRLR 288, HL and *O'Neill* at para 2.74 above.

115　See *West Midlands Passenger Transport Executive v Singh* [1988] IRLR 186, CA where the Court of Appeal held that if a practice is being operated against a racial group then, in the absence of a satisfactory explanation in a particular case, it is reasonable to infer that the complainant, as a member of the group has himself been treated less favourably on grounds of race. This reasoning should also apply to maternity cases, so that treatment of other pregnant woman will be relevant.

Indirect sex discrimination

2.82   Indirect discrimination is concerned with practices which have the effect of discriminating against women (or men) and which cannot be justified by the needs of the job. In the context of this book, such practices are usually connected to the fact that, in reality, women still have primary responsibility for children (see chapters 13 and 14).

2.83   The EAT has held that refusal to allow a woman to return to work part-time is not direct but indirect discrimination. It would only be direct discrimination if a man in a similar job was allowed to work part-time and a woman in a similar situation was not. Thus, where a woman is bringing a claim for indirect sex discrimination because she is not allowed to work reduced hours, a man could claim that, if the woman won, it would be direct discrimination not to allow him to reduce his hours.

2.84   Where a practice is found to be indirectly discriminatory against women, it should not be applied to men either. In *Jesuthasan*[116] the Court of Appeal held that legislative measures that have been declared a breach of EC law because they are indirectly discriminatory to women must be disapplied in respect of both women and men. The same reasoning should apply to measures imposed not only by legislation but by employers.

2.85   Note that where a woman or man is treated less favourably than a comparable full-time worker, because s/he is working part-time, this may be a breach of the Part-time Workers Regulations[117] (see chapter 14).

Direct and indirect marital (civil partnership) discrimination

2.86   It is not only sex discrimination that is unlawful but also discrimination on grounds of marital and civil partnership status. Refusal to appoint or promote a woman (or man) because s/he is married (or a civil partner) will be direct marital discrimination. The comparison no longer has to be between a married woman and an unmarried

---

116 *Jeruthasan v Hammersmith & Fulham LBC* [1998] IRLR 372, CA.
117 Part-time Workers (Prevention of Less Favourable Treatment) Regulations 2000 SI No 1551.

woman or a married man and an unmarried man, but is between a person who is married or a civil partner and person who is not married or a civil partner. The circumstances must be similar so there is a 'like with like' comparison. Unmarried people are not protected unless it is sex discrimination.

2.87 A requirement to work full-time or long or anti-social hours may be indirect marital discrimination. The requirement is likely to disadvantage a substantially higher proportion of married women than single women because they are more likely to have children than single women (see chapter 13). A claim of marital discrimination might be made by a male claimant (who is not able to argue indirect sex discrimination to get time off for child care).

Harassment

2.88 The provisions of the SDA 1975 which prohibit discrimination on grounds of pregnancy and maternity leave do not explicitly prohibit harassment on grounds of pregnancy or maternity leave.

There is a separate definition of harassment under the SDA 1975, which provides:

> 4A(1) a person subjects a woman to harassment if–
> (a) on the ground of sex, he engages in unwanted conduct that has the purpose or effect–
> (i) of violating her dignity, or
> (ii) of creating an intimidating, hostile, degrading, humiliating or offensive environment for her,
> (b) he engages in any form of unwanted verbal, non-verbal or physical conduct of a sexual nature that has the purpose or effect–
> (i) of violating her dignity, or
> (ii) of creating an intimidating, hostile, degrading, humiliating or offensive environment for her, or
> (c) on the ground of her rejection of or submission to unwanted conduct of a kind mentioned in paragraph (a) or (b), he treats her less favourably than he would treat her had she not rejected, or submitted to, the conduct.
> (2) Conduct shall be regarded as having the effect mentioned in subparagraph (i) or (ii) of subsection (1)(a) or (b) only if, having regard to all the circumstances, including in particular the perception of the woman, it should reasonably be considered as having that effect.

Points to note are:

- There are three definitions of harassment: the first on the ground of the woman's sex (which will be most common in pregnancy cases); it is no defence that a man would be subjected to the same abusive behaviour. The second type is where there is conduct of a 'sexual nature', such as offensive sexual jokes or pornography in the office. The third type is where the worker has been treated less favourably on the grounds of her rejection of or submission to harassment;
- In most cases harassment against a pregnant woman or new mother will be less favourable treatment under SDA 1975 s3A (see para 2.40), though it may be advisable to argue harassment in the alternative as the position is not clear. Harassment is separate from discrimination, there being no overlap between the two. There have been no appeal decisions on the new definitions of harassment;
- The type of conduct which will constitute harassment includes verbal comments, offensive material on display, ridiculing a woman over her appearance (see, eg, para 3.154), asking a woman about her sex life, etc;
- Conduct must be *unwanted*, which it usually will be in pregnancy cases, for example where a pregnant woman was told 'no one wants to be with a fat bird';[118]
- The conduct must have the purpose or effect of violating the woman's dignity or creating an intimidating, hostile, degrading, humiliating or offensive environment for her. If there is an intention to harass the woman, this is sufficient. If intention is not proved the question is then whether, having regard to all the circumstances, including in particular the perception of the woman, it should reasonably be considered as having that effect;
- SDA s20A provides that ex-employees are protected from harassment where this arises out of or is closely connected with a previous employment relationship;
- Principles of vicarious liability apply (see para 2.15);
- The EOC have published advice about harassment on their website.

---

118 As happened in *Gilbank v Miles* [2006] IRLR 538, CA. For more details see Palmer et al, *Discrimination Law Handbook* (2nd edn, forthcoming, 2006, Legal Action Group).

Victimisation

2.89 It is unlawful to treat a person less favourably because s/he has either:

- brought a complaint under the SDA 1975, EPA 1970, or Pensions Act (PA) ie issued proceedings; or
- given evidence or information in connection with proceedings (such as supporting a claim); or
- done anything else under or by reference to the SDA 1975, EPA 1970 or PA (this is very wide); or
- made allegations against the employer that it has acted unlawfully under the SDA 1975, EPA 1970 or PA (such as stating that it is discriminatory not to allow the woman to work part-time).[119]

2.90 In *Coote v Granada Hospitality*[120] the claimant settled her pregnancy discrimination claim and subsequently her employers refused to provide her with a reference. She claimed that the refusal was due to the fact that she had claimed discrimination so she had been victimised for bringing a discrimination claim. The ECJ held that the ETD required member states to ensure protection for workers whose employer, after the employment relationship has ended, refuses to provide references as a reaction to a discrimination claim. The claim was successful in the tribunal and settled for the equivalent of £185,000. The SDA 1975 has now been amended to protect employees and others where the relationship has come to an end.[121]

2.91 In *Visa International Service Association v Paul*[122] the claimant brought proceedings complaining of unfair dismissal, wrongful dismissal, pregnancy-related detriment, pregnancy-related dismissal and sex discrimination. Following these proceedings the employers brought a counterclaim seeking recoupment of enhanced maternity benefit the claimant had received during her period of leave. Ms Paul claimed this was victimisation as the respondent did not seek to

---

119 SDA 1975 s4.
120 [1998] IRLR 656, ECJ and [1999] IRLR 452, EAT.
121 SDA 1975 ss20Aand 35C. For ex-employees it is unlawful to discriminate against a woman by subjecting her to a detriment where the discrimination arises out of, and is closely connected to, the relevant relationship. See Palmer et al, *Discrimination Law Handbook* (2nd edn, forthcoming, 2006, Legal Action Group).
122 [2004] IRLR 42, EAT.

recover recoupment from two other people who had left employment. The EAT upheld the tribunal's finding of victimisation.

2.92 For example, if a woman asks to work part-time, complains of discrimination, and, as a result, is denied the opportunity to do particular work, or refused promotion or otherwise treated less favourably, this will be victimisation if the reason for her treatment is the allegation of discrimination.

Unfair dismissal

2.93 A woman may have a claim for discriminatory dismissal under the SDA 1975 and for automatically unfair dismissal (for pregnancy/maternity reasons) or ordinary unfair dismissal under ERA 1996 s99. A discriminatory dismissal will generally also be an unfair one, giving rise to a claim for compensation under the ERA 1996.[123] However, compensation is not payable twice (see para 18.25).

2.94 Where there has been a breach of the terms of the woman's contract by the employer, this may entitle the woman to resign and claim constructive dismissal (see chapter 15).

Discrimination related to parental and dependants' leave

2.95 Where an employee has been treated less favourably for a reason related to paternity, parental or dependants leave, s/he may also have a discrimination claim. However, the principles are different because both male and female employees are entitled to such leave. If, for example, a female employee is allowed more favourable time off than a male employee, that would be direct discrimination against the man. He would have to show that the reason was because of his sex and the principles set out at paras 2.28–2.33 above would apply.

2.96 If, however, male and female employees are treated equally, but a practice has a disproportionate adverse impact on women (because they are more likely to take parental and dependants' leave) this may be indirect discrimination (see *Lewen v Denda* at para 5.87 onwards).

123 *Clarke v Eley (IMI) Kynock Ltd* [1982] IRLR 482.

Equal Pay Act 1970

2.97 The EPA 1970 only covers contractual terms, whether pay or other benefits. The statutory provisions require a worker to show that s/he is doing similar work, work rated as equivalent under a job evaluation scheme or work of equal value to an actual worker of the opposite sex (see para 2.98). However, where a worker is paid less or receives other less favourable contractual terms for a reason related to her pregnancy or maternity leave (apart from pay during leave which is replaced by SMP), arguably she does not need to rely on a comparator. The EPA 1970 has been amended to give effect to the narrow provisions relating to pay rises which needed to be implemented following *Alabaster* (see para 2.108 onwards) but not to the broader principle established by the Court of Appeal that a comparator is not needed in pregnancy or maternity cases (see para 2.103).[124]

2.98 Where a woman is doing either:

• like work or work of a similar nature; or
• work rated as equivalent under a job evaluation scheme; or
• work of equal value,
with a comparable man in the same employment,[125] she is entitled to the same pay and contractual terms, provided there is no material difference between the two workers under EPA 1970 s1(3). An equality clause is implied into the woman's contract. The details are beyond the scope of this book except in relation to the less favourable treatment of part-timers (see chapter 14).

2.99 The definition of 'pay' is very wide, as it must comply with the EC definition under article 141 of the Treaty of Rome 1957 (which provides for equal pay). It includes:

• salary and wages;
• overtime;[126]
• redundancy pay;[127]

---

124 Section 1(2)(d).
125 This includes a predecessor or successor
126 *Arbeiterwohlfahrt der Stadt Berlin eV v Botel* [1992] IRLR 423, ECJ.
127 *Hammersmith and Queen Charlotte's Special Health Authority v Cato* [1987] IRLR 483, EAT; *Secretary of State for Scotland and Greater Glasgow Health Board v Wright and Hannah* [1991] IRLR 187, SEAT.

- contractual and statutory sick pay;[128]
- maternity pay;[129]
- compensation for unfair dismissal;[130]
- any other payments made, directly or indirectly, by the employer as a result of the employee's employment;
- any other terms of the contract, not just pay. For example, a dispute relating to a contractual bonus must be brought under EPA 1970 (see para 1.14 onwards), whereas issues relating to non-contractual bonuses are governed by the SDA 1975 (see paras 2.108 onwards and 5.83 onwards).

2.100   The Pensions Act and Occupational Pension Schemes (Equal Treatment) Regulations 1995[131] provides that men and women doing equal work are entitled to equality in pensions. This is enforceable by a claim under the EPA 1970. This is outside the scope of this book but see para 5.112 onwards for treatment of pensions during maternity leave.

Who is protected under the EPA 1970?

2.101   All workers (irrespective of age and length of service) who are employed at an establishment in United Kingdom are covered, including employees, the self-employed and contract workers.[132] The definition is the same as under the SDA 1975 (see para 2.9 onwards).[133] Workers previously excluded are now protected, including:

- House of Commons and House of Lords staff;[134]
- armed forces personnel[135] (however, a complainant must usually first use the internal service redress procedures);
- all public employees including those in Crown employment;[136]
- office holders.[137]

---

128   *Rinner-Kuhn v FWW Spezial-Gegaudereinigung GmbH* [1989] IRLR 493, ECJ; *HK (acting on behalf of Hoj Pederson) v Faellesforeningen for Fanmarks Brugsforeninger (Acting on behalf of Kvickly Skive)* [1999] IRLR 55, ECJ.
129   *Gillespie v Northern Health and Social Services Board* [1996] IRLR 214, ECJ.
130   *R v Secretary of State for Employment ex p Seymour Smith* [1999] IRLR 253, ECJ.
131   SI No 3183.
132   EPA 1970 s1(1).
133   SDA 1975 s82(1).
134   EPA 1970 s1(10A), (10B).
135   Armed Forces Act 1996 (Commencement No.3 and Transitional Provisions) Order 1997 SI No 2164 which repealed EPA 1970 s1(9) and inserted s7A. The SDA 1975 also applies (see para 2.9). The ERA 1996 does not (see para 1.31).
136   EPA 1970 s1(8)(a), (b).
137   EPA 1970 ss6A–6C as from 1 October 2005.

Exceptions

2.102 Workers employed at establishments outside United Kingdom[138] (the exception is the same as under the SDA 1975) (see para 2.23);

- special provisions apply to employment on ships, hovercraft and aircraft[139] (this is the same as under the SDA 1975) (see para 1.31);
- illegal contracts though this will depend on the nature of the illegality. An employee may still complain of discrimination where the contract is tainted by illegality as the claim is not based on the contract of employment; however, the position may be different if the employee is actively involved in the illegality so that the claim is inextricably bound up with the illegality[140] (see para 2.23);
- special treatment given to women in connection with pregnancy or childbirth;[141]
- contractual terms affected by laws regulating the employment of women (see EPA 1970 s6(1)(a)); this is largely obsolete.

When can an equal pay claim be made by a worker who is pregnant or on maternity leave?

2.103 A pregnant worker can make a claim under the EPA 1970 (and/or article 141) if she receives lower pay or other contractual terms for a reason related to her pregnancy. In *Alabaster v Barclays Bank plc (No 2)*[142] the Court of Appeal held that in order to give effect to EC law, it was appropriate to disapply those parts of section 1 of the EPA 1970 which impose a requirement for a male comparator. Thus, where a claim is made under the EPA 1970 and this relates to pregnancy or maternity leave, there is no need for the claimant to show that a male comparator was paid more. It is sufficient to show that there was less favourable treatment and it was on grounds of pregnancy or maternity leave. The approach should be that set out in *Webb v EMO Air Cargo (UK) Ltd (No 2)* where it was held that any less favourable treatment related to pregnancy is automatically sex

---

138 SDA 1975 s10; EPA 1970 s1(1), (12).
139 SDA 1975 s10(2); this applies to both the SDA 1975 and EPA 1970 s1.
140 *Hall v Wooston Leisure Ltd* [2000] IRLR 578, CA.
141 EPA 1970 s6(1); see also provisions of section 1(2)(d)–(f) as from 1 October 2005.
142 [2005] IRLR 576, CA.

discrimination without the need to rely on a male comparator (see para 2.42 onwards).

2.104   For example, in *Hoj Pedersen*[143] the ECJ held that it was a breach of article 141 and the EPD to deprive a woman of her full pay when she has pregnancy-related sickness prior to going on maternity leave, when a worker (with non pregnancy-related sickness) was entitled to sick pay (see para 3.125). The position would be different if other workers in a similar situation would not receive sick pay. In *North Western Health Board v McKenna*[144] the ECJ held that it was not a breach of EU law for a sick pay scheme to treat women off work with a pregnancy-related illness in the same way as employees with an illness that is unrelated to pregnancy, so long as the amount of payment made is not so low as to undermine the objective of protecting pregnant workers (see chapter 3).

2.105   It is also a breach of article 141 to deny a woman the benefit of a pay rise which she receives at any time prior to her leave and up to the end of the paid part of her leave (see *Alabaster* para 5.74). This must be reflected in her pay (before leave) and earnings-related statutory maternity pay (during leave).[145]

2.106   On the other hand, a woman is not entitled to pay during her maternity leave. This is governed by the PWD which simply provides for an 'adequate allowance'. In *Gillespie* the ECJ held that women taking maternity leave are in a special position, which requires them to be afforded special protection, but which is not comparable with that of a man or a woman actually at work (see para 5.39 onwards). Therefore it is not contrary to either the EPA 1970 nor to the PWD not to pay full pay during leave. The position with bonuses is covered at para 2.108 and chapter 5.

2.107   Similarly, it is not discrimination against men to make a lump sum payment to female workers when they return from maternity leave, and not to men who become fathers (see para 5.94).[146]

143   *Handels-og Kontorfunktionaerernes Forbund I Danmark acting on behalf of Hoj Pederson v Faellesforeningen for Danmarks Brugsforeninger acting on behalf of Kvickly Skive* [1999] IRLR 55, ECJ.
144   [2005] IRLR 895.
145   *Gillespie v Northern Health and Social Services Board* [1996] IRLR 214, ECJ and *Alabaster v Woolwich plc* [2000] IRLR 754.
146   *Abdoulaye v Regie Nationale des Usine Renault* [1999] IRLR 811, ECJ.

Provisions relating to pay rises and bonuses in the EPA 1970

2.108 There are special provisions in the EPA 1970 dealing with pay rises and bonuses. These provide:

a) Where a term of a woman's contract relating to contractual maternity-related pay provides for such pay to be calculated by reference to her pay at a certain date[147] then any increase in pay, between that date up to the end of maternity leave, must be reflected in her contractual maternity related pay. This would not apply if she is receiving full pay, which includes the benefit of her pay rise, as this would be the same as she would have received if she had been at work.[148]

b) An employee is entitled to the benefit of a bonus in respect of her compulsory leave period of maternity leave and must be paid it even if it falls to be paid during a later part of her maternity leave.[149] Any pay or bonus in respect of a period prior to the woman's maternity leave must be paid as if she had not taken maternity leave and must be paid it even if it falls to be paid during a later part of her maternity leave.

c) Any pay or bonus in respect of the period after the woman returns to work must be paid at the same time as if she had not been on maternity leave.[150]

d) Any pay increase which the woman would have received if she had not been on maternity leave must be paid to her on her return. Thus if employees have had a pay rise while she was on leave, she must benefit fully from that pay rise when she returns.[151]

2.109 This means that any bonus in respect of the period of leave after the compulsory maternity leave period is not payable under EPA 1970 and this was confirmed by the Court of Session in *Hoyland v Asda Stores Ltd.*[152] However, it may be that EPA 1970 has again not given full effect to ECJ case-law. In *Lewen v Denda*[153] the ECJ left open the possibility that some bonuses that fell to be paid during maternity or

---

147 Which is usually the same date used for statutory maternity pay.
148 EPA 1970 s1(2)(d), (5A), (5B).
149 EPA 1970 s1(2)(e).
150 EPA 1970 s1(2)(e), s1(2)(f), (5A), (5B).
151 EPA 1970 s1(2)(f), (5A), (5B).
152 [2005] IRLR 438.
153 [2000] IRLR 67, ECJ.

parental leave and after the compulsory maternity leave period should be paid in full. In *Lewen*, as in *Hoyland*, however, the ECJ did not think that the full bonus was payable (see para 5.83 onwards for a more detailed discussion).

2.110   Chapters 16 and 17 cover tribunal procedure, including time limits and the SDA 1975 questionnaire, and chapter 18 covers remedies for sex discrimination.

CHAPTER 3

Rights before birth and health and safety protection

Key points

- Employers have general duties to protect the health and safety of workers, including the common law duty of care and a statutory duty under the Health and Safety at Work Act (HSWA) 1974.
- Employers have specific duties towards pregnant women and new and breastfeeding mothers which include a duty to carry out a risk assessment to assess the risks to the health and safety of a new or expectant mother or that of her baby. If the assessment reveals a risk the employer must:
  - consider whether preventive or protective action can be taken;
  - if this would not avoid the risk, vary the woman's working conditions to avoid the risk;
  - if that is not possible, and once the employer has been informed in writing of her situation, offer the pregnant woman or new mother suitable alternative work;
  - if this is not possible, suspend her on full pay for as long as necessary to avoid the risk.
- Where a pregnant woman or new mother doing night work obtains a medical certificate stating that she should avoid such work, the employer must offer suitable available work or suspend her on full pay.
- All pregnant women are entitled to reasonable paid time off for antenatal classes, which includes relaxation classes.
- It is unlawful to dismiss a woman for a reason connected with her pregnancy.
- Any less favourable treatment of a woman because she is absent from work as a result of her pregnancy is unlawful.
- Any less favourable treatment of a woman because she is pregnant will be sex discrimination.
- The exclusion of pregnancy-related sickness from a contractual sick pay scheme is unlawful.

Background and statutory framework

3.1   There is very strong protection for pregnant workers against discrimination. This protection comes mainly from European directives and case-law. The aim of the legislation, which was prompted by the European Pregnant Workers Directive (PWD), is to ensure that:

- an employee and her baby are protected against health and safety risks by getting adequate care and protection from risks during the pregnancy;
- she and her baby do not suffer distress or poverty as a result of dismissal; and
- she is not forced into having an abortion because she fears dismissal (see also para 15.50).

3.2 The preamble to the PWD states:

> . . . pregnant workers, workers who have recently given birth or who are breastfeeding must be considered a specific risk group in many respects, and measures must be taken with regard to their safety and health . . .
> . . . the risk of dismissal for reasons associated with their condition may have harmful effects on the physical and mental state of pregnant workers, workers who have recently given birth or who are breastfeeding; . . . provision should be made for such dismissal to be prohibited.

3.3 This chapter summarises:

- employers' duties to protect the health and safety of pregnant employees and new mothers;
- pregnant employees' entitlement to reasonable paid time off for antenatal care;
- issues relating to pregnancy-related sickness;
- other less favourable treatment of pregnant workers.

Pregnancy-related dismissal is covered in detail in chapter 15.

3.4 Any unfavourable treatment of a worker because of her pregnancy, including pregnancy-related sickness, will be unlawful discrimination, without the need to show that she has been treated less favourably than a comparable man (see chapter 2).

Health and safety

Background

The importance in European law of health and safety protection for workers

3.5   A key element of the protection offered under the social provisions of the European Treaty of Rome is the 'improvement in particular of the working environment to protect workers' health and safety'.[1] This commitment to improve health and safety measures resulted in the PWD.[2] This Directive 'on the introduction of measures to encourage improvements in the safety and health of pregnant workers and workers who have recently given birth or are breastfeeding' places health and safety protection at the very centre of the protective regime for pregnant women and new mothers. Far from treating health and safety as an afterthought, employers must take their responsibilities in this area very seriously and must remember that the primary responsibility for health and safety protection rests with them and not with the individual woman. The European Commission's health and safety guidelines are in appendix D. These have to a large extent been adopted by the Health & Safety Executive ('the HSE') in their guidance to employees and employers.[3]

3.6   The specific health and safety provisions in the PWD were implemented into UK law by (a) the Management of Health and Safety at Work Regulations (MHSW Regs) 1999[3a] and (b) the Employment Rights Act (ERA) 1996.[4]

3.7   The preamble to the PWD demonstrates its important relationship with the Equal Treatment Directive (ETD), saying that 'the protection of the safety and health of pregnant workers . . . should not treat women on the labour market unfavourably nor work to the detriment of Directives concerning equal treatment for men and women'. The PWD has been incorporated into the Recast Directive 2006/54/EC, 5 July 2006. It is to be implemented by August 2008.

---

1   Treaty of Rome article 137.
2   92/85/EEC.
3   See note 28 below.
3a   1999 SI No 3242. A full copy can be found on the HMSO website: www.hmso.gov.uk/si/si1999/19993242.htm.
4   ERA 1996 ss66–70.

A statutory framework and common law duties

3.8 An employer[5] has both general duties to protect the health and safety of all workers and specific duties towards pregnant women and new mothers. These are set out below.

Employer's general duty of care to the employee and her child

3.9 Employers are under a general duty (both in tort and through an implied term in employees' contracts) to take reasonable care for the health and safety of their workers. This is an implied contractual term in every contract. Workers who are injured as a result of their employer's breach of this duty can sue for damages in the county court or High Court.

3.10 Where an employer is in breach of its duty of care towards a pregnant worker (whether statutory or common law duty) and as a result her child is born with a disability, the child can bring an action for damages against the employer under Congenital Disabilities (Civil Liability) Act (CDA) 1976 s1.

A general statutory duty to protect the health and safety of workers

3.11 Employers have a statutory duty, under the HSWA 1974[6] and the MHSW Regs 1999, to 'ensure so far as is reasonably practicable' the health, safety and welfare at work of their employees. This includes women of childbearing age. The duty extends to those who are not employees but who may be affected by the way the employer runs the workplace, for example agency workers. Enforcement is by the HSE or the local authority.[7] In summary, the duty is to take reasonable care to lay down safe systems of work, to provide a safe place of work, to provide safe plant and equipment and a safe working environment.

Specific duties towards women of childbearing age under the MHSW Regs 1999[8]

3.12 The MHSW Regs 1999 set out the steps that an employer must take

---

5 The term 'employer' is used in the sense of 'the person who engages the services of the worker'. Exactly who is covered by health and safety protection is dealt with below.
6 HSWA 1974 s2(1).
7 HSWA 1974 s18; see para 4.73.
8 See note 3 above.

where there are women of childbearing age at work and in relation to new mothers or pregnant workers, see para 3.18 onwards.[9]

3.13   Other regulations set out restrictions on when a woman may return to work after having a baby (see paras 3.72 and 4.63). The MHSW Regs 1999 can apply to specified activities and premises outside Great Britain.[10]

The Workplace (Health, Safety and Welfare) Regulations 1992[11]

3.14   These require that the workplace should provide 'suitable rest facilities for pregnant women and nursing mothers'. This might include a bed or sofa of an appropriate size on which a pregnant woman can rest.

Duties under the ERA 1996 and the MHSW Regs 1999

3.15   The MHSW Regs 1999 set out the duties to carry out a risk assessment and take specified preventative action. The ERA 1996[12] imposes an obligation on the employer to pay an employee her full pay if she is suspended from work for health and safety reasons, and a duty to offer any suitable alternative work first before suspending. The employer's duties under the ERA 1996 and MHSW Regs 1999 are summarised below. A breach of the implied contractual term to provide a safe workplace or a breach of the duties under the ERA 1996 or MHSW Regs 1999 could lead to a claim by an employee for constructive dismissal and/or sex discrimination (see para 18.23 onwards).

3.16   In some circumstances (set out in ERA 1996 s100) – for example, where there is a health and safety danger – the dismissal of an employee who takes preventative action or refuses to work, will be automatically unfair (see para 3.87).[13]

Who is protected and who is excluded?

3.17   The table below summarises the position.

9   MHSW Regs 1999 regs 3, 16.
10   MHSW Regs 1999 reg 23.
11   SI No 3004.
12   ERA 1996 ss66–70.
13   ERA ss95 and 100.

Who?	Protection	Legislation
All new and expectant mothers and their babies, eg, employees, agency workers	• Common law duty of care • Right to risk assessment and general steps to protect health and safety	• HSWA 1974 and MHSW Regs 1999 reg 16(1)
'Employees' only (ERA 1996 definition)	All the above, plus: • implied term in contract • right not to be dismissed for a health and safety reason; • right to be offered suitable alternative work • right to be suspended from work on full pay	• ERA 1976 s100 • MHSW Regs 1999 reg 16(2) and ERA 1996 s67 • MHSW Regs 1999 reg 16(3) and ERA 1996 s68
A child of the worker or employee	• Right to sue in respect of a disability • Right to risk assessment and general steps to protect health and safety	• CDA 1976 • MHSW Regs 1999 reg 16(1)
Master and crew of a sea-going ship	• Common law duty of care • No protection in respect of shipboard activities from MHSW Regs 1999 but protection under merchant shipping legislation	• MHSW Regs 1999 reg 2 • Merchant Shipping and Fishing Vessels (Health and Safety at Work) Regulations 1997 SI No 2962

Protection for pregnant women and new mothers

3.18 The four steps prescribed in the MHSW Regs 1999 are set out below.

HEALTH AND SAFETY FOR WOMEN OF CHILDBEARING
AGE: THE FOUR STEPS

Step 1: Carry out a risk assessment, take any necessary steps to
avoid or reduce the risk and inform the employees of what
risks exist and what measures are being taken to deal with
them.

Step 2: Once an employee has notified her employer in writing of
her pregnancy, the fact that she has given birth within the
last six months or is breastfeeding and supplied proof if
requested,[14] if it is reasonable to do so, alter working conditions or hours of work.[15]

Step 3: If the risk cannot be avoided that way, or where a doctor or
midwife recommends that an employee should not work
at night,[16] offer suitable alternative work.[17]

Step 4: If there is no available alternative work, suspend on full
pay.[18]

Step 1: The risk assessment

3.19   Employers have a general duty to safeguard health and safety.[19] The
aim of the risk assessment is to identify the protective or preventive
measures necessary to ensure health and safety of mothers and
children.

When must a risk assessment be carried out?

3.20   A risk assessment must be carried out where there are women of
childbearing age in the workplace and the work is of a kind which
could involve risk, by reason of her condition, to a new or expectant
mother or to her baby. A 'new or expectant mother' is an employee
who is pregnant, who has given birth within the previous six months,
or who is breastfeeding (even if breastfeeding lasts for longer than six

14   MHSW Regs 1999 reg 18.
15   MHSW Regs 1999 reg 16(2).
16   MHSW Regs 1999 reg 17.
17   ERA 1996 s67.
18   MHSW Regs 1999 reg 16(3) and ERA 1996 s68.
19   MHSW Regs 1999 reg 3(1).

months). This includes women whose babies have died or who have been stillborn.[20]

3.21   The obligation to carry out this general risk assessment arises not because the employer is aware of any particular pregnancy but simply because of there being women of child bearing age in the workforce. Once the employer has been told in writing that a woman is pregnant, the duty to carry out a specific risk assessment applies to that particular individual (see Step 2).[21] Both types of risk assessment must assess any general risk or risk specific to an individual and take the necessary steps to remove or reduce the risk.[22] The duty to assess risks and review the risk assessment never ends.

3.22   In *Day v T Pickles Farms Ltd*[23] the Employment Appeal Tribunal (EAT) confirmed that the duty to have a risk assessment in place applies irrespective of whether there actually is a new or expectant mother working in the establishment.[24] Mrs Day, who was of child-bearing age, was an assistant in a sandwich shop where food was cooked and no risk assessment had been carried out. She began to suffer from severe morning sickness which was made worse by the smell of food cooking and by having to handle food in the shop. The EAT said that this might have been avoided if a risk assessment had been in place, which it should have been at the start of Mrs Day's employment at the very latest. The EAT also commented that a failure to carry out a risk assessment can amount to a detriment entitling the claimant to make a successful sex discrimination claim.

3.23   In *Hardman v Mallon*[25] the claimant was employed as a care assistant and her job involved lifting residents. She produced a medical certificate stating that she needed to avoid heavy lifting but she was only offered a cleaner's job. The EAT held that the employer discriminated when it failed to carry out a risk assessment and it was

---

20 MHSW Regs 1999 reg 1(2). 'Given birth' means delivered a living child or after the 24th week of pregnancy a stillborn child.
21 As the EAT said in *Page v Gala Leisure & others* EAT 1398/99 there are two types of risk assessment when the employer employs women of childbearing age. The first is the general duty to assess risk under MHSW Regs 1999 regs 3(1) and 16(1). The second type arises when an employee gives notice to the employer in writing of being pregnant, of having given birth within the last six months or of breastfeeding (regs 16 and 17).
22 MHSW Regs 1999 reg 16(1).
23 [1999] IRLR 217, EAT.
24 MHSW Regs 1999 reg 16 appears to have improved upon the protection offered by the PWD.
25 [2002] IRLR 516, EAT.

no defence that the employer had not produced risk assessments in respect of any of their employees regardless of their sex. The EAT held that a failure to carry out a risk assessment in respect of a pregnant woman is sex discrimination as it is one way in which a woman's biological condition during and after pregnancy is given special protection in accordance with the requirements of the PWD and the obligations of the MHSW Regs 1999.

In *Brocklebank v Silveira*, UKEAT/0571/05/MAA, 11 January 2006 the end-user, ie the prospective employer, asked the employment agency to be responsible for carrying out a risk assessment but this was not done and the claimant was not appointed. She claimed that the failure of the agency to assist her in obtaining employment was sex discrimination. The EAT upheld the tribunal's decision that the failure to carry out the assessment was discrimination.

What does the risk assessment have to consider?

3.24   The general risk assessment must identify hazards which could pose a health and/or safety risk to new or expectant mothers. The risk can come from any processes or working conditions, or physical, biological or chemical agents including those set out in Annexes I and II to the PWD (see below).[26] In order for there to be a workplace risk from any infectious or contagious disease (eg, German measles) the risk must be such that it is greater at work than it would be outside the workplace.[27]

Pregnant Workers Directive (92/85/EEC)

Annex I – Non-exhaustive list of agents, processes and working conditions regarded as posing a potential risk

A. Agents

1. *Physical agents* where these are regarded as agents causing foetal lesions and/or likely to disrupt placental attachment, and in particular:

(a) shocks, vibration or movement;
(b) ionising radiation;

---

26   MHSW Regs 1999 reg 16(1)(b).
27   MHSW Regs 1999 reg 16(4).

(c) non-ionising radiation;

(d) extremes of cold or heat;

(e) movements and postures, travelling – either inside or outside the establishment – mental and physical fatigue and other physical burdens connected with the activity of the worker.

2. *Biological agents*

Set out in the EC Biological Agents Directive No 90/679, in so far as it is known that these agents or therapeutic measures necessitated by such agents endanger the health of pregnant women and the unborn child and in so far as they do not appear in Annex II.

3. *Chemical agents*

So far as they do not appear in Annex II:

(a) substances listed in the Carcinogens at Work Directive No 90/394

(b) mercury and derivatives

(c) antimitotic drugs

(d) carbon monoxide

(e) chemical agents of known and dangerous percutaneous absorption.

B. Processes

Industrial process listed in the Carcinogens at Work Directive.

C. Working conditions

Underground mining work.

Annex II – Non-exhaustive list of agents, processes and working conditions to which the PWD prohibits exposure

A. Pregnant workers

1. *Agents*

(a) Physical agents. Work in hyperbaric atmosphere eg pressurised enclosures and underwater diving.

(b) Biological agents. Toxiplasma, rubella virus – unless the pregnant workers are proved to be adequately protected against such agents by immunisation.

(c) Chemical agents. Lead and lead derivatives in so far as these agents are capable of being absorbed by the human organism.

2. *Working conditions*
Underground mining work.

B. Workers who are breastfeeding

1. *Agents*

(a) *Chemical agents.* Lead and lead derivatives in so far as these agents are capable of being absorbed by the human organism.

2. *Working conditions*
Underground mining work.

General risk assessment

3.25   In carrying out the general risk assessment an employer must consider the following:

- *Current knowledge about hazards.* The list in the PWD is the starting point and the HSE has a range of advisory booklets including *New and Expectant Mothers at Work – a guide for employers.*[28] Employers also need to bear in mind the fact that hazards occur before as well as during pregnancy and a pregnant woman is most vulnerable during early pregnancy when she may not be aware she is pregnant. Preventative measures may need to be taken in respect of women of childbearing age. Unfortunately, there is a need for much more research before the full effect of certain risks is known. For example, it is still not clear exactly what are the risks from heavy lifting in early pregnancy. See also the guidelines drawn up by the European Commission at appendix D.
- *The extent of the risk.* The more serious the hazard, the more careful the employer must be and the more precautions s/he must take.
- *The assessment must be reviewed* if there is reason to suspect that it is no longer valid or there is significant change in the matters to which it relates.[29] It must also be reviewed once the employer knows a particular employee is pregnant (see para 3.21).

---

28   ISBN 0717625834 £9.50 from the HSE. They also produce a 'Guide for new and expectant mothers who work', INDG373; a guide on 'Infection risks to new and expectant mothers in the workplace' ISBN 0717613607, £10.50 and a 'Guide for health professionals'. For further information on possible risks call the health and safety InfoLine on 0845 345 0055 or look on their website www.hse.gov.uk and search 'new and expectant mothers'.

29   MHSW Regs 1999 reg 3(3).

Duty to record findings of assessment

3.26   Where an employer employs five or more employees, it must record the significant findings of the assessment and note any groups of employees who have been identified as especially at risk.[30]

Necessary steps to prevent or avoid the risk following a general risk assessment

3.27   The employer has a duty to make appropriate arrangements, having regard to the nature of its activities and the size of its business, for the effective planning, organisation, control, monitoring and review of the preventive and protective measures required by statute. Such measures, if effective, would allow all those in the workplace to continue working without any further action being taken until such time as an employee informs her employer of her pregnancy, and not even then if sufficient steps have already been taken to protect from risk. For example, if the only risk identified was one to posture arising from the design of a typist's chair, and if the chair had already been replaced by a better one before she became pregnant, there would be no need to take further action. If, however, the woman was a deep-sea diver, probably no adaptations could be made to protect her from risk as if she became pregnant she would need to be moved to other work. Until she is pregnant her employer should allow her to continue to work but should inform her of the risks and make it clear that she should not continue diving if pregnant.

3.28   The MHSW Regs 1999 set out the general principles of prevention to be applied.[31] They include:

- avoiding risks;
- evaluating the risks which cannot be avoided;
- adapting the work to the individual, especially as regards the design of workplaces, choice of equipment and the choice of working and production methods to suit the individual;
- developing a coherent overall prevention policy which covers technology, organisation of work, working conditions, social relationships etc;
- giving appropriate instructions to employees.

---

30 MHSW Regs 1999 reg 3(6).
31 MHSW Regs 1999 reg 4 and Sch 1.

This last point means, for example, that employees who are not pregnant and not facing a risk from too much lifting may have to be instructed to take on more lifting work in order that a pregnant woman could do less. Of course the health and safety of nonpregnant employees would also have to be protected.

3.29   Guidance on general health and safety risks which must be considered, such as the Manual Handling Regulations, is also available from the HSE.

3.30   An employer must strike a balance between the need to protect potentially pregnant employees as far as possible and the importance of not preventing women for working in certain roles because they might be at risk if pregnant. To prevent a woman doing a particular job because she might get pregnant would be unlawful sex discrimination.

Information for employees of what risks exist and what measures are being taken to deal with them

3.31   The employer must provide its employees with comprehensible and relevant information on the risks to their health and safety identified by the assessment. This includes any preventive and protective measures taken. The information must be capable of being understood and account should be taken of an employee's training, knowledge and experience. Special consideration should be given to employees with language difficulties.[32]

Step 2: The duty to alter working conditions or hours of work and specific duties to individual employees who are pregnant or new mothers

The need for an ongoing risk assessment for a pregnant employee

3.32   Once the employee notifies the employer of her pregnancy it must consider any specific health and safety risks she may suffer. The HSE's advisory leaflet[33] says that: 'advice to a pregnant woman that she should or should not continue to work on a particular job

---

32   MHSW Regs 1999 reg 10 and see paras 53–56 of the approved code of practice.
33   *Occupational Health Aspects of Pregnancy*, HSE.

depends upon a mixture of social, medical and occupational factors which can only be assessed on a case-by-case basis. Moreover, since pregnancy is a dynamic state these factors probably vary in their impact throughout its course. Continual assessment is therefore suggested in cases where difficulties are anticipated.' Thus, for example, a woman with a back problem may become even more vulnerable in the later stages of pregnancy and a woman who does not have a back problem at all in the early stages of her pregnancy may develop one as her pregnancy progresses.

Duty to notify employer of pregnancy

3.33　The duties set out below to alter the woman's working conditions or hours of work and, if this is not possible, to suspend her on full pay, only apply where the employee has notified the employer in writing of her pregnancy or the fact that she has given birth in the previous six months, or is breastfeeding.[34]

3.34　　In *Day v T Pickles Farms Ltd*[35] the EAT concluded that the employer had known of Mrs Day's pregnancy because she had submitted sick notes which indicated that her illness was pregnancy-related. Several of her sick notes had said that she was suffering from 'hyperemesis gravidarum' but the use of Latin did not deter the EAT from concluding that the definition (of 'severe vomiting associated with pregnancy') in *Black's Medical Dictionary* 'makes it quite plain that it relates, and it relates only, to a condition of pregnancy'!

3.35　　Lindsay J observed that the employment tribunal (ET), 'had it looked at the issue not as a matter of burden of proof but as a matter of the common-sense assessment of the facts, could not have concluded other than that written notice had been given or, at any rate, technically looking at it as a matter of burden, that the burden had switched to the employer to show that that was not the case'.

3.36　　If the employer makes a written request that the employee provide the employer with a certificate from a doctor or midwife confirming that she is pregnant, the employee must produce this within a reasonable time of the request.[36] If she fails to do so the employer is not obliged to maintain the actions described below at para 3.43 onwards. In addition, the obligations cease once the employer knows that the

---

34　MHSW Regs 1999 reg 18(1).
35　[1999] IRLR 217 EAT.
36　MHSW Regs 1999 reg 18(2)(a).

woman is no longer a new or expectant mother or if the employer cannot establish whether she remains a new or expectant mother.[37]

Common risks for pregnant women

3.37   Common risks identified by the PWD and by the HSE in its guidance and which are likely to occur in office or shop-based jobs as well as in more obviously dangerous environments, are as follows:

- Lifting/carrying of heavy loads
- Standing or sitting for long lengths of time (eg, too much standing can cause varicose veins and haemorrhoids)
- Exposure to infectious diseases and lead
- Work-related stress
- Long working hours
- Lone working
- Working at heights
- Postures in awkward spaces and workstations
- Cigarette smoke from other people at work
- Vibration
- Excessive noise
- Radiation (covered by specific legislation)
- Chemical handling (drugs or specific chemicals such as pesticides, lead etc)
- Extreme temperatures
- Too much travelling (which may lead to tiredness)
- Inadequate facilities (including rest rooms)

Does the risk come from work or from the pregnancy?

3.38   In some cases it will be hard to tell whether the risk – which may be a risk to health as much as to safety – arises from a process, working condition or 'agent' at work or simply from the fact that a woman is pregnant. For example, there will be times in pregnancy when the woman may be very tired and is not able to be as productive at work.[38] If there is no particular working condition which has caused or contributed to the fatigue, she will not fall within the protection of health

---

37 MHSW Regs 1999 reg 18(2)(b) and (c).
38 Her pay and bonus should not be reduced if she is less productive as this would be sex discrimination (see chapter 2).

and safety legislation. However, she must not be disadvantaged for being less productive (for example, in relation to her pay or bonus).

3.39   Similarly, if she suffers from morning sickness and her main difficulty is coping with the long trip to work on the train in the morning, there will be no risk for which the employer has responsibility. The woman would probably have either to negotiate different working hours with her employer to avoid the rush hours or take sick leave, although she might be able to argue that a refusal to change her working hours was indirect sex discrimination (see chapter 13). It would be different if she had to do excessive travelling for work as this would be the employer's responsibility, for which adjustments should be made.

3.40   Where, however, a woman such as Mrs Day[39] is prone to morning sickness and faces strong cooking smells at work which appear to increase her nausea, or if she works very early shifts, her working conditions may be affecting her health and the employer should take the necessary steps to avoid the risk. The employer's duty is to protect the health as well as the safety of the employee.

Disagreement over the findings of the risk assessment

3.41   If an employer has carried out a risk assessment and finds there to be no risk but the woman disagrees, she may have to decide whether to remove herself from the workplace. This is risky as she faces being disciplined for being absent without leave and she should try and reach a compromise with her employer. Her doctor may be able to advise and may be willing to write to the employer with appropriate advice on how to deal with the risk. Alternatively the doctor might issue a sick note if the woman has become unwell due to stress or physical symptoms.[40] Large employers have occupational health departments to advise in such cases, but many small employers may rely on the guidance that a woman can produce for them from her doctor or they could bring in a freelance occupational health consultant to advise. In either case, an employer may need to revise the risk assessment in the light of the medical information. The risk, for example from lifting, faced by a woman with a history of miscarriage may be very different from that faced by a woman with no such history. An employee may be unreasonable or wrong in her belief

39 See para 3.22 above.
40 See the guidance for health professionals on the HSE website.

that a risk exists. If she were to cease working because of her concern about a risk then whether or not any disciplinary action would be unlawful or discriminatory is likely to depend on whether the employer has carried out a proper risk assessment and taken appropriate action. It would not be advisable for a woman to resign in these circumstances unless she felt she had no alternative. She should try to resolve the problem with the help of her GP, a health expert and through internal grievance procedures.

3.42   If an employer refuses to agree that a risk exists, where no proper assessment has been carried out, or ignores a risk that has been identified by the assessment, a woman who resigns or who is dismissed or disciplined as a result of her absence from work may well have a claim for sex discrimination, detriment and 'automatically' unfair dismissal (see para 3.57 and chapter 15).[41]

The duty to alter working conditions or hours of work

3.43   Once an assessment has revealed a risk, which in itself cannot be prevented, or avoided, the employer must, 'if it is reasonable to do so, and would avoid such risks, alter her working conditions or hours of work'.[42] Such an alteration may be effective even where there is an absolute prohibition on the woman working with particular risks. If the woman's working conditions or hours are altered, she should continue to receive the same pay and benefits.

> EXAMPLE: Joy is a pregnant sales assistant. She finds standing for long periods on the sales floor exhausting. Following a risk assessment, her employers decide that although they could offer her a chair, this might affect sales, but what they can do is alter her working patterns so that instead of working one long shift on the sales floor before going into the office to do her paperwork at the end of the day, they will ask her to alternate between short periods of standing and short periods of office work all day.

3.44   Whether it is reasonable to alter working conditions should take account of what the woman needs to protect the health and safety of her and her baby and whether it is reasonable for the employer to make the adjustments. Thus, it would not be reasonable to change

---

41 See, in particular, *New Southern Railway Ltd v Quinn* [2006] IRLR 266.
42 MHSW Regs 1999 reg 16(2) and PWD article 5(1).

the woman's hours if that made it impossible for her to continue working.

> EXAMPLE: Another option for Joy's employers would be to adjust her working hours so that she works 9 to 5 rather than 10 to 6 because the first hour is usually quiet and she could sit down. This is not possible because she has to drop a child off at school in the morning before coming into work and so the alteration would not be reasonable and may be indirect sex discrimination.

3.45 A health professional can help point the employer in the right direction by writing advice on how to deal with the risk on the Med 3 (usually called the 'sick note') and, rather than signing a woman off sick, certifying her as fit to work subject to the advice being followed.[43] From a financial point of view it is usually important to avoid being signed off sick when this is not necessary as it will affect pay and, depending when the absence occurs, entitlement to statutory maternity pay (SMP) (see para 6.34 onwards).

Step 3: If the risk cannot be avoided by altering working conditions or hours of work, the employer must offer suitable alternative work

3.46 If it is not possible to alter an employee's working conditions or hours of work, her employer must offer the woman suitable alternative work where this is available. The work must be:

- of a kind which is both suitable and appropriate for her to do in the circumstances; and
- where the terms and conditions are not substantially less favourable to her than her existing terms and conditions. In other words, slight differences in the work are acceptable so long as they do not make the new role 'substantially less favourable'.[44]

---

43 The HSE has advice to health professionals available on their website: www.hse.gov.uk/pubns/indg373hp.pdf.
44 ERA 1996 s67.

3.47   Account should be taken of the following:

- status or grade;
- pay and other remuneration or payments in kind;
- working conditions, hours of work, location;
- travelling time to work.

3.48   The employee's condition should be taken into account, so it may be unreasonable to expect her to travel further or work anti-social hours even though the job offered is in every other respect 'suitable'. To this extent at least, the test may be different from the test applied in redundancy situations.

Alternative work which is not 'suitable'

3.49   In *British Airways v Moore and Botterill*[45] the EAT upheld the ET decision that pregnant cabin crew, who were transferred to ground work following a risk assessment, had not been offered suitable alternative work under ERA 1996 s67(2) as they were given only their basic pay and not their flying allowances. The EAT concluded that the difference in pay meant that the ground-based job was substantially less favourable than their normal job so that it was not suitable.

3.50   Where the work offered is not suitable, the woman must be suspended and paid remuneration calculated at her normal rate.[46] Even if a woman continues to work in the *un*suitable alternative job at lower wages, she must be paid her normal remuneration since, if she is not performing the work she normally performed before the suspension, she is to be treated as if she is suspended.[47]

3.51   In *McMurray v Mytravel Airways Ltd*[48] part of the flight allowances included payment of out of pocket expenses which were only paid when the employee was away from home. The tribunal held that a pregnant employee was not entitled to be paid them when she was suspended and on ground duties. In the *British Airways* case all of the flight allowances had been remuneration and not expenses so were payable.

3.52   If a woman has been given alternative work, there is no reason why she should not continue doing this right up to the time of the birth if she is suspended she may have to start her maternity leave

---

45   [2000] IRLR 296, EAT.
46   ERA 1996 s69 and s220ff.
47   ERA 1996 s66(3)(b).
48   ET: 2305708/04.

four weeks before the expected week of childbirth (EWC) which may be earlier than planned (see para 4.17).

3.53   If the employee unreasonably refuses suitable alternative work, she will be suspended and she will forfeit her right to be paid while she is suspended.[49] Ultimately it will be up to an ET to decide whether the refusal was unreasonable.

Failure to offer suitable alternative work before suspension

3.54   Under ERA 1996 s70(4) an employee (and only an employee) can complain to an ET if she is not offered suitable alternative work. She is then entitled to such compensation as the tribunal considers just and equitable bearing in mind the employer's infringement and any loss suffered. The tribunal can award compensation for lost earnings and also injury to feelings in the same way as it can under the similarly worded ERA 1996 s49 in relation to protection from detriment.[50]

Step 4: If there is no available alternative work the employer must suspend the employee on full pay

3.55   If, and only if, there is no suitable alternative work, the MHSW Regs 1999 require the employer to suspend the employee from work on full pay for so long as is necessary to avoid the risk.[51]

The right to full pay whilst suspended

3.56   The ERA provides that an employee (and only an employee) is entitled to be paid whilst suspended if she is suspended as a result of a 'relevant' requirement or recommendation.[52] The secretary of state

---

49 ERA 1996 s68(2).

50 *Virgo Fidelis v Boyle* [2004] IRLR 268 (see para 18.139).

51 MHSW Regs 1999 reg 16(3). The PWD has similar provisions. Article 5 states that if the risk cannot be avoided by preventive measures the employer must temporarily adjust the woman's working conditions or working hours. If this is not 'technically and/or objectively feasible or cannot reasonably be required on duly substantiated grounds', the employer must take the necessary measures to move the worker concerned to another job. Failing this, she must be granted leave for the whole of the period necessary to protect her safety or health.

52 ERA 1996 s66(1) and (2).

has specified a suspension under the MHSW Regs 1999 as a suspension under a 'relevant' requirement.[53]

3.57   In *New Southern Railway v Quinn*[54] the claimant was promoted to duty station manager, following which she informed her employer she was pregnant. A risk assessment by the employers' safety strategy manager found that there were some risks, but he decided that she could continue in her post as manager. Subsequently, at the end of her probationary period, the station manager and others decided the risk to Mrs Quinn was too high (saying they would never be able to forgive themselves if anything happened to her baby) and she was returned to her previous post at a lower salary. She claimed she had suffered a detriment by reason of her pregnancy because of the reduction in her salary and failure to offer her alternative employment. She then resigned and claimed there had been an unlawful deduction from her salary. The tribunal noted the main concern was of physical assault but this was low, saying 'in reality, these managers jumped to the conclusion that the claimant could not continue in her position because of their personal feelings, and attached to it a label of health and safety concern. They did not carry out a proper or reasonable analysis of the risk assessment at any time ... She was removed from her post because of the patronising and paternalistic attitude of those managers, rather than in consequence of an appropriate analysis of the draft risk assessment'. Her claims for sex discrimination, detriment under ERA 1996 s47C, unlawful deduction and constructive dismissal were upheld.

3.58   The EAT held that the term 'avoid the risk' cannot mean the complete avoidance of all risks, but means 'reduced to its lowest possible level'. As the implementation of regulation 16 of the MHSW Regs 1999 involves the restriction on the right of a pregnant woman to carry out her normal role, thus giving rise to a potential automatic sex discrimination claim, there must be a balancing exercise. The employer must be able to show that it is necessary for health and safety reasons to treat a pregnant woman unfavourably. The EAT upheld the ET finding that when Mrs Quinn was moved from her trial post as a duty manager to her former post as a PA on lower pay when she became pregnant, she had been discriminated against.

---

53   Suspension from Work (on Maternity Grounds) Order 1994 SI No 2930 specified suspensions under MHSW Regs 1999 regs 16(3) and 17 as suspensions under a relevant requirement.
54   [2006] IRLR 266, EAT.

This was not a suspension but an act of discrimination. It was not appropriate to move her because in fact only a very low level of risk existed and in any event the same level of risk applied to her in the lower graded post so there was a fundamental flaw in the employer's case.

3.59   Not all suspensions from work are as a result of the MHSW Regs 1999 and therefore are not as a result of a relevant requirement or recommendation. For example, until the secretary of state specified a suspension under the Merchant Shipping and Fishing Vessels (Health and Safety at Work) Regulations 1997[55] as a 'relevant' requirement,[56] pregnant seafarers were excluded from full health and safety protection. However, despite the exclusion, the EAT held in *Iske v P&O Ferries (Dover) Ltd*[57] that although the employee was not entitled to the protection of the ERA 1996, she had suffered sex discrimination when she was suspended from work at sea on no pay because she was pregnant and, unlike men who were not fit for seagoing work, was not offered suitable alternative shore work. She was therefore entitled to compensation.

3.60   In *Bannigan, Petinaud and Nembhard v United Airlines*[58] the employer unsuccessfully argued in the ET that its employees were not entitled to full pay because although they had stopped working because of pregnancy, this was not as a result of a suspension under a relevant requirement but because of an agreement with their union. The union had allegedly agreed that in order to protect their health and safety, pregnant cabin crew would cease flying after the 27th week of pregnancy. The ET rejected this argument and found that there had been a suspension under ERA 1996 s66.

3.61   An employee is to be treated as suspended only as long as she continues to be employed by her employer but is not provided with work or (disregarding alternative work for the purposes of Step 3 above) does not perform the work she normally performed before her suspension.[59] In other words, if she is performing suitable alternative work she will not be treated as suspended but if, for example, she is working odd days or working in a lower paid job which is not a suitable alternative, she must be treated as suspended.

---

55   SI No 2962.
56   Suspension from Work on Maternity Grounds (Merchant Shipping and Fishing Vessels) Order 1998 SI No 587.
57   [1997] IRLR 401, EAT.
58   ET 10471, 21107, 20119/96, London (North).
59   ERA 1996 s66(3).

3.62   An employee who is suspended is entitled to be paid the same remuneration as though she was working unless she has refused suitable alternative work.[60]

Calculation of pay during suspension

3.63   An employee who is entitled to be paid will be entitled to full remuneration at the normal rate[61] until her maternity leave period begins (see paras 4.30–4.37). In the absence of any contractual provision, this is calculated in accordance with ERA 1996 s220 et seq which define a 'week's pay'. The calculation date depends on when the suspension occurs. If an employee is suspended at the end of her maternity leave so that the day before the suspension is within the employee's maternity leave period, it is the day before the beginning of the maternity leave period that is relevant. If the suspension takes place at any other time, the relevant day is the day before the suspension.[62] If an employee has a contractual right to be paid whilst suspended, she must not receive less than she would receive using the statutory calculation. She is not entitled to claim both her contractual and her statutory entitlement.[63] Expenses are probably not included in the definition of remuneration.[64]

Time limits for an ET claim relating to suspension

3.64   An employee can complain to an ET within three months of:

- her employer's failure to pay her whilst she is suspended from work; or
- the first day of the suspension from work if she is not offered suitable alternative work.

3.65   The time limit may be extended if it was not reasonably practicable for the complaint to be presented in time (see para 16.131 onwards). The statutory grievance procedure does not apply to these claims but will apply where the claim is for sex discrimination or detriment (see para 16.13 onwards).

---

60   ERA 1996 s68.
61   ERA 1996 s69.
62   ERA 1996 s225(5)(b).
63   ERA 1996 s69(3).
64   *S & U Stores v Wilkes* [1974] IRLR 283.

Rights during suspension

3.66   Whilst she is suspended, an employee's contractual and statutory rights as an employee continue.[65] A woman who suffers a detriment as a result of a suspension by, for example, being denied access to promotion or being refused a bonus or commission that is due can make a complaint to an ET that she has suffered a detriment because of her pregnancy.[66] She can also make a complaint of sex discrimination. In *Lewen v Denda*[67] the European Court of Justice (ECJ) held that periods during which a mother is prohibited from working must be taken into account when calculating the bonus payable to her for work done during the year. To fail to take these periods into account would be to discriminate against a female worker in her capacity as a worker because, had she not been pregnant, the periods of suspension would have been periods worked. This has now been incorporated in the Equal Pay Act 1970 but only in relation to compulsory maternity leave, not maternity suspension, so employees will have to rely on EC law (see para 1.21 onwards).[68]

Effect of suspension on commencement of maternity leave

3.67   A woman who is suspended in the last four weeks of her pregnancy will almost certainly be treated as absent on account of her pregnancy (see paras 4.35–4.40). She will therefore have to start her maternity leave at the beginning of the four weeks before the EWC. Her maternity pay period would start at the same time (see para 4.45).[69]

Sickness or health and safety suspension?

3.68   A woman who is experiencing a health and safety problem may not be aware of her right to health and safety protection, or her employer

65   The government spokesman said, during the debates on the Trades Union Reform and Employment Rights Act 1993, 'the employee's contract continues while she is suspended . . . Her contractual rights are maintained. No special provision for that is required.' (HC Standing Committee F, cols 430–431, 14 January 1993).
66   ERA 1996 s47C, MHSW Regs 1999 reg 19(2)(c).
67   [2000] IRLR 67 ECJ.
68   EPA 1996 s1(2)(e)(ii).
69   MPL Regs 1999 reg 6.

may have refused to suspend her. If she is off sick rather than on a health and safety suspension, she may suffer the following consequences:

- she will receive sick pay. If she does not receive contractual sick pay, statutory sick pay (SSP) is probably far lower then her weekly wage;
- if she is receiving SSP during all or part of the calculation period for SMP she may not satisfy the earnings condition for SMP so that it will be refused and she will have to fall back on maternity allowance instead (see chapters 6 and 7);
- if her sick note does not state that her illness is pregnancy-related (in which case she should not be treated less favourably as a result), and for example it just says 'stress', her sickness record will be affected and her employer may come to regard her as an unreliable employee (see para 3.118 onwards for protection from unfavourable treatment on account of pregnancy related sickness).

3.69   In *Hickey v Lucas Service UK Ltd*[70] an ET found that a woman who had been absent during her pregnancy on sick leave certified by her doctor had in fact been suspended from work due to a health and safety risk. She was therefore entitled to be paid her normal pay rather than SSP during that period. Mrs Hickey's employer had failed to carry out a risk assessment on her job as a stores person although the work involved heavy lifting and despite the fact that she and her representative had raised her concerns. Her absence was therefore clearly pregnancy-related due to a health and safety risk and the ET decided that this fell within the meaning of 'suspension on maternity grounds' set out in ERA 1996 s66.

3.70   The success of such a claim will depend on whether the absence was in fact due to health and safety reasons even if there was no actual suspension. Medical advice will be relevant. It would be difficult to argue that there was a health and safety suspension if the employer has carried out a proper health and safety risk assessment which found that there were no risks.

---

70 Bristol ET 1400979 6 May 1997.

Special provisions relating to night work

3.71   If a pregnant woman or new mother doing night work obtains a certificate from her doctor or midwife stating that it is necessary for her health and safety to avoid night work, the employer must follow Steps 3 and 4 above and consider offering her suitable alternative work where it is available. If none is available she must be suspended on full pay.[71] Thus a woman who was unable to undertake day work, because she was not available to work those hours, would be treated as suspended because no suitable alternative was available to her. Many women cannot work during the day because of their childcare responsibilities. 'Suitable' work would be work at the same level of pay as night work even if other daytime workers were paid less than night workers.[72] 'Night work' is not defined in MHSW Regs 1999 but in the Working Time Regulations a night worker is defined as working for at least three hours between 11pm and 6am. HSE guidance on pregnant workers in the catering industry says that night work of itself presents no particular risk to pregnant women.[73]

Compulsory leave after the birth

3.72   It is a criminal offence for an employer to permit an employee who is entitled to maternity leave to work within two weeks of the birth[74] (or four weeks if she works in a factory or workshop[75]). The HSE has responsibility for enforcing this.

Breastfeeding

3.73   A woman cannot postpone her return to work because she is breast-feeding, although she can ask to take some parental leave provided she gives adequate notice (see chapter 10).

3.74   There is also no power for an employer to delay a woman's return to work against her will because she is breastfeeding and a refusal to

---

71   MHSW Regs 1999 reg 17 and PWD article 7.
72   See *British Airways v Moore and Botterill*, note 55 above.
73   HSE Information sheet 19 at www.hse.gov.uk/pubns/cais19.pdf.
74   ERA 1996 s 72 and MHSW Regs 1999 reg 8.
75   Public Health Act 1936 s205 (as amended).

allow her to return may be a detriment or an unfair dismissal and discriminatory (see chapter 15).

3.75   An employer should, however, do a risk assessment to ensure that there is no health and safety risk to a mother who has given birth in the last six months or who is breastfeeding, or to her baby. The MHSW Regs 1999 impose no cut-off date after which the employer's specific responsibility for the protection of a woman who is breast-feeding ends.[76] PWD Annex II lists risks to which a breastfeeding mother must not be exposed, such as lead and underground mining work (see appendix D). There has been little research into the effect of other potential risks to breastfeeding mothers so a full range of risks is not known. A woman may want to seek advice from a health professional or information from the HSE.

Can the employer refuse to allow a woman to breastfeed on her return to work?

3.76   Many women express milk at work and a few go home in breaks or have the baby brought into work so that they can continue feeding her/him. Both arrangements are 'breastfeeding'. Medical evidence shows that generally it is advisable to breastfeed a baby and in some cases a baby's health may be put at risk if the mother does not breast-feed the baby, particularly if the baby has allergies. For example, there is a greater risk of the baby suffering from gastro-enteritis if the baby is not breastfed in the first 6 to 12 months. Many women do not breastfeed their babies at all because they are worried that they will have to stop when they return to work.

3.77   The extent to which health and safety legislation protects the pro-cess of breastfeeding rather than the product (ie, the contamination of breast milk) is debatable. There have been no cases that have estab-lished the extent of the protection available, although there is a clear obligation on the employer to provide breastfeeding workers with the facilities to rest (see para 3.14 above).

3.78   The MHSW Regs 1999 refer to the risk to a new mother or her baby from 'processes or working conditions, or physical, biological or chemical agents'. If, for example, a woman was doing a very stressful job which resulted in her supply of milk drying up or in her being unable to find the time to express, it is arguable that fatigue at work resulted in a risk to the baby and that the employer should take steps

76   See the definition in MHSW Regs 1999 reg 1.

to avoid this. On the other hand, it is rarely possible to show that a particular baby is at risk from not being breastfed. The argument would be strengthened if, for example, the baby was at risk of suffering from allergies and a doctor was recommending that the baby be breastfed exclusively for a period of time.

3.79 The PWD is clearer than the MHSW Regs 1999 in this regard. Article 5, for example, says that an employer should take steps to avoid 'an effect on . . . the breastfeeding of a worker' thus apparently envisaging the protection of the process. The European Commission's guidelines on risks include an assessment of 'hazard due to unsuitable or absent facilities', which inhibit breastfeeding. Recommended protective measures include access to a private room; secure, clean refrigerators for storing milk; and to time off to express milk or breastfeed. Whilst these guidelines will not have statutory force, they should encourage employers and ETs to apply the legislation in a way that supports breastfeeding at work (see appendix D).

3.80 Although the Workplace (Health, Safety and Welfare) Regulations 1992[77] require that the workplace should provide 'suitable rest facilities for pregnant women and nursing mothers', they do not specifically require the provision of facilities for breastfeeding. However the accompanying guidance says that the rest facilities should be near sanitary facilities and, where necessary, should include the facility to lie down. HSE guidance goes further and reflects EC guidance by saying that other facilities, such as a clean environment and a fridge for expressing and storing milk, should be provided.

Breastfeeding, indirect sex discrimination, detriment and dismissal

3.81 A refusal to allow a woman the flexibility she needs to breastfeed at work may be indirectly discriminatory where, for example, there is an unjustified provision, criterion or practice that a woman work long hours or a pattern of hours that make it impossible for her to breastfeed (see chapter 13).[78] In addition, if she suffers a detriment because she is breastfeeding, resigns or is dismissed she may have a claim

---

77 SI No 3004.
78 This argument was used successfully in *Squillaci v WS Atkins (Services) Ltd* ET 68108/94, 21 January 1997, London South.

under the ERA. The dismissal may be 'ordinarily' or automatically unfair (see chapter 15).[79]

Breach of the health and safety provisions

3.82   The sections above have dealt with claims relating to specific provisions. The table below summarises the range of causes of action and remedies available in general. A failure to protect the health and safety of a pregnant woman, a new mother, a woman who is breastfeeding or her child may lead to criminal prosecution as well as to civil proceedings in the High Court, county court or ET.

Health and safety claims in the ET: sex discrimination

3.83   A failure to carry out a specific risk assessment or to act appropriately in the face of the risks which exist will be automatic sex discrimination on the ground of pregnancy under Sex Discrimination Act (SDA) 1975 s3A if the woman suffers a detriment as a result (see chapter 2). In *Hardman v Mallon*[80] Mrs Hardman worked in a care home for frail elderly women and as a care assistant had to do heavy lifting which she was not able to continue once she became pregnant. Her employer did not do a risk assessment but offered her another job as a cleaner which she refused as it was less favourable. Her claim for failure to offer suitable alternative work under the health and safety provisions in the ERA 1996 was upheld. The EAT held that it was sex discrimination to fail to carry out a risk assessment in that situation.

3.84   SDA 1975 s2(2) (discrimination against men) states that no account shall be taken of special treatment afforded to women in connection with pregnancy and childbirth. Thus, a man cannot claim discrimination in similar circumstances.

3.85   In *Taylor v Thomas Bee Ltd*[81] the ET found that there were very serious shortcomings in the way the risk assessment had been

---

79 MPL Regs 1999 regs 19(5) and 20(4) say that a dismissal which is connected to the fact that a woman has had a baby is only automatically unfair if it occurs during maternity leave so that 'automatic' protection under the ERA 1996 may not be available although a woman may have an 'ordinary' unfair dismissal claim.
80 [2002] IRLR 516.
81 (1996) DCLD 28, No 63877/95, ET.

carried out. Thus, the instruction to a pregnant woman to continue working with cleaning materials which made her unwell was unreasonable and her dismissal when she refused to do so was unfair. In addition, the dismissal was for a reason connected with the pregnancy and so was automatically unfair and discriminatory (see para 2.34 onwards).

3.86   In *Tapp v Chief Constable of Suffolk*[82] a pregnant trainee police constable was taken off an important training course because of her pregnancy and suspended from work. This meant that she could not complete her training. The ET, upholding her sex discrimination claim, said that as a pregnant woman she had suffered a detriment because a risk assessment was not carried out. A risk assessment would have shown that it was not necessary for her to be suspended as with minor adjustments she could have carried on with the training course and successfully completed it (see also para 3.153).

3.87   In *Anderson v Belcher Food Products*,[83] the claimant, who was a meat packer, was asked to work in very cold temperatures but was moved when she protested because of her pregnancy. She was then told to do a job involving lifting heavy boxes. When she asked to be moved to another line she was told to go home. She took this as being a dismissal. She complained of unfair dismissal and sex discrimination. The ET held that she was dismissed either because she was pregnant or for reasons connected with her pregnancy, ie, her absences and her inability to work on the line which involved lifting heavy boxes. The dismissal was therefore automatically unfair and discriminatory. She could also have claimed that it was automatically unfair because she was dismissed/subjected to detriment for raising health and safety concerns and because she removed herself from the workplace believing herself to be in danger[84] (see paras 15.117–15.118).

Failure to appoint a pregnant woman because she cannot take up her post due to a health and safety risk

3.88   In *Mahlburg v Land Mecklenburg-Vorpommern*[85] a pregnant employee was refused a job because she would not be able to take it up before the end of her maternity leave. She was applying for a job as a nurse

---

82   EOR Digest 37.
83   S1571195, 9 August 1995, Glasgow ET. Note that each case will be decided on its own facts and tribunal decisions are not binding.
84   ERA 1996 s100.
85   [2000] IRLR 276, ECJ.

in the Rostock University Heart Surgery Clinic operating theatre which involved handling surgical instruments during operations which she temporarily could not do due to risk of infection. The employer said that the refusal was not directly because of her pregnancy (which would have been sex discrimination) but because health and safety law prohibited a pregnant woman from doing that job. The ECJ, making the point that a job was permanent whereas a pregnancy was not, said that the protection due to a pregnant woman overrode such considerations. The employer had discriminated against her. The ECJ also pointed out that an employer cannot justify direct sex discrimination on the grounds that it would be too expensive to wait for a woman to finish her maternity leave.

Is it lawful to discriminate in order to protect a woman's health and safety?

3.89   SDA 1975 s51 states that an employer is permitted to discriminate against a woman where the act of discrimination was done in circumstances where it was necessary in order to comply with:

- an existing statutory provision concerning the protection of women;[86] or
- the requirement of a relevant statutory provision (within the HSWA 1974 Part I)[87] and it was done in order to protect the woman;

where, in either case, the provision is necessary for the purpose of protecting women as regards:

- pregnancy or maternity; or
- other circumstances giving rise to risks specifically affecting women.

3.90   Despite this exception, it is rarely, if ever, lawful under the SDA 1975 to dismiss or subject a woman to more than a minor detriment because of a need to protect her health and safety. Where section 51 applies in relation to pregnant women, new mothers or breastfeeding women, the specific duties to protect their health and safety and that

---

86   This includes the Factories Act 1961, and the Offices, Shops and Railway Premises Act 1963.
87   This includes the prohibition on employing a woman in a factory within four weeks of the birth.

of their babies, as well as the need, under discrimination law, to protect pregnant women from unfavourable treatment, override this exception.[88]

3.91   Thus, the MHSW Regs 1999 provide for positive duties (such as temporary redeployment or suspension) to avoid the need to dismiss or disadvantage expectant or new mothers as a result of health and safety risks. However, section 51 might apply, for example, where a woman refuses to move to suitable alternative work, following the identification of a risk, and her employer dismisses her because there is no other way of protecting her health and safety. This is only likely to arise where the employer has carried out a proper risk assessment which has revealed a significant risk but the employee is not prepared to agree to any action to avoid the risk.

3.92   The ETD provides that there shall be 'no discrimination what-soever on grounds of sex' and it will be discriminatory to treat a pregnant woman or new mother less favourably on health and safety grounds. In *Habermann-Beltermann*[89] the claimant was employed as a night worker and German law prohibited pregnant women working at night. As a result, the claimant was dismissed. The ECJ held that the termination of a contract (without a fixed term) on account of a woman's pregnancy cannot be justified on the ground that a statutory prohibition, imposed because of pregnancy, temporarily prevents the employee from performing night work. The court held that to allow an employer to dismiss a woman because of the temporary inability of the pregnant employee to perform night work would be contrary to the objective of protecting women. This approach was confirmed in *Mahlburg* (see para 3.88).

3.93   In *Quinn* the EAT said that as a suspension on full pay involved the restriction on the right of a pregnant woman to carry out her normal role, this could give rise to a claim for potential automatic sex discrimination claim. Unless it is necessary to vary the employee's working conditions in order to protect her health and safety, it will be discrimination to do so – unless this is agreed. *Quinn* is a good illustration of the relevance of section 51 (see para 3.57). It permits protective measures where any detriment will be minor (such as

---

88 The ETD exempts 'provisions concerning the protection of women, particularly as regards pregnancy and maternity', article 2(7); this means only that such provisions will not be treated as discriminating against men.
89 *Habermann-Beltermann v Arbeiterwohlfahrt, Bezirksverband Ndb/Opf eV* C-421192 [1994] IRLR 364, ECJ.

missing the satisfaction of being at work) but if the employer gets the balance wrong and, as in this case, removes her from work when it was not necessary, this will be discrimination. SDA 1975 does not give the employer permission to ignore or mis-apply the statutory protective measures. Arguably, all that section 51 does is allow employers to implement them appropriately, thus giving rise to a small degree of disadvantage to women who may for some reason, perverse or otherwise, prefer to live with a risk rather than have their work adjusted. The key, however, for employers is to carry out a proper risk assessment and not make unsubstantiated assumptions about what is necessary to protect women in these circumstances.

Detriment and automatic unfair dismissal

3.94   ERA 1996 ss47C and 99 and MPL Regs 1999 regs19 and 20 make it unlawful to subject a woman to detriment or to dismiss her for a reason connected with suspension on health and safety grounds.[90] It is also unlawful to dismiss her or subject her to detriment for a reason connected with pregnancy or maternity leave, which will include a health and safety reason, see chapter 15. Further, if an employee is dismissed because she has alleged an infringement of right to alternative employment under ERA 1996 s67 or to be paid while suspended, she can claim she has been dismissed for asserting a statutory right under ERA 1996 s104 (see para 15.122).

The grievance procedure

3.95   Where an employee is making a claim relating to suspension or failure to offer alternative work under ERA 1996 s70, the statutory grievance procedure does not apply, so there is no requirement to put in a written complaint prior to commencing proceedings and time limits are not extended. However, where the claim is for unlawful detriment or dismissal or for unlawful deduction of wages under ERA 1996 s23 or sex discrimination, the employee must first put in a written complaint to the employer and wait 28 days before lodging a claim. In these circumstances the normal three-month time limit for bringing a claim is extended by three months (see chapter 16).

---

90   MPL Regs 1999 regs 19(2)(c) and 20(3)(c). See also ERA 1996 s100 and para 15.116.

Criminal proceedings

3.96   The HSE and the local authority environmental health department are the enforcing agencies; the size of the workplace and the level of risk to health and safety will determine which one is appropriate. With low risk workplaces, eg retail, the environmental health department is the prosecuting authority. With high risk workplaces, eg chemical factory, the HSE is the prosecuting authority. The maximum penalty on conviction in the magistrates' court is set at a specific limit. Conviction in the Crown Court can lead to an unlimited fine and/or in respect of certain offences (including failure to comply with a prohibition or improvement notice), up to two years' imprisonment.

3.97   In addition to the power to prosecute, local authority and HSE inspectors are given wide-ranging powers under this Act. These relate to the right of entry to premises, making examinations and investigations (including risk assessments); taking measurements, photographs and samples; the production and inspection of books and documents; the provision of facilities and assistance; questioning people; and the rendering harmless of articles and substances. Inspectors also have the power to issue improvement and prohibition notices to employers. The enforcing authorities appear to prefer to work collaboratively with employers and in practice prosecutions are rare.

Civil proceedings

3.98   An employee could take civil proceedings if the woman or her baby is injured as a result of the employer's failure to carry out a risk assessment.[91] In addition, any breach of the MHSW Regs 1999 would be taken into account in assessing the employer's duty of care. Enforcement through civil proceedings is expensive, time-consuming and depends on the woman having suffered an injury. Arguably, it is an inadequate remedy under the PWD, which requires member states to implement measures which enable workers who have suffered by a breach of the directive to pursue their claims by judicial process.[92]

---

91 A breach of MHSW Regs 1999 does not usually confer a right of action in civil proceedings but reg 22(2) says that the general exclusion does not apply where the employer has failed to carry out a risk assessment under reg 16(1).
92 PWD article 12.

Health and safety duty to a pregnant woman or new mother breached	Remedy if breached	Relevant section or regulation
Common law duty of care	Damages claim in High/county court	
Implied duty of care in contract of employment	Damages claim in High/county court Constructive dismissal claim in ET	ERA 1996 s95
Congenital Disabilities (Civil Liability) Act 1976	Damages claim in High/county court	CDA 1976 s1
Failure to carry out a risk assessment, to take appropriate preventative measures, to inform the employee of what steps have been taken and to alter working conditions or hours of work	Prosecution in magistrates' or Crown Court. Claim for compensation for detriment/dismissal and sex discrimination in ET (see chapter 15) If dismissed for raising health and safety concerns claim for compensation in ET (see para 3.87) If injury results, damages claim in High/county court	HSWA 1974 s33 ERA 1996 s47C SDA 1975 s6 ERA 1996 s100
Failure to offer an employee suitable alternative work before suspension	Compensation claim in ET. The compensation payable shall be what the ET considers to be just and equitable in the circumstances having regard to the infringement of the rights to be offered alternative work and any loss sustained as a result If injury results, damages claim in High/county court	ERA 1996 s70(4)

Unreasonable refusal of suitable alternative work	No right to claim full pay during suspension	ERA 1996 s68(2)
Failure to suspend a woman where suspension is necessary	Prosecution in magistrates' or Crown Court	HSWA 1974 s33
	Claim for compensation for detriment/dismissal and sex discrimination in ET (see paras 3.83, 3.94 and chapter 15)	ERA 1996 s47C, s99 SDA 1975 s6
	If dismissed for raising health and safety concerns, claim for compensation in ET (see para 15.116)	ERA 1996 s10C
	If injury results, damages claim in High/county court	ERA 1996 s100
Failure to pay an employee who is suspended	Compensation claim in ET. The ET will award the amount of remuneration which it finds is due	ERA 1996 s70(1), (3)
	Claim for unlawful deduction from wages in ET	ERA 1996 ss13 and 27(1)(f)
Detriment because of suspension from work on maternity grounds	Compensation claim in ET	ERA 1996 s47C MPL Regs 1999 reg 19(2)(c)
Dismissal connected with suspension from work on maternity grounds	Reinstatement, re-engagement or compensation claim in ET	ERA 1996 s99 MPL Regs 1999 reg 20(3)(c)
Dismissal for asserting a statutory right to health and safety protection	Compensation claim in ET	ERA 1996 s104

Remedies

3.99   See chapter 18 for compensation and other remedies for unfair dismissal and sex discrimination.

Right to reasonable paid time off for antenatal care

3.100   All pregnant employees, irrespective of length of service or hours of work, whether permanent or temporary, are entitled to paid time off during working hours for antenatal care (for definition of 'employee', see para 1.28).[93] There are a few exceptions, including those employed in the armed forces,[94] those employed in share fishing and the police.[95] Special provisions apply to seafarers (see para 1.31). The PWD contains a similar right to time off, without loss of pay, in order to attend antenatal examinations.[96] A woman worker who is not an employee is not entitled to paid time off but she may have a sex discrimination claim if she suffers a disadvantage such as losing a contract as a result of taking time off. She will not be entitled to claim her lost pay under ERA 1996 but this may be included in a compensation claim under SDA 1975.

3.101   A pregnant employee has a right to reasonable paid time off work for antenatal care provided she has made an appointment to receive such care on the advice of a registered medical practitioner, midwife or nurse.[97]

What is antenatal care?

3.102   Antenatal care is care of a pregnant employee who 'has, on the advice of a registered medical practitioner, registered midwife or registered nurse, made an appointment to attend at any place for the purpose of receiving antenatal care'.[98] The legislation is no more specific than this. The Under-Secretary of State for Employment said in parliamentary debates that antenatal care would include relaxation

---

93   ERA 1996 ss55–57.
94   ERA 1996 s192.
95   ERA 1996 s200.
96   Article 9. This does not provide any greater protection than exists under the ERA 1996.
97   ERA 1996 s55(1).
98   ERA 1996 s55(1)(b).

classes.[99] As the government pointed out, there is no need to show the specific reason for an antenatal appointment. This was the interpretation adopted in *Satchwell Sunvic Ltd v Secretary of State for Employment*,[100] when the EAT held that antenatal care covered non-medical care such as relaxation classes.[101] The Department of Trade and Industry (DTI) guide[102] states that antenatal care can include relaxation and parentcraft classes as long as these are advised by a registered medical practitioner, registered midwife or registered nurse.

Requirement for appointment for antenatal care and certificate

3.103 There is no obligation for the employee to provide proof of the appointment in relation to the first visit, though she should obtain the employer's permission to attend.[103] For subsequent appointments, however, if the employer so requires, the employee must provide:

- written proof of the appointment (such as an appointment card); and
- a certificate or note from a registered medical practitioner, midwife or nurse stating that she is pregnant.[104]

3.104 An employer can refuse paid time off if the employee fails to comply with these requirements, after being requested to do so by the employer.

Can the employer refuse time off for antenatal care?

3.105 Time off cannot otherwise be unreasonably refused. The amount of time off needed for antenatal care is fairly standard for most women who have uncomplicated pregnancies. There are unlikely, therefore, to be many situations when an employer could justify refusing time off. Clearly, it would not be reasonable for a woman to take part of every day off in order to attend relaxation classes, nor to take off more

---

99 HC Standing Committee F, cols 291–292, 12 January 1993; HL Debates, cols 531–532, 25 March 1993 (Trades Union Reform and Employment Rights Bill 1993).
100 [1979] IRLR 455, EAT.
101 See also *Gregory v Tudsbury Ltd* [1982] IRLR 267, ET.
102 Maternity Rights PL 958 (Rev 8) January 2003, p14.
103 ERA 1996 s55(3).
104 ERA 1996 s55(2).

than a few hours at a time. Time should be allowed for waiting and travelling to and from the appointment. For example, in *Dhamrait v United Biscuits Ltd*[105] the appointment lasted longer than expected and as a result the woman missed the works bus (her only means of transport). The ET held she was entitled to be paid for the whole shift.

3.106   It would not generally be reasonable to expect a woman to attend work for as little as half an hour before or after the appointment. Thus, in *Edgar v Giorgione Inns Ltd*[106] the woman worked from 9 am to 3 pm. The tribunal expected her to work before an appointment fixed at 3 pm (she had to leave at 2 pm) and after an appointment at 9.05 am, but said it was not reasonable for her to attend work before or after appointments fixed between 10.30 am and 11.15 am. It will be a question of fact in each case and the type of work may be a relevant factor.

3.107   There is no obligation on the woman to arrange antenatal care outside working hours or to make up the time.[107] In *Gregory v Tudsbury Ltd*[108] the tribunal suggested that an employer could reasonably refuse time off if a woman worked part-time and could arrange antenatal care outside working hours. This is not binding. A decision about what is reasonable will depend on the particular facts of the case. Women are frequently not able to choose the time of their appointment. The statute states that there is entitlement to time off during working hours and there is no proviso that this is subject to the woman not being able to attend outside working hours. In *Sajil v Carraro t/a Foubert's Bar*[109] the ET said it was important not to allow employers scope for requiring women to change their working hours or make up for lost time.

3.108   A casual worker who is an employee is also entitled to time off to attend an antenatal appointment at a time when it was normal for the employee to work. The employer cannot avoid paying her by saying

105   ET 10128/83.
106   ET 20961/86.
107   *Edgar v Giorgione Inn* ET 20961/86; *Bland v Laws (Confectioners) Ltd* ET 31081/84 and *Sajil v Carraro t/a Foubert's Bar*. See also *Holmwood v Smith & Gardner Ltd* ET 6001899/98 where the ET held that the employer could not insist that the woman take her weekly day off on the days when she had an antenatal appointment.
108   See note 106 above.
109   COIT 1890/34.

she was not obliged to attend work on the day of the appointment, where it is usually a day when she would attend.[110]

The right to be paid for time off

3.109 An employee who takes time off for antenatal care is entitled to be paid as though she was still at work.[111] Once the employer has allowed time off, it must be paid at the normal hourly rate, which should be clear from the agreed terms and conditions or contract of employment.

3.110 Pay is calculated as follows:

a) if a week's pay is always the same, the hourly rate is calculated by dividing the week's pay by the hours worked;[112] or

b) if the pay varies, it should be averaged over a 12-week period, ending with the last complete week before the day on which the time off is taken;[113] or

c) if the pay varies and the woman has not been employed for 12 weeks, the pay should be calculated by taking into account:[114]
   - the average number of normal working hours a week which the employee could expect, and
   - the average number of such hours of other employees engaged in relevant comparable employment with the same employer.[115]

3.111 Normal working hours and a week's pay are defined by the ERA 1996.[116]

- Pay includes overtime only where it is compulsory under the contract.
- There is no maximum limit on a week's pay.
- The date when pay is calculated is the day of the antenatal appointment.[117]

---

110 *Pollard v Greater Manchester Passenger Transport Executive* ET 2402582/96.
111 ERA 1996 s56.
112 ERA 1996 s56(2); the hourly rate is the amount of one week's pay divided by the number of normal working hours in a week.
113 ERA 1996 s56(3)(a).
114 ERA 1996 s56(3)(b).
115 ERA 1996 s56(4).
116 ERA 1996 s220 onwards.
117 ERA 1996 s225(3).

3.112   Payment made by the employer under the contract of employment discharges liability under statute and vice versa.

Breach of antenatal provisions

3.113   An employee can complain to an ET on the following grounds:

- Where an employee has been unreasonably refused time off.[118]
- Where the employer refused to pay the employee for the time off.[119]
- Where an employee has been dismissed (including selection for redundancy) because she has taken time off (which must by definition be for a reason connected to her pregnancy).[120] The dismissal will be automatically unfair under ERA 1996 s99. For example, where a woman was dismissed at the end of a probationary period because of poor attendance and this was caused by her antenatal appointments, the dismissal was for a reason connected with pregnancy and automatically unfair.[121] A woman refused time off for antenatal appointments may be able to resign and claim constructive dismissal (which may be ordinary or automatically unfair and discriminatory). In *Wainwright v Halton t/a Hair Talk*[122] the employer refused to allow the woman time off for antenatal appointments and treated her badly because of her pregnancy. There was a breach of the implied duty of trust and confidence which entitled her to resign (see para 15.23).
- Dismissal of an employee where the reason or principal reason for dismissal is that she has alleged that she has been denied the right to paid time off will be automatically unfair on the grounds that she has alleged a breach of a statutory right under ERA 1996 s104. This will apply even if there has been no breach provided the allegation was made in good faith. Note, however, that there cannot be two 'reasons' or 'principal reasons' so that an ET could not uphold a claim under ERA 1996 s104 *and* s99. It must find one of the reasons is the principal one.
- Any less favourable treatment of a woman (falling short of dismissal) because she has either taken or tried to take paid time off

---

118   ERA 1996 s57(1)(a).
119   ERA 1996 s57(1)(b).
120   ERA 1996 s99 and MPL Regs 1999 reg 20(3)(a).
121   *Mains v MD Homes* ET 22031/96.
122   ET 11642/96.

for antenatal care may amount to 'subjecting her to a detriment'. This would be a breach of MPL Regs 1999 reg 19 (see para 15.22 onwards).

- Refusal to pay a woman who takes time off is also likely to be an unlawful deduction of wages under ERA 1999 Part II. Thus, where the employee's bonus was reduced solely because of her attendance at antenatal appointments, this was held to be an unlawful deduction.

- In all the above situations, there is likely to be sex discrimination (see chapter 2). In *Dixon v Motorcise (Torbay) Ltd*[123] the claimant was told that she was expected to make antenatal appointments out of working hours and this together with the failure to carry out a risk assessment and pay her contractual sick pay led her to resign. She then returned to work but was told that antenatal appointments were to be taken in her own time. The tribunal found that the claimant was constructively dismissed, resigning in response to two fundamental breaches of contract: the failure to pay her contractual sick pay and a course of conduct that undermined trust and confidence.

Remedies relating to antenatal care

3.114   Where an employer refuses to give time off for antenatal care or refuses to pay (in full or in part), the woman can complain to a tribunal within three months from the date of the appointment (see para 18.132).[124]

3.115   If the tribunal upholds the woman's complaint, it must make a declaration to that effect and award compensation equal to the amount the woman should have received had she been given the time off.[125]

3.116   See chapter 18 for compensation and other remedies for unfair dismissal and sex discrimination.

The grievance procedure

3.117   Where an employee is making a claim under ERA 1996 s57, the statutory grievance procedure does not apply, so there is no

123 21 October 2004; case no 1702438/03, ET.
124 ERA 1996 s57(2).
125 ERA 1996 s57(3), (4), (5).

requirement to put in a written complaint prior to commencing proceedings and time limits are not extended. However, where the claim is for unlawful deduction of wages under ERA 1996 s23 or sex discrimination, the employee must first put in a written complaint to the employer and wait 28 days before lodging a claim. In these circumstances the time limit for bringing a claim is extended by three months (see chapter 16).

Pregnancy-related sickness and discrimination

3.118   Any less favourable treatment of a woman, because of pregnancy-related sickness, is sex discrimination. SDA 1975 s3A(3)(b) provides that where a person's treatment of a woman is on grounds of illness suffered by her as a consequence of a pregnancy of hers, that treatment is to be taken to be on the ground of the pregnancy. This is in line with the ECJ decision in *Brown v Rentokil*[126] where the ECJ held that the ETD prevents the dismissal of a woman at any time during her pregnancy for absences due to incapacity for work caused by an illness resulting from pregnancy.

3.119   In *Brown* the claimant was absent for 26 weeks, from almost the beginning of her pregnancy until she went on maternity leave. Her contract provided that an employee who was off sick continuously for 26 weeks would be dismissed and at the end of her 26 weeks' absence she was accordingly dismissed. The ECJ held that the contractual rule was discriminatory, pointing out that the Pregnant Workers Directive was introduced precisely because of:

> . . . the harmful effects which the risk of dismissal may have on the physical and mental state of women who are pregnant, women who have recently given birth or women who are breastfeeding, including the particularly serious risk that pregnant women may be prompted voluntarily to terminate their pregnancy.

3.120   The ECJ held that the ETD gives a woman protection against dismissal on grounds of her absence throughout the period of pregnancy and during the maternity leave given to her under national law. The fact that she was unable to work or that a man would have been dismissed for a similar period of sickness, was not relevant. Thus, the court held:

126   [1998] IRLR 445 ECJ.

Where a woman is absent owing to illness resulting from pregnancy or childbirth, and that illness arose during pregnancy and persisted during and after maternity leave, her absence not only during maternity leave but also during the period extending from the start of her pregnancy to the start of her maternity leave cannot be taken into account for computation of the period justifying her dismissal.

3.121 The SDA 1975 and the decision in *Brown* means that it will be discriminatory, for example:

- To dismiss a woman for any absence related to her pregnancy.
- Not to consider a woman for an appraisal (and as a result a pay rise) because she is absent as a result of her pregnancy (see *CNAVTS v Thibault* (paras 5.76–5.78) where the ECJ held that denial of an appraisal during a woman's absence on maternity leave was discriminatory where the result of the appraisal determined a subsequent pay review).
- Not to consider a woman for promotion because she is absent as a result of her pregnancy (or maternity leave).
- To refuse to give a woman a bonus because of pregnancy-related absence. In *GUS Home Shopping Ltd* [127] the employer did not pay a 'loyalty bonus' (in respect of co-operation and goodwill while work was transferred from the appellant's location to another place of work) to two women who were either off work with pregnancy-related illness or on maternity leave throughout the whole of the period covered by the loyalty bonus. The EAT upheld the ET's decision that this was due to pregnancy or absence on maternity leave and so was discrimination contrary to SDA 1975. [128]
- To treat a woman less favourably at any time (ie, during or after her pregnancy or maternity leave) as a result of pregnancy-related absence which occurs during her pregnancy. Thus, any period when a woman has a pregnancy-related absence should be left out of account. For example, even if sickness is a factor in a redundancy selection exercise, pregnancy-related absence during pregnancy must be ignored, irrespective of when the redundancy takes place.
- To dismiss a woman following a disciplinary hearing which she was incapable of attending because of a pregnancy-related condition. Where an employee is prevented from defending herself at a

127 *GUS Home Shopping Ltd v Green and McLaughlin* [2001] IRLR 75, EAT.
128 The position of a woman on maternity leave is more uncertain (see paras 5.91–5.93).

disciplinary hearing due to her absence for a pregnancy-related reason, that is sex discrimination.[129]

What is pregnancy-related sickness?

3.122 It includes morning sickness, fatigue, threatened or actual miscarriage or any other illness connected with the pregnancy. It is often difficult to distinguish between pregnancy-related sickness and health problems arising out of health and safety risks.

3.123 If pregnancy has exacerbated an existing condition, this should be sufficient to establish that it is 'related to pregnancy'. If the employee would not have been dismissed 'but for' the pregnancy-related sickness absence, the dismissal will be unfair. In *George v Beecham Group*[130] the claimant received two written warnings about her sickness absences followed by a final warning after she went into hospital for a gynaecological operation. She then told her manager she was pregnant. Soon after, she was admitted to hospital after a miscarriage and was dismissed on her return to work. The tribunal held that her dismissal was automatically unfair because the main reason for the dismissal was her absence caused by the miscarriage.

Sick pay during absence

3.124 Where the employer has a contractual sick pay scheme that provides that sick pay is generally payable to sick employees but not to those with pregnancy-related sickness, this is a breach of European law.

3.125 In *Hoj Pedersen*[131] employees absent from work due to illness were entitled to full pay. A pregnant employee who was ill before her maternity leave was not entitled to any pay. The ECJ held that it was a breach of article 141 of the Treaty of Rome 1957 to deny a pregnant woman the same sick pay as other workers because she was unfit for work because of her pregnancy.

3.126 There is no legal obligation to continue to pay an employee full pay where she is absent as a result of her pregnancy in circumstances where a man or other worker would not receive full pay. In *North-Western Health Board v McKenna*[132] the ECJ held that a sick leave

---

129 *Abbey National plc v Formoso* [1999] IRLR 222, EAT.
130 [1977] IRLR 43 ET.
131 *Handels-og Kontorfunktionaerernes foribund I Danmark*, acting on behalf of *Hoj Pedersen v Faellesforeningen for Danmarks Brugsforeninger* [1999] IRLR 55 ECJ.
132 [2005] IRLR 895 ECJ.

scheme which treats female workers suffering from a pregnancy-related illness in the same way as other workers suffering from an illness that is unrelated to pregnancy is pay within article 141.[133] However a rule which provides for a reduction in pay where the absence exceeds a certain duration and which applies to pregnancy-related sickness and sickness unrelated to pregnancy is not discrimination provided the amount of payment is not so low as to undermine the objective of protecting pregnant workers. The ECJ's rationale for the decision was that if it was not discrimination to deprive a woman on maternity leave of full pay, then it was not discrimination to deprive pregnant women of full pay when absent with pregnancy-related sickness.

3.127 An unanswered question is what is the minimum income to which a woman off with pregnancy related illness is entitled. The likelihood is that this is statutory sick pay. However SSP is not paid:

- to those with earnings below the lower earnings limit;
- after the SSP payment period has expired; and
- for the first three days of sickness.

3.128 It is not clear whether the employer should pay the woman an equivalent amount if she is not entitled to sick pay. Arguably, since the statutory regime provides for these exclusions a woman cannot challenge this, particularly as she would be able to claim means tested benefit if her earnings fell below a certain level (see chapter 7). The analogy would be with PWD article 11(3) which says that maternity pay will be adequate if it guarantees income at least equivalent to the national sick pay scheme, albeit that the article refers to the 'ceiling laid down under national legislation' and not the minimum level.

3.129 The ECJ further held that a pregnancy-related illness can be offset against the maximum total number of days of paid sick leave to which a worker is entitled over a specified period. However, such offsetting should not mean that during a sickness absence occurring after her return from leave she receives pay that is below the minimum amount to which she was entitled over the course of the illness which arose during her pregnancy. For example, an employee's statutory right to sick pay and incapacity benefit must not be affected by her pregnancy (see chapter 7). Her contractual sick pay may, however, be reduced if she has already used up part of it during pregnancy, whatever the reason for her sick leave.

---

133 The ETD was not relevant.

Effect of sickness on entitlement to SMP

3.130   If a woman is sick during the eight weeks or two months before the qualifying week (and is on unpaid leave or only getting statutory sick pay or incapacity benefit), she may not be entitled to SMP because she will not have earned enough during this crucial period (see para 6.34 onwards).

3.131   Note also the triggering provisions whereby a woman who has a pregnancy-related absence in the four weeks before the EWC will be forced to start her maternity leave and pay (see para 4.17).

Other less favourable treatment of pregnant women

Detriment

3.132   There are two separate statutory provisions which deal with detriment to a woman for pregnancy/maternity related reasons. There is likely to be a substantial overlap between the two and in most cases both should be argued in the alternative.

Subjecting a woman to a detriment under the MPL Regs 1999

3.133   Under the MPL Regs 1999[134] an employee is entitled not to be subjected to any detriment by any act (or deliberate failure to act) by her employer because:

- she is pregnant;
- she has given birth;
- she is the subject of a relevant health and safety requirement or recommendation relating to suspension from work; or
- other reasons relating to maternity, parental or dependants' leave (for details see para 15.128).

This does not apply where there is a dismissal, as this is covered by ERA 1996 s99 and MPL Regs 1999 reg 20.

Detriment under the SDA 1975 and EPA 1970

3.134   The SDA 1975[135] makes it unlawful not only for an employer to dismiss a woman for a pregnancy-related reason, but also to discriminate against her in relation to promotion, transfer, training or other

---

134   ERA 1996 s47C, MPL Regs 1999 reg 19.
135   SDA 1975 s6(2).

benefits or to subject her to any other detriment (see para 2.25. Harassment is also prohibited under SDA 1975 s4A (see para 2.88)).

3.135 Where there is discrimination in pay or contractual terms, there may be a breach of the Equal Pay Act (EPA) 1970 (see para 2.53 onwards). For the difference between the SDA 1975 and EPA 1970 see paras 2.5–2.8 onwards. Note that where a claim is made under European provisions, this must be also based on a domestic statute. To avoid relying on the wrong statute, it is advisable to argue any relevant statute in the alternative (see the table on pp671–672).

Examples of detriment

3.136 Any less favourable treatment of a pregnant woman, for a reason relating to her pregnancy, which results in a detriment will be unlawful. This might include the following situations:

- where a woman is criticised for being pregnant or taking time off for antenatal appointments;
- where a woman is given less interesting or less responsible work because of her pregnancy;
- where a woman is excluded from meetings or otherwise marginalised or ignored because she is pregnant;
- where an employer does not consider a woman for transfer, training or promotion because she is pregnant;
- where, for a pregnancy-related reason, a woman is unable to attend a disciplinary hearing and is, as a result, dismissed (see para 3.121).[136]

3.137 A detriment need not be physical or economic (see chapters 2 and 15). During pregnancy, intangible disadvantages such as distress can amount to a detriment. In *Gilbank v Miles*[137] there was particularly shocking treatment of a pregnant employee which the tribunal found was 'an inhumane and sustained campaign of bullying and discrimination' which was 'targeted, deliberate, repeated and consciously inflected. It not only demonstrated to the claimant a total lack of concern for the welfare of the claimant herself, but a callous disregard or concern for the life of her unborn child'. It included:

- refusing to allow another employee to get the claimant something to eat from a local shop while the claimant worked on;

---

136 *Abbey National v Formoso* above, para 3.121.
137 [2006] IRLR 538, CA.

- ignoring the claimant's attempt to discuss what her doctor advised her;
- laughing at the claimant when she raised a complaint.

3.138   The EAT, in upholding the tribunal's award of £25,000 for injury to feelings against the owner of the hairdressing salon, Ms Miles, said that:

> . . . the Tribunal found very clearly that this claimant was put through the anxiety and distress of being prevented from doing things needed to protect the child. Anyone who has any knowledge of these matters, knows that women, following the imperative needs of their own body, are primarily concerned with the child they are carrying. A woman will suffer great anguish if she is denied doing that, without good cause, which she knows is in the child's best interests and has been advised as such.

3.139   The EAT decision was upheld by the Court of Appeal.

Refusal to recruit

3.140   Refusal to recruit a woman because she is pregnant or because of the consequences of her pregnancy will be sex discrimination under the SDA 1975 interpreted in accordance with the ETD.

3.141   In *Dekker v Stichting Vormingscentrum voor Jonge Volwassenen (VJV-Centrum) Plus*[138] the ECJ held that it was a breach of the ETD for an employer to refuse to employ a suitable female claimant on the ground of 'possible adverse consequences for him arising from employing a woman who is pregnant at the time of the application'. The employers had refused to employ Mrs Dekker as a training instructor because they would not be reimbursed the sickness benefits which the employer would have to pay her during her maternity leave. As a result they would lose some of their training places. The ECJ held that a refusal to employ a woman because of the financial consequences of absence connected with pregnancy must be deemed to be based principally on the fact of the pregnancy and was as such discriminatory (see also *Mahlburg* at para 3.88). It was irrelevant that there was no male candidate. The ECJ stressed that no account could be taken of justification provided under national law.

3.142   In *Tele Danmark*[139] the ECJ said that:

138   [1991] IRLR 27.
139   [2001] IRLR 853.

. . . a refusal to employ a woman on account of her pregnancy cannot be justified on grounds relating to the financial loss which an employer who appointed a pregnant woman would suffer for the duration of her maternity leave [see *Dekker*] and that the same conclusion must be drawn as regards the financial loss caused by the fact that the woman appointed cannot be employed in the post concerned for the duration of her pregnancy.

Discriminatory questions at interview

3.143 The Equal Opportunities Commission (EOC) Code of Practice (see para 26) recommends that interview questions should relate to the requirements of the job. In *Woodward v (1) Corus Hotels plc (2) Rushton* the opening question at the interview was to ask the claimant if she had any children. When she said she was a single parent with a 12-year-old he asked what arrangements she would make for her son when required to stay away overnight for training and she was told about employees with children who had left after six weeks' employment. The tribunal concluded that a hypothetical male applicant would not have been asked such questions and there was direct discrimination in the questions asked in the interview and in the refusal to appoint Ms Woodward to the post.[140]

3.144   Where it is necessary to assess whether personal circumstances will affect performance of the job (for example, where it involves unsocial hours or extensive travel) this should be discussed objectively without detailed questions based on assumptions about marital status, children and domestic obligations. Questions about marriage plans or family intentions could be construed as showing bias against women.

3.145   For example, in *Johnston v Fultons Fine Furnishing Ltd,*[141] an ET held that a woman who was asked at her job interview questions aimed at filtering out female candidates of childbearing age (such as whether she intended to have any more children) suffered unlawful discrimination. The tribunal found she was better qualified than two candidates invited to a second interview who were aged 38 and 43, at which age the tribunal considered it was uncommon for women to have children.

140   14 July 2005; Case no 1800398/05 The tribunal awarded £5,000 for injury to feelings but this was reduced by the EAT to £4,000. There was no appeal against the liability decision and as Bean LJ said in the EAT 'the interview was conducted in a crassly sexist manner' [2006] UKEAT 0536 17 March 2006.
141   (1995) DCLD 25, p7 No 02087/94, ET.

3.146   Arguably, any questions about childbearing are themselves discriminatory after *Webb* and as found in *Woodward* above. The only question which needs to be asked is whether the claimant can do the hours.[142] Even if the questions are not in themselves discriminatory,[143] they will be strong evidence of discrimination if a male claimant is not asked similar questions and the woman fails to get the job, particularly if the woman is better qualified.[144]

3.147   A refusal to recruit a woman because she has children (and so is assumed to be unreliable) was held to be discriminatory in *Hurley v Mustoe*.[145] The EAT said there were other ways of establishing whether the claimant was reliable such as by taking up references.

Demotion

3.148   An employment tribunal held, in *Bushby v Connect Personnel Ltd*[146] that the demotion of the claimant without warning shortly after she told her employer that she was pregnant was unlawful discrimination. The tribunal did not accept the respondent's argument that the demotion was on grounds of performance. However, the tribunal dismissed her constructive dismissal claim saying that although the demotion was a fundamental breach of contract she did not resign because of the demotion but because, on her solicitor's advice, she was not allowed to return to work as branch manager and the failure to send her flowers after her baby died, which she found deeply upsetting.

Training

3.149   In *Ministry of Defence v Williams*[147] the claimant had been unable to attend a training course in September 2000 due to her pregnancy. There was no complaint in relation to this refusal but she expected to be pre-selected for the next course in September 2001, but this did not happen. The tribunal held that as pregnancy was the causative

---

142   Though in *Woodhead v Chief Constable of West Yorkshire Police* EAT 285/89 the EAT held that it may be legitimate for an employer to ask questions about whether the claimant's circumstances would affect her performance in the job.

143   See *Saunders v Richmond upon-Thames BC* [1977] IRLR 362, EAT.

144   See *Smith v North Western Regional Health Authority* COIT 1842/176.

145   [1981] IRLR 208 EAT. It was held to be direct sex discrimination and indirect marital discrimination (see chapters 2 and 13).

146   31 October 2005; Case no 1101068/05; EOR No 152 p26, ET.

147   EAT/0833/02 8 October 2003.

factor of her being deprived of the September 2000 course, in not being offered pre-selection for the 2001 course (having found that pre-selection would cause no practical problems in her particular case) she had suffered direct discrimination. The tribunal rejected a submission by the respondent that this would amount to impermissible positive discrimination. The EAT upheld the tribunal's decision stating that it was 'entirely consistent with *Webb v EMO* principles' (see para 2.61).

Transfer

3.150   If a woman is transferred because she is pregnant or refused a transfer because she is pregnant, this is likely to be discrimination.

3.151   In *McLachlan v Central Scotland Health Care NHS Trust*,[148] for example, the tribunal held that a decision to transfer the claimant was made because she was female, part-time and due to go on maternity leave. This was direct discrimination, because it was related to the claimant's maternity leave, and indirect discrimination in that she was selected because she worked part-time (see chapter 13).[149]

3.152   In *Iske v P & O European Ferries (Dover) Ltd*[150] the EAT held that failure to offer a pregnant woman, for whom it was no longer considered safe to work at sea, a transfer to shore-based work, which would have delayed the start of her maternity leave, was sex discrimination. The EAT said that no comparison was necessary between a pregnant woman and a man. It was only necessary to show that she was not offered a transfer because of her pregnancy. Because a man (or non-pregnant woman) would have been offered alternative work if unfit for seagoing work, it must be inferred that the reason Mrs Iske was not offered it was because she was pregnant. Mrs Iske was not entitled to the direct protection of the health and safety provisions because they did not relate to seafarers at the time she brought her claim.

3.153   The removal of a pregnant probationer constable from her training and her transfer to clerical duties, purportedly to protect her health and safety but without carrying out any risk assessment, was held to be unlawful sex discrimination in *Tapp v Chief Constable*

---

148 S/4932/94, 14 June 1995, Glasgow ET.
149 Although the move was cancelled, and the claimant incurred no financial loss she was awarded £500 for injury to feelings.
150 DCLD 34.

of Suffolk Constabulary.[151] The ET held that the employer 'made a paternalistic decision based upon the stereotypical assumption that someone who was pregnant could not do any physical activity whatsoever and would be better off in an office'. See also para 3.86.

Appearance

3.154   It is likely to be unlawful to move a woman to a different job because she is pregnant and 'would not look good' dealing with customers. For example, in *O'Neill v Walthamstow Building Society*[152] Ms O'Neill was told that her attempt to conceal her stomach by wearing her shirt outside her skirt made her look a mess and if she did not wear her uniform properly she would be transferred out of sight of the public. Feeling humiliated, the claimant resigned and the tribunal upheld her complaint of discrimination (see also para 2.88 on harassment).

3.155   In *Martin v McConkey*[153] the claimant was told she would have to leave when her pregnancy showed 'because he did not want people talking in the shop'. She won her sex discrimination claim.

Promotion

3.156   In *Pearson v Swindells and British Telecommunications Ltd*[154] the ET held that the claimant failed to obtain promotion because of her absence on maternity leave. She had attended an interview while eight months pregnant and no account had been taken of the possibility that her poor performance at interview might have been affected by being eight months pregnant and on leave (see also *CNAVTS v Thibault* at para 2.66). An employer should make every effort to arrange the interview at a time when the woman can attend. This will depend on the employee's situation but the timing should be discussed with her. Similar principles apply to promotion as to recruitment.

---

151   DCLD 37, p5.
152   DCLD 6, No 27886/89.
153   DCLD 5, 1577/89, NI Tribunal.
154   ET 48222/93; see also *Abbey National and Formoso* above.

Maternity leave and return to work

Key points

- All women employees are entitled to 26 weeks' ordinary maternity leave (OML) irrespective of length of service, hours of work or whether they have a permanent or temporary contract.
- Women whose expected week of childbirth (EWC) is before 1 April 2007 need to have been employed by the same employer for 26 weeks by the beginning of the 14th week before childbirth in order to qualify for additional maternity leave (AML). All women employees whose EWC is on or after 1 April 2007 will qualify for OML and AML. AML begins at the end of OML and lasts for 26 weeks.
- The earliest maternity leave can start is the beginning of the eleventh week before the EWC (unless the baby is born earlier).
- Otherwise the employee can choose when to start her leave unless:
  - she is absent because of her pregnancy in the four weeks before the EWC, in which case her leave will start then; or
  - the baby is premature, in which case her leave starts then.
- Entitlement to OML and AML usually depends on giving notice by the end of the 15th week before the baby is due:
  - of her pregnancy;
  - of the EWC;
  - of the date she intends to start leave (which may be in writing if requested by the employer).

    An employer must confirm the date a woman's maternity leave will end within 28 days of receiving her notice.
- If a woman wants to return earlier than the end of her OML or AML, she must give notice. Otherwise it is assumed that she will return at the end of her OML or AML, ie the date notified by her employer.
- A woman returning after OML is entitled to the same job on the same terms and conditions.
- A woman returning after AML is entitled to return to the job in which she was previously employed:
  - with the same pay package;
  - with preserved seniority and other rights;
  - on no less favourable terms and conditions.
- If it is not reasonably practicable to allow the woman to return

> to the same job after AML, she must be given another job which is both suitable for her and appropriate for her to do in the circumstances. She may have a sex discrimination claim if she would have kept the same job had she not taken her maternity leave.
>
> - If a woman takes two or more consecutive periods of leave which includes a period of AML, additional adoption leave or parental leave of more than four weeks, she will have the same rights to return as a woman returning from AML unless she returns to work between periods of leave.
> - Where a woman has a contractual as well as a statutory right to return, she can take advantage of whichever right is, in any particular respect, more favourable.
> - If there has been a transfer of business during a woman's maternity leave, she is entitled to return to her job with the new employer.
> - If a woman is dismissed or forced to resign before the start of maternity leave, she will not be entitled to her leave but may have qualified for statutory maternity pay (SMP). If she is dismissed during her leave, her leave will end but she will still be entitled to receive SMP. She may have a claim for automatic unfair dismissal and sex discrimination if her dismissal is related to her pregnancy, childbirth or maternity leave.
> - If a woman is made redundant during OML or AML she is entitled to any suitable alternative work with equivalent terms and conditions.

Background and statutory framework

4.1 The Employment Rights Act (ERA) 1996, as amended by the Employment Act (EA) 2002, and the Maternity and Parental Leave etc Regulations (MPL Regs) 1999, as amended by the Maternity and Parental Leave (Amendment) Regulations (MPL (Amend) Regs) 2002, contain the main provisions relating to maternity leave for women whose EWC was on or after 6 April 2003.

4.2 These regulations have been amended by the Maternity and Parental Leave etc and the Paternity and Adoption Leave (Amendment) Regulations 2006. They apply to employees whose EWC is on or after 1 April 2007 and made the following main changes:

- removed the service qualification for AML;

- changed the notice period from 28 days to 8 weeks for early return from maternity leave; and
- introduced a right for employers to make reasonable contact with employees during maternity leave and enabled employees to work for up to 10 days during maternity leave without losing rights to leave and pay.

Who is entitled to OML and AML

4.3   Only employees are entitled to maternity leave. Non-employees, such as agency workers, bank nurses or homeworkers who are classified by their employers as 'self-employed' may in fact be employees, but if they are not they will not be entitled to maternity leave. See para 1.28 for who is an employee. A woman who is not an employee may still be entitled to maternity pay even if she is not entitled to maternity leave. See chapters 6 and 7.

4.4   A limited number of employees are excluded from the protection of the ERA 1996 in relation to rights such as the right to maternity leave (see para 1.31). Note that parental leave may be taken at the end of OML or AML (see chapter 10 and para 4.76 onwards for rights to return after consecutive periods of leave).

4.5   It is important to distinguish between the two types of leave. The term OML refers to the 26-week period which runs from the start of maternity leave. The term AML is the period which commences the day after the end of OML (26 weeks) and lasts up to a further 26 weeks. Employees whose EWC is before 1 April 2007 are only entitled to additional maternity leave if they have sufficient service. In addition, women's rights during OML and AML are different irrespective of the date of the EWC.

Contractual rights

4.6   Employees may be entitled, under their contract of employment or by agreement with their employer, to more favourable terms than the statutory minimum, such as a longer period off work or higher pay. It is always important to establish whether there is any such agreement (written or oral) between employer and employee and the terms of any agreement. Where there is a statutory and a contractual right to maternity leave, the employee may take advantage of whichever right is, in any particular respect, the more favourable (see para 4.96). This is called a *composite right*.[1] For example, if an employee is entitled to 26 weeks' paid maternity leave under her contract, if she qualifies she will still be entitled to AML even if the contract does not mention this, but only 26 weeks of her leave will be paid. The rest of the time off will be unpaid.

Women with more than one job

4.7 Women with more than one employer can exercise their maternity rights separately in relation to each employment. There is no reason why maternity leave should not start at different times for each job, subject to the normal notice rules. An employee's maternity pay may be affected by the fact that she is working for someone else during her maternity leave, see paras 6.79–6.80.

Entitlement to OML and AML

OML

4.8 Provided the appropriate notice is given, all employees[2] are entitled to maternity leave of 26 weeks, irrespective of the hours they work, length of service, and whether permanent or temporary. Where a woman's fixed term contract expires during OML and is not renewed, this will be a dismissal. As with any dismissal it will bring her contract and maternity leave to an end. However, she will still be entitled to SMP, if she qualifies, for up to 26 or 39 weeks (depending on her EWC) – see chapter 6 and paras 4.103–4.108 on dismissal. For rights on dismissal, see chapter 15.

AML

Employees whose EWC is before 1 April 2007

4.9 An employee is entitled to AML if she is entitled to OML (ie, gives the required notice) and she has been continuously employed by the same employer for 26 weeks by the beginning of the 14th week before the EWC.[3] Note: This is the same service condition as for SMP, see para 6.12 for how to calculate the relevant weeks.

1 MPL Regs 1999 reg 21.
2 But not other types of workers (see para 1.28).
3 MPL Regs 1999 reg 5.

Continuous employment

4.10 Continuous employment includes any week in which the employee has a contract of employment (written or oral) with her employer. An employee may be on sick leave, on holiday, or on unpaid leave and still have a contract of employment.[4]

4.11 There are also special rules as to when an absence from work, when there is no contract, may still be treated as continuous employment. These absences between contracts include up to 26 weeks' sickness absence, and leave of absence by arrangement or custom. This may apply, for example, to seasonal workers who have successive short-term contracts with gaps in between.

4.12 Even if the woman stopped working for her employer before the beginning of the 14th week (ie, has been dismissed or resigned), she may still have a contract of employment (to which she can return) if this was the intention of the parties. For example, in *Satchwell Sunvic Ltd v Secretary of State for Employment*[5] the woman stopped work before the required date (which at that time was 11 weeks before the EWC) but, as the employers expected her to return (and kept her on the payroll, retaining her P45) her contract was held to continue.

Women whose EWC is on or after 1 April 2007

4.13 All women employees whose EWC is on or after 1 April 2007 who are entitled to OML (ie, give the required notice) are also entitled to AML.[6]

Notice provisions for OML and AML

Normal notice

4.14 Normally an employee must notify her employer by the end of the 15th week before her EWC (see para 6.12 for how to find the 15th week) or, if that is not reasonably practicable (see para 4.22), as soon as reasonably practicable, of:

- the fact that she is pregnant;
- the EWC; and

---

4 ERA 1996 ss210 and 212(3).
5 [1979] IRLR 455, EAT.
6 MPL Regs 1999, reg 4 as amended by the Maternity and Parental Leave etc and the Paternity and Adoption Leave (Amendment) Regulations 2006 reg 5.

- the date on which she intends to start her OML (which cannot be earlier than the beginning of the 11th week before the EWC). An employer can ask for notice of the date she intends to start her OML to be given in writing. If her employer asks, she must provide a certificate from her medical practitioner or midwife stating her EWC.[7]

Changing the start of maternity leave

4.15   If an employee has given her employer notice of the date she intends to start her maternity leave, she can subsequently change that date providing she gives her employer at least 28 days' notice before the new date or the original date, whichever is earliest (and the new date is not earlier than the beginning of the 11th week before the EWC). If that is not reasonably practicable, she must give notice as soon as reasonably practicable. Again, an employer can ask for this notice to be given in writing. See table on p141 for notice requirements.

EXAMPLE: Nina's baby is due on Monday 14 May 2007. She notifies her employer on Friday 2 February 2007 (ie, in the 15th week before her EWC) that she wishes to start her maternity leave on 15 April 2007, four weeks before her baby is due. Her partner is made redundant and she decides to work closer to her EWC in order to earn as much money as possible before her maternity leave and pay starts. She notifies her employer on 15 March 2007 (ie, at least 28 days before the original date of 15 April) that she wishes to start her leave on Monday 7 May 2007, one week before her baby is due. If her baby is born early, before her maternity leave has started, her leave will start on the day after childbirth, see para 4.18.

4.16   The various elements of the notice may be given at different times if the employee wishes and she can give notice earlier than the 15th week before the EWC. For example, it is generally best to give earlier notice of pregnancy as the woman is then protected from sex discrimination (see chapter 2) and health and safety provisions apply (see chapter 3). For failure to give notice correctly see para 4.24.

---

7   MPL Regs 1999 reg 4(1)(b).

Trigger rule

4.17   Different provisions apply if the employee is triggered on to leave by pregnancy-related absence. Where the woman is absent wholly or partly because of pregnancy at any time after the beginning of the fourth week before the EWC, her employer may (but does not have to) insist that her maternity leave begins on the day after her first day of absence (see para 4.30 onwards). She must inform her employer, as soon as reasonably practicable, that she is absent from work wholly or partly because of pregnancy and of the date on which her pregnancy-related absence began (see table on page 141).[8] The employer may ask for this notice to be in writing.[9] It is important to distinguish pregnancy-related absence (which will often be sickness) and ordinary sickness (see para 4.39).

Early birth

4.18   Where the woman gives birth before the start of her maternity leave, her OML will start on the day after the day of childbirth. Regardless of whether she has already informed her employer of the date she intends to start her maternity leave, she must inform her employer, as soon as reasonably practicable, that she has given birth and the date of childbirth (see table on page 141). The employer may ask for the notice to be in writing. For failure to give notice correctly see para 4.24.

4.19   Note that the ERA 1996 requirements for notice of maternity leave are different from the requirements under the maternity pay legislation (para 6.49 onwards). Most women will claim both maternity leave and pay, so the table on page 141 shows the minimum requirements for a woman claiming both.

Medical certificate

4.20   In all cases where a woman is asking for SMP or, if she only requires leave, where requested by the employer, the woman must provide a medical certificate signed by a doctor or registered midwife giving the EWC.[10] The employer's request must clearly require a certificate, which will generally be a MAT B1. The MPL Regs 1999 do not specify

---

8   MPL Regs 1999 reg 4(3).
9   MPL Regs 1999 reg 4(5).
10   MPL Regs 1999 reg 4(1)(b).

What is the notice for?	Notice period required	Contents of notice
OML/OML and AML and SMP	By the end of the 15th week before the EWC or as soon as reasonably practicable (see para 6.12 for how to find the 15th week before the EWC)	I am pregnant My EWC is . . . I intend to start my leave on . . . (in writing if requested) Medical evidence of EWC (must supply this for SMP)
To change the start of OML/OML and AML and SMP	At least 28 days before the new and the old date, whichever is earliest, or as soon as reasonably practicable	I wish to change the start of my maternity leave. My leave will now start on . . . (in writing if requested)
OML/OML and AML and SMP when leave triggered by pregnancy-related absence in last four weeks of pregnancy	As soon as reasonably practicable	I am absent from work because of pregnancy and my absence began on . . . (in writing if requested) Medical evidence of EWC (must supply this for SMP if not already done so)
OML/OML and AML and SMP when baby born (stillborn) before notice of leave given	As soon as reasonably practicable after the birth (stillbirth)	I was pregnant My EWC was . . . I have given birth and my baby was born (stillborn) on . . . (in writing if requested) Medical evidence of EWC and evidence of birth/stillbirth, eg, birth certificate or certificate of stillbirth (must supply this for SMP within 21 days of birth or as soon as practicable)
OML/OML and AML and SMP when baby born (stillborn) after notice given but before leave began	As soon as reasonably practicable after the birth (stillbirth)	I have given birth and my baby was born (stillborn) on . . . (in writing if requested) Medical evidence of EWC and evidence of birth/stillbirth, eg, birth certificate or certificate of stillbirth (must supply this for SMP within 21 days of birth or as soon as practicable)

a time limit for producing a certificate, though it should be produced within a reasonable timescale. However, there is a strict timescale for SMP purposes (see para 6.49). There is no obligation to provide a certificate if it is not requested, except that it is required to claim SMP (see para 6.49). For failure to comply with an employer's request see para 4.24.

Notice required for contractual rights

4.21   Where the woman claims the benefit of more favourable contractual terms but there is no provision in the contract (or by agreement with the employer) for notice, then the statutory provisions regarding notice will apply (see *Kolfor Plant Ltd v Wright*[11]).

Not reasonably practicable

4.22   An employee is not entitled to maternity leave until the correct notice has been given or it was not reasonably practicable to give notice. It will be a question of fact whether it was reasonably practicable to give the correct notice. Absence from work because of pregnancy complications may constitute a good reason, particularly if the woman was unaware of her obligations, as well as complications following a premature birth or where the baby was stillborn.

4.23   However, notice should *always* be given on time where possible; it is never safe to assume that it can be given late.

Failure to give notice about pregnancy and start of leave

4.24   A woman is only entitled to her statutory right to OML and AML and the benefit of her terms and conditions during OML if she gives the required notice and medical certificate (if requested) before going on leave or as soon as reasonably practicable after leave has started as a result of a pregnancy-related absence or childbirth.[12]

4.25   Even if no notice is given, the woman's contract should not come to an end unless and until terminated by the employer or employee (see para 5.14). If the employer terminates a woman's contract for a reason related to her pregnancy, childbirth or maternity leave, this will be automatically unfair under ERA 1996 s99 (see para 15.58). It

11   [1982] IRLR 311, EAT.
12   MPL Regs 1999 reg 4.

may also be an ordinary unfair dismissal (see para 15.70 onwards) and discriminatory (see paras 2.34 and 15.40). Because an employer cannot terminate a woman's employment (by dismissing her or by treating her employment as at an end), it is probable that in practice a woman who does not give the correct notice will lose nothing more than her right to accrue her contractual rights during her time off, although this may be sex discrimination and a breach of the EU Pregnant Workers Directive (PWD).

4.26 A refusal to allow a woman to return to work would be unfair dismissal and sex discrimination (ERA 1996 s71) and a breach of the PWD which provides for a minimum period of leave. In *Rashid v Asian Community Care Services* the EAT decided that a woman who failed to return from leave on time had not repudiated her contract. A woman who took time off to have a baby without giving proper notice could also argue that she had not repudiated her contract.[13]

Employer's failure to advise about rights

4.27 There is no statutory obligation on employers to inform employees of their rights. However, there may be circumstances in which an employer cannot insist on strict compliance with the law where they have not given their employees any guidance on their maternity rights.[14] In *Thurisamy v Alma Enterprises Ltd*,[15] the employee gave notice just before going on maternity leave. Her employer wrote to say that her job would not be kept open for her. The ET held that the dismissal was unfair as the employee had given notice before going on leave and the company had not taken satisfactory steps to inform their employees, many of whom spoke English as a second language, of their rights. (See para 4.62 on employer's failure to notify end of maternity leave.)

Notice provisions relating to AML

4.28 There are no additional notice provisions for AML. Once a woman has given the correct notice for OML she will be entitled to take AML, providing she qualifies for it (see paras 4.9–4.13). Note: An

---

13 IDS Brief 678, February 2001.
14 *Gray v Smith* [1996] DCLD 30, No 03216/95.
15 ET Case No 27627/94.

employer may no longer write to a woman 21 days before the end of her ordinary maternity leave period asking for written confirmation of whether she intends to return to work at the end of her AML period,[16] but see para 4.48 on keeping in touch during maternity leave.

Employer's notice of the end of maternity leave

4.29   Once an employer has received notice of the date a woman wants to start her OML, the employer must write to the woman within 28 days,[17] notifying her of the date her OML will end, if she is only entitled to OML, or, if she is entitled to OML and AML, the date her AML will end.[18] If a woman has given notice to vary the date her maternity leave starts, see para 4.15, her employer must write to her within 28 days of the date her OML started.[19]

Commencement of leave

4.30   A woman cannot start her OML before the start of the 11th week before the EWC (unless the baby is born before the 11th week). The EWC is the date on the MATB 1 certificate or any other certificate from the midwife or doctor (see para 6.49).

4.31   It is generally up to the woman to decide when her OML starts. It will be either:

- the date she notifies to her employer (see para 4.14); or
- the day after the date on which she gives birth; or
- where she has a pregnancy-related absence during the four weeks before the EWC, the day after her first day of absence (see para 4.35).[20]

4.32   To calculate the earliest date the woman can give for the start of her OML:

- start with the Sunday before the baby is due (ie, at the beginning of the EWC);

---

16   MPL Regs 1999 reg 12, revoked by the MPL (Amend) Regs 2002 in respect of women whose EWC is on or after 6 April 2003.
17   MPL Regs 1999 reg 7(7).
18   MPL Regs 1999 reg 7(6).
19   MPL Regs 1999 reg 7(7).
20   MPL Regs 1999 reg 6.

- count back 11 weeks (to the 11th Sunday – a week ends on a Saturday);[21]
- the earliest leave can start is the 11th Sunday.

For example, if the baby is due on Thursday 23 November 2006, the EWC began on Sunday 19 November, and 11 Sundays before this date will be 3 September 2006. Maternity leave could commence on any day from 3 September 2006. See the table at appendix C, column 4 for the start of the 11th week before the EWC.

4.33 Even where there is a provision in the contract stating that the woman must start her maternity leave at a specified time, this is overridden by the statute which allows women to choose the start date.[22] Many women will want to start their OML as close as possible to the EWC in order to maximise the number of weeks off after the birth. OML lasts for 26 weeks from the actual day it starts.[23]

4.34 If a woman is entitled to AML (see para 4.9), her AML begins on the day after the last day of her OML period.[24] AML lasts for 26 weeks from the day it started.[25]

Absence due to pregnancy during four weeks before EWC

4.35 A woman who, in the four weeks before the EWC, is absent wholly or partly because of her pregnancy (for example, because she has high blood pressure) will have to commence her OML on the day after the first day of absence from work, unless her employer agrees otherwise (see para 4.42).[26] If she has given birth, her leave will start on the day after the day of childbirth.

4.36 It is not clear whether a woman who is off work for as little as half a day because of her pregnancy may, in theory, have to start her leave or whether the trigger rule only applies if she is absent for a whole day.

4.37 If the woman is not aware of these provisions, she may return to work for a few days only to discover that, when she tells her employer she was off for a pregnancy-related reason, she is informed that her maternity leave started from the time she was off. If this happens she will lose some of her paid leave (see para 6.62).

---

21 See *Secretary of State for Employment v A Ford & Son (Sacks) Ltd* [1986] ICR 882, EAT.
22 *Inner London Education Authority v Nash* [1979] ICR 229, EAT.
23 MPL Regs 1999 reg 7(1).
24 MPL Regs 1999 reg 6(3).
25 MPL Regs 1999 reg 7(4).
26 MPL Regs 1999 reg 6(1)(b) and (2).

Sickness unrelated to pregnancy does not trigger maternity leave

4.38   If the absence is not related to the woman's pregnancy, it does not trigger maternity leave and she can take sick leave (and receive statutory or contractual sick pay or incapacity benefit) until the date of the birth or start of her maternity leave. It is therefore very important to distinguish between ordinary sickness and pregnancy-related sickness.

What is pregnancy-related absence?

4.39   This will generally depend on the doctor's opinion. There are some conditions which are clearly pregnancy-related, such as high blood pressure, and others where the illness is linked to and exacerbated by pregnancy, such as backache. The woman may need to get a medical certificate to confirm whether or not the absence is pregnancy-related. Absence at an antenatal class should not count.

4.40   Although not explicit, it is likely that a woman who has been suspended for health and safety reasons will be treated as absent because of her pregnancy and therefore forced to start her maternity leave from the fourth week.

No obligation to provide medical certificate showing fitness to work

4.41   There is no obligation on the woman to provide a medical certificate to show she is fit. If the employer asks for such a certificate, the woman would be entitled to refuse. The onus is on the employer to carry out a health and safety risk assessment to determine if the working conditions pose any risk (see para 3.19 onwards).

Right of woman to work following pregnancy-related absence

4.42   An employer need not force the woman to start her maternity leave if she has a pregnancy-related absence. The contract of employment may give the woman the right to choose when her leave starts, irrespective of pregnancy-related absences, in which case this overrides the statutory provisions. Alternatively, the employer may agree to the woman starting it later. It is advisable, if possible, to get such agreement in writing. Department of Trade and Industry (DTI) guidance says that odd days of pregnancy-related illness may be disregarded at the employer's discretion if the employee wishes to defer the start of her maternity leave period.[27]

27 DTI Guide to Maternity Rights, PL 958 p55.

4.43   If the employer allows a woman to return to work after pregnancy-related absence and nothing is specifically agreed, there may have been a waiver of these triggering provisions. This will only apply if the woman informed her employer, as she is obliged to do, that the absence was pregnancy-related (see para 4.17). In such a case, maternity leave should start at the date given in the original notice.

4.44   The trigger provisions have been unsuccessfully challenged as being a breach of EU law. In *Boyle v EOC*[28] the European Court of Justice held that it was for the member state to fix periods of maternity leave and the rule was not a breach of the PWD nor the ETD (Equal Treatment Directive).

Commencement of SMP period

4.45   The SMP period is automatically triggered if there is a pregnancy-related absence in the four weeks before the EWC and this cannot be overridden. This poses a problem for employers who wish to ignore odd days of absence from work (see para 6.60 onwards).

Premature births

4.46   The maternity leave period will automatically start on the day after the day on which the baby is born.[29] There is no right to postpone all or part of maternity leave unless this is negotiated with the employer. Some employers allow the employee to split her leave by taking some when the baby is born and then returning to work and taking the rest of her leave when the baby comes out of hospital. However, there is no provision for splitting the SMP period. Other employers consider extending leave when a baby is premature. An employee may also be entitled to take parental leave, see chapter 10.

Stillbirths

4.47   Childbirth is defined as the birth of a living child (however premature) or of a child (whether living or dead) after 24 weeks of pregnancy.[30] A woman who gives birth to a live baby is entitled to maternity leave whenever the baby is born and even if the baby only lives for a very short time. A woman who has a stillbirth after 24 weeks will

---

28   *Boyle v Equal Opportunities Commission* [1998] IRLR 717, ECJ.
29   MPL Regs 1999 reg 6(2).
30   MPL Regs 1999 reg 2(1).

also be entitled to maternity leave. When the birth or stillbirth occurs, her OML will start on the day after the birth or stillbirth. For the purposes of calculating 26 weeks' service by the 14th week before the baby is due (for entitlement to AML), any week of absence after the birth but before the 11th week will count toward continuous service and so will entitle the woman to AML.

Keeping in touch during maternity leave

Reasonable contact

Employees whose EWC is on or after 1 April 2007

4.48　Where the EWC is on or after 1 April 2007, an employer may make reasonable contact with the employee.[31] This is to enable the employer and employee to keep in touch during maternity leave. Guidance on 'reasonable contact' is expected from the DTI by the end of 2006.

Work during maternity leave

4.49　An employee may work for up to 10 keeping in touch (KIT) days during OML or AML without bringing her maternity leave to an end[32] However, an employee may not work during the two weeks of compulsory maternity leave immediately after the birth of her baby,[33] see para 4.63 for compulsory maternity leave. Factory workers are prohibited from working during the four weeks immediately after the birth. The work can be consecutive or not and can include training or any other activity (for example, a staff meeting) that enables the employee to keep in touch with the workplace. Working for part of a day will count as one day's work.[34] Any such work must be by agreement and neither the employer nor the employee can insist on it. Any days of work will not extend the maternity leave period.[35] An employee is protected from detriment and unfair dismissal for working or refusing to work during maternity leave, see para 4.109. An employee may work for up to 10 KIT days during her maternity leave

31　MPL Regs 1999 reg 12A(4) inserted by the Maternity and Parental Leave etc and the Paternity and Adoption Leave (Amendment) Regulations 2006 reg 9.
32　MPL Regs 1999 reg 12A(1).
33　MPL Regs 1999 reg 12A(5).
34　MPL Regs 1999 reg 12A(2) and (3).
35　MPL Regs 1999 reg 12A(6) and (7).

without losing her SMP or MA, see paras 6.77 and 7.35. There are no specific provisions in the regulations in relation to pay for KIT days, therefore it will be a matter for agreement between the employer and employee. SMP can be offset against any payments of contractual maternity pay, see para 6.107.

4.50   Note: These provisions do not apply where the EWC is before 1 April 2007.

4.51   See chapter 5 for rights during maternity leave.

Returning to work

Returning at the end of maternity leave

4.52   An employee should return to work on the first working day after the end of her 26-week OML or, if she qualifies for AML (all employees whose EWC is on or after 1 April 2007), the first working day after the end of her 52-week AML. Her employer should have notified her of the date of return within 28 days of her notice to take maternity leave, see para 4.29. If her employer failed to notify her of her return date and she does not return to work on time, she may have protection against dismissal.

Notice of return to work

4.53   Unless a woman gives notice that she wants to return earlier, the assumption is that a woman who is *only* entitled to OML will return to work at the end of her OML (see below). If she is also entitled to AML it is assumed she will return at the end of her AML.[36] If she wishes to take all of the leave to which she is entitled, she does not need to give notice of return to work if she returns on the day after the end of the OML and/or AML period to which she is entitled. This is provided there is no health and safety reason which prevents her from working[37] and she has not been dismissed[38] (see para 15.33). If she is dismissed, her leave ends at the time of the dismissal (see para 4.107 on dismissal).

4.54   Note that an employee who wants to take parental leave after the

---

36   MPL Regs 1999 reg 7(1), (4) and reg 11.
37   MPL Regs 1999 reg 7(2), (3) and reg 8.
38   MPL Regs 1999 reg 7(5).

end of OML must give appropriate notice (see chapter 10), see para 4.76 for rights to return after consecutive periods of leave.

Return at the end of OML for women who are entitled to AML

4.55   It is likely that an employee who is entitled to AML cannot return at the end of the 26-week OML period without giving notice to return early. The assumption is that she will return *at the end of the AML period* to which she is entitled *unless she gives notice* as she is effectively returning to work early. A woman who is entitled to AML should give 28 days' or eight weeks' notice (depending on her EWC, see paras 4.56–4.59) if she intends to return at any time before the end of AML. DTI guidance states that an employee entitled to AML, who only wishes to take 26 weeks' OML, must give her employer notice of her return to work because she will be returning to work before her full maternity leave entitlement has ended.[39] If she is only taking OML, she has a clear right to return to the same job (see para 4.65) as she has not taken AML.

Notice of early return

Notice of early return where an employee's EWC is before 1 April 2007

4.56   A woman who wants to return to work before the end of her OML or AML must give her employer at least 28 days' notice of the date she intends to return.[40] The notice need not be in writing, but it is advisable to put it in writing to avoid any doubt.

4.57   If the employee returns to work without giving 28 days' notice, the employer is entitled to postpone her return until she has given 28 days' notice. An employer cannot postpone her return to work beyond the end of her maternity leave period (OML or AML).[41] Where the employer has postponed the woman's return and informed her of this, the employer is entitled to refuse to pay the woman until she has given the required notice or the maternity leave period has expired.[42] For example, if a woman (who is not entitled to AML) returns three

---

39   DTI Guide to Maternity Rights PL 958, p63.
40   MPL Regs 1999 reg 11(1).
41   MPL Regs 1999 reg 11(2) and (3).
42   MPL Regs 1999 reg 11(4).

days before the expiry of her OML, having given only two weeks' notice, the employer can refuse to pay her until the day after the end of the 26 weeks.

Notice of early return where an employee's EWC is on or after 1 April 2007

4.58   If an employee wants to return to work before the end of AML (to which all employees whose EWC is on or after 1 April 2007 are entitled, see para 4.13), she must give at least eight weeks' notice of the date she wishes to return.[43] Notice of early return does not have to be in writing, but it is advisable.

4.59   If she returns to work without giving eight weeks' notice, an employer is entitled to postpone her return for the full notice period, but an employer cannot postpone it beyond the end of the AML period.[44] If her employer notifies her that her return date has been postponed and she returns to work anyway, she is not entitled to be paid.[45] This does not apply if her employer did not notify her of the date her AML ends. In that case, she does not have to give notice of early return and the employer has no right to delay her return or refuse to pay her for returning early.[46]

More than one change of return date

4.60   If an employee has given eight weeks' notice to return to work before the end of her AML on date X but she changes her mind and wants to go back earlier than date X, she must give at least eight weeks' notice of the date she now intends to return. If she wants to go back later than date X she must give at least eight weeks' notice before date X.[47] These notice requirements also apply where an employer has postponed an employee's return because she returned to work before the end of her eight-week notice period and she wishes to change the return date.

---

43 MPL Regs 1999 reg 11(1) as amended by the Maternity and Parental Leave etc and the Paternity and Adoption Leave (Amendment) Regulations 2006 reg 8(a).
44 MPL Regs 1999 reg 11(3).
45 MPL Regs 1999 reg 11(4).
46 MPL Regs 1999 reg 11(5).
47 MPL Regs 1999 reg 11(2A) as amended by the Maternity and Parental Leave etc and the Paternity and Adoption Leave (Amendment) Regulations 2006 reg 8(c).

EXAMPLE: Mary's AML ends on 15 March 2007. She decides to go back to work early and on 15 September 2006 gives her employer notice that she will return to work on 1 January 2007. She has difficulty finding suitable childcare and decides that it may not be possible to return to work on 1 January. Therefore, on 1 November 2006 she gives notice to her employer that she will now return on 1 February 2007. Because she is returning later than originally notified, Mary has given her employer notice on 1 November 2006 of a new date at least eight weeks before the date of 1 January 2007 originally notified.

4.61　Note: Where the EWC is before 1 April 2007, there are no specific notice provisions allowing an employee to change her mind once she has given notice to return to work early or had her return postponed after returning to work without giving sufficient notice.

Employer's failure to notify end of maternity leave

4.62　An employee does not have to give notice of early return from maternity leave if her employer failed to notify her of the date her maternity leave would end, see para 4.29. Her employer also has no right to postpone her return or to refuse to pay her in these circumstances.[48] An employee is protected from detriment and dismissal for failing to return at the end of maternity leave where her employer did not notify her of the end of maternity leave and it was reasonable for her to believe that her leave had not ended or where her employer gave her less than 28 days' notice of the date her leave would end and it was not reasonably practicable for her to return by that date.[49]

EXAMPLE: Mary contacted her employer on 15 March 2007 to say that her doctor had signed her off work for two weeks because of high blood pressure. Her baby was born early on 30 March 2007 and she contacted her employer the following day to say that her baby had been born. Mary's maternity leave began on 16 March 2007 as a result of a pregnancy-related illness in the last four weeks

---

48　MPL Regs 1999 reg 11(5).
49　MPL Regs 1999 regs 19(2)(ee) and 20(3)(ee).

of her pregnancy. However, her employer did not notify her of the date her maternity leave would end.

Mary met with her employer in February 2008 to discuss returning to work part-time and her employer agreed.

On 5 March 2008 her employer wrote to her to confirm that she would return on a part-time basis and that she was due back on 16 March 2008 (52 weeks after her leave started) but giving less than the required 28 days' notice. Mary thought that her maternity leave had started on 31 March 2007, the day after the day her baby was born. Her employer cannot dismiss her for failing to return on 16 March 2008, as they should have given her at least 28 days' notice of her return and Mary should return by 1 April 2008 at the latest, which is when she believed her leave ended.

Statutory prohibitions on working after leave

4.63   The only situations where a woman cannot return to work after the end of OML are where:

a) There is some other statutory prohibition on working, in which case the OML will continue for as long as there is a statutory provision which prohibits her from working,[50] eg:
   – Health and safety legislation provides that a woman working in a factory or workshop must not return to work within four weeks of childbirth.[51] This covers people doing manual work involving the making, repairing or cleaning of any goods. Breach of the prohibition by the employer is a criminal offence punishable by a fine on level 1. The woman is not entitled to be paid.
   – A woman is not allowed to work for two weeks after the birth.[52] This period (which is called 'compulsory maternity leave') begins with the day the baby was born. It is an offence for an employer to allow an employee to return to work within these two weeks, punishable by a fine not exceeding level 2 on the standard scale. The Health and Safety Executive has the

---

50   MPL Regs 1999 reg 7(2) and (3).
51   Public Health Act 1936 s205 (as amended).
52   MPL Regs 1999 reg 8.

responsibility for enforcing these provisions. The woman is not entitled to be paid.

b) There is a health and safety risk to the woman (because she has recently given birth or is breastfeeding) and the employer has suspended her[53] (see para 3.55). The woman is entitled to full pay during her suspension (see para 3.56).

Situations a) and b) are mutually exclusive. Situation b) does not apply where there is a statutory prohibition on working (see chapter 3).

Employee becomes pregnant while on maternity leave

4.64   Where an employee who becomes pregnant while on maternity leave wants to return to work early (from her existing maternity leave) there is no obligation to inform her employer that she is pregnant again. This applies even if she will be unable to carry out all of her duties because of statutory prohibitions imposed because of pregnancy.[54] The reason is because it would be unlawful discrimination for the employer to treat her unfavourably because of her pregnancy, so it is irrelevant. See also para 4.82.

Right to return to the same job after OML

4.65   The right to return is the right to return to exactly the same job on the same terms and conditions of employment as if she had not been absent[55] (unless a redundancy situation has arisen, in which case she is entitled to be offered a suitable alternative vacancy if the redundancy occurs during leave – see para 4.110). 'Job' means 'the nature of the work which she is employed to do in accordance with her contract and the capacity and place in which she is so employed'.[56] This means she is entitled to benefit from any general improvements to the rate of pay, or other terms and conditions, which may have been introduced for her grade or class of work while she has been away.

---

53   ERA 1996 s66.
54   *Busch v Klinikum etc* [2003] IRLR 625, ECJ.
55   ERA 1996 s71(4)(c).
56   ERA 1996 s235(1). 'Job', in relation to a return after AML and parental leave, is also defined in MPL Regs 1999 reg 2. It is identical.

4.66 An employee has different rights to return where she takes two or more consecutive periods of leave which include additional maternity leave, additional adoption leave or parental leave of more than four weeks. See *Consecutive periods of leave* at para 4.76 onwards.

4.67 Where an employee is not allowed to return at all, or where she is not given her old job back at the end of OML, she will be treated as having been dismissed. She may have a claim for unfair dismissal, automatically unfair dismissal and/or discrimination, depending on the reason for the dismissal (see chapter 15). If her old job has changed for the worse, she may have a detriment claim (see para 15.127 onwards) or may be able to resign and claim constructive dismissal (see para 15.23 onwards).

Right to return to same or equivalent job after AML

4.68 A woman who returns to work after AML is entitled to return from leave to the job in which she was employed before her absence or if it is not 'reasonably practicable', for a reason other than redundancy, for the employer to allow her to return to that job she must be given another job which is:

- suitable for her; and
- appropriate for her to do in the circumstances.[57]

4.69 For the position where an employee combines other periods of leave with AML, eg parental leave or a second period of ordinary maternity leave, see *Consecutive periods of leave* at para 4.76.

4.70 'Job' in relation to an employee returning after AML means 'the nature of the work which she is employed to do in accordance with her contract and the capacity and place in which she is to be employed'.[58] Thus, whether or not the work is exactly the same, the nature of the work, the contract, capacity and place should be the same.

4.71 Where it is not reasonably practicable for the woman to return to exactly the same job because, for example, there has been a

57 MPL Regs 1999 reg 18(2) and (4).
58 MPL Regs 1999 reg 2 and ERA 1996 s235(1).

reorganisation (falling short of redundancy)[59] during her absence, she must be given a similar job which has the same or better status and terms and conditions as the old job. In these circumstances, the woman should be consulted about any changes in the same way as other employees, and failure to do so may be discriminatory.[60] Similarly, if the reason for the change in job is because she has been absent on maternity leave, this will be discriminatory.

4.72   The onus is on the employer to show that it is not reasonably practicable to allow the woman to return to her old job. In *Stelfox v Westco Building Components Ltd*[61] the claimant's temporary replacement was made permanent and the claimant was offered a different job. The employment tribunal held that the employer had not proved that it was not practicable to give the claimant back her job. Her dismissal was automatically unfair. It would also have been discriminatory as 'but for' her absence on maternity leave, she would not have lost her job. There is a potential conflict between the right to return after AML and protection from discrimination. If the reason the employer says that it is not reasonably practicable for the woman to return to exactly the same job is that the work has been reallocated in her absence, this may fall within the ERA exception but it would be discrimination; 'but for' her maternity leave she would have retained exactly the same job (see para 2.57).

4.73   The other exception to the right to return to the same job after AML is where the employee's job has been made redundant. If the redundancy occurred during her maternity leave she is first entitled to be offered a suitable alternative vacancy. This is discussed in para 15.100 and see para 4.110 on redundancy during maternity leave.

Terms and conditions of job on return

4.74   Whether the woman returns to the same or an equivalent job, it must be:

- with her seniority, pension rights and similar rights as they would have been if the period prior to her AML were continuous with

---

59   It is often difficult to determine whether there has been a reorganisation or whether there has been a redundancy situation. How it is defined by the employer is not necessarily conclusive (see para 15.77).
60   See *McGuigan v TG Baynes* EAT 1114/97, 24 November 1998 (see para 15.94).
61   ET 15083/95.

her employment following her return from work (see para 5.125).[62] This is subject to the special provisions relating to pensions (see 5.112 onwards). This means that the period of AML will not count unless the contract provides otherwise but is arguably sex discrimination and contrary to the PWD[63] (see para 5.42 onwards); and

- on terms and conditions no less favourable than she would have received if she had not been absent.[64]

4.75 An employee returning to work after AML is entitled to benefit from any general improvements to the rate of pay, or other terms and conditions, which may have been introduced for her grade or class of work while she has been away.[65] If terms and conditions have been validly altered she will suffer the same disadvantage as other employees. She should however be consulted about any changes in the same way as other employees.

Consecutive periods of leave

4.76 If a woman returns to work after a single period of OML, parental leave of four weeks or less, or OML followed by parental leave of four weeks or less, she has the right to return to exactly the same job she was doing before she started her leave (see para 4.65 on return from OML and chapter 10 on parental leave). If the OML or parental leave of four weeks or less is at the end of two or more consecutive periods of leave which does not include any period of AML, additional adoption leave (AAL) or parental leave of more than four weeks, she retains the right to return to the same job.[66]

EXAMPLE: If a woman takes OML and two weeks' parental leave immediately afterwards (this might be because she gets some paid parental leave from her employer, but not paid AML), she has the right to return to the job she was doing before she started her OML.

---

62 MPL Regs 1999 reg 18A(1)(a).
63 *Land Brandenburg v Sass* [2005] IRLR 147, ECJ.
64 MPL Regs 1999 reg 18A(1)(b).
65 See DTI Guide to Maternity rights PL958, p77.
66 MPL Regs 1999 reg 18(1).

4.77   If a woman returns to work after a period of AML or parental leave of more than four weeks and it is not reasonably practicable for her to return to the same job, she can be offered a suitable alternative job on similar terms and conditions (see para 4.68 on return from AML and chapter 10 on parental leave). Where a woman takes two or more consecutive periods of leave, which includes a period of AML, AAL or parental leave of more than four weeks (regardless of whether her leave begins or ends with AML, AAL or parental leave of more than four weeks) she is entitled to return to the job she was doing immediately before her first period of leave started[67] but, if it is not reasonably practicable for her to return to that job, she must be offered a suitable alternative job on similar terms and conditions.[68]

> EXAMPLE: If a woman takes OML and AML, followed by a further consecutive period of OML in respect of a second baby, she will not have the right to return to exactly the same job after her second period of OML if it is not reasonably practicable, but will have the right to return to a suitable alternative job on similar terms and conditions.

4.78   Note: If a woman returns to work, even for just one day, between periods of leave, she maintains the rights that apply to each individual leave period. Also, once her leave has ended, if she is on sick leave or annual leave, she is counted as having returned to work.

> EXAMPLE: A woman with a young child takes five weeks' parental leave in order to settle her child into nursery school and spend some time with her before the arrival of her new baby. She returns to work for a week and then starts her maternity leave. At the end of her OML she returns to work and has the right to return to exactly the same job. If she had taken the parental leave of more than four weeks immediately before her OML, with no break, she could be offered a suitable alternative job if it was not reasonably practicable for her to return to the same job.

---

67 MPL Regs 1999 reg 18(3).
68 MPL Regs 1999 reg 18(2).

4.79   Thus the right to return to exactly the same job (as with OML) applies where the employee returns in the following circumstances:

- after OML (or OAL) on its own or OML (or OAL) plus parental leave of four weeks or less, taken either before or after the OML (or OAL);
- after parental leave of four weeks or less.

4.80   The employer can only argue that it is not reasonably practicable for her to return to the same job where she returns:

- after AML (or AAL), or any period longer than OML (or OAL), which for these purposes is treated as being a return after AML;
- after parental leave of more than four weeks;
- after AML, followed immediately by OML or parental leave (irrespective of length).

4.81   A woman who is not allowed to return to the same job or is not offered suitable alternative employment on similar terms and conditions may have a claim for unfair dismissal, detriment or sex discrimination, see chapter 15.

Two consecutive periods of maternity leave

4.82   If a woman becomes pregnant again during her maternity leave she will be entitled to any further leave and pay that she qualifies for, see paras 4.8–4.13 for leave and para 6.10 for maternity pay. Her maternity leave counts as continuous employment for leave and pay purposes. She may qualify for SMP in respect of her second pregnancy if she has average earnings of at least £84 a week (the lower earnings limit from April 2006 to April 2007) in the relevant period, see para 6.81 onwards. She can include previous payments of SMP as earnings, if it falls within the relevant period, but not MA. If she has taken additional maternity leave she may not have high enough earnings in the relevant period in order to qualify for SMP for her second period of leave. However, she may qualify for MA, see para 7.12.

4.83   If a woman takes two consecutive periods of maternity leave which includes a period of AML – for example, OML and AML in respect of her first pregnancy, immediately followed by OML in respect of her second pregnancy – she will have the right to return to her original job or, if this is not reasonably practicable, to a suitable alternative job on similar terms and conditions. If she returns to work between her periods of maternity leave, even for just one day, she will have the right to return to her original job if she just takes OML in respect of her second pregnancy.

Exceptions to the right to claim automatically unfair dismissal at the end of AML

Small employers exemption

For women whose EWC is before 1 April 2007

4.84   A woman will not have a right to return to work after AML where the employer can show that:

- immediately before the end of the woman's AML (or if she is dismissed, immediately before the dismissal), the total number of employees employed by her employer (and any associated employer) did not exceed five; and
- it is not reasonably practicable for the employer or any successor to allow the woman to return to the same job or to offer a job which is suitable for her and appropriate in the circumstance.[69]

4.85   The small employer must first consider whether the employee can return to the same job and then whether there is a similar job. Only if the employer can show that there is no such job and no suitable alternative, will the exception apply. Although the dismissal will not be automatically unfair, the employee may still be able to claim unfair dismissal and sex discrimination.

4.86   In *Stewart and Gower t/a Gowers v Male*[70] the Employment Appeal Tribunal (EAT) stressed that the employer had to show it was not reasonably practicable for the woman to return. The employer had restructured to cover for the claimant's absence but had not considered whether other employees could cover for her, as they had done when she had been off sick. The dismissal was therefore unfair.

---

69   MPL Regs 1999 reg 20(6).
70   EAT 813/93, 19 May 1994.

Women whose EWC is on or after 1 April 2007

4.87 The small employer's exemption has been removed for employees whose EWC is on or after 1 April 2007. An employee can claim automatic unfair dismissal if she is prevented from returning to the same job or a suitable alternative job, regardless of the size of the organisation.[71]

Offer of suitable alternative work

4.88 The woman will lose her right to return to work and will not be able to claim automatically unfair dismissal where:

- it is not reasonably practicable for a reason *other than redundancy* for the employer or any successor to permit the woman to return to the same job or to offer a job, which is suitable for her and appropriate for her to do in the circumstances; and
- an associated employer offers her a suitable and appropriate job; and
- she accepts or unreasonably refuses that offer.[72]

4.89 This situation might arise where there has been a business reorganisation, which is not a redundancy (where separate rules apply – see para 15.77). The alternative work must be suitable for the employee and appropriate in the circumstances. Other terms and conditions of the contract must not be substantially less favourable. Thus, a move to a different location which would involve more travelling is unlikely to be suitable (see para 15.104 onwards). In this situation employees may want to argue that there is a redundancy because they are then automatically entitled to a suitable job or redundancy pay.

4.90 Although an employer might argue that this exception applies if it has employed a permanent replacement, it will be difficult for the employer to show that it was not 'reasonably practicable' for the employer to allow the woman to return both to her former job *and* a

---

71 MPL Regs 1999 reg 20(6) as amended by the Maternity and Parental Leave etc and the Paternity and Adoption Leave (Amendment) Regulations 2006 reg 11(b).
72 MPL Regs 1999 reg 20(7). See ERA 1996 s231 for the definition of 'associated employer'.

suitable alternative. Even if the replacement was about to complete a complex piece of work and it would not be practicable for the returning employee to take it over, the employer should agree to allow a woman returning from maternity leave to have her job back when the project has been completed. Refusal to do so is likely to be discriminatory. In *Rees v Apollo Watch Repairs plc*[73] a woman was refused the right to return to her job as the employer had found her replacement more efficient. The EAT held that this was unlawful discrimination as the effective reason for the employee's dismissal was pregnancy since, but for her absence through pregnancy, the unfavourable comparison with her replacement would not have arisen. This would also be an ordinary unfair dismissal claim.[74]

4.91　The flowchart at para 4.92 illustrates the steps an employer must take when an employee is returning from AML.

Sick leave or annual leave at the end of maternity leave

4.92　If a woman takes sick leave or annual leave immediately after her maternity leave it does not affect her rights to return, see para 5.95 for rights to accrue annual leave during maternity leave. She is entitled to take sick leave and/or annual leave and should be treated the same as any other employee. If she is not well enough to return to work at the end of her maternity leave she should follow her employer's normal sickness reporting procedures. She is entitled to any contractual sick pay that she would normally receive, see para 7.53 onwards for entitlement to statutory sick pay (SSP). If she wishes to take annual leave, she should agree her leave with her employer in the normal way. It may be a good idea to confirm the arrangement in writing to avoid any confusion, ie confirm in writing the day the woman's maternity leave ends, the dates that have been agreed for annual leave and the date she will actually be returning to work.

73　[1996] ICR 466, EAT.
74　Under ERA 1996 s98.

Return to work at the end of AML

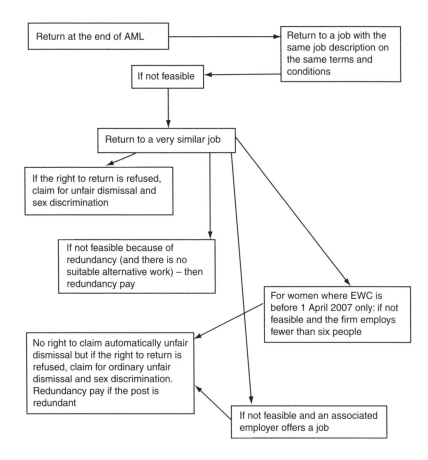

Late return

4.93   In some circumstances a woman may be unable to return to work at the end of her maternity leave, for example, she has had difficulty in finding childcare, her baby is taking a long time to settle into childcare or a breastfed baby will not take a bottle. There are a number of options for extending her time off work. A woman may take parental leave at the end of her maternity leave, providing she gives the appropriate notice, see chapter 10 for parental leave and para 4.76 for rights to return after consecutive periods of leave. She can also ask to take annual leave, see para 4.92 or ask her employer to agree to a further period off work. It is advisable to put any such agreement in writing to avoid any dispute or in case she is dismissed for failing to return to work on time.

4.94   A woman may also find it difficult to return to work on time where there is a dispute over the job she is returning to or where she and her employer have been unable to come to an agreement over her application for flexible work, see para 12.69 for options after refusal of flexible work. If an employee's job is changing, she is entitled to be consulted and the employer can make reasonable contact with her during her maternity leave to discuss such changes, see para 4.48. If an employee wishes to change her working hours she should make an application for flexible work in plenty of time – government guidance suggests that it can take up to four months for an employer to consider an application and to make any changes necessary in the workplace, eg recruiting a jobshare partner or training staff. However, where it has not been possible to reach agreement before the return date, the employee must ensure that any further time off work is agreed with her employer so that she is not treated as absent without leave. Any such arrangement should be confirmed in writing to avoid a dispute. If her job has been changed and it is unclear what job she is returning to or if her employer is still considering her application for flexible work (see paras 12.56–12.58 for time limits for considering flexible work applications) she may be entitled to be on full pay and treated as working after the end of her maternity leave. If possible, this should be clarified in writing. For discussion of what is a dismissal and whether it is discriminatory and/or unfair, see chapter 15.

Not returning to work after maternity leave

4.95   If a woman decides not to return to work after her maternity leave, she should resign giving the notice period required by her contract of employment, if she has one. If she does not have one, she should give at least one week's notice.[75] Her employment will end at the end of the notice period and she is entitled to any contractual and statutory rights that apply during that period. She is also entitled to be paid for

75   ERA 1996 s86(2).

any annual leave that she has accrued up to the end of the contract. See chapter 5 on accrual of annual leave, notice pay and other rights during maternity leave. If she resigns during her SMP period, she is still entitled to receive it for the full 26 or 39 weeks (depending on her EWC) regardless of when her contract comes to an end.

Contractual rights – 'composite rights'

4.96 An employee may have both a statutory right to return and a contractual right; this is known as a composite right. ERA 1996 s79(1)(f) provides that an employee who has both the right to return to work under the ERA 1996 and another right to return to work after absence because of pregnancy or childbirth (under a contract of employment or otherwise) may not exercise the two rights separately. She may, however, in returning to work, take advantage of whichever right is, in any particular respect, the more favourable.[76] It is not clear what the words 'or otherwise' mean, but presumably they would cover, for example, an oral agreement between employer and employee.

4.97 In *Bovey v Board of Governors of the Hospital for Sick Children*,[77] Ms Bovey wanted to return to work part-time but her employers gave her the option of returning to her original job full-time or to a lower grade job part-time. She argued she was entitled to return to her original job part-time. The EAT held that there was a limit to the extent to which the right (in this case to return to work) could be subdivided so as to identify the particular respects in which it was more favourable. The EAT upheld the ET finding that the contractual right to work part-time on the lower grade was indivisible.[78]

4.98 If the contractual right is less favourable than the statutory right, the statutory right will apply.

---

76 MPL Regs 1999 reg 21. The regulation also provides that where the composite right applies the provisions of the statutory scheme (for example, concerning notice for maternity leave) apply unless more favourable contractual rules exist.
77 [1978] IRLR 241, EAT.
78 The applicant could have argued that she had a right to return to her original job and refusal to allow her to return part-time was indirectly discriminatory (see chapter 13).

Transfer of undertakings

4.99   If there has been a transfer of the business or a service provision change, eg outsourcing, the new employer takes over the responsibilities of the old employer and the woman has a right to return with the new employer. The transfer does not terminate the contract but transfers it to the transferee organisation, including all the rights and obligations under or in connection with the contract.[79] This means that if there is a transfer during the time when a woman is exercising her maternity rights, she has the same rights against the new employer. If there is a transfer to a new employer while the woman is on OML or AML, her right to return is to the new employer. She is entitled to the benefit of her terms and conditions during leave (see chapter 5) and her service will be treated as continuous.[80]

4.100   It is unlawful to dismiss an employee as a result of the transfer unless there is an 'economic, technical or organisational reason entailing changes in the workforce of either the transferor or the transferee before or after a relevant transfer'.[81] Any reason connected with maternity leave would not be an economic, technical or organisational reason, and would also be discriminatory.

4.101   A TUPE transfer would not entitle the new employer to argue that it was an 'associated employer' with no absolute obligation to allow an employee to return.

4.102   The woman must enforce her rights against the new employer even if the breach was by the old employer.[82]

---

79   Transfer of Undertakings (Protection of Employment) Regulations 2006 (TUPE) SI No 246 reg 4(1) which came into force on 6 April 2006. The only exception is rights and obligations under or in connection with an occupational pension scheme (reg 10).
80   Even if not preserved by TUPE, continuity of service is preserved by ERA 1996 s218.
81   TUPE reg 7.
82   TUPE reg 4(2)(b).

Remedies

Dismissal or resignation before the start of maternity leave

4.103 A woman who is dismissed or forced to resign because her employer will not let her take the leave she is entitled to, or to avoid paying SMP, can claim unfair dismissal, detriment and sex discrimination (see chapter 15).

4.104 If an employee is dismissed or resigns before the start of her OML, she loses the right to maternity leave.[83] However, any dismissal for a reason related to pregnancy or maternity leave will be automatically unfair and sex discrimination, see chapter 15. She may be entitled to compensation (and possibly reinstatement or re-engagement) for unfair dismissal, which should include an amount for loss of maternity pay (see para 6.119).

4.105 If the dismissal or resignation takes place after the 15th week before the EWC (the qualifying week for SMP) the woman may have qualified for SMP and will still be entitled to receive it, see para 6.45.

4.106 Where a woman has a fixed-term contract that is not renewed, there is no right to return but the failure to renew the contract on the same terms will be a dismissal, which may be discriminatory, automatically unfair or an ordinary unfair dismissal (see para 15.21). If the reason for the failure to renew the fixed-term contract is the woman's absence on maternity leave this will be sex discrimination.

Dismissal during or at the end of maternity leave

4.107 If a woman is dismissed during OML or AML this will bring her leave to an end.[84] The woman will still be entitled to SMP for up to 26 or 39 weeks (depending on her EWC, see para 6.57) but not to the benefit of other contractual terms and conditions (see para 15.33). She may be entitled to her notice pay (see para 15.34). Note that grievance or disciplinary procedures apply during maternity leave (OML or AML).

---

83 However, if she merely says that she does not intend to return, this should not count as a resignation. If she then complies with all the notice provisions, she should be entitled to maternity leave and to return to work (*Hughes v Gwynedd Area Health Authority* [1977] IRLR 436, EAT).
84 MPL Regs 1999 reg 7(5).

4.108   If the dismissal is related to the woman's pregnancy, childbirth or maternity leave, it will be automatically unfair and discriminatory and any compensation should include her loss of benefits during OML (see para 18.12 onwards).

Women whose EWC is on or after 1 April 2007

4.109   It is automatically unfair to dismiss a woman for working or refusing to work for her employer during her maternity leave.[85] She also has protection from detriment for working or refusing to work for her employer during her maternity leave. See para 4.48 for keeping in touch during maternity leave.

Redundancy during maternity leave

4.110   Where it is not practicable, because of redundancy, for the woman to return to the same job, she must be offered a suitable vacancy, if available.[86] She has priority over other employees who may be candidates for the alternative job (see para 15.100 onwards). The new contract must take effect at the end of the previous one (see para 15.104). Note that failure to consult a woman about redundancy because she is on maternity leave is likely to be unfair and discriminatory (see para 15.92 onwards). Redundancy and unfair dismissal are covered in chapter 15.

4.111   Chapter 5 covers rights during maternity leave and chapter 15 covers dismissal, detriment and protection from discrimination where a woman's job has been changed on return from maternity leave or she has not been allowed to return to work. Chapter 3 covers the situation where an employee cannot return to work for health and safety reasons.

85 MPL Regs 1999 reg 20(3)(eee) as inserted by the Maternity and Parental Leave (Amendment) Regulations 2006 reg 11.
86 MPL Regs 1999 reg 10.

CHAPTER 5

Rights during maternity leave

Key points

- Rights during maternity leave are determined under:
  - the Employment Rights Act (ERA) 1996 and the Maternity and Parental Leave etc Regulations (MPL Regs) 1999;
  - the Sex Discrimination Act (SDA) 1975 and the Equal Pay Act (EPA) 1970;
  - contractual rights;
  - the Working Time Regulations (WT Regs) 1998;
  - European law when it provides better protection than UK law.
- An employee is not entitled to receive her full normal pay while on maternity leave (ordinary maternity leave (OML) or additional maternity leave (AML)) unless the contract provides for this.
- During OML an employee's terms and conditions of employment (other than full normal pay) continue.
- During compulsory maternity leave an employee is entitled to the benefit of any bonus, but not full pay.
- During AML an employee continues to be an employee but only some of her terms and conditions apply, such as notice and redundancy pay.
- An employee's statutory holiday entitlement (under the Working Time Regulations) accrues during OML and AML.
- It is unlawful to discriminate against a woman on grounds of her absence on maternity leave, in relation to her working conditions, eg, consulting her about redundancy, denying her opportunities for promotion.
- Where the expected childbirth or placement is on or after 1 April 2007 there will be provision for contact with employees on maternity leave and 'keeping in touch' days when employees may agree to work.
- Although an employee on maternity leave is not entitled to full normal pay, nor a contractual bonus, she must not be disadvantaged in respect of pay and benefits when she returns to work.
- Where an employee receives a pay rise after the qualifying period and before the end of her maternity leave, this must usually be included in her statutory and contractual maternity pay.

- Continuity of service continues during OML for both contractual and statutory rights. During AML service accrues only for statutory rights.
- European law (eg, Pregnant Workers Directive (PWD) and Equal Treatment Directive (ETD)) may provide greater rights during maternity leave.

Background and overview

5.1 This chapter only covers women's rights and protection during maternity leave, OML and AML. Rights during other types of leave are set out in the chapter dealing with the particular leave in question although statutory ERA rights during adoption leave are very similar to those during maternity leave.

5.2 Although a woman on maternity leave continues to be an employee, she is not entitled to receive normal full pay during OML or AML unless the contract of employment makes provision for it. Most employees with sufficient service will receive statutory maternity pay (see chapter 6). Employees whose EWC is on or after 1 April 2007 will be entitled to 52 weeks' leave (irrespective of length of service) and 39 weeks' pay (see chapter 6). However, OML and AML will remain as two 26-week periods with different rights in each (see chapter 4).

5.3 The extent to which an employee retains her other rights and benefits under the ERA 1996 and MPL Regs 1999 will depend on whether she is on OML or AML. Apart from wages or salary, the ERA and MPL Regs 1999 provide that most rights and benefits, apart from normal pay, continue during OML but not AML. The failure to maintain rights during AML (apart from pay) may be a breach of EC law (see below).

5.4 This distinction between OML and AML is not generally relevant in equal pay and sex discrimination claims. However, there is an important distinction between how discrimination law treats working conditions and non-contractual terms (covered by the SDA 1975) and pay and contractual terms (covered by the EPA 1970). The European Court of Justice (ECJ) have repeatedly said that, during her maternity leave, a woman must not be treated less favourably 'in her capacity as a worker'. This means that she should not be disadvantaged as a result of her pregnancy and taking maternity leave. However, this does not mean that, while she is on maternity leave, she is entitled to the same pay and pay related benefits as other workers not on leave (para 5.65). Thus, the rights and protection of employees on maternity leave are different from those prior to leave as prior to leave women must not be treated less favourably on grounds of pregnancy or impending maternity leave in relation to either pay, benefits or working conditions.

5.5 This chapter starts with a discussion of the relevant statutory provisions and broad principles. The second part of the chapter explains the likely position in relation to each right or benefit.

Rights during maternity leave under ERA 1996 and MPL Regs

5.6 Only employees are entitled to maternity leave and rights during maternity leave under the ERA 1996. See para 1.28 for who is an employee. An agency worker, bank nurse, contract worker or home-worker who is classified by her employer as 'self-employed' may still be an employee as the classification is not conclusive.[1] A limited number of employees are excluded from the protection of the ERA 1996 (see para 1.31).

5.7 If the woman is not an employee she will not be entitled to maternity leave.[2] However, she may be entitled to maternity allowance (see chapter 6) and to some protection under the discrimination legislation.

Summary of rights during maternity leave

Entitlement	Duration	Statutory reference
Contract of employment continues	Throughout maternity leave	ERA 1996 ss71 and 73, MPL Regs 1999 reg 17
Maternity leave counted as continuous service for statutory rights	Throughout maternity leave	Ditto
Maternity leave counted as continuous service for statutory *and* contractual rights	OML only	Ditto (NB this may be discrimination)

1   See *Dacas v Brook Street Bureaux (UK) Ltd* [2004] IRLR 358, CA and *Cable & Wireless plc v Muscat* [2006] IRLR 354 and *Ncube and Others v 24/7 Support Services and Others* ET/2602005/05 (see para 1.29).
2   Though may be entitled to maternity allowance or incapacity benefit (see chapter 7).

Entitlement	Duration	Statutory reference
Right not to be dismissed for a reason relating to maternity leave	Throughout maternity leave	SDA 1975, ERA 1996 s99, MPL Regs 1999 reg 20
Right not to be discriminated against 'in her capacity as a worker'	Throughout maternity leave	SDA 1975
Right not to be subjected to detriment	Throughout maternity leave	ERA 1996 s47C, MPL Regs 1999 reg 19
Right to trust and confidence, notice, redundancy pay, disciplinary and grievance procedures	Throughout maternity leave	MPL Regs 1999 regs 9 and 17, ERA 1996 s87
No right to 'remuneration'	Throughout maternity leave (for SMP entitlement see chapter 6)	EPA 1970, MPL Regs 1999 regs 9 and 17
Right to have a pay rise reflected in maternity pay	Throughout maternity leave	EPA 1970
Right to accrue statutory holiday	Throughout maternity leave	WT Regs 1998
Right to accrue contractual holiday	OML only	MPL Regs 1999 regs 9 and 17
Right to a bonus paid to the rest of the workforce	Pro rata amount paid to reflect the employee's time at work and compulsory maternity leave (two weeks) only	EPA 1970
Right to day to day terms and conditions, such as to keep the company car	During OML (it may be sex discrimination for these to be refused during AML)	MPL Regs 1999 regs 9 and 17

5.8   Many workers who are not employees are protected from discrimination by the SDA 1975, EPA 1970 and EC law (see, for example, *Fletcher* at paras 2.58–2.59). For example, a contract worker can bring a claim that she had been discriminated against by a principal in not allowing her to return to work after absence due to childbirth.[3] In addition, the agency may provide for the continuation of some rights during the time she is off work. For as long as she is engaged under a contract with her 'employer', a worker is entitled to accrue holiday under the WT Regs 1998 (see para 5.95 onwards onwards). In addition to maternity pay, if she has been paying national insurance she may be able to claim incapacity benefit if she is off work and is unwell (see para 7.8).

Overview of the ERA 1996 and MPL Regs 1999

5.9   The ERA 1996 and MPL Regs 1999 set out employees' contractual position and statutory employment protection rights during maternity leave. These are subject to overriding discrimination law. However, the amendments to the SDA 1975 and EPA 1970 in October 2005 aim to exclude discrimination and equal pay claims where there are specific provisions for such rights in the ERA 1996 and MPL Regs 1999 (see para 5.28 onwards).

5.10   An employee on OML or AML is also entitled to protection from unfair dismissal and from detriment (see chapter 15).[4] If she is made redundant during leave she is entitled to any suitable available vacancy in preference to other employees[5] (see para 15.100).

Reasonable contact during maternity leave

5.11   Where the EWC is on or after 1 April 2007 employers will be able to make 'reasonable contact with an employee while she is on maternity leave from time to time' (see para 4.48).[6] There is to be guidance about what is 'reasonable contact' but this has not yet been published. This strengthens the argument that employers should inform employees of any changes that arise during their absence on leave

---

3   *BP Chemicals Ltd v Gillick* [1995] IRLR 128 EAT (see para 2.52).
4   Under MPL Regs 1999 regs 19 and 20.
5   MPL Regs 1999 reg 10.
6   MPL Regs 1999 reg 12A(4) (as amended, see below).

including any reorganisation, redundancy situation, promotion prospects or jobs being advertised (see *Visa International v Paul* at para
2.91). Failure to do so may be discrimination.

Keeping in touch days

5.12   From April 2007 employees will be able to work for 10 days during
their statutory maternity/adoption leave period without losing statutory payments for that week or ending their leave.[7] Such work must
be agreed between employer and employee. An employee is protected
from any detriment or dismissal for undertaking, considering undertaking or not undertaking to work (see para 4.48 onwards). Forcing
an employee to work during her leave may also be sex discrimination.

5.13   Where a woman wants to take part in training or specified meetings the employer should give serious consideration to her doing so.

Employees' rights during OML under the ERA 1996 and MPL Regs 1999

5.14   The ERA 1996 and MPL Regs 1999 provide that during OML an
employee is entitled to the benefit of any statutory or other terms and
conditions of employment[8] (apart from remuneration)[9] which would
have applied if she had not been absent.[10] 'Terms and conditions of
employment' cover the monetary elements of remuneration such as
for example, health insurance, life insurance, participation in a share
ownership scheme, accrued holiday, health club membership, professional subscriptions and personal use of company car, whether
contractual or non-contractual. Equal access to promotion and other
working conditions must also be guaranteed (see para 5.122).
Pensions are covered at para 5.112 onwards.

5.15   The employee is also bound by her obligations under her contract

---

7   MPL Regs 1999 reg 12A as amended by the Maternity and Parental Leave etc and
Paternity and Adoption Leave (Amendment) Regulations 2006 SI No 2014 in
force from 1 October 2006. Similar amendments have been made to the PAL
Regulations. See reg 21A.

8   ERA 1996 s71(5) defines terms and conditions of employment; it '(a) includes
matters connected with an employee's employment whether or not they arise
under her contract of employment, but (b) does not include terms and
conditions about remuneration'.

9   MPL Regs 1999 reg 9(3) states that 'only sums payable to an employee by way of
wages or salary are to be treated as remuneration'.

10 MPL Regs 1999 reg 9(1)(a).

(except the obligation to work).[11] She is entitled to return from leave to the same job (see chapter 4).[12]

Rights during compulsory maternity leave

5.16 During compulsory maternity leave, which is the two weeks immediately following the birth, or four weeks for factory employees, the employer must not allow the employee to work. It is an offence to do so.[13] The employee is entitled to the benefit of any bonus payable in respect of this period, but probably not during the rest of her maternity leave (see para 5.84 onwards).[14] Otherwise her rights are the same as during OML.

Rights during AML under the ERA 1996 and MPL Regs 1999

5.17 During AML the position is more complex. An employee is not entitled to remuneration but unlike OML, this is not defined so could cover a wider category of benefits.[15] Although the contract continues,[16] the ERA 1996 and MPL Regs 1999 provide that the employee is only entitled to the benefit of the employer's implied obligation to her of trust and confidence and any terms and conditions of her employment relating to:

- her contractual notice period (and possibly notice pay – see below);
- compensation if she is made redundant;
- disciplinary or grievance procedures.[17]

5.18 The employee is bound by her implied obligation to her employer of good faith and any terms and conditions of employment relating to:

- notice of the termination of the contract;

11 MPL Regs 1999 reg 9(1)(b).
12 ERA 1996 s71(4)–(7) and MPL Regs 1999 reg 18 and 18A which was amended with effect from 6 April 2003. The regulations set out the rights in detail.
13 ERA 1996 s72. See chapter 3.
14 EPA 1970 s1(2)(e)(ii).
15 ERA 1996 s73(5).
16 MPL Regs 1999 reg 17 does not explicitly state that the contract continues but this is its effect and the DTI guidance confirms this.
17 MPL Regs 1999 reg 17(a): Terms and conditions of employment are defined in the same way as for OML, see ERA 1996 s73(5).

- the disclosure of confidential information;
- the acceptance of gifts or other benefits; and
- the employee's participation in any other business.[18]

Continuity of service during OML and AML

5.19 The ERA provides that, in relation to statutory rights based on length of service, the whole of maternity leave is counted for the purpose of determining service. For contractual rights based on length of service, OML counts as continuous service but the period of AML is ignored. Thus, the period from the end of OML is treated as continuous with the period after the end of AML, ie when the date the woman returns to work[19] (but see paras 5.58 and 5.126 for how this is likely to be a breach of EC law).

Notice pay during OML and AML

5.20 The ERA 1996 provides for a right to paid notice during both OML and AML, irrespective of whether the notice is given by the employer or the employee,[20] but only where the employee is entitled to the minimum statutory notice period. Where the employer is required to give at least a week's longer notice under the contract, these provisions do not apply and so the employee will not be entitled to paid notice under the ERA 1996.[21] Ironically, therefore, it appears that those with better contractual rights than the legal minimum will not benefit from the statutory right to notice pay under the ERA 1996.[22] The employer is entitled to deduct from the notice pay, any payment being made in respect of SMP or other family leave pay.[23]

5.21 It is not entirely clear how the above notice provisions under the ERA 1996 (set out above) relate to the right to notice during OML or

---

18 MPL Regs 1999 reg 17(b).
19 MPL Regs 1999 reg 18A(1)(a). The same applies to additional adoption leave.
20 The ERA 1996 provides for payment of notice pay 'in respect of any period during which the employee is absent from work wholly or partly because of pregnancy or childbirth': sections 86(1)–(3), 88(1)(c), 89(1), (3)(b); the same provisions apply to adoption, parental or paternity leave.
21 ERA 1996 s87(4).
22 The position was confirmed by the EAT in *Scotts Company (UK) Ltd v Budd* EAT 823/01.
23 ERA 1996 ss88(2), 89(4).

AML.[24] During OML employees are entitled to the benefit of all terms and conditions of employment but not remuneration which may include notice pay.[25] During AML (and parental leave) employees are entitled to (and must give) 'notice of termination of the employment contract'.[26] Unless an employee only has a statutory right to paid notice (see para 5.20), it is doubtful if the regulations entitle her to *paid* notice during maternity leave. This is partly because the courts have held that an employee on maternity leave is not entitled to the benefit of her pay and this may include notice pay (see para 5.69). However, it is also arguable that, following the decisions in *Alabaster* and *Sass* employees will be able to pursue a right to notice pay (given during leave) through a claim relying on EC law (see para 5.82).

Other benefits not within the MPL Regs 1999

5.22   In relation to other benefits (apart from those guaranteed under the MPL Regs 1999), the position will depend on the terms of the contract or agreement between the employer and employee. However, the general principle under UK law is that employers are not obliged to provide other contractual benefits during AML, such as health insurance and access to a company car and the SDA now makes this clear (see para 5.28 onwards).[27] EC law is discussed in para 5.39 onwards.

Social Security Act (SSA) 1989 Sch 5: pensions

5.23   This entitles an employee on *paid* maternity leave (whether OML or AML)[28] to receive the same pension contributions from her employer, as when she was working and receiving normal pay.[29] The employee has to pay a proportion of her contributions based on her actual income (ie maternity pay). Further, the ECJ held, in *Boyle*,[30] that

24   Although MPL Regs 1999 reg 17 refers to the employee's entitlement to notice of termination it is very unlikely that notice pay would be payable during AML but not OML.
25   MPL Regs reg 9(1)(a).
26   MPL Regs reg 17.
27   SDA 1975 s6A.
28   The same applies to paid paternity and adoption leave (see chapters 8 and 9).
29   SSA 1989 Sch 5 paras 5 and 6; the same principles apply to paid paternity and adoption leave.
30   *Boyle v Equal Opportunities Commission* [1998] IRLR 717, ECJ.

pension rights must be maintained during OML, whether paid or unpaid (see para 5.112 onwards).

SDA 1975

5.24   SDA 1975 s6(1)(b) and (2) provides that a woman must not be treated less favourably on ground of her sex in relation to the terms on which she is offered employment or in respect of her working conditions, such as access to promotion, training, transfer, other benefits, facilities or services, dismissal, detriment etc. This protection continues (for employees) during both OML and AML (see para 2.38 onwards).

5.25   The SDA 1975 (as amended, with effect from 1 October 2005) makes it clear that, subject to specified exceptions, less favourable treatment of a woman where it is on the ground of her pregnancy or maternity leave is unlawful sex discrimination without the need to establish less favourable treatment than a comparator.[31]

5.26   SDA 1975 s3A states:

> . . . a person discriminates against a woman if–
> (a) at a time in a protected period, and on the ground of the woman's pregnancy, the person treats her less favourably than he would treat her had she not become pregnant; or
> (b) on the ground that the woman is exercising or seeking to exercise, or has exercised or sought to exercise, a statutory right to maternity leave, the person treats her less favourably than he would treat her if she were neither exercising nor seeking to exercise, and had neither exercised nor sought to exercise, such a right.

5.27   The protected period, during which the automatic protection exists, is the start of pregnancy until the end of maternity leave or the employee's return to work (see para 2.40 onwards). This is explained in detail in chapter 2.

Exceptions to the SDA 1975 relating to terms and conditions during maternity leave

5.28   SDA 1975 s6A sets out the exceptions relating to terms and conditions during maternity leave. It provides (at section 6A(1)):

---

31 The Employment Equality (Sex Discrimination) Regulations 2005 SI No 2467 reg 4 which inserts section 3A after SDA 1975 s3.

Subject to subsections (2) and (5), section 6(1)(b) and (2) [ie offer of terms of employment and discrimination at work, eg promotion, training, dismissal] does not make it unlawful to deprive a woman who is on ordinary maternity leave of any benefit from the terms and conditions of her employment relating to remuneration.

5.29 Section 6A(7) defines 'remuneration' for these purposes as 'benefits (a) that consist of the payment of money to an employee by way of wages or salary, and (b) that are not benefits whose provision is regulated by the employee's contract of employment'. Thus, remuneration (for the purposes of section 6A(1)) covers only non-contractual benefits, such as a discretionary bonus. This is consistent with the MPL Regs 1999 and the fact that the SDA 1975 does not cover contractual matters (see paras 2.4–2.6). It is also clear that an employee is not entitled to contractual pay.[32]

5.30 Section 6A(2) states: 'Subsection (1) does not apply to benefit by way of maternity-related remuneration.'

'Maternity-related remuneration' is defined by s6A(7) as 'remuneration to which she is entitled as a result of being pregnant or being on ordinary or additional maternity leave'. This would cover maternity pay. Thus, of course, an employee will be entitled to maternity pay during her leave; it is not excepted under section 6A(1).

5.31 Section 6A(3) states:

Subject to subsections (4) and (5), section 6(1)(b) and (2) [see para 5.28] does not make it unlawful to deprive a woman who is on additional maternity leave of any benefit from the terms and conditions of her employment.[33]

Although it is not clear, section 6A(3) appears to cover not only financial benefits, such as a car allowance, health insurance, bonus, but also other terms and conditions which could include the right to an appraisal, the right to be consulted about a reorganisation or redundancy, the right to be considered for promotion, ie, her rights as a worker. Section 6A(3) should be interpreted to cover only financial benefits and not working conditions. Failure to do so would be inconsistent with ECJ decisions such as *Thibault, Sass* and *Herrero* and so be a breach of EC law (see para 5.56 onwards).

5.32 Section 6A(4) states that subsection (3) does not apply to

---

32 *Gillespie v Northern Health and Social Services Board* [1996] IRLR 214, ECJ, *Alabaster v Barclays Bank and Secretary of State for Social Security* [2000] IRLR 754.
33 Of course, the woman will still be entitled to her statutory maternity rights contained in ERA 1996 and MPL Regs 1999, as discussed above.

maternity pay or the terms and conditions which continue to apply during AML, ie those set out in regulation 17 and membership of a pension scheme.[34] These are not within the exception in section 6A(3).

5.33   Subsection (5) states that 6A(1) and (3) do not apply to pay outside the maternity leave period or to pay increases that must be reflected in maternity pay (see *Alabaster*). Thus, where such payments are due during leave, they will be payable and do not fall within the exceptions.

5.34   The aim of the amendments to the SDA 1975 is to bring discrimination law in line with the rights set out in the ERA 1996 and MPL Regs 1999 and to prevent discrimination claims being made in relation to benefits during maternity leave which are governed by the statutory scheme. However, the amendments should be interpreted consistently with long established rights established by UK and ECJ case-law.

5.35   In summary, the SDA 1975 provides that:

a) A woman on OML is entitled to maternity pay (subject to complying with the qualifying conditions) and to the benefit of any pay increase awarded after the qualifying period and before the end of maternity leave (see para 2.108) but not to any discretionary payments, such as a bonus.[35]

b) During both OML and AML employees are entitled to any pay, pay increases and bonuses payable in respect of periods outside maternity leave, even if payable during the period of leave.[36] Note that a bonus is also payable in respect of the compulsory leave period (see para 2.108).

c) During AML, apart from any maternity pay to which she is entitled, membership of a pension scheme and the terms set out in MPL Regs 1999 reg 17(a) (see para 5.17), an employee is not entitled to any benefit from the terms and conditions of her employment.

5.36   The amended SDA 1975 is discussed in detail at para 2.40 onwards and 5.28 onwards.

---

34 SDA 1975 s6A(4) which excludes from section 6A(3) maternity pay, the implied obligation of trust and confidence, notice, redundancy compensation, disciplinary or grievance procedures or membership of a pension scheme.

35 MPL Regs 1999 reg 9(1)(a) also provides that she will also be entitled to the benefit of all the terms and conditions of employment which would have applied if she had not been absent; this is not affected by these SDA provisions.

36 SDA 1975 s6A(5).

EPA 1970

5.37 The EPA 1970 provides that a man and woman doing similar work, work rated as equivalent under a job evaluation scheme or work of equal value, must receive the same pay and *contractual* terms unless there is a material factor defence (see para 2.98 onwards). Where the woman is arguing that she receives lower pay or less favourable contractual terms on grounds of her pregnancy and/or maternity leave there is no need for her to rely on a comparator.[37] However, the extent to which a woman can make a claim under the EPA 1970, in relation to contractual benefits payable during maternity leave is limited as the courts have generally held that a woman on maternity leave is in a special position which is not comparable to other workers (see paras 5.39 and 5.47). The EPA 1970 is subject to the overriding provisions of article 141 of the Treaty of Rome (which provides for equal pay).

5.38 In relation to bonuses and pay rises the EPA 1970 (as amended) provides, in summary, that:

- Where an employee receives a pay increase after the qualifying period[38] and before the end of her maternity leave and her maternity pay is calculated by reference to a particular period (usually the qualifying period) the pay increase must be reflected in her maternity pay. This would apply to her contractual and statutory maternity pay. This only applies if her maternity pay is less than what her full pay would have been but for her maternity leave.
- Any pay or bonus relating to periods outside maternity leave must be paid as normal.
- An employee on compulsory maternity leave is entitled to any bonus payable in respect of this period.
- Any pay rise which would have been awarded to a woman on maternity leave must be reflected in her salary on her return.[39]

---

37 *Alabaster* [2004] IRLR 486 ECJ, [2005] IRLR 576, CA.
38 Which is approximately eight weeks or two months before the 15th week before the EWC (see para 6.11).
39 EPA 1970 s1(2)(d)–(f) and s1(5A), (5B) inserted with effect from 1 October 2005.

European Law

Article 141

5.39   Article 141 of the Treaty of Rome establishes the principle of 'equal pay for male and female workers for equal work or work of equal value'. Pay is very widely defined and includes all emoluments in cash or kind paid or payable as a result of the worker's employment. It includes, for example, pension, bonuses, payments on dismissal, sick pay, maternity pay. It covers contractual and non-contractual pay. However, the ECJ has held that women on maternity leave are in a different and special position; they are unable to make a claim for equal pay under article 141 as they cannot compare themselves with a man or woman at work or on sick leave.[40] However, if the woman is outside the protected period because, for example, she is not an employee so has no entitlement to pay or leave, then she can, under UK law, compare herself with a sick man (see *Fletcher* para 2.59 onwards). Cases brought under article 141 include *Gillespie,*[41] *Alabaster,*[42] *Lewen v Denda,*[43] *McKenna,*[44] *Hoj Pedersen,*[45] *Abdoulaye*[46] and *Rinner-Kuhn.*[47]

Equal Treatment Directive

5.40   The ETD provides that there shall be 'no discrimination whatsoever on grounds of sex either directly or indirectly by reference in particular to marital or family status'. Article 2 specifically provides that 'Less favourable treatment of a woman related to pregnancy or maternity leave ... shall constitute discrimination'. It applies, in relation to both public and private bodies, to conditions for access to employment, promotion, training, employment and working conditions, including dismissal and pay (for effect of ETD see para 1.22). Cases brought under the ETD include *Webb,*[48] *Dekker,*[49]

40   See *Gillespie v Northern Health and Social Services Board and others* [1996] IRLR 214 and *Boyle v EOC* [1998] IRLR 71.
41   *Gillespie v Northern Health and Social Services Board and others* [1996] IRLR 214.
42   *Alabaster v Woolwich plc* [2004] IRLR 486, ECJ.
43   *Lewen v Denda* [2000] IRLR 67, ECJ.
44   *North Western Health Board v McKenna* [2005] IRLR 895, ECJ.
45   *HK (acing on behalf of Hoj Pedersen) v Faelleforeningen for Danmarks Brugsforeninger (acting on behalf of Kvickly Skive)* [1999] IRLR 55 ECJ.
46   *Abdoulaye v Regie Nationale des Usine Renault* [1999] IRLR 811 ECJ.
47   *Rinner-Kuhn v FWW Spezial-Gegañdereinigung GmbH* [1989] IRLR 493 ECJ.
48   *Webb v EMO Air Cargo (UK) Ltd* [1994] IRLR 482, ECJ.
49   *Dekker v VJV-Centrum* [1991] IRLR 27, ECJ.

Hertz,[50] *Brown v Rentokil,*[51] *Thibault,*[52] *Jiménez Melgar,*[53] *Haberman-Beltermann,*[54] *Mahlburg v Land Mecklenburg Vorpommern,*[55] *Busch*[56] *and Herrero.*[57]

5.41 Although the ECJ held, in *Gillespie*, that the ETD did not cover pay, with the inclusion of pay in the ETD with effect from 5 October 2005,[58] this is no longer the case. One of the differences between article 141 and the ETD (as between the EPA 1970 and SDA 1975) is that an actual comparator is usually needed under the former, but not the latter (see also 14.10 onwards). Thus, a woman on maternity leave can claim pay benefits under the ETD (as well as article 141) (apart from her full wages or salary). The ETD will be replaced by the Recast Directive 2006/54/EC (5 July 2006) from August 2008. Article 2, para 2(c) is similar to Article 2 of ETD. It also covers pay (see Article 1(6)).

Pregnant Workers Directive 92/85/EEC

5.42 The purpose of the PWD is to encourage improvements in the safety and health at work of pregnancy workers and new and breastfeeding mothers. It provides for a minimum period of leave, maintenance of an adequate allowance for pregnant workers and recent mothers and the maintenance of rights during leave as well as protection from dismissal (for effect of PWD see para 1.23).

5.43 The PWD provides that during maternity leave the following must be ensured:

a) the rights connected with the employment contract of workers within the meaning of article 2 (ie pregnant workers, workers who have recently given birth and breastfeeding workers), other than those rights referred to in point (b) below;

---

50 *Handels-og Kontorfunktionaererernes Forbund I Danmark (acting for Hertz) v Dansk Arbejdsgiverforening (acting for Aldi Marked K/S)* [1991] IRLR 31, ECJ.
51 *Brown v Rentokil Ltd* [1998] IRLR 445, ECJ.
52 *CNAVTS v Thibault* [1998] IRLR 399, ECJ.
53 *Jiménez Melgar v Ayuntamiento de Loss Barrios* (C-438/99) [2003] 3 CMLR 67; [2001] IRLR 848, ECJ.
54 *Habermann-Beltermann v Arbeiterwohlfahrt, Bezirksverband Ndb/Opf e V* [1994] IRLR 364, ECJ.
55 *Mahlburg v Land Mecklenburg Vorpommern* [2000] IRLR, ECJ.
56 *Busch v Klinikum Neustadt GmbH & Co Betriebs-KG* [2003] IRLR 625, ECJ.
57 *Sarkatzis Herrero v Instituto Madrileno de la Salud* [2006] IRLR 296, ECJ.
58 Article 3 which was substituted by Council Directive 2002/73.

b) maintenance of a payment to, and/or entitlement to an adequate allowance for, workers within the meaning of article 2.

5.44   The ECJ have now held that this protection applies not only to the 14 weeks (being the minimum maternity leave under the PWD) but to any statutory period of maternity pay laid down by the Member State. In *Land Brandenburg v Sass*[59] the ECJ held that the fact that legislation grants women maternity leave of more than the minimum period of 14 weeks laid down by the PWD does not preclude that leave from being considered to be maternity leave as referred to in article 8 and therefore a period during which the rights connected with the employment contract must be ensured. The ECJ distinguished the decision in *Boyle*, which concerned additional leave granted by an employer rather than statutory leave.[60]

5.45   In *Merino Gomez* the ECJ held that article 11(2)(a) of the PWD provides that rights connected with the employment contract (apart from pay) must be ensured during maternity leave[61] which included entitlement to paid annual leave (see para 5.100 onwards).

Relationship between statutory maternity rights, discrimination and equal pay

5.46   There is potential conflict between:

- first, the limited statutory rights during AML set out in the ERA 1996 and the principles of non-discrimination as developed under the SDA 1975 and EC law;
- second, the exceptions set out in the amended SDA 1975 (see para 5.28 onwards) and principles of non-discrimination during maternity leave developed under the unamended SDA 1975 and EC law.

---

59   [2005] IRLR 147 para 44.
60   The ECJ decision in *Boyle* also made it clear that employees were not entitled to contractual holiday during any period of supplementary maternity leave granted by the employer. The ECJ did not deal with the position during a period of statutory maternity leave in excess of the 14 weeks laid down by the PWD.
61   Which must include any statutory leave provided by the member state, ie, ordinary and additional maternity leave in the UK: *Merino Gomez v Continental Industries Del Comcho SA* [2004] IRLR 407, ECJ.

The main principles under UK discrimination law and EU law

5.47 Although it is difficult to extract consistent principles, we start by analysing the UK and EU case-law. Many decisions make it clear that a pregnant worker and woman on maternity leave must not be disadvantaged in relation to her *working conditions* by virtue of her pregnancy or absence on maternity leave or the consequences of her pregnancy and absence. This does not mean, however, that she is entitled to *normal pay* during maternity leave (unless guaranteed by the contract of employment or by agreement). Thus, a distinction has emerged between:

- *working conditions*, which affect a woman in her capacity as a worker, where protection from discrimination continues from the beginning of pregnancy through to the end of maternity leave (OML and AML) and in some circumstances her return to work; and

- *normal pay during the maternity leave period* which does not continue during maternity leave (OML and AML), although the period of absence should not disadvantage the employee in respect of pay and benefits when she returns to work. It is the definition of 'pay' which has caused so much confusion.

5.48 This analysis takes into account European law since regrettably UK sex discrimination law does not fully reflect the European position.

5.49 The Employment Appeal Tribunal (EAT) said in *Hoyland*,[62]

> . . . when a woman returns from maternity leave she must be treated for the purposes of future pay and working conditions as though she had never been away. Thus if the workforce has received a pay rise during her absence the pay rise is applicable to her. If she would have moved into a higher seniority band, she must be given that benefit on her return. If she would have been assessed for promotion, she must be assessed anyway. But none of these is the same as saying that she must be paid for the period of the maternity leave as if she had never been on leave.

5.50 First, it is often difficult to distinguish between pay and working conditions particularly in relation to benefits that could be described as part of both pay and working conditions, such as holiday

---

62 *Hoyland v Asda Stores Ltd* [2005] IRLR 438; this decision was upheld by the Court of Session [2006] IRLR 468 CS.

entitlement, health insurance, company car. This stems mainly from the decision in *Gillespie*[63] where the ECJ distinguished between non-payment of full 'pay', which it held was not discrimination and non-payment of a 'pay rise' and other unfavourable treatment of the woman 'in her capacity as a worker' which the ECJ held was discrimination.[64] As the Advocate General pointed out in *Alabaster* (para 66) these two principles seem to be somewhat contradictory.

5.51   Second, it is difficult reconciling EU and UK law. UK law distinguishes between contractual terms (EPA 1970) and non-contractual terms (SDA 1975) but EU law does not make this distinction. Instead EU law has in the past distinguished between pay, which is very widely defined (article 141) and working conditions (ETD). However, the ETD now also covers pay as does the Recast Directive (see para 1.23). In addition, a worker may have rights under the PWD, which provides for the maintenance of rights connected with the employment contract during statutory maternity leave.

5.52   Third, there is now the amended SDA 1975 which provides explicit protection on grounds of pregnancy and maternity leave and sets out exceptions to this protection. However, tribunals and courts will need to interpret these somewhat restrictive provisions, which could be interpreted regressively (see paras 2.40 onwards and 5.28 onwards), in accordance with pre-existing EC case-law to avoid further challenges in the ECJ.

Protection of an employee 'in her capacity as a worker'?

5.53   There is a long line of ECJ decisions which state that there must be no discrimination at any time, either prior to or during maternity leave, in respect of working conditions which affect a pregnant woman or new mother in 'her capacity as a worker' (see for example *Webb*,[65] *Brown v Rentokil*,[66] *Gillespie*,[67] *Thibault*,[68] *Sass*,[69] *Herrero*[70]). A

---

63 *Gillespie v Northern Health and Social Services Board* [1996] IRLR 214, ECJ; see also the amended EPA 1970.

64 A woman on maternity leave is not entitled to full pay but is entitled to have a 'pay rise' reflected in her earnings related maternity pay.

65 *Webb v EMO Air Cargo Ltd* [1994] IRLR 482 ECJ and [1995] IRLR 645, HL.

66 *Brown v Rentokil* [1998] ILR 445, ECJ.

67 [1996] IRLR 214, ECJ.

68 *CNAVTS v Thibault* [1998] IRLR 399, ECJ.

69 *Land Brandenburg v Sass* [2005] IRLR 147, ECJ.

70 *Sarkatzis Herrero Instituto Madrileño de la Salud* Case C-294/04; [2006] IRLR 296, ECJ.

woman claiming sex discrimination in these circumstances has automatic protection against unfavourable treatment and does not need to rely on how a comparable man would be treated. This protection is sometimes known as 'protected status' and the less favourable treatment related to pregnancy or maternity leave is 'automatic sex discrimination'.

5.54   Thus, any less favourable treatment which affects a woman in the longer term, before or after her maternity leave, is unlawful discrimination (see also chapter 2). This would apply, for example, to less favourable treatment during maternity leave in relation to:[71]

* entitlement to the same pay rise as other employees; this is now provided for in the EPA 1970 (see para 2.108);
* the right to the same appraisals and pay reviews (see *CNAVTS v Thibault* at para 5.76);
* the same right to be re-graded;
* consideration for promotion or any other job (see *Visa International v Paul* at para 15.25);
* protection from dismissal, including redundancy (see chapter 15);
* protection from detriment;
* rights to consultation about changes in the workforce, including redundancy (see *McGuigan v T G Baynes* at para 15.94);
* continuous service during maternity leave (following *Sass* and *Herrero*. See paras 5.57–5.64).

5.55   In *Brown v Rentokil* (see para 3.118) the ECJ confirmed that the ETD affords a woman protection both from the beginning of her pregnancy and during the period of maternity leave given to her under national law. Thus unequal treatment, such as dismissal, failure to promote or award a pay rise, for a reason connected with the fact that a woman is either pregnant or on maternity leave, constitutes sex discrimination. The same principles apply to dismissal for a reason related to her absence on maternity leave (see chapter 15).[71]

5.56   In *Gillespie* the ECJ concluded that despite the fact that a woman is not entitled to full pay during maternity leave, she should still receive the benefits and protection she acquires 'in her capacity as a worker' (see paras 5.50 and 5.65). In *CNAVTS v Thibault* the ECJ held that European law is intended 'to ensure substantive equality between

---

71 Note that the amended SDA 1975 refers to discrimination being 'on the ground of' the woman's pregnancy but it is clear from the case-law that it need only be related to her pregnancy or maternity leave (see chapter 2).

men and women regarding both access to employment and working conditions'. Thus, it was discrimination to deny a woman a performance appraisal because she was on maternity leave. Following *CNAVTS v Thibault*, protection from discrimination covers (at least) the 'long-term' rights of an employee so that their absence should not affect detrimentally their pay, status or other benefits on return (see also para 5.76 onwards).

5.57   In *Land Brandenburg v Sass*[72] part of the claimant's maternity leave (12 out of the 20 weeks' leave) was not taken into account as qualifying service for the purposes of re-grading, which was based on length of service. Ms Sass was re-graded 12 weeks later than her contemporaries who had not taken maternity leave. The ECJ held this was a breach of the ETD as rights connected with the employment contract must be ensured during all of statutory maternity leave, where that leave is to protect women as regards pregnancy and maternity.[73] It is not just limited to the 14 weeks set out in the PWD. It is for the national court to determine if the leave had the purpose of protecting women. The ECJ pointed out that:

> . . . a female worker is protected in her employment relationship against any unfavourable treatment on the ground that she is or has been on maternity leave . . . [para 35]

> . . . a woman who is treated unfavourably because of absence on maternity leave suffers discrimination on the ground of her pregnancy and of that leave. Such conduct constitutes discrimination on the grounds of sex within the meaning of Directive 76/207 [para 36].

5.58   The ECJ held in *Sass* in relation to rights under the PWD that:

> . . . under its Article 11, [the PWD] provides that, in order to guarantee the protection of pregnant workers, workers who have recently given birth or are breastfeeding, the rights connected with the employment contract must be ensured 'in the case referred to in Article 8'. [Article 8 provides for 'a continuous period of maternity leave of at least 14 weeks'.]

> Therefore, the fact that a piece of legislation grants women maternity leave of more than 14 weeks does not preclude that leave from being considered to be maternity leave as referred to in Article 8 of Directive 92/85 and, therefore, a period during which the rights

72   ECJ [2005] IRLR 147.
73   Under UK law this would have been a contractual matter as it was part of a collective agreement so would come within the EPA 1970.

connected with the employment contract must, under Article 11 be ensured.[74]

5.59 It held further that the ETD provides that where the maternity leave was for the protection of a woman's biological condition and the special relationship between her and her child:

> . . . Community law requires that taking such statutory protective leave should interrupt neither the employment relationship of the woman concerned nor the application of the rights derived from it and cannot lead to discrimination against that woman.[75]

5.60 It is clear from *Sass* that the period of AML, to the extent that the national courts consider this to be a period for the protection of woman as regards pregnancy and maternity (which should include the special relationship between mother and child), must be treated as continuous employment for the purpose of both statutory and contractual rights. Thus, any contractual rights based on service must not exclude this period of maternity leave. This will override the provisions of the ERA 1996 which only treat AML as continuous employment for statutory not contractual rights (see para 5.19).

5.61 *Sass* was followed by the ECJ decision of *Sarkatzis Herrero v Instituto Madrileño de la Salud*[76] where the claimant, who was a temporary employee, was appointed to a permanent position while she was on maternity leave. She was told that she had to take up the post within one month. She was allowed to start the job at a later date but her seniority was not calculated from the date of appointment but the date she started the job. Ms Herrero claimed this was discrimination as a result of her having taken maternity leave.

5.62 In *Herrero* the ECJ held that the claim came within the ETD 76/207, not the PWD as it concerned the appointment of a woman, not dismissal. The ECJ held:

> Directive 76/207 prohibits any discrimination whatsoever on grounds of sex . . . Thus, direct and indirect discrimination are prohibited as regards conditions for access to employment, including selection criteria and recruitment conditions, access to all types and to all levels of vocational guidance, vocational training, . . . and also as regards work experience, conditions of employment, working conditions and participation in an organisation which represents workers or others . . . [para 36]

---

74 Paras 43, 44.
75 Para 48.
76 [2006] IRLR 296, ECJ.

> ... the aim of Directive 76/207 is substantive, not formal equality, [that] Directive must be interpreted as precluding any unfavourable treatment of a female worker on account of maternity leave or in connection with such leave, which aims to protect pregnant women, and that is so without it being necessary to have regard to whether such treatment affects an existing employment relationship or a new employment relationship ... [para 41]
>
> The fact that other people, in particular men, may, on other grounds, be treated in the same way as Ms Herrero has no bearing on an assessment of her position since the deferment of the date on which her career is deemed to have started stemmed exclusively from the maternity leave to which she was entitled [para 46].

5.63   Thus the ECJ have said in both *Sass* and *Herrero* that a woman who is treated unfavourably because of absence on maternity leave suffers discrimination on the ground of her pregnancy and of that leave. Arguably, the decision in *Sass*, followed by *Herrero*, means that contractual rights as well as all other benefits given to workers, apart from pay, should be maintained during not only OML but also AML.

5.64   If this is correct, based on the ECJ decisions in *Thibault*, *Sass* and *Herrero* then all contractual rights except remuneration should continue to be provided during AML and the exceptions set out in the SDA 1975 are in breach of EU law (either the ETD or PWD). The next crucial and difficult question is how 'remuneration' is defined.

Pay and pay-related benefits during maternity leave

5.65   Women on maternity leave cannot claim equal pay with workers not on leave in respect of wages or salary. They are, however, entitled to maternity pay (see chapter 6). In *Gillespie* it was argued that women should receive their full pay for the duration of maternity leave. Failure to pay would, it was argued, be discrimination against them because they would receive it 'but for' their pregnancy and absence on maternity leave. At this point the ECJ, appreciating no doubt the costs to member states (and the conflict with the maternity pay provisions in the PWD),[77] drew the line. It held that a woman on leave was in a special protected position and could not compare herself with an employee at work, so could not claim equal pay. The claimant was, however, entitled to have a pay rise reflected in her maternity pay and

---

77   The PWD does not impose an obligation on member states to pay full pay as long as an 'adequate allowance' is paid (article 11) (see para 5.42).

this was a benefit payable to her in her capacity as a worker. This is now set out in the EPA 1970 (see paras 2.108–2.109).

5.66   Arguably, the principle in *Gillespie*, which was followed by the ECJ in *Boyle* and *Alabaster*, that no equal pay claim can be made by a woman on maternity leave, should be limited to wages and salary which are replaced by statutory maternity pay. This is supported by *Edwards v Derby City Council*[78] where a school teacher argued that it was contrary to article 141 to pay her only half-pay during a school holiday at a time when she was on maternity leave, when other teachers, who were not working, received full pay. The EAT held that arrangements for maternity pay are a matter for member states and the provision of a rate less than full pay does not fall foul of article 141, adding 'We do not think that more of relevance can be taken from *Gillespie* than that'. Note that in *Merino Gomez*, the ECJ took a different view to a woman's entitlement during maternity leave in relation to holidays (see para 5.100 onwards).

5.67   Thus, a logical distinction, which has yet to be argued in the courts, is between those elements of pay that are reflected in SMP (based on earnings during the reference period) and benefits which are not reflected in SMP. This is consistent with the finding by the ECJ in *Lewen v Denda* that receipt of a bonus earned outside the maternity leave period was not part of the allowance (under article 11(2)(b) of the PWD) intended to ensure a minimum level of income during maternity leave (see para 5.87 onwards). The Court of Session in *Hoyland* have held that a contractual bonus is not payable in respect of the period actually covered by the maternity leave period (except the first two weeks of compulsory maternity leave).

5.68   There are often inconsistencies between statutory provisions and case-law in relation to:

- the ERA 1996 and MPL Regs 1999 – ie, the statutory maternity scheme;
- cases developed under UK discrimination and equal pay law pre October 2005,
- UK discrimination law post October 2005, which does not apparently reflect discrimination law before October 2005 in every respect; and
- ECJ decisions under article 141, the ETD and PWD.

This makes it very difficult to extract any consistent principles.

78   [1999] ICR 114, EAT.

5.69   For example, in *Clark v Secretary of State for Employment*,[79] a claim brought under article 141 (and the now repealed Employment Protection (Consolidation) Act 1978), the Court of Appeal held that when pregnant women were in receipt of payments under the separate code (relating to maternity pay) their position could not be compared with that of a man or woman at work so that they could not claim that they had been discriminated against. The claimant was not therefore entitled to full notice pay which she was claiming.[80] Following a number of subsequent ECJ decisions where discrimination and equal pay claims were upheld (such as *Thibault, Gomez, Sass* and *Alabaster*) arguably *Clark* is no longer good law. In *Thibault* the ECJ held that if the claimant had not taken maternity leave she would have had a performance assessment in accordance with a collective agreement and failure to give her an appraisal was a breach of the ETD.[81] In *Gomez* the ECJ held that the claimant was entitled to her holiday, which she was prevented from taking because of her absence on maternity leave. The Court of Appeal in *Alabaster* held that a woman on maternity leave can bring a claim under the EPA, in relation to a pay rise, by disapplying the requirement for a comparator, as was done in *Webb* and is not barred from doing so because she cannot compare herself to others. Further, even if *Clark* is still correct, arguably it is limited by its facts to notice pay, which, it could be argued, is in fact full contractual pay which is not payable.[82]

5.70   The general rule under article 141 established by *Gillespie*, and, more recently, by the ECJ in *Alabaster*, is that women cannot rely on the provisions of article 141 to argue that they should continue to receive *full normal pay* while on maternity leave as though they were actually working. The statutory regime, both in the UK and the EU (under the PWD) makes it clear that *full pay* is replaced by a statutory maternity pay regime. What is not clear is whether other terms and conditions (contractual or discretionary) relating to benefits during leave must be maintained in order to comply with the principles of non-discrimination and the PWD (see paras 5.57–5.64).

---

79 [1997] IRLR 578, CA.
80 ERA 1996 ss86–91 were subsequently amended to entitle a woman to notice pay in certain circumstances (see para 5.20) but the principle in *Clark* may still be relevant.
81 This claim, if brought in the UK, would have been made under the EPA 1970 as it concerned a contractual entitlement under the collective agreement.
82 Parliament showed its intention to limit the effect of *Clark* by implementing ERA 1996 s86.

5.71   The principles set out in *Gillespie* do not apply to women who are completely outside the protective regime (because they are not entitled to either maternity leave or pay). In *Fletcher*, the EAT held that, in relation to a claim under the ETD, *Gillespie* does not prevent a woman benefiting, at least to some extent, from facilities (such as a bursary) during the time she was off having a baby (see paras 2.58–2.59).

Specific rights during maternity leave

5.72   This section looks at the range of various rights and benefits that a woman might expect to receive during maternity leave.

Pay accrued or acquired prior to maternity leave is protected

5.73   The SDA 1975 now provides that pay acquired or accrued *prior to* maternity leave must be preserved and, if it becomes payable to the rest of the workforce, paid during OML and AML (see para 5.33). This includes a pay rise or bonus relating to the period prior to, or following, the leave.[83]

Pay increase

5.74   Where an employee receives a pay rise at any time after the qualifying period (in a case where maternity pay is calculated on the basis of a reference period as it is in the UK)[84] and before the end of her maternity leave this must be reflected in her earnings related maternity pay, whether statutory or contractual (see para xx).

Pay review and re-grading

5.75   Where a woman's pay review or appraisal, which may lead to a pay review, is due to be carried out during her OML or AML, failure to carry it out is likely to be discrimination and/or a breach of contract.

5.76   In *CNAVTS v Thibault*, a collective agreement provided that any

---

83   SDA 1975 s6A(5) this implemented the ECJ judgment in *Alabaster.*
84   During which pay is averaged for the purposes of calculating earnings related SMP.

employee present at work for at least six months of the year must receive a performance assessment. Employees receiving a satisfactory assessment received a merit increase of 2% per year, up to a maximum of 24%. Mrs Thibault had been absent on maternity and childcare leave for five months and off sick for a further period. Her employer refused to carry out an assessment of her performance because she had not been present at work for six months. She did not, therefore, receive a performance pay increase.

5.77   The ECJ held that depriving a woman of the right to an annual assessment, because she was on maternity leave, and therefore of the opportunity of qualifying for promotion, was discrimination and a breach of the ETD. Arguably, carrying out an appraisal over the telephone during an employee's maternity leave is also less favourable treatment if she would have had a meeting had she not been on maternity leave.

5.78   Employers should carry out a review before the woman goes on leave or it should take place immediately on her return but she should not be put at a disadvantage because of any delay. If it is based on productivity, this should be assessed on the basis of an average over a period which does not include the maternity leave period or a period where the woman's earnings are unusually low because of her pregnancy. The Advocate General pointed out in *Gillespie* that 'the fact that a woman is pregnant cannot be relied on in order to reduce her pay on the grounds that she has become less productive or that her pregnancy entails special arrangements justifying a pay cut'.

5.79   In *Athis v The Blue Coat School*[85] a teacher was on maternity leave when the school decided not to promote her on the pay spine. A notice was put in the staff common room setting out the criteria for promotion but Ms Athis did not see this as she was on leave. The school argued that no teachers were consulted so she was not treated differently. The EAT held that the tribunal did not consider the critical point that Mrs Athis was not informed of the contents of the circular so she was not aware that she could make representations or provide further material to the Head before he made his recommendation to the Salary Review Committee of the Governing Body. The school therefore failed to provide her with relevant information which was available to other teachers. This was sex discrimintion.

---

85 [2005] UKEAT/0541/04 27 April 2005 judgment 11 August 2005.

Payment of salary during school holidays

5.80   Following the principles set out in *Gillespie* and *Clark* the EAT has held that where a teacher's maternity leave coincides with school holidays, she is only entitled to maternity pay, not full pay, even though other teachers, who are not working, are on full pay. In *Edwards v Derby City Council*[86] a teacher took 18 weeks' contractual maternity leave as from 17 August 1997. She claimed full pay during the October half-term at a time when other teachers were not working but they still received full pay. The EAT held that the teacher, being a woman on maternity leave, was in a special position and cannot be compared either with a man or woman 'actually at work' – ie, someone working normally, although not necessarily at the workplace. Provided the maternity pay was not so low as to jeopardise the purpose of maternity leave, it was up to member states to determine maternity pay. As in *Gillespie* she could not make a claim under the EPA 1970 for full pay.

5.81   The position of women claiming full pay in respect of bank holidays or annual shutdowns that fall during maternity leave is probably the same but see para 5.95 onwards. Note, however, that in *Gomez* the ECJ held that where a woman was on maternity leave during the annual shutdown she was entitled to take holiday at a different time.

Notice pay during OML and AML

5.82   The ERA 1996 provides for a right to paid notice during both OML and AML, but only where the employee is entitled to the minimum statutory notice (see para 5.20).[87] Where there is entitlement to longer notice under the contract, the statutory provisions do not apply. Under EU and UK discrimination law, if notice pay is treated as 'pay' then according to *Gillespie* and *Boyle* it will not be payable during maternity leave (see para 5.69). If, however, it is treated as a 'right connected with the employment contract' then, following *Sass*, arguably it should be paid (see para 5.57 onwards). Alternatively, it may be possible to rely on the amended ETD, which provides for the principle of equal treatment in 'pay'. However, the courts may well hold

---

86   [1999] ICR 114.
87   The difficult question is whether regulation 17 overrides ERA 1996 s86 to provide for paid notice.

that the same principles apply under the ETD as under article 141 so as to exclude women on maternity leave claiming discrimination in notice 'pay'.

Bonuses and commission

5.83   The position of bonuses and commission is not entirely clear and is likely to depend on whether they are contractual or discretionary, the type of bonus and the period to which it relates.

During OML: under ERA 1996

5.84   Contractual terms, apart from remuneration, are maintained during OML (see para 5.14). A contractual bonus or commission that is part of a woman's wages or salary, so would be classified as 'remuneration' is unlikely to be payable (except during the compulsory leave period) unless it relates to the period prior to or following maternity leave (see paras 2.108 and 5.86 onwards). Thus, productivity pay or a bonus based on the individual's performance is likely to be classified as part of the woman's salary or wages.

During AML: under ERA 1996

5.85   Under the ERA 1996 a bonus or commission is not payable during AML unless it is payable in respect of a period either before or after AML when it should be paid as normal, at least on a proportionate basis. This is also the position under the amended SDA 1975 (s6A) and EPA 1970 (s1(2)(e)).

Discrimination and equal pay

5.86   Entitlement to a bonus must also be considered under UK and EC equal pay and discrimination law, where there is no distinction between OML and AML. The type of bonus will also be relevant.

5.87   In *Lewen v Denda*[88] a woman on *parental* leave was not given a Christmas bonus. Although the claim was brought under article 141, the PWD and the Parental Leave Directive (PLD), the ECJ found that only article 141 was relevant as it was 'pay', even if paid voluntarily by the employer as an exceptional allowance.

5.88   The ECJ held that failure to pay a bonus to a woman on parental

88   [2000] IRLR 67, ECJ.

leave could not be direct discrimination as it applied without distinction to male and female workers. The ECJ then considered indirect discrimination as female workers were more likely to be on parental leave. It held that if a Christmas bonus is retroactive pay for work performed, refusal to award a bonus, even one reduced proportionately, to workers on parental leave who worked during the year in which the bonus was granted, on the sole ground that their contract was suspended when the bonus is granted, may be indirect discrimination. However, in fact there was no indirect discrimination if the sole condition attached to the payment of the bonus was active attendance at work when the bonus was payable and where it was paid in order to encourage a worker's loyalty and hard work *in the future* as opposed to reward for past work. In this situation, a worker who exercises a statutory right to take parental leave, which carried a parenting allowance, is in a special situation, not comparable to a person at work since the leave involves suspension of the contract of employment. The relevance of this part of the decision to UK law is doubtful as the contract continues during parental leave and the leave is unpaid.

5.89   The ECJ also held that, in relation to *maternity* leave if the bonus was payable for a period in which the woman was unable to work for health and safety reasons relating to her pregnancy, she should be credited with the bonus in the same way as if she had been working. This is probably referring only to the period of compulsory maternity leave (see also para 2.108 which summarises the position under EPA 1970).

5.90   In summary, *Lewen* establishes that failure to pay a woman on parental leave a bonus where it relates to work done either before or after parental leave may be indirect discrimination. However, where the bonus relates to the parental leave period, at least where parental leave is paid and the contract is suspended (as in *Lewen*) there can be no comparison with a person at work as the worker is in a 'special' position.

5.91   In *Hoyland v Asda Stores Ltd* employees were paid an annual bonus based on the sales achieved by the workforce as a whole; it was not related to individual productivity. The bonuses were to reward employees for their work and continued contribution to the financial performance of the business during the calendar year. Payments were reduced in respect of any absences of more than eight consecutive weeks. Mrs Hoyland's bonus was reduced on account of her being absence on OML for 26 weeks. The claimant relied on the SDA

1975 and article 141 and also argued that it was a pregnancy-related detriment under the ERA 1996. Both the employer and employee called the bonus discretionary but the tribunal found that it was contractual as it was paid to all employees. It was therefore outside the scope of the SDA 1975 (s6(6)).

5.92   The EAT held, in *Hoyland*, that a worker who takes maternity leave during a bonus year must be paid a bonus in respect of the periods when she is at work and the fortnight of compulsory maternity leave. But a proportionate reduction to reflect absence on ordinary maternity leave is permitted. The EAT said that what was 'surely significant is the period during which the entitlement accrues'.[89] This would apply to OML and AML. This decision was upheld by the Court of Session,[90] who said that the entitlement to a bonus arose out of the contract of employment and was regulated by it, thus excluding any claim under the SDA.[91]

5.93   However, a different result was reached in the older decision of *GUS Home Shopping Ltd v Green and McLaughlin*[92] where the EAT held that a discretionary loyalty bonus should have been paid to women absent due to pregnancy-related sickness and maternity leave and failure to pay it was sex discrimination. In *GUS Home Shopping* payment was contingent upon an orderly and effective transfer of the marketing operation over the preceding six months, co-operation and goodwill of the individual employee and the employee remaining in the post until a specified date. The EAT, in *Hoyland*, considered that *GUS Home Shopping* was 'a long way from the present case.' Despite this assertion, it is difficult to distinguish the two situations, except that *Hoyland* concerned a contractual bonus and *GUS* a non-contractual one. In *Gus Home Shopping* the employees were not at work to contribute to the 'orderly and effective transfer' nor to show the co-operation and goodwill any more than the employees in *Hoyland* were at work to contribute to the financial performance of the business. In both cases the bonus was paid in relation to work carried out which would contribute to the success of the business. The unresolved question, under UK law, is whether a discretionary bonus

---

89 Para 15.
90 [2006] IRLR 468.
91 The Court of Session questioned whether there was any discrimination as a man on paternity leave would not be entitled to a bonus, thus misunderstanding the protection provided to women on maternity leave and the different principles that apply during maternity and paternity leave.
92 [2001] IRLR 75.

is payable where it relates to the maternity leave period. Similarly, under EC law it is not clear whether or not a contractual or discretionary bonus is payable.

Maternity bonus: discrimination against men?

5.94 Payment of a bonus only to female employees who take maternity leave will not generally be discrimination against men. The ECJ, in *Abdoulaye v Regie Nationale des Usines Renault SA*,[93] held that it was not a breach of article 141 to make such a payment exclusively to female workers as it was designed to offset the occupational disadvantages identified by the employers. Although the decision may be correct the reasoning is at odds with the fundamental principle that it is discrimination if a woman suffers any occupational disadvantages by reason of her maternity leave. There is no statutory right to such a payment in the UK and in practice it is rare for employees on maternity leave to receive such a bonus apart from a 'returner's bonus' although this is usually paid on return to work.

Holidays

During OML and AML: minimum holiday entitlement under the WT Regs 1998 and MPL Regs 1999

5.95 Under the ERA 1996 and MPL Regs 1999 an employee on OML is entitled to accrue paid statutory and contractual holidays exactly as if she were at work. During AML she only accrues her statutory holiday of 20 days a year (or pro rata if she works part-time).

5.96 All employees are entitled to a minimum of four weeks' paid holiday every year (or pro rata if they work part-time).[94] The employer may specify when the leave may be taken and it can only be taken in the leave year to which it relates (though the employer may agree otherwise) and may not be replaced by a monetary payment unless the woman resigns. Although bank holidays may be included as part of the statutory four weeks, many employers choose to give them in addition. The government is proposing to increase the minimum amount of statutory annual leave so that workers can take eight

---

93 [1999] IRLR 811, ECJ.
94 WT Regs 1998 regs 13–17.

further days to take into account public holidays. There is also a proposal to allow leave to be carried over to the next year.[95]

5.97   The DTI confirms that entitlement to the 20 days accrues during both OML and AML. This is because in order to be entitled to paid annual leave, a woman must simply be a 'worker'. She does not need to have worked a specific amount of working time in the year in order to accrue it.

5.98   Thus, under the WT Regs 1998 if a woman takes OML followed by 26 weeks' AML she will get four weeks' statutory holiday during the holiday year. If she is entitled to more than the statutory minimum, for example six weeks a year, her statutory entitlement will be untouched but the contractual balance, two weeks, may be reduced (though this may be discrimination or a breach of the PWD, see below). This is because contractual leave does not accrue during AML. Many employers allow full holiday to accrue throughout maternity leave.

5.99   AML will often span two holiday years. Many employers require employees to take their holiday entitlement during the holiday year. There is no right, under the WT Regs 1998, to carry over unused statutory holiday entitlement. The best option is to take holiday prior to and/or after the end of the leave. If this is not been possible, the woman should ask for the holiday leave to be carried over into the following year or to be paid instead. However, there is no right under the WT Regs 1998 to paid holiday during maternity leave so an employee must return to work first.[96]

5.100   The right to carry over leave or to receive pay in lieu will depend on the terms of the contract and the employer's normal practice. If different rules, relating to when holiday can be taken and if it can be carried over, are applied to women on maternity leave this may be discrimination. It is also arguable that if a woman cannot take her holiday entitlement during her leave, then it would be discrimination

---

95   Work and Families Act 2006 contains a power for the secretary of state to increase statutory leave. The DTI is also consulting as to whether, if leave is not taken during the appropriate leave year, there should be a possibility of paying in lieu or carrying the extra days over to another leave year.

96   In *Commissioners of Inland Revenue v Ainsworth and others* [2005] IRLR 465, the CA held, overruling the EAT decision in *Kigass Aero Components Ltd v Brown* [2002] IRLR 312, that employees who are absent from work on long-term sick leave are not entitled to claim holiday pay under the WT Regs 1998. The same principle is likely to be applied to maternity leave – at least under the WT Regs 1998.

to refuse to allow her to carry it over until the following holiday year. In *Merino Gomez v Continental Industrias Del Caucho SA*[97] the ECJ held that a worker must be able to take the paid statutory annual leave to which she is entitled during a period other than her maternity leave. In *Gomez* the collective agreement provided that staff could take leave from 16 July to 12 August and from 6 August to 2 September. These periods coincided with Ms Gomez's maternity leave so she asked to take her holiday during a period after her maternity leave. This was refused. The ECJ considered, in relation to holiday entitlement, the relationship between the Working Time Directive (WTD) (which guarantees a minimum of four weeks' holiday), the PWD and the ETD.

5.101   First, the ECJ held that where the dates of a worker's maternity leave coincide with those of the annual leave of the workforce, the requirements of the WTD cannot be regarded as met; a woman must be able to take holiday outside the prescribed leave period. Where the employer includes bank holidays within the 20 days' entitlement, women should not be forced to take these during their maternity leave.

5.102   Second, the ECJ held that the purpose of annual leave is different to maternity leave. PWD article 11(2)(a) provides that the rights connected with the employment contract of a worker (apart from pay) are preserved during maternity leave and this applied to entitlement to paid annual leave. Thus, the same principles apply to both statutory and contractual holiday.

5.103   Third, the ECJ held that the determination of when paid annual leave is to be taken comes under the ETD (see *Boyle*). This must be interpreted, following the decision in *Thibault*,[98] as meaning that a worker must be able to take her annual leave outside her maternity leave. The decision did not, however, determine whether a woman is entitled to carry over any untaken annual leave into the next holiday year. Arguably, in many situations this is a necessary corollary in order to enable a woman to take her holiday outside her maternity leave period. In *Federatie Nederlandse Vakbeweging v Staat Der Nederlanden* [2006] IRLR 561 the ECJ held that the carrying forward of annual leave guaranteed by the WTD may be inevitable. Pay in lieu of holiday may only be paid where the employment relationship is terminated. At para 24 the ECJ said 'Thus, in the event of the

97   [2004] IRLR 407, ECJ.
98   [1998] IRLR 399, ECJ.

aggregation of several periods of leave guaranteed by Community law at the end of a year, the carrying forward of annual leave, or part thereof to the following year may be inevitable'. This only applies to the 20 days guaranteed by the WT Regs.

5.104   The ECJ, in *Boyle*,[99] held that an employee does not accrue annual leave during any period of supplementary maternity leave granted by the employer. It is now clear that this only applies to maternity leave which is more generous than the statutory minimum, so does not fall within the protection of the PWD.

School holidays

5.105   If maternity leave for teachers and school staff (OML or AML) falls during school holidays there is no statutory entitlement to take leave to make up for missing the holidays (see para 5.66). However, it is arguable that the principles in *Gomez* also apply to school holidays. The position is unclear. If, however, a woman returns to work before the beginning of the holidays, she will get paid for them in the normal way. It remains to be seen how far the UK courts will interpret the ECJ decision in *Gomez*.

Time off in lieu for missed bank holidays

5.106   If there is a bank holiday during the woman's maternity leave, there is normally no entitlement to take a day off at a later stage, unless it is treated as part of the minimum 20-day entitlement under the WT Regs 1998 (see para 5.95 onwards above). If, however, employees who are sick on a bank holiday are entitled to take a day off in lieu then arguably, following *Boyle*, it would be discriminatory to refuse to allow a woman on maternity leave to do the same, but see *Edwards* for the contrary argument (see para 5.66).

Other benefits

OML

5.107   Under the ERA 1996 and MPL Regs 1999 an employee is entitled to retain benefits during OML. These would include private use of company car or mobile phone,[100] health and life insurance, mortgage

---

99   [1998] IRLR 717, ECJ.
100   Where the car and/or phone are for personal use only or both personal and business use, the woman should be entitled to use it during OML.

subsidies, luncheon vouchers, payment of professional subscriptions, health club membership, benefits of share schemes. Where a company car or mobile phone (or other perk) is restricted to business use only, there is no entitlement to continued use of it during OML (or AML).

5.108   Arguably this entitlement applies even where a cash allowance is paid to an employee instead of the benefit. If the employer pays a car allowance or a contribution towards a car or phone (such as rental, insurance, repairs), these payments should not be classified as 'remuneration' where they are for personal or both personal *and* business use. This is because they appear separately from the 'wages or salary' item on the pay slip and so probably do not fall within the definition of 'remuneration', nor are they the 'adequate allowance' referred to in the PWD (see para 5.42).

AML

5.109   There is no statutory right under either the ERA 1996, MPL Regs 1999 or the SDA 1975 to retain these contractual benefits during AML although an employer may be prepared to allow an employee to do so. However, arguably this is discrimination and/or a breach of the PWD (see para 5.57).

During both OML and AML: discrimination, equal pay and PWD rights

5.110   A grey area is the extent to which *Sass* and other EC decisions (*Gillespie, Alabaster, Gomez*) can be relied on by employees to claim, under the ETD and/or PWD, that contractual rights (apart from pay) should be maintained during AML as well as during OML. Although *Sass* was decided on its own facts (relating to continuous service) the ECJ held that rights associated with the contract of employment should be continued during statutory maternity leave (see para 5.57 onwards).

Private health insurance: discrimination by an employer who fails to provide it

5.111   Where a private health insurance scheme excludes pregnancy-related illness, the insurance company may refuse to insure the woman, relying on the exception in the SDA 1975 that allows differential treatment for actuarial reasons.[101] There is no equivalent exception for an employer. If an employer fails to provide an equivalent benefit, the woman may arguably have an equal pay claim against the employer.

Occupational pensions

During OML and AML: under ERA 1996, SSA 1989 and sex discrimination

5.112   During OML the employer must continue to pay pension contributions as though the woman was working normally and irrespective of whether she receives maternity pay or returns to work at the end of the leave (or absence).[102] In *Boyle* the ECJ held that the accrual of pension rights was one of the rights connected with the employment contracts of workers under PWD article 11(2)(a) and must be maintained during the 26-week period. The employee must also pay contributions but these are based on the maternity pay she receives.

5.113   In addition, under SSA 1989 Sch 5, a woman on paid maternity leave (whether ordinary or additional) must be treated for all purposes (except her liability to pay contributions) as though she was at work and receiving full pay. The provisions apply to final salary and money purchase schemes, whether or not the woman returns to work at the end of her OML or AML and whether she is in receipt of statutory or contractual pay.

5.114   These provisions are enforced in the civil courts (usually the county court). The SSA 1989 provides that where any provision of the pension scheme is in breach of the principle of equal treatment in the Act it may be overridden. Thus, for example, if the employer fails to maintain the pension contributions during OML or paid AML an application can be made (by an 'interested person') to the county court for payment to be made.

5.115   The woman herself is only required to pay contributions on the maternity pay she actually receives.

5.116   Where the pension is a money purchase scheme (ie, based on actual contributions made as opposed to the final salary), an employee who has been on maternity leave and has paid (or had paid

---

101   SDA 1975 s45 which excludes treatment in relation to an annuity, life assurance policy, accident insurance policy, or similar matter involving the assessment of risk where the treatment was effected by reference to actuarial date and was reasonable having regard to the data and any other relevant factors.

102   SSA 1989 Sch 5.

on her behalf) fewer contributions will receive a lower pension than an employee who has not. As with a final salary scheme, she will also have accrued less service because under the ERA 1996 and MPL Regs any time on AML is not taken into account when calculating length of service (see para 5.19). It is not clear what, if any, remedy she would have for this loss of pension benefit. Arguably, the exclusion of the AML period from the calculation of the length of service is discriminatory against a woman as a worker, particularly after the ECJ decision in *Sass* and *Herrero* (see para 5.57 onwards).

5.117   Although there is no statutory entitlement to receive pension contributions from the employer after the end of OML or any paid AML, there may be a contractual entitlement. Usually, however, employers' contributions are based on earnings so, if the woman is on unpaid leave, the employer will not pay contributions. Pension schemes have different rules and it is worth checking these.

Statutory and contractual sick pay

5.118   There is no entitlement to *statutory* sick pay during the maternity pay period see para 6.67 onwards).[103]

5.119   A woman who is unwell during her maternity leave will not be entitled to *contractual* sick pay as this would count as 'remuneration'. In *Todd v Eastern Health and Social Services Board*[104] the claimant argued that she was entitled, while absent from work during pregnancy, to the benefit of her contractual sick pay scheme which was more favourable than the maternity pay she would receive. The Court of Appeal (Northern Ireland) held that a healthy pregnancy did not come within the contractual provisions relating to sickness and disability and pregnancy could not be compared with sickness. This decision, delivered at the same time as *Gillespie* is consistent with *Gillespie*. A woman on maternity leave cannot claim more than her statutory or contractual right to maternity pay by relying on UK or EU discrimination or equal pay law and so cannot claim contractual sick pay.

5.120   An employee may be entitled to contractual sick pay if she returns to work before the end of her maternity leave (having given the appropriate notice). The question then is whether she can return to

---

103 Social Security Contributions and Benefits Act 1992 Sch 13.
104 [1997] IRLR 410, CA (NI).

maternity leave after taking sick leave. In *Boyle* the ECJ held that if a woman becomes ill during the minimum maternity leave provided for by the PWD, and places herself under the sick leave arrangements, and the sick leave ends before the end of the 14 weeks, she can then continue with her maternity leave up until the end of the 14-week period.[105] At the time of *Boyle* the minimum provided by the PWD and the statutory leave was the same, so it is not clear whether the same principle would now apply to the whole period of statutory maternity leave (ie the 52 weeks). However, how this would operate in practice is very unclear, particularly as a woman has to give notice to return to work early and there is no provision for terminating maternity leave and then returning to it after the end of the sick pay period (see paras 4.56–4.61 for notice of early return). Notice of early return is 28 days if her EWC is before 1 April 2007 and eight weeks if her EWC is on or after 1 April 2007. It would not be advisable for an employee to risk returning to work solely in order to claim contractual sick pay and then attempt to continue her maternity leave.

5.121   Chapter 7 covers sick pay, incapacity benefits and other benefits payable during maternity leave.

Rights 'in her capacity as a worker' during OML and AML: protection from sex discrimination

5.122   It will be discriminatory not to consider a woman on maternity leave for opportunities given to other staff members, for example, a performance assessment or opportunities for promotion (see para 5.53 onwards). In *McGuigan v TG Baynes*[106] the EAT upheld a finding of sex discrimination in favour of an employee who was not consulted about her impending redundancy because she was on maternity leave (see para 15.94). An employee should be informed of any changes that affect her job and vacancies for which she may wish to apply. She should also be considered for training opportunities if she wants to work for some days during her maternity leave (see para 4.48 onwards).

---

105   In particular, the ECJ has held that protection of rights applies during the whole of statutory maternity leave, not just the 14-week minimum laid down by the PWD.
106   EAT 1114/97, 24 November 1998.

Duty of trust and confidence and continuance of entitlement to disciplinary and grievance procedures

5.123 The MPL Regs 1999 provide that an employer is bound, throughout the maternity leave period, by the notice provisions, the obligation of trust and confidence, and by an obligation to apply the disciplinary and grievance procedures (see para 5.17). This would include an obligation not only to act fairly in any disciplinary or grievance matter but also not to discriminate. Duties in relation to redundancy are covered in chapter 15.

Continuity of service

5.124 During the OML period the contract of employment continues, irrespective of pay, length of service or hours of work.[107] Thus, this period counts towards her period of continuous employment for the purposes of qualifying for statutory employment rights (for example, towards two years' service for redundancy pay). It also counts as service for contractual rights, such as assessing seniority, pension rights and other personal length-of-service payments and pay increments under her contract of employment (see DTI guidance on maternity rights[108]).

5.125   The ERA provides that an employee continues to be an employee of her employer throughout the time that she is absent on maternity leave, including AML, although many of the terms of her contract are suspended during AML. For the purposes of calculating length-of-service-related *statutory* benefits (such as redundancy pay) each week of AML is taken in account. However, for the purposes of the woman's seniority and similar contractual rights (including pensions) the period of employment after AML is to be treated as continuous with the period of employment immediately before AML (leaving out the period of AML itself).[109] This applies where the employee is returning from or consecutive periods of statutory leave which include AML or AAL. The period of additional leave (ie, from the end of ordinary maternity leave until the date the woman returns to work) does not itself count (except for pensions during paid leave, see para 5.113 onwards).

---

107   ERA 1996 s71, MPL Regs 1999 reg 18A(1)(a)(ii).
108   Available on the DTI website.
109   MPL Regs reg 18A(1)(a)(i). This also applies if there is a consecutive period of statutory leave which included AML or AAL.

5.126   The ECJ have held, in *Sass*, that it is discrimination not to include an employee's statutory maternity leave as continuous service for contractual rights. Thus, the regulations are in breach of EC law (see para 5.57).[110]

5.127   Some employers give employees on maternity leave the right to retain all their terms and conditions of service throughout the time they are off work in order to offer consistent and simplified rights. The cost is not high since most employees do not benefit from an extensive range of terms and conditions. Indeed, since the WT Regs 1998 have already given workers the right to continue to accrue the statutory 20 days' holiday throughout maternity leave, most employers need concede little in order to achieve simplicity.

Remedies

5.128   If the employer refuses to provide a benefit to which the woman is entitled, she may have the following claims in the employment tribunal:

- under the ERA 1996 for an unlawful deduction of wages; in *Moxley and Cherowbrier v Governors of St Edward's School*[111] the tribunal held that failure to give the claimants a single lump sum (awarded to all teachers as part of a pay review) because they were on maternity leave was an unlawful deduction under the Wages Act 1986 (the predecessor of ERA 1996 Part II). Where the total wages paid are less than those due, the amount of shortfall will be treated as a deduction.[112] Thus, failure to pay statutory maternity pay, sick pay or holiday pay, where payments are due, is likely to be an unauthorised deduction;
- there is no specific remedy for failure to provide the benefit of all terms and conditions of employment under MPL Regs 1999 reg 9, so the claim must be made under the ERA 1996 Part 11 or SDA 1975 or EPA 1970;
- under the SDA 1975 where there has been discrimination in relation to non-contractual terms, such as failure to consult a woman about redundancy or failure to give her a pay rise;

---

110   *Land Brandenburg v Sass* [2005] IRLR 147.
111   48132/93 and 48735/93, 18 February 1994, Southampton ET.
112   ERA 1996 s13(3).

- under the EPA 1970 in relation to contractual terms, such as the failure to provide contractual benefits during OML (and possibly AML relying on EC law); there is no need for a comparator where discrimination is on grounds of pregnancy or maternity leave;
- under article 141 for pay related benefits, except full pay;
- under the PWD and/or ETD but only in relation to public sector employees (see para 1.23);
- breach of contract but this claim can only be made in the tribunal once the employment has been terminated.

5.129 An action can be brought in the county court for:

- breach of contract, where the woman has not received the benefit of her contractual terms during her leave (and, where she is entitled to them, during her absence); or
- breach of SSA 1989 Sch 5 (see para 5.114).

Statutory maternity pay

Key points

- An employed woman will be entitled to statutory maternity pay (SMP) where she:
  - has 26 weeks' continuous service with the same employer by the end of the qualifying week; and
  - has average earnings of at least the lower earnings limit for national insurance (NI) (£84 per week for April 2006 to April 2007) during an eight-week or two-month calculation period ending with the qualifying week. There are detailed provisions for the calculation of average earnings.
- The qualifying week (QW) is the 15th week before the expected week of childbirth (EWC) or approximately the 26th week of pregnancy.
- SMP is payable for 26 weeks for women whose EWC is before 1 April 2007 and for 39 weeks for women whose EWC is on or after 1 April 2007. SMP is paid at the rate of 90% of her average earnings for the first six weeks and a flat rate for the remaining period. The flat rate is currently £108.85 (April 2006 to April 2007).
- The woman can choose when SMP is payable except that:
  - it cannot be paid before the 11th week before the EWC, unless the baby is born before then;
  - it is not payable while she is still working for the employer liable to pay it;
  - if she has a pregnancy-related absence in the four weeks before the EWC her SMP will start the day after her first day of absence.
- If a woman is awarded a pay rise between the start of the calculation period for SMP and the end of her maternity leave, she is entitled to have her SMP recalculated and receive any extra SMP due.
- SMP is payable even if the woman does not intend to return to work after the birth. She does not have to repay any SMP if she resigns.
- No employers are exempt from paying SMP. Employers can recover all or most of the SMP they pay.
  - If an employer thinks SMP is not due they must issue form SMP1 stating the reasons why SMP is not payable. If the woman disagrees with her employer she can ask her local

> HMRC (Her Majesty's Revenue and Customs) officer for a formal decision and ultimately HMRC will pay the SMP she is entitled to if the employer refuses to comply. She may also have a claim for unlawful deduction of wages.
> - If a woman is dismissed before the qualifying week (QW) in order to avoid liability for SMP she will have a claim for automatic unfair dismissal and sex discrimination. She may still qualify for SMP or any loss of SMP will form part of her claim for compensation.
> - A woman who does not qualify for SMP may qualify for maternity allowance or incapacity benefit. A family on reduced earnings may be entitled to tax credits (see chapter 7 on maternity allowance and other benefits).

Background and statutory framework

6.1   SMP is payable instead of a woman's full salary since, in the absence of a contractual right, a woman is not entitled to be paid her full salary while on maternity leave (see para 5.14). If she does not meet the qualifying conditions for SMP a woman may be entitled to maternity allowance (MA) or incapacity benefit. She may also be entitled to a means-tested benefit such as income support or tax credits (see chapter 7).

6.2   The first maternity payment to be introduced was MA, which was paid at a weekly rate with an earnings-related supplement. A payment similar to SMP was introduced in 1975. The Employment Protection Act 1975 introduced the concept of income replacement and gave women with at least two years' service with their employer six weeks' maternity pay at 90% of normal pay. The Social Security Act (SSA) 1986 introduced SMP administered by employers.

6.3   The Social Security Contributions and Benefits Act (SSCBA) 1992, the Statutory Maternity Pay (General) Regulations (SMP Regs) 1986[1] and the Statutory Maternity Pay (General) (Modification and Amendment) Regulations 2000[2] set out the main provisions. These have been amended a number of times but the principal amendments have been made by the Social Security, Statutory Maternity Pay and Statutory Sick Pay (Miscellaneous Amendments) Regulations

---

1   SI No 1960 (as amended).
2   SI No 2883.

2002 SI No 2690 which incorporated the changes to SMP for women whose EWC began on or after 6 April 2003, and the Statutory Maternity Pay (General) (Amendment) Regulations 2005 SI No 729 which provided for the inclusion of pay increases in the calculation of average earnings. Further amendments have been made by the Statutory Maternity Pay and Maternity Allowance (Amendment) Regulations 2006 which extended SMP to 39 weeks for women whose EWC is on or after 1 April 2007. The regulations also enabled women to work for up to 10 days during the SMP period without losing SMP and made provision for SMP to start on any day of the week.

6.4   Note: The Work and Families Act 2006 contains powers to extend maternity and adoption pay to 52 weeks and to introduce a new entitlement to additional paternity leave (APL) which could be taken within the second six months of the child's life. Some of the APL could be paid if the child's mother or adopter has returned to work and has some of her entitlement to SMP, MA or SAP (statutory adoption pay) left at the time of her return. The government intends to introduce these new measures by the end of this Parliament which is expected to be by 2010 but is still consulting on the details of the new scheme.

6.5   HMRC publishes a Help Book for Employers called 'Pay and time off work for parents E15' ('the Help Book') which provides information about calculating, paying and reclaiming SMP, as well as SPP (statutory paternity pay) and SAP.[3] The SMP legislation is the responsibility of the Department for Work and Pensions (DWP) but the employer's local HMRC office oversees the payment of SMP and deals with complaints.

Who may claim SMP?

6.6   The woman must be an employee. The definition of 'employee' for the purposes of a claim for SMP is different from the definition under the Employment Rights Act (ERA) 1996. A woman may be an employee for SMP purposes and therefore entitled to maternity pay but not an employee under the ERA 1996 and so not entitled to maternity leave (see para 1.27 onwards). In such a case, she would

---

3   The Employer's Help Book can be obtained from the Employer's Orderline on 0845 7 646 646 or from the website: www.hmrc.gov.uk/employers.

have to rely on a contractual right to maternity leave or agree some time off. A refusal of time off might be discrimination.

6.7 To be an employee for SMP purposes a woman must be an 'employed earner', ie earnings that attract a liability for employer's class 1 NI contributions, or would if they were high enough, and are chargeable to income tax under schedule E (any tax due is deducted by her employer under the PAYE system).[4] A woman does not have to pay NI regularly in order to qualify for SMP (see para 6.34). In practice, this definition covers anyone who pays tax under PAYE.

6.8 Provided they satisfy the above two conditions, women who work under a contract of apprenticeship are employees for the purposes of SMP[5] as are Crown employees.[6] Agency workers (the agency who pays the worker is the employer for SMP purposes), continental shelf workers, workers employed on government training schemes, part-time workers and married women and widows who pay reduced rate NI can all qualify for SMP providing they meet the qualifying conditions, see below. Office holders including police officers, members of parliament, the judiciary and some company directors can qualify.[7]

Women excluded from the right to claim SMP

6.9 Few women are excluded, but SMP is not payable to the following:

- Some foreign-going mariners employed by a UK employer who pays a special rate of NI contributions;[8] but mariners employed on a British ship or whose employer has a place of business in the UK are usually entitled to SMP.[9]

- A woman who works outside the UK where the employer is not resident or present in Great Britain or does not have a place of business in Great Britain, and is not liable to pay NI contributions.[10] However, if a woman has worked for the same employer

---

4 SSCBA 1992 s171(1) and SMP Regs 1986 reg 17 as amended by the Employment Equality (Age) Regulations 2006 SI No 1031 which came into force on 1 October 2006 and removed the age restriction.
5 SMP Regs 1986 reg 17(2).
6 SSCBA 1992 s169; SSA 1989 Sch 6 para 25.
7 SMP Regs 1986 reg 17.
8 SSCBA 1992 s170 and SMP (Persons Abroad and Mariners) Regulations 1987 SI No 418.
9 The Help Book E15 (Supplement) (2006) p2.
10 SMP Regs 1986 reg 17(3) and Social Security (Contributions) Regulations 2001 reg 145(1)(b).

inside Great Britain and the European Economic Area (EEA) (but not outside it), her employment can count towards the 26-week continuous employment rule even if the employer has not been liable to pay class 1 NI during the whole period, providing she worked for the employer in the UK in the 15th week before the EWC and the employer was liable to pay class 1 NI on her earnings for that week.[11]

- A woman detained in custody or sentenced to imprisonment; this includes detention in prison or a police station, but does not include a suspended sentence. SMP ceases in the week she is detained and does not resume when she is released.[12]
- SMP is not payable for any week after a woman's death.[13]

The main qualifying conditions for SMP

6.10   To qualify for SMP the woman must:

- have been continuously employed for at least 26 weeks continuing into the 15th week before the EWC (this 15th week is known as the qualifying week);
- have average weekly earnings of not less than the lower earnings limit for the payment of NI (£84 per week from April 2006 to April 2007);
- have stopped working;
- be pregnant and, in order to claim SMP, she must have reached the 11th week before the EWC or have given birth before that date;
- produce medical evidence and give the required notice to her employer.

The flowchart on p221 summarises the main qualifying conditions.

11 The Help Book E15 (Supplement) (2006) p5.
12 SMP Regs 1986 reg 9.
13 SMP Regs 1986 reg 10.

Who qualifies for SMP?

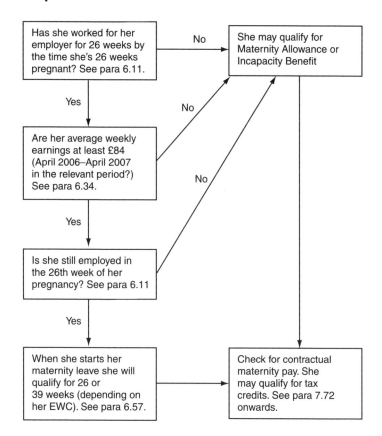

The woman must have continuous service with the same employer for a period of at least 26 weeks continuing into the QW

6.11   The QW is the 15th week before the EWC.[14] A woman will have sufficient qualifying service if she only works for a day or part of a day in the QW but she must be employed in the QW.[15] The only exception to this is that if the baby is born before the QW a woman can still

14   SSCBA 1992 s164(2)(a) (which actually says '26 weeks ending with the week immediately preceding the 14th week before the EWC', which amounts to the same thing).
15   SMP Regs 1986 reg 11(4).

qualify for SMP (see para 6.27). If the woman started work in the 26th week before the end of the QW, she need only have worked part of that week.[16]

6.12   The Help Book contains tables which set out the QW in relation to a woman's EWC and also the latest start date for 26 weeks' employment which avoids the need to use a calendar.[17] Part of the SMP tables for 2006/7 is reproduced in appendix C. To see if a woman has sufficient service:

- Identify the week of the EWC using column 1 of the tables (week baby due) or a calendar. The week must start on a Sunday. The MAT B1 gives the date the baby is due (see para 6.49).
- Identify the start of the qualifying week using the SMP tables in appendix C, column 2, (start of 15th week before baby due). Alternatively, use a calendar and start with the Sunday at the beginning of the week the baby is due. Then find the previous Sunday and count back 14 more Sundays from there.
- Identify the 26-week period using the SMP tables, column 3 (latest start date for employment with you) or start with and include the QW and count back 25 more weeks using a calendar.

EXAMPLE: Nina's baby is due on Monday 14 May 2007. Her EWC is therefore the week beginning Sunday 13 May 2007. If you count back one Sunday from there to Sunday 6 May and 14 more Sundays, the QW will start on Sunday 28 January 2007 and end on Saturday 3 February 2007. This is the week in column 2 of the tables (start of 15th week before baby due). The 26th week before 3 February ends on Saturday 12 August 2006 (column 3 in the tables). Nina has to have worked for the same employer throughout this 26 week period to qualify for SMP but if she did not start her job until Saturday 12 August and ended it on Sunday 28 January she will still have enough continuous service to qualify for SMP.

Rules of thumb

6.13   Since the 15th week before the EWC is roughly the start of the last three months of pregnancy, the QW is about the 26th week or the end of the sixth month of pregnancy. This means that, as a rule of thumb,

---

16   SMP Regs 1986 reg 16A.
17   See note 3 above.

if a woman has been working for her employer since before she got pregnant, even if only just before, she will have at least 26 weeks' service by the 26th week of her pregnancy. She will therefore have sufficient service and it will not be necessary to reach for calendar or tables. In borderline cases the date on the MAT B1 is critical, the later the better (see para 6.49).

What counts as continuous employment?

6.14 Employment is continuous if there has been a contract of service (written or unwritten) in existence for the whole period (see para 1.28). If some work was done during any week, it counts as a full week. The contract may be deemed to continue even where the employee is not working.[18] In *Secretary of State for Employment v Doulton Sanitaryware Ltd*[19] the employee left to have a baby and the employers put her on their list of 'prolonged absentees'. The EAT held that the contract continued.

6.15 However, even where there is no contract of service in existence, employment will be deemed to be continuous in some circumstances. Under SMP Regs 1986 reg 11, the following breaks in the relevant period (ie, the 26 weeks up to the qualifying week) do not count:

- up to 26 weeks' absence due to sickness or injury;[20]
- where there is a temporary cessation of work because the employer was unable to offer the employee work;[21]
- absence from work in circumstances such that, by arrangement or custom, the woman is regarded as continuing in employment (eg, a public holiday or annual shutdown);[22] thus, if the employee worked before and after a week with a public holiday (such as Christmas), that week is treated as a week of employment;
- absence due wholly or partly to pregnancy or childbirth;[23]
- absence from work as a result of taking paternity leave, adoption leave or parental leave.[24]

18 *Satchwell Sunvic Ltd v Secretary of State for Employment* [1979] IRLR 455, EAT.
19 [1981] ICR 477, EAT.
20 SMP Regs 1986 reg 11(1)(a) and (2) and the Help Book (Supplement) (2006) p3.
21 SMP Regs 1986 reg 11(1)(b).
22 SMP Regs 1986 reg 11(1)(c).
23 During the maternity leave period the contract normally subsists; this provision assists women whose contract does not continue during a period of absence not exceeding 26 weeks; see SMP Regs 1986 reg 11(1)(d) and (3).
24 SMP Regs 1986 reg 11(1)(e).

In the above situations the woman must normally return to work for her employer after the absence, otherwise continuity will not be preserved.[25] For example, a woman is employed on a series of short-term contracts with breaks between contracts on account of a 'temporary cessation of work'. She returns to work for the same employer under a new contract and her continuity of employment is preserved despite her absence between contracts.

6.16   In the majority of cases, a contract is not brought to an end because of absence on the grounds mentioned above, eg employment continues during parental leave or sickness absence. The provisions above only apply where breaks in employment occur in which there is no contract of employment such as between short-term or term-time only contracts.

Agency workers and other contractors without permanent contracts

6.17   Agency workers and other workers can qualify for SMP even if they cannot establish that they work under a contract of service (see paras 1.28 and 6.7) since they are an employee for SMP purposes if they pay NI. The 'employer' is whoever pays the worker and is liable for the employer's NI contribution. This is usually the agency.

Continuous service for agency workers

6.18   Agency workers, like other employees, must have been working for the agency for a continuous period of 26 weeks up to and into the QW. Some agency workers will be employed by the agency on a contract of service (in other words they will be 'employees' of the agency under the ERA 1996). Other agency workers, particularly those on long-term placements, may be regarded as employees of the end-user.[26] If there is a continuing contract of service, the agency worker will have continuous service despite any interruptions in her work (see para 6.14).

6.19   If the agency worker does not have a continuing contract of service she will only be an employee when she is working for the agency. When she has periods when she does not work for the agency, the SMP rules say that she may still have continuity of employment, see

---

25   SMP Regs 1986 reg 11(1). See also reg 11(3A) which contains a limited exception to the need to return to work for women who are unable to do so, such as seasonal workers or women who are unwell.

26   *Brook Street Bureau v Dacas* [2004] EWCA (Civ) 217.

para 6.15 above. In addition, the rules say that continuity is not broken for agency workers where:

- the agency had no work for the woman in any particular week;
- she was on paid leave under the Working Time Regulations (WT Regs) 1998;
- the agency offered her work but the woman could not take it because of sickness, injury or pregnancy (if she decided not to accept the work for any other reason, continuity would be broken); and
  she returned to work for the agency after the absence. If a woman has up to 26 weeks off sick, she will still be treated as continuously employed, providing she did some work within the 26 weeks.[27]

Agency workers who take time off for other reasons

6.20 Only employees have statutory rights to paid time off for antenatal care, parental leave and time off for dependants (see chapters 3, 10 and 11) so if a worker who is not an employee takes such time off it is not clear whether her continuity will be preserved. Continuity of employment would probably not be broken where she takes time off for antenatal care as she is not working because of pregnancy, see para 6.19. She would need to agree the time off and notify the agency of the reason for not working. If she needed time off to care for a sick child, and her 'employer' agreed to her taking time off, continuity would probably not be broken as she would be regarded as continuing in employment 'by arrangement and custom'.[28] If the 'employer' did not agree, a woman would be in a more difficult position because continuity might be broken, although if she worked for other days in that week it would not be.

No employment in the QW for agency worker

6.21 If there is no work in the QW, the agency worker can be treated as employed if:

- she was not intending to start her leave at that time and was available for work after the QW, and

---

27 The Help Book E15 (Supplement) (2006) p5.
28 See note 22.

- she returns to work for the agency before taking maternity absence.[29]

6.22   If she stopped working before the QW because of sickness (but had intended to continue working), she will be treated as working into the QW (and thus be eligible for SMP), but only if she does some work within 26 weeks of the first day of her sickness absence.[30] Thus, no decision can be made about entitlement to SMP until after she has returned to work with the agency.[31]

6.23   Where the woman has chosen to stop work for the agency before the QW, she will not be entitled to SMP (see para 6.11).

Seasonal and regular temporary workers

6.24   There are special rules about continuity for these workers which are similar to those for agency workers. A seasonal or regular temporary worker is one where it is the employer's practice:

- to offer work for a fixed period of not more than 26 consecutive weeks; and
- to offer such work for two or more times a year for periods which do not overlap; and
- to offer the work to the same people.

6.25   A seasonal or regular temporary worker who is absent because of her pregnancy or is otherwise sick throughout the QW is not required to return to work afterwards in order to preserve continuity because, of course, there may be no work available at that particular time. She can be treated as having worked into the QW even though she does not return to work.[32]

6.26   Supply teachers, seasonal and other temporary workers who regularly work for fixed periods may still have continuous employment if they were not working for one of the reasons in the SMP Regs 1986 reg 11, see para 6.15. For example, a temporary worker may have continuous employment if she did not work in a week because of paid leave under the WT Regs 1998 or there was no work available.[33]

---

29 The Help Book E15 (Supplement) (2006) p5.
30 Ibid.
31 SMP Regs 1986 reg 11(3)(a).
32 SMP Regs 1986 reg 11(3A).
33 The Help Book E15 (Supplement) (2006) p5.

Birth before QW

6.27 Where the baby is born in or before the QW the woman will be entitled to SMP if she would have been employed for 26 weeks by the end of the QW, had the baby not been born early (see also para 6.54).[34]

Industrial action and stoppage of work

6.28 Where a woman takes part in a strike, the day or week when she does not work will not break her continuity of employment. However, the whole of the week (even if she was on strike for only one day) will be disregarded when working out whether she has worked for 26 weeks.[35] This does not apply if the woman can prove that at no time did she have a direct interest in the trade dispute.[36] Continuous employment is not broken by a lockout. If the woman is dismissed during a stoppage of work, her continuity of employment is deemed to have ceased on the day she stopped work, unless she can prove that at no time did she have a direct interest in the trade dispute in which case her continuity continues until the day she is dismissed.[37]

Return from the armed forces

6.29 If a woman returns to her former employer after a period in the armed forces, her previous employment with the former employer will count provided the break is no more than six months.[38]

Transfer of the undertaking

6.30 Where the business has been taken over by another employer and this is a transfer of the undertaking, continuity of employment will not be broken.[39] Account must be taken of her continuous employment with the former employer.

Other transfers

6.31 Continuity of employment may also be preserved if there are other transfers, such as:

34 SMP Regs 1986 reg 4(2).
35 SMP Regs 1986 reg 13(1).
36 SMP Regs 1986 reg 13(3).
37 SMP Regs 1986 reg 13(2).
38 SMP Regs 1986 reg 15.
39 As defined by Transfer of Undertakings (Protection of Employment) Regulations (TUPE) 2006 reg 4.

- under a statute;
- on the death of the employer, where the personal representatives take over;
- where a teacher moves from employment by a local education authority to employment in another school maintained by that authority or to a school where the governors of the school are the teacher's employer (or vice versa); or
- where the employee moves to an associated employer (ie, a company which is directly or indirectly controlled by the other).[40]

Suspension for health and safety reasons

6.32   A woman who has been suspended for health and safety reasons will still be employed and so she will be treated as still working (see para 3.66).

Termination of contract in order to avoid liability for SMP

6.33   If the employer terminates the woman's contract in order to avoid liability for SMP then it may still be payable (see para 6.119).

The woman must have average weekly earnings of not less than the lower earnings limit for the payment of NI (£84 per week from April 2006 to April 2007)

6.34   A woman does not have to pay NI regularly or at all to claim SMP. The calculation is based on an assessment of her *average* earnings, not on her NI contributions. It does not matter if her pay falls below the lower earnings limit in any one week, provided the average pay does not fall below it. There is also no requirement for the woman to be working for a minimum number of hours per week; but the lower earnings limit excludes many women who work part-time because their weekly earnings are not high enough (see chapter 7).

6.35   Average weekly earnings are calculated over the 'relevant period' which is the period between the last normal pay day before the Saturday at the end of the QW and the last normal pay day falling at least eight weeks before that (see para 6.81 for calculation of average pay).

6.36   The calculation of average pay is based on actual gross pay paid during the relevant period. This includes overtime, bonuses, sick pay and any other payment subject to NI. If a pay rise is awarded that

40 SMP Regs 1986 reg 14.

applies between the start of the relevant period and the end of a woman's maternity leave, her average earnings should be recalculated, see para 6.97. What constitutes pay is dealt with in more detail in para 6.82 onwards.

6.37 The lower earnings limit for the payment of NI increases in April every year. From April 2006 to April 2007 it is £84. Employees whose earnings are equal to or just over the lower earnings limit will not always actually pay NI as the earnings of low earners are zero-rated. Therefore, even if an employee does not pay any NI at all in the relevant period she may still be entitled to SMP. It is the lower earnings limit in force immediately before the end of the QW which counts.

Rules of thumb

6.38 The relevant period for assessing average earnings is roughly the 18th to 26th weeks of a woman's pregnancy (although the relevant period for irregularly paid employees may be very different). If she regularly pays NI and either receives full pay when she is off sick or is not off sick in those weeks, her earnings will be high enough to qualify for SMP. For how to calculate average earnings see para 6.89.

Where the woman has more than one contract with the same employer

6.39 The employer must treat the contracts as one contract where they are aggregated for the purpose of NI contributions. The woman's earnings under both contracts are added together in order to calculate pay.[41] There is an exception where it is not reasonably practicable to aggregate the earnings for the purposes of NI contributions. In such a case, SMP is payable separately under each contract if the woman qualifies under each contract.[42] The contracts may also be aggregated where the woman works for different but associated employers.

6.40 Where, as a result of the establishment of National Health Service Trusts, the woman who works in more than one hospital or unit is treated as having two contracts, she can choose whether or not they are treated as one for the purposes of SMP.[43]

41 SMP Regs 1986 reg 5.
42 Social Security (Contributions) Regulations 1979 SI No 591 reg 11 provides that there will not be aggregation where aggregation is not reasonably practicable because the earnings in the respective employments are separately calculated.
43 SMP (National Health Service Employees) Regulations 1991 SI No 590 and see the Help Book E15 (Supplement) (2006) p14.

Working for more than one employer

6.41 The contracts will not be aggregated where the woman works for two separate employers. If the woman's earnings are below the lower earnings limit in each employment, she will not be entitled to SMP. If she satisfies the qualifying conditions in each job (including earning above the lower earnings limit), she will be entitled to SMP from both employers.[44]

Lower earnings threshold unlawful?

6.42 The European Pregnant Workers Directive (PWD) provides that a woman taking maternity leave must receive her full pay or be guaranteed an 'adequate allowance'.[45] Under the PWD the allowance is deemed adequate if it is at least equal to the amount an employee would receive if off work because of sickness.[46]

6.43 It has been argued that making SMP dependent on earning more than the lower earnings limit is a breach of article 141 of the Treaty of Rome and of the PWD. This was because in *Gillespie* the European Court of Justice (ECJ) held that the amount of maternity pay could not be 'so low as to undermine the purpose of maternity leave, namely the protection of women before and after giving birth' and the exclusion of women earning less than the lower earnings limit arguably *does* undermine the protection offered by maternity leave.[47] The Employment Appeal Tribunal (EAT) has rejected this argument.[48] However, in a later case on annual leave, the ECJ has said that preconditions for entitlement should not prevent a certain class or group of workers from benefiting from the general right.[49] As a class of workers is prevented from getting SMP, and indeed MA, it may be that another test case would successfully challenge the rule. MA has been extended to workers earning less than the lower earnings limit but more than £30 a week (see chapter 7). There is no upper limit on pay taken into account when assessing entitlement to SMP.

44 SSCBA 1992 s164(3).
45 Article 11(2)(b).
46 Article 11(3).
47 *Gillespie v Northern Health and Social Services Board* [1996] IRLR 214, ECJ.
48 *Banks v Tesco Stores Ltd and Secretary of State for Social Security* [2000] ICR 1141.
49 *R v Secretary of State for Trade and Industry ex p BECTU* [2001] IRLR 559, ECJ.

A woman's maternity pay must be equivalent to a man's paternity pay

6.44 In *Banks* the employment tribunal (ET) held that because Mrs Banks received less pay during maternity leave than a male employee on contractual paternity leave would have received, she had been discriminated against. Tesco gave male staff a week's fully paid paternity leave but paid nothing to women whose earnings were so low that they did not qualify for SMP. It was held that Mrs Banks should have received one week's full pay. Presumably even employees who are paid SMP should receive full pay, rather than 90% of their pay, for as long as fathers on paternity leave receive full pay.

The woman must have stopped work for the employer

6.45 A woman will qualify for SMP if she satisfies the conditions set out in para 6.10 and then stops work for the employer.[50] The woman can stop work for any reason after the start of the QW and she will be entitled to SMP if she satisfies the other conditions. In most cases a woman will stop work in order to start her maternity leave. Maternity leave may start no earlier than the start of the 11th week before the EWC unless the baby is born before then (in which case maternity leave will start the day after the birth, see para 4.30). A woman is still entitled to SMP if she resigns or is dismissed after the QW or if she does not intend to return to work for the employer. If she does any work for her employer in the maternity pay period she will lose SMP for any week in which she works (if her EWC is before 1 April 2007), see para 6.74.

A woman must be pregnant and have reached the 11th week before the EWC or have given birth before that date

6.46 The woman must be pregnant and have reached the 11th week before the EWC, or have given birth before that date. SMP is not payable before then. SMP does not increase if a woman has a multiple birth.[51]

---

50 SSCBA 1992 s164(2)(a).
51 SSCBA 1992 s164(2)(c) and s171(1).

Stillbirths and miscarriages

6.47 A woman is still entitled to SMP if:

- she has a live birth at any stage in the pregnancy, even if the baby only lives for a very short time; or
- she has a stillbirth, which is defined as a baby born dead after 24 weeks of pregnancy.

6.48 If she miscarries, which means her baby is born dead before the end of the 24th week of pregnancy, SMP is not payable, but if she is off work she may be entitled to sick pay, statutory or contractual.

A woman must produce medical evidence and give the required notice

6.49 The woman must produce medical evidence (usually a maternity certificate, form MAT B1) showing the EWC. The form must be signed by a doctor or midwife not earlier than the beginning of the 20th week before the EWC.[52] The MAT B1 must be given to the employer by the end of the third week of the maternity pay period. If the woman has a good reason for not providing the evidence earlier, it must be produced no later than the end of the thirteenth week of the maternity pay period (see para 6.60 onwards for maternity pay period).[53] The date on the MAT B1 is all-important when it comes to deciding whether a woman has sufficient service to qualify for SMP. If the MAT B1 certifies that the baby is due on a Saturday, the start of the EWC will be the previous Sunday. However, if the midwife certifies the baby as being due a day later, a Sunday, the EWC will start on that day and this may make all the difference to whether a woman qualifies for SMP or not. This is because her QW will start a week later than the QW of a woman whose baby is due on a Saturday.

6.50 If the baby is premature, the woman will also need to provide evidence of the date the baby was born; this will be necessary so that the employer knows that SMP has become payable.[54]

6.51 The woman must give at least 28 days' notice to her employer of the date she wants SMP to begin. The notice must be in writing if the employer requests it.[55] If it is not reasonably practicable to give 28

---

52 Statutory Maternity Pay (Medical Evidence) Regulations 1987 SI No 235 reg 2 (as amended).
53 SMP Regs 1986 reg 22(3).
54 SMP Regs 1986 reg 22(1).
55 SSCBA 1992 s164 (4) and (5).

days' notice, because, for example, the baby is born early or maternity leave is triggered by a pregnancy-related absence from work (see para 4.35 onwards), the woman must give as much notice as possible.[56] SMP may be refused if 28 days' notice is not given and it was reasonably practicable for her to give it. If this happens, the woman is entitled to a written statement giving reasons and she may refer the dispute to her local HMRC (National Insurance Contributions) Office (see para 6.124).

6.52   A woman entitled to maternity leave and pay may give notice for both together by the 15th week before the EWC (providing she has still met the requirement for 28 days notice for SMP), see para 4.14 onwards. The SSCBA 1992 prescribes slightly different notice requirements from those prescribed for maternity leave by Maternity and Parental Leave etc Regulations (MPL Regs) 1999.[57] A woman who expects to receive SMP from her employer should ask specifically for SMP when she gives notice of maternity leave to be sure that her employer knows that she expects to receive it. The table on p141 (see chapter 4 sets out what notice is required by a woman claiming both leave and pay.

Where the woman gives birth before the date given in the notice

6.53   The woman must give further notice to her employer stating the date the baby was born and that this is the reason for her absence.[58] This notice must be given within 28 days of childbirth or, if this is not practicable, as soon as practicable. The notice must be in writing if the employer so requests.

Where the baby is born before the QW or before notice has been given

6.54   The woman must give the employer notice stating her EWC, the date the baby was born and that this is the reason for her absence. Notice must be given within 28 days of the birth or, if that is not practicable (because, for example, she is ill), as soon as reasonably practicable. The notice must be in writing if the employer asks for it to be.[59]

6.55   Where the birth is premature, notice contained in a properly

---

56 SSCBA 1992 s164(4)(b).
57 SI No 3312.
58 SMP Regs 1986 reg 23(2).
59 SMP Regs 1986 reg 23(1).

addressed and stamped envelope is deemed to be given on the day it was posted – not when it arrives.[60]

Where the woman leaves her job after the QW

6.56   If a woman leaves her job or is dismissed after the QW but before the start of her maternity leave she does not have to give notice for maternity leave and pay (providing she has already given her employer her MAT B1 or medical evidence, see para 6.49). She will be entitled to SMP from the 11th week before the EWC or from when her employment ends (whichever is later), see para 6.60 onwards for the start of the MPP. However, if she has her baby before the 11th week before the EWC she must give her employer notice within 28 days specifying the date of the birth so that her employer knows when to start paying her SMP.[61]

The maternity pay period (MPP)

6.57   SMP is payable for a maximum of 26 weeks for women whose EWC is before 1 April 2007 and for a maximum of 39 weeks for women whose EWC is on or after 1 April 2007.[62] This is the MPP. Once a woman has qualified for SMP it is paid at the rate of 90% of her average earnings for the first six weeks and then at a flat rate (or 90% of her average earnings if that is lower) for the remaining 20 or 33 weeks. The flat rate increases in April every year and is currently £108.85 a week (April 2006 to April 2007). A woman will be entitled to the increase in the flat rate if it rises during her MPP. Note: The increase in the length of SMP applies for women whose baby is DUE on or after 1 April 2007. The woman will still be entitled to the increase if her baby is born prematurely, however, a woman whose baby is due before 1 April 2007 but born after 1 April will not qualify for the longer period of SMP. When SMP is paid for 39 weeks the maternity leave period will still be divided into 26 weeks OML and 26 weeks AML. There will be no change to an employee's rights to return to work after OML and AML, see para 4.65 onwards and no

---

60   SMP Regs 1986 reg 23(3).
61   SMP Regs 1986 reg 23(4) and (5).
62   SMP Regs 1986 reg 2(2) as amended by the Statutory Maternity Pay, Social Security (Maternity Allowance) and Social Security (Overlapping Benefits) (Amendment) Regulations 2006 SI No 2379 reg 3(2) which came into force on 1 October 2006.

change to an employee's rights during the OML and AML period, see chapter 5.

6.58   The MPP cannot start before the 11th week before the EWC, unless the baby is born before the 11th week. Otherwise the woman can choose when it starts (unless she gives birth or is triggered onto SMP because of a pregnancy-related absence in the four weeks before the EWC; see para 6.60 onwards). A woman who qualifies for SMP from more than one employer may choose to start her two MPPs at different times (see para 6.41).

The start of the MPP

6.59   The rules on when the MPP will start differ according to when a woman's baby is due.

The start of the MPP for women whose EWC is before 1 April 2007

6.60   For women whose EWC is before 1 April 2007, the MPP usually starts at the beginning of a week, ie, on a Sunday. Therefore, SMP usually starts on the Sunday *after* the woman stops working and starts her maternity leave (or gives birth), including the situations:

- where the woman gives her employer notice that she intends to stop work and does stop work in that week;[63]
- where she leaves employment or is dismissed after the 11th week before the EWC, but not later than the week of birth.[64]

6.61   Once she has qualified for SMP, if she is dismissed before the start of the 11th week before EWC her MPP will start when she reaches the 11th week.[65]

6.62   However, SMP will start on any day of the week in the following situations:

- where she gives birth before the 11th week, SMP will start on the day after the birth;[66]
- where she gives birth after the 11th week before the EWC but before the date she notified to her employer that she intended to give up working, SMP will start on the day after the birth;[67]

63   SMP Regs 1986 reg 2(1).
64   SMP Regs 1986 reg 2(6).
65   The Help Book E15 (2006) p17.
66   SMP Regs 1986 reg 2(3)(a).
67   SMP Regs 1986 reg 2(3)(b).

- the woman stops working because of a pregnancy-related absence during the four weeks before the EWC, SMP starts on the day after the first day of absence.[68] Note: the 'trigger' rule only applies to pregnancy-related absence. Other sickness does not trigger the start of the MPP and the woman can choose when her SMP period starts.

6.63   If the woman works until the birth, SMP is payable from the day after the birth.

The start of the MPP for women whose EWC is on or after 1 April 2007

6.64   For women whose EWC is on or after 1 April 2007, the MPP can start on any day of the week including the following situations:

- where the woman gives her employer notice that she intends to stop work and does stop work in that week, the MPP will start on the day stated in her notice;[69]
- where she leaves employment or is dismissed after the 11th week before the EWC, but not later than the day of the birth, the MPP will start on the day after her employment ends.[70] Once she has qualified for SMP, if she is dismissed before the start of the 11th week before EWC her MPP will start when she reaches the 11th week.
- where she gives birth before the 11th week, SMP will start on the day after the birth;[71]
- where she gives birth after the 11th week before the EWC but before the date she notified to her employer that she intended to give up working, SMP will start on the day after the birth;[72]
- the woman stops working because of a pregnancy-related absence during the four weeks before the EWC, SMP starts on the day after the first day of absence.[73]

6.65   If the woman works until the birth, SMP is payable from the day after the birth.

68   SMP Regs 1986 reg 2(4).
69   SMP Regs 1986 reg 2(1) as amended by the Statutory Maternity Pay, Social Security (Maternity Allowance) and Social Security (Overlapping Benefits) (Amendment) Regulations 2006 SI No 2379 reg 3(2) which came into force on 1 October 2006.
70   SMP Regs 1986 reg 2(5).
71   SMP Regs 1986 reg 2(3)(a).
72   SMP Regs 1986 reg 2(3)(b).
73   SMP Regs 1986 reg 2(4).

6.66   Where necessary, SMP can be calculated at a daily rate, see para 6.103.

Sickness during MPP

6.67   A woman who is unwell during her MPP is not entitled to either SSP or contractual sick pay. This is the case even if she does not qualify for SMP or MA. She is in the 'disqualifying period' for SSP which ceases to be payable when SMP or MA begin. Where a woman *qualifies* for SMP or MA the disqualifying period lasts for 26 or 39 weeks (depending on the woman's EWC).

6.68   Even if she does *not* qualify for either SMP or MA, there is a disqualifying period but it lasts for 18 weeks and begins:

- at the start of the week in which the baby is born; or
- at the start of the fourth week before the EWC if she is absent for a pregnancy-related reason.

6.69   If SSP is already being paid to a woman because of sickness starting before the MPP or for non pregnancy-related sickness absence, SSP will stop:

- on the day of childbirth; or
- on the day she is absent with a pregnancy-related illness on or after the start of the four weeks before the EWC.[74]

6.70   Following *Gillespie* it is clear that it is not sex discrimination for an employer to refuse to pay contractual sick pay even when the latter would be higher than her maternity pay. In *Boyle v Equal Opportunities Commission,*[75] the ECJ held that a woman may interrupt her OML to take sick leave and so claim contractual sick pay and then revert back onto the remainder of her OML later (see chapter 4), however, the difficulties involved make this impractical.

6.71   A woman who is ill during her MPP who does not qualify for SMP or MA or who does not receive SSP or contractual sick pay from her employer, may be able to claim incapacity benefit if she is incapable of work and has sufficient NI contributions in recent years.

6.72   A woman may be entitled to SSP after her MPP if her period of sick leave begins on the day after the end of the MPP, see para 7.56 onwards.

---

74 Statutory Sick Pay (General) Regulations 1982 SI 894 reg 3(4) and (5).
75 [1998] IRLR 717.

Working in the MPP

6.73   The rules on working during the MPP differ according to when a woman's baby is due.

Women whose EWC is before 1 April 2007

6.74   For women whose EWC is before 1 April 2007, SMP is not payable for any week where, during any part of that week, she works for the employer liable to pay SMP.[76]

6.75   If a woman continues to work after the MPP has started, she will lose SMP, at the lower rate first, for every week she works. The MPP will not be extended to compensate for the weeks in which the woman has worked. She will lose SMP for the whole week even if she only works for a few hours during the week. The employer cannot choose to ignore this rule. Thus, if a woman starts her MPP in the eleventh week before the EWC and is absent from work during that week, but works for part of the following week, she will lose one week's SMP.

6.76   If a woman works for her employer after the birth but before the end of the MPP, she will again lose a week's SMP for every week or part week she works, starting with the lower rate. If she has ended her maternity leave and returned to work but is off sick for a whole week during the MPP, she will receive SMP. If she is not sick for a whole week she will not be entitled to SMP or SSP but will be entitled to any contractual sick pay or means-tested benefits available.

Women whose EWC is on or after 1 April 2007

6.77   A woman whose EWC is on or after 1 April 2007 may work for up to 10 days during her MPP, without losing SMP.[77] The days on which work is done may be consecutive or not. An employer may make reasonable contact with an employee during maternity leave and, by agreement, she may work for up to 10 days without losing her entitlement to leave and pay, for more on 'keeping in touch (KIT) days' see para 4.48. Once she has worked for more than 10 KIT days she will lose a week's SMP for every week in which she works, even if she only works for a day or part of a day. So, if a week in the SMP period contains only KIT days, SMP will be retained. If a week

76   SSCBA 1992 s165(4).
77   SMP Regs 1986 reg 9A as amended by the Statutory Maternity Pay, Social Security (Maternity Allowance) and Social Security (Overlapping Benefits) (Amendment) Regulations 2006 SI No 2379 reg 3(3).

contains, for example, the last of the KIT days and also another day of work, the employee will once again lose that week's SMP.

6.78   If a woman receives contractual maternity pay she will still be entitled to it if she works for up to 10 KIT days during her maternity leave. There are no specific provisions in the regulations in relation to pay for KIT days, therefore, it will be a matter for agreement between the employer and employee. SMP can be offset against any payments of contractual maternity pay, see para 6.107.

Working for another employer

Before the birth

6.79   If a woman works for another employer (employer B) before the baby is born, it does not affect her entitlement to SMP from her original employer (employer A). This is the case even if she starts work for employer B after employer A has begun to pay her SMP. If a woman qualifies for SMP with more than one employer, each must pay her SMP.

After the birth

6.80   If the woman starts work or returns to work for employer B after the birth and during the MPP, her entitlement to SMP from employer A ceases from the week she starts work, *unless* she was working for employer B in the QW.[78] If she returns to work for employer B after the birth and she *was* working for that employer in the QW, her entitlement to SMP from employer A is not affected. She must, within seven days of starting work, inform the employer who is paying her SMP.[79]

Calculation of average earnings for SMP

6.81   The calculation has two purposes:

1) To assess whether a woman earns enough to qualify for SMP (see para 6.34).

2) To calculate her average earnings. Ninety per cent of her average pay is paid during the first six weeks of her MPP. If a woman has a multiple birth she does not receive more SMP (SSCBA 1992

---

78   SSCBA 1992 s165(6) and SMP Regs 1986 reg 8.
79   SMP Regs 1986 reg 24.

s171(1)). Average earnings are calculated using the pay received in the 'relevant period'.

Pay

6.82   'Pay' is defined as earnings on which NI contributions are payable. The gross figure is used.

6.83   'Pay' includes:

- gross earnings which are liable to class 1 NI contributions;
- any profit from the woman's employment in the eight-week period, including bonuses or overtime (however large);[80]
- contractual sick pay or payments for injury;[81]
- SSP;[82]
- SMP;[83]
- SPP;[84]
- SAP;[85]
- arrears of pay whether under an order for reinstatement or reengagement or generally;[86]
- pay which is paid under an order under the ERA 1996 for the continuation of a contract of employment;[87]
- pay in pursuance of a protective award;[88]
- earnings paid in a PAYE settlement agreement which attracted class 1B NI liability should be taken into account if the employee did not otherwise qualify for SMP.[89]

6.84   Note: Pay rises awarded after the relevant period are also taken into account, see para 6.97.

6.85   Certain payments are expressly excluded from earnings that may be taken into account for SMP purposes. These mirror the payments that are excluded from earnings for NI purposes.[90]

---

80 SMP Regs 1986 reg 20(2). A bonus paid during the eight-week period will be included even if it relates to earnings over a longer period.
81 SMP Regs 1986 reg 19(b).
82 SMP Regs 1986 reg 20(4)(d).
83 SMP Regs 1986 reg 20(4)(e).
84 SMP Regs 1986 reg 20(4)(f).
85 SMP Regs 1986 reg 20(4)(g).
86 SMP Regs 1986 reg 20(4)(a).
87 SMP Regs 1986 reg 20(4)(b).
88 SMP Regs 1986 reg 20(4)(c).
89 The Help Book E15 (Supplement) (2006) p14.
90 SMP Regs 1986 reg 20(2) with the details set out in Schedule 3 to the Social Security (Contributions) Regulations 2001 SI No 1004.

6.86   The main payments that are excluded from 'pay' for SMP purposes are:

- payments on account;
- money drawn by directors in anticipation of voting;[91]
- holiday payments, where the sum is from a fund to which more than one employer pays;
- tips and gratuities unless paid directly or indirectly by the employer;
- payments in kind or board or lodging or other services or facilities;
- pension payments;
- fees to a minister of religion which are not part of her salary or stipend;
- travelling and relocation expenses;
- payments from profit-sharing schemes;
- sick pay derived from contributions made by the woman into a sickness fund;
- redundancy payments;
- childcare vouchers (up to £50 per week);
- payments in respect of training.

Childcare vouchers

6.87   Some employers operate a childcare voucher scheme which employees can use to pay for registered or approved childcare. From April 2005 childcare vouchers up to £55 per week supplied by employers are exempt from tax and NI for employees.[92] Employees have to sign a contractual agreement confirming that they agree to sacrifice part of their salary in return for childcare vouchers. The agreement must usually be for a fixed period but most schemes offer an early review of the agreement in the event of an unexpected lifestyle change linked to birth, death and marriage.

6.88   As childcare vouchers are not included as 'pay' (see para 6.86), a woman's average earnings will be reduced when calculating her entitlement to SMP. As pregnancy is considered a 'life changing' event she would be entitled to leave the scheme but would need to do so before the relevant period (see para 6.89 onwards) in order to increase her average earnings.

91 The Help Book E15 (Supplement) (2006) p9.
92 Social Security (Contributions) Regulations 2001 Sch 3 as amended by the Social Security (Contributions) (Amendment No 3) Regulations 2006.

The relevant period for calculation of average earnings varies depending on whether the employee is paid weekly, monthly or irregularly

The 'relevant period' for weekly paid employees

6.89   If the woman is regularly paid weekly, she must have been paid (in the eight pay days up to and including the pay day in the QW) on average a sum at least equivalent to the lower earnings limit (£84 per week from April 2006 to April 2007). The woman's normal weekly earnings are calculated by adding together the pay received for the eight pay days before the end of the QW and dividing by eight. If the woman has been off sick and on SSP, this will count as earnings. However, as SSP is £70.05 (April 2006 to April 2007) it may mean that her average earnings fall below the lower earnings limit in the relevant period thus making her ineligible for SMP (see paras 6.34–6.37).[93]

EXAMPLE: Sunita's EWC begins on Sunday 18 March 2007 (the baby being due on 22 March), her QW is the week beginning 3 December 2006. She is paid every Friday so the last pay day before the end of her QW will be 8 December. 8 December and the previous seven Fridays before that will make up the relevant period. Her employer adds together her earnings in the eight weeks from and including 14 October to 8 December and divides by eight. If Sunita is sick during one week in the relevant period and so receives only £70.05 SSP for that week, but in all other weeks her gross pay is £85, she will qualify for SMP because her earnings average £84.90 which takes her over the lower earnings limit of £84. If she is sick for two weeks and receives her normal gross wage of £85 only in the remaining six weeks, her average will be £80.80 and she will miss out on SMP. She may well qualify for MA.

6.90   If a normal payment is made early or late so that the eight-week relevant period contains more or less than eight weeks' pay, the payments should be divided by the number of weeks they represent.[94] See para 6.97 for how a pay rise should be treated.

---

93   This will be the case even though her earnings are usually above the limit.
94   The Help Book E15 (Supplement) (2006) p9.

6.91   Where the woman's contract specifies a day on which she is paid, the eight-week period runs from the last pay day before the end of the QW. If there is no contractual pay day, the eight-week period runs from the day on which she is normally paid. If there is no 'normal pay day', the period is calculated from the last date the woman was actually paid (before the end of the QW).[95]

Rounding to the nearest whole pence

6.92   When calculating average earnings in the relevant period, there is no provision in the legislation for rounding up or down to the nearest whole pence. However, when calculating the earnings-related payment (six weeks at 90% of average earnings) ie the amount the woman will actually be paid, her average earnings should be rounded to the next whole number of pence at this stage[96] (see the example in para 6.93).

The 'relevant period' for monthly paid employees

6.93   If a woman is paid once every calendar month, the average weekly earnings are calculated by:

- adding the gross payments made on the last normal pay day falling before the end of the QW and adding any other payments made after (but not including) the last normal pay day which was at least eight weeks before – this will therefore usually mean adding together the last two monthly pay cheques;
- multiplying the total by six – which gives annual earnings;
- dividing by 52 – to give average weekly earnings.[97]

EXAMPLE: Holly's EWC begins on Sunday 18 March 2007 (the baby being due on 22 March), her QW is the week beginning 3 December 2006. She is paid on the 30th of every month so the last pay day before the end of her QW will be 30 November. The last normal pay day at least eight weeks before that will be 30 September so the period from 1 October to 30 November will make up the relevant period. Holly's employer adds her gross pay of £450 paid on 30 November to her £450 gross pay of 30 October. This comes to

---

95 SMP Regs 1986 reg 21(4).
96 SMP Regs 1986 reg 28.
97 The Help Book E15 (Supplement) (2006) p15.

£900. She then multiplies by six to make £5,400 and divides by 52 to come to a weekly average of £103.84615. Holly will qualify for SMP and receive £93.47 for the first six weeks of her MPP which is 90% of £103.84615 (rounded up, see para 6.92).

The 'relevant period' for irregularly paid employees

6.94   Where a woman is paid at irregular intervals, for example, because she is paid by bonus or commission periodically, the average weekly earnings are calculated by:

- Establishing the relevant period. This is the period between:
  1) the last normal pay day falling before the end of the QW; and
  2) the last normal pay day at least eight weeks before that.
- Adding together the gross earnings paid after the date in 2) above up to and including those paid in 1) above.
- Dividing the total by the number of days in the relevant period.
- Multiplying by seven to give an average week's pay.[98]

EXAMPLE: Freda is paid irregularly and according to the hours she works which vary from week to week. Her EWC begins on Sunday 18 March 2007 (the baby being due on 22 March), her QW is the week beginning 3 December 2006. She is paid £400 on 1 December, £500 on 5 November and £300 on 4 October. The relevant period will be 5 October to 1 December inclusive (58 days). The payment on 4 October does not count as it is the last pay day which is at least eight weeks before the pay day of 1 December and only payments received after that date are taken into account. Freda's total earnings for the relevant period are therefore £900. £900 is divided by 58 and multiplied by seven for average earnings of £108.62068. Freda will qualify for SMP.

6.95   Employees who work term-time only or do sporadic agency work may have pay days which are several months apart resulting in a long calculation period. However, as their earnings are divided by the number of days within the relevant period, this could significantly reduce their average earnings.

---

98 The Help Book E15 (Supplement) (2006) p10.

Where the baby is born before the end of the QW

6.96 The relevant period will be the eight weeks or two months ending with the last complete week before the week in which the baby is born.[99]

Pay rises

6.97 Prior to 5 April 2005, only pay rises backdated into the 'relevant period' had to be taken into account in the SMP calculation. However, as a result of *Alabaster*,[100] if a woman is awarded a pay increase after 6 April 2005, and that new figure applies at any point between the beginning of the 'relevant period' and the end of her maternity leave, her average weekly earnings for SMP must be recalculated as if she has earned this new, higher sum throughout the relevant period and the employer must pay any extra SMP due.[101] Maternity leave includes ordinary and additional maternity leave. It would be sex discrimination to refuse to award a pay rise to a woman because she was on maternity leave although she is not entitled to be paid it in full during her leave. She is only entitled to have it reflected in her SMP. Note: There is no statutory definition of a 'pay increase'. This is yet to be tested in a tribunal.

6.98 If a woman receives more than one pay rise during this period, she is entitled to receive the benefit of all increases in her SMP. This applies if she is awarded the pay rise in the last week of her maternity leave even though her earnings in the relevant period will be based on only one week's pay. It also applies to women who are paid irregularly.

6.99 If a woman who was not entitled to SMP receives a pay increase which means her average earnings are now high enough for her to qualify for SMP, the employer must calculate the amount of SMP she is entitled to.[102] If she received Maternity Allowance (see chapter 7) she is entitled to the difference between the MA and the SMP she now qualifies for. A woman should still benefit from a pay increase even if she does not intend to return to work.

---

99 SMP Regs 1986 reg 4(2).
100 *Alabaster v Barclays Bank plc* [2005] EWCA Civ 508.
101 Statutory Maternity Pay (General) (Amendment) Regulations 2005 SI No 729 and the Help Book (Supplement) (2006) p18.
102 SMP Regs 1986 reg 21B as amended by the Statutory Maternity Pay (General) (Amendment) Regulations 2005 SI No 729.

6.100　　Note: There is no provision to decrease SMP if a woman's pay is decreased.

How SMP is paid

6.101　SMP is usually paid in the same way as contractual pay.[103] It is rounded up to the nearest penny.[104] Tax and NI contributions are payable on SMP. She may be entitled to a tax rebate and should contact HMRC. SMP can be paid in a lump sum by agreement but this could lead to an overpayment if circumstances change during the SMP period and may result in employer and employee paying more NI.

6.102　　Employees can receive SMP even if they go outside the European Economic Area during their MPP.[105]

Calculating a daily rate

Women whose EWC is on or after 1 April 2007

6.103　For women whose EWC is on or after 1 April 2007, an employer may, where necessary, calculate SMP at a daily rate by paying one-seventh of the weekly rate.[106] This is intended to simplify the administration of SMP and could be used where, for example, a woman's MPP overlaps a monthly payroll or where her MPP starts in the middle of the week, see para 6.64 for the start of the MPP for women whose EWC is on or after 1 April 2007. This does not mean that SMP is payable for odd days – the woman is still entitled to SMP for each week of the 39-week SMP period. However, the weekly rate is capable of being divided by seven in order to fit SMP more easily into the employer's payroll.

6.104　　Where SMP is paid on a weekly or daily basis it is rounded up to the nearest whole penny.[107]

6.105　　Note: For women whose EWC is before 1 April 2007 there is no provision for calculating a daily rate, therefore, SMP can only be paid on a weekly basis.

103　SMP Regs 1986 reg 27.
104　SMP Regs 1986 reg 28.
105　Social Security Contributions, SMP and SSP (Miscellaneous Amendments) Regulations 1996 SI No 777.
106　SSCBA 1992 s166(4) as amended by the Work and Families Act 2006 Sch 1 para 8(3).
107　SMP Regs 1986 reg 28 as amended by the Statutory Maternity Pay, Social Security (Maternity Allowance) and Social Security (Overlapping Benefits) (Amendment) Regulations 2006 SI No 2379 reg 3(4).

Resignation during or at the end of the MPP

6.106 SMP is payable by the employer even if the woman does not intend to return to work after maternity leave and even if she resigns during her maternity leave. A woman does not have to repay SMP if she resigns. Her contract may require her to repay any pay she receives on top of SMP but the SMP itself cannot be repaid.[108]

Overlap with contractual maternity pay

6.107 The employer is not obliged to pay both contractual maternity pay and SMP. SMP will usually be offset against contractual maternity pay depending on the terms of the contract. However, the minimum she must receive is her SMP; if in any week the SMP exceeds contractual maternity pay, then the difference must be paid.[109] If an employee chooses to take advantage of a KIT day (employees whose EWC is on or after 1 April 2007 only, see para 6.73 onwards for KIT days) she retains her SMP for that week and her employer is entitled to offset her SMP against any contractual pay agreed for the work done.

EXAMPLE: If a woman earns £50 for a KIT day, she will be able to retain her SMP. The £50 earned will be offset against her SMP, meaning she will receive £108.85 for the week (the flat rate for SMP from April 2006 to April 2007). If she works for three KIT days in the same week and earns £150 she will receive £150 – her SMP being offset against contractual pay paid for the same week. In both cases the employer will be able to reclaim the normal amount of SMP from HM Revenue and Customs.

No contracting out of the SMP scheme

6.108 Any agreement between an employer and employee to exclude, limit or modify the statutory provisions relating to SMP or to require an employee to contribute to the costs is void and illegal.[110] Deductions such as overpayments may be made from SMP where the employer is authorised to make deductions from the contractual pay.[111]

---

108 In *Boyle v EOC* [1998] IRLR 717 the ECJ said that it is not sex discrimination for an employer to require repayment of contractual maternity pay.
109 SSCBA 1992 s168, Sch 13 para 3.
110 SSCBA 1992 s164(6).
111 SSCBA 1992 s164(7).

Effect on other benefits

6.109   SSP and SMP are mutually exclusive. An employee who *is* entitled to SMP or MA cannot get SSP for 26 or 39 weeks (depending on her EWC) from the beginning of the MPP.

6.110   Where the woman is *not* entitled to SMP or MA, she still cannot get SSP for 18 weeks (see para 6.68) but she may qualify for incapacity benefit or other means-tested benefits, see chapter 7.

6.111   The first £100 of SMP is disregarded as income for the purposes of calculating entitlement to tax credits but it is counted in full for income support or jobseeker's allowance. SMP has no effect on guardian's allowance, disability living allowance or widow's benefits.

Administration of SMP by employers

6.112   The employer must keep, for three years after the end of the tax year in which the MPP ends, a record of:

- the notified date of absence (because of pregnancy or childbirth) and, if different from the actual date she was first absent, the date of her first absence;
- the weeks in which SMP was paid (in each tax year) and the amount paid each week; and
- any week within the woman's MPP when no SMP was paid and the reasons no payments were made.[112]

6.113   The employer must also keep for three years any medical certificate or other evidence relating to the EWC or the childbirth. Where the woman needs the medical certificate back, the employer should keep a copy[113] and the employer should only keep a copy of the birth certificate, not the original if this has been produced for any reason.

6.114   There are standard forms (available from the Employer's Order-line) for SMP purposes:

- SMP1: this must be sent to an employee employed in the QW but who is not eligible for SMP;
- SMP2: this is a record sheet of SMP payments;
- SP32: claim form for recovery of SMP paid in a previous tax year.

---

112   SMP Regs 1986 reg 26(1).
113   SMP Regs 1986 reg 26(3).

Recovery of SMP by employers

6.115 All employers can recover payments of SMP by making a deduction from the money they have to pay to HMRC. This includes:

- NI contributions;
- PAYE tax;
- student loan deductions; and
- Construction Industry Scheme deductions.

There is a different rate of recovery according to the size of the employer, see paras 6.117 and 6.118.

Advance funding

6.116 Employers can apply to their HMRC Accounts Office for advance funding of SMP payments where the amount they have to pay out exceeds the amount they have available in the same tax month or quarter.[114]

Small employers

6.117 No employers are exempt from paying SMP: small employers must also pay SMP (including private families employing nannies, cleaners, etc). Where the employer's gross employer and employee class 1 NI contributions for the previous tax year (excluding class 1A and class 1B payments) do not exceed £45,000, the employer can deduct from those contributions 100% of the gross SMP paid to employees. The employer can also deduct an additional 4.5% of the total gross SMP paid as a contribution towards the administration costs.[115]

Other employers

6.118 All other employers can recover 92% of the total gross SMP they have paid in the tax month by deducting it from their NI contributions and tax.[116]

---

114 The Help Book E15 (Supplement) (2006) p24.
115 The Help Book E15 (Supplement) (2006) p21.
116 Ibid.

Remedies

Termination of contract in order to avoid liability for SMP

6.119   If a woman is dismissed and her contract terminated before the QW (taking account of any notice period during which the contract subsists) she will not satisfy the service condition. If the employer terminates the woman's contract in order to avoid liability for SMP and the woman has been employed by the employer for a continuous period of at least eight weeks, the employer will still be liable to pay SMP. The woman will be deemed to have been employed by the employer from the date her employment ended until the end of the QW on the same terms and conditions as those subsisting immediately before her employment ended. Her earnings are calculated by reference to what she was earning in the eight weeks before her contract was terminated.[117] She will also have a claim for automatically unfair dismissal under ERA 1996 s99 and for sex discrimination.

6.120   If the woman is dismissed by her employer wholly or partly to avoid their liability for SMP but either:

- she has been employed for less than eight weeks; or
- she has been employed for more than eight weeks but cannot prove that the dismissal was in order to avoid liability for SMP,

she will not be entitled to be paid SMP. However, her loss of SMP will be part of her claim for compensation for dismissal. She will need to show that she would have fulfilled all the conditions for SMP had she not been dismissed.

Ordinary unfair dismissal

6.121   Where a dismissal is clearly not related to the woman's pregnancy, she will not be able to make a claim under ERA 1996 s99. The dismissal may nevertheless be an ordinary unfair dismissal; if it is, the compensation awarded should reflect the loss of SMP.

Reinstatement or re-engagement

6.122   Where there has been an order for re-engagement or reinstatement by an employment tribunal,[118] continuity of employment will be

---

117   SMP Regs 1986 reg 3.
118   This includes a compromise agreement or agreement reached with the help of ACAS.

maintained for all weeks between the date the contract was terminated and the date of reinstatement or re-engagement.[119] Following the introduction of dispute resolution procedures in October 2004, if a woman is reinstated or re-engaged by her employer as a result of following the statutory procedure, her employment is regarded as continuous and any break in service is disregarded for calculating qualifying service for SMP.[120]

Fair dismissal

6.123   If the dismissal was fair and not related to pregnancy (for example, if the employee was found to have been dishonest), there will be no entitlement to SMP where the contract has been terminated before the QW. She will be entitled to SMP if the contract ends after the QW and she meets all the conditions.

Refusal of the employer to pay SMP

6.124   The woman should first ask the employer for the reasons why they will not pay. An employer who thinks that a woman is not entitled to SMP must give her written reasons on form SMP1. A woman who disagrees with this decision can then ask her local HMRC officer for a formal decision.[121] If HMRC decide against the employer and the employer still fails to pay and does not appeal, this is an offence and the employer will be liable to a civil penalty in the form of a fine.[122] Ultimately, HMRC will pay SMP to the employee if the employer defaults.[123] There is, however, a further right of appeal on a point of law to a tax appeal commissioner.[124]

6.125   Alternatively, or in addition, a woman can apply to an ET for an order for payment of SMP under ERA 1996 Part II in respect of an unlawful deduction of wages. SMP is defined as 'wages' in ERA 1996 s27.

---

119 SMP Regs 1986 reg 12.
120 SMP Regs 1986 reg 12(1)(d) as amended by the Statutory Maternity Pay (General) and the Statutory Paternity Pay and the Statutory Adoption Pay (General) (Amendment) Regulations 2005 SI No 358.
121 Both parties will be asked for written observations and supporting evidence.
122 The Help Book E15 (Supplement) (2006) p20.
123 SMP Regs 1986 reg 7.
124 On appeals procedure, see *Welfare benefits and tax credits handbook*, Child Poverty Action Group.

Insolvency of employer

6.126   If the employer has been declared bankrupt, has made a composition or arrangement with his/her creditors, has died or the company has been wound up, HMRC is liable to pay SMP from the week the employer becomes insolvent.[125] The employee should contact HMRC Statutory Payments Disputes Team if she thinks her employer is insolvent.

6.127   If the employer has not paid SMP, for whatever reason, HMRC must first determine by formal decision that the employer is liable to pay SMP. HMRC is liable for SMP once the period for any appeal has expired (with no appeal having been lodged) or the appeal has been resolved in the woman's favour.[126] HMRC is also liable to pay any SMP due if the employer fails to pay after a formal decision has been made even if the employer is not legally insolvent (see para 6.124).

125   SMP Regs 1986 reg 7(3).
126   SMP Regs 1986 reg 7.

Maternity allowance and other benefits

Key points

- A woman may qualify for maternity allowance (MA) if she:
  - has been employed or self-employed for at least six months in the 15 months before the baby is due, not necessarily for the same employer; and
  - sometimes earns £30 a week or more.
  The flowchart at para 7.12 summarises the qualifying conditions for MA.
- MA is paid by the Department for Work and Pensions (DWP) through Jobcentre Plus offices for 26 weeks for women whose expected week of childbirth (EWC) is before 1 April 2007 and for 39 weeks for women whose EWC is on or after 1 April 2007.
- Women who do not qualify for MA may qualify for incapacity benefit (IB) which is payable for eight weeks.
- Most parents will be entitled to child tax credit (CTC). Families on a low income may also receive working tax credit (WTC) to top up their income which can include help with the cost of registered childcare and may qualify for the Sure Start Maternity Grant.

Background and statutory framework

7.1   If a woman is not entitled to statutory maternity pay (because, for example, her earnings are too low or she has not worked for long enough), she may be entitled to MA or IB.

7.2   MA was the first weekly maternity payment available to working women and was introduced in 1948 at a time when there was no right to maternity leave. Before that, only a one-off flat rate maternity grant had been paid.[1] An earnings-related supplement to MA was added in 1966, but a payment similar to today's statutory maternity pay (SMP) was not introduced until 1975, at the same time as the Employment Protection Act 1975 gave women who had worked for their employer for two years the right to return to work after having a baby.

7.3   The Social Security Contributions and Benefits Act (SSCBA) 1992 as amended by the Welfare Reform and Pensions Act 1999 sets out the framework for MA and IB. Detailed provisions on maternity allowance are contained in the Social Security (Maternity Allowance)

---

1   The maternity grant was introduced in 1911 when it was 30 shillings.

Regulations (MA Regs) 1987 as amended;[2] and the Social Security (Maternity Allowance) (Earnings) Regulations (MA (Earnings) Regs) 2000.[3] Further amendments have been made by the Statutory Maternity Pay and Maternity Allowance (Amendment) Regulations 2006, which extended MA to 39 weeks for women whose EWC is on or after 1 April 2007. The regulations also enabled women to work for 10 days during the MA period without losing MA.

7.4   Detailed provisions on IB are contained in the Social Security (Incapacity Benefits) Regulations 1994 as amended.[4]

7.5   Note: The Work and Families Act 2006 contains powers to extend maternity and adoption pay to 52 weeks and to introduce a new entitlement to additional paternity leave (APL) which could be taken within the second six months of the child's life. Some of the APL could be paid if the child's mother or adopter has returned to work and has some of her entitlement to SMP, MA or SAP (statutory adoption pay) left at the time of her return. The government intends to introduce these new measures by the end of this Parliament which is expected to be by 2010, but is still consulting on the details of the new scheme.

Who qualifies for MA and other benefits?

Maternity allowance

7.6   All women who work, either as employed earners or as self-employed earners, can qualify for MA. An 'employed earner' is someone whose earnings attract a liability for employer's class 1 national insurance (NI) contributions, or would if they were high enough, and are chargeable to income tax under schedule E (any tax due is deducted by her employer under the PAYE system). In practice, this definition covers anyone who pays tax under PAYE. A self-employed earner is one who is gainfully employed and is not an employed earner. She should have registered as self-employed with Her Majesty's Revenue and Customs (HMRC) and either pay class 2 NI or have been granted a small earnings exception.[5]

7.7   Entitlement to MA is not conditional on payment of NI and women who work but who do not pay NI because their earnings are

2   SI No 416.
3   SI No 688.
4   SI No 2946.
5   SSCBA 1992 s2(1).

too low can still qualify. Agency workers who pay tax under PAYE and NI, or who would do if their earnings were high enough, can qualify for MA if they do not qualify for SMP. Women who work 'off the books' and do not have proof of their earnings will not be able to claim successfully.

Incapacity benefit

7.8 To qualify for IB a woman must have paid sufficient class 1 or class 2 (self-employed) NI during recent years.

7.9 Workers who are unemployed or who are covered by a medical certificate will usually be 'credited' with a NI contribution for the week in which they are not earning and actually paying NI. Home responsibilities relief can also be treated as a credit for IB purposes, see para 7.51. These credits will assist a woman to claim IB but she must also have worked as well (see para 7.43).

Means-tested benefits for parents who are either low earners or unemployed

7.10 Apart from asylum-seekers, most people resident in the UK are entitled to claim welfare benefits and tax credits if their income is low enough. For full information on who is entitled to claim and who is excluded, see the Child Poverty Action Group's *Welfare benefits and tax credits handbook.*

Maternity allowance

7.11 MA is paid by the DWP for 26 weeks for women whose EWC is before 1 April 2007 and for 39 weeks for women whose EWC is on or after 1 April 2007. The flowchart on p259 sets out the qualifying conditions which are also described below.

Qualifying conditions

7.12 In order to qualify for MA, the woman must:[6]

- be pregnant and have reached the 11th week before the EWC or have given birth before the EWC;[7] and

---

6 SSCBA 1992 ss35 and 35A.
7 SSCBA 1992 still uses the term 'confinement' but this book uses the term 'childbirth' throughout.

- satisfy the employment condition; and
- satisfy the earnings condition; and
- not be entitled to SMP.

A woman must be pregnant and have reached the 11th week before the EWC, or have given birth before the EWC

7.13   MA is not payable until the 11th week before the EWC unless the woman has already given birth. If the woman has already given birth MA is payable if either:

- the baby is born alive, however premature, even if the baby lives only for a very short time; or
- the baby is stillborn after the 24th week of pregnancy.

It is not payable if the woman miscarries earlier than the end of the 24th week.[8]

The employment condition: a woman must have worked for 26 out of 66 weeks (approximately 6 out of 15 months)

7.14   The period of 66 weeks before the EWC is known as the 'test period'.[9] As long as she works for 26 weeks in the test period, a woman can work in any of the 66 weeks and she will satisfy the employment condition. She does not have to have worked for several weeks in a row and she could have worked for 26 different employers or have worked in a combination of employed and self-employed employment and still qualify. She does not have to have worked for the whole week as long as she has worked for part of it. She has to be 'engaged in employment' rather than actually physically at work, so periods of absence during her employment, such as sick leave and annual leave, will assist her in fulfilling the employment condition. She can also count any periods in which she was in receipt of SMP, SAP or SPP (statutory paternity pay) but not previous periods in which she received MA.[10]

7.15   This condition is so flexible that as long as a woman has worked in each of the 26 weeks before she got pregnant, she could do no work at all during her pregnancy and still qualify for MA. At the other extreme, she may only have worked for 15 weeks in the 66-week

---

8 SSCBA 1992 ss35(1)(a) and 35(6).
9 MA (Earnings) Regs 2000 reg 1.
10 SSCBA 1992 s35(1)(b).

Who qualifies for Maternity Allowance?

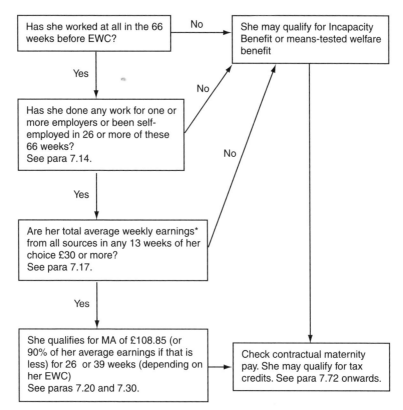

* Earnings are:

Earnings from employment: the gross sum earned (proof needed).

Paying class 2 NI: treated as earning £120.94 a week.

Holding a certificate of small earnings exception: treated as earning £30 a week.

period by the time she reaches the 11th week before the EWC. As long as she then works in each of the next 11 weeks, right up to the EWC, she will qualify. However, there is a danger that if she has her baby early she will not be able to meet the employment condition. If she starts maternity leave or her leave is triggered by pregnancy-related sickness in the last four weeks of her pregnancy, she may be able to meet the employment condition as her maternity leave will count as a week of work (providing her baby is not born early) (see para 4.30 onwards).

> EXAMPLE: Jane works for two years. She then gives up her job to look after her mother who is unwell and discovers that she is six weeks pregnant. Since she has worked for the first 34 weeks of the test period she will satisfy the employment condition for MA even if she does not work during the rest of her pregnancy, a period of 32 weeks.

7.16   A woman must actually be in employment or self-employment during these 26 weeks. If she is signing on, claiming home responsibilities relief or receiving NI credits this will not count towards her target of 26 weeks' work during the test period.

The earnings condition: a woman's average weekly earnings must be not less than the MA threshold[11]

7.17   The threshold is currently £30 and the secretary of state may increase it by order from time to time.[12] The average is calculated using gross rather than net earnings. If the threshold increases during the test period the relevant threshold is the one in place at the beginning of the 66-week test period.[13]

7.18   The SSCBA 1992 and the MA (Earnings) Regs 2000 set out how average earnings are calculated in a particular 'specified period'. The specified period is 13 weeks (whether consecutive or not) within the test period.[14] A woman can choose the 13 weeks in which she earned the most. See paras 7.26–7.28 for how to calculate average earnings.

---

11   SSCBA 1992 s35(1)(c).
12   There has been no change to the MA threshold since 2000.
13   SSCBA 1992 ss35(1)(c) and 35A(4).
14   MA (Earnings) Regs 2000 reg 6.

A woman must not be entitled to SMP

7.19   The DWP will not pay MA if a woman is entitled to SMP and has not claimed it from her employer.[15] If she is working, they will require a SMP1 form from her employer explaining why she is not entitled to SMP before they will process the claim (see para 6.124). If the employer wrongly refuses to pay SMP and issues a SMP1, a woman can claim MA whilst she is in dispute with her employer. If an employer refuses to issue a SMP1, a woman should apply to the DWP for MA and explain with the application why she is not submitting a SMP1 with her claim and why she believes she is not entitled to SMP. Failure to supply a SMP1 may delay the claim. If necessary, a woman should apply for means-tested benefits during the delay.

The 'earnings condition': average earnings and calculating entitlement to MA

7.20   MA is payable at the rate of £108.85 per week (April 2006 to April 2007)[16] or 90% of average earnings if less than £108.85.

What counts as earnings?

Earnings from employment

7.21   An employed earner's gross earnings are used to calculate her average earnings. 'Earnings' are defined in the same way as for SMP and include SSP, SMP, SPP and SAP as well as bonuses, commission and car allowances, not just basic pay (see para 6.82).[17] See para 7.26 onwards for how to calculate average earnings.

---

15 SSCBA 1992 s35(1)(d).
16 This is the same as the flat rate for SMP, SPP and SAP and rises in April each year.
17 MA (Earnings)Regs 2000 reg 2 sets out which payments are to be taken into account for the purposes of SSCBA 1992 s35A(4)(a). These include payments under Employment Rights Act (ERA) 1996 ss114, 115 and 129, under Trade Union Act 1992 s189, any sum payable by way of SSP including sums payable by the Inland Revenue Commissioners under SSCBA 1992 s151 and any sum payable by way of SMP including sums payable by the Inland Revenue Commissioners and any sums payable by way of SPP and SAP. The only payments specifically not to be counted are those excluded from the computation under Social Security (Contributions) Regulations 1979 SI No 591 regs 19, 19A and 19B.

7.22   Any payment that is backdated into the specified period must also be taken into account.[18] NI credits during periods of unemployment and home responsibilities relief are irrelevant when calculating whether a woman has satisfied the earnings condition.

7.23   Employed earners need to prove their earnings by producing a pay slip or equivalent.

Earnings from self-employment

7.24   A self-employed woman is treated as having the following earnings regardless of the amount she actually earns:

- If she pays a class 2 NI contribution she will be treated as earning £120.94 a week (from April 2006 to April 2007) entitling her to MA of £108.85 per week.
- If she holds a small earnings exception certificate from NI she will be treated as earning £30 a week (the MA threshold) entitling her to MA of £27 per week (90% of her deemed average earnings, as this is less than £108.85).[19] She can only receive a higher rate of MA if she can add any employed earnings.

7.25   Self-employed women do not need to prove their exact earnings when claiming MA as the Jobcentre Plus will check their NI contribution record. A woman can pay a class 2 NI contribution for any week (£2.10 per week April 2006 to April 2007) in which she does work as a self-employed person even if she holds a certificate of small earnings exception.[20] However, for any week that she holds a certificate of small earnings exception and pays a class 2 NI contribution (to protect her pension record, for example), she will only be treated as having earnings of £30 per week for MA purposes.[21]

EXAMPLE 1: Kim is self-employed and pays class 2 NI every week. She qualifies for MA of £108.85 per week

---

18 MA (Earnings) Regs 2000 reg 6(2).
19 MA (Earnings) Regs 2000 reg 3.
20 Social Security (Contributions) Regulations 2001 SI No 1004 reg 46.
21 Social Security (Maternity Allowance) (Earnings) Regulations 2000 SI No 688 reg 3(a).

EXAMPLE 2: Gloria has two jobs. She is a self-employed piano teacher earning £50 a week and she holds a small earnings exception certificate for that job. She is also employed part-time at a school teaching music for which she earns £50 a week in term-time. She can find 13 weeks (she can choose any 13 weeks in term-time) in which her average salary will be £80 (she is treated as earning £30 as a self-employed earner and £50 as an employed earner). She will receive MA of £72 (90% of £80).

Calculating average earnings and the rate of MA payable

7.26   The worker may select the weeks during which her earnings were highest.[22] The weeks do not have to be consecutive.

7.27   Earnings from all employments may be aggregated and taken into account however low the earnings from each individual job and irrespective of whether some jobs were done on an employed basis and others on a self-employed basis.[23] Workers who earn the same every week will thus be able to tell how much MA they will receive simply by identifying their total gross weekly earnings.

7.28   For women whose earnings are irregular, the average is calculated by taking the total earnings in the 13 chosen weeks and dividing by 13.[24] If a woman is not paid weekly, divide the payments received by the nearest number of weeks in the period for which they were paid.[25] If her average earnings are at least £30 per week or more (the MA threshold) she will receive MA of £108.85 per week or 90% of her average earnings if the 90% rate is less than £108.85.

EXAMPLE 1: Janet started her new job when she was already pregnant so she does not have enough service to qualify for SMP. Her regular weekly earnings are £200 and she receives full pay when she is off sick. She qualifies for MA of £108.85 per week.

22   MA (Earnings) Regs 2000 reg 6(1)(b).
23   MA (Earnings) Regs 2000 reg 4(1).
24   MA (Earnings) Regs 2000 reg 6(1).
25   MA (Earnings) Regs 2000 reg 6(3).

> EXAMPLE 2: Bernice has three cleaning jobs; she earns £20 a week
> from two employers and £25 a week from a third. This means that
> her total earnings are usually £65 a week but over the Christmas
> fortnight she earns £150 a week. When she chooses her 13 weeks
> she includes the Christmas fortnight so that her average earnings
> are £78 (£65 × 11 + £150 × 2 = £1015; £1015 divided by 13 = £78).
> She is entitled to MA of £70.26 (90% of £78).

Adult dependant

7.29   An increase of MA may be paid for one adult dependant. The adult
dependant increase is £36.60 (April 2006 to April 2007). If an adult
dependant is looking after the claimant's children then she can claim
the increase if:

- the claimant is entitled to child benefit; and
- the children normally live with her or she is contributing at least
  as much to their maintenance as she would get from the increase
  or she lives with the dependant, and
- her dependant's earnings are not too high.

If in doubt, a woman should tick the relevant box on her MA claim
form and the DWP will send a form for claiming the increase (see
para 7.36).

The MA payment period

7.30   MA is not payable before the eleventh week before the EWC. The MA
period (MAP) is the same as for SMP – 26 weeks for women whose
EWC is before 1 April 2007 and 39 weeks for women whose EWC is
on or after 1 April 2007 (see para 6.57).[26] Payment can begin at the
11th week before the EWC but not earlier unless the woman has
already given birth. The latest it can start is the beginning of the week
following the week of the birth.

For women with an EWC before 1 April 2007

7.31   Where a woman has not qualified for MA at the 11th week before
the EWC but subsequently becomes entitled before giving birth, the

---

26 SSCBA 1992 s35(2).

MAP will be the 26 weeks commencing with the week after she stopped work.[27] She must, of course, work up until the time she satisfies the employment and earnings tests. If her baby is born prematurely and she is unable to satisfy the employment and earnings tests she will not qualify for MA.

For women with an EWC on or after 1 April 2007

7.32 The MAP will start the day after the day she stopped work and last for 39 weeks, providing she has worked for long enough to satisfy the employment and earnings conditions.[28]

The start of the MAP

7.33 The MAP begins according to the following rules which are the same as for the SMP maternity pay period (see para 6.59 onwards). Where the woman is unemployed at the 11th week before her EWC her MAP will start then. She cannot choose to start it later.

7.34 Where the woman is working or in employment her MAP may, if she chooses, start later than the 11th week (this includes a situation where she is receiving SSP, IB or severe disablement allowance). There are two exceptions to this:

- *Premature birth* If the birth occurs before the date the woman intended to start her leave, MA is automatically payable from the day after childbirth.[29] Note that if the baby is born later than expected the MAP will not change.

- *Pregnancy-related absence in the four weeks before the EWC* Where a woman is absent from work after the fourth week before the EWC and this is because of her pregnancy, she will automatically be transferred onto MA. MA will be payable from the day after the first day of absence.[30]

She should notify the DWP if her baby is born early or she has a pregnancy-related absence from work in the four weeks before her EWC.

27 MA Regs 1987 reg 3(2A).
28 MA Regs 1987 reg 3(2A) amended by the Statutory Maternity Pay, Social Security (Maternity Allowance) and Social Security (Overlapping Benefits) (Amendment) Regulations 2006 SI No 2379, reg 4(3).
29 SSCBA 1992 ss35(2), 165 and Statutory Maternity Pay (General) Regulations 1986 SI No 1960 reg 2(3).
30 SSCBA 1992 ss35(2), 165 and Statutory Maternity Pay (General) Regulations 1986 SI No 1960 reg 2(4).

Disqualification from entitlement to MA

7.35   A woman is not entitled to MA in the following circumstances:

- *Working during the MAP*
  - **Women whose EWC is before 1 April 2007** A woman whose EWC is before 1 April 2007 will not be paid MA in any week when she works either as an employed or a self-employed earner during the 26 weeks MAP. The disqualification will last 'for such part of the maternity allowance period as may be reasonable in the circumstances'. This might mean that she does not get any MA for all or part of each week in which she works. The DWP decides.
  - **Women whose EWC is on or after 1 April 2007** A woman whose EWC is on or after 1 April 2007 can work for up to 10 days as an employed or self-employed earner without losing any MA during the 39 week MAP. However, she will be disqualified from receiving MA for any days that she works during the MAP over and above the 10 days that are designated as 'keeping in touch' days (see para 4.48).[31]
- *Women in custody*
  MA is not payable to a woman in prison or in legal custody. MA is not affected if a woman becomes a hospital in-patient.[32]
- *Claiming whilst abroad*
  MA is not usually payable for a period when the woman is temporarily abroad, either inside or outside the European Economic Area (EEA), unless she has gone abroad for medical treatment. A woman who has gone to live permanently in another EEA state can continue to receive MA there. A British citizen who lives abroad may be able to claim MA or its equivalent in another EEA state or in a non-EEA state if there is a reciprocal agreement.[33]

31 MA Regs 1987 reg 2(1)(a) as amended by the Statutory Maternity Pay, Social Security (Maternity Allowance) and Social Security (Overlapping Benefits) (Amendment) Regulations 2006 SI No 2379, reg 4(2). A woman can also be disqualified under the regulations if she fails to take care of her health or to attend a medical examination which she has been required to attend.

32 See the Child Poverty Action Group's *Welfare benefits and tax credits handbook* for more information.

33 A claimant may also go temporarily to another EEA state without penalty if she has been incapable of work (for a reason unrelated to pregnancy) for 26 weeks at the date of departure and is still incapable of work. For more information contact the DSS Overseas Directorate at either Tyneview Park, Whitley Road, Benton, Newcastle, NE98 1YX (0191 213 5000) or Castle Court, Royal Avenue, Belfast, BT1 1SN (028 9033 6000).

Women who are ordinarily resident in Great Britain but who have worked abroad may qualify for MA.[34]

- *If a woman dies her entitlement to MA ends*[35]

Claiming MA

7.36　A claim cannot be made before the end of the qualifying week (the end of the 15th week before the EWC – see para 6.11).[36] It is advisable to claim as soon as possible after that. This applies even if the woman is still working. If she is working, she should first claim SMP from her employers. If she is not entitled to SMP, the employer must give her a form SMP1 within one week of refusal of SMP (see para 6.124). The woman must then submit the following to the Jobcentre Plus:

- Form MA1 which is available from her local JobCentre Plus office, online or sometimes from the antenatal clinic.
- Medical evidence (usually form MAT B1) signed by the doctor or midwife; this states the week the baby is due. If the baby has been born, the birth certificate should also be sent.[37]
- Form SMP1.
- If the woman receives SSP up to the start of her MA she must also ask her employer for form SSP1, stating that her SSP has stopped, and send it to the DWP. SSP is not payable during the MA period. It is up to the woman to decide when she wishes to stop receiving SSP and start her MA.

7.37　If the claim is made before the woman stops working, the Jobcentre Plus will send her a form BM 25A notifying her of her entitlement and asking to be informed of the date she stops working. See para 7.30 onwards for the MA payment period.

Backdating a claim

7.38　A claim can only be backdated by three months so it is very important to claim in time. If the claim is made more than three calendar months after a woman has stopped work and started her MAP then MA will not be paid for the full period, see paras 7.30–7.34 for the

---

34 Social Security (MA) (Work Abroad) Regulations 1987 SI No 417, as amended by Social Security (MA) (Work Abroad) (Amendment) Regulations 2000 SI No 691.
35 SSCBA 1992 s35(4).
36 Social Security (Claims and Payments) Regulations 1987 SI No 1968 reg 14.
37 Social Security (Medical Evidence) Regulations 1976 SI No 615 reg 2(3).

start of the MAP. She does not need to show 'good cause' why her claim is late but there is no discretion to allow a claim to be backdated more than three months.[38]

> EXAMPLE: Mia's MAP began on 1 May 2006. She claims MA five months later on 2 October. She can only backdate her claim three months to 2 July, which means she has lost nine weeks of her 26 week MAP and will only get MA for the balance of the period, 17 weeks. If she had claimed three months after the end of the MAP she would not receive any MA at all.

Payment of MA

7.39   MA is paid either directly into a bank or building society or by Giro, which can be cashed at the post office. Any dependant's allowance will be included. Payment can be made to an appointee.

Tax and NI

7.40   Tax and NI are not payable on MA. NI contribution credits will be awarded automatically for each week the woman receives MA.

Appeals against refusal of MA

7.41   If a woman wishes to dispute a decision about her entitlement to MA she can ask the decision-maker at her local Jobcentre Plus office to give her an explanation of why the decision was made. If she is not satisfied, the decision-maker will look at the decision again and must consider any further information provided. The decision must be disputed within one month of the decision being given.

7.42   There is an appeal against most decisions made by a decision-maker to an independent appeal tribunal. An appeal should be made in writing, preferably on a form attached to leaflet GL24, available from the DWP, the Revenue and some Citizens' Advice Bureaux. It must be sent to the DWP within a month of notification of the decision. There is a further appeal on a point of law to the social security commissioners.

---

38   See note 36, reg 19(2).

Incapacity benefit

7.43   IB may be payable if there is no entitlement to SMP or MA. However, the woman has to have paid or been credited with sufficient NI contributions in the last three years that do not overlap the current calendar year. This means that she must have paid sufficient class 1 or class 2 NI in one of the last three tax years before the current one and paid or been credited with sufficient NI contributions in one out of the last three years before the current one (see para 7.50 for NI credits).

7.44   Where a claim is made for MA, and is unsuccessful, her local Jobcentre Plus office will automatically consider it as a claim for IB. The MAT B1 or other medical evidence that was sent in with the MA claim will be taken as evidence of incapacity for work from six weeks before the start of the EWC until 14 days after the date the baby is born.

7.45   IB is £59.20 (April 2006 to April 2007). It is paid for six weeks before the start of the EWC until two weeks after the birth. It is not paid for any week that the woman works.

7.46   IB can be claimed up to three months before the woman expects to qualify for it. A claim for IB can be backdated for up to three months. Where a claim is made after the birth IB will only be payable from the date of the birth.[39]

7.47   IB can also be paid to men and women who are incapable of work and are not entitled to SSP, providing they have paid (or been credited with) sufficient NI contributions.[40]

Other benefits

7.48   Both women who do not qualify for SMP or MA and women who do but who are still on a very low income may be able to claim a range of means-tested and non-means-tested benefits which ensure a basic level of welfare and income. Broadly speaking, the benefits available fall into the following main categories.

---

39 For more details see the Child Poverty Action Group's *Welfare benefits and tax credits handbook.*
40 For more details see the Child Poverty Action Group's *Welfare benefits and tax credits handbook.*

Universal benefits

7.49   These are benefits available to all parents regardless of their financial position. They are:

- *Child benefit* This is paid to all parents at the rate of £17.45 per week for the eldest (or only) child and £11.70 for each other child in the family (rates apply until April 2007). Claim forms are available from the local Jobcentre Plus office, the post office or in the 'bounty bag' from the post-natal ward after the woman has had her baby.
- *Free prescriptions* All women are entitled to free prescriptions during their pregnancy and for the year after the birth of the baby. The woman's GP will issue her with a form FW8 that is sent to the Family Health Services Authority for an exemption certificate. Children under 16 are also entitled to free prescriptions.
- *Free NHS dental care* All women are entitled to free NHS dental treatment during their pregnancy and for 12 months after the birth. A woman claims by ticking a box on a form provided by the dentist or showing her certificate for free prescriptions.

National insurance credits

7.50   These are available to a woman or man who is claiming SMP, MA or SAP. They count towards various, but not all, benefits s/he may need to apply for in the future. For example, they help her/him qualify for a pension but not for jobseeker's allowance. Credits for women claiming MA are automatic. Credits for the SMP and SAP period are not automatic and a woman or man will have to apply to the DWP for them especially if s/he has been receiving SMP or SAP at a rate less than the lower earnings limit (£84 a week from April 2006 to April 2007). A woman receiving SMP at 90% of her average earnings may have paid NI on her SMP anyway. The Contributions Agency should notify an individual whose NI record is deficient in any year. Most working women and men do not need to claim credits, as their NI payment record for the year will be high enough without them. Only a certain amount of NI needs to be paid/credited each year.

7.51   If a woman or man is away from work for a whole tax year caring for her/his children s/he will qualify for home responsibilities relief which means that s/he will not need to pay NI in that year. Home responsibilities relief becomes automatic for all women or men once they are claiming child benefit. Again, home responsibilities relief will only count towards some benefits, for example, part of the qualifying condition for incapacity benefit and contribution-based jobseeker's allowance.

Contributory and in-work benefits

7.52 These are benefits for women and men who have worked and who satisfy the particular qualifying conditions in respect of earnings or payment of NI. Relevant benefits are as follows.

Statutory sick pay (SSP)

7.53 SSP is paid at the rate of £70.05 per week (April 2006 to April 2007) for a maximum of 28 weeks in one period or linked period of incapacity for work. It is a daily benefit and can be paid for periods of less than a week. SSP is not paid for the first three days of sickness. Entitlement to SSP depends on the employee having normal weekly earnings of at least the lower earnings limit (£84 per week for 2006/07) during the eight weeks immediately before the period of entitlement. An employee for SSP purposes is the same as for SMP and MA, see para 7.6. Normal weekly earnings are calculated by averaging the employee's gross earnings between the last normal pay day before entitlement to SSP began and the day after the last normal payday at least eight weeks before that. Earnings can include SMP, SPP and SAP, but not MA. An employee who does not qualify for SSP may be entitled to IB. S/he will also be entitled to contractual sick pay if it is payable.

When SSP is not payable

7.54 If a woman *is* entitled to SMP or MA, SSP is not payable during the 26- or 39-week MPP or MAP irrespective of whether the woman actually returns to work during the pay period (see para 6.67) (the length of her pay period depends on her EWC, see para 7.30 above). If she *is not* entitled to SMP or MA she cannot receive SSP for 18 weeks.

Sickness before or after a SAP or SPP period

7.55 An employee is not entitled to SPP or SAP in respect of any week in which s/he is entitled to SSP, see paras 8.67 and 9.96. However, an employee who is sick before or after a statutory adoption or statutory paternity pay period can claim SSP from her/his employer providing they meet the qualifying conditions (see para 7.53). An employee may be able to qualify for SSP at the end of the SAP period, but an employee who had received SSP then SPP for two weeks would probably not meet the earnings condition to re-qualify for SPP.

Sickness before or after a MPP or MAP

7.56   As the MPP or MAP can start at any time from the 11th week before the EWC up to the week after the birth, SSP is payable during this period if the woman has not started her MPP or MAP. A woman who does not start her MPP or MAP until her baby is born can receive SSP up to that date *unless* the start of her MPP/MAP is triggered earlier than she expected because she is away from work with a pregnancy-related illness (see para 4.17). Where a woman is claiming SSP when she reaches her MPP or MAP, the employer should give her form SSP1(T) stating that she is not entitled to SSP.

7.57   A woman will be entitled to SSP after the end of the MPP or MAP if the period of sick leave begins on the day after the end of the 26- or 39-week maternity pay period and providing s/he meets the qualifying conditions (see para 7.53). A period of entitlement to SSP can only arise after the MPP or MAP has ended. This means that any sick note, for example, must be dated after the end of the MPP or MAP.

7.58   Note also that an employee who was in receipt of MA (which is not counted as earnings for the purposes of SSP) or who has taken additional maternity leave or a long period of unpaid parental leave may not have earned enough in the previous eight weeks to qualify for SSP.

Contribution-based jobseeker's allowance (JSA)

7.59   JSA is not means-tested and is different from income-based JSA. JSA is not payable at the same time as SMP or MA. If a woman is claiming JSA at the 11th week, her MAP will start immediately. If she is not entitled to SMP or MA, she can continue to claim JSA as long as she is available for and capable of work. If a woman gave up her job voluntarily in order to have a baby rather than taking maternity leave, her JSA might be suspended for up to six months. The woman would have to show 'just cause' for voluntarily leaving her job. A constructive dismissal might well be 'just cause'.

Means-tested benefits

7.60 Each year the DWP publishes target income levels for people on low incomes. These figures reflect the minimum level of income that an individual or family unit should receive. If a family's actual income falls below that level they may be entitled to income support (IS) or income-based JSA. These benefits are means-tested, which means that:

- the income of both co-habiting partners; and
- savings

are taken into account when assessing eligibility. Eligibility for a particular benefit also depends on how many hours each week the claimant and her partner works. Couples living together (whether married or not) must make joint claims for means-tested benefits.

7.61 Women who receive a means-tested benefit are then 'passported' onto a range of other benefits. These include the Sure Start Maternity Grant and housing benefit.

Income support or income-based JSA

7.62 IS is for people aged 16 and over who are not working and are not obliged to seek work or who work less than 16 hours per week and are on a very low wage. Those not obliged to seek work include:

- A single parent. She can claim IS from 11 weeks before the EWC until the time she resumes work or her child reaches 18.
- A woman who is pregnant. She can claim for 11 weeks before the EWC (or sooner if she is incapable of working because she is pregnant) until 15 weeks after the birth.[41] She can claim IS even if she is living with a partner who is not working, but not if her partner is claiming JSA or working more than 24 hours a week and/or his income is too high.
- A parent taking parental leave where the other partner is not working (or also on parental leave) and before the start of parental leave s/he was receiving working tax credit (WTC), child tax credit (CTC) of at least the family element, housing benefit or council tax benefit (see below).
- A parent taking paternity leave who is not entitled to SPP or any

---

41 Income Support (General) Regulations 1987 Sch 1B as amended by the Social Security (Paternity and Adoption) Amendment Regulations 2002 reg 2(5)(a).

paternity pay, who was entitled to WTC, CTC of at least the family element, housing benefit or council tax benefit on the day before paternity leave began.

- A parent on adoption leave is treated as not working. Any SAP is taken into account for IS.
- Pregnant women aged 16 or 17 from 11 weeks before the EWC (as long as they are no longer in education or treated as being in education). Alternatively they may be able to claim JSA.

7.63   A mother aged less than 16 cannot claim IS, but her parents may be able to claim for the family including the new baby.

7.64   Income-based JSA is payable at the same rates as IS to families where one partner is available for and seeking work.

Housing benefit and council tax benefit

7.65   Both these benefits are means-tested and paid to those on IS (or means-tested JSA), or a low income. Housing benefit helps to pay the rent. Council tax benefit covers all or some of council tax. Families on IS or income-based JSA can get some help with the interest on the mortgage, but usually only after a waiting period of about 40 weeks.

Sure start maternity grant

7.66   If the woman or her partner is receiving IS, income-based JSA or CTC of at least the family element (see tax credits below), she is entitled to a maternity grant of £500 for each child. This includes an adopted child aged less than 12 months. The claim should be made on form SF100 (Sure Start), available from local Jobcentre Plus offices, and can be made in the 11 weeks before the baby is due until three months after the birth. If the claim is made before the baby is due, the MAT B1 or a note from the doctor or midwife must be submitted. If the claim is made after the birth, a birth or adoption certificate must be provided. A midwife, GP or health visitor must complete part of the form and they must confirm that the woman has received advice about the health and welfare of herself and her baby.

Social fund loans

7.67   The social fund provides discretionary grants and loans.

Free milk and vitamins

7.68   Women on IS, income-based JSA or CTC (providing they do not work more than 16 hours a week and have an annual household income of less than £14,155), who are at least 10 weeks pregnant or breastfeeding or who have children aged less than five years can claim:

- tokens to exchange for milk (where the baby is under one a woman can claim for dried milk formula instead);
- free vitamins (these are available from the antenatal or child health clinic).

There is also cheap formula milk for a woman on a low income who is caring for a child under one.

7.69   Claim forms are available from the woman's midwife or GP who will need to sign the form before the claim can be processed.

Help with fares to hospital

7.70   Women on IS or income-based JSA, and some women on CTC or on a low income, can get help with fares to the antenatal clinic or hospital. Proof of benefit entitlement should be taken to the hospital where fares will be reimbursed.

Low income scheme

7.71   Women who are not exempt from payment on other grounds but who are on a low income may be able to get help with NHS health costs eg dental treatment, eye tests or hospital fares through the Low Income Scheme. Claims can be made on form HC1 from local Jobcentre Plus offices, Post Offices or local health centres. If the woman's income is low enough, she may be exempt from any charges and will be sent an HC2 certificate. If she does not qualify for free services, she may be able to get some help towards health costs and will be sent an HC3 certificate telling her the maximum she will have to pay for any services. Both certificates usually last for six months and the woman can reapply at the end if her income is still low. If her income falls during the period she can apply for a reassessment.

Tax credits

7.72   Child tax credit (CTC) is paid to families with children regardless of whether the parent is working. Working tax credit (WTC) is paid to low income workers to top up their wages. It is not necessary to pay NI to qualify for tax credits.

7.73   The amount of CTC and/or WTC a family will receive will depend on their income, how many children they have, their age and whether they pay for registered childcare. Any child benefit, child mainten-ance, MA or the first £100 of SMP, SPP and SAP is ignored as income.

Child tax credit

7.74   CTC is financial support for children paid to the main carer. Extra CTC is paid to families with a baby under one. Families on a low income who receive CTC of at least the family element (£10.45 per week from April 2006 to April 2007 or £20.90 per week with a baby under one) will qualify for other benefits, eg Sure Start Maternity Grant, see para 7.66.

Working tax credit

7.75   WTC is financial support for low-income workers paid through their salary. WTC is payable to workers without children who are at least 25 and work at least 30 hours a week. Parents with children have to be at least 16 and must work at least 16 hours a week. A parent is 'treated as working' during ordinary maternity leave, paternity leave and ordinary adoption leave providing they were working at least 16 hours a week on average before they started their leave. A parent cannot claim WTC during AML/AAL but if they have a part-ner who is working at least 16 hours a week their partner can claim WTC.

7.76   Extra WTC is also paid to help with the cost of registered child-care. To qualify for help with childcare costs a single parent must be working at least 16 hours a week or, if living in a couple, both parents must work at least 16 hours a week. This means that help with child-care costs may be available to low income parents during OML or OAL but not during AML or AAL (because a parent is not treated as working during AML or AAL). For example, a family on a low income receiving help with the cost of a nursery for their first child, will not be able to continue to receive help with those childcare costs if the woman takes AML to care for her new baby. If she returns to work after OML she can continue to receive help with registered childcare costs for both of her children.

7.77   Because more women than men claim WTC, a woman who is dismissed for claiming WTC would have an indirect sex discrimination claim (see paras 2.82 and 15.54).

7.78   Tax credits are administered by HMRC.[42] Claims for CTC and WTC (including help with costs of childcare) are made on the same claim form. Applications are based on the previous year's household income and are revised at the end of the tax year. If there is a change of circumstances during the year, for example, if a woman goes on maternity leave and her income falls, she can notify HMRC and her tax credit award can be revised.

---

42   For more help and an application form contact the Tax Credits help line on 0845 300 3900.

Paternity leave and pay

Key points

- An employee is entitled to up to two weeks paternity leave if he has been continuously employed for at least 26 weeks by the 15th week before the expected week of childbirth (EWC) and is the father of the child or is the mother's husband, civil partner or partner and has, or expects to have, responsibility for the upbringing of the child.
- An employee can start his leave on the day the baby is born, or a specified number of days/weeks after the birth, or a predetermined date after the start of the EWC.
- An employee must give notice to take paternity leave in or before the 15th week before the EWC, stating:
  - the EWC;
  - whether he is taking one or two weeks' paternity leave;
  - the date he intends to start his leave; and
  - a signed declaration (if requested by his employer).
- An employee taking paternity leave is entitled to his normal terms and conditions, as if he was at work, except remuneration.
- An employee is entitled to return to exactly the same job on the same terms and conditions after taking paternity leave.
- Employees taking paternity leave are protected from detriment and unfair dismissal.
- Statutory paternity pay (SPP) is payable to an employed father who:
  - has 26 weeks' continuous service by the 15th week before the EWC and is still employed by the same employer until the day the baby is born;
  - is the father of the child or is the mother's husband, civil partner or partner and has, or expects to have, responsibility for the upbringing of the child;
  - has been earning at least the lower earnings limit (£84 a week for April 2006 to April 2007) during an eight-week or two-month calculation period ending with the 15th week before the EWC.
- SPP is payable for up to two weeks at a flat rate of £108.85 per week from April 2006 to April 2007.
- To qualify for SPP, he must give his employer at least 28 days' notice in writing stating:

- his name;
- the EWC;
- when he wants his SPP to start and whether he wants SPP for one or two weeks; and
- a signed declaration.
- If an employer refuses to pay SPP the employer must give the employee form SPP1 explaining why SPP is not payable. If the employee disagrees, he can ask a local HMRC (Her Majesty's Revenue and Customs) Officer to make a formal decision.
- If he is dismissed to avoid liability for SPP, he may still qualify. He may have a claim for automatic unfair dismissal and he can claim any loss of SPP as part of compensation.

Introduction

8.1   This chapter covers paternity leave and pay for fathers and partners following the birth of a child. The next chapter covers adoption leave and pay, including paternity leave and pay following the adoption of a child.

8.2   Note: For simplicity we refer to the person entitled to take paternity leave as the father or 'he', however, civil partners and partners, including same sex partners, can take paternity leave, see para 8.9.

Background and statutory framework

8.3   The Employment Act 2002 introduced a new right for fathers or partners to take up to two weeks' paid paternity leave on the birth of a child by inserting some new provisions into the Employment Rights Act (ERA) 1996 and the Social Security Contributions and Benefits Act (SSCBA) 1992. These provisions apply to babies born or expected to be born on or after 6 April 2003. The Paternity and Adoption Leave Regulations (PAL Regs) 2002 govern the right to paternity leave and the Statutory Paternity Pay and Statutory Adoption Pay (General) (SPP and SAP Regs) Regulations 2002 as amended by the Statutory Paternity Pay and Statutory Adoption Pay (General) and the Statutory Paternity and Adoption Pay (Weekly Rates) (Amendment) Regulations 2006 govern the right to pay.

8.4   Note: The Work and Families Act 2006 contains powers to extend maternity and adoption pay to 52 weeks and to introduce a new entitlement to additional paternity leave (APL) and additional statutory paternity pay (ASPP). APL and ASPP will be in addition to the current entitlement to two weeks' paternity leave and pay. The government intends to introduce these new measures by the end of this Parliament which is expected to be by 2010. Employed fathers or partners of an adopter will be able to take up to 26 weeks' APL within the first year of the child's life, usually during the second six months. Some of it could be paid if the child's mother or adopter has returned to work and has some of her entitlement to statutory maternity pay (SMP), maternity allowance (MA) or statutory adoption pay (SAP) left at the time of her return to work.

8.5 HMRC publishes a Help Book for Employers called 'Pay and time off work for parents E15' ('the Help Book') which provides information about calculating, paying and reclaiming SMP and SPP.[1]

Who is entitled to paternity leave?

8.6 Only employees are entitled to paternity leave, not workers or the self-employed. Non-employees, such as agency workers, bank nurses or homeworkers who are classified by their employers as 'self-employed' may in fact be employees, but if they are not they will not be entitled to maternity leave. See para 1.28 for who is an employee. A father who is not an employee may still be entitled to paternity pay even if he is not entitled to leave. See para 8.27 onwards for paternity pay.

8.7 Members of the armed forces, share fishermen and the police are excluded from the right to take paternity leave.[2] Seafarers are entitled, providing the ship is registered under the Merchant Shipping Act 1995 s8, belongs to a port in Great Britain and they are ordinarily resident in Great Britain and do not work wholly outside Great Britain.[3]

Entitlement to paternity leave

8.8 An employee is entitled to take paternity leave in order to care for a

---

1 The Employer's Help Book can be obtained from the Employer's Orderline on 0845 7 646 646.
2 ERA 1996 ss192, 199 and 200.
3 ERA 1996 s199(7) and (8).

newborn child or to support the child's mother.[4] An employee qualifies for paternity leave if he:

- has been continuously employed for at least 26 weeks by the 15th week before the EWC;[5]
- is the father of the child, or is the mother's husband, civil partner or partner (including same sex partners) but is not the child's father;[6] and
- has, or expects to have, responsibility for the upbringing of the child.[7]

8.9 A 'partner' includes a person of the same or different sex, who lives with the mother and the child in an 'enduring family relationship'.[8] The mother's relatives are expressly prohibited from being a partner. This includes her parents, grandparents, sisters, brothers, aunts and uncles, of full or half blood, but they could be entitled to parental leave if they have parental responsibility.[9]

Continuous employment

8.10 As with maternity leave, continuous employment includes any week in which the employee has a contract of employment, whether written or oral, with his employer which includes periods of sick leave, annual leave or unpaid leave.[10] An employee will be treated as having been continuously employed for 26 weeks by the 15th week before the EWC if the child is born before the 15th week and he would have continued in employment until then.[11]

Stillbirth

8.11 An employee will still be entitled to paternity leave if the child is stillborn after the end of the 24th week of pregnancy or is born alive and dies afterwards.[12]

---

4 PAL Regs 2002 reg 4(1).
5 PAL Regs 2002 reg 4(2)(a).
6 PAL Regs 2002 reg 4(2)(b) as amended by Schedule 17 of the Civil Partnership Act 2004 (Amendments to Subordinate Legislation) Order 2005 SI No 2114.
7 PAL Regs 2002 reg 4(2)(c).
8 PAL Regs 2002 reg 2(1).
9 PAL Regs 2002 reg 2(2) and (3)(a).
10 PAL Regs 2002 reg 2(5).
11 PAL Regs 2002 reg 4(3).
12 PAL Regs 2002 reg 4(5).

Commencement and length of paternity leave

8.12   An employee can take one or two weeks' consecutive leave, but not odd days or two separate weeks.[13] He is not entitled to any more paternity leave in the case of a multiple birth,[14] however, if he qualifies for *parental* leave, he would be entitled to 13 weeks' parental leave for each child see chapter 10 on parental leave.

8.13   Paternity leave cannot begin before the birth. It must be completed within 56 days of the birth.[15] If the baby is born before the EWC, paternity leave can be taken within 56 days of the birth or within 56 days of the EWC.

8.14   The employee can choose to start his leave on:

- the date the baby is born; or
- a fixed number of days or weeks after the birth, as specified in his notice; or
- a fixed date after the EWC, as specified in his notice.[16]

When an employee has chosen to start his leave on the day of birth and he is at work that day, his leave will start the following day.[17] If he needs time off immediately, he can take time off for dependants, see chapter 11 on time off for dependants.

Notice provisions for paternity leave

8.15   An employee must give notice to take paternity leave, in writing if requested by his employer, stating:[18]

- the EWC;
- whether he wishes to take one or two weeks leave; and
- the date he has chosen to start his leave.

8.16   If his employer requests it, he must also provide a signed declaration stating that the purpose of his absence is to take care of a child or to support the child's mother, that he is the father of the child, or the

---

13 PAL Regs 2002 reg 5(1).
14 PAL Regs 2002 reg 4(6).
15 PAL Regs 2002 reg 5(2).
16 PAL Regs 2002 reg 5(3).
17 PAL Regs 2002 reg 7(2).
18 PAL Regs 2002 reg 6(1).

mother's husband, civil partner or partner and that he has or expects to have responsibility for the upbringing of the child.[19]

8.17 Notice must be given in or before the 15th week before the baby is due, or as soon as reasonably practicable.[20] See appendix C for a table of relevant dates for SMP and SPP; including how to find the 15th week before the EWC.

Changing the start of paternity leave

8.18 An employee can vary the start of his leave providing he gives notice at least 28 days before the EWC, if he intended to take his leave from the birth, or at least 28 days before the date specified in his notice. If it is not reasonably practicable to give 28 days' notice, he should give notice as soon as reasonably practicable.[21] If he gave his employer a predetermined date for starting his leave and the baby has not been born yet, he must choose a new date or select one of the other options for starting his leave,[22] see paras 8.12–8.14 for commencement and length of leave. He must give notice of the variation as soon as reasonably practicable.

Notice of birth

8.19 An employee must give his employer notice, in writing if requested, of the child's birth as soon as reasonably practicable.[23]

Early birth

8.20 If the baby is born before any notice has been given, the father or partner should give notice as soon as reasonably practicable, see paras 8.15–8.17, notice for paternity leave, and state the date the baby was born. He can take his leave any time between the birth and 56 days after the first day of the week the baby was *due*, see paras 8.12–8.14.

Terms and conditions during paternity leave

8.21 An employee on paternity leave is entitled to his normal contractual

19 PAL Regs 2002 reg 6(3).
20 PAL Regs 2002 reg 6(2).
21 PAL Regs 2002 reg 6(4).
22 PAL Regs 2002 reg 6(6).
23 PAL Regs 2002 reg 6(7) and (8).

terms and conditions[24] as if he was at work, apart from remuneration.[25] Remuneration means an employee's normal salary or wages. An employee is also bound by the obligations in his contract providing they are not inconsistent with his absence on paternity leave. His seniority, pension and other service-related rights continue to accrue as if he had not been absent. An employee on paid paternity leave is entitled to receive the same pension contributions from his employer as if he was working and receiving normal pay.[26] The employee is only required to pay contributions based on the remuneration (ie, SPP or contractual paternity pay) he actually receives.[27]

8.22   Note: These provisions are the same as for women taking ordinary maternity leave, see chapter 5 for more details on 'remuneration' and rights during leave.

Right to return after paternity leave

8.23   An employee is entitled to return to exactly the same job as he was doing immediately before he started his paternity leave[28] on the same terms and conditions[29] providing he is returning from a single period of paternity leave or his paternity leave is at the end of two or more consecutive periods of leave that do not include a period of additional maternity leave, additional adoption leave or parental leave of more than four weeks.

> EXAMPLE: If Gus takes paternity leave and two weeks' parental leave immediately afterwards, he has the right to return to the job he was doing before he started his paternity leave.

Right to return after consecutive periods of leave

8.24   If he returns from two or more consecutive periods of leave that include a period of AML, AAL or parental leave of more than four

---

24 PAL Regs 2002 reg 12(1).
25 PAL Regs 2002 reg 12(2).
26 Social Security Act (SSA) 1989 Sch 5 para 5A(4). The pension provisions apply to paternity leave (birth) and paternity leave (adoption).
27 SSA 1989 Sch 5 para 5A(3).
28 PAL Regs 2002 reg 13(1).
29 PAL Regs 2002 reg 14(1).

weeks, regardless of whether he took paternity leave before or after one of those periods of leave, he is entitled to return to the job he was doing immediately before his first period of leave started[30] but if it is not reasonably practicable, he must be offered a suitable alternative job on similar terms and conditions. If he returns to work, even for one day, his periods of leave are not treated as consecutive and he would have the right to return to work appropriate to the individual period of leave. If he takes sick leave or annual leave he is treated as returning to work.

EXAMPLE: Adam takes six weeks' parental leave over the summer school holiday to spend time with his children. After five weeks' parental leave, his partner gives birth to a premature baby. His paternity leave starts on the day of birth and he takes two weeks' paternity leave immediately after five weeks' parental leave. He does not have the right to return to the same job if it is not reasonably practicable but he must be offered a suitable alternative on similar terms and conditions. If his baby had been born nearer to the EWC or he had delayed the start of his paternity leave, he would have returned to work after parental leave of six weeks and he would have had the right to return to exactly the same job after a single period of paternity leave.

8.25 His seniority, pension and other service-related rights do not continue to accrue during the period of additional maternity or additional adoption leave but they are treated as if the two periods of leave either side of the leave were continuous.[31]

8.26 The position may alter if the employee is paid during any part of the additional maternity or additional adoption leave period and, if he is taking paid leave, he should be treated as if he is working and receiving normal pay during that period. This means that any pension contributions by the employer should be based on normal pay. The employee's contributions should be based on the amount of remuneration (ie maternity or adoption pay) actually received.[32] This is the same as the rules on maternity leave, see para 5.112 onwards.

---

30 PAL Regs 2002 reg 13(3).
31 PAL Regs 2002 reg 14(1).
32 PAL Regs 2002 reg 14(2).

Statutory paternity pay

Who can claim SPP?

8.27   In most cases employees who qualify for paternity leave will also be entitled to SPP and vice versa but there are a few exceptions. To be eligible for SPP, he must be an employee. The definition of 'employee' for SPP purposes is different to that for entitlement to leave. He is an employee for SPP purposes if he is treated as an 'employed earner'.[33] He is an employed earner if his employer is liable to pay class 1 national insurance (NI) contributions or who would pay NI if his earnings were high enough. A man earning less than the lower earnings limit for NI (£84 a week for 2006/7) is not entitled to SPP, but see *Low income parents* below. A man employed under a contract of apprenticeship may be an employed earner and eligible for SPP.

8.28   Office holders, such as members of the police, judiciary, armed forces, MPs, some company directors and many agency and casual workers, will be eligible for SPP as employed earners but may not be eligible for paternity leave if they are not employees. They may have a contractual right to paternity leave or may be able to agree time off work.

Low income parents

8.29   Low income parents taking paternity leave can receive income support if they are:

*   not entitled to SPP or any other kind of pay during paternity leave; and/or
*   are entitled to working tax credit, child tax credit paid at a rate higher than the family element, housing benefit or council tax benefit on the day before their paternity leave begins.[34]

---

33   SPP and SAP Regs 2002 reg 32(1) as amended by the Employment Equality (Age) Regulations 2006 SI No 1031 which came into force on 1 October 2006 and removed the age restriction.
34   The Income Support (General) Regulations 1987 SI No 1967 reg 2(5)(b) as amended by the Social Security (Paternity and Adoption) Amendment Regulations 2002 SI No 2689.

The main qualifying conditions for SPP

Continuous employment

8.30   To qualify for SPP an employee must have 26 weeks' continuous employment by the end of the 15th week before the EWC and he must remain continuously employed by the same employer until the day the baby is born.[35] This is different from SMP, where the woman does not have to remain employed after the qualifying week, see para 6.45. The flowchart below summarises the main qualifying conditions for SPP. See appendix C table of relevant dates for SMP and SPP.

Who qualifies for SPP?

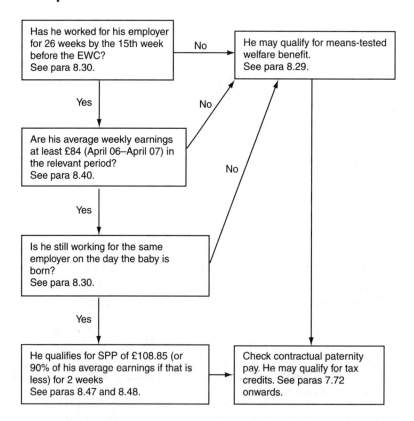

35   SSCBA 1992 s171ZA(2).

What counts as continuous employment

8.31 Work for part of a week will count towards continuous employment. Any weeks in which he is not under a contract of employment will not count apart from any week or part of a week in which he is:

- absent through sickness or injury up to a maximum of 26 weeks;
- absent on account of a temporary cessation of work; or
- regarded as continuing in employment by arrangement or custom[36]

providing he returns to work for his employer after the period of illness or absence.

8.32   Note: This is the same as for SMP, see para 6.14 onwards.

Seasonal and regular temporary workers

8.33 There are special rules about continuity for seasonal and regular temporary workers who work at certain times of the year and not others. An employee will not normally lose his continuity of employment if he is absent from work for one of the reasons stated above, see para 8.31, providing he returns to work after the absence.

8.34   However, where it is customary for an employer to offer work for a fixed period of less than 26 weeks on two or more occasions a year which do not overlap and offers work to the same people, an employee who is absent because of sickness or injury is not required to return to work afterwards and will be regarded as having continuity of employment.[37]

Industrial action and stoppage of work

8.35 There is no break in continuity of employment if there is a stoppage of work due to a trade dispute. However, any weeks of stoppage do not count towards the continuous employment and if the person is dismissed during the stoppage his continuity of employment stops and is not restored if he is re-employed unless he can show that he had no direct interest in the trade dispute.[38]

36   SPP and SAP Regs 2002 reg 33(1).
37   SPP and SAP Regs 2002 reg 33(3).
38   SPP and SAP Regs 2002 reg 35.

Transfer of undertaking

8.36   There are a number of circumstances in which a change of employer does not break continuity, including where the business is transferred to a new employer or employment is transferred to an associated employer.[39]

Reinstatement or re-engagement

8.37   Where there has been an order for re-engagement or reinstatement,[40] continuity of employment will be maintained for all weeks between the date the contract was terminated and the date of reinstatement or re-engagement.

8.38   Following the introduction of dispute resolution procedures in October 2004, if a man is reinstated or re-engaged by his employer as a result of following the statutory procedure, his employment is regarded as continuous and any break in service is disregarded for calculating qualifying service for SPP.[41] This only applies to reinstatements and re-engagements which take place on or after 6 April 2005.

Early birth

8.39   If the baby is born in or before the 15th week before the EWC and the employee would have met the continuous employment provisions had his baby not been born early, he is treated as having satisfied it providing his average earnings are not less than the lower earnings limit in the eight weeks immediately before the week in which the baby is born.[42]

Average earnings

8.40   To qualify for SPP, an employee must have average earnings of at least the lower earnings limit (£84 per week for 2006/7) in the eight

---

39   SPP and SAP Regs 2002 reg 36.
40   This includes compromise agreements or agreement reached with the help of ACAS.
41   SPP and SAP Regs 2002 reg 34 as amended by the Statutory Maternity Pay (General) and the Statutory Paternity Pay and Statutory Adoption Pay (General) (Amendment) Regulations 2005 SI No 358.
42   SPP and SAP Regs 2002 reg 5.

weeks, if paid weekly, or two months, if paid monthly, before the end of the 15th week before the EWC[43].

8.41 Earnings includes any remuneration subject to tax and NI and includes statutory sick pay, SMP, SPP and SAP[44].

8.42 Calculation of average earnings is exactly the same as for SMP, see para 6.81 onwards with the exception of the rules on pay rises. If an employee receives a pay rise after the calculation period for SPP and before the end of his paternity leave he is not entitled to have his SPP recalculated to take account of the increase unless it is a pay rise which has been backdated into the calculation period for SPP.

8.43 Employees whose average earnings are too low to receive SPP, should check their contract to see if they have any contractual entitlement to paternity leave and pay. See also para 8.29, low income parents above.

More than one employer or contract

8.44 If an employee has two or more contracts for different employers he may qualify for SPP from one or all of his employers. If his earnings are aggregated and treated as a single payment for NI purposes, liability for SPP is apportioned between the employers.[45]

8.45 If an employee works under more than one contract for the same employer, or two associated employers, the contracts must be treated as one for SPP purposes unless the earnings cannot be aggregated for NI contribution purposes.[46]

Relationship to the child

8.46 As with paternity leave, in order to qualify for SPP an employee must be the father of the child or the mother's husband, civil partner or partner and have, or expect to have responsibility for the upbringing of the child.[47] See para 8.8 above, entitlement to paternity leave.

---

43 SSCBA 1992 s171ZA(2).
44 SPP and SAP Regs 2002 reg 39(3).
45 SPP and SAP Regs 2002 reg 38(2).
46 SPP and SAP Regs 2002 reg 38(3).
47 PAL Regs 2002 reg 4.

Rate of SPP

8.47   From 6 April 2006 to 5 April 2007, SPP is £108.85 per week or 90% of average earnings if that is less. Rates change in April each year.

The paternity pay period

8.48   SPP is payable for one week or two consecutive weeks.[48] The SPP period must be within 56 days of the baby's date of birth or, where a baby is born before the EWC, up to 56 days from the first day of the EWC.[49]

8.49   As with paternity leave, it is up to the employee to decide when he wishes to receive SPP and it may start on:

- the day the baby is born or, if he is at work that day, the following day;
- a specified number of days after the day the baby is born; or
- a specified date which must be after the start of the EWC.[50]

8.50   Note: SPP is not payable if his employment has ended before his baby is born, see para 8.30.

Notice provisions for SPP

8.51   An employee must give at least 28 days' notice of when he wants his SPP to begin or as soon as reasonably practicable.[51] The notice must be in writing if requested.[52] An employee can change the start of his SPP, and choose any of the options in the paragraph above, providing he gives at least 28 days' notice before the date he wants SPP to begin or, if not reasonably practicable, gives notice as soon as reasonably practicable.

8.52   If the employee chose to start his SPP on the day of birth or a specified number of days after the birth he must give his employer further notice of the date the baby was born as soon as reasonably practicable after the birth.[53]

---

48 SPP and SAP Regs 2002 reg 6(3).
49 SPP and SAP Regs 2002 reg 8.
50 SPP and SAP Regs 2002 reg 6(1).
51 SSCBA 1992 s171ZC(1).
52 SSCBA 1992 s171ZC(2).
53 SPP and SAP Regs 2002 reg 7(1).

8.53   If the employee chose to start his SPP on a specified date after the EWC and the baby has not been born yet, he must give notice as soon as reasonably practicable that SPP will begin on a different date and he can choose a new date in accordance with any of the options in the paragraph above.[54]

Evidence of entitlement to SPP

8.54   To claim SPP the employee must give his employer evidence of his entitlement in writing, stating:

- his name;
- the EWC, or the date of birth if the baby has already been born;
- the date he wishes to start receiving SPP; and
- whether he wants SPP for one or two weeks.[55]

8.55   He must also provide a written declaration that he is the father of the child or the civil partner, partner or husband of the child's mother and that he is taking the leave in order to care for the child or to support the mother and that he has, or expects to have, responsibility for the child's upbringing.[56] A model self-certificate of entitlement to paternity leave and pay is available on the HMRC website (www.hmrc.gov.uk).

8.56   The written evidence and declaration must be given at least 28 days before the employee wishes SPP to start or as soon as reasonably practicable.[57] The employee can give his employer notice of both leave and pay in the 15th week before the EWC, as long as he fulfills all the notice requirements for SPP, see para 8.15 onwards, notice for paternity leave.

8.57   An employer can ask an employee to inform him of the date of the baby's birth within 28 days or as soon as reasonably practicable[58] but he does not have to provide medical evidence of the pregnancy or birth.

No contracting out of SPP scheme

8.58   Any agreement to exclude, limit or modify the SPP provisions or to

---

54   SPP and SAP Regs 2002 reg 7(2) and (3).
55   SPP and SAP Regs 2002 reg 9(2).
56   SPP and SAP Regs 2002 reg 9(1)(b).
57   SPP and SAP Regs 2002 reg 9(3).
58   SPP and SAP Regs 2002 reg 9(4).

require the employee to contribute to the costs is illegal.[59] Deductions can be made from SPP such as overpayments, subscriptions and loans providing the employer is authorised to make the same deductions from contractual pay. SPP cannot be replaced by any form of payment in kind.[60]

Recovery of SPP

8.59   As with SMP, all employers can reclaim 92% of SPP (small employers with a NI liability of less than £45,000 can reclaim 104.5%) by making a deduction from the money they have to pay to the Inland Revenue. This includes:

- NI contributions;
- PAYE tax;
- student loan deductions; and
- Construction Industry Scheme deductions.

Advance funding

8.60   Employers can apply to their HMRC Accounts Office for advance funding of SMP payments where the amount they have to pay out exceeds the amount they have available in NI contributions etc. in the same tax month or quarter.[61]

How SPP is paid

8.61   SPP should be paid on the normal pay day or a day that has been agreed. If there is no normal pay day or agreed date, it should be paid on the last day of a calendar month.[62] SPP is treated as earnings and is subject to tax and NI. As with SMP, SPP can be paid in a lump sum by agreement.

Calculating a daily rate

EWC on or after 1 April 2007

8.62   Where the EWC is on or after 1 April 2007, an employer may, where necessary, calculate SPP at a daily rate by paying one-seventh of the

---

59   SSCBA 1992 s171ZF.
60   SPP and SAP Regs 2002 reg 41.
61   The Help Book E15 (2006) p24.
62   SPP and SAP Regs 2002 reg 42.

weekly rate.[63] This is intended to simplify the administration of SPP and could be used where, for example, an employee's SPP period overlaps a monthly payroll or where the SPP period starts in the middle of the week.

Rounding up payments

8.63 Where SPP is paid on a weekly or daily basis it is rounded up to the nearest whole penny.[64]

8.64 Note: Where the EWC is before 1 April 2007 there is no provision for calculating a daily rate, therefore SPP can only be paid on a weekly basis.

Administration of SPP by employers

8.65 The employer must keep, for three years after the end of the tax year in which SPP is paid, a record of:[65]

- the date the pay period began;
- the payment dates and the amounts paid; and
- any unpaid SPP and the reasons no payments were made.

The employer must also keep for three years the declaration of family commitment or a copy if it was given back to the employee with form SPP1.

8.66 There are standard forms (available from the Employer's Order-line) for SPP purposes:

- SPP1: this must be sent to an employee who is not eligible for SPP;
- SPP2: this is a record sheet of SPP payments;
- SP32: claim form for recovery of SPP paid in a previous tax year.

Disentitlement to SPP

8.67 An employee is not entitled to receive SPP for any week that he

---

63 SSCBA 1992 s171ZE as amended by the Work and Families Act 2006 Sch 1 para 16(3).
64 Statutory Paternity Pay and Statutory Adoption Pay (Weekly Rates) Regulations 2002 SI No 2818 reg 4 as amended by the Statutory Paternity Pay and Statutory Adoption Pay (General) and the Statutory Paternity Pay and Statutory Adoption Pay (Weekly Rates) (Amendment) Regulations 2006 reg 7.
65 The Help Book E15 (2006) p25.

receives statutory sick pay (SSP) (see para 7.55), or is in custody. It is not payable following his death.[66]

Work during the SPP period

8.68   An employee cannot receive SPP during any week in which he works for the employer liable to pay his SPP or for another employer.[67] The employee must inform the employer paying SPP within seven days of the start of his work for another employer and the employer can ask for it in writing.[68] However, the employee can receive SPP from an employer (employer A) and work for another employer (employer B) who is not liable to pay him any SPP, providing he worked for employer B in the 15th week before the EWC.[69]

8.69   Note: The rules on working during the maternity and adoption pay period for babies due or expected to be placed for adoption on or after 1 April 2007 do not apply to SPP.

Contractual rights to leave and pay

8.70   Where an employee has a contractual right to paternity leave and pay that is more favourable than the statutory scheme, he cannot take each right separately but is entitled to take whichever right is more favourable.[70] If he combines elements of a contractual and statutory right, the statutory provisions are modified to give effect to the more favourable contractual terms.[71] This is known as a composite right.

Remedies relating to SPP

Refusal to pay SPP

8.71   If an employee is not entitled to SPP, his employer must give him form SPP1 explaining why he does not qualify. If the employee does not agree with those reasons he can ask HMRC for a formal decision, see refusal of the employer to pay SMP at para 6.124. An employer can be fined for failure to pay SPP following a decision by HMRC.

---

66 SPP and SAP Regs 2002 reg 18.
67 SPP and SAP Regs 2002 reg 17.
68 SPP and SAP Regs 2002 reg 17(2) and (3).
69 SPP and SAP Regs 2002 reg 10.
70 PAL Regs 2002 reg 30(2).
71 PAL Regs 2002 reg 30(2)(b).

Termination of contract to avoid SPP

8.72 If an employee's contract is terminated in order to avoid liability for SPP and he has been employed by that employer for a continuous period of at least eight weeks, the employer will still be liable to pay SPP. The employee will be treated as having been employed for a continuous period ending with the baby's birth and his average earnings will be calculated by reference to his normal weekly earnings for eight weeks ending with the last day for which he was paid.[72]

8.73 He may also have a claim for automatic unfair dismissal and sex discrimination, see para 15.58. Any loss of SPP can form part of his claim for compensation.

Insolvency

8.74 As with SMP, if the employer is insolvent, HMRC Statutory Payments Disputes Team will pay any SPP owing.[73]

Protection from detriment and unfair dismissal

8.75 An employee is protected from detriment for taking or trying to take paternity leave. He should not be subjected to any detriment by any act, or deliberate failure to act, by his employer, for any reason which relates to paternity leave.[74]

8.76 Employees who are dismissed for taking or trying to take paternity leave will be regarded as unfairly dismissed.[75]

8.77 Dismissal for any reason which relates to paternity leave is automatically unfair.[76] The dismissal is not automatically unfair if it is not reasonably practicable, for a reason other than redundancy, for the employer to allow the employee to return to the same job or a suitable alternative job and an associated employer offers the employee a suitable job and the employee accepts it or unreasonably refuses it.[77]

8.78 An employee who is made redundant will be treated as unfairly dismissed if the circumstances of the redundancy applied equally to

---

72 SPP and SAP Regs 2002 reg 20.
73 SPP and SAP Regs 2002 reg 43.
74 ERA 1996 s47C, PAL Regs 2002 reg 28.
75 PAL Regs 2002 reg 29(1) and (3)(a).
76 ERA 1996 s99.
77 PAL Regs 2002 reg 29(5).

one or more employees who had similar positions to the employee but have not been dismissed and the reason, or main reason, for redundancy was that the employee took or tried to take paternity leave.[78]

8.79   An employee who is dismissed or made redundant during paternity leave is entitled to paid statutory notice as well as any statutory or contractual redundancy pay that he qualifies for. However, if he is entitled to contractual notice of at least a week more than his statutory notice, he is not entitled to statutory notice but must rely on his contractual rights.[79] He will not be entitled to contractual notice pay during paternity leave unless the contract provides for it, but see para 5.20 onwards as the same provisions apply during maternity leave. Any SPP or contractual paternity pay may be offset against notice pay.[80] If he is receiving SPP, he is entitled to continue to receive it for two weeks.

8.80   All the above provisions are the same as for women made redundant during maternity leave, see para 15.86.

Protection from sex discrimination

8.81   A man would be able to claim direct sex discrimination if he was treated less favourably than a woman taking paternity leave, and vice versa, see para 2.28 onwards on sex discrimination. This would also apply where a woman taking paternity leave was treated less favourably than a man taking paternity leave.

Other rights for fathers

8.82   Fathers who have worked for the same employer for at least a year are entitled to take up to 13 weeks' parental leave before their child's fifth birthday (see chapter 10 on parental leave) and they are entitled to time off for dependants where they need urgent time off to care for a dependant (see chapter 11 on time off for dependants). This can include the care of a spouse or partner who goes into labour, as well as a child or parent who is ill or injured.

---

78   PAL Regs 2002 reg 29(2).
79   ERA 1996 s87(4).
80   ERA 1996 ss88 and 89.

Adoption leave and return to work

Key points

- An employee is entitled to 26 weeks' ordinary adoption leave (OAL) if she has been continuously employed for at least 26 weeks by the week in which she was notified of having been matched with the child.
- She is also entitled to 26 weeks' additional adoption leave (AAL) immediately after the OAL period.
- An employee can start her leave on the day the child is placed for adoption, or a predetermined date no more than 14 days before the expected date of placement.
- An employee must give notice to take adoption leave no more than seven days after being notified of having been matched with a child, stating:
  - the expected date of placement;
  - the date she intends to start her leave; and
  - evidence of the adoption (if requested by her employer).
- After receiving notice of adoption leave, an employer must write to the employee confirming the date her additional adoption leave will end.
- If the adoption placement is disrupted, an employee can remain on adoption leave for a further eight weeks.
- An employee taking OAL is entitled to her normal terms and conditions, as if she was at work, except remuneration. During AAL she is only entitled to some of her contractual terms and conditions.
- An employee is entitled to return to exactly the same job on the same terms and conditions after taking OAL. After taking AAL she is entitled to return to exactly the same job but, if it is not reasonably practicable, she is entitled to a suitable alternative job on equivalent terms and conditions.
- Employees taking adoption leave are protected from detriment and unfair dismissal.
- A woman taking adoption leave who suffers less favourable treatment may have a claim for indirect sex discrimination. A man on adoption leave may have a claim for direct sex discrimination.
- Statutory adoption pay (SAP) is payable to an employee who:
  - has 26 weeks' continuous service by the week in which she was notified of being matched with a child for adoption;

- has stopped work; and
- has average weekly earnings of not less than the lower earnings limit for the payment of NI (£84 per week from April 2006 to April 2007).

• SAP is payable for 26 weeks for a child expected to be placed for adoption before 1 April 2007[1] and for 39 weeks for a child expected to be placed for adoption on or after 1 April 2007.[2] SAP is paid at a flat rate of £108.85 per week (April 2006 to April 2007) or 90% of average earnings if less than £108.85.

• To qualify for SAP, she must give her employer at least 28 days' notice, in writing if requested, stating:
  - when she wants her SAP to start;
  - the expected date of placement;
  - evidence of the adoption from the adoption agency; and
  - a declaration that she wishes to receive SAP not SPP.

• If an employer refuses to pay SAP they must give the employee form SAP1 explaining why SAP is not payable. If the employee disagrees she can ask a local HMRC (Her Majesty's Revenue and Customs) Officer to make a formal decision.

• If she is dismissed to avoid liability for SAP, she may still qualify. She may have a claim for automatic unfair dismissal and can claim any loss of SAP as part of compensation.

• The adopter's spouse, civil partner or partner may be entitled to two weeks' paternity leave and pay. A couple may choose who takes adoption leave and who takes paternity leave.

• There are some additional provisions for parents adopting a child from overseas.

Introduction

9.1 For simplicity, we refer to the parent who takes adoption leave and pay as 'she' in this chapter. A 'partner' includes a person of the same or different sex, who lives with the adopter and the child in an 'enduring family relationship'.[3] The adopter's relatives are expressly prohibited from being a partner. This includes her parents, grand-

1   SPP and SAP Regs 2002 reg 21.
2   SPP and SAP Regs 2002 reg 21 as amended by the Statutory Paternity Pay and Statutory Adoption Pay (General) and the Statutory Paternity Pay and Statutory Adoption Pay (Weekly Rates) (Amendment) Regulations 2006 SI No 2236 reg 4.
3   PAL Regs 2002 reg 2(1) and (2).

parents, sisters, brothers, aunts and uncles, of full or half blood. However, they may be entitled to parental leave if they have parental responsibility.

Background and statutory framework

9.2 The Employment Act 2002 introduced a new right for employees who are newly matched with a child for adoption to take paid adoption leave by inserting some new provisions into the Employment Rights Act (ERA) 1996 and the Social Security Contributions and Benefits Act (SSCBA) 1992. The Paternity and Adoption Leave Regulations (PAL Regs) 2002 govern the right to adoption leave and the Statutory Paternity Pay and Statutory Adoption Pay (General) Regulations (SPP and SAP Regs) 2002 govern the right to pay. They apply to children matched or placed for adoption on or after 6 April 2003.[4] These regulations have been amended by the Maternity and Parental Leave etc and the Paternity and Adoption Leave (Amendment) Regulations 2006 and the Statutory Paternity Pay and Statutory Adoption Pay (General) and the Statutory Paternity Pay and Statutory Adoption Pay (Weekly Rates) (Amendment) Regulations 2006. They apply to employees with a child expected to be placed for adoption on or after 1 April 2007 (regardless of when the child is actually placed) and made the following main changes:

- increased SAP from 26 to 39 weeks;
- changed the notice period from 28 days to eight weeks for early return from adoption leave;
- introduced a right for employers to make reasonable contact with employees during adoption leave and enabled employees to work for up to 10 days during adoption leave without losing rights to leave and pay.

9.3 The Work and Families Act 2006 contains powers to extend maternity and adoption pay to 52 weeks and to introduce a new entitlement to additional paternity leave (APL) which could be taken within the second six months of the child's life. Some of the APL could be paid if the child's mother or adopter has returned to work and has some of her entitlement to SMP, MA (maternity allowance) or SAP left at the time of her return. The government intends to introduce these new

4   PAL Regs 2002 reg 3(2).

measures by the end of this Parliament which is expected to be by 2010, but is still consulting on the details of the new scheme.

9.4   HMRC publishes a Help Book for Employers called 'Pay and time off work for adoptive parents E16' ('the Help Book') which provides information about calculating, paying and reclaiming SAP and SPP (adoption).[5] There is also an interactive SAP calculator available at www.hmrc.gov.uk/calcs/sap.htm.

Who is entitled to adoption leave?

9.5   Only employees are entitled to adoption leave, not workers or the self-employed. Non-employees, such as agency workers, bank nurses or homeworkers who are classified by their employers as 'self-employed' may in fact be employees (see para 1.28 for who is an employee). An adoptive parent who is not an employee may still be entitled to adoption pay even if she is not entitled to leave. See para 9.54 for adoption pay.

9.6   Members of the armed forces, share fishermen and the police are excluded from the right to take adoption leave.[6] Seafarers are entitled, providing the ship is registered under the Merchant Shipping Act 1995 s8, belongs to a port in Great Britain and they are ordinarily resident in Great Britain and do not work wholly outside Great Britain.[7]

Entitlement to OAL

9.7   An employee qualifies for OAL if she:

- is the child's adopter;[8]
- has been continuously employed for at least 26 weeks ending with the week in which she was notified of having been matched with the child[9] (note: this is different from ordinary maternity leave (OML), where there is no service requirement);
- has notified the agency that she agrees that the child should be placed with her and the date of placement.[10]

5   The Help Book can be obtained from the Employer's Orderline on 0845 7 646 646.
6   ERA 1996 ss192, 199 and 200.
7   ERA 1996 s199(7) and (8).
8   PAL Regs 2002 reg 15(2)(a).
9   PAL Regs 2002 reg 15(2)(b).
10   PAL Regs 2002 reg 15(2)(c).

An adopter

9.8   An adopter means a person who has been matched with a child for adoption or, where a couple adopts a child, whichever of them has elected to be the adopter for the purpose of taking adoption leave.[11] Only one of the adoptive parents can take adoption leave and pay. Her spouse, civil partner or partner can take up to two weeks' paternity leave and pay (see para 9.117 onwards).

Matched with a child

9.9   A person is matched with a child for adoption when the adoption agency decides that the individual or couple would be suitable adoptive parents for the child.[12] She is notified of having been matched on the date she receives the agency's decision.[13] The PAL Regs 2002 apply to children matched and placed for adoption within the UK. See para 9.131 onwards for children adopted from overseas.

9.10   This means that adoption leave is only available to parents who have been newly matched with a child through an agency. It is not available to step fathers or mothers, for example, who wish to adopt a stepchild, but they could be entitled to parental leave.

Placement of a child

9.11   A placement occurs when a child goes to live with the adopter permanently with a view to being formally adopted in the future. The exact date of placement can often be unpredictable and at very short notice.

Continuous employment

9.12   Continuous employment includes any week in which the employee has a contract of employment, whether written or oral, with her employer which includes periods of sick leave, annual leave or unpaid leave.[14]

9.13   There are also special rules as to when an absence from work, when there is no contract, may still be treated as continuous

---

11   PAL Regs 2002 reg 2(1) and (4)(c).
12   PAL Regs 2002 reg 2(4)(a).
13   PAL Regs 2002 reg 2(4)(b).
14   PAL Regs 2002 reg 2(5).

employment. See para 9.61 for more on continuous employment in relation to SAP.

Entitlement to AAL

9.14   An employee is entitled to AAL if:[15]

- the child was placed with her;
- she took OAL in respect of the child; and
- the OAL period has not ended by dismissal or disruption of the placement, see disrupted placement during adoption leave below.

Commencement and length of adoption leave

OAL

9.15   OAL lasts for 26 weeks.[16] An employee is not entitled to any more adoption leave where she adopts more than one child,[17] however, if she qualifies, she would be entitled to 13 weeks *parental* leave for each child see chapter 10 on parental leave.

AAL

9.16   AAL lasts for 26 weeks beginning with the day after the last day of OAL.[18]

9.17   If an employee is dismissed during OAL or AAL, her leave will end on the date of dismissal.[19]

9.18   The employee can choose to start her adoption leave on:

- the day the child is placed with her for adoption (whenever that occurs); or
- a fixed date, as specified in her notice, no more than 14 days before the expected date of placement.[20]

When an employee has chosen to start her leave on the day of placement and she is at work that day, her leave will start the following

15 PAL Regs 2002 reg 20(1).
16 PAL Regs 2002 reg 18(1).
17 PAL Regs 2002 reg 15(4).
18 PAL Regs 2002 reg 20(2).
19 PAL Regs 2002 reg 24.
20 PAL Regs 2002 reg 16(1).

day.[21] If she needs time off immediately she can take time off for dependants, see chapter 11 on time off for dependants.

Notice provisions for adoption leave

9.19 An employee must give notice to take adoption leave, in writing if requested by her employer,[22] stating:

- the expected date of placement; and
- the date she has chosen to start her leave.[23]

9.20 If her employer requests it, she must also provide evidence of her entitlement to adoption leave[24]. Evidence must be in the form of documents issued by the adoption agency that confirm:

- the name and address of the agency;
- the date on which the employee was notified that she had been matched with the child; and
- the date the agency expects to place the child with the employee.

9.21 Notice must be given to the employer no more than seven days after the date the employee is notified of having been matched with a child for adoption or, where that is not reasonably practicable, as soon as reasonably practicable.[25]

Changing the start of OAL

9.22 An employee can vary the start of her OAL providing she gives her employer at least 28 days' notice:

- before the date of placement, if she intended to take her leave on the date of placement; or
- before the fixed date, if she intended to start her leave on a fixed date within 14 days prior to the placement.[26]

If it is not reasonably practicable to give 28 days' notice, she should give notice as soon as reasonably practicable.[27]

21 PAL Regs 2002 reg 18(3).
22 PAL Regs 2002 reg 17(6).
23 PAL Regs 2002 reg 17(1).
24 PAL Regs 2002 reg 17(3).
25 PAL Regs 2002 reg 17(2).
26 PAL Regs 2002 reg 17(4).
27 PAL Regs 2002 reg 17(4).

EXAMPLE: Jane is notified that she has been matched with a child on 1 June 2007. She gives notice to her employer on 8 June 2007 that she wishes to start her adoption leave on the date of placement. The expected date of placement is 7 July 2007. On 12 June Jane is notified that the placement will happen five days earlier on 2 July. Jane talks to her employer about the situation and gives 20 days' notice before the new date which her employer accepts.

Employer's notice of the end of adoption leave

9.23   Once an employer has received notice of the date an employee wants to start her adoption leave, the employer must write to the woman within 28 days of receiving her notice, notifying her of the date her adoption leave will end.[28] If a woman has given notice to vary the date her adoption leave starts, see para 9.22, her employer must write to her within 28 days of the date her OAL started.[29] The employer's notice must take account of AAL.

9.24   If the employer does not notify the employee of the date her adoption leave will end, the employer loses the right to postpone her return if she does not give adequate notice to return to work early, see notice of return to work, para 9.42 onwards. She is also protected from detriment or dismissal if the employer does not notify the employee of the date her adoption leave will end and, for example, she is dismissed for failing to return at the end of her leave, see protection from detriment and unfair dismissal at paras 9.107 and 9.109.

Disrupted placement during adoption leave

9.25   There is an eight-week period which allows adoptive parents to come to terms with the ending of the placement. This applies in the following three circumstances:[30]

- if an employee has started OAL before the placement and the adoption agency notifies her that the child will not be placed with her, her OAL will end eight weeks after the end of the week in which she is notified that the placement will not take place;

---

28   PAL Regs 2002 reg 17(8)(a).
29   PAL Regs 2002 reg 17(8)(b).
30   PAL Regs 2002 reg 22(1) and (3).

312 Maternity and parental rights / chapter 9

- if the child dies during adoption leave, leave will end eight weeks after the end of the week in which the child dies; or
- if the child is returned to the adoption agency, leave will end eight weeks after the end of the week in which the placement ends.

9.26 She should give notice to her employer that she is returning to work earlier than expected, see notice of return at paras 9.43 and 9.45. If her OAL ends during the eight-week period, she is entitled to AAL until the end of the eight-week period.[31] However, if her AAL ends during the eight-week period, her AAL is not extended and she is due back to work at the end of the 26 weeks AAL period.[32] An employee may take annual leave, by agreement with her employer, if she wishes to have more time off, see para 9.27 onwards for accrual of annual leave during adoption leave.

Terms and conditions during OAL and AAL

OAL

9.27 An employee's contract of employment continues during OAL. An employee on OAL is entitled to her normal contractual terms and conditions[33] as if she was at work, apart from remuneration.[34] Remuneration means an employee's normal salary or wages. An employee is also bound by the obligations in her contract providing they are not inconsistent with her absence on adoption leave. Her seniority, pension and other service-related rights continue to accrue as if she had not been absent.[35] An employee on paid adoption leave is entitled to receive the same pension contributions from her employer as if she was working and receiving normal pay.[36] The employee is only required to pay contributions based on the remuneration (ie SAP or contractual adoption pay) she actually receives.[37]

9.28 These provisions are the same as for women taking OML, see chapter 5 for more details on 'remuneration' and rights during maternity leave.

---

31 PAL Regs 2002 reg 22(2)(b).
32 PAL Regs 2002 reg 22(2)(c).
33 PAL Regs 2002 reg 19(1).
34 PAL Regs 2002 reg 19(2) and (3).
35 PAL Regs 2002 reg 27(1)(a)(ii).
36 SSA 1989 Sch 5 para 5B(4).
37 SSA 1989 Sch 5 para 5B(3).

AAL

9.29 During AAL, the contract of employment continues but an employee is only entitled to the benefit of some of the terms and conditions, including:

- the employer's implied obligation of trust and confidence;
- notice of termination of employment;
- redundancy pay; and
- disciplinary or grievance procedures.[38]

9.30 The employee is bound by her implied obligation of good faith and terms and conditions of employment relating to:[39]

- notice of termination of employment;
- disclosure of confidential information;
- acceptance of gifts and benefits;
- participation in any other business.

9.31 These statutory provisions are the same as for women taking additional maternity leave, see chapter 5 on rights during maternity leave.

9.32 Her seniority, pension and other service-related benefits, such as sickness, invalidity or death benefits, do not continue to accrue during the period of AAL but they are treated as if her employment before and after the leave were continuous.[40] However, if the employee is paid during any part of the AAL period, any pension contributions by the employer should be based on her normal salary and any pension contributions by the employee should be based on the amount of remuneration actually received.[41] This is the same as the rules on maternity leave, see para 5.112.

9.33 For protection from dismissal and less favourable treatment during adoption leave, see para 9.107.

38 PAL Regs 2002 reg 21(a).
39 PAL Regs 2002 reg 21(b).
40 PAL Regs 2002 reg 27(1)(a)(i) and (2).
41 PAL Regs 2002 reg 27(2) and SSA 1989 Sch 5 para 5B.

Keeping in touch during adoption leave

Reasonable contact

Child expected to be placed for adoption on or after 1 April 2007

9.34   If a child is expected to be placed for adoption on or after 1 April 2007, an employer may make reasonable contact with the employee.[42] This is to enable the employer and employee to keep in touch during adoption leave. These provisions are the same as for maternity leave, see para 4.48 onwards.

Work during adoption leave

9.35   An employee may work for up to 10 keeping in touch (KIT) days during OAL or AAL without bringing her adoption leave to an end. The work can be consecutive or not and can include training or any other activity, for example, a staff meeting, that enables the employee to keep in touch with the workplace. Working for part of a day will count as one day's work. Any such work must be by agreement and neither the employer nor the employee can insist on it. Any days of work will not extend the adoption period.[43] An employee is protected from detriment and unfair dismissal for working or refusing to work during adoption leave, see paras 9.108 and 9.112. These provisions are the same as for maternity leave, see para 4.48 onwards.

9.36   An employee may work for up to 10 KIT days without losing her SAP, see para 9.98. There are no specific provisions in the regulations in relation to pay for KIT days, therefore, it will be a matter for agreement between the employer and employee. SAP can be offset against any payments of contractual adoption pay, see para 9.102.

9.37   Note: These provisions do not apply for a child expected to be placed for adoption before 1 April 2007.

Redundancy during adoption leave

9.38   If an employee is made redundant during OAL or AAL, she is entitled to be offered any suitable alternative employment on terms and conditions that are not substantially less favourable.[44] She should

---

42   PAL Regs 2002 reg 21A(4) inserted by the Maternity and Parental Leave etc and the Paternity and Adoption Leave (Amendment) Regulations 2006 reg 14.
43   PAL Regs 2002 reg 21A(6).
44   PAL Regs 2002 reg 23.

be offered any suitable alternative employment without having to attend an interview or selection process and she takes priority over other employees. A new contract should take effect immediately after the end of the previous one.

9.39   If a suitable alternative vacancy does exist and the employer does not offer it to her, the dismissal will be automatically unfair if the reason, or principal reason, for the dismissal is redundancy.[45] See para 9.111 on protection from detriment and unfair dismissal. If she unreasonably refuses a suitable alternative vacancy she will lose the right to a redundancy payment.

9.40   If there is no suitable alternative vacancy, her adoption leave will end on the date of dismissal. She is entitled to paid statutory notice during OAL and AAL as well as any statutory or contractual redundancy pay that she qualifies for. However, if she is entitled to contractual notice of at least a week more than her statutory notice, she is not entitled to statutory notice but must rely on her contractual rights.[46] She will not be entitled to contractual notice pay during adoption leave unless the contract provides for it, but see para 5.20 onwards as the same provisions in respect of notice pay apply during maternity leave. Any SAP or contractual adoption pay may be offset against notice pay.[47] If she is receiving SAP, she is entitled to continue to receive it for the full 26- or 39-week period, see *SAP* below.

9.41   All the above provisions are the same as for women made redundant during maternity leave, see para 15.86.

Notice of return to work

9.42   If an employee returns to work at the end of her AAL she does not have to give any notice of return. She returns on the first working day after her AAL ends which should be the date notified by her employer, see para 9.23.

Changing the date of return

Changing the date of return where a child is expected to be placed for adoption before 1 April 2007

9.43   If she wants to return to work before the end of AAL or if she only wants to take OAL, she must give at least 28 days' notice of early

---

45   ERA 1996 s99 and PAL Regs 2002 reg 29(1)(b).
46   ERA 1996 s87(4).
47   ERA 1996 ss88 and 89.

return.[48] Notice of early return does not have to be in writing. She must also give 28 days' notice if she is returning early because of a disrupted placement, see para 9.25.[49]

9.44   If she returns to work without giving 28 days' notice, an employer is entitled to postpone her return for the full notice period, but an employer cannot postpone it beyond the end of the AAL period.[50] If she returns to work anyway, she is not entitled to be paid.[51] This does not apply if an employer did not notify her of the date her AAL ends. In that case, she does not have to give notice of early return and the employer has no right to delay her return or refuse to pay her for returning early.[52] This is the same as for maternity leave, see para 4.57.

Changing the date of return where a child is expected to be placed for adoption on or after 1 April 2007

9.45   If an employee wants to return to work before the end of AAL or if she only wants to take OAL, she must give at least eight weeks' notice of early return.[53] Notice of early return does not have to be in writing but it is advisable to avoid any misunderstanding. She must also give eight weeks' notice if she is returning early because of a disrupted placement, see para 9.25. As her adoption leave will end eight weeks after a disrupted placement, this means that she must notify her employer on the day the placement ends that she will be returning to work in eight weeks' time. In many cases the employee will have advance warning that the placement is likely to come to an end, but where there is no warning the employee should give notice that she is returning to work early on the day the placement ends or as soon afterwards as possible, otherwise the employee could face a delayed return to work, see below.

9.46   If she returns to work without giving eight weeks' notice, an employer is entitled to postpone her return until eight weeks' notice has been given but an employer cannot postpone it beyond the end of the AAL period.[54] If she returns to work anyway she is not entitled to be paid. This does not apply if an employer did not notify her of the

---

48 PAL Regs 2002 reg 25(1).
49 PAL Regs 2002 reg 25(6).
50 PAL Regs 2002 reg 25(2) and (3).
51 PAL Regs 2002 reg 25(4).
52 PAL Regs 2002 reg 25(5).
53 PAL Regs 2002 reg 25(1) as amended by the Maternity and Parental Leave etc and the Paternity and Adoption Leave Regulations 2006 reg 15(a).
54 PAL Regs 2002 reg 25(2).

date her AAL ends. In that case, she does not have to give notice of early return and the employer has no right to delay her return or refuse to pay her for returning early. This is the same as for maternity leave, see para 4.59.

More than one change of return date

9.47   If an employee has given eight weeks' notice to return to work before the end of her AAL on date X but she changes her mind and wants to go back earlier than date X, she must give at least eight weeks' notice of the date she now intends to return. If she wants to go back later than date X, she must give at least eight weeks' notice before date X.[55] These notice requirements also apply where an employer has postponed an employee's return because she returned to work before the end of her eight-week notice period and she wishes to change the return date. This is the same as for maternity leave, see para 4.60.

9.48   Note: Where a child is expected to be placed for adoption before 1 April 2007, there are no specific notice provisions allowing an employee to change her mind once she has given notice to return to work early or had her return postponed after returning to work without giving sufficient notice.

Right to return after adoption leave

OAL

9.49   An employee is entitled to return to exactly the same job as she was doing immediately before she started her leave[56] on the same terms and conditions,[57] providing she is returning from a single period of OAL or from a period of OAL at the end of two or more consecutive periods of leave that does not include AML, AAL or parental leave of more than four weeks. The job she was doing before her leave is the job she was doing immediately before her single period of OAL or immediately before the first of consecutive periods of leave.[58]

---

55 PAL Regs 2002 reg 25(2A) inserted by the Maternity and Parental Leave etc and the Paternity and Adoption Leave Regulations 2006 reg 15(c).
56 PAL Regs 2002 reg 26(1).
57 PAL Regs 2002 reg 27(1)(b).
58 PAL Regs 2002 reg 26(3).

> EXAMPLE: If a woman takes OAL and two weeks' parental leave immediately afterwards (this might be because she gets some paid parental leave from her employer, but not paid AAL) she has the right to return to the job she was doing before she started her OAL.

Right to return after consecutive periods of leave

9.50   If she returns from two or more consecutive periods of leave that includes a period of AML, AAL or parental leave of more than four weeks, regardless of whether OAL is at the beginning or end of the leave period, she is entitled to return to the same job but, if it is not reasonably practicable for her to return to that job she is entitled to a suitable alternative job[59] on terms and conditions that are not less favourable.[60] If she returns to work, even for one day, between periods of leave, her leave is not counted as continuous and she would have the right to return which applies to that individual period of leave. If she takes sick leave or annual leave on return she is treated as returning to work.

> EXAMPLE: If a woman takes OAL and AAL, followed by a further consecutive period of OAL in respect of a second adoption, eg, a sibling, she will not have the right to return to exactly the same job after her second period of OAL if it is not reasonably practicable, but will have the right to return to a suitable alternative job on similar terms and conditions. If she returned to work for a short period between her AAL and second period of OAL, she would have the right to return to exactly the same job following her second isolated period of OAL.

AAL

9.51   An employee who returns from AAL (regardless of whether it is at the beginning or end of consecutive periods of leave) is entitled to return to the job she was doing immediately before her leave[61] but if it is not reasonably practicable for her to return to that job, to a suitable

---

59 PAL Regs 2002 reg 26(2)(b).
60 PAL Regs 2002 reg 27(1)(b).
61 PAL Regs 2002 reg 26(3).

alternative job[62] on terms and conditions that are not less favourable.[63] An employee who is not allowed to return to her job after AAL may have a claim for automatic unfair dismissal but there are exceptions if she works for a small employer or she is offered a suitable alternative job, see paras 9.113 to 9.115. She may also have a claim for indirect sex discrimination.

Other rights to time off for adoptive parents

9.52   If she is an employee with at least one year's service, an adoptive parent can take up to 13 weeks' parental leave up to the fifth anniversary of the child's placement for adoption or up to the child's 18th birthday if that is sooner or the child is disabled. See chapter 10 on parental leave. Adoptive parents are also entitled to time off for dependants in an emergency, see chapter 11.

9.53   Adoptive parents of a child under six or a disabled child under 18, who meet the qualifying conditions, have the right to ask for flexible work, see chapter 12.

Statutory Adoption Pay

Who can claim SAP?

9.54   In most cases employees who qualify for adoption leave will also be entitled to SAP and vice versa, but there are a few exceptions. To be eligible for SAP, she must be an employee. The definition of an employee for SAP purposes is different to that for entitlement to leave. She is an employee for SAP purposes if she is treated as an 'employed earner'.[64] She is an employed earner if her employer is liable to pay class 1 national insurance (NI) contributions or who would pay NI if her earnings were high enough. A woman earning less than the lower earnings limit for National Insurance (£84 a week from April 2006–April 2007) is not entitled to SAP but see *Low income parents*, para 9.57. A woman employed under a contract of apprenticeship may be an employed earner and eligible for SAP.

---

62 PAL Regs 2002 reg 26(2)(a).
63 PAL Regs 2002 reg 27(1)(b).
64 SPP and SAP Regs 2002 reg 32(1) as amended by the Employment Equality (Age) Regulations 2006 SI No 1031 which removed the age restriction with effect from 1 October 2006. Note: A person must be 21 before they may adopt in any event.

9.55　Office holders, such as members of the police, judiciary, armed forces, MPs, some company directors and many agency and casual workers, will be eligible for SAP as employed earners but may not be eligible for adoption leave if they are not employees. They may have a contractual right to adoption leave or may be able to agree time off work.

Who is excluded from claiming SAP?

9.56　Few groups are excluded, but SAP is not payable to the following:

- mariners employed on a ship whose employer does not have a place of business in the UK;
- a woman who works outside the UK where the employer is not resident or present in Great Britain or does not have a place of business in Great Britain, and is not liable to pay NI contributions. However, she can qualify for SAP if she has worked in the European Economic Area (EEA) but she works for the employer in the UK in the week in which she was notified of having been matched with a child for adoption and she had worked for the same employer in the EEA for 26 weeks prior to that week.

Low income parents

9.57　Adoptive parents should first contact their adoption agency for an assessment of financial support.

9.58　Parents taking adoption leave may be entitled to income support if they have a low income or no income at all, providing they have savings under £8,000 and the employee's partner is not working. A person is not treated as being 'in work' during any period of adoption leave for income support purposes.[65] Any remuneration received whilst on adoption leave is counted as earnings for income support or jobseeker's allowance (JSA). Employees receiving Income Support (IS) or on a low income may be entitled to housing benefit or council tax benefit. If they are already receiving those benefits, they may be entitled to an increase if their income stops or is reduced during adoption leave.

9.59　Employees receiving SAP are treated as being 'in work' for tax

---

65　Income Support (General) Regulations 1987 SI No 1967 as amended by the Social Security (Paternity and Adoption) Amendment Regulations 2002 SI No 2689.

credit purposes, as long as they were working at least 16 hours a week immediately before starting SAP. The first £100 of SAP is ignored as income for tax credit purposes. Adoptive parents on JSA, IS or getting at least the family element of Child Tax Credit (CTC) can claim the Sure Start Maternity Grant. See chapter 7 on maternity allowance and other benefits.

The main qualifying conditions for SAP

9.60   To qualify for SAP the woman must:

- have had a child placed for adoption, or expected to be placed for adoption with her;
- have been continuously employed for at least 26 weeks ending with the week in which she is notified of having been matched with a child for adoption;
- have stopped working;
- have average weekly earnings of not less than the lower earnings limit for the payment of NI (£84 per week from April 2006 to April 2007); and
- have elected to receive SAP, not SPP, and given the required notice to her employer.[66] A woman may not elect to receive SAP if she has chosen to receive SPP or her spouse, civil partner or partner has chosen to receive SAP.[66a]

The flowchart on page 322 summarises the main qualifying conditions for SAP.

An employee must have 26 weeks' continuous employment ending with the week in which she is notified of having been matched with a child for adoption

What counts as continuous employment?

9.61   Work for part of a week will count towards continuous employment.

9.62   Any weeks in which a woman is not under a contract of employment will not count apart from any week or part of a week in which she is:

---

66   SSCBA 1992 s171ZL(1).
66a SSCBA 1999 s171ZL(4) as amended by the Adoption and Children Act 2002 (Consequential Amendment to Statutory Adoption Pay) Order 2006 SI No 2012 in respect of a child expected to be placed for adoption on or after 1 October 2006.

Who qualifies for SAP?

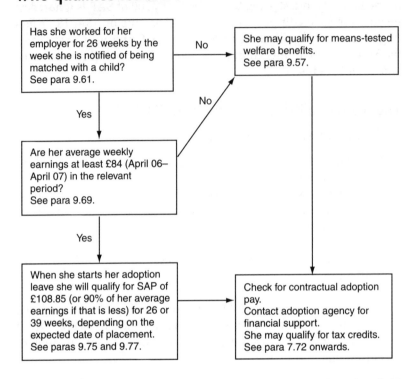

- absent through sickness or injury up to a maximum of 26 weeks;
- absent on account of a temporary cessation of work; or
- regarded as continuing in employment by arrangement or custom,[67]

providing she returns to work for her employer after the period of illness or absence.

9.63   Note: These provisions are the same as for SMP, see para 6.14 onwards.

Seasonal or regular temporary workers

9.64   There are special rules about continuity of employment for seasonal and regular temporary workers who work at certain times of the year and not others. A woman will not normally lose her continuity of

67 SPP and SAP Regs 2002 reg 33(1).

employment if she is absent from work for one of the reasons stated above, see para 9.61, providing she returns to work after the absence. However, where it is customary for an employer to offer work for a fixed period of less than 26 weeks on two or more occasions a year which do not overlap and offers work to the same people, a woman who is absent because of sickness or injury is not required to return to work afterwards and will be regarded as having continuity of employment.[68]

Industrial action and stoppage of work

9.65   There is no break in continuity of employment if there is a stoppage of work due to a trade dispute. However, any weeks of stoppage do not count towards the continuous employment and if the person is dismissed during the stoppage her continuity of employment stops and is not restored if she is re-employed unless she can show that she had no direct interest in the trade dispute.[69]

Transfer of undertaking

9.66   There are a number of circumstances in which a change of employer does not break continuity, including where the business is transferred to a new employer or employment is transferred to an associated employer.[70]

Reinstatement or re-engagement

9.67   Where there has been an order for re-engagement or reinstatement,[71] continuity of employment will be maintained for all weeks between the date the contract was terminated and the date of reinstatement or re-engagement.[72] Following the introduction of dispute resolution procedures in October 2004, if a woman is reinstated or re-engaged by her employer as a result of following the statutory procedure, her employment is regarded as continuous and any break in service is disregarded for calculating qualifying service for SAP.[73]

68 SPP and SAP Regs 2002 reg 33(3).
69 SPP and SAP Regs 2002 reg 35.
70 SPP and SAP Regs 2002 reg 36.
71 This includes an agreement reached through a compromise agreement or agreement reached with the help of ACAS.
72 SPP and SAP Regs 2002 reg 34.
73 SPP and SAP Regs 2002 reg 34 as amended by the Statutory Maternity Pay (General) and the Statutory Paternity Pay and the Statutory Adoption Pay (General) (Amendment) Regulations 2005 SI No 358.

An employee must have stopped work

9.68   The woman must stop work in order to receive SAP, this will usually be because she has started her adoption leave. See para 9.97 onwards on work during the SAP period. If she leaves her job or is dismissed after she has qualified for SAP she is still entitled to it, see para 9.104 on termination of contract before start of SAP.

An employee must have average weekly earnings of not less than the lower earnings limit for the payment of NI

9.69   To qualify for SAP, an employee must have average earnings of at least the lower earnings limit (£84 a week from April 2006 to April 2007) in the eight weeks, if paid weekly, or two months, if paid monthly, ending with the week in which she is notified of being matched with a child for adoption.[74]

9.70   Earnings includes any remuneration subject to tax and NI and includes statutory sick pay, SMP, SPP and SAP.[75]

9.71   Calculation of average earnings is exactly the same as for SMP, see para 6.81 onwards on SMP, with the exception of the rules on pay rises. If an employee receives a pay rise after the calculation period for SAP and before the end of her AAL, she is not entitled to have her SAP recalculated to take account of the increase unless it is a pay rise which has been backdated into the calculation period for SAP.

9.72   Employees whose average earnings are too low to receive SAP should check their contract to see if they have any contractual entitlement to adoption leave and pay. See also para 9.57 on low income parents.

More than one employer or contract

9.73   If an employee has two or more contracts for different employers, she may qualify for SAP from one or all of her employers. If her earnings are aggregated and treated as a single payment for NI purposes, liability for SAP is apportioned between the employers.[76]

9.74   If an employee works under more than one contract for the same employer, or two associated employers, the contracts must be treated

74   SPP and SAP Regs 2002 reg 40(2).
75   SPP and SAP Regs 2002 reg 39(3).
76   SPP and SAP Regs 2002 reg 38(2).

as one for SAP purposes unless the earnings cannot be aggregated for NI contribution purposes.[77]

Rate of SAP

9.75   From 6 April 2006 to 5 April 2007, SAP is £108.85 per week or 90% of average earnings if that is less. Rates change in April each year.

9.76   Note: There is no higher rate as with SMP. There is no additional SAP if more than one child is adopted.[78]

The adoption pay period

9.77   SAP is payable for 26 weeks for a child expected to be placed for adoption before 1 April 2007[79] and for 39 weeks for a child expected to be placed for adoption on or after 1 April 2007.[80] When SAP is paid for 39 weeks the adoption leave period will still be divided into 26 weeks OAL and 26 weeks AAL. There will be no change to an employee's rights to return to work after OAL and AAL, see para 9.49 onwards, and no change to an employee's rights during OAL and AAL, see para 9.27 onwards.

9.78   The employee can choose when she wishes to receive SAP and it may start on:

- the day the child is placed with her or, if she is at work that day, the following day; or
- a specified date which must be no more than 14 days before the expected date of placement.[81]

9.79   If she has left her job, for whatever reason, after qualifying for SAP, her SAP will begin 14 days before the expected date of placement or on the day after the last day of employment, if her contract ends within 14 days before the expected date of placement.

---

77   SPP and SAP Regs 2002 reg 38(3).
78   SSCBA 1992 s171ZL(5).
79   Statutory Paternity Pay and Statutory Adoption Pay (General) Regulations 2002 reg 21(5).
80   SPP and SAP Regs 2002 reg 21(5) as amended by the Statutory Paternity Pay and Statutory Adoption Pay (General) and the Statutory Paternity Pay and Statutory Adoption Pay (Weekly Rates) (Amendment) Regulations 2006 reg 4.
81   SPP and SAP Regs 2002 reg 21(1).

Disruption of adoption

9.80   If the adoption is disrupted, the adoption pay period will end:

- eight weeks after the end of the week in which the child dies; or
- eight weeks after the week in which the child is returned to the adoption agency; or
- eight weeks after the adoptive parent is notified that the placement will not now take place, where the adoption pay period had begun before the adoption was expected to take place.[82]

Notice provisions for SAP

9.81   An employee must give at least 28 days' notice stating:

- when she wants her SAP to begin, and
- the expected date of placement.[83]

If she cannot give 28 days' notice she must give notice as soon as reasonably practicable.[84] The notice must be in writing if requested.[85]

Change of start of SAP

9.82   An employee can change the start of her SAP, and choose either of the options for when she starts her leave, see adoption pay period above, providing she gives at least 28 days' notice before the date she wants SAP to begin or, if not reasonably practicable, gives notice as soon as reasonably practicable.

9.83   If she chose to start her SAP on the date the child is placed for adoption, she must give notice to her employer of the actual date of placement, as soon as reasonably practicable.[86]

Evidence of entitlement to SAP

9.84   To claim SAP the employee must give her employer the following documents as evidence of her entitlement:

- the name and address of the adoption agency;
- her name and address;

---

82 SPP and SAP Regs 2002 reg 22.
83 SPP and SAP Regs 2002 reg 23(1).
84 SSCBA 1992 s171ZL(6).
85 SSCBA 1992 s171ZL(7).
86 SPP and SAP Regs 2002 reg 23(2).

- the date the child is expected to be placed for adoption, or the date of placement if it has already happened; and
- the date she was notified by the adoption agency of having been matched with a child.[87]

9.85 She must also provide a written or oral declaration that she has chosen to receive SAP and not SPP (adoption).[88] The evidence can be in the form of documents from the adoption agency or a matching certificate that can be used for giving notice for adoption leave and pay is available on the DTI website (www.dti.gov.uk/er) which is completed by the adoption agency.

9.86 The evidence and declaration must be given at least 28 days before the employee wishes SAP to start or as soon as reasonably practicable.[89] The employee can give her employer notice of both leave and pay together as long as she fulfills all the notice requirements for SAP, see notice for adoption leave above. There is sometimes very little time between the date the adoption agency tells the employee that they have been matched with a child and the date of placement. An employee should provide evidence 28 days before the start of the SAP period but if the employee is late because of this, the employer should accept it as it was not reasonably practicable to give 28 days' notice.[90]

How SAP is paid

9.87 SAP should be paid on the normal pay day or a day that has been agreed. If there is no normal pay day or agreed date, it should be paid on the last day of a calendar month.[91] SAP is treated as earnings and is subject to tax and NI. As with SMP, SAP can be paid in a lump sum by agreement.

Calculating a daily rate

Child expected to be placed for adoption on or after 1 April 2007

9.88 Where a child is expected to be placed for adoption on or after 1 April 2007, an employer may, where necessary, calculate SAP at a daily rate

---

87 SPP and SAP Regs 2002 reg 24(1) and (2).
88 SPP and SAP Regs 2002 reg 24(1)(b).
89 SPP and SAP Regs 2002 reg 24(3).
90 The Help Book E16 (2006) p14.
91 SPP and SAP Regs 2002 reg 42.

by paying one-seventh of the weekly rate.[92] This is intended to simplify the administration of SAP and could be used where, for example, a woman's SAP period overlaps a monthly payroll or where her SAP starts in the middle of the week.

Rounding up payments

9.89   Where SAP is paid on a weekly or daily basis it is rounded up to the nearest whole penny.[93]

9.90   Note: Where a child is expected to be placed for adoption before 1 April 2007 there is no provision for calculating a daily rate, therefore, SAP can only be paid on a weekly basis.

No contracting out of SAP scheme

9.91   Any agreement to exclude, limit or modify the SAP provisions or to require the employee to contribute to the costs is illegal.[94] Deductions can be made from SAP such as overpayments, subscriptions and loans providing the employer is authorised to make the same deductions from contractual pay. SAP cannot be replaced by any form of payment in kind.[95]

Recovery of SAP

9.92   As with SMP, all employers can reclaim 92% of SAP (small employers with a NI liability of less than £45,000 can reclaim 104.5%) by making a deduction from their NI contributions, PAYE tax, student loan deductions, and Construction Industry Scheme deductions.

Advance funding

9.93   Employers can apply to their HMRC Accounts Office for advance funding of SAP payments where the amount they have to pay out exceeds the amount they have available for NI contributions etc in the same tax month or quarter.[96]

---

92 SSCBA 1992 s171ZN as amended by the Work and Families Act 2006 Sch 1 para 21(3).
93 Statutory Paternity Pay and Statutory Adoption Pay (Weekly Rates) Regulations 2002 reg 4 as amended by the Statutory Paternity Pay and Statutory Adoption Pay (General) and the Statutory Paternity Pay and Statutory Adoption Pay (Weekly Rates) (Amendment) Regulations 2006 reg 7.
94 SSCBA 1992 s171ZO.
95 SPP and SAP Regs 2002 reg 41.
96 The Help Book E16 (2006) p20.

Administration of SAP by employers

9.94 Employers must keep records of any SAP paid for three years. There are standard forms (available from the Employer's Orderline) for SAP purposes:

- SAP1: this must be sent to an employee who is not eligible for SAP;
- SAP2: this is a record sheet of SAP payments;
- SP32: claim form for recovery of SAP paid in a previous tax year.

9.95 Employers must keep the evidence of adoption provided by the adoption agency.[97] If employers give the evidence back with form SAP1, they should keep a copy.

Disentitlement to SAP

9.96 An employee is not entitled to receive SAP for any week that she receives statutory sick pay (SSP) (see para 7.55 for more on SSP) or is in custody and it is not payable following her death.[98] HMRC will pay SAP if she has been released from custody or is subsequently found not guilty or is given a non-custodial sentence.[99]

Work during the SAP period

Child expected to be placed for adoption before 1 April 2007

9.97 Where a child is expected to be placed for adoption before 1 April 2007, an employee cannot receive SAP during any week in which she works for the employer liable to pay her SAP or for another employer.[100]

Child expected to be placed for adoption on or after 1 April 2007

9.98 Where a child is expected to be placed for adoption on or after 1 April 2007, an employee may work for up to 10 KIT days, consecutively or not, without losing SAP.[101] An employer may make reasonable contact with an employee on adoption leave and she may work for up to

---

97 The Help Book E16 (2006) p21.
98 SPP and SAP Regs 2002 reg 27.
99 SPP and SAP Regs 2002 reg 44.
100 SSCBA 1992 s171ZN.
101 SPP and SAP Regs 2002 reg 27A inserted by the Statutory Paternity Pay and Statutory Adoption Pay (General) and the Statutory Paternity Pay and Statutory Adoption Pay (Weekly Rates) (Amendment) Regulations 2006 reg 5.

10 KIT days by agreement without losing her rights to leave and pay, see para 9.34 onwards. Any pay over and above SAP should be agreed between the employer and employee. An employer can offset payment for the days worked against SAP (see para 9.102 below). This is the same as for SMP, see paras 6.77 and 6.78. If she works for more than 10 days she will lose a week's SAP for every week in which she does some work, even if she only works for a day or part of a day. So, if a week in the SAP period contains only KIT days, SAP will be retained. If a week contains, for example, the last of the KIT days and also another day of work, the employee will once again lose that week's SAP.

Working for more than one employer

9.99   An employee can receive SAP from an employer (employer A) and work for another employer (employer B) who is not liable to pay her any SAP, providing she worked for employer B in the week in which she was notified of being matched with a child for adoption.[102] This applies both before and after 1 April 2007.

Contractual rights to leave and pay

9.100   Where an employee has a contractual right to adoption leave that is more favourable than the statutory scheme, she cannot take each right separately but is entitled to take whichever right is more favourable.[103]

9.101   If she combines elements of a contractual and statutory right, the statutory provisions are modified to give effect to the more favourable contractual terms.[104] This is known as a composite right.

9.102   If she is entitled to SAP, she can also receive any contractual remuneration she is entitled to.[105] However, SAP can be offset against any contractual remuneration, adoption pay or sick pay owing if the employer wishes to do so.[106] If an employee chooses to take advantage of a KIT day (employees whose child is expected to be placed for adoption on or after 1 April 2007 only, see para 9.34 onwards for KIT days) she retains her SAP for that week and her employer is entitled

---

102 SPP and SAP Regs 2002 reg 25.
103 PAL Regs 2002 reg 30(2).
104 PAL Regs 2002 reg 30(2)(b).
105 SSCBA 1992 s171ZP(4).
106 SPP and SAP Regs 2002 reg 28.

to offset her SAP against any contractual pay agreed for the work done.

EXAMPLE: If a woman earns £50 for a KIT day, she will be able to retain her SAP. The £50 earned will be offset against her SAP, meaning she will receive £108.85 for the week (the flat rate for SAP from April 2006 to April 2007). If she works for three KIT days in the same week and earns £150 she will receive £150 – her SAP being offset against contractual pay paid for the same week. In both cases the employer will be able to reclaim the normal amount of SAP from HM Revenue and Customs.

Remedies relating to SAP

Refusal to pay SAP

9.103   If an employee is not entitled to SAP, her employer must give her form SAP1 explaining why she does not qualify. As with SMP, if the employee does not agree with those reasons she can ask her local HMRC Officer for a formal decision. The employer can be fined for refusing to pay SAP following a formal decision by HMRC, see para 6.124 refusal of the employer to pay SMP.

Termination of contract before start of SAP

9.104   If an employee who is entitled to SAP is dismissed or she leaves employment for whatever reason, the employer will still be liable to pay SAP. Her SAP will begin 14 days before the expected date of placement or on the day after the last day of employment, if her contract ends within 14 days before the expected date of placement.[107]

9.105   If the employer terminates the woman's contract in order to avoid liability for SAP and the woman had been employed for a continuous period of at least eight weeks, the employer will still be liable to pay SAP. The woman will be deemed to have been employed for a continuous period ending with the week in which she was notified of having been matched for adoption. Her average weekly earnings are calculated by reference to what she was earning in the eight weeks before her contract was terminated.[108] She may also have a claim for

---

107 SPP and SAP Regs 2002 reg 29.
108 SPP and SAP Regs 2002 reg 30.

automatic unfair dismissal and sex discrimination, see paras 9.107 onwards and para 15.58. Any loss of SAP can form part of her claim for compensation.

Insolvency

9.106   As with SMP, if the employer is insolvent, the HMRC Statutory Payments Disputes Team will pay any SAP owing.[109]

Protection from detriment and unfair dismissal

Protection from detriment

9.107   An employee should not be subjected to any detriment by any act, or deliberate failure to act, by her employer, for any reason which relates to adoption leave.[110] She is protected from detriment for taking or trying to take adoption leave. She is also protected from detriment for not returning after AAL if:

- her employer did not notify her of the date the AAL would end and she had good reason to believe that AAL had not ended; or
- her employer gave her less than 28 days' notice of when her adoption leave would end and it was not reasonably practicable for her to return on that date.

Child expected to be placed for adoption on or after 1 April 2007

9.108   An employee is protected from detriment for working or refusing to work for her employer during her adoption leave.[111] See para 9.34 onwards for keeping in touch days. For example, if an employee cannot attend a training course while on adoption leave and as a result is denied the opportunity of attending when she returns to work, this would be a detriment.

Unfair dismissal

9.109   Employees who are dismissed where the reason or principal reason is for taking or trying to take adoption leave will be regarded as unfairly

---

109   SPP and SAP Regs 2002 reg 43.
110   ERA 1996 s47C, PAL Regs 2002 reg 28.
111   PAL Regs 2002 reg 28(1)(bb) as amended by the Maternity and Parental Leave etc and the Paternity and Adoption Leave (Amendment) Regulations 2006 reg 16.

dismissed.[112] It will also be unfair dismissal if she is dismissed for not returning after AAL, if:

- her employer did not notify her of the date the AAL would end and she had good reason to believe that AAL had not ended, or
- her employer gave her less than 28 days' notice of when her adoption leave would end and it was not reasonably practicable for her to return on that date.

9.110 An employee who is made redundant will be treated as unfairly dismissed if the circumstances of the redundancy applied equally to one or more employees who had similar positions to the employee but have not been dismissed and the reason, or main reason, for redundancy was that the employee took or tried to take adoption leave.[113] See para 9.38 onwards for rights to redundancy and notice pay.

Automatic unfair dismissal

9.111 Dismissal for any reason which relates to adoption leave is automatically unfair.[114] If a woman is redundant and an employer does not offer her any suitable alternative vacancy that exists, the dismissal will be automatically unfair,[115] see para 9.38 for redundancy during adoption leave.

Child expected to be placed for adoption on or after 1 April 2007

9.112 It is also automatically unfair to dismiss a woman for working or refusing to work for her employer during her adoption leave.[116] See para 9.34 onwards for keeping in touch during adoption leave.

Offer of alternative employment

9.113 The dismissal is not automatically unfair if it is not reasonably practicable, for a reason other than redundancy, for the employer to allow the employee to return to the same job or a suitable alternative job

---

112 PAL Regs 2002 reg 29(1) and (3)(a).
113 PAL Regs 2002 reg 29(2).
114 ERA 1996 s99.
115 PAL Regs 2002 reg 29(1)(b).
116 PAL Regs 2002 reg 29(1)(bb) as amended by the Maternity and Parental Leave etc and the Paternity and Adoption Leave (Amendment) Regulations 2006 reg 17.

and an associated employer offers the employee a suitable job and the employee accepts it or unreasonably refuses it.[117]

Small employer's exemption

Child expected to be placed for adoption before 1 April 2007

9.114　A woman cannot claim automatic unfair dismissal if she works for a small employer (who employs five or fewer employees immediately before the end of her AAL or her dismissal if sooner) and it was not reasonably practicable for her employer to allow her to return to the same job or a suitable alternative job.[118]

Child expected to be placed for adoption on or after 1 April 2007

9.115　The small employer's exemption has been removed for a child expected to be placed for adoption on or after 1 April 2007.[118a] An employee can claim automatic unfair dismissal if she is prevented from returning to the same job or a suitable alternative job, regardless of the size of the organisation.

Protection from sex discrimination

9.116　If a female employee is treated less favourably for taking adoption leave, this may be indirect sex discrimination (see para 15.54). She would have to show that it is disproportionately female employees who take adoption leave so they are particularly disadvantaged by the treatment compared to men. The employer may be able to justify such treatment in a case of indirect sex discrimination. If a male employee is treated less favourably than a woman taking adoption leave and the treatment is on grounds of his sex, this would be direct discrimination (see para 15.53). This is different from the protection from discrimination that applies during pregnancy and maternity leave as it is only pregnant women and women on maternity leave who have automatic protection from unfavourable treatment during the protected period (see para 15.42).

117　PAL Regs 2002 reg 29(5).
118　PAL Regs 2002 reg 29(4).
118a Maternity and Parental Leave etc and the Paternity and Adoption Leave (Amendment) Regulations 2006 reg 17(b).

Paternity leave and pay (adoption)

9.117 The adopter's spouse, civil partner or partner can take one or two weeks' paternity leave and pay, if they meet the qualifying conditions, in order to care for the child or support the adopter. A partner includes a person who lives with the adopter and child in an enduring family relationship. This includes same sex partners but does not include relatives of the adopter, eg, the adopter's parents, grandparents, sister, brother, aunt or uncle.

9.118 Note: For simplicity we refer to the person taking paternity leave as 'he', but a woman can take paternity leave.

9.119 Chapter 8 on paternity leave and pay contains the full provisions. The following provisions apply to an adoptive parent taking paternity leave and pay.

Entitlement to paternity leave

9.120 An employee is entitled to paternity leave if he:

- has been continuously employed for 26 weeks ending with the week in which the child's adopter is notified of having been matched with a child;
- he is married to, the civil partner or the partner of the child's adopter; and
- has, or expects to have, responsibility for the upbringing of the child.[119]

Start of paternity leave

9.121 He can choose to take one or two weeks' consecutive leave on:

- the date the child is placed with the adopter;
- a fixed number of days after the date the child is placed with the adopter; or
- a predetermined date which is later than the date the child is expected to be placed.[120]

Leave must be taken within 56 days of the date the child is placed for adoption.[121]

---

119 PAL Regs 2002 reg 8 as amended by Schedule 17 of the Civil Partnership Act 2004 (Amendments to Subordinate Legislation) Order 2005 SI No 2114.
120 PAL Regs 2002 reg 9(3).
121 PAL Regs 2002 reg 9(2).

Notice for paternity leave

9.122   An employee must give his employer notice no more than seven days after the adopter is notified of being matched with a child, or as soon as reasonably practicable,[122] stating:

- the date the adopter was notified of being matched with a child;
- the date the child is expected to be placed with the adopter;
- whether he wishes to take one or two weeks' leave; and
- when he wishes his leave to begin.[123]

He must give his employer further notice of the date the child was placed, as soon as reasonably practicable.[124]

Changing the start of paternity leave

9.123   He can change the start of his paternity leave, see para 8.18. If he chose to start his leave on a predetermined date and the child has not yet been placed for adoption, he can substitute a later date or choose another option and notify his employer as soon as reasonably practicable.[125]

9.124   If he has chosen to start his leave on the day of placement and is at work that day, his leave will start the following day.[126]

Statutory paternity pay (SPP) (adoption)

Entitlement to SPP (adoption)

9.125   An employee is entitled to SPP if he:

- is married to, or the civil partner or partner of, the child's adopter;
- has, or expects to have, responsibility for the upbringing of the child;
- has been continuously employed for at least 26 weeks ending with the week in which the adopter is notified of being matched with a child;
- has average weekly earnings of more than the Lower Earnings Limit (£84 a week from April 2006 to April 2007) in the eight

---

122   PAL Regs 2002 reg 10(2).
123   PAL Regs 2002 reg 10(1).
124   PAL Regs 2002 reg 10(7).
125   PAL Regs 2002 reg 10(6).
126   PAL Regs 2002 reg 11.

weeks before the end of the week in which the adopter is notified of being matched with a child;

- he is still employed by the same employer on the day the child is placed for adoption; and
- he has chosen to receive SPP (not SAP).[127]

Notice for SPP

9.126 He must give at least 28 days' notice of the start of SPP or as soon as reasonably practicable and can choose when it starts, see paras 8.49–8.53 on start of paternity pay. If he chooses to start his SPP on the date the child is placed for adoption or a fixed number of days afterwards, he must give his employer notice of the date the placement happened as soon as reasonably practicable.[128] If he chose to start his pay on a predetermined date and the placement has not yet happened, he must give his employer notice as soon as reasonably practicable and choose a different date.[129]

9.127 An employee must give notice at least 28 days before he wants his SPP to start,[130] stating:

- his name;
- the expected date of placement;
- the date he wants to start his SPP;
- whether he wants SPP for one or two weeks; and
- the date the adopter was notified of being matched with a child.[131]

He must also provide a written declaration that:

- he is married to, or is the civil partner or partner of the adopter;
- he has responsibility for the child's upbringing;
- he wishes to take paternity leave and pay in order to care for the child or support the adopter;
- he has chosen to receive SPP (Adoption) and not SAP.[132]

A model self-certificate of entitlement to paternity leave and pay[133] is available on the HMRC website (www.hmrc.gov.uk) which an

---

127 SSCBA 1992 s171ZB(2) and (3).
128 SPP and SAP Regs 2002 reg 13(2).
129 SPP and SAP Regs 2002 reg 13(2) and (3).
130 SPP and SAP Regs 2002 reg 15(3).
131 SPP and SAP Regs 2002 reg 15(2).
132 SPP and SAP Regs 2002 reg 15(1).
133 Form SC4 Becoming an adoptive parent: SPP/Paternity Leave.

employee can use or he can provide all the information required above in writing.

9.128　If the employer asks, he must inform the employer of the date of the child's placement within 28 days or as soon as reasonably practicable.[134]

Working for two employers

9.129　SPP is still payable if an employee works for an employer from whom he does not qualify for SPP and he worked for that employer in the week the adopter was notified of being matched with a child.[135]

Disrupted placement

9.130　If the adopter is told that the adoption will not take place before paternity leave and pay has started, the employee will not be able to have leave or pay. If the child dies during the SPP period or the placement ends, he is entitled to continue to receive his paternity leave and pay.[136]

Overseas adoptions

9.131　The Paternity and Adoption Leave (Adoptions from Overseas) Regulations 2003[137] came into force in April 2003 and gave rights in respect of children adopted from overseas. These regulations modify the PAL Regs 2002. An adoption from overseas means the adoption of a child who enters Great Britain from outside the UK for adoption.[138] To qualify for adoption leave and pay, an employee who adopts from overseas must have received 'official notification'. This must be written notification issued by a domestic authority confirming that it is prepared to issue a certificate to the overseas authority concerned with the adoption, that the adopter is eligible to adopt and has been approved as being a suitable adoptive parent.[139]

9.132　The provisions in this chapter apply but with the following modifications for parents adopting a child from overseas. The DTI

134　SPP and SAP Regs 2002 reg 15(4).
135　SPP and SAP Regs 2002 reg 16.
136　The Help Book E16 (Special Cases) (2006) p20.
137　SI No 921.
138　PAL (Adoption from Overseas) Regs 2003 reg 4.
139　PAL (Adoption from Overseas) Regs 2003 reg 4.

produces a guide for employers and employees: *Adoptive parents: rights to leave and pay when a child is adopted from overseas.*[140]

Entitlement to adoption leave

9.133 A parent is entitled to OAL and AAL if she has been continuously employed for at least 26 weeks ending with the week in which she received official notification or 26 weeks from the start of her employment.[141] She can choose to start her OAL on the date the child enters Great Britain or a predetermined date no more than 28 days after the date the child enters Great Britain.[142]

9.134 An employee must give her employer notice within 28 days of receiving official notification or within 28 days of completing 26 weeks' continuous employment, whichever is later, stating:

- the date she received official notification;
- the date the child is expected to enter Great Britain.

She must give at least 28 days' notice before:

- the date she has chosen to start her leave.

Within 28 days of the child entering GB she must give notice stating:

- the date the child actually entered Great Britain[143]

The employer can ask for a copy of the official notification and evidence of the date the child entered Great Britain.

9.135 OAL can continue for up to eight weeks where the child dies or stops living with the adoptive parent. If it becomes known that the child will not enter Great Britain, the employee must notify the employer as soon as reasonably practicable.

Entitlement to adoption leave and pay on change of employment

9.136 It can take up to 18 months from receipt of official notification for a child to enter Great Britain. A former employer remains liable to pay SAP for up to six months after an employee has left or been

---

140 Also available on the DTI website www.dti.gov.uk/er/overseas.
141 PAL (Adoption from Overseas) Regs 2003 reg 9.
142 PAL (Adoption from Overseas) Regs 2003 reg 9.
143 PAL (Adoption from Overseas) Regs 2003 reg 9.

dismissed from her job providing she qualified for SAP and her adoption leave and pay starts within six months of leaving. If the SAP period does not start within six months of leaving, the Inland Revenue will pay SAP unless she qualifies with her new employer.[144]

> EXAMPLE: Meg has received official notification. She gives her employer notice within 28 days that she would like to take adoption leave and when she expects the child to arrive in Great Britain. Six months later she changes jobs. Once she has completed 26 weeks employment she has 28 days to give her new employer notice. If the child enters Great Britain before she completes 26 weeks' service with her new employer she will not be eligible for OAL and SAP. Her old employer remains liable for paying SAP up to six months after her old employment ended.

SAP

9.137 In addition to the notice above for OAL, an employee claiming SAP must give at least 28 days' notice of the date she wants her SAP to start. She must give her employer her name and address, a copy of the official notification at least 28 days before SAP starts and a declaration that she is claiming SAP not SPP. Within 28 days of the child entering Great Britain, she must provide evidence of entry, such as a plane ticket or copies of entry clearance documents.[145]

Paternity leave (adoption)

9.138 The adopter's spouse, civil partner or partner must have worked for at least 26 weeks ending with the week official notification was received or 26 weeks from the start of his employment. He must continue working up to the date the child enters Great Britain.

9.139   He can choose to start his leave on the date the child enters Great Britain or a chosen date within 56 days after the child enters Great Britain. Paternity leave must be completed within 56 days of the date the child entered Great Britain.

9.140   An employee must give his employer notice within 28 days of

---

144 SPP etc (Adoptions from Overseas) (No 2) Regs 2003 reg 17.
145 SPP etc (Adoptions from Overseas) (No 2) Regs 2003 reg 14.

receiving official notification or within 28 days of completing 26 weeks' continuous employment, stating:

- the date the adopter received official notification;
- the date the child is expected to enter Great Britain.

He must give at least 28 days' notice stating:

- the date he has chosen to start his leave; and
- whether he wishes to take one or two weeks.

Within 28 days of the child entering Great Britain he must give notice stating:

- the date the child actually entered Great Britain.[146]

9.141 If the employer asks for it, he must provide a written declaration that his partner, civil partner or spouse, has received official notification and he is married to, or the civil partner or partner of the child's adopter and has, or expects to have, responsibility for the child's upbringing.

SPP (adoption)

9.142 In addition to the notice for paternity leave above, an employee must give at least 28 days' notice of the date he wants his SPP to start.

9.143 He must give the following written declaration to his employer stating that:

- he is married to, or the civil partner or partner of the child's adopter;
- he is taking leave to care for the child or to support the adopter;
- his partner, civil partner or spouse has received official notification;
- he has or expects to have responsibility for the child's upbringing, and he has chosen to receive SPP and not SAP.[147]

146 PAL (Adoption from Overseas) Regs 2003 reg 7.
147 SPP etc (Adoptions from Overseas) (No 2) Regs 2003 reg 9.

Parental leave

Key points

- Each parent who is an employee and has one year's service with the employer is entitled to a total of 13 weeks' unpaid parental leave for each child under 5, or under 18 if disabled.
- Parental leave must be taken:
  - before the child is five; or
  - within five years of when s/he is placed for adoption; or
  - if the child is entitled to disability living allowance, before the child is 18.
- A default scheme sets out the detail of procedure where there is no workforce or collective agreement.
- Under the default scheme, a parent is only entitled to take a maximum of four weeks' parental leave in any one year in relation to the same child.
- It is unlawful to subject an employee to a detriment or dismiss him/her for taking parental leave.
- Parental leave is unpaid, although a parent taking time off might be entitled to claim means-tested benefits.
- It may be indirect sex discrimination to treat a woman less favourably because she has taken parental leave.

Background and statutory framework

10.1 Employees with one year's service can take unpaid parental leave of 13 weeks to look after a child (under 5, or under 18 if disabled) or make arrangements for the child's welfare. The European Parental Leave Directive (PLD)[1] has been implemented by the Employment Rights Act (ERA) 1996[2] and the Maternity and Parental Leave etc Regulations (MPL Regs) 1999.[3] There are explanatory leaflets published by the government.[4]

10.2 There are effectively three parts to the scheme. First, there are the basic legal minimum provisions covering amount of leave, definition

---

1 96/34. This directive also covers time off for dependants, see chapter 11.
2 ERA 1996 ss76 to 80.
3 SI No 3312 regs 13–22, Schs 1 and 2. Parallel regulations were introduced in Northern Ireland.
4 Parental leave: a guide for employers and employees URN No: 06.567. See www.dti.gov.uk/employment.

of parent and age of child in respect of whom leave may be taken. These can be improved on by agreement but cannot be reduced. Thus an employer cannot restrict parental leave to children of, say, three years old and younger, but could give it to parents of children over 5.

10.3   Secondly, subject to the statutory minimum set out above, workplaces can construct their own detailed scheme for how and when parental leave may be taken. This must be agreed through a collective or workforce agreement between employer and employee. The collective or workforce agreement can, unlike statutory maternity rights, be more *or less* favourable than the default provisions, which only apply in the absence of such an agreement (see para 10.37 onwards).

10.4   The default provisions, or fallback scheme (set out in a schedule to the regulations) form the third part of the scheme. If, and only if, they apply (ie, where there is no workplace scheme) they provide a further part of the legal minimum framework. They set out arrangements for how and when parental leave may be taken which may be improved on by agreement but cannot be reduced.[5]

10.5   There is nothing to stop an individual employee negotiating more favourable terms with the employer on a one-to-one basis. However, an individual agreement must not be less favourable than the default scheme.

Who is entitled to parental leave?

10.6   Only employees are entitled to take parental leave. An agency worker, bank nurse, casual worker or homeworker who is classified by his/her employer as 'self-employed' may, despite the label, be an employee but if s/he is not s/he will not be entitled to parental leave (see para 1.28 onwards for who is an employee). The right is available to all employees, male and female, irrespective of their hours of work, whether full-time or part-time, on a permanent or temporary contract. A limited number of employees are excluded from the protection of the ERA 1996 (see para 1.31).[6]

---

5   Except where there is a workforce or collective agreement in which case the default scheme would not apply anyway.
6   Members of the armed forces, share fishermen and women and the police.

Legal minimum provisions

10.7 An employee is entitled to take time off to care for his/her child if:

- s/he has at least one year's service with the same employer by the time s/he wants to take the leave; and
- the leave is for the purpose of caring for that child and either:
  - s/he has or expects to have responsibility for a child under 5; or
  - s/he has or expects to have parental responsibility for a child entitled to disability living allowance who is under 18; or
  - s/he is an adoptive parent who has had a child placed with her/ him for adoption.

10.8 Employees have the right to limited terms and conditions of employment during parental leave and a right to return to work, but not always to exactly the same job (see para 10.30 onwards).

Who has responsibility for the child?

10.9 To take parental leave the employee must have or expect to have parental responsibility. This means that leave may be taken to care for a child before the employee actually has parental responsibility, provided the employee expects to have it. The definition of parental responsibility is wider than under the Children Act (CA) 1989.[7] A person has responsibility for a child if:

- the employee has parental responsibility under the CA 1989. A mother and father (if married to the mother) and civil partner automatically have parental responsibility;
- an unmarried father has parental responsibility if he registered the birth jointly with the mother.[8] He can acquire parental responsibility either by entering into a legal agreement with the mother or through a court order;
- the employee has adopted a child, in which case parental responsibility is given from the date of placement;[9]

---

7 CA 1989 s3 (or Children (Scotland) Act 1995).
8 CA 1989 as amended by Adoption and Children Act 2002 s111.
9 Adoption and Children Act 2002 s25(3).

- the employee is a step-parent[10] and enters into an agreement with both natural parents or obtains a court order if this is not possible;[11]
- the employee is a guardian with parental responsibility.

10.10   A parent does not have to be living with the child to take parental leave as long as they have parental responsibility. Neither grandparents nor other carers are entitled to parental leave unless they have a parental responsibility order which is hard to acquire if the child does not live with them at least part of the time. However, the Department of Trade and Industry (DTI) says that it is good practice for employers to extend entitlement to parental leave to individuals with informal responsibility for looking after a child, such as grandparents, step-parents or long-term foster parents.

10.11   The employee needs a year's continuous service by the time s/he takes her/his parental leave, not by the time s/he applies to take it.[12] Absence from work because of sickness, pregnancy or temporary layoff do not break continuous employment. However, if an employee starts with a different employer s/he will have to wait a further year before s/he can take parental leave.

10.12   The DTI says that good practice employers can waive the one-year qualifying period if they so wish, or set a lower qualifying period. This may particularly help parents who are returning to the labour market and could help the employer attract more candidates for a vacancy.

The age of the child

10.13   An employee is only entitled to parental leave while his/her child is under 5,[13] unless:

- the child is placed for adoption, in which case parental leave can be taken for up to five years after the placement or up to the date of the child's 18th birthday, whichever is earlier.[14] Placement is the date the child is 'placed' in the family home prior to formal adoption, usually through an adoption agency.[15] Where a child is

---

10   CA 1989 s4A(1); see Civil Partnership Act 2004 s75 which amends section 4A to include civil partners aswell as persons married to the parent.
11   CA 1989 as amended by Adoption and Children Act 2002 s112; this is known as a parental responsibility order.
12   MPL Regs 1999 reg 13(1).
13   MPL Regs 1999 reg 15(1).
14   MPL Regs 1999 reg 15(1).
15   See DTI guidance para 2.4.

adopted but there is no placement, for example because a step-parent adopts a child, the period for taking parental leave starts when the step-parent acquires parental responsibility and ends on the child's fifth birthday;[16]

- the child is entitled to receipt of disability living allowance, in which case parental leave can be taken up to the date of the child's 18th birthday;[17]
- where the default scheme applies and the employer has postponed parental leave, in which case parental leave can be taken after the end of the period to which the leave was postponed (see below).[18]

The purpose of leave

10.14   The time must be taken to care for the child,[19] which may include, according to the DTI guidance:

- settling a child into new childcare or into a nursery or school;
- spending more time with the child;
- visiting new schools;
- accompanying a child during a stay in hospital;
- enabling the family to spend more time together.

10.15   However, if the default provisions apply (see below), parental leave cannot in practice be used for some of these occasions as it cannot be taken for a period of less than a week. If an employee needed to visit a new school s/he would have to take a whole week's parental leave for the sake of a short appointment. In practice it would be better for her/him to take half a day's holiday and take a week's parental leave during for example the summer holiday if necessary.

10.16   Note that if a child is suddenly sick or there is an emergency, the employee may be able to take a short period of dependants leave (see chapter 11).

Length of leave

10.17   The maximum leave an employee can take is 13 weeks in total per child unless the child qualifies for disability living allowance in which

---

16 See DTI guidance para 2.4.
17 MPL Regs 1999 reg 15(1)(b).
18 MPL Regs 1999 reg 15(4)(b), in which case entitlement to leave is exercisable until the end of the period to which the leave was postponed.
19 MPL Regs 1999 reg 13(1).

case the parent is entitled to 18 weeks.[20] The 13 weeks is per child which applies to each twin and where more than one child is adopted. The right is non-transferable between parents.

10.18   The clock does not start to run again if the employee changes jobs. Although employers are not obliged to keep records, a new employer may want to know how much parental leave the employee has taken so that it knows what remaining entitlement the employee has. Employers should not ask questions at the interview stage about how much parental leave an employee has taken as this might indicate an unwillingness to take on an employee with outstanding entitlement. This could be indirect discrimination if it impacts on female employees who are more likely to take such leave (see para 10.73).

10.19   If the default scheme applies, unless the employer agrees, or the child is entitled to disability living allowance, parental leave can only be taken one week at a time.[21] If the employee takes one day, this will count as one week (see also para 10.54 onwards). In *Rodway v South Central Trains Ltd*[22] the Court of Appeal held that parental leave under the statutory default scheme can only be taken for a minimum of one week or in blocks of weeks (see para 10.71).

10.20   A week is calculated as follows:

- Where an employee works the same hours each week, a week's leave will be the equivalent to these hours. Thus, if an employee works 16 hours per week, a week's leave will be 16 hours.[23]
- Where an employee's hours vary each week, or s/he works some weeks but not others, these hours will be calculated by averaging them out over 52 weeks.[24]
- If there is a workplace agreement (see para 10.39 below) and an employee takes leave of less than a week – calculated as above – s/he completes a week's leave when s/he has taken the period which is equivalent to a week's leave.[25] Note, however, that if the default provisions apply (see below) parental leave can only be

20   MPL Regs 1999 reg 14(1A).
21   MPL Regs 1999 Sch 1 para 7 which provides that an employee may not take parental leave in a period other than the period which constitutes a week's leave for him or a multiple of that period except in a case where the child is entitled to a disability living allowance.
22   [2005] IRLR 583.
23   MPL Regs 1999 reg 14(2).
24   MPL Regs 1999 reg 14(3).
25   MPL Regs 1999 reg 14(4).

taken one week at a time and odd days may not be taken (see para 10.54).

Terms and conditions during parental leave

10.21 These are the same as during additional maternity leave (AML) and additional adoption leave (AAL) (see chapters 5 and 9). The contract of employment continues, and the period of leave must be counted for the purposes of seniority, pension and simliar contractual and statutory rights. An employee is entitled to:

- the benefit of the employer's implied obligation to her/him of trust and confidence; and
- any terms and conditions of her/his employment relating to:
  - notice of the termination of the employment contract (the position in relation to paid notice is the same as for AML – see para 5.20);
  - compensation in the event of redundancy (although there is nothing in the legislation, the employee's salary for the purposes of calculating redundancy should be that received immediately before parental leave);
  - the disciplinary or grievance procedures.[26]

10.22 The employee is bound:

- by her/his implied obligation to the employer of good faith;
- any terms and conditions of her/his employment relating to:
  - notice of the termination of the employment contract by her/him;
  - the disclosure of confidential information;
  - the acceptance of gifts or other benefits; or
  - the employee's participation in any other business.[27]

10.23 Any other contractual matters are subject to agreement between the employer and employee so that the employee cannot expect to benefit from them just because they are in her/his contract unless the contract specifically provides for a continuation of terms during parental leave. In practice, if an employee takes a week's parental leave the employer is unlikely, for example, to require the company car to be returned for that week.

---

26 MPL Regs 1999 regs 17, 18 and 18A.
27 MPL Regs 1999 reg 17(b).

Holiday

10.24   Entitlement to paid annual holiday under the Working Time Regulations (WT Regs) 1998[28] accrues during parental leave in the same way as it does during AML (see para 5.95 onwards). Other contractual holiday entitlement does not accrue unless agreed between employer and employee.

Pensions

10.25   Any period of parental leave taken after April 2003 and not taken in association with AML or AAL must be counted for the purposes of pension rights, as if the employee had not been absent. Usually, employees on unpaid parental leave are not entitled to pension contributions from their employer. However, if it is a final salary scheme, as the employers' contributions depends on actuarial advice, not on the employee's earnings, the employer may have to continue making contributions to keep the fund at an appropriate level. In any event, if the leave is paid, the pension contributions must be paid but only on the amount of pay actually paid (unlike maternity leave where they are based on normal pay).[29] The employee is only liable to pay her/his contributions on the salary received during parental leave.

Bonuses

10.26   The statutory parental leave scheme does not cover bonuses. In practice, the employee will be entitled to a performance-related bonus for work done outside, but not generally during, the parental leave period.

10.27   In *Lewen v Denda*[30] the ECJ held that failure to pay a bonus to a woman on parental leave may be indirect sex discrimination because more women than men are likely to take parental leave. Whether a woman will be entitled to a bonus will depend on the nature of the bonus. The ECJ has held that it is not directly discriminatory to deny a woman on parental leave a Christmas bonus where the sole condition of the bonus was that the employee was in active employment at the time the bonus was awarded and it did not constitute retroactive

---

28   SI No 1833.
29   MPL Regs 1999 reg 18A. Social Security Act 1989 Sch 5 provides that during paid maternity and family leave the employee should be treated as working normally. The same provisions apply as for any part of paid AML (see paras 5.113–5.114).
30   [2000] IRLR 67, ECJ.

pay for work performed. However, if the bonus relates to work done outside the parental leave period, the employee should receive an amount proportionate to the period s/he worked and failure to pay this may be indirect sex discrimination (see para chapter 13). The purpose of the bonus and period to which it relates is therefore crucial. Note that a man would not be able to argue indirect discrimination (as parental leave is mainly taken by women), but if a woman was given a bonus whilst on parental leave it would be direct discrimination to refuse to pay a man in similar circumstances on parental leave.

Redundancy while on parental leave

10.28 Where a redundancy situation arises during the employee's parental leave, s/he should be treated in the same way as any other employee. S/he must not be selected for redundancy because s/he is on parental leave and s/he must be consulted like every other employee. If s/he is selected because of his/her absence on parental leave, s/he would have a claim for automatic unfair dismissal and a female employee might have a claim for indirect sex discrimination. There is no automatic entitlement to a suitable alternative job for an employee who is on parental leave.[31]

Promotion opportunities

10.29 Apart from the decision in *Lewen v Denda*[32] (see para 10.27), there have been no cases looking at the extent to which a parent on parental leave is protected from discrimination. However, s/he must not be discriminated against directly or indirectly on the grounds of sex or marital status and it is advisable for employers to ensure that employees on parental leave are informed of any jobs that become available so that they are not disadvantaged because of their absence on parental leave (see para 10.69). Failure to do so may be a detriment or discrimination or, if she resigns, constructive unfair dismissal.

---

31 MPL Regs 1999 reg 10 and 18(4).
32 [2000] IRLR 67, ECJ.

Right to return after parental leave

Parental leave of four weeks or less except immediately after AML

10.30   An employee who takes parental leave for a period of four weeks or less, except where it is taken immediately after AML or AAL, is entitled to return from leave to the job in which s/e was employed before her/his absence. This also applies where parental leave of four weeks or less is taken immediately after OML, OAL, paternity leave (but not AML, AAL or parental leave of more than four weeks).[33] The position is the same as returning from OML[34] (see para 4.65).

Parental leave of more than four weeks

10.31   Where an employee takes parental leave of:

- more than four weeks (whether or not preceded by any other statutory leave);[35] or
- a period of four weeks or less following AML or AAL,

s/he is entitled to return to the job in which s/he was employed before her/his parental leave, or, if it is not reasonably practicable for the employer to permit her/him to return to that job, to another job which is:

- suitable for her/him; and
- appropriate for her/him to do in the circumstances.[36]

These provisions are exactly the same as a woman's entitlement after AML (see para 4.68 onwards).

10.32   The onus is on the employer to show that it is not reasonably practicable for the employee to return to the same job.

10.33   An employee may therefore want to take a maximum of four weeks' parental leave at any one time to maintain her/his entitlement to return to the same job. Under the default scheme s/he will only be able to take four weeks in any one year in relation to the same child. It is not clear whether, if a woman takes eight weeks in relation to two children (or 12 weeks for three children), this counts as four weeks

---

33   MPL Regs 1999 reg 18(1).
34   'Job' is defined under regulation 2(1) as being the nature of the work that the employee is employed to do in accordance with the contract and capacity and place in which the employee is employed.
35   Which could be OML, OAL, AML, AAL, paternity leave.
36   MPL Regs 1999 reg 18(2) and (3).

per child and so she therefore maintains her right to return to the same job. Arguably, it should and if an employee is concerned about her/his job changing, it would be better to take only four weeks at a time in relation to each child.[37]

10.34 Whether the employee is returning to the same job or a suitable and appropriate alternative job, the right to return is to return on terms and conditions not less favourable than those which would have applied if the employee had not been on parental leave. MPL Regs 1999 reg 18A provides that the employee's right to return is:

- with her seniority, pension rights and similar rights; and
- on terms and conditions not less favourable than those which would have applied if she had not been absence.

Any changes that took place during parental leave will apply to the employee. Parental leave must be included when calculating service for seniority, pensions or other simliar rights, whether statutory or contractual.

No notice required for return from parental leave

10.35 Under the default scheme, an employee must give notice of the start and length of parental leave. There is no need to give notice of the date of return. If the employee is sick following parental leave s/he should be treated in the same way as any other sick employee and not treated less favourably because the sickness follows from a period of parental leave.

Protection from detriment or dismissal

10.36 An employee who takes parental leave has protection from dismissal and from being subjected to a detriment (see chapter 15).

Collective and workplace agreements

10.37 Although an employer cannot reduce the legal minimum require-ments set out above, other contractual arrangements may be more or less favourable than the default provisions (see para 10.43), provided

---

37 There is no reason why a period of holiday should not be taken, if agreed between employer and employee, between two periods of parental leave.

they are made via a collective or workforce agreement which complies with the statutory requirements. The agreement applies instead of the default provisions. So, for example, the agreement may allow employees to book and take their parental leave in exactly the same way as they make holiday arrangements.

10.38   A collective agreement is negotiated between an employer and an independent trade union or other representative body (in accordance with Trade Union and Labour Relations (Consolidation) Act 1992 s178).[38]

10.39   A workforce agreement is an agreement between an employer and employees or their representatives, where the following conditions are satisfied:[39]

• the agreement is in writing;[40]
• it has effect for a specified period not exceeding five years;[41]
• it applies to all relevant members of the workforce or to all relevant members of the workforce who belong to a particular group;[42]
• the agreement is signed by representatives of the workforce (or the relevant group)[43] or, where there are 20 or fewer employees, either the appropriate representatives or a majority of employees; and
• before the agreement was signed the employer has provided all employees to whom the agreement is to apply, with copies of the agreement and guidance so they can understand it.

The requirements concerning elections of representatives must satisfy the following conditions, namely:

– the number of representatives must be determined by the employer;
– candidates must be relevant members of the workforce (or group);
– no employee should be excluded from standing;
– all relevant members must be entitled to vote for as many candidates as there are representatives to be elected;

---

38 MPL Regs 1999 reg 2(1). The details are outside the scope of this book.
39 MPL Regs 1999 Sch 1.
40 MPL Regs 1999 Sch 1 para 1(a).
41 MPL Regs 1999 Sch 1 para 1(b).
42 MPL Regs 1999 Sch 1 para 1(c).
43 Group refers to employees doing particular work or those at a particular workforce or a unit within the business (Sch 1 para 2).

– the election is conducted to ensure, if reasonably practicable, that voting is in secret and the votes are fairly and accurately counted.[44]

10.40 Workforce representatives have protection from detriment and dismissal as a result of their activities or functions.

10.41 Collective and workforce agreements must be incorporated into an employee's contract.

10.42 In order to displace the default scheme, the employee's contract of employment must include a provision which:

- gives entitlement to parental leave in order to care for a child; and
- incorporates or operates by reference to all or part of a collective agreement or workforce agreement.[45]

This means that existing employees will have to agree to the terms of the agreement unless their contract provides for automatic incorporation of a term negotiated on their behalf.

The default provisions

10.43 The default provisions, or fallback scheme, apply where the employee's contract of employment does not include a provision which:

- gives entitlement to absence for the caring of a child (ie, parental leave); and
- incorporates or operates by reference to a collective or workforce agreement.[46]

Thus, where there is entitlement to parental leave in the employee's contract and the contract either incorporates or operates by reference to such an agreement, the default scheme does not apply.

10.44 MPL Regs 1999 Sch 2 sets out the default provisions that cover:

- evidence requirements;
- notice requirements;
- length of leave to be taken at any one time;
- postponement of leave.

44 MPL Regs 1999 Sch 1 para 3. Note that these provisions are very similar to those relating to the provisions on workforce agreements on working time.
45 MPL Regs 1999 reg 16.
46 MPL Regs 1999 reg 16(a),(b).

Evidence

10.45 The employer may require reasonable evidence of:

- the employee's responsibility or expected responsibility for the child;
- the child's date of birth, or date on which the placement began; or
- where appropriate, the child's entitlement to disability living allowance.[47]

10.46 The employee must provide this information which may include, for example, birth certificate, parental responsibility order or adoption papers. This kind of proof is not always available, of course, since the baby may not yet have been born. Failure to provide information that is reasonably required means that the employee is not entitled to parental leave.

Notice requirements

10.47 Except where the father is taking leave at the time of the birth or the child is being placed for adoption, the notice (which need not be in writing) must:

- specify the dates on which the leave is to begin and end; and
- be given at least 21 days before the beginning of the leave.

Parental leave cannot be taken unless the correct notice is given.

10.48 Where the father is to take leave from the date of the child's birth, the notice must:

- specify the expected week of childbirth and duration of leave; and
- be given to the employer at least 21 days before the beginning of the expected week of childbirth.[48]

10.49 Parental leave should then be able to start on the day the child is born, even if the baby is early or late so the employer does not have exact notice of the date. In this case, the father should produce a copy of the maternity certificate, the Mat B1, as proof of his expected parental responsibility.

---

47 MPL Regs 1999 Sch 2 para 1(a).
48 MPL Regs 1999 Sch 2 para 4.

10.50   Where the child is to be placed for adoption and the leave is to be taken on the date of the placement, the notice must:

- specify the week in which the placement is expected to occur;
- give duration of the leave; and
- be given to the employer at least 21 days before the beginning of the expected week of placement, or, if that is not reasonably practicable, as soon as is reasonably practicable.[49]

10.51   Again, the employee need not take leave to be present when the child is placed for adoption at exactly the time given in the notice; the time may be taken when it is necessary to take it, ie the date of placement if it occurs earlier or later than anticipated.

10.52   An employee may want to take parental leave after paternity leave. However, he will then have to give 21 days' notice of the specific start and end dates. The flexibility around the start of parental leave only applies where parental leave is due to start on the date of birth or placement.

10.53   Note that parental leave cannot be postponed by the employer where fathers are taking leave at the time of the birth or in respect of either adoptive parent where leave is taken at the time of placement even if the actual event does not take place on the planned date.

Periods of leave

10.54   Parental leave must be taken either a week at a time or in multiples of a week. Thus, under the default scheme, it is not possible to take a day or two at a time, unless the child is in receipt of a disability living allowance when it may be taken a day at a time or in multiples of less than a week.[50] If an employee takes only two days it will still be treated as a week, unless the child is entitled to disability living allowance.

10.55   Note that in some situations an employee who needs only a day off may be able to take dependants leave and there is no minimum period of notice as it is intended to cover unforeseen events (see chapter 11). However, situations such as school visits or pre-arranged hospital appointments almost certainly do not merit dependants leave so that the employee would need to take a whole week's leave for the sake of a few hours off. The only practical option would be for the employee to take holiday at a time when s/he might otherwise

49 MPL Regs 1999 Sch 2 para 5.
50 This is now clear from the Court of Appeal decision in *Rodway*. See para 10.71.

take parental leave, as this can usually be taken a day at a time. Parental leave could then be taken when the employee might otherwise have taken a longer holiday. However, the parental leave must be for the purpose of caring for a child under 5.

10.56　An employee may not take more than four weeks' leave in respect of any child during a particular year.[51] Thus, if an employee has three children under 5, s/he can take 12 weeks in the year.

10.57　A year runs from the date on which the employee first became entitled to take parental leave in respect of the child in question. If the employee's entitlement has been interrupted at the end of a period of continuous employment, the year runs from the date on which the employee most recently became entitled to take parental leave.[52] Thus the year will run from a different date for each employee.

Postponement of leave

10.58　In the case of parental leave, which is *not* taken by the father at the time of the birth or by either parent at the time of placement for adoption, an employer may postpone a period of parental leave to a period no later than six months later. This may be done where the employer considers that 'the operation of his business would be unduly disrupted if the employee took leave during the period identified in his notice'.

10.59　Where the employer postpones the leave, s/he must:

- within seven days of the employee's notice to the employer, give the employee notice in writing of the postponement, stating the reason and giving the dates when the leave can be taken. These dates may include a period after the child's fifth birthday but must be before the child's 18th birthday.
- allow the employee to take leave of the same length no later than six months after the leave was due to commence. The employer can decide the date but must consult the employee.[53]

10.60　The employee would therefore be advised not to commit to any arrangement such as an expensive holiday until the seven days have elapsed. The problem with this is that if s/he has only given 21 days' notice s/he will then only have 14 days to make arrangements, which

---

51　MPL Regs 1999 Sch 2 para 8.
52　MPL Regs 1999 Sch 2 para 9.
53　MPL Regs 1999 Sch 2 para 6.

may be inadequate time. The way round this is for the employee to give notice for parental leave well in advance if possible. If the employer does not give notice postponing the leave seven days later, the employee can take the leave as planned. There is no provision in the default scheme for more than one postponement.

10.61　The DTI guidance gives examples of when an employer may want to postpone leave:

- when there is a peak in work;
- where a significant proportion of the workforce asks for parental leave at the same time;
- where the employee's role is such that her/his absence at the time would unduly harm the business.

10.62　Where an employer has unreasonably postponed leave, the employee can complain to a employment tribunal. The tribunal will then balance the needs of the employer and the business against those of the employee. If the employee takes that leave anyway and is dismissed s/he may also have a claim for automatically unfair dismissal. However, if the postponement was reasonable it will not be an automatically unfair dismissal, though, depending on the circumstances, it may be an ordinary unfair dismissal.

Record keeping

10.63　There is no obligation on employers to keep records though, in practice, they are likely to want to do so.

Individual agreement

10.64　Where the default provisions apply, they act as a legal minimum set of rules. There is still, however, room for individual agreement between employer and employee but only to the extent that the individual agreement provides more favourable rights.[54] This is confirmed by paragraph 3.8 of the DTI guidance. The provisions are the same as the composite rights in relation to maternity leave (see para 4.96).

54　MPL Regs 1999 reg 21.

Rights and remedies

Postponement/refusal of parental leave

10.65   An employee can, within three months, make a complaint to a tribunal that the employer has:

- unreasonably postponed a period of parental leave; or
- prevented or attempted to prevent the employee from taking parental leave.[55]

10.66   The statutory grievance procedure does not apply to a claim for breach of any of the statutory rights to parental leave. However, it does apply to claims for detriment (as a result of taking or seeking to take parental leave) and constructive dismissal, whether automatically unfair, ordinary unfair or discriminatory.

10.67   The tribunal, if it upholds the complaint, must make a declaration to that effect and may award such compensation as is 'just and equitable' having regard to the employer's behaviour and the loss suffered.[56]

10.68   The DTI guidance states that the employee should first try and resolve the matter with the employer. This will include using any grievance or appeal procedure. Note, however, that an employee should not miss the three-month time limit. The statutory grievance procedure does not apply so time is not extended (see chapter 16).

Dismissal and detriment

10.69   It is unlawful to subject to a detriment or where the reason or principal reason for dismissal is because:

- the employee took or sought to take parental leave; or
- refused to sign a workforce agreement; or
- carried out (or proposed to carry out) any activities as a workforce representative or candidate in an election to be a representative.[57]

10.70   'Detriment' is widely interpreted and covers any disadvantage but it must be related to the taking of parental leave.

10.71   In *South Central Trains Ltd v Rodway*[58] the claimant sought to take

---

55   ERA 1996 s80(1).
56   ERA 1996 s80(4).
57   ERA 1996 s99; MPL Regs 1999 reg 20(e),(f) (dismissal); ERA 1996 s47C; and MPL Regs 1999 reg 19(e),(f) (detriment).
58   [2005] IRLR 583.

one day's parental leave to look after his child and argued that he was subjected to a detriment when he was disciplined after he took the day off anyway when permission was refused. The Court of Appeal held that he was only entitled to take parental leave for a minimum of one week in the absence of any workforce agreement providing to the contrary. As the claimant was not entitled to take one day's parental leave, but had to take five days, the subsequent disciplinary action taken against him was lawful (see also chapter 15 on dismissal and detriment).

Sex discrimination

10.72 Where a woman is treated less favourably than a man, or vice versa, in relation to parental leave, s/he may have a claim for direct sex discrimination if the employee is treated less favourably on grounds of her or his sex. The parental leave provisions should be the same for men and women.

10.73 There may be circumstances where a woman can claim indirect sex discrimination. It is likely that a significantly larger proportion of women than men will take parental leave and this was recognised in *Lewen v Denda*[59] (see para 5.87). Indirect discrimination is covered in chapter 13 and similar principles will apply. The provision, criteria, practice or requirement will be 'not to take parental leave' or 'not to be absent on parental leave' or 'not to take family-related time off'.

Dismissal for asserting a statutory right

10.74 An employee who is dismissed because s/he exercised or tried to exercise the right to parental leave, may have a claim under ERA 1996 s104. The dismissal will be automatically unfair if the principal reason for dismissal was that:

- the employee brought proceedings to enforce the right to parental leave; or
- the employee alleged that the employer had infringed her/his right, although following *Rodway* this right only applies to requests for parental leave in multiples of a week where there is no workforce agreement.

This is covered in para 15.22.

59 [2000] IRLR 67, ECJ.

CHAPTER 11

Time off for dependants

Key points

- An employee can take time off to care or arrange care for a dependant where:
  - the dependant is ill, injured, assaulted, gives birth or dies;
  - arrangements for the care of a dependant break down;
  - there is an unexpected incident involving a child at school.
- A 'dependant' includes a spouse, civil partner, child, parent, person living in the same household as the employee (other than as an employee, tenant, lodger).
- The time off is unpaid.
- The employee is allowed 'a reasonable amount of time off'.
- An employee who takes time off is protected against dismissal and detriment.

Background and statutory framework

11.1   The Parental Leave Directive (PLD)[1] introduced the right to unpaid dependants leave. The PLD refers to 'time off from work on grounds of *force majeure*', saying it is (along with parental leave) 'an important means of reconciling work and family life and promoting equal opportunities and treatment between men and women'. The right is to reasonable time off to deal with certain unexpected or sudden emergencies and to make any longer term arrangements (see Department of Trade and Industry (DTI) guidance).

11.2   The right is contained in Employment Rights Act (ERA) 1996 ss57A and 57B. The DTI guidance can be obtained from their website. Although the provisions enable an employee to take time off to look after dependants other than children and women giving birth, these are not covered in detail in this chapter.

Who is entitled to time off?

11.3   Only employees are entitled to take time off for dependants. An agency worker, bank nurse, casual worker or homeworker who is classified by her/his employer as 'self-employed' may, in fact, be an

---

1   96/34. This was implemented by Employment Relations Act 1999 s8 and Sch 4 Part II which inserted sections 57A and 57B into ERA 1996.

employee, but if s/he is not s/he will not be entitled to time off (see para 1.28 for who is an employee). The right is available to all employees, male and female, irrespective of their hours of work, whether full-time or part-time, on a permanent or temporary contract. There is no qualifying period, so the right to time off is available from day one of starting a job.

11.4   A limited number of employees are excluded from the right to time off for dependants under the ERA 1996 (see para 1.31).[2]

What events are covered?

11.5   The right is to take 'a reasonable amount of time off during the employee's working hours in order to take action which is necessary in five specified circumstances set out below.

(a) 'to provide assistance on an occasion when a dependant falls ill, gives birth or is injured or assaulted'[3]

11.6   This applies where a dependant, such as a child, is ill or has been injured. The DTI guidance says that the illness need not necessarily be serious or life-threatening, and may be mental or physical. It may also apply as a result of a deterioration of an existing condition. In *Morancie v PVC Vendo plc*[4] the claimant had to take her one-year-old daughter to hospital and stayed with her overnight until the Monday. She said she hoped to return to work Wednesday or Thursday but was dismissed on Monday afternoon. The tribunal held that the claimant's presence was necessary to provide assistance as defined by ERA 1996 s57A(1)(a).

11.7   Where necessary an employee can also take time off to help a dependant when she is having a baby. This does not include taking time off after the birth to care for the child and this would be covered by parental leave if the employee is entitled to parental leave (see chapter 10). Time off for dependants would be useful if the employee either did not qualify for parental leave or had not given enough notice to entitle him/her to be present at the birth.

---

2   Those employed in armed forces (ERA 1996 s192), share fishing (ERA 1996 s199(2)) and the police (ERA 1996 s200).
3   ERA 1996 s57A(1)(a).
4   ET Case No 3300938/01.

11.8   In *Qua v John Ford Morrison Solicitors*[5] the Employment Appeal Tribunal (EAT) said that the provisions do not enable employees to take time off in order themselves to provide care for a sick child, beyond the reasonable amount necessary to enable them to deal with the immediate crisis. Leave to provide longer-term care would be covered by parental leave entitlement (see chapter 10). The EAT also said that an employee is not entitled to unlimited amounts of time off work under this section, but only time to deal with a child who is ill unexpectedly, ie, where it is unforeseen. Once it is known that the child is suffering from an underlying medical condition, which is likely to cause him to suffer regular relapses, it does not fall within ERA 1996 s57A. Whether the condition is such that a relapse is fore-seeable – so not unexpected – will be a question for the tribunal to decide.

11.9   The disruption to the business caused by the absence is not rele-vant. The right is to time off to deal with the unexpected.

(b) Time off 'to make arrangements for the provision of care for a dependant who is ill or injured'

11.10   This is to enable a parent to make longer-term arrangements for the care of a dependant, such as employing a temporary carer or taking a sick child to stay with relatives.[6] It would cover making care arrange-ments for an elderly parent.[7] There is likely to be an overlap between (a) and (b). In many situations, the employee may need to do both. For example, a child with a cold may be left with a carer but if s/he develops a high fever, this may require the parent to take time off at least until the fever is under control. Alternatively, a child may be very ill and need a parent during the serious illness but during the period of recovery could be looked after by another carer.

11.11   If a child is likely to be ill for a substantial period, the parent should try to make arrangements for care, provided the child is well enough to be left with a carer. For example, a child with chicken pox may be very ill for the first few days but then be in quarantine. It may be reasonable for the parent to stay with the child while s/he is very ill but s/he will then need to make arrangements for the week or so of quarantine.

5   [2003] IRLR 184.
6   ERA 1996 s57A(1)(b).
7   See *MacCulloch & Wallis Ltd v Moore* [2003] UKEAT 51/02 11 February 2003.

11.12　It is not clear how much time off would be reasonable, but the PLD talks about the entitlement applying in cases of 'force majeure'[8] so that on-going pre-planned care such as a hospital appointment would probably not be permitted as time off for dependants. This is problematical, as it would not be possible to take parental leave for the appointment. The only option may be to take holiday.

11.13　There is nothing in the legislation that requires a medical certificate to show that the child is ill. If the employee has asked for a lengthy period of time off where the child is very ill, it may not be unreasonable for the employer to ask for a doctor's certificate or letter as to the length of the illness in order to establish that it is still necessary to allow the time off. The DTI guidance states that employers who think that an employee is abusing the right to time off should deal with the situation according to their normal disciplinary procedures, which would include asking for a doctor's certificate or letter.

(c) To take action 'in consequence of the death of a dependant'[9]

11.14　The guidance states that time off to make funeral arrangements and attending the funeral would be covered. The DTI guidance says that if the funeral is overseas, then the employer and employee will need to agree a length of absence that is reasonable in the circumstances.[10]

(d) 'Because of the unexpected disruption or termination of arrangements for the care of a dependant'[11]

11.15　The DTI guidance says that time off can be taken where the normal carer of the dependant is unexpectedly absent, for example if the

8　Clause 3(1) which refers to 'on grounds of *force majeure* for urgent family reasons in cases of sickness or accident making the immediate presence of the worker indispensable'.

9　ERA 1996 s57A(1)(c).

10　See, for example, *Forster v Cartwright Black Solicitors* [2004] UKEAT 0179 25 June 2004 where the EAT quoted Lord Sainsbury in the debates who said: 'We intend the right to apply where a dependant becomes sick or has an accident, or is assaulted, including where the victim is distressed rather than physically injured. It provides for reasonable time off if an employee suffers a bereavement of a family member, to deal with the consequences of that bereavement, such as making funeral arrangements, as well as to take time off to attend the funeral.'

11　ERA 1996 s57A(1)(d).

childminder fails to turn up or the nursery is unexpectedly closed.[12] This should also cover a situation where, for example, the other parent, who is normally the carer, is ill or suddenly leaves the family. In *Giles v Tyco Healthcare UK Ltd*[13] the claimant's son was ill and could not go to his childminder. The employer refused time off unless the claimant made it up in the evening. She could not do this as she needed to be at home with her son, so she resigned. The tribunal held this was a breach of ERA 1996 s57A and upheld her unfair constructive dismissal claim.

(e) 'To deal with an incident which involves a child of the employee and which occurs unexpectedly in a period during which an educational establishment which the child attends is responsible for him[14]

11.16 This only covers a child or adopted child. The DTI guidance says that an employee can take time off to deal with a serious incident involving his/her child during school hours. For example, if the child has been involved in a fight, is distressed, or is being suspended from school.

Who is a dependant?[15]

11.17 A 'dependant' is a spouse, a civil partner, a child, a parent, or a person living in the same household as the employee, other than his/her employee, tenant, lodger or boarder.[16] It covers, for example:

- unmarried partners including same sex partners;
- children, including those who are not the employee's children but who live in the same house, such as step-children whatever their age;
- an elderly relative who lives in the employee's household, such as a grandparent or aunt/uncle.

11.18 For the purposes of (a) or (b) above (sickness or injury of dependant),

12 See *Qua* para 16.
13 ET Case No 1701470/01.
14 ERA 1996 s57A(1)(e).
15 ERA 1996 s57A(3)–(6).
16 ERA 1996 s57A(3).

'dependant' also includes, in addition, 'any person who reasonably relies on the employee':

- for assistance when the person falls ill, is injured or assaulted;
- to make arrangements for the provision of care in the event of illness or injury.[17]

11.19   For the purposes of (d) (disruption of care arrangements), 'dependant' includes a person who reasonably relies on the employee to make arrangements for the provision of care.[18]

11.20   For the purposes of (e) (incidents at school), only a child, including an adopted child, is a dependant.

How much time off is allowed?

11.21   An employee is allowed a 'reasonable amount of time during the employee's working hours in order to take action which is necessary'.[19] In *Qua* the EAT held that factors to be taken into account will include:

- the nature of the incident which has occurred;
- the closeness of the relationship between the employee and the dependant;
- the extent to which anyone else was available to help out.

11.22   There is no maximum period of time that is reasonable in any particular circumstances as this will depend on:

- the individual circumstances;
- the number and length of previous absences, as well as the dates when they occurred.

11.23   The employer should take account of the employee's individual circumstances. For example, there may be times where it would be reasonable to allow one employee more time off than another, even though both employees' children have the same illness. Thus, where a child is cared for by a childminder or goes to a nursery, it may not be possible to leave him/her with the childminder or nursery if s/he has conjunctivitis or is recovering from chicken pox, as they are highly infectious. However, where the employee employs a nanny who does

---

17   ERA 1996 s57A(4).
18   ERA 1996 s57(5).
19   ERA 1996 s57A(1).

not look after other children, there is no reason why the nanny cannot continue to care for the child. It will be a question of fact and what is 'reasonable' in every situation.

11.24 The problem is that arranging childcare for a sick child may be expensive as the parent is likely to have to continue paying the child-minder or nursery in order to keep the place. The better paid parent is likely to be able to afford to make such arrangements, but the lower paid employee may find this difficult or impossible. Arguably, the employer should take this into account when deciding what is 'reasonable' time off. For example, in *Darlington v Allders of Croydon*[20] the claimant's 11-year-old daughter had a fractured skull so had to stay at home for five weeks to ensure she had no bumps. The claimant, having had two weeks' unpaid 'domestic leave', asked for a further two to three weeks, but was refused and she was dismissed. The tribunal held that since the claimant had no friends or family who could help with caring for her daughter and no resources to employ replcement childcare, the refusal of the request for further time was unreasonable. As this was the principal reason for her dismisal, it was automatically unfair.

11.25 There is no formal limit on the number of occasions the employee can take time off, as the question is whether it is reasonable on each occasion. However, if the dependant has an underlying medical condition as a result of which s/he is ill periodically, the employer can take into account the number and length of previous absence in deciding what is reasonable. In such circumstances, the employee may be expected to make appropriate care arrangements to avoid having to take time off.

11.26 The DTI guidance says that there may be times when both parents should be able to take time off work at the same time. This might be, for example, where the child was having an operation, had an accident or was very ill. It would not be reasonable for both parents to take time off if the childminder was ill.

11.27 The guidance also says that in most cases one or two days should be sufficient to deal with the problem, though this will depend on individual circumstances.[21] It may not be possible to arrange alterna-

---

20 ET Case No 230421/01.
21 See also *Qua* where the EAT said that in the vast majority of cases, no more than a few hours or, at most, one or possibly two days would be regarded as reasonable to deal with the particular problem which has arisen. However, the EAT said it was not possible to specify maximum periods of time which are reasonable in any particular circumstances.

tive childcare in one or two days, particularly for families on low incomes. If the child is under 5, a parent may be able to take parental leave, though if 21 days' notice is required this will be difficult.

Notification duties

11.28 It will often not be possible to tell the employer in advance, but if the employee is at work s/he should generally be able to tell the employer before leaving. If this is not feasible, because, for example, a child becomes sick during the night, the employee must tell his/her employer the reason for his/her absence as soon as reasonably practicable and tell the employer for how long s/he expects to be absent. The notice need not be in writing.[22]

11.29 Normally, it will be possible to inform the employer of the reason for the absence without delay. The guidance suggests that there would have to be exceptional circumstances before it would be considered not reasonably practicable to contact the employer until the employee's return. Although not mentioned in the guidance, this could be where the employee had to take the child to casualty and could not easily telephone, but then returned to work after leaving the child with the other parent.

11.30 In *Qua* the EAT held that there is no continuing duty on an employee to update the employer as to her situation.[23]

11.31 In *Truelove v Safeway Stores plc*[24] the claimant told the employer that there was no one to look after his daughter the following day. EAT held that this indicated a clear expression to the employer of a reason why he would be absent. It was not necessary for the 'reason' in ERA 1996 s57A(2) to be articulated with any formality. There must be a communication which imparts an understanding into the mind of the respondent that something has happened to cause what would otherwise be a stable arrangement affecting a child and making it necessary for the employee to leave work.

11.32 Failure to give appropriate notice means that the employer can treat the leave as any other unauthorised leave. However, if the employer wrongly decides that inadequate notice has been given, this may amount to a detriment or unreasonable refusal of time off.

22 ERA 1996 s57A(2).
23 *Qua v John Morrisons Solicitors* [2003] IRLR 184.
24 UKEAT/0295/04 1 November 2004. The EAT applied *Qua*.

Ultimately, only the ET will be the judge of this. An employee can complain to an ET that her/his employer has unreasonably refused time off.[25]

Reasonable refusal?

11.33 It may be reasonable to refuse time off if the employee's spouse or partner is not working and is available to care for the child. However, it will depend on the circumstances and this might not apply if, for example, the spouse or partner had a job interview or the child needed his/her mother because s/he was ill and needed breastfeeding. However, if possible, an employer may expect the other parent to share in the care of a child, even if working, though this may depend on the nature of both parents' jobs.

11.34 If the condition of the dependant changes, the employee should make this clear if further time off is requested. For example, in *MacCulloch & Wallis Ltd v Moore*[26] the claimant was dismissed without notice after she told her employer that she would be away for a further week as her father was in hospital, though at the time she informed them he was apparently not critically ill. The employer told her, on the Friday, that if she was not back by the Monday it was likely she would be dismissed with immediate effect. The respondents did not accept that she was entitled to the time off, so she was dismissed for taking unpermitted time off. The condition of the claimant's father deteriorated further over the weekend and as a result he died the following Friday. The EAT held that the tribunal was wrong to say that where circumstances change an extension to a previous permitted period can be taken without notice, as the employer should have been informed of the change in his circumstances. However, because the tribunal did not consider whether, when the time off was requested (on the Friday), time was necessary to provide assistance, it was remitted to another tribunal. Further, it was acknowledged that if the employer had been informed that the father's condition was so much worse on the Monday, it may have reacted differently.

---

25 ERA 1996 s57B.
26 See note 7 above.

Rights and remedies

Refusal of time off

11.35 Where the employee complains that the employer has unreasonably refused her/him time off[27] the ET can:

- make a declaration that the complaint is well-founded;
- award compensation which is 'just and equitable', having regard to the employer's default in refusing to allow time off and any loss sustained by the employee.

Automatically and ordinary unfair dismissal

11.36 It will be automatically unfair to dismiss an employee (or select her/ him for redundancy) if the only principal reason is that s/he sought to take or took time off for dependants leave (see para 15.58).[28] It may also be an ordinary unfair dismissal.

11.37 For example, if in response to being told that an employee cannot attend work because her husband walked out on her and there is no one to look after the children, the employer dismisses her, this will be automatically unfair.

11.38 In *Qua v John Morrison Solicitors* the EAT held that when determining whether the reason for an employee's dismissal was that she had taken, or had sought to take, time off under ERA 1996 s57A, the tribunal should ask the following questions:

1) Did the claimant take time off or seek to take time off from work during her working hours? If so, on how many occasions and when?

2) If so, on each of those occasions did the claimant (a) as soon as reasonably practicable inform her employer of the reason for her absence; and (b) inform him how long she expected to be absent; (c) if not, were the circumstances such that she could not inform him of the reason until after she had returned to work?

3) If the claimant had complied with these requirements then the following questions arise:
   a) Did she take or seek to take time off work in order to take action which was necessary to deal with one or more of the five situations listed at paragraphs (a) to (e) of subsection (1)?

---

27 ERA 1996 s57B.
28 ERA 1996 s99 and Maternity and Parental Leave etc Regulations 1999 SI No 3312 reg 20.

b) If so, was the amount of time off taken or sought to be taken reasonable in the circumstances?

4) If the claimant satisfied questions (3)(a) and (b), was the reason or principal reason for her dismissal that she had taken/sought to take that time off work?

If the tribunal answers that final question in the affirmative, then the claimant is entitled to a finding of automatic unfair dismissal.[29]

11.39   If the claimant had not complied with the requirements, the right to take time off work does not apply, the absences would be unauthorised and the dismissal would not be automatically unfair. There may be a claim for ordinary unfair dismissal. In *Rodway* the claimant had not complied with the conditions for taking parental leave which is why it was found that the action taken against him was not unlawful (see para 10.71).

Detriment

11.40   Employees must not be subjected to a detriment for taking time off.

11.41   'Detriment' means putting at a disadvantage (for example, being given a warning, a reduction in pay, refusal of training etc). Detriment is explained in more detail in chapter 15.

Dismissal for asserting a statutory right under ERA 1996 s104

11.42   If an employee is dismissed because s/he tried to take time off this may be a breach of ERA 1996 s104. It makes the dismissal automatically unfair if the reason or principal reason for the dismissal was that:

- the employee brought proceedings against the employer to enforce a statutory right; or
- the employee alleged that the employer had breached a statutory right.

11.43   The claim must be made in good faith and the nature of the right must be clear but it is not necessary to show that there has been an actual breach.[30]

29   *Qua* was followed by *MacCulloch & Wallis Ltd v Moore*. See para 11.34.
30   ERA 1996 s104(2), (3).

Sex discrimination

11.44   Where a woman is treated less favourably than a man, or vice versa, this will be direct discrimination. However, as significantly more women than men have primary responsibility for childcare there may also be a claim by a woman for indirect sex discrimination. For example, a requirement not to take any time off when a child is sick is likely to be one which has a disproportionate adverse impact on women. Whether the requirement is justified will be mainly a question of fact. There are no known reported cases.

Procedure

11.45   A complaint must be made within three months from the date when the refusal, detriment or dismissal occurred, or if not practicable to do so, within such further period as is reasonable (see chapter 16). The statutory grievance procedure does not apply to a refusal of time off under ERA 1996 s57A. It does apply in cases of constructive dismissal or discrimination claims (apart from discriminatory dismissal), in which case a written grievance must first be lodged and the claimant must wait 28 days before lodging a claim (see chapter 16). Where the employee is dismissed for taking time off, the statutory disciplinary and dismissal procedure applies (see chapter 16).

Remedies

11.46   If the tribunal upholds the claim under ERA 1996 s57B it:

a) shall make a declaration to that effect; and
b) may make an award of compensation to be paid by the employer to the employee.[31]

11.47   The compensation shall be such as the tribunal considers just and equitable in all the circumstances having regard to:

a) the employer's default in refusing to permit time off; and
b) any loss sustained by the employer which is attributable to the matters complained of.[32]

11.48   Remedies for detriment, dismissal and discrimination are covered in chapter 18.

31   ERA 1996 s57B(3).
32   ERA 1996 s57B(4).

CHAPTER 12

The right to request flexible working for parents and carers

Key points

- The 'right to request' procedure under the Employment Rights Act (ERA) 1996 is a right to use the procedure set out by statute to request flexible hours; it is not an entitlement to flexible hours.
- The employee and the employer must follow the statutory procedures.
- The remedies, which are very limited, are only available for breach of the procedure, not in respect of a refusal of flexible working.
- Men as well as women may use it.
- Where an employee's request is refused, they may be able to bring a direct or an indirect (usually women) sex or marital discrimination claim for flexible working. This can result in substantial compensation being awarded and recommendations made (see chapter 13). So it is advisable for an employer to give serious and objective consideration to a request.
- In April 2007 the right to request flexible working will be extended to carers.

Background and legal framework

12.1   Many women returning from maternity leave want to adjust or reduce hours to enable them to combine work and family commitments. Some men also seek similar changes. Working hours which are compatible with childcare responsibilities are referred to below as flexible working. These are also known as child-friendly working or family-friendly hours. Flexible working includes part-time work, job sharing and flexible work patterns. It may also cover seeking predictable and regular work schedules.

12.2   In summary, the rights to flexible working are:

- for women and men employees, with at least 26 weeks' service, the right to request flexible working to care for a child under 6 (or under 18, if disabled), and to have their request considered in accordance with a prescribed procedure under the ERA 1996. In April 2007, the right to request flexible working will be extended to employees caring for certain adults; and/or

- for women workers regardless of length of service, the right to bring a claim for indirect discrimination under the SDA 1975 (on the grounds of sex and/or marital and civil partnership (see para 13.159) status) in relation to an unjustified refusal to allow a change in working hours or patterns. This claim may be brought where an existing work pattern disadvantages a woman worker due to her childcare (or other caring) responsibilities and includes a woman returning from maternity leave (see para 13.4). Because of the way such a claim must be framed, it is unlikely to be available to men. However, a man may claim direct sex discrimination if his request is refused on the grounds of his sex, ie, where a woman's request would be accepted (see para 13.160 onwards).

12.3 This chapter looks at the 'right to request' flexible working procedure and chapter 13 at indirect discrimination and flexible working. There is no obligation to follow the 'right to request' procedure before making a claim for indirect discrimination, but it is strongly advisable as it may be possible to reach agreement. This procedure helps to achieve a cheap, quick and mutually agreeable outcome.

Relevant statutory provisions

12.4 The right is referred to by the ERA 1996 as the 'statutory right to request a contract variation' and is set out in the ERA 1996 ss80F–80I (inserted by the Employment Act 2002 and amended by the Work and Families Act (WFA) 2006 s12 to come into force on 6 April 2007) and the two following sets of regulations:

- Flexible Working (Procedural Requirements) Regulations 2002,[1] referred to as the Procedural Regs 2002;
- Flexible Working (Eligibility, Complaints and Remedies) Regulations 2002,[2] referred to as the Eligibility Regs 2002[3] as amended by the draft Flexible Working (Eligibility, Complaints and Remedies) (Amendment) Regulations 200[ ][4] referred to as the Eligibility Amendment Regs. The amendments are proposed to come into force on 6 April 2007 as published in draft. They will extend the right to request flexible work to employees caring for certain adults.

1 SI 2002 No 3207.
2 SI 2002 No 3236.
3 The legislation came into force on 6 April 2003.
4 SI No not yet available.

The focus of this chapter is on women using the 'right to request' procedure for childcare reasons but the procedural requirements are the same for carers of certain adults except as described.

12.5 The DTI has published a Guide on the right to request[5] and suggested model forms to use.[6] These are referred to below where relevant. The Guide, though useful, is not legally binding. It does not have the status of a statutory code which must be taken into account by an employment tribunal (ET) when reaching its decision.

Statutory grievance and disciplinary procedures

12.6 The statutory grievance and disciplinary procedures do not apply to claims under the 'right to request' procedure. However, they will apply to some of the claims mentioned in this chapter. For example, an employee is likely to have to raise a statutory grievance prior to bringing a discrimination or constructive dismissal claim (see chapter 16 and paras 12.81–12.82 on statutory grievance procedure).

Other relevant provisions

12.7 These are:

- *the Equal Opportunities Commission (EOC) code of practice on sex discrimination, equal opportunity policies, procedures and practices in employment.*[7] Employers and tribunals must take account of the code.[8] It recommends that employers consider with their employees whether certain jobs can be carried out on a part-time or flexi-time basis;
- *the EC Recommendation on Childcare*[9] which is intended to provide a work environment that takes into account the needs of working parents, suggests flexible working practices. It is not binding but is aimed at helping translate policy into practice. The European Court of Justice (ECJ) has ruled that domestic courts

---

5 See 'Flexible working: The right to request and the duty to consider: guidance for employers and employees (PL520)' at: www.dti.gov.uk/employment/workandfamilies/flexible-working/index.html.
6 See the DTI website for model forms at: www.dti.gov.uk/employment/balancing-work-family-responsible/flexible-working/flexforms/index.html.
7 See at: www.eoc.org.uk/Default.aspx?page=15577&lang=en.
8 SDA 1975 s56A. See also para 2.26.
9 92/241/EEC.

are bound to take such Recommendations into account in deciding disputes;[10]

- *the contract of employment.* Where it includes a provision that the employer will try to accommodate requests for part-time/flexible work and lays down a procedure for employees to follow, failure to follow the policy may amount to a breach of the employment contract and could lead to a constructive dismissal claim;[11]
- the *Part-time Workers (Prevention of Less Favourable Treatment) Regulations 2000*[12] which provide that an employer must not treat part-time employees (men and women) less favourably unless this can be 'objectively justified' (see chapter 14).

The 'right to request' procedure and indirect discrimination

12.8   An employee should first consider raising the possibility of a change in hours or working patterns on an informal basis to see whether it can be agreed without going through the formal procedure. If this is not successful, it is advisable for an employee to use the 'right to request' procedure, where they are eligible to do so. If this fails, a claim for indirect sex discrimination under the SDA 1975 should be considered (see paras 12.2 and 12.3). For more about the differences between the 'right to request' procedure and an SDA claim, see the table at para 12.39. A chart at the end of this chapter summarises the 'right to request' procedure.

Who is eligible to use the 'right to request' procedure?

12.9   The employee may be a man or woman and must satisfy all the following conditions:

- They must be an employee.[13] Agency workers[14] and other workers

---

10   *Grimaldi v Fonds des Maladies*, Case 322/88, [1990] IRLR 400, ECJ.
11   In *Taylor v Secretary of State for Scotland* [2000] IRLR 502, the House of Lords found that an equal opportunities policy which had been negotiated with the trade union formed part of employees' individual contracts of employment. But in this case the employer had not breached the policy.
12   SI 2000 No 1551 as amended.
13   ERA 1996 s80F(1), (8); Eligibility Regs 2002 reg 2(1). This is a narrower definition than in SDA 1975 s82(1). See paras 2.9–2.14 for eligibility to bring an SDA claim.
14   ERA 1996 s80F(8)(a)(ii), (b).

386 Maternity and parental rights / chapter 12

who are not employees (see para 1.29) and members of the Armed Forces[15] cannot apply.

- They must have 26 weeks' continuous service with the employer at the date of the application.[16]
- They must have, or expect to have, responsibility for the upbringing of a child[17] who must be under 6[18] or, if disabled, under 18, and entitled to a disability allowance[19] and/or be caring for, or expect to care for, a person who is 18 or over.[20] There are certain conditions as to relationship in respect of the adult or child, see below.
- They must make the application with the purpose of enabling the employee to care for a child or adult who meets the conditions as to relationship.[21]
- For an application for flexible work to care for a child, the employee must be either the mother, father, adopter, guardian or foster parent of the child, or married to, or the civil partner[22] or a partner (including same-sex partner) of, one of the above.[23] 'Partner' means a member of a couple who are not married to each other but are living together as if they were husband and wife or two people of the same sex who are not civil partners but are living together as if they were civil partners.[24] It may be sufficient that the child lives with the partner for the part of the week when they want flexible working. A relative such as a grandparent or aunt of the child is not eligible to make a request, even if living in the same house and caring for the child, unless they are also, for

15 ERA 1996 s192.
16 Eligibility Regs 2002 reg 3(1)(a), reg 3B(1)(a) inserted by the Eligibility Amendment Regs.
17 Eligibility Regs 3(1)(c) ER. There is no statutory definition of what this means.
18 Eligibility Regs 2002 reg 3A, inserted by the Eligibility Amendment Regs. Until 6 April 2007, see ERA 1996 s80F(3) (repealed by the WFA 2006 s12(4)).
19 Eligibility Regs 2002 regs 2(1) and 3A inserted by the Eligibility Amendment Regs. Until 6 April 2007, see ERA 1996 s80F(3), (7) (repealed by the WFA 2006 s12(4)).
20 Eligibility Regs 2002 reg 3B(1)(b) inserted by the Eligibility Amendment Regs.
21 ERA 1996 s80F(1)(b) amended by the WFA 2006 s12(2) to include caring for adults.
22 Inserted into the Eligibility Regs 2002 by Civil Partnership Act 2004 (Amendments to Subordinate Legislation) Order 2005, SI No 2114 Sch 17 from December 2005.
23 Eligibility Regs 2002 regs 3(1)(b) and 2(1).
24 Eligibility Regs 2002 reg 2(1), amended by the Eligibility Amendment Regs. Until 6 April 2007, the definition is that the partner lives with their partner and the child in an enduring family relationship but is not a relative (as defined) of their partner.

example, the child's guardian. The application must be made before the day on which the child reaches the age of 6 or, if disabled, 18.[25]

- For an application for flexible work to care for an adult (see para 12.2), the person to be cared for must be either married to the employee or the employee's partner[26] or civil partner, or a relative of the employee or a person living at the same address as the employee.[27] 'Relative' will be defined either as a mother, father, adopter, guardian, parent-in-law, son, son-in-law, daughter, daughter-in-law, including adoptive relationships or such of those relationships as would exist but for adoption, OR may also include brother, brother-in-law, sister, sister-in-law, uncle, aunt or grandparent, including adoptive relationships and relationships of the full blood or half blood, or, in the case of an adopted person, such of those relationships that would exist but for the adoption.[28]

12.10 The employee must not have made an application to the same employer under the procedure during the previous 12 months.[29]

What changes to the contract can be requested?

12.11 The employee can request changes to:

- the hours the employee is required to work[30] (eg, to part-time work or to fewer hours than their existing part-time work). A change may be requested to extend rather than reduce working hours, provided the above requirements are met (eg, once a child reaches school age, a two day per week employee may seek to work five days during school hours); and/or
- the times when they are required to work (eg, to begin and/or stop work half an hour later/earlier to fit in with childcare);[31] and/or

---

25 Eligibility Regs 2002 reg 3A, inserted by the Eligibility Amendment Regs. Until 6 April 2007, the application must be made prior to the 14th day before the child's sixth birthday or if the child is disabled, their 18th birthday, ERA 1996 s80F(3) (repealed, see note 18).
26 See note 24.
27 Eligibility Regs 2002 reg 3B (1) (b) inserted by the Eligibility Amendment Regs.
28 Eligibility Regs 2002 reg 2(1) one or other definition to be inserted by draft Eligibility Amendment Regs from 6 April 2007.
29 ERA 1996 s80F(4).
30 ERA 1996 s80F(1)(a)(i).
31 ERA 1996 s80F(1)(a)(ii).

- where, as between their home and a place of business of their employer, they are required to work[32] (eg, to provide for working from home). A request to limit or stop travelling for work is not covered whether travelling to different work sites or overnight (but see chapter 13 for a possible SDA claim in such a situation); and/or
- the employment terms and conditions specified in regulations (none so specified as at summer 2006).[33]

12.12 The Explanatory Notes to the Employment Act 2002 state that the above provisions are intended to cover work patterns such as flexi-time, job-sharing, working from home, teleworking, staggered hours, term-time working, compressed hours, shift working, self-rostering and annualised hours.[34] Note that a request to reorganise and not necessarily reduce hours may be made.

The change made is usually permanent

12.13 Unless there is an agreement limiting the period during which the flexible work arrangement will apply, a change agreed under the procedure will be a permanent change to the employee's terms and conditions of employment. The employee should therefore be clear that they can manage the change requested both in terms of finances (loss of wages and any reduction in tax credits or benefits) and child-care arrangements. Further, if there is any danger of a redundancy situation the reduced pay will result in a proportionately reduced redundancy payment.

12.14 There is nothing to prevent the employee requesting a return to her former hours at a subsequent date but she has no entitlement to return to full-time working. Both employer and employee may prefer a limited arrangement, possibly on a trial basis and there is nothing to prevent such an agreement. However, this must be made clear before the change is finalised under the procedure, otherwise it will be permanent though, of course, it can be revised at a later stage by agreement. The change continues in effect regardless of when the child for whom it was sought becomes 6 (or 18 if the child is disabled).

---

32 ERA 1996 s80F(1)(a)(iii).
33 ERA 1996 s80F(1)(a)(iv).
34 See the Guide (note 5) for descriptions of some of these work patterns.

Timing of the application

12.15 The application can only be made after the birth of the child to whom it relates (not while pregnant) but it must be made before the day on which the child reaches the age of 6 or, if the child is disabled, 18.[35] An employee making an application to care for an adult can make the application at any time providing they meet all the conditions.

12.16 In all cases, the application should be made well before the new work pattern is proposed to come into effect. A woman on maternity leave can apply whilst on leave, after her baby is born. She should make the application sufficiently early in her maternity leave to ensure that the procedure can be completed (it may take about 10–14 weeks) before her maternity leave expires. This will also enable the employer to make any arrangements necessary to manage the changed working pattern.

12.17 If the employee does not have enough time to complete the procedure before her maternity leave ends, the employer and employee can informally agree to a limited period of flexible working. Alternatively, the employee could seek to delay her return by taking holiday or unpaid parental leave, provided she gives sufficient notice (see chapter 10).

No further requests within a year

12.18 A further request under the procedure may not be made to the same employer within 12 months from the date when the previous application was made.[36] There is no similar restriction under the SDA 1975 so it may be possible to bring an SDA indirect discrimination claim based on a refusal of flexible working (see chapter 13).

The application

12.19 The form of the application must comply with all the statutory requirements which are that it:

- be in writing, whether handwritten or typed;[37]
- be dated;[38]

---

35 See note 25, especially regarding timing before 6 April 2007.
36 ERA 1996 s80F(4).
37 Eligibility Regs 2002 reg 4(a).
38 Eligibility Regs 2002 reg 4(c).

- state whether and if so, when, a previous application has been made to the employer;[39]
- state that it is an application for a change in working times/hours/location (see paras 12.11–12.12).[40] It is advisable to be as specific as possible and say that it is an application under the statutory right to request a contract variation in relation to flexible working under ERA 1996 s80F, that the employee is making the request to enable them to care for an adult or for a child and that they have (or expect to have) responsibility for the child's upbringing (see para 12.9);
- explain the relationship the employee has with the adult or child which falls within para 12.9;[41]
- specify the change in working pattern sought (see paras 12.11–12.12 for options);[42]
- state the date on which the claimant proposes the change should become effective (it is advisable to bear in mind the points made in paras 12.15–12.17 under timing of the application);[43]
- explain what effect, if any, the employee thinks making the change would have on the employer and how, in their opinion, any such effect may be dealt with.[44]

12.20   The DTI model Form FW(A)[45] for making an application could be used, though an employee should check whether the employer has a preferred form. Alternatively a letter, fax or email will be sufficient. There is no legal requirement to use a particular form or to sign the application.

Incomplete applications

12.21   Where an application is incomplete, the Guide[46] suggests that the employer should inform the employee:

- what they have omitted and ask them to resubmit the application when complete;
- that they are not obliged to consider the application until it is complete and resubmitted.

---

39   Eligibility Regs 2002 reg 4(b).
40   ERA 1996 s80F(2)(a).
41   ERA 1996 s80F(2)(d) as amended by WFA 2006 s12(3) to include adult.
42   ERA 1996 s80F(2)(b).
43   ERA 1996 s80F(2)(b).
44   ERA 1996 s80F(2)(c).
45   See DTI website, note 6.
46   See note 5.

12.22 The employer does not have to do this and could refuse to consider it as incomplete, but it is good practice to do so. In any event, the employee could start the application again, as an incomplete application is not caught by the bar on submitting one application every 12 months. In addition, a claim for indirect discrimination under the SDA 1975 could be made if the request is refused or has not been considered even if the application was incomplete (see chapter 13).

Request for further information

12.23 Even if the application is otherwise complete, the employer has the right to request any further information it needs in order to assess the application. This need not be done in writing. The employee should make every effort to supply this as if they have no reasonable excuse for refusing, the employer may treat the application as withdrawn (see paras 12.35 and 12.63–12.68).[47] The employer must confirm in writing that they are treating an application as withdrawn to the employee[48] (see para 12.66). The employee may be able to answer the employer's request briefly and without any difficulty, but if the response is complex or if there is a reason why information cannot be supplied, it is advisable for the employee to provide a written response and keep a copy.

How much detail must the employee include to justify the proposed change?

12.24 Employees must explain what effect, if any, they think making the change would have on the employer and how, in their opinion, any such effect may be dealt with. The DTI Guide[49] suggests:

> This does not mean that the employee is expected to know every factor that might influence the employer's decision. It simply means that they should show that they have considered the factors that they are aware of that are likely to influence their employer's decision. Evidence shows that applications for flexible working patterns succeed where they are soundly based on the business needs of the employer.

> See paras 12.30–12.32, 'Preparing for the meeting' and paras 12.34–12.39, 'Negotiating positively', for ideas about how to proceed.

47 Procedural Regs 2002 reg 17(1)(c).
48 Procedural Regs 2002 reg 17(2).
49 See note 5.

Date when an application is taken as made

12.25   This is the date which sets the timetable for the rest of the procedure. The application is taken as having been made on the date when it is received by the employer.[50]

12.26   That is, the day:

- on which it is given in person to the employer;
- on which it is sent if sent electronically;[51] or
- on which it would be delivered in the ordinary course of the post, if sent by post.[52]

12.27   If there is proof that it was received on a different date, that is the relevant date.[53] So it is advisable to send the application by recorded delivery or otherwise ensure there is proof of its receipt by the employer. It is also a good idea for the employer to acknowledge receipt of a request in writing to the employee, stating the date on which it was received. DTI Form FW(A)[54] provides a tear-off slip on which to do this.

Procedure once the application is made

Employer may agree to the request without meeting

12.28   The employer may agree to the request to work flexibly without a meeting. If the employer does this, it must notify the employee of the decision in writing within 28 days of when the application was made,[55] setting out the agreed contract variation and the date from which it is to take effect.[56] The start date for the new arrangement need not be the one requested by the employee but must be an agreed date. If the date is after the employee's return from maternity leave, she may have to negotiate holiday or parental leave in the meantime (see chapter 10). The employer cannot impose a new arrangement on the employee which is different from the one requested. An attempt to do so could be a breach of contract and a detriment and could lead to an unfair dismissal and a sex discrimination claim (see chapters 2 and 15).

---

50 Eligibility Regs 2002 reg 5(1).
51 Eligibility Regs 2002 reg 5(2)(a).
52 Eligibility Regs 2002 reg 5(2)(b).
53 Eligibility Regs 2002 reg 5(1).
54 See note 6.
55 Procedural Regs 2002 reg 3(2).
56 Procedural Regs 2002 reg 3(3).

Meeting must be held within 28 days

12.29 Unless the employer agrees to the employee's request, it must organise a meeting to discuss the application within 28 days of when it is made.[57] This is subject to specific exceptions relating to postponing a meeting or extending time limits (see paras 12.56–12.58). The time and place of the meeting must be convenient to the employer and employee.[58] The procedure envisages an actual meeting not just a telephone discussion.[59] The DTI Guide suggests that particular consideration should be given to the meeting place where an employee is on maternity leave as she may find it difficult to travel to the workplace. Failure to hold a meeting within 28 days may give rise to a claim to an employment tribunal for breach of the procedure (see para 12.76). The employee is entitled to bring a companion[60] (see paras 12.59–12.62 for details about this right). The aim of the meeting is to explore the request, and if necessary, consider other options.

Preparing for the meeting[61]

12.30 The Guide[62] suggests the following preparation for the employee:

- be prepared to expand on any points within the application;
- be prepared to be flexible. For example, respond to any employer request as to whether other working patterns are possible, or another start date, or a trial period;
- read up on the Guide and other sources of information on flexible working (see paras 12.99–12.100 and appendix E for useful addresses and websites).

12.31 If taking a companion, the employee should:

- tell the employer that a companion will attend;

---

57 Procedural Regs 2002 reg 3(1); see paras 12.25–12.27 for when an application is taken as made.
58 Procedural Regs 2002 reg 11.
59 In *Humphrey v Hardings Estate Agency Ltd*, ET Case 2701793/03, the employee gave her application for flexible working personally to a human resources manager and had a discussion. Contrary to the employer's contention, the tribunal held this did not constitute the statutory meeting (reported IDS Brief 801, March 2006).
60 Procedural Regs 2002 reg 14.
61 See also: Working Families, Flexible Working checklist, in para 12.100, Useful addresses.
62 See note 5.

- ensure that the companion has seen the application and is fully briefed about it and about their role (see paras 12.59–12.62 about the companion).

12.32   The Guide suggests the following preparation for the employer:

- prepare all the issues you want to discuss at the meeting;
- check with the personnel section, if there is one, about options and see if any other worker wants to cover any extra hours created if the request is granted;
- inform the employee as to who will be at the meeting;
- be familiar with the Guide and other sources of information on flexible working (see paras 12.99–12.100 and appendix E for useful addresses and websites);
- be open to the possibility of involving external expertise.

Procedure at the meeting

12.33   There is no set procedure. However, the employee must attend the meeting unless there is a good reason why s/he cannot do so.[63] The Guide[64] provides that the meeting 'will provide the employer and the employee with the opportunity to explore the desired work patterns in-depth and discuss how it might be accommodated. It will also provide an opportunity to consider alternative working patterns should there be problems in accommodating the desired work patterns outlined in the employee's application.'

Negotiating positively

12.34   The DTI Guide says that both sides should approach the suggestions of the other with an open mind and consider a trial period. The employee should present his/her proposal and set out in detail how his/her preferred working pattern would work in practice, proposing solutions to any employer concerns as to how it will affect the job and how practical issues such as cover can be resolved. Questions to consider are:

- Will colleagues be able to manage the change in hours?

---

63   Procedural Regs 2002 reg 17(1)(b). One failure to attend without reasonable excuse does not entitle the employer to treat the application as withdrawn (see paras 12.63–12.68) but it is strongly advisable to provide a good reason for non-attendance.
64   See note 5.

- Can any of them confirm that the planned new pattern is workable, for example, those already working flexibly?
- Could a job share arrangement be implemented?
- Can any positive advantages be shown for the employer's business if the change is implemented?

12.35   The employee must supply information required by the employer which the employer needs to assess before making a decision. This may include whether the employee could occasionally vary their hours with notice, or work days other than those proposed. Failure to do this without reasonable cause[65] may lead to the application failing as it may be 'deemed' to have been withdrawn[66] (see paras 12.63–12.68). A positive and flexible approach by the employee will make any subsequent SDA claim for flexible working more likely to succeed.

12.36   The employee must also give serious consideration to any alternative suggestions made by the employer or to concerns it expresses, for example by investigating a range of childcare options. Whether and, if so, when the employee should raise the possibility of alternative work patterns to their first preference depends upon whether the employee thinks his/her preferred option will be acceptable and whether the employee can manage a compromise (eg, four days per week instead of three). If the employee does not talk about alternatives at the first meeting s/he could do so at an appeal.

12.37   An employer should deal with an application on an individual basis and not refuse one by reference to generalisations (eg 'part-time work always disrupts continuity') or create arbitrary policies limiting flexible working (eg, making it unavailable to managerial staff). The more thoroughly the employer addresses the job done by the individual and the individual's concerns, the more clearly it can see whether flexible working might work and make a decision which can be justified in any discrimination claim. It should suggest alternatives which it considers more practicable to the employee. This approach may well lead to a request being granted.

12.38   The request can be refused for specified reasons (see paras 12.43 onwards) which need not be objectively justified. However, with an

---

65   In the case of an SDA claim for flexible working, the employer could then claim its failure to make a decision is because of lack of co-operation. See *Barancewicz v RAC Motoring Services* ET, Case 5200086/01 and 1201690/99 (claimant failed to consider options offered by the employer); *Hill v Staffordshire Sentinel Newspapers Ltd* ET Case 2900163/01 (claimant resigned without responding to employer's genuine invitation to make positive suggestions).

66   Procedural Regs 2002 reg 17(1)(c).

Key differences between the rights to flexible working under the SDA 1975 and the ERA 1996 (for provisions relating to adults see paras 12.4 and 12.9)

	Indirect sex discrimination **SDA**	Indirect marital and civil partnership discrimination **SDA**	Right to request different working pattern **ERA**
Qualifying period	None	None	26 weeks
Who can claim	Mother or carer	Married person Civil partner	Parents, civil partners, adopters, foster parents, guardians and partners (same or different sex)
Employee or worker	Worker and job applicant	Worker and job applicant	Employee only
Age of child	No age limit	No age limit	Child under 6 If disabled under 18
When can request be made	Any time, including before or after maternity leave or when applying for a job	As for indirect discrimination	Up to the day before the child's 6th birthday or 18th if disabled
Restriction on number of requests	None	None	Only one request can be made every year
Procedure (see also para 12.8)	No set procedure	No set procedure	Prescribed procedure must be followed by employer and employee

On what basis can the employer refuse the request	Where it is objectively 'justifiable' to refuse	As for indirect sex discrimination	Where the employer decides to refuse on a specified ground
Time limit for making claim (see also chapter 16)	3 months less one day but may extend if just and equitable	As for indirect sex discrimination	3 months less one day, subject to reasonably practicable extension
Remedies on refusal	Declaration Recommendation Compensation (uncapped) including injury to feelings/ additional compensation if recommendation not implemented	As for indirect sex discrimination	8 weeks' pay subject to the statutory maximum of a week's pay (£290 up to the end of Jan 2007) Order to reconsider the application

SDA indirect discrimination claim for flexible working an employer must **objectively** justify a refusal. Failure to approach the request in an objective and thorough fashion means that an employer may refuse a request for flexible working under the 'right to request' procedure in a perfectly valid way but then fail to defend successfully a subsequent discrimination claim. Thus full reasons should be given, as if there is a claim for indirect discrimination the tribunal will expect the employer objectively to justify the refusal. A refusal must also be based on correct facts (see para 12.46 onwards).

12.39   See the table above regarding the differences between the two types of claim.

Procedure after the meeting

Employer acceptance of request: procedure

12.40   If the employer accepts the request, it must state this specifying the changes to the contract which have been agreed and giving a starting date in a written dated notice to the employee within 14 days of the date of the meeting.[67] DTI Form FW(B) can be used.[68]

Employer refusal of request: obligation on employer to give reasons

12.41   If the employer refuses the application, it must provide a written dated notice[69] to the employee within 14 days of the date of the meeting[70] setting out:

- which of the grounds for refusal (see para 12.43 onwards below) apply;[71]
- a sufficient explanation as to why those grounds apply in relation to the application; and
- the appeal procedure (see para 12.49).[72]

DTI Form FW(C) can be used.[73]

12.42   Failure to comply with these requirements may entitle the claimant to make a tribunal claim (see para 12.76 onwards).

---

67 Procedural Regs 2002 regs 4, 5(a), (b)(i), (c). The date need not be the one requested by the employee but it must be an agreed date.
68 See note 5.
69 Procedural Regs 2002 reg 5(a), (c).
70 Procedural Regs 2002 reg 4.
71 The grounds are set out in ERA 1996 s80G(1)(b).
72 Procedural Regs 2002 reg 5(b)(ii).
73 See note 6.

Grounds for an employer refusal of request for change

Refusal on a specified ground

12.43 The employer can only refuse the application on one of the following grounds.[74] Refusal on grounds other than these will entitle the employee to bring a claim to the ET[75] (see para 12.73) but only after an appeal has been made and rejected and the employee notified of this rejection[76] (see para 12.74):

- the burden of additional costs;
- detrimental effect on ability to meet customer demand;
- inability to reorganise work among existing staff;
- inability to recruit additional staff;
- detrimental impact on quality;
- detrimental impact on performance;
- insufficiency of work during periods the employee proposes to work;
- planned structural changes;
- other grounds as may be set out in regulations (none as at summer 2006).

12.44 There is no further clarification as to the extent of the explanation required other than it must be 'sufficient' and this will be for the tribunal to decide. The Guide[77] suggests:

> The explanation should include the key facts about why the business ground applies . . . An explanation of around two paragraphs will usually be sufficient, although the actual length of explanation necessary to demonstrate why the business ground applies will differ depending on each individual case . . . The aim is for the employer to explain to the employee, in terms that are relevant, why the requested working pattern cannot be accepted as a result of the business ground applying in the circumstances. If the argument does not look convincing to the employer it is unlikely to look convincing to the claimant.

12.45 The Guide provides an example of a refusal. The DTI TIGER website[78]

---

74 Set out in ERA 1996 s80G(1)(b)(i)–(ix).
75 ERA 1996 s80H(1)(a).
76 ERA 1996 s80H(3)(a).
77 See note 5.
78 See para 12.99.

also gives examples of a refusal on each of the above grounds. Both give examples of what might be expected, although what is sufficient will be up to the tribunal to decide in any particular case. However, it should not be assumed that the reasons for refusing a request which are sufficient for the 'right to request' procedure would be adequate to defend an SDA 1975 claim (see para 12.38 and chapter 13 for flexible working).

Refusal must be based on correct facts

12.46 The employer's reasons must be based on correct facts. If they are not, the employee may bring a claim to the tribunal[79] (see para 12.73), but only after an appeal has been made to the employer and rejected and the employee notified of this rejection[80] (see para 12.74). The employee must be able to provide evidence to support this allegation. The DTI Guide says that facts provided in the explanation must be accurate and capable of being backed up should they subsequently be disputed. Examples of incorrect facts may be:

- that the employer could not provide cover from 9–9.30 am for the telephones when other employees were willing and able to do this;
- where a decision is based on the burden of additional costs, there arc in fact no extra costs.

12.47 If an employee is aware of incorrect facts in the employer's decision, they should raise these at the appeal hearing. If the employer fails to address them then or includes other incorrect facts in the appeal decision, then this would be the basis for a tribunal claim (see para 12.73).

12.48 In *Commotion Ltd v Rutty*,[81] the employer had refused the 'right to request' flexible work application of Ms Rutty, a warehouse packer, alleging it would impact detrimentally on performance.[82] No evidence was put before the tribunal that part-time work was not feasible nor that the employers had properly investigated this. The Employment Appeal Tribunal (EAT) upheld the tribunal decision that the employer had breached the procedure as the reason given for turning down the application was based on incorrect facts. Although the tribunal is not

---

79 ERA 1996 s80H(1)(b).
80 ERA 1996 s80H(3)(a).
81 [2006] IRLR 171.
82 A permissible reason under ERA 1996 s80G(1)(b)(vi).

entitled to examine the fairness and reasonableness of the employer's decision, it may examine objectively the circumstances surrounding a flexible work application (eg, what would be the effect of granting the application) to test whether its rejection was based on correct facts. If it could not, this ground for complaint would have no use.

Right of appeal

Notice and grounds of appeal

12.49 The employee must be notified of the right to appeal in the notice refusing their application.[83] They must appeal within 14 days after the date on which the notice of the decision is given,[84] unless an extension of time is agreed with the employer (see para 12.58). A notice of appeal must:

- set out the grounds of appeal, which are not limited in any way;
- be in writing;
- be dated.[85]

DTI Form FW(D)[86] can be used.

12.50 According to the Guide:[87]

> There are no constraints to the grounds under which an employee can appeal. It may be that they wish to bring to attention something the employer may not have been aware of when they rejected the application, e.g. that another member of staff is now willing to cover the hours the claimant no longer wishes to be at work. Or it may be to challenge a fact the employer has quoted to explain why the business reason applies.

12.51 It is advisable for the employee to address directly the reasons for the refusal given by the employer in the decision notice, though there is no requirement to give other than brief details of the appeal grounds in the notice of appeal.

---

83 Procedural Regs 2002 reg 5(b)(ii).
84 Procedural Regs 2002 reg 6.
85 Procedural Regs 2002 reg 7.
86 See note 6.
87 See note 5.

Employer may agree to the request without an appeal meeting

12.52   If the employer decides to allow the appeal, it does not need to hold an appeal meeting but must notify the employee in writing, within 14 days after the notice of appeal is given, of this decision, specifying the contract variation agreed to and the date it is to take effect.[88]

The appeal meeting

12.53   Unless the employer has allowed the appeal, it must hold an appeal meeting within 14 days after the employee's notice of appeal is given.[89] Where an appeal meeting is held, it must be at a time and place convenient for the employer and the employee.[90] The employee is, as at the initial meeting, entitled to bring a companion (see paras 12.59–12.62).[91] Failure to hold a meeting within 14 days may give rise to a claim to an employment tribunal for breach of the procedure (see para 12.76).

12.54   There are no requirements as to who should hold the appeal meeting. The DTI Guide[92] states:

> Experience shows that an employee is far more likely to feel that their appeal has been taken seriously when a manager senior to the one who originally considered the application hears it.

It states that this is not always necessary, nor may it be possible in small businesses. Where it is possible, it will usually be advisable to have a fresh view to ensure any rejection is, for example, sufficiently explained and based on correct facts.

Notification of decision after appeal

12.55   The employer must provide a written dated notice to the employee of the outcome of the appeal within 14 days of the appeal meeting.[93] DTI Form FW(E)[94] could be used. If the appeal is upheld, the employer

---

88   Procedural Regs 2002 reg 8(2). The date need not be the one requested by the employee but it must be an agreed date.
89   Procedural Regs 2002 reg 8(1).
90   Procedural Regs 2002 reg 11.
91   Procedural Regs 2002 reg 14.
92   See note 5.
93   Procedural Regs 2002 regs 9, 10(a), (c).
94   See note 6.

must specify the contract variation agreed and the date it is to take effect.[95] If the appeal is dismissed, the employer must set out in the written notice the grounds on which the dismissal is based and give a sufficient explanation as to why those grounds apply.[96] Failure to comply with these requirements may entitle the claimant to make a tribunal claim (see para 12.76).

Meetings and other general provisions

Can the meetings be postponed or other time limits extended?

12.56   If the individual who would ordinarily consider the application is on holiday or sick leave on the day when it is received by the employer, the 28-day period for holding the initial meeting starts to run only from the day when that individual returns to work, or 28 days after the application was made, whichever is sooner.[97] For example, if the relevant manager is on holiday for another seven days when the application is submitted, the 28 days begins to run on their return. If they have just begun five weeks' holiday, the 28-day period begins to run 28 days after the application was made. See also para 12.65, regarding an employee's failure to attend a meeting.

Postponement of initial or appeal meeting: if the companion is unavailable

12.57   If the employee's chosen companion is not available, the employer must postpone (only once) the meeting, but only if the employee has proposed an alternative time convenient to the employer, employee and companion. This must be within seven days, beginning with the first day after the day proposed by the employer.[98]

---

95   Procedural Regs 2002 reg 10(b)(i). The date need not be the one requested by the employee but it must be an agreed date.
96   Procedural Regs 2002 reg 10(b)(ii).
97   Procedural Regs 2002 reg 13.
98   Procedural Regs 2002 reg 14(4) and (5).

Extension of certain time limits by agreement

12.58   The employer and employee may agree to an extension of time limits for the initial meeting including the period referred to in para 12.56. Other extensions may also be agreed regarding notifying the decision on the application, the date by which a notice of appeal must be submitted, the date by which an appeal meeting must be held and the date by which the appeal decision must be notified.[99] The agreement must be recorded in writing by the employer[100] and must:

- specify what period the extension relates to;
- specify the date on which the extension is to end;
- be dated; and
- be sent to the employee.[101]

DTI Form FW(F) may be used.[102]

The right to be accompanied at the meetings

12.59   An employee who reasonably requests to be accompanied at the initial and/or appeal meetings by a worker[103] chosen by the employee and who is employed by the same employer (wherever they work), must be allowed to bring this companion. The companion's role is limited to conferring with the employee during the meeting and addressing it.[104] The companion may not answer questions on behalf of the employee unless the employer agrees.

Why a companion?

12.60   The presence of a companion at the meeting can be beneficial to both employer and employee. This may be particularly true of an external representative with experience of flexible working. Such a person may attend even if they are not a co-worker of the employee, provided the employer agrees. The Guide[105] highlights the value of a com-

---

99   Procedural Regs 2002 reg 12(1).
100   Procedural Regs 2002 reg 12(2).
101   Procedural Regs 2002 reg 12(3).
102   See note 6. Although the form does not mention the extensions available under Procedural Regs 2002 regs 6 and 13, it can be adapted for use in such cases.
103   Procedural Regs 2002 reg 2 defines 'worker' to cover many self-employed and contract workers.
104   Procedural Regs 2002 reg 14(1)–(3).
105   See note 5.

panion from outside the workplace where this would help reach an acceptable outcome. This may be particularly important where the employee needs a companion with particular skills, for example one who can translate or who understands the needs of a disabled employee.

The rights of the companion

12.61 The companion is entitled to reasonable[106] paid time off during working hours,[107] if they are one of the employer's workers. This is to accompany the employee at the meeting and arguably to consult with the employee beforehand.[108] The employee is not entitled to paid time off for such a consultation, but good practice would be for the employer to agree a period of time with the employee as well as the companion for this purpose. The employer's agreement must be obtained before taking the time off.

12.62 Remedies available for breach of this right and detriment or dismissal as a result of exercising it are covered in paras 12.78–12.79, 12.85–12.86 and 12.87 onwards.

Applications withdrawn or unresolved

12.63 If an actual or deemed withdrawal occurs, the employee will not be able to make another application for 12 months from the date the withdrawn application was made.[109]

12.64 An employee can withdraw an application:

- by notifying the employer that the employee is withdrawing the

---

106 In deciding 'reasonable' time off (eg, in terms of the time allowed and the occasions when and any conditions subject to which, it is taken,) regard must be had to the ACAS Code of Practice 3: Time off for trade union duties and activities ('the ACAS Code') at: www.acas.org.uk. This provides a summary of the legal provisions about time off and practical advice, eg, about the factors affecting reasonableness, such as the size and nature of the business and the need to provide as much notice as possible about the time off required: Procedural Regs 2002 reg 14(7); Trade Union and Labour Relations (Consolidation) Act 1992 (TULRCA) 1992 s168(3).
107 Procedural Regs 2002 reg 14(6) and (7) applying specified sections of TULRCA 1992.
108 See para 12 of the ACAS Code.
109 ERA 1996 s80F(4); Procedural Regs 2002 reg 17.

application, whether orally or in writing.[110] If the employee makes an oral notification, the employer must confirm the withdrawal to the employee in writing.[111]

12.65 An employer is entitled to treat the application as withdrawn (that is 'deem' it to be withdrawn) in certain circumstances because the employee has failed to comply with the procedure. This may be done where the employee has:

- without reasonable cause failed, more than once, to attend a meeting under the procedure (or in accordance with any agreed variation of the procedure).[112] The Guide[113] points out that if an employee misses a meeting because their child is ill and informs the employer, this should be treated sympathetically and it is likely to constitute a reasonable cause for not attending the meeting; or
- without reasonable cause, refused to provide the employer with information which the employer requires in order to assess whether a contract variation should be agreed.[114] The Guide gives as an example of this a situation where the employer may wish to ensure that the working space of an employee who wishes to work at home meets health and safety standards, but the employee refuses to co-operate with doing this (see also paras 12.23 and 12.34 onwards). It will be for the tribunal to decide if the employee has unreasonably refused to provide the required information (see paras 12.67–12.68).

12.66 Once the employer decides that there has been a deemed withdrawal, it must confirm the withdrawal to the employee in writing.[115] DTI Form FW(G)[116] can be used.

Disputed withdrawal

12.67 There may be a dispute about whether the application has been withdrawn. For example, the employer may say it has not received sufficient information so it will not hold a meeting and is treating the application as withdrawn under Procedural Regs 2002 reg 17(1)(c),

---

110 Procedural Regs 2002 reg 17(1)(a).
111 Procedural Regs 2002 reg 17(2).
112 Procedural Regs 2002 reg 17(1)(b).
113 See note 5.
114 Procedural Regs 2002 reg 17(1)(c).
115 Procedural Regs 2002 reg 17(2).
116 See note 6.

whereas the employee denies that there has been a withdrawal and considers that the employer has breached the procedure by refusing to hold a meeting.

12.68 In these circumstances the employee will have to proceed with a claim to the tribunal that the employer has breached the procedure (eg, not held a meeting, see para 12.76), but the tribunal will first have to decide if there has been a withdrawal. If it finds there was not (eg, decides that there was no unreasonable refusal of required information) it must then find a breach of the procedure. However, if the tribunal finds there has been a withdrawal, the claim can be taken no further as no complaint can be made after withdrawal.[117] No further application can be made for 12 months (see para 12.18, no further requests in a year).[118]

Unresolved applications

12.69 The Guide[119] recommends that unresolved applications (eg where an appeal has been unsuccessful, but the employee feels it was not dealt with satisfactorily) be dealt with by:

- an informal discussion;
- using the employer's grievance procedure (which is compulsory since October 2004, if the employee intends to bring an SDA claim or certain other proceedings, see para 12.81 onwards and chapter 16);
- seeking third party involvement, eg, ACAS, union representative;
- agreeing with the employer to seek formal arbitration by ACAS;[120]
- a formal complaint to the tribunal where the employer has failed to follow the procedure properly, or the decision by the employer to reject the application was based on an unspecified ground or incorrect facts (see para 12.70 onwards).

---

117 ERA 1996 s80H(2).
118 ERA 1996 s80F(4).
119 See note 5.
120 In this case, ACAS can make a binding arbitration, see www.acas.org.uk and SI 2004 No 2333.

Tribunal claims relating to the 'right to request' procedure

12.70 An employee (and/or the companion) can make a complaint to a tribunal where an employer has:

- breached specified aspects of the 'right to request' procedure;
- contravened the right of the employee to be accompanied or refused the companion paid time off;
- subjected to a detriment or dismissed, the employee in connection with exercising the employee's right to request, and the employee and/or the companion in connection with the right to be accompanied;
- discriminated on the grounds of sex/marital status and civil partnership in relation to any of the above conduct.

12.71 An employee considering a claim should be aware of the very limited powers of a tribunal, see table at para 12.39 and para 12.83 onwards (unless there has been a detriment, dismissal or discrimination, see paras 12.96–12.98). Under the 'right to request' procedure, provided an employer follows the procedure, gives a prescribed reason, provides a sufficient explanation of the reason and bases its decision on correct facts, the employer is not required to justify its decision objectively.

12.72 The procedure must be complied with by both employer and employee and the employer must consider the application genuinely. For example, it should not make its mind up in advance (see *Clarke*[121]) and must base its decision on accurate information (see *Commotion*[122]). Although procedural breaches are not subject to substantial sanctions of themselves, they may sometimes be sufficient to found successful discrimination and/or constructive dismissal claims.

Breach of the 'right to request' procedure

12.73 An employee can make a complaint to the tribunal where the employer:

- has breached specified procedural requirements to hold meetings or notify decisions set out in the regulations;[123] (see para 12.76).

121　*Clarke v Telewest Communications plc*, ET 1301034/2004, Birmingham, reported in IDS Brief 790.
122　See note 81.
123　ERA 1996 ss80H(1)(a) and 80G(1)(a); Eligibility Regs 2002 reg 6.

The complaint can be made at the time of the breach though it is not advisable as agreement may be reached (but note time limits, see para 12.80 onwards);

- has refused the application on a ground other than those specified under ERA 1996 s80G(1)(b) (see para 12.43);[124]
- has rejected the application based on incorrect facts (see para 12.46);[125]

12.74 The second and third complaints can only be made once the employer has notified the employee of a decision to reject the application on appeal.[126]

12.75   No complaint can be made if the application has been disposed of by agreement or withdrawn (including a 'deemed' withdrawal).[127] If the employer alleges a deemed withdrawal and the employee contests this a tribunal must decide if there has been a withdrawal or not before going on to decide if the complaint succeeds (see paras 12.67–12.68).

Breach of specified aspects of the 'right to request' procedure

12.76 An employee can make a complaint to the tribunal where the employer has breached certain aspects of the 'right to request' procedure in considering a request. The employee can do this during the procedure once the breaches have occurred, ie, without waiting for the application to be finalised by refusal (see para 12.73), provided the application has not been agreed or withdrawn (see para 12.75). In practice, the employee will not want to bring a claim if there is still a chance that the employer will grant the request. Complaints can only be made about the following breaches:[128]

- failure to comply with the 28-day time limit for holding the initial meeting to discuss the employee's application;[129]
- failure to comply with the 14-day time limit for holding an appeal meeting;[130]

---

124   ERA 1996 s80H(1)(a) and 80G(1)(b).
125   ERA 1996 s80H(1)(b).
126   ERA 1996 s80H(3)(a).
127   ERA 1996 s80H(2).
128   ERA 1996 s80H(3)(b); Eligibility Regs 2002 reg 6.
129   ERA 1996 ss80G(1)(a), 80H(3)(b); Eligibility Regs 2002 reg 6(a).
130   ERA 1996 ss80G(1)(a), 80H(3)(b); Eligibility Regs 2002 reg 6(a).

- failure to give a written dated notice to the claimant of the decision made after the initial meeting within the 14-day time limit containing the information set out in paras 12.40 and 12.41;
- failure to give a written dated notice to the claimant of its decision after an appeal hearing within the 14-day time limit containing the information set out in para 12.55.[131]

12.77   Where one or more of these procedural defects occurs, whether or not it results in a complaint, the employer should rectify it as soon as possible to minimise the chance of a complaint being made (eg, hold a meeting or provide an adequate notice). If a complaint is made, this should be done before the tribunal hearing so as to minimise the amount of compensation which may be awarded for the breach. The employee should ensure s/he has made the application in full compliance with the 'right to request' procedure before complaining of an employer's breach.

Complaints relating to the right to be accompanied

12.78   An employee can complain where the employer has breached the employee's right to be accompanied or has threatened to do so.[132] The nature of the breaches are not specified in the legislation but will cover:

- a refusal to allow the employee the right to be accompanied by their chosen companion (a worker working for the same employer);
- a refusal to allow the companion to address the meeting;
- a refusal to allow the companion to confer with the employee during the meeting (see para 12.59);
- a refusal to allow a postponement within the specified time limit to enable the companion to be present (see para 12.57).

12.79   The companion can also bring a claim for a refusal to allow him/her reasonable, paid time off during working hours to act as a companion (see para 12.61).[133]

---

131   ERA 1996 ss80G(1)(a), 80H(3)(b); Eligibility Regs 2002 reg 6(b).
132   Procedural Regs 2002 reg 15(1).
133   Procedural Regs 2002 reg 14(6) and (7) applying TULRCA 1992 ss168(4), 169(5).

Time limits

12.80 A complaint must be made three calendar months less one day:

- from the date on which the employee was notified of the decision on his/her appeal (see para 12.74);[134] or
- from the date on which the breach complained of was committed (see para 12.76);[135] or
- from the date of the failure or threat in relation to the right to be accompanied;[136] or
- from the failure to permit a companion to take time off or pay them for it;[137]
- within such further period as the ET considers reasonable, where it is satisfied that it was not reasonably practicable for the complaint to be presented within three months.[138]

Statutory grievance procedure

12.81 The statutory grievance procedure (GP) (see para 12.6 and chapter 16) does not apply to any of the tribunal claims listed in para 12.70 onwards for breaches of the 'right to request' procedure. It:

- does apply where an employee alleges under ERA 1996 s47E or the Procedural Regs 2002 being subjected to a detriment in relation to any aspect of the application to work flexibly (see paras 12.92–12.94);
- does apply to making a claim for discrimination (whether direct or indirect – but not a discriminatory dismissal) or constructive dismissal arising out of a refusal of a request to work flexibly, whether made formally or informally. This includes bringing an SDA claim for flexible working (see chapter 13). It also applies to any other allegation of discriminatory conduct (including victimisation) occurring at any point during the 'right to request' procedure.

12.82 In *Commotion*,[139] the EAT upheld the tribunal decision that an

---

134 ERA 1996 ss80H(5)(a), 80H(6)(a).
135 ERA 1996 ss80H(5)(a), 80H(6)(b).
136 Procedural Regs 2002 reg 15(2)(a).
137 Procedural Regs 2002 reg 14(7) applying TULRCA 1992 s171.
138 ERA 1996 s80H(5)(b); Procedural Regs 2002 reg 15(2)(b), reg 14(7) applying TULRCA 1992 s171(b).
139 See note 81.

application under the 'right to request' procedure was a step 1 grievance as it followed the employer's refusal of an informal request. Therefore no further grievance was required before Ms Rutty lodged her constructive dismissal claim. The position is likely to have been different if she had not previously made an informal request before the formal 'right to request' application. The EAT also said that paragraph 2(2) of the Employment Act 2002 (Dispute Resolution) Regulations 2004[140] meant that a grievance could be raised in the same letter as a statutory 'right to request' flexible working application. However, in order to avoid any argument it will usually be advisable, where a discrimination or constructive dismissal claim is likely, to raise a separate grievance if a flexible working application is turned down. In cases where this has not been possible tribunals have shown themselves to be willing to be flexible in their interpretation of what constitutes a grievance (see chapter 16).

Remedies

Remedies on breach of the 'right to request' procedure (other than the right to be accompanied)

12.83   Where a complaint is upheld in relation to a breach of the 'right to request' procedure (see paras 12.73–12.77) the tribunal:

- must make a declaration that the complaint has been upheld;[141] and
- may make an order for the employer to reconsider the application[142] (this means that the application is treated as being made on the date of the order, so that the time limits set out in the regulations run from that date;[143] arguably this is the date the tribunal informed the parties of the order, not when the written decision was dated, unless the decision was reserved); and/or
- may make an award of compensation to be paid to the employee, which is just and equitable in all the circumstances.[144] This is

---

140   SI 2004 No 752.
141   ERA 1996 s80I(1).
142   ERA 1996 s80I(1)(a).
143   ERA 1996 s80I(4).
144   ERA 1996 s80I(1)(b), (2).

subject to a maximum of eight weeks' pay, with a cap on a week's pay of £290 (up to the end of January 2007), that is £2,320.[145]

12.84 Where the procedure has been completed, it is unlikely that it is worth complaining about procedural defects unless a claim is also made on other grounds eg for unfair dismissal, discrimination, or detrimental treatment. It is in both parties' interest to avoid litigation solely over breaches to the 'right to request' procedure. The remedies for the employee are weak; for the employer, although the penalties where a breach is held to have occurred are not likely to be severe, it will have to meet the (easily avoidable) time and financial costs of litigation.

Remedies on beach of the right to be accompanied

12.85 Where a complaint is upheld in relation to the right to be accompanied (see para 12.78), the tribunal:

- must make an award of compensation of not more than two weeks' pay to be paid to the employee. This is subject to the statutory cap (up to the end of January 2007) on a week's pay (£290).[146]

12.86 In addition, the companion is protected by specified provisions of the Trade Union and Labour Relations (Consolidation) Act (TULRCA) 1992 relating to paid time off for trade union duties.[147] Complaint to a tribunal may be made where the employer fails to permit reasonable time off during working hours or to pay the companion (see para 12.79). The tribunal:

- shall make a declaration and may award compensation such as the tribunal considers just and equitable having regard to the employer's default and the employee's loss.[148] The tribunal must order an employer to pay wages unpaid but held to be due under these provisions.[149]

---

145 Eligibility Regs 2002 reg 7; ERA 1996 s227; Employment Rights (Increase of Limits) Order 2005 SI No 3352 in force from 1 February 2006.
146 Procedural Regs 2002 reg 15(3), (5).
147 Procedural Regs 2002 reg 14(7).
148 This will be the loss of the companion who may be a worker rather than an employee (see para 12.59).
149 Procedural Regs 2002 reg 14(7) applying TULRCA 1992 s172(1)–(3).

Protection from dismissal or other detriment

Dismissal

12.87   There are no length of service or age requirements in order to claim automatically unfair dismissal or detriment.[150] It is automatically unfair under ERA 1996 s104C (see also para 15.58) to dismiss an employee if the reason or the principal reason is that the employee:

- made (or proposed to make) an application for flexible working under s80F;
- exercised (or proposed to exercise) a right under the procedure under s80G;
- brought proceedings against the employer for breach of the procedure under s80H (ie improperly refused a request for flexible working or breached the statutory procedures, see paras 12.73–12.77);
- alleged the existence of any circumstance which would constitute a ground for bringing such proceedings.

12.88   It is automatically unfair under Procedural Regs 2002 reg 16(3)(a) and (b) to dismiss an employee for exercising his/her right to accompaniment or a worker for being a companion. This claim arises where an employee (or a worker, in the case of a companion[151]):

- exercised or sought to exercise his/her right to be accompanied or to ask for a postponement because of the unavailability of the companion;[152]
- accompanied or sought to accompany another employee following a request under the right to request procedure.[153]

12.89   Interim relief is available to the employee and companion in the above situation, but an application must be made within seven days of the dismissal (see para 16.54 for the effect of such an application on a DDP implemented by the employer).[154]

12.90   It is automatically unfair under ERA 1996 s104 to dismiss an employee if the reason or the principal reason is that the employee:

---

150   ERA 1996 ss108, 109.
151   Procedural Regs 2002 reg 16(6).
152   Procedural Regs 2002 reg 16(3)(a).
153   Procedural Regs 2002 reg 16(3)(b).
154   Procedural Regs 2002 reg 16(5), ERA 1996 ss128–132.

- brought proceedings against the employer to enforce a specified statutory right which includes the right to request flexible work; or
- alleged that the employer had infringed such a right of theirs.

12.91   It does not matter whether the employee has the right or whether it has been infringed (provided the claim to the right and that it has been infringed are made in good faith). In certain circumstances this protection adds to the ones mentioned above. In *Horn v Quinn Walker*[155] an employee referred to the 'right to request' legislation and sought a change in work pattern but did not use the correct procedure, during a meeting with his employer. A tribunal found that he had asserted a statutory right when he alleged at the meeting that the employer had infringed his right to request flexible work. Since this was the reason for his subsequent dismissal, the dismissal was automatically unfair under ERA 1996 s104 (see paras 12.90 and 15.122–15.124).

Detriment

12.92   An employee has the right under ERA 1996 s47E and the Procedural Regs 2002 not to be subjected to any detriment (less favourable treatment) by any act, or deliberate failure to act, by his employer done on the grounds that the employee:

- made (or proposed to make) an application for flexible working under s80F;
- exercised (or proposed to exercise) a right under the procedure under s80G;
- brought proceedings against the employer for improper refusal of a request or for breach of the statutory procedure under s80H (see paras 12.73–12.77);
- alleged the existence of any circumstance which would constitute a ground for bringing such proceedings;[156]
- exercised or sought to exercise his/her right to be accompanied or to ask for a postponement because of the unavailability of the companion.[157]

12.93   A worker has an identical right if the employer acts on the grounds that the worker:

155   ET 2505740/03, reported in IDS Brief 802, April 2006.
156   ERA 1996 s47E.
157   Procedural Regs 2002 reg 16(1)(a).

- accompanied or sought to accompany another employee follow-ing a request under the right to request procedure.[158]

12.94   A tribunal claim under any of the above detriment provisions must be brought only after a statutory grievance has been raised, see chap-ter 16 for the procedure for doing this and applicable time limits (see also chapter 15).

Time limits and remedies

12.95   A complaint must be made:

- three months less one day from the effective date of termination,[159] or the date of the act or the failure to act or the last of a series of similar acts or failures,[160] or within seven days, in the case of seek-ing interim relief;[161]
- within such further period as the ET considers reasonable, where it is satisfied it was not reasonably practicable for the complaint to be presented within three months.[162]

12.96   For remedies in relation to dismissal, see chapter 18. In relation to a contravention of ERA 1996 s47E or Procedural Regs 2002 reg 16(1), a tribunal which finds a complaint justified shall make a declaration to that effect and may make an award of compensation which is just and equitable (which may include injury to feelings) taking into consider-ation the factors listed in ERA 1996 s49 (see paras 18.152–18.155).

Other potential claims

Discrimination

12.97   Where any of the conduct above is done in a discriminatory manner, there may be a discrimination claim (see para 12.98 and chapters 2 and 15).

---

158   Procedural Regs 2002 reg 16(1)(b).
159   ERA 1996 s111(2)(a).
160   ERA 1996 s48(3)(a) but see also s48(4).
161   ERA 1996 s128(2).
162   ERA 1996 ss111(2)(b), s48(3)(b).

Unfair dismissal

12.98 Where dismissal occurs (including a constructive dismissal where an employee/worker is forced to resign because the employee cannot work the hours required of him/her[163]) in any of the circumstances described above, there may also be claims for ordinary unfair dismissal under the ERA 1996 and discriminatory dismissal under the SDA 1975 (see chapter 15).

Useful information

Government websites

12.99 Department of Trade and Industry

See 'Flexible working: The right to request and the duty to consider: guidance for employers and employees (PL520)' at:
www.consumer.gov.uk/er/individual/flexible-pl516.htm

See 'Right to request' model forms at:
www.dti.gov.uk/employment/balancing-work-family-responsible/flexible-working/flexforms/index.html
TIGER (Tailored Interactive Guidance on Employment Rights, see also 'Directgov') concerning applications to work flexibly at:
www.tiger.gov.uk/flexible/index.htm

Working families

12.100 Flexible working checklist – interactive guide, at:

workingfamilies.org.uk/asp/family_zone/flex_work_guide/f_flex_work_guide_step1.asp

See also their flexible work factsheets at:
www.workingfamilies.org.uk/asp/family_zone/f_factsheets.asp

---

163 See, eg, *Commotion Ltd v Rutty*, note 81 and *Clarke v Telewest Communications plc*, note 121.

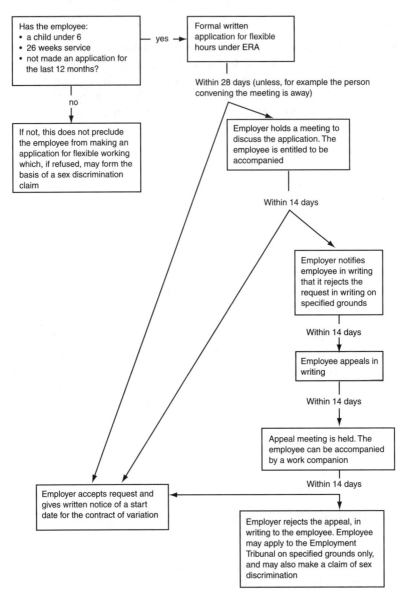

Source: Equal Opportunities Commission Website www.eoc-law.org.uk

CHAPTER 13

Indirect discrimination and flexible working hours

13.149 Evidence

Evidence from the employer • Evidence from the claimant • Evidence from other employees/of the employer's policy • Evidence from employee in another organisation doing similar work part-time/on a job share basis • Expert evidence

13.158 No right to return to full-time work

13.159 Indirect marital/civil partnership discrimination

13.160 Can men claim?

13.163 Remedies

13.164 Useful information

Key points

- It will be unlawful indirect sex discrimination to refuse a woman the right to work part-time or other flexible working hours if:
  - a provision, criterion, practice, requirement or condition to work full-time or inflexible hours puts or would put women at a particular disadvantage compared to men;
  - it puts the woman at that disadvantage; and
  - the employer cannot justify the refusal.
- Provisions, criteria or practices which are likely to disadvantage women more than men are those requiring full-time working, long hours, overtime, a full-time presence in the office, travelling over a long period.
- Proof that such practices disadvantage women disproportionately to men may be obtained from:
  - the workforce, if, as is common, more women than men work part-time;
  - labour market statistics;
  - research reports.
- Where a man is refused flexible working hours where a woman would be allowed them, this may be direct discrimination if he is treated less favourably than a woman has been or would be in similar circumstances.

Indirect sex discrimination and child-friendly hours

13.1   Many women with childcare and other caring responsibilities want to adjust or reduce their hours to enable them to combine work and family. Whether or not a woman is eligible to make a request under the statutory 'right to request' flexible working procedure (the 'right to request' procedure) (see chapter 12), she may still be able to make a claim under the Sex Discrimination Act (SDA) 1975 (see para 2.9 for who is covered). This is because an unjustified refusal to allow a change or reduction in hours may be indirect sex discrimination under the SDA 1975. It is generally advisable to make a request under the 'right to request' procedure first (where eligible), but this is not mandatory.

13.2   Indirect discrimination is concerned with unjustified employment practices (applied equally to men and women) which have the effect of disadvantaging women compared to men (or vice versa), or married people and civil partners compared to unmarried people and those not in a civil partnership (see para 13.59 for a discussion about marital and civil partnership discrimination).

13.3　　The disadvantage suffered by women is usually due to women's primary role in childcare which is difficult to combine with traditional working such as full-time work, long hours, variable shifts and overtime. Refusal of flexible working hours which are compatible with childcare responsibilities (such as part-time work) place women at a particular disadvantage. Where the refusal cannot be objectively justified, this may amount to indirect sex discrimination. Flexible working is the term used to cover work patterns which are also known as child-friendly working or family-friendly hours (see paras 12.1 and 12.12 for examples). The same principles apply to the disadvantage women suffer due to their role in caring for adults.

13.4　　Note that in order to avoid a claim under SDA 1975 an employer should, if possible, allow a woman to return to the same job as she held prior to her maternity leave, but on flexible working hours. Only if the job cannot be done on flexible working hours might the woman want to negotiate a different job which can be done on suitable hours.

13.5　　A woman may also have a claim for indirect sex discrimination if she is treated less favourably because she is working part-time or other child-friendly hours. In addition, the Part-time Workers (Prevention of Less Favourable Treatment) Regulations (PTW Regs 2000) 2000[1] provide that an employer must not treat part-time employees (male and female) less favourably unless this can be 'objectively justified'. These provisions are covered in chapter 14.

13.6　　Some reduction of hours could also be achieved by taking parental leave if the employer were to allow such leave to be taken in periods of less than a week (see chapter 10 onwards).

13.7　　See paras 13.60–13.62 for the position regarding claims by men.

Background

13.8　　The current definition of indirect sex discrimination is the third to apply since 1975.

1　　SI 2000 No 1551. Note regs 3 and 4 which protect the terms and conditions of a woman reducing her hours in certain circumstances even if there is no full-time comparator.

1. The definition in force to 12 October 2001

13.9 The pre-2001 definition of indirect discrimination said that:

> ... a person discriminates against another if he applies to her a requirement or condition which he applies or would apply equally to a man but–
> - which is such that the proportion of women who can comply is considerably smaller than the proportion of men who can comply with it; and
> - which he cannot show to be justifiable irrespective of the sex of the person to whom it is applied; and
> - which is to her detriment because she cannot comply with it.[2]

2. The definition in force from 12 October 2001 to 30 September 2005

13.10 This provided that:

> ... a person discriminates against another if he applies to her a provision, criterion or practice which he applies or would apply equally to a man but–
> - which is such that it would be to the detriment of a considerably larger proportion of women than men; and
> - which he cannot show to be justifiable irrespective of the sex of the person to whom it is applied; and
> - which is to her detriment.[3]

3. The current definition of indirect sex discrimination[4]

13.11 Under the SDA 1975 as amended on 1 October 2005,[5] an employer[6] indirectly discriminates against a worker if:

2 This was the original definition.
3 SDA 1975 s1(2)(b) and s3(1)(b) regarding indirect marital discrimination were amended from 12 October 2001 to contain this definition by the Sex Discrimination (Indirect Discrimination and Burden of Proof) Regulations 2001 SI No 2660 so as to comply with the Burden of Proof Directive (97/80/EC) (the BPD).
4 The definition of indirect marital discrimination is the same except the comparison is between married people and civil partners compared to unmarried people and those not in a civil partnership (SDA 1975 ss3(1)(b) and (2) as amended by Civil Partnership Act 2004 s251, in force from 5 December 2005 (SI 2005 No 3175). See further para 13.159.
5 Employment Equality (Sex Discrimination) Regulations 2005 SI No 2467 amended SDA 1975 s1(2)(b) (and s3(1)(b) regarding indirect marital discrimination, subsequently amended as described in note 4) to comply with the Equal Treatment Amendment Directive (2002/73/EC) (ETAD) amending the Equal Treatment Directive (76/207/EEC) (ETD).
6 Or other body.

. . . he applies to her a provision, criterion or practice:[7]
which he applies or would apply equally to a man, but–

- which puts, or would put women at a particular disadvantage when compared with men,
- which puts her at that disadvantage, and
- which he cannot show to be a proportionate means of achieving a legitimate aim.[8]

13.12   All the sex discrimination cases referred to in this chapter were decided under the previous law when one of the two earlier definitions set out above applied.

13.13   The government guidance[9] to the 2005 amendments to the SDA 1975 states that they do not change existing sex discrimination law. European legal principles provide that it is not possible to take away existing rights and these must be followed by UK courts. Thus where pre-existing law is more favourable to complainants, it must be followed.[10] In certain respects, despite what the government guidance says the new definition will be more advantageous to claimants in some respects (particularly points 1 and 2 at para 13.15). As a result, although many of the cases decided under previous definitions will remain relevant in interpreting the new law, it cannot be assumed that their outcome would have been the same if they had been decided under the current definition. In particular, those decided under the pre-2001 more restrictive definition[11] must be approached with more caution.

---

7   See SDA 1975 s82, which includes requirement and condition but is referred to in this chapter as 'PCP'.
8   See SDA 1975 s1(2).
9   See 'Changes to Sex Discrimination Legislation in Great Britain: Explaining the Employment Equality (Sex Discrimination) Regulations 2005' at: www.womenandequalityunit.gov.uk/publications/ sda_change_explanation_051603.doc.
10   By virtue of the non-derogation provision in article 6 of the BPD and article 8(e) of the ETD (see further paras 1.22 and 1.23). See also *Starmer v British Airways* 2005 IRLR 862, where the EAT said the definition of a PCP will be at least as wide as to include anything that would previously have qualified as a requirement or condition.
11   The most significant differences between the pre-2001 definition and the subsequent one was that the application of a 'requirement or condition' rather than a PCP had to be shown and that rather than just showing 'detriment' the claimant had to show she could not comply with it in practice.

Codes of practice

13.14 Codes of practice and EC recommendations are not legally binding but the tribunal must take them into account in reaching its decision. The following are relevant to flexible working and indirect discrimination:

- the European Council recommendation on childcare;
- the EC childcare good practice guide;
- the EOC Code of practice under the SDA 1975 (see paras 2.26–2.27).

The four main questions

13.15 There are four main questions to address in order to decide if indirect sex discrimination has occurred:

1) Is there a provision, criterion, practice (PCP), requirement or condition applied to work inflexible hours?
2) Does it, or would it, put women at a particular disadvantage when compared with men?
3) Is the claimant put at that disadvantage?
4) Can the employer justify the PCP[12] by showing it to be a proportionate means of achieving a legitimate aim?

Question 1: Is there a PCP?

Introduction

13.16 The claimant must show that a PCP has been applied to her. PCP is wider in scope than the pre-2001 wording[13] and is interpreted broadly.[14] As well as written provisions found eg, in a letter of appointment, a job contract or a collective agreement, it includes informal human resources and workplace practices. In *Rutherford v Secretary of State for Trade and Industry*,[15] the House of Lords charac-

---

12 Which includes requirement and condition, which is the old definition, see SDA 1975 s82(1).
13 See notes 10 and 12 above.
14 See, eg, *Cross v British Airways* [2005] IRLR 423. In *Allonby v Accrington and Rossendale College* [2001] IRLR 364, the Court of Appeal said the pre-2001 wording was not to be narrowly construed.
15 [2006] UKHL 19.

terised Pcps as encompassing measures which are 'formal and general or informal and particular'.

What is a provision, criterion or practice?

13.17 A PCP:

- may apply to all aspects of the employment relationship, eg, recruitment, promotion, training, transfer, dismissal, detriment;
- may apply to all or some workers or only the claimant;
- may allow for exceptions;
- need not be essential for doing a job, eg, a preference for an employee to work late;
- can be oral as well as written;
- can be a single instruction, such as a requirement to work one weekend;[16]
- includes anything which was a requirement or condition;[17]
- can be a discretionary decision applied only to the claimant and not to all those in broadly similar jobs;[18]
- may be implied from the facts of a situation rather than made explicit.[19]

The questionnaire procedure (para 17.28 onwards) is useful to identify the PCP.

13.18 Examples of PCPs include:

- to work full-time;[20]
- to work a particular number of hours if working part-time;[21]
- to work inflexible hours[22] or be fully flexible;[23]

---

16 *Banner Business Supplies v Greaves* EAT/0420/04, 4 November 2004; [2005] AER(D) 26 (Feb).
17 SDA 1975 s82(1); see also *British Airways v Starmer*, note 10.
18 *Starmer*, note 10.
19 *British Medical Association v Chaudhary* EAT/1351/01, 24 March 2004 (unreported) (a Race Relations Act 1976 case).
20 *Home Office v Holmes* [1984] IRLR 299 EAT (a refusal to permit part-time work); *Hardys and Hansons plc v Lax* [2005] IRLR 726 CA (a refusal to permit the job share of a full-time job); *British Telecommunications plc v Roberts* [1996] IRLR 601 (to avoid unsocial hours working, employees had to work full-time).
21 *Starmer*, note 10.
22 *Commotion Ltd v Rutty* [2006] IRLR 171.
23 *Manning v Wick Hill* ET 2300178/02 (PCP to work full-time and fully flexibly); *Oddbins v Robinson* EAT 188/96 (unreported) (a requirement to work such hours as may be necessary).

- to work overtime/anti-social hours/rotating shifts;[24]
- to change shift patterns;[25]
- to be office-based rather than work from home;[26]
- to change hours;[27]
- a mobility clause providing that the worker must work in another part of the country at the employer's discretion;[28]
- to work long hours;[29]
- a change of hours imposed by the employer;
- a refusal to allow other child-friendly work patterns (see para 13.3).

13.19   If different PCPs are applied to women than to men, this will be direct discrimination. Thus, refusing to allow a man to work part-time where a woman would be allowed to, is direct discrimination (see further para 13.160 onwards).[30]

Identifying the PCP

13.20   Defining the PCP carefully is important as it must particularly disadvantage women (see para 13.28 onwards for how this is decided):

- It is for the claimant to define the PCP; it is irrelevant if her

24 *Briggs v North Eastern Education and Library Board* [1990] IRLR 181 NICA (requirement to work one hour in the evening each week); *London Underground v Edwards (No 2)* [1998] IRLR 364, CA (the introduction of an anti-social rotating shift system); *Hale and Clunie v Wiltshire Healthcare NHS Trust* (1999) DCLD 39, ET 1401250198 and 1401251/98 (nurses made redundant because they could not work rotating shifts, held to be indirect marital discrimination).

25 *Smith v High Table* ET 2000 (introduction of a shift pattern of 6 am–2 pm and 1 pm–9 pm); *Williams-Drabble v Pathway Care Solutions Ltd and another*, ET 2601718/04, reported in IDS Brief 776 (a religious discrimination case, where a rota change was imposed which prevented the claimant attending her church) and see the *South African Airways* case, note 28.

26 *Unn v Presentation Services Ltd* ET 2301439/00 (requirement to work only in the office rather than from home); *Lockwood v Crawley Warren Group Ltd* EAT 1176/99, 28 June 2000, DCLD 47 (refusal to consider working from home); *Castleton v Department for Work and Pensions* EAT 0715/02, 30 October 2002 (unreported) (requirement to work two days a week in the office instead of one out of ten days).

27 *Banner Business Supplies*, note 16 (a provision to work a particular weekend); *Smith v Greyfriars Taverns Ltd* ET 2801894/01 (a requirement to work varied hours at short notice); *Rollinson v Baldwin (t/a United Colours of Benetton)* EAT 0873/04, 22 March 2004 (unreported) (a requirement to cover for other employees' holidays and sickness).

28 *Meade-Hill v British Council* [1995] IRLR 478, CA.

29 *Cowley v South African Airways* ET 1999 (a requirement to work back to back double shifts).

30 *Walkingshaw v The John Martin Group*, ETS 401126/00, Edinburgh (unreported).

employer identifies a different one which is unobjectionable, from the same facts.[31]

- The PCP need not be specified in the claim but it must be clear that it is an indirect sex discrimination claim. The employer also may ask for further details of it from the claimant.

- There may be more than one PCP if the claimant is requesting an adjustment to more than one working pattern, for example if there is a request to work part-time (say three days a week instead of five) and partially from home. The employer may ask the employee to suggest alternative options or may propose other possibilities, such as a four-day week instead of the three-day week requested, in which case the PCP would be to work a four-day week. These different PCPs may be argued in the alternative.

Has the PCP been applied to the claimant?

13.21   A PCP must be applied to the worker before she can make a claim; the request for different hours must have been refused. The PCP (for example, full-time hours) is applied if a request for part-time work is refused or the employer imposes a new working pattern incompatible with the claimant's childcare arrangements and refuses to make any adjustment.

13.22   If an employee has made a request under the 'right to request' procedure (see chapter 12) the identity of the PCP(s) will be clear.

13.23   If the worker gets no response to her request for flexible working, whether made under the 'right to request' procedure or not, she should repeat her request, preferably in writing,[32] setting a time limit for a response. She should say that if none is received, she will assume that her request has been refused. If the employer fails to respond this will probably be deemed to be a refusal.

13.24   A PCP is unlikely to have been imposed if:

- the employer is still genuinely considering the request;[33]
- the employer has agreed to the claimant's request, even only on a trial basis;[34]
- there is only the possibility of a PCP (such a contractual mobility clause) being imposed in the future; an exception will be

---

31 *Allonby v Accrington and Rossendale College* [2001] IRLR 364.
32 If it is made under the 'right to request' procedure, she must apply in writing and follow the procedure carefully, see chapter 12.
33 *Hill v Staffordshire Sentinel Newspapers Ltd* ET 2900163/01.
34 *Benson v Mr S P Johnson* ET 1900059/02.

where the contract has already been altered to make provision for this.[35]

Statutory grievance and disciplinary procedures

13.25 The statutory grievance and disciplinary procedures (see chapter 16 for full details including time limits) apply, although only to employees.

13.26 Although the grievance procedure does not apply in relation to claims for breach of the 'right to request' procedure (see chapter 12), it does apply for most claims under the SDA 1975.

Advice to employers and employees negotiating different working patterns

13.27 Whether an informal or formal procedure is being used, the advice given in 'Negotiating positively' (see para 12.43 on 'right to request') should be followed. Note that although the flexible working procedure is available only to employees, workers can still ask for flexible working before taking action under the SDA 1975 provisions described in this chapter.

Question 2: Does the PCP put, or would it put, women at a particular disadvantage when compared with men?

13.28 The claimant must show that the PCP puts or would put women at a particular disadvantage when compared with men (or vice versa). Under the previous definitions it was usually necessary to carry out a detailed statistical analysis of the ability of women to meet the PCP compared to men.[36] However, different tribunals and courts took varying approaches towards the evidence required to show 'disproportionate adverse impact'. Some accepted that it was 'common knowledge' that women work part-time in order to care for children and so find it harder to work full-time, so that statistics were not

---

35 *Meade-Hill v British Council*, note 28.
36 Under the first definition, many tribunals took the view that it was necessary to have actual male comparators in order to show disparate impact in the workforce.

always necessary. This flexible approach to statistical evidence taken by many tribunals in the past (see para 13.34) should be increasingly followed by tribunals under the current definition.

13.29   There are broadly three ways of identifying whether women are put at a particular disadvantage. They are not mutually exclusive and should be argued in the alternative where possible. These are:

1) that the disadvantage is common knowledge and/or demonstrated by other general evidence;
2) that national/international labour market statistics demonstrate the disadvantage; and/or
3) that workplace statistics demonstrate the disadvantage.

1. Common knowledge and other evidence

13.30   Government guidance states that the current test should mean that reliance will be placed less on statistical evidence than in the past and more on expert and other evidence to establish particular disadvantage:

> Statistics can be helpful in ascertaining relative disadvantage, however they are not essential . . . evidence could come from experts or other witnesses.[37]

13.31   Where common knowledge or other evidence such as labour market statistics (see para 13.45 onwards) show that a PCP 'would put'[38] women at a particular disadvantage compared to men, this enables the tribunal to hypothesise about the affect of the PCP on women generally, thereby applying the general impact to the particular case without the need to rely on actual workplace comparators. This may be useful where there are no men in the claimant's workplace or no men doing similar work.[39]

13.32   Common knowledge and a tribunal's own expertise may enable it to draw inferences as to why women are less able and therefore less likely to work unchild-friendly hours than men, and how they would suffer a particular disadvantage were they required to do so. This may

---

37 Note 9.
38 Such a comparator has been possible since the October 2001 amendments to the SDA 1975. Similarly, the current wording asks whether the PCP puts or *would* put women at a particular disadvantage.
39 In *Shamoon v Chief Constable of the Royal Ulster Constabulary* [2003] IRLR 285, HL, a direct sex discrimination case, the use of hypothetical comparisons was approved.

be accepted as sufficient evidence in itself, but more commonly is used to reinforce other evidence of disparate impact, such as labour market statistics.

13.33   For example, in *London Underground v Edwards*[40] the Court of Appeal said that the tribunal was entitled to take into account their own knowledge and experience that the burden of childcare falls upon many more women than men and that a far greater proportion of single parents with care of children are women rather than men. Thus, the fact that only one woman was affected by the PCP was likely to represent a minimum impact on the female workforce, in other words it was the tip of the iceberg.

13.34   Tribunals and courts have acknowleged that:

- a far greater proportion of sole parents undertaking childcare are women;[41]
- a considerably larger proportion of women than men may have to take time off work to care for a sick child;[42]
- the majority of those who work part-time do so for childcare reasons which disproportionately fall on women;[43]
- part-time work is overwhelmingly done by women;[44]
- it is more difficult for women to work full-time when they have childcare responsibilites;[45]
- a tribunal is entitled to take into account, where appropriate, a more general picture than is specifically displayed by statistics put in evidence;[46]
- a higher proportion of women than men are secondary earners.[47]

13.35   However, other tribunals have taken a different approach and:

- refused to take judicial notice of the disparate impact the running of family life has on women to show, in the absence of any

---

40   Note 24.
41   *Edwards*, note 24.
42   *McCrimmon v Quality Fare* ET S/103350/02, 21 March 2003, reported EOR 121.
43   *Chief Constable of Avon and Somerset Constabulary v Chew*, EAT/503/00, 28 September 2001 (unreported).
44   *Allonby* note 31.
45   *Mitchell v David Evans Agricultural Ltd.*, EAT/0083/06, 15 March 2006 (unreported).
46   *Starmer*, note 10.
47   *Meade-Hill v British Council*, note 28.

evidence, the disparate impact on women of the requirement to work full-time;[48]

- refused to accept, at least in relation to highly paid City jobs (the claimant was a partner in a legal firm), that a considerably larger proportion of women than men could not work full-time due to childcare responsibilities, without specific evidence to this effect.[49]

13.36 These cases, however, were decided when there was a more restrictive definition of disparate impact.

Expert and evidence other than statistics

13.37 Specific evidence should be used where particular disadvantage may not be common knowledge or evident from statistics for the reasons described below (paras 13.45–13.47 on labour market statistics and para 13.55 on where workplace statistics may not be available or representative). For example:

- where statistics show that the proportions of men and women working a particular pattern of hours are similar; or
- where statistics about particular work patterns and their effect on women with children's workforce participation are not readily available.

13.38 An expert in sociology, economics or demography can explain the gender-based reasons why women work particular hours. For example, as many more women than men take primary responsibility for children, any hours which do not accommodate a woman's childcare needs arguably put women at a particular disadvantage. The differing reasons why women and men work, for example, evenings and weekends may be explained in research data or statistics not readily available.

13.39 Experts in workplace organisation, eg Working Families, may also be able to provide expert evidence about the impact of specific working patterns on women and men, though expert evidence may be expensive.

---

48 *Ministry of Defence (Royal Navy) v Macmillan*, EATS/0003/04, 22 September 2004 (unreported), a refusal to allow a Royal Navy employee to work part-time in her existing job.

49 *Sinclair Roche and Temperley v Heard* [2004] IRLR 763, EAT per Burton J who distinguished it in deciding *Starmer*, note 10 though in *Starmer* workplace and national labour force statistics were produced but not much emphasis placed on them.

13.40   Research reports can be used as evidence, for example, those on the EOC's website.[50]

13.41   In addition, the claimant can give evidence about her knowledge of patterns of work in the workplace even if she does not have detailed knowledge of the breakdown of male and female employees.

13.42   Arguably, where it is well known that the PCP particularly disadvantages women (such as a full-time work requirement) this should be accepted by tribunals and courts without the need for further proof on the basis of common knowledge. This is because there is ample research showing that it is primarily women who work part-time (and other flexible hours) in order to combine work with childcare. Thus, for example:

- 81% of part-timers are women;[51]
- 97% of part-time workers who gave domestic reasons for working part-time were women;[52]
- the main earner in most families is the man so women are more likely to reduce their hours for childcare reasons.

13.43   However, despite the greater emphasis which should now be placed on evidence other than statistics (see para 13.65 onwards) statistics may still be needed, particularly where the impact of a PCP is not well documented or obvious (for example see *Secretary of State for Trade and Industry v Rutherford*,[53] see para 13.64).

13.44   Even in 'obvious' cases, because of the different views adopted by the courts, it is advisable to provide at least labour market statistics and not just rely on common knowledge. If available and representative, workplace statistics should also be produced. Where these are used, case-law prior to the definition change about how they show disparate impact is likely to remain relevant (see para 13.48 onwards on workplace statistics).

2. Labour market statistics

13.45   It is always advisable to produce labour market statistics and/or research reports, because even though they may not be job specific,

50 See the EOC website for its work on research and statistics at: www.eoc.org.uk/Default.aspx?page=18682.
51 From EOC website, based on Spring 2004 Labour Force Survey, at: www.eoc.org.uk/Default.aspx?page=17922.
52 From EOC website, based on Spring 2004 Labour Force Survey, at: www.eoc.org.uk/Default.aspx?page=17923.
53 See note 15.

they more accurately represent the differences between men and women as they are based on larger samples of workers than a workplace. It is particularly important to consider labour market statistics or other evidence of women's working constraints, where workforce statistics are not representative (see para 13.55 onwards).

13.46   Figures compiled annually by the EOC show statistics for part-time, flexitime, home working, annualised hours, job share, term-time working,[54] evening and weekend working.[55] For example, according to their 2006 report only 58% of women work full-time but 91% of men do so.[56]

13.47   Even labour market statistics are not always available particularly for the less common types of flexible working arrangements. Relying on common knowledge and seeking expert and other evidence may assist (see para 13.30 onwards).

3. Workplace statistics

Defining the pool

13.48 First, it is important to identify the relevant group (ie pool) from which the statistics are taken. The courts have generally said that the pool should be those workers whose circumstances are similar, ie, who are doing similar work or who have the same qualifications and experience, regardless of whether they meet the PCP. In *Allonby v Accrington and Rossendale College*,[57] where the redundancy of hourly paid part-time lecturers was challenged, the Court of Appeal said that once the PCP has been defined, identifying the pool is a matter of logic and there is likely to be only one correct pool. It is not a question of fact. The tribunal decision about the pool will therefore be critically scrutinised by the EAT.

13.49   Depending on the facts of the case and their availability, statistics may come from:

• in recruitment decisions, those eligible for the job;
• the workplace;

54 EOC: Facts about women and men in Great Britain 2006, at: www.eoc.org.uk/ Default.aspx?page=14895.
55 EOC: Working arrangements statistics 2004 at: www.eoc.org.uk/ Default.aspx?page=17910.
56 EOC: Facts about women and men in Great Britain 2006, note 54; see also working arrangements statistics for reasons for working part-time at: www.eoc.org.uk/Default.aspx?page=14893.
57 Note 31.

- evidence from the claimant and other witnesses;
- information provided by the employer under the statutory questionnaire procedure (see para 17.28 onwards).

Statistics in recruitment decisions

13.50 Where a claimant has applied for a job and seeks, for example, part-time hours, the workplace pool is those men and women who, but for the disputed requirement (eg to work full-time) are qualified for the advertised job.[58] However, such statistics may not be easily or comprehensively available so that a flexible approach to the statistics which are available should be taken and other evidence may be needed.[59]

Statistics in decisions affecting existing workers

13.51 Where a worker requests a different working pattern, the pool generally comprises all workers, male and female, whatever their hours, in the same or broadly similar jobs[60] to the claimant's.[61] It could comprise the whole workforce, particularly if it is small, or a department in a large organisation or, in a very large organisation, a section of the department (see para 13.57 for the situation in the leading case of *Edwards*[62]). For example, if a secretary wishes to work part-time, the pool could consist of all secretaries in her section, or those in her department, or (less likely unless the other figures are unrepresentative, see para 13.55 onwards) those in the organisation.

13.52 The questionnaire should ask the employer for the relevant details from which the statistics can be compiled (see para 17.28 onwards).

13.53 The resulting figures should be examined in the light of relevant national labour market statistics (see paras 13.45–13.47). If the workplace statistics are significantly different to the national labour market ones, this may indicate their unreliability and the need to emphasise the national statistics and to rely on other evidence (see paras 13.30–13.44).

---

58 *University of Manchester v Jones* [1993] IRLR 218.
59 *Greater Manchester Police Authority v Lea* [1990] IRLR 372.
60 SDA 1975 s5(3).
61 If a claimant must satisfy several criteria, only one of which is being challenged, the pool comprises those who can comply with the criteria with which the applicant can comply apart from the one which is challenged, *Taylor v Inland Revenue Commissioners* EAT/498/98, 28 September 1999.
62 Note 24.

The calculation

13.54 The calculation of the proportions is done as follows where, for example, the PCP is to work full-time. The same would apply to other PCPs:

a) take the number of women in the pool identified as above (say there are 100 female clerks in the workforce); and
b) take the number of women in the group who work full-time (say there are 75 full-time female clerks); and
c) calculate b) as a percentage of a); this gives the proportion of women in the pool who satisfy the PCP, ie, 75%; and
d) take the number of men in the group (say 100 clerks); and
e) take the number of men in the group who work full-time (say 95); and
f) calculate e) as a percentage of d); this gives the proportion of men in the pool who satisfy the PCP, ie, 95%.

The proportion of women who comply (75%) is compared to the proportion of men who comply (95%) and if the difference is considerably smaller (see paras 13.59–13.64), disproportionate impact has been proved.

Where workplace statistics are not available or representative

13.55 In many workplaces, the statistics will be inadequate or not accurately reflect the reality of the effect of the PCP on women. If so, either the pool should be widened to cover a larger section of the workplace (if appropriate) or to cover the national labour market (see paras 13.45–13.47). It is no longer necessary for the comparative exercise to be based on actual men and women in the workplace as SDA 1975 s1(1)(b) only requires that women are or 'would' be put at a disadvantage. Thus, the tribunal can look at what would have been the position had there been comparable men, ie, make a hypothetical comparison. This will be needed where, for example:

- there is a women-only workplace or where there are no men doing similar work as there will be no relevant workplace statistics relating to women and men;
- in small workplaces (for example, if one person joins or leaves the organisation, this may change the balance);[63]

63 *White v Timbmet Ltd* EAT 1125/99, 27 June 2000 (unreported) said that a tribunal may assess the significance of statistics yielded by a very small pool in the light of national labour force and social statistics.

- where the statistics are unusual viewed in the context of labour market statistics because of special factors (for example, in predominantly male workplaces where non-complying women may be rare,[64] or where a large number of part-timers are men);
- where part-time working is never allowed.

13.56   Workforces which do not reflect national statistics may be indicative of discriminatory practices, for example where part-time working is not allowed, where no men are disadvantaged by the disputed practice and/or very few women are employed. The workplace pool may, in these circumstances, be 'tainted by discrimination', and so unreliable.

13.57   In *London Underground v Edwards (No 2)*,[65] a requirement to work a new anti-social rotating shift system was imposed on underground train drivers of whom 21 were women and 2,023 men. One female sole parent (the claimant) could not work the new system, whereas all the men could. The correct pool was the employer's workforce to whom the new arrangements were to be applied, that is the existing train drivers. The proportional difference between the men who could comply (100%) and the women (95.2%) was small. The Court of Appeal accepted that the tribunal was right to have regard to the large discrepancy in numbers between male and female operators. A figure of 100 men to one woman indicated that it was either difficult or unattractive for women to work as train operators, so the proportion of women not complying with the PCP represented a minimum figure, not a maximum. It was also significant that there were no men disadvantaged by the practice. The new roster was found to have disproportionately disadvantaged women (see further para 13.61).

13.58   Where other employees have difficulty in complying with a PCP but do not challenge it, they should be treated as part of the disadvantaged group, along with other women non-compliers. The questionnaire procedure (see para 17.28 onwards) can be used to get information about the proportion of flexible work applications made by women, the number refused,[66] complaints about lack of flexibility (and whether they are mainly made by women) and whether any employees (male or female) have left as a result. In *Edwards*[67] the court took account of the fact that another woman applied to opt out

---

64   For example, *Edwards*, note 24.
65   Ibid.
66   See *British Airways plc v Starmer*, note 10.
67   Note 24.

where an increase in one woman unable to comply with the PCP would have substantially widened the proportional gap between the men and women compliers.[68]

Assessment of whether there is a 'particular' disadvantage

Where statistics are used

13.59 Prior to October 2005, the tribunal had to assess whether the difference in the proportion of women adversely affected by a PCP was 'considerably larger' than the proportion of men.

13.60 Where statistics were used, many tribunals accepted that since this issue had to be resolved in an infinite number of different employment situations,[69] a flexible approach was required as to whether a particular percentage was to be regarded as 'substantially smaller' in any given case (see paras 13.61–13.63). Tribunals should be more willing to use this approach to statistical evidence which is produced, in view of the new wording, particularly as it is a threshold provision and the threshold has now arguably been lowered by the most recent definition.

13.61 The Court of Appeal decision in *Edwards*[70] and other cases has provided important guidelines. These include:

- The PCP must produce a substantial and not merely a marginal discriminatory effect.[71] A persistent, though lesser, disparity may be sufficient.[72]
- Its disparate impact should be inherent in its application and not simply a result of unreliable statistics or fortuitous circumstances.[73]
- There is no rule of thumb as to the correct percentage difference.[74]

---

68 See also *Chief Constable of Avon and Somerset Constabulary v Chew*, note 43. The EAT in *Ministry of Defence (Royal Navy) v Macmillan*, note 48, accepted the potential validity of such evidence.

69 *Edwards*, note 24.

70 Note 24.

71 Note 24.

72 *R v Secretary of State for Employment, ex p Nicole Seymour-Smith and Laura Perez*, Case number C 167/97, [1999] IRLR 253, ECJ; *R v Secretary of State for Employment, ex p Nicole Seymour-Smith and Laura Perez (No 2)* [2000] IRLR 263, HL.

73 *Edwards*, note 24; Seymour-Smith ECJ and HL, note 72.

74 *Edwards*, note 24.

- When assessing the significance of a particular percentage difference, the tribunal is entitled to take a flexible approach. In *Edwards*, 4.8% satisfied the test and could be seen as representing a minimum rather than the maximum figure as far as discriminatory effect is concerned. The relevant factors included:
  - the fact that not even one man was disadvantaged by the practice;
  - the fact that the small number of women train drivers indicated that it was either a difficult or unattractive job for women;
  - national statistics about the disproportionate childcare responsibilities of sole parents;
  - indications that another woman employee had difficulty with the requirement.

13.62　In *Chew*,[75] 99.96% of male officers could comply with the required shift roster and 97.7% of women, a difference of 2.26%. The EAT said this was not enough to show disparate impact of itself but that the tribunal was correct to have regard to other factors including the fact that the majority of those who could not do the required shifts had childcare responsibilities and generally the overwhelming burden of childcare responsibilities falls on women. In addition the effect of the PCP was supported by statistics, which were not fortuitous. The small difference was therefore explicable in terms of the impact of variable shifts on women, so demonstrating disparate impact.

13.63　　In *British Airways plc v Starmer*[76] a woman pilot was allowed to work 75% of full-time but not 50%. Following the Court of Appeal in *Edwards*[77] and *Allonby*,[78] the EAT upheld the tribunal's decision that a 3.66% difference[79] constituted a disproportionate impact saying that the tribunal was entitled to take into account, where appropriate, a more general picture than is specifically displayed by statistics put in evidence. Evidence was also brought that most part-time work applications were from women and were usually for childcare reasons, women generally having primary childcare responsibility. These reflected national labour force statistics also placed before the tribunal. The EAT concluded that 'that there was evidence, over and

---

75　Note 43.
76　Note 10.
77　Note 24.
78　Note 31.
79　The percentage of men working 75% or full-time was 99.816% and the women who worked 75% or full-time was 96.15%.

above the limited statistics, upon which the tribunal was entitled to and did reach its conclusion . . . as to disparity'. Therefore, the tribunal was 'entitled to find that requiring her to work 75% if she wished to do part-time working, was one which "would be to the detriment of a considerably larger proportion of women than of men" '.[80]

13.64   The House of Lords in *Rutherford*[81] a case also decided under the pre-2005 definition, said that when examining statistical evidence the focus should usually be on the relative proportions of men and women in the advantaged group. This was particularly so in cases involving national legislation of general application and where the vast majority of the pool are in the advantaged group.[82] It did not rule out examining the disadvantaged group in appropriate cases. It also gave cautious endorsement to the general guidance given in *Harvest Town Circle Ltd v Rutherford*[83] which recommended using more than one type of comparison when assessing statistical evidence, if only as a check. The approach in *Harvest Circle* is likely to remain useful in less 'obvious' cases under the new definition.

Where statistics are not produced

13.65   Although similar wording to the new definition has been in force in race, religious and sexual orientation discrimination law since 2003[84] there is little case-law as yet about how it will be interpreted. In two indirect religious discrimination cases,[85] decided under wording identical in the relevant respect to the amended SDA 1975, claimants have been successful. They argued that a PCP hindering the exercise of their religion put persons of the same religion at a particular disadvantage (compared with those not of that religion), without producing statistical evidence of this effect.

80 Paras 29 and 30.
81 Note 15, per Walker LJ, with whom Nicholls LJ agreed.
82 The PCP was derived from a legislative provision (the exclusion of workers of 65 and over from unfair dismissal rights) with implications for the entire workforce rather than an employer-imposed one. Whether or not it had a disparate adverse impact on men was not self-evident.
83 [2001] IRLR 599, EAT.
84 Race Relations Act 1976 (Amendment) Regulations 2003, SI 2003 No 1626; Employment Equality (Religion or Belief) Regulations 2003 SI No 1657; Employment Equality (Sexual Orientation) Regulations 2003 SI No 1661; similar provisions are contained in the Employment Equality (Age) Regulations 2006 SI No 1031, in force from October 2006.
85 *Williams-Drabble v Pathway Care Solutions and Rehman* ET 2601718/04, reported in IDS Brief 776; *Fugler v MacMillan-London Hairstudios Limited* ET 2205090/04, reported in IDS Brief 795.

13.66   By analogy with nationality discrimination case-law, if requirements of certain (unchild-friendly or inflexible) working patterns are
'intrinsically liable' to affect women more than men and there is
therefore a risk that women would be placed at a particular disadvantage compared to men, that disadvantage should be established. In
O'Flynn v Adjudication Officer,[86] the European Court of Justice (ECJ)
held (subject to objective justification) that a national law must be
regarded as indirectly discriminatory and subject to the prohibition
on discrimination on the basis of nationality (of a member state) 'if it
is intrinsically liable to affect migrant workers more than national
workers and if there is a consequent risk that it will place the former
at a particular disadvantage. It is not necessary in this respect to find
that the provision in question does in practice affect a substantially
higher proportion of migrant workers. It is sufficient that it is liable
to have such an effect'. This was followed by the Court of Appeal in
Secretary of State for Work and Pensions v Bobezes[87] where statistical
proof of indirect nationality discrimination was not required. The
court commented that sex discrimination cases were quite different
where discrimination will often not be obvious and statistical evidence of disparate impact will be necessary. Many PCPs in indirect
sex discrimination flexible hours claims will increasingly be accepted
as obvious, and in such cases the approach taken in *O'Flynn,*[88] should
be used to reinforce the use of common knowledge by tribunals.

13.67   In *R (on the application of Elias) v Secretary of State for Defence*[89] the
claimant was excluded from a non-statutory payment for those
interned by the Japanese during the war because she could not meet
the criteria of having been born in the UK or having a parent
or grandparent born here. She succeeded in her judicial review
application alleging the scheme was indirectly discriminatory against
those of non-British national origins. Her claim was made under the
Race Relations Act 1976.[90] The disparate impact of the scheme was
conceded. Referring to *Bobezes*, the Court said that where (as here

---

86   C237/94.
87   [2005] EWCA Civ 111 16 February 2005, was an indirect nationality
     discrimination case challenging a condition of entitlement to a social security
     benefit. The court held that it could find the condition was intrinsically liable to
     affect a significant number of migrant workers on the ground of nationality
     without statistical proof being available.
88   Note 86.
89   [2005] EWHC 1435 (Admin), HC.
90   As amended in 2003 (see para 13.65) though in this case the court considered the
     changes did not add to the protection available.

where the extent of the discrimination was very marked) the effects are obvious or intrinsic to the scheme being adopted, specific statistical evidence of disparate impact was unnecessary.

Is there a disadvantage where the woman has been offered a different flexible working pattern than the one she has asked for?

13.68 It may be difficult to show that working hours proposed by the employer particularly disadvantage women, for example where it requires the employee to work four days instead of a requested three days per week. This occurred in *Starmer*.[91] The EAT accepted that women were generally disadvantaged by being required to work longer hours and looked at statistics which showed that those able to work more than three days a week (ie, 75% or full time) were mainly men whilst those not able to do so were mainly women. Statistically this was still not very significant but other evidence (see para 13.63) meant that disproportionate impact was found. In such cases, using other evidence as well as common knowledge will be important.

Question 3: Has the PCP put the claimant at the particular disadvantage complained of?

13.69 The ETD definition of indirect discrimination does not require proof of 'disadvantage' by the claimant, only that the PCP would put women in general at a particular disadvantage compared to men. However, it will be advisable for the claimant also to show that she herself suffers a disadvantage because of the application of the PCP as this is required by the SDA.[92] In flexible hours cases, the disadvantage will be the difficulty in combining the required work hours with her childcare responsibilities. This does not mean that the claimant must show she *cannot* work these hours.

13.70 'Disadvantage' should be interpreted at least as broadly as 'detriment'.[93] The Court of Appeal has said that 'subjecting to ... detriment' does not mean anything more than 'putting under a

---

91 Note 10.
92 Prior to October 2005, a claimant had to show that the PCP was to her detriment. Pre-October 2001, it was also necessary to show that she could not comply with it in practice.
93 See note 10.

disadvantage'.[94] In *Gill v El Vino*,[95] the Court of Appeal held that the deprivation of choice was sufficient to amount to less favourable treatment. In *Shamoon*[96] the House of Lords said the correct question was whether 'a reasonable worker would or might take the view that in all the circumstances it [the treatment complained of] was to [her] detriment'. It made it clear that there was no need to show physical or economic loss. A detriment is more, however, than 'an unjustified sense of grievance'.

13.71   The definition before 1 October 2005 involved showing that the worker suffered a 'detriment' and this was interpreted in the same way as the SDA 1975 s6(2)(b) definition of detriment. It is likely that the same broad interpretation will be given to 'disadvantage'.

Personal choice

13.72   Refusal of the desired hours or working pattern is arguably sufficient to show disadvantage. A woman is disadvantaged when she is deprived of the choice of the reqested hours to enable her to care for her children in the way she wants and which is in the child's interests.[97] However, under the old law tribunals sometimes held that the denial of 'choice' was not sufficient to cause a detriment. Therefore, it is advisable for the claimant to give evidence of her need for the requested hours. Relevant factors are the affordability[98] of childcare and its availability including by other family members, the need to attend a particular nursery[99] and the opening and closing times which might limit her ability to start early or work late. Also relevant are any particular needs of the child such as the need to attend regular

---

94 *Jeremiah v Ministry of Defence* [1979] IRLR 436.
95 [1983] IRLR 206.
96 *Shamoon v Chief Constable of the Royal Ulster Constabulary*, note 39.
97 See, eg, *Dolan v Radio Clyde Ltd*, EOR No 146, October 2005, where the tribunal said that full-time working prevented the claimant from exercising her choice to place her son in nursery care on only three days a week and that consequently she had suffered a detriment.
98 Note that even under the compliance test (see note 11), in *Zurich Insurance Co v Gulson* [1998] IRLR 118 the EAT said that the financial questions about whether the claimant could afford childcare in order to be able to work full-time was only one of many considerations that was relevant.
99 In *Ducasse v Links of London*, ET 2303190/98, the tribunal accepted that the claimant was entitled to choose the nursery which she considered would provide the best care for her child, even if it was not convenient to where she worked resulting in her request to leave work early to collect her child.

medical appointments and the desirability of spending more time with the child.

13.73   Even in 1978 the EAT stated a woman:

> . . . is not obliged to marry, or to have children, or to mind children; she may find somebody to look after them and as a last resort she may put them into care. However to say that for those reasons she can comply with the requirement to work full-time would be wholly out of sympathy with the spirit and intent of the Act . . . it is relevant in determining whether a woman can comply with the condition to take into account the current usual behaviour of women in this respect as observed in practice, putting aside behaviour and responses which are unusual.[100]

Examples of detriment/disadvantage

13.74   Examples include:[101]

- continuing full-time work which resulted in 'excessive demands on [the claimant's] time and energy';[102]
- the strain on the worker's relationship and/or illness caused by the stress of combining long hours and childcare;[103]
- being forced to resign (see paras 15.23–15.26, constructive dismissal);
- having to accept a lower paid job in order to work part time (see also chapter 14 on part-time worker's rights);
- loss of a hoped-for benefit (rejection of a request to be posted to a location nearer home so as to meet childcare responsibilities);[104]
- covering for the absence of a job share partner and working rotating shifts, as organising childcare in both situations would be extremely difficult;[105]
- it not being feasible to work full-time and continue to run the home;[106]

---

100 *Price v Civil Service Commission* [1977] IRLR 291, EAT.
101 The cases referred to in the following paragraph were all decided under the wordings described in paras 13.9–13.10 (pre-2005).
102 *Home Office v Holmes*, note 20.
103 *Barrett v Newport Borough Council* ET 34096/91.
104 *Steel v Chief Constable of Thames Valley Police* EAT/0793/03, 17 March 2004, a direct SDA case.
105 *Golding v Honda of the UK Manufacturing Ltd*, EOR No 133, September 2004 (unreported), ET Case 1402282/03.
106 *Smith v Ingram Motoring Group Ltd*, EOR No 126, February 2004, ET Case S/105095/020.

• being subject (as a female soldier) to an unlimited liability to deploy at the same time as her (soldier) partner.[107]

Commuting

13.75   Where a woman has to commute a long distance the EAT has held that this caused the disadvantage, not the requirement to work full-time.[108] However, arguably, when the question is 'is there is a disadvantage?' it is wrong to look at one element of a woman's arrangements in isolation. The EAT has also said both that the loss of a hoped-for benefit may be a detriment if the loss is a material and substantial benefit[109] and that whether a long commute can affect the feasibility of a flexible arrangement should be judged as part of justification.[110] Moreover, a PCP which requires a woman to relocate could itself be challenged as being discriminatory.[111]

Burden of proof

13.76   The effect of the burden of proof in indirect discrimination cases is not clear. Arguably, once the claimant has provided some evidence of a PCP and adverse impact, it is for the employer to prove that there was no such PCP or impact.

13.77   It is clear that once the above questions have been answered in the claimant's favour the burden of proof then shifts to the employer to objectively justify the PCP (see para 17.124 onwards). If the employer does not do this, the tribunal must uphold the complaint.

107   *Boote v Ministry of Defence*, Northern Ireland Industrial Tribunals Case 01846/00, 29 September 2003.
108   *MoD(RN) v MacMillan*, note 48; see also *Finnigan v MoD Police* EAT/0019/05, 1 September 2005 (unreported).
109   *Steel* note 104.
110   In *Pryce v Blair Travel and Leisure Ltd*, EAT/443/01, 26 April 2002 (unreported), the EAT warned against giving excessive attention to the claimant's travel difficulties which were considered under justification. But it said that they were relevant to some extent in that had she lived closer to work so as to be able to offer more flexibility, justification might not have been made out.
111   *Meade-Hill*, note 28.

Question 4: Is the PCP a proportionate means of achieving a legitimate aim?

13.78   The employer must show that the PCP is a 'proportionate means of achieving a legitimate aim'.[112] Prior to October 2005, the employer had to show the measure to be 'justifiable irrespective of the sex of the person to whom it is applied' and the relevant test is still often referred to as 'the justification defence'.

13.79   The ETD states that the employer must show that the PCP is 'objectively justified by a legitimate aim, and the means of achieving that aim are appropriate and necessary'.[113]

13.80   Tribunals should not interpret the present law more narrowly than the previous definition, as under EC law a member state cannot reduce a claimant's existing rights when implementing directives.[114] Although the current wording under the SDA 1975 does not reflect the wording of the European directive, the SDA 1975 should be interpreted in line with the ETD. In *Elias*[115] (see para 13.67), the High Court said that there was no difference between the European '*Bilka*' test for justification (see paras 13.84–13.85) and the Race Relations Act 1976 definition which is the same as the current SDA 1975 definition.

13.81   The onus of proving justification falls on the employer (see para 13.77 on the burden of proof).[116] It is decided on the facts of each case, though the legal test must be applied in analysing these.

Greater margin of appreciation for the state

13.82   If their aim is legitimate, governments have a 'broad measure of discretion' when choosing the method to achieve their social and employment policy objectives.[117] Thus, is it easier for the state to justify legislative measures which have a disproportionate adverse

---

112   See para 13.11.
113   Directive 2002/73, article 1(2).
114   See para 13.13 and note 10.
115   Note 89.
116   SDA 1975 s63A.
117   See *R v Secretary of State ex p Seymour-Smith*, ECJ and HL, note 72. The House of Lords held that the government was entitled to allow a reasonable period to elapse before deciding whether the two-year qualifying period had achieved its objective. The Lords said that the 'burden placed on the government in this type of case is not as heavy as previously thought. Governments must be able to govern'.

impact than it is for employers. Policy aims are unlikely to apply in a flexible hours employer–employee case, so the burden on employers to justify hours that are not child-friendly will be heavier. This means that indirect discrimination cases involving government decisions may be less relevant if based on policy objectives.

13.83   The legal test has two key elements, which are set out below.

Objective justification

13.84   Most cases have adopted the legal test set out in *Bilka-Kaufhaus GmbH v Mrs K Weber Von Hartz*,[118] where the ECJ held that the employer must show that the PCP:

- can be objectively justified on grounds other than sex; and
- corresponds with a real need of the business; and
- is appropriate to meet that need; and
- is necessary to do this.[119]

13.85   The terms 'appropriate' and 'necessary' in *Bilka* correspond with the definitions under the ETD and the EC law principle of proportionality.[120]

13.86   This should continue to be the test applied even though the UK courts have not always interpreted 'justification' consistently with *Bilka*. For example, in *Cadman* the Court of Appeal said that 'the test does not require the employer to establish that the measure complained of was "necessary" in the sense of being the only course open to him'.[121] However, in *Lax*[122] the Court of Appeal emphasised the objective nature of the 'reasonably necessary' test and its role in the application of the principle of proportionality. It said that:

> . . . the word 'necessary' used in *Bilka* is to be qualified by the word 'reasonably'. That qualification does not, however, permit the margin of discretion or range of reasonable responses . . . The presence of the word 'reasonably' reflects the presence and applicability of the principle of proportionality. The employer does not have to demonstrate that no other proposal is possible. The employer has to show that the proposal, in this case for a full-time appointment, is

---

118 [1986] IRLR 317.
119 Followed in, for example, the Court of Appeal in *Allonby*, note 31; *Hardys and Hanson plc v Lax* [2005] IRLR 726.
120 See for example, Steiner, J and Woods, L, *Textbook on EC Law*, 8th edn, OUP.
121 *Cadman v Health and Safety Executive* [2004] IRLR 971, CA at 31.
122 Note 119.

justified objectively notwithstanding its discriminatory effect. The principle of proportionality requires the tribunal to take into account the reasonable needs of the business. But it has to make its own judgment, upon a fair and detailed analysis of the working practices and business considerations involved, as to whether the proposal is reasonably necessary.[123]

Balancing the needs of the two parties

13.87 The other additional element in the justification defence is that the employee's situation should be put into the balance alongside the employer's reasons for justifying the imposition of the PCP. That way the ET can decide whether the justification amounts to a 'proportionate means' of achieving the employer's aim. For example, in *Hampson v Department of Education*,[124] the Court of Appeal said that ' "justifiable" requires an objective balance between the discriminatory effect of the condition and the reasonable needs of the party who applies the condition'.[125] In *Allonby*[126] the Court of Appeal said that what is required of the tribunal at a minimum is a critical evaluation of whether the employer's reasons demonstrate a real need; if there was such a need, consideration of the seriousness of the disparate impact on women including the claimant; and an evaluation of whether the former were sufficient to outweigh the latter.

13.88 The tribunal will weigh up the reasonable needs of the employer to achieve the legitimate business aim and the effect of the PCP on the employee. The more serious the impact on the claimant or on a group of women, the harder it will be to justify the PCP. In *Barry v Midland Bank plc*,[127] the House of Lords referring to the ECJ judgment in *Enderby*,[128] interpreted the EC principle of proportionality as meaning: 'the more serious the disparate impact on women or men as the case may be, the more cogent must be the objective justification'.[129] Thus, where the effect of the PCP means that the employee will lose her job, the employer will need more persuasive reasons to prove justification. The measure adopted should have only such disparate

---

123 Para 32.
124 [1989] IRLR 69, approved by the House of Lords in *Webb v EMO Air Cargo (UK) Ltd* [1990] IRLR 302; [1993] IRLR 27.
125 See also the House of Lords in *Barry v Midland Bank* [1999] IRLR 581.
126 Note 31.
127 Note 125.
128 *Enderby v Frenchay Health Authority* [1993] IRLR 591.
129 Relied on in *Allonby*, note 31.

impact as is proportionate to the legitimate aim; where it is possible to do so, a less discriminatory alternative should be adopted.[130]

13.89   In *Craddock*,[131] where a teacher was refused part-time working, the EAT said that they did not consider that the requisite balancing act took place between weighing the discriminatory effect of the condition against the justification, commenting:

> To say that employing part time employees can be inconvenient in that it requires an employer to make adjustments is a glimpse of the obvious. Yet the failure to make such adjustments to enable posts to be part time has a public as well as a private consequence in that it denies society the services of a wider pool of potential employees and in the context of school teaching reduces the number of parents; normally mothers, who can bring to their work the insight and experience which parenting can confer.[132]

13.90   The main legal principles relevant to the justification defence are set out below.

Employers should have regard to their policies

13.91   Where an employer has a policy which covers access to part-time or other flexible working, it should follow this. Failure to do so will be considered by the tribunal when assessing whether the PCP is justified and may undermine the employer's arguments. In *Amos v IPC Magazines*,[133] the tribunal held that a refusal to allow the claimant to job share could not be justified in the light of the respondent's significant failures to follow its own maternity policy. Not following such a policy may also lead to a finding of breach of the employment contract if the obligations are contractual and may lead to a claim for constructive dismissal.[134]

Generalised statements and blanket assertions are not sufficient

13.92   Generalised statements or blanket assertions, such as that part-timers are more time consuming to manage or cost more, will not

130   *Elias*, note 89.
131   EAT/0367/05, 19 December 2005, All ER (D) 278 (Dec).
132   Para 14.
133   ET 2301499/00, 4 April 2001.
134   In *Taylor v Secretary of State of Scotland* [2000] IRLR 502, the House of Lords examined an equal opportunities policy which was part of the claimant's contract. Here it decided that, looking at the contract as a whole, the policy did not enable the claimant to succeed in this particular type of age discrimination claim.

constitute objective justification. In *Hill*,[135] where the length of service of job sharers was treated as half that of full-timers, the ECJ held that generalised assertions, such as 'job-sharers have less experience than full timers' did not establish justification.[136] An argument against flexible working must be supported by evidence relating to the specific job and claimant.

13.93   For example, in *Starmer*,[137] the employer alleged that it would be unsafe if the airline pilot claimant flew less than 75–100% of full-time hours, based on a generalised standard requiring a minimum number of flying hours. The EAT said that the employer had failed to justify that requirement in relation to the particular claimant's skills and competence. In *Craddock v Cornwall County Council*,[138] the EAT criticised the implicit assumption by the tribunal that the only proper work is full-time work. See also *Caswell v Advance Travel Partners UK Ltd* (para 13.119).

13.94   It is different if the employer can show that a job sharer/part-timer is less experienced or less effective. In *Rinke v Arztekammer Hamburg*[139] a requirement for doctors to do part of their training full-time was justified because it enabled them to acquire sufficient experience in the various situations likely to arise in general practice. Similarly, if the employer can show that flexible working undertaken by the claimant in the past was not successful and can provide substantial evidence of this, refusal may be justifiable.

Critical evaluation

13.95   A tribunal must make its own critical evaluation of whether the PCP is reasonably necessary.[140] This must be based on a fair and detailed analysis of the employer's working practices and the business considerations which it produces to justify the measure preventing flexible working.[141] As the Court of Appeal said in *Lax*:[142]

> The statute requires the employment tribunal to make judgments upon systems of work, their feasibility or otherwise, the practical

135 *Hill and Stapleton v Revenue Commissioners* [1998] IRLR 466.
136 See also *Nimz v Freie und Hansestadt Hamburg* [1991] IRLR 222; *Gerster v Freistaat Bayern* [1997] IRLR 699.
137 Note 10.
138 Note 131.
139 C 25/02, ECJ.
140 *Allonby*, note 31.
141 *Lax*, note 119; *Allonby*, note 31.
142 Note 119, at 33.

problems which may or may not arise from job sharing in a particular business, and the economic impact, in a competitive world, which the restrictions impose upon the employer's freedom of action. The effect of the judgment of the employment tribunal may be profound both for the business and for the employees involved. This is an appraisal requiring considerable skill and insight. As this court has recognised in *Allonby* and in *Cadman*, a critical evaluation is required and is required to be demonstrated in the reasoning of the tribunal.

13.96   The test is not the same as in unfair dismissal cases, where the tribunal need only consider whether an employer's decision was within the range of reasonable responses in the particular circumstances.[143]

Justification must not be discriminatory

13.97   The justification must not be tainted by discrimination. Thus, to argue that it was justified to pay part-time workers less as this would encourage employers to recruit part-timers would be inherently discriminatory.[144] In *Allonby*,[145] the Court of Appeal said that if the aim of a dismissal is itself discriminatory, it could never be justified – for example, where the purpose of the dismissals was to deny part-time workers, a predominantly female group, benefits provided by the legislation. The High Court in *Elias*[146] said that despite the wide margin of discretion to be afforded to the government to adopt criteria having a discriminatory disparate impact, the criteria must not be the unlawful grounds nor 'consist of factors which in practice are closely related to them'.

Justification should be judged at the time the PCP is applied

13.98   The tribunal must consider the justification at the time when the PCP was applied.[147] Thus, if a woman is refused flexible working, it is at the time of refusal that the justification has to be judged. In

---

143   *Lax*, note 119; applied eg in *Mitchell*, note 45.
144   *R v Secretary of State ex p EOC* [1995] IRLR 464; see also *Ratcliffe and others v North Yorkshire County Council* [1995] IRLR 439 HL where the HL found that women were paid less because they could not find other work to fit round their childcare responsibilities and this was the kind of pay discrimination which the EPA was designed to prohibit.
145   Note 10.
146   Note 89.
147   Eg, in *Taylor*, note 61, it was when the regrading exercise was carried out.

Seymour-Smith,[148] the relevant time was when the two-year qualifying condition was applied to the two claimants.

Factors not in the employer's mind at the time of the decision

13.99 However, the employer can later (ie, in a tribunal) rely on reasons which were not considered at the time the claimant's request was refused.[149] However, such reasons are less likely to be as persuasive. The EAT in *Cadman*[150] commented that the absence of evidence that the justification was in the mind of the employer at the time the PCP was established, might be relevant as evidence as to the degree of the strength of the justification. In *Starmer*[151] the EAT also said 'after the event' justification must be particularly carefully scrutinised. The Court of Appeal in *Hockenjos*[152] referred to the need for appropriate evidence to establish this and commented, 'afterthoughts are allowed but they are seldom convincing'.[153]

Factors which no longer exist

13.100 However, a PCP that was once justified might cease to be so over time if circumstances changed.[154] In *Benveniste v University of Southampton*,[155] a woman was appointed at a lower salary scale than men doing like work due to financial constraints, but this did not constitute valid justification once the financial constraints were removed.

Obligations on employer to consider other options

13.101 The employer does not have to show that there is no alternative to the current PCP.[156] However, the possibility of achieving its aim by other

---

148 HL, note 72.
149 *Schonheit v Stadt Frankfurt am Main* [2004] IRLR 983, where the ECJ said: '. . . difference in treatment between men and women may be justified, depending on the circumstances, by reasons other than those put forward when the measure introducing the differential treatment was adopted'; *Cadman v Health and Safety Executive*, note 121.
150 *Health and Safety Executive v Cadman* [2004] IRLR 29, EAT
151 Note 10.
152 *Hockenjos v Secretary of State for Social Security*, [2001] EWCA Civ 624, [2001] ICR 966, CA.
153 See also *Elias*, note 89.
154 In *Hockenjos* (at 60), note 152. The Court of Appeal did not doubt such a submission made by the claimant.
155 [1989] IRLR 123, CA.
156 *Cadman*, note 121; *Lax*, note 119. For an interesting article see M Connolly, 'Discrimination law: justification, alternative measures and defences based on sex', ILJ, September 2001.

means is one of the factors relevant to assessing justification.[157] Without considering this, it will be hard to demonstrate that it has analysed whether the PCP is reasonably necessary to the extent that this outweighs its discriminatory effect on the claimant. In *Allonby*,[158] the Court of Appeal said the 'obvious question' of how the employer could meet its aims other than by dismissals should have been asked. 'Other fairly obvious measures short of dismissal', which had been proposed and could have achieved the employer's objectives, should have been considered. An employee who offers other viable options herself will therefore make it harder for the employer to justify a refusal whilst at the same time improving her chances of negotiating a successful resolution.

13.102   In *Hockenjos*,[159] a child premium for the jobseeker's allowance was paid to the parent in receipt of child benefit, ie, the mother.[160] This was challenged by the father who had equal care of the child as indirect sex discrimination.[161] The Court of Appeal held, in considering whether it was justified, that there was no evidence that the secretary of state or anyone on his behalf, ever applied their mind to the question of whether there was a better or different way of achieving the policy aim that would avoid, or diminish, the considerable discrimination. The Court of Appeal held:

> Where there may be alternatives that do not offend a fundamental principle of Community law but the Secretary of State has simply not explored them, he could not be held to have discharged the burden of establishing justification. It was not up to the appellant to show that there is an obviously better alternative.

13.103   Whereas governments have a margin of appreciation (see para 13.82) in justifying a discriminatory law, the burden on employers will be heavier.

13.104   In most child-friendly cases, the claimant puts forward at least one proposal for a new working pattern which differs from her present one (see paras 12.34 onwards: negotiating positively). The employer will have to explain why it is not feasible as part of its overall justification of the PCP testing it against the principles

---

157 *Seymour-Smith*, ECJ, note 72; *Kutz-Bauer v Freie und Hansenstadt Hamburg*, [2003] IRLR 368.
158 Note 31.
159 Note 152.
160 It is generally the mother who receives child benefit.
161 Under Directive 79/7/EEC regarding statutory social security schemes.

described in this chapter. An employer may propose an alternative in response, for example working four days per week instead of the requested three. This will be a new PCP (to work four days per week) as well as part of the justification of the previous one. It too will have to be justified independently if it particularly disadvantages women.

13.105   If an employee has explained to his/her employer his/her difficulties with the PCP, whether or not the employee makes other proposals, it is arguable that the employer should take the initiative to, at the least, canvass obvious alternatives.[162] What is 'obvious' should be a wide range of flexible work practices in view of the publicity given to these over recent years.[163] An obvious example, as an alternative to part-time working, is a job share.

13.106   The burden of proof on the employer is not to demonstrate 'indispensability [but to provide] proof of a real need'.[164] For example, in *Lax*[165] the job share proposal was 'insufficiently explored and objections overstated' by the employer. In *Craddock*,[166] the EAT criticised 'the general tenor of the decision . . . that it was up to the employee to put forward proposals'.

13.107   In *Smith v Penlan Club*[167] the ET found that a requirement for a barperson to work until 6pm was not justified as the employer failed to look at a range of alternatives that might accommodate the claimant's difficulties. In *Kaur v David Lloyd Leisure Ltd*[168] a dismissal due to the claimant's inability to work a duty manager's shifts was unjustified as the employer gave no or little consideration to sharing or splitting shifts and did not consult the applicant's colleagues. In *Commotion Ltd v Rutty*,[169] the tribunal found that there was no evidence to show that working as a part-time warehouse assistant as the claimant proposed, was not feasible for the employer's business. It found the refusal of these hours unjustified. In *Dickie v Talbot House School*[170] a part-time French teacher was told that instead of working mornings only she had to work one or more afternoons. No attempt

---

162   In *Hockenjos*, note 152, evidence of alternatives not considered by the government was heard by the Court which it considered to be 'obvious possibilities'.
163   See the EAT's criticism in *Commotion*, note 22.
164   *Allonby*, note 31.
165   *Lax*, note 119.
166   Note 131.
167   ET 1602995/01.
168   ET 2600421/02 (Nottingham).
169   Note 22.
170   ET 3104539/99.

was made to get other morning teachers to do any afternoons or swap round other lessons/teachers. The ET held that the requirement to work afternoons was not justified.

Trial period/Have similar hours worked in the past?

13.108   If the same or a similar job is being done or has previously been done successfully on similar hours, the claimant will be in a stronger position, provided other factors in the workplace remain the same.

13.109   Agreeing a trial period, if it works well, can assist the claimant's case; if the employee refuses a trial period without good reason,[171] this may make it easier for the employer to justify rejecting the requested hours.[172] If the employer refuses a trial period this may make its refusal of flexible hours harder to justify, although in *Pryce*,[173] the EAT accepted the tribunal's finding that not trialling part-time work or a job share was justified given the nature of the business. Thus the feasibility of a trial period must be considered in view of the needs of both employer and employee.

13.110   In *Lowe v Peter Bainbridge Optometrist*,[174] the tribunal found that the job had been shared perfectly satisfactorily while the woman was on maternity leave and could continue to be. In *Dillon v Rentokil Initial UK Ltd*[175] the refusal to allow a supervisor of seven technicians to work her hours 9.15am to 3pm or 5.15pm (instead of 8am to 5pm) for 50% of the time, and to be available by telephone when not at work, was not justified. A reasonable employer would have afforded a trial period, particularly for a long serving and highly regarded employee.

13.111   If the employer agrees to a trial period, it must assess the trial period appropriately or the worker may have a claim. In *Terry v ICM Computer Solutions plc*,[176] a claimant was successful where her employer terminated the agreed trial of working shorter days. The employer failed to test its assumption that the arrangement would have an adverse effect on the business during the six-month trial and there was no evidence of this. The situation may be different where

---

171   The difficulty of arranging childcare on a temporary basis could be a reason to reject a trial period though every attempt should be made to try a trial period as the alternative may be a refusal.
172   *Southall v London Chamber of Commerce and Industry*, ET 2204702/00.
173   Note 110.
174   ET 5202334/99.
175   ET 2700899/01.
176   ET 2409119/03.

there is sufficient evidence to demonstrate that when the claimant had undertaken a similar job part-time in the past, this presented difficulties resulting in the employer requiring a return to full-time work.[177]

Examples of justification put forward by employers

Costs and economic considerations

13.112 Where an employer seeks to justify indirect sex discrimination, it cannot do this on the basis of cost considerations alone. This is clear from the ECJ in *Hill*,[178] an equal pay case, where it stated that an employer cannot justify discrimination arising from a job sharing scheme solely on the ground that avoidance of such discrimination would involve increased costs (see para 13.92, it rejected other justifications put forward).

13.113   Subsequent ECJ cases have reiterated this approach. In *Kutz-Bauer v Freie und Hansenstadt Hamburg*,[179] the ECJ said that although budgetary considerations may underlie a member state's choice of social policy and influence the nature or scope of social protection measures which it wishes to adopt, they do not in themselves constitute an aim pursued by that policy and cannot therefore justify discrimination against one of the sexes. To concede this would mean that the fundamental EC law principle of equal treatment might vary according to the state of the public finances of member states. The respondent public employer could not rely solely on the costs argument either as public authority or as employer.[180]

13.114   As employers do not have the margin of appreciation available to governments (see para 13.82), costs arguments should be even less available to them if they would undermine a fundamental principle of EC law such as gender equality. They could, for example, lead to the variable application of discrimination law across different workplaces arguably benefiting the least efficient and innovative firms. Tribunals must seek detailed evidence in support of such arguments applying the principle of critical evaluation described above (paras 13.95–13.96).

177   *Bryce v R Glasgow and Associates Public Relations Ltd.*
178   Note 135.
179   Note 157.
180   See also *Steinicke v Bundesanstalt fur Arbeit* [2003] IRLR 892, ECJ; *Jorgensen v Foreningen af Specialaeger and Sygesikringens Forhandlingsudvalg* [2000] IRLR 726, ECJ.

13.115   In *Home Office v Holmes*,[181] the employers argued that if the claimant worked part-time, their costs would rise. The EAT preferred the
claimant's evidence as to the savings and efficiency gains which part-
time work gave rise to. In *Edwards*,[182] the employer sought to justify its
new discriminatory shift patterns as a means of cutting costs. The
EAT held that this did not justify their application to the claimant as it
could have made arrangements which would not have damaged their
business plans. The Court of Appeal in *Allonby*[183] criticised the tribunal's failure to explore alternatives to the discriminatory measure
by which the costs saving required by the employer might have been
made.

13.116   In *Cross v British Airways*[184] the EAT considered whether costs
savings can justify discrimination. After reviewing ECJ case-law, it
decided that an employer cannot rely solely on costs considerations,
although it may put cost into the balance, together with other justifications if there are any. In the weighing exercise, costs may be valued
less, particularly if the discrimination is 'substantial, obvious and
even deliberate'. However, economic justification must be considered. It would need clear reasoning and binding authority to prevent that occurring. Thus employers cannot rely on costs arguments
alone as justification. However, despite *Cross* it does remain unclear
how far an employer can use even thoroughly presented economic
justification to justify discrimination in the light of ECJ statements in
cases such as *Kutz-Bauer* (see para 13.113).

The job cannot be done in any other way

13.117   Resistance to change is often based on arguments such as: continuity
must be guaranteed, duplication of work will occur, there will be no
cover at a particular time of day if reduced or compressed hours are
worked, the job requires someone to be present in the office at all
times. These arguments require the critical evaluation described in
Lax.[185] The nature of the job, the rhythm of the work and the size of
the workforce will be factors affecting their relevance. Varied working
practices and extended business hours are now common in many

---

181   Note 20.
182   *London Underground Ltd v Edwards (No 2)* [1997] IRLR 157, EAT.
183   Note 31.
184   [2005] IRLR 423.
185   Note 119.

industries where workplaces are used to arranging very complex work patterns/shifts, such as the health service.

13.118   Negotiating positively about change will be important (see para 12.34 onwards). The evidence claimants should produce to a tribunal in support of their claim, should negotiations fail, is outlined below (para 13.149 onwards)

Customer preference

13.119 In *Caswell v Advance Travel Partners UK Ltd*[186] the employment tribunal held that the employer had failed adequately to explain why the claimant's requested reduction in daily working hours would have the alleged detrimental impact on customer service. The reasons for refusal put forward were 'vague and unspecific'. In *Rentokil*,[187] the need for the claimant to work fixed hours to satisfy customers' requirements (as well as to be available to the technicians she was supervising) was rejected by the tribunal.

13.120   In contrast, in *Colman Coyle v Georgiou*,[188] the EAT accepted that commercial clients expected prompt access to the person dealing with their matter, as one of a number of reasons justifying the refusal of part-time work to an assistant solicitor. The EAT in *Pryce v Blair Travel*,[189] accepted that the full-time work requirement was justified because of the one-to-one relationship which the claimant and other travel consultants had with their clients.

Setting a precedent

13.121 Some employers seek to justify refusal on the basis that it would open the floodgates to flexible work requests. As a refusal of flexible hours must be justified in relation to the individual request, this type of generalised assumption will be insufficient justification unless the employer can show actual problems in that particular case. An example might be if many employees work away from the premises so that it is already difficult to arrange essential meetings, and the hours proposed by the claimant would make it much more so.

13.122   In *Scanlon v G Plan Upholdstery Ltd*[190] the ET held that to allow the claimant to leave work ten minutes earlier each day to pick up her

---

186 ET 2304832/04.
187 Note 175.
188 EAT/535/00, 13 December 2001 (unreported).
189 See note 10.
190 ET 1401871/99.

child from school would not set a precedent, as argued by the employer, and therefore the refusal was not justified.

13.123   In *Wright v Rugby BC*[191] the claimant wanted half an hour for lunch and to leave half an hour earlier. The ET rejected the council's argument that this would affect their flexitime policy and set an undesirable precedent.

13.124   In *Parry v De Vere Hotels and Leisure Ltd*[192] a tribunal rejected the employer's justification for refusing a woman's request to alter her working hours on the basis that this would open the floodgates for women to ask for fewer hours to suit their childcare.

Other employees' attitudes

13.125   The fact that other employees object to one employee doing flexible hours may be relevant if this imposes an unreasonable extra burden on those employees. It will depend on the facts and will not necessarily amount to justification. For example, in *Rothwell v Noble t/a DC's Chuckwagon and Pizza Pi*,[193] the claimant had been allowed to leave work 15 minutes early at 2.45 pm so that she could collect her son. She was then told she had to work until 3 pm because other employees were not happy that the claimant finished earlier than they did. The tribunal did not consider this amounted to justification. (But see paras 13.145–13.146, shifts, regarding requiring other employees to change hours.) An employee who is badly treated as a result of working flexibly may have a claim for indirect sex discrimination as less favourable treatment of part-time workers must be justified in the same way as a refusal of a request for flexible working. She may also have a claim under the Part-time Workers Regulations 2000 (see chapter 14).[194]

Part-time or job sharing

Need for continuity and avoiding duplication of work

13.126   Continuity is a common argument for opposing job sharing. However, many round-the-clock industries have devised satisfactory

191   ET 23528/84.
192   ET 2101853/04.
193   ET 2902130/99.
194   SI No 1551. Where she is treated less favourably as a result of asking for flexible working this may be an unlawful detriment or if the reason for the treatment is an allegation that there has been sex discrimination this may be victimisation.

handover systems to maintain continuity. In some jobs, computerisation will make it harder for an employer to argue that the need for continuity cannot be met under flexible working arrangements. Difficulties in coordinating the start and finish times or problems arising where an employee is not in the office at all times may also arise with full-time employees. They are unlikely to amount to justification for refusing flexible work in the absence of convincing evidence relating to the specific job. However, it is important for the employee to suggest ways that any potential problems could be resolved.

13.127   In *Given v Scottish Power plc*[195] the claimant successfully rebutted the employer's argument about the need for continuity by saying that, if a customer phoned to speak to her, the matter could be dealt with by someone else because notes were kept and everything was dealt with under laid-down procedures. In *Squillaci v WS Atkins (Services) Ltd,*[196] the employer argued that time would be wasted in job sharers liaising. The tribunal felt the employer had not discussed this with the employee and unsubstantiated assumptions were made.

13.128   The Court of Appeal, in *Lax,*[197] upheld the tribunal decision that the full-time requirement could not be justified. It considered that the job functions could be split between job-sharers, that concerns over duplication of effort were not convincing and that appropriate liaison mechanisms between the job sharers could be devised. However, the claimant in *Bryce*[198] was unsuccessful in arguing for a job share. The employer said this would be impractical because the job required close and continuous co-ordination with the directors and the claimant had not suggested any specific proposals that would have properly addressed employer concerns.

Managers cannot work part-time or job share

13.129   Some employers consider that a job that involves managing or supervising staff cannot be done part-time. In *Given v Scottish Power plc,*[199] the claimant (who managed 10 to 12 team members) was told that a policy applied at her grade preventing job sharing. The tribunal held that the need for continuity and certain 'operational' matters did not amount to justification, as the employers had not assessed the

195 ET S/3172/94.
196 ET 68108/94, 21 January 1997, London South.
197 Note 119.
198 Note 177.
199 Note 195.

claimant's duties and any difficulties that might be encountered in job sharing.

13.130   In *Oddbins Ltd v Robinson*,[200] the employers refused a job share on the basis that it was necessary for one person to do the job, the post required leadership and motivation of the junior staff and responsibility for the general running of the business. The tribunal heard evidence that very senior jobs had been job shared successfully and held that the employers had failed to justify the condition. See also *Lax*,[201] where the employers also argued unsuccessfully that a management post could not be split.

13.131   In *Webster v Princes Soft Drinks*[202] the tribunal found that although the employer had complied with the 'right to request' procedure,[203] a refusal to allow a senior financial accountant to job share in her post amounted to indirect sex discrimination. The respondent's concerns about the risk of different management styles interfering with the management of direct reports did not justify refusal and the respondent should have considered delegating routine tasks to other members of staff.

Difficulty in finding a job share partner or other person to cover work

13.132   The EAT in *Brown v McAlpine and Co Ltd*[204] upheld the tribunal decision that the employer's failure in its attempts to find a job share partner for the claimant could justify its refusal of part-time work (full-time cover being needed). The EAT implied that in most similar cases the employer should take reasonable steps to find a job share partner. However in some cases urgency or financial constraint (particularly for small employers) will preclude undertaking a search.

13.133   A request for flexible hours that involves starting late and/or leaving early will be easier to accommodate in an organisation where the hours at the beginning and end of the day can be covered by other workers. In *Armstrong v Boots the Chemist*[205] the tribunal accepted that requiring the claimant to work until 5 pm rather than 4 pm was justified. The earlier finish time would have left a gaping hole in the

---

200   Note 23.
201   Note 119.
202   ET 1803942/04.
203   See chapter 12.
204   EATS/0009/05, 22 September 2005 (unreported).
205   ET 5301767/00, 1400472/01.

pharmacy management at the end of the day, which could not be covered by other employees.

13.134   However, in *Ducasse v Links (London) Ltd t/a Links of London*[206] there were two other members of staff to cover an earlier finish. The tribunal held that the refusal to allow the claimant to change her working hours to leave before 6 pm to pick her child up was therefore not justified. She was the shop manageress but she could not in any event be present throughout the entire opening hours of the shop.

There is a need to be in the office all the time

13.135 If the employer maintains a need for the employee to be in the office full-time but there is evidence that this has not been the case in the past, either for her or other employees in a similar position, the employer will find it difficult to justify the need for a full-time presence. It is worth drawing the employer's (and tribunal's) attention to any previous periods when there may have been no full-time presence and how these were dealt with, for example during maternity leave or holidays.

13.136   In *Howe v Fisher Rosemount Ltd*[207] the tribunal rejected the employer's argument for refusing the claimant part-time work on the basis that she needed to be in the office full-time and needed to travel. If she was away on business obviously she could not always be in the office and short notice travel was rare. Thus, both arguments was unconvincing.

Working from home

Need to attend meetings in office

13.137 In *Castleton v Department for Work & Pensions*,[208] the employer required the employee to cease working at home on a nearly full-time basis and attend the office two days per week. The tribunal found the requirement to be justified because employees were needed in the office for meetings and discussions and to sort out which cases needed to be taken home to work on.

---

206   See note 99.
207   ET 1100337/98.
208   ET 1803569/01, confirmed on appeal EAT/0715/02, 30 October 2002 (unreported).

Need to be in the office all the time

13.138   See paras 13.135–13.136.

Taking confidential documents home

13.139   It is common for an employer to try and justify a refusal of home working because it may undermine confidentiality to take documents home. However, it is rare for there to be documents that are too confidential to take home and it is often the case that other employees do in practice take documents home.

A home office: safety and cost

13.140   With new technology it is much easier to work at home. Emails, phone calls and faxes can be directly diverted to home and it is possible to access networks remotely. However, an employee will need a proper dedicated space and equipment. See the Health & Safety Executive's (HSE's) guidance on health and safety for homeworkers (see HSE website).

13.141   In *Unn v Show Presentation Services Ltd*[209] an accountant was dismissed because she would not undertake to work full-time at the office within a year, instead of working at home one day a week. The ET upheld her claim, as the small costs of upgrading her home computer so that she could email documents was far outweighed by the discriminatory effect of not being allowed to work at home.

13.142   In another case an ET rejected arguments that health and safety considerations prevented an employee from working at home. The employer had made no effort to identify risks and had not considered simple measures such as asking an occupational health adviser to visit.[210]

13.143   However, there is no obligation upon an employer to provide a fully equipped office at home and it may be in the employee's interests to install some of the necessary equipment herself if that is the sole obstacle to her working at home. If, however, the employee can show that the costs of providing equipment at home are not disproportionate or not much more expensive, because, for example, it would save providing the equipment at work, this may make it more difficult for the employer to refuse. In addition, the employee can

209   ET 2301439/00.
210   *Giles v Geach and Jones* Southampton ET Case 310072/2005.

point to the cost of recruiting and training a replacement if she was to leave, which may be considerably more.

13.144 Note:

- Working from home is not a substitute for child care.
- If working from home, workers should make clear the hours they will be available for receiving phone calls or checking emails.

Shift work

13.145 Many women with chilcare responsibilities find it difficult to do variable shift patterns as it is difficult to arrange childcare. They may request fixed shifts or the ability to swap with other employees. An employer will not be expected to change other workers' contracts or to impose different hours on them, to accommodate the claimant's request. Nevertheless, the employer should consult other workers, who may be willing to voluntarily accept changes. Failure to do this or make other reasonable arrangements may lead to a finding that the refusal to vary shifts patterns is not justified.

13.146 In *Kaur v David Lloyd Leisure Ltd*,[211] the tribunal found that the employer gave no consideration to splitting shifts or any other practice which could have sustained the claimant's employment. The EAT in *London Underground v Edwards*[212] upheld the tribunal decision that the claimant's need to work 'social hours' only shifts could have been accommodated without damaging the employer's business plan.

Compressed hours

13.147 A worker undertakes compressed hours when they work full-time weekly hours over fewer days. Where the employer is concerned about the unavailability of an employee for part of the day and the job is not necessarily office-based, the employee may be able to allay the employer's concerns by offering to be contacted by phone or email (as in *Rentokil*[213]) or by offering to be flexible (as in *Lax*[214]).

13.148 Where cover is necessary during office hours, it may be possible to make the appropriate arrangements (see paras 13.152–13.154). This very much depends upon the facts of the case and the claimant

---

211 See note 168.
212 Note 182.
213 Note 175.
214 Note 119.

should be prepared to suggest practical ways of dealing with the employer's business concerns.

Evidence

13.149 As described above and emphasised by the Court of Appeal in *Lax*,[215] the employer's arguments of justification must be substantiated by detailed evidence about its working practices and business considerations. The claimant should ask for this from the employer, for example by using the questionnaire procedure (see para 17.28 onwards).

Evidence from the employer

13.150 It must show:

- the importance of the PCP to meet real business needs and that it is appropriate for doing this; and
- why it is necessary to apply the PCP to the claimant (and any others) in the form or manner which disadvantaged the claimant (and others); and
- that the need for it outweighs its discriminatory effect.

Evidence from the claimant

13.151 The claimant's detailed knowledge of her job and the workplace will enable her to give evidence as to how the work could be done in the hours she proposes and/or how it could be done as a job share (see, for example, *Lax*). Her evidence of her willingness to be flexible where this is appropriate will also be helpful to her case. In *Craddock*,[216] the EAT commented that anecdotal evidence from the claimant that similar jobs are done successfully on a job sharing basis in the same occupation was valid evidence.

Evidence from other employees/of the employer's policy

13.152 Other employees may be able to give evidence about when reduced hours or job sharing have worked satisfactorily in similar jobs to the claimant's in the past. They may be able to reinforce the claimant's

---

215 Note 119.
216 Note 131.

evidence that the job can be done in a different way. If a co-worker is willing to rearrange their job so as to facilitate the claimant's request, this evidence should be produced.

13.153 An employer's own formal policy where this exists and provides for flexible working should be produced and evidence provided as to whether it has been followed (see para 13.91).

Evidence from employee in another organisation doing similar work part-time/on a job share basis

13.154 If an employee can show that other employers have allowed flexible working in similar jobs, this will help to show that it is possible. In *Kane v Kerr-McGee Oil (UK) plc,*[217] the ET took into account the fact that three other oil companies had part-time female petroleum engineers. It found that the claimant's request to work a three-day week could have been accommodated without insurmountable problems.

13.155 In *Barrett v Newport BC,*[218] the claimant pointed out that a neighbouring borough, Cardiff, had introduced job sharing and described the benefits. The ET held that the policy against job sharing was not justified. In *Craddock,*[219] the EAT did not consider that evidence as to the positive effect of job sharing which occurred elsewhere in the same occupation, should be rejected simply because it was anecdotal.

Expert evidence

13.156 General information about the advantages of part-time work, job sharing and other child-friendly work patterns is useful. Expert evidence from, for example, Working Families has assisted claimants and they have a number of useful publications.[220]

13.157 In *Oddbins*[221] (see para 13.130 above) where the claimant was successful, the tribunal had heard expert evidence from the organisation New Ways to Work (now Working Families) to the effect that there are very few managerial jobs which cannot be shared.

217 ET 2201015/98.
218 See note 103.
219 Note 131.
220 See para 13.163.
221 Note 23.

No right to return to full-time work

13.158 If the worker negotiates reduced hours, she cannot then use the SDA 1975 to argue that she should be allowed to return to full-time work, though this may be agreed with the employer.

Indirect marital/civil partnership discrimination

13.159 As married persons are more likely to have responsibility for children than unmarried persons, any unjustified working pattern may also be indirect marital/civil partner discrimination.[222] The comparison must be made between all persons who are married and in a civil partnership, comprising men and women together as a group and those who are unmarried and not in a civil partnership, as a group (see footnote 4 and para 2.86). For example, in a women-only workplace there will be no relevant workplace statistics relating to women and men. However, a claimant who is married or in a civil partnership may be able to show that more unmarried workers than married workers can comply with an unchild-friendly PCP (see para 12.162 for figures showing more married persons than unmarried have children). A claimant who is a civil partner will be able to rely on the statistics relating to married and unmarried persons. This is because the definition of the person who has a claim for discrimination comprises those in marital and civil partner relationships. The statistics relating to the proportion of civil partners having care of children as opposed to those who are not civil partners do not need to be provided.

Can men claim?

13.160 It is unlikely that a man will be able to prove indirect sex discrimination as he will not be able to show that a requirement to work full-time has a disproportionate impact on men. The adverse impact is on women, who take the main responsibility for childcare. However, a

---

222 For example, *Hale and Clunie*, note 24, where nurses were made redundant because they could not work rotating shifts. This was held to be indirect marital discrimination, decided under the definition prior to 5 December 2005, which compared married and unmarried persons of the same sex.

man (or a woman) can claim direct sex discrimination where a woman (or a man) is or would be granted flexible working hours for family reasons, but a similar request from a man (or a woman) is refused. Hypothetical comparators will be particularly useful in male-only workplaces (see para 13.31).

13.161   In *Walkingshaw v The John Martin Group*,[223] the male claimant was successful in alleging that a refusal to grant him reduced hours to look after his son was direct sex discrimination. He compared himself to a hypothetical female comparator as there were no women in his technical grade. However, female employees in other work areas had been granted part-time work for childcare reasons.[224]

13.162   It may also be possible for a man to argue indirect marital discrimination if he has not been successful in a job application because he has small children.[225] As 42% of children are born out of wedlock but 58%[226] in wedlock, it can be argued that a requirement not to have children disadvantages a considerably larger proportion of married than unmarried persons. However a man will usually not be able to use indirect marital discrimination to obtain child-friendly hours as the reality is that most married men work long hours so that a PCP to work full-time, from the office etc will not disadvantage the majority of married men.

Remedies

13.163   In *Craddock* the EAT said that 'the two matters of sex discrimination and constructive dismissal are inherently connected' and allowed the claimant's appeal as to the dismissal of both the sex discrimination and constructive dismissal actions.[227] See chapter 15 for more detail

---

224   See also *Jervis v Hertfordshire Partnership NHS Trust*, ET 3302614/02 (EOR No 141, May 2005). A male claimant succeeded in his sex discrimination claim as his employer did not insist that a female comparator carry out nightshifts (she needed to work days for childcare reasons) to the same extent as it insisted that the claimant carry out dayshifts (instead of nightshifts which suited his caring responsibilities for his ailing wife). See also *Jesuthasan v London Borough of Hammersmith and Fulham* [1998] IRLR 372, CA (para 2.84: practices found to be indirectly discriminatory against women should not be applied to men either).
225   *Gleed v Pricewaterhouse Coopers* ET 6400323/01, Newcastle upon Tyne, decided as a preliminary issue that such claim could be pursued.
226   Figure for 2004.
227   Para 18, see note 131.

(and for protection from dismissal and other detriment; para 2.89 onwards for victimisation). Apart from compensation, the tribunal that finds indirect discrimination may make a declaration and a recommendation (see chapter 18).

Useful information

13.164   DTI summary of right to request
www.dti.gov.uk/er/individual/flexible-pl516.htm

DTI guidance PL520
www.dti.gov.uk/er/individual/flexwork-pl520.pdf

DTI flexible work application form – suggested model
www.dti.gov.uk/er/individual/flexA.pdf

Working Families website (see para 12.100)
www.workingfamilies.org.uk/asp/home_zone/m_welcome.asp

EOC website
www.eoc.org.uk

EOC Guidance for employers: 'How to manage flexibility in the workplace'
www.eoc.org.uk/EOCeng/EOCcs/Advice/
how_to_manage_flexibility_in_the_sworkplace.asp

EOC for legal advisers, includes summaries of useful cases including ET ones:
www.eoc-law.org.uk/

The rights of part-time workers

Key points

- The Part-time Workers (Prevention of Less Favourable Treat-ment) Regulations (PTW Regs) 2000 give part-time workers pro rata rights with full-time workers.
- The PTW Regs 2000 protect workers, whether permanent or temporary and irrespective of their hours of work, length of service or age.
- The part-time worker can only compare her/himself to a full-time worker with a similar contract, doing broadly similar work.
- The comparison can be with a person of the same or different sex.
- There is special protection for full-time workers who become part-time workers; the provisions are slightly different depend-ing on whether the change is immediate or after a gap of less than 12 months.
- The regulations cover pay, terms and conditions, benefits and any other detriment.
- The employer may justify the difference between the part-time and full-time worker on objective grounds.
- A part-time female worker can also claim indirect sex and marital and civil partnership status discrimination or equal pay (in respect of contractual terms) if treated less favourably than a male full-time worker.

Introduction and statutory framework

14.1   The EU Part-time Workers Directive[1] (PTWD) prohibits discrimin-ation against part-time workers unless it is justified on objective grounds. This was implemented in July 2000 by the PTW Regs 2000.[2] To the extent that it provides greater protection, the PTWD should be taken into account when applying the PTW Regs.[3] The Department of

1   97/81/EC extended to the UK by 98/23/EC.
2   Part-time Workers (Prevention of Less Favourable Treatment) Regulations 2000 SI No 1551 in force 1 July 2000, amended by the Part-time Workers (Prevention of Less Favourable Treatment) Regulations 2000 (Amendment) Regulations 2002 SI No 2035 in force from 1 October 2002.
3   For example, *Matthews and Others v Kent and Medway Towns and Fire Authority and Others* (at 7) [2006] UKHL 8; [2006] IRLR 367, HL.

Trade and Industry (DTI) has published guidance notes on its website.

14.2   The PTW Regs 2000 give part-time male and female workers rights to the same terms and conditions (usually pro rata, see para 14.48 onwards) as full-time workers, with a similar contract, doing broadly similar work. In addition, where a full-time worker becomes part-time, they should retain their full-time terms and conditions on a pro rata basis (see paras 14.34–14.36). The regulations do not allow workers to challenge full-time working practices. How to do this is covered in chapter 13.

14.3   Before the regulations came into force, women who were treated less favourably because of their part-time status could only bring a claim for indirect sex or marital discrimination under either the Sex Discrimination Act (SDA) 1975 or the Equal Pay Act (EPA) 1970.

14.4   This chapter summarises workers' rights under the PTW Regs 2000 and compares these to rights under the EPA 1970 and SDA 1975. A brief overview of the EPA 1970 (which mainly covers contractual matters) and the SDA 1975 (which covers non-contractual matters) is set out in chapter 2; how to prove indirect sex discrimination is set out in chapter 13.

14.5   In some respects the PTW Regs 2000 are broader and simpler to use. For example, comparisons between same sex workers can be made and men as well as women may bring claims. In others ways the rights under the EPA 1970 and SDA 1975 are more extensive. For example, the range of comparators is wider, though they must be of the opposite sex. The following table sets out the main differences.

PTW Regs 2000	EPA 1970	SDA 1975
Apply to contractual and non-contractual discrimination where an actual (narrowly defined) comparator exists	Only applies to pay and contractual terms where a comparator exists (but see paras 14.11 and 14.13)	Applies to non-contractual terms and requires only a hypothetical comparator
Applies to men and women workers, including many self-employed, contract workers and apprentices.	Applies to men and women workers, but indirect discrimination provisions protect only women in this context	Applies to men and women workers and job applicants, but indirect discrimination provisions protect only women in this context

PTW Regs 2000	EPA 1970	SDA 1975
Comparator can be same sex	Comparator must be opposite sex	Comparator must be opposite sex
Comparator must be engaged in the same or broadly similar work for the same employer	Comparator must be doing like work, work rated as equivalent, or work of equal value, for the same or an associated employer	Comparator, real or hypothetical, must be a man in similar circumstances, not necessarily one doing the same or similar work
Employer may justify a difference in treatment between a part-time and a full-time worker on objective grounds	Employer may defend direct discrimination with the 'GMF' defence and may justify indirect sex discrimination on objective grounds (but check current case-law)	Employer may not justify direct discrimination but may justify indirect sex discrimination on objective grounds
Three-month time limit with just and equitable extension	Six-month time limit (usually) with no power to extend	Three-month limit with just and equitable extension
Worker can request written statement giving reasons for less favourable treatment	May use equal pay questionnaire	Applicant may serve a sex discrimination questionnaire
Power for ET to order: – declaration – recommendation – compensation excluding injury to feelings	The ET may award back pay and damages for (usually) up to six years from date claim lodged. (But for pension claims see para 14.83 onwards)	No cap on compensation which can include injury to feelings
The statutory grievance procedure need not be implemented before lodging a claim (except in dismissal cases)	The statutory grievance procedure must usually be implemented before lodging a claim	The statutory grievance procedure must usually be implemented before lodging a claim

Who is protected?

14.6 The PTW Regs 2000 cover the following workers (male and female),[4] whether permanent or temporary and irrespective of the number of hours worked, age or length of service:

- employees working under a contract of employment (or who have worked under a contract of employment) whether written or oral;
- individuals who work (or have worked) under a contract, express or implied, where the person undertakes to do personally any work or services for another (this would cover, for example, many self-employed and contract workers, but does not apply to contracts where the individual is a profession or business providing services to clients or customers);[5]
- trainees and apprentices.

Exclusions and special categories

Crown employees and workers

14.7 They are protected in the same way as other employees and workers.[6]

Armed forces

The PTW Regs 2000 apply to the armed forces[7] except in relation to service as a member of the reserve forces in so far as that service consists in undertaking certain training obligations.[8] Complaints by members of the armed forces must first be made to an officer under the service redress procedures and must not be withdrawn.[9]

---

4 For definitions see PTW Regs 2000 reg 1(2).
5 PTW Regs 2000 reg 1(2). Note the wider definitions in s82(1) of the SDA 1975 and s1(6)(a) of EPA 1970.
6 PTW Regs 2000 reg 12.
7 PTW Regs 2000 reg 13.
8 PTW Regs 2000 reg 13(2). In *Manson v the Ministry of Defence*, EAT/0289/02, 30 October 2002 (unreported), the EAT applied this exclusion to reject a claim brought by a part-time major in the Territorial Army. The Court of Appeal in *Manson v the Ministry of Defence*, [2005] EWCA Civ 1678 (related judicial review proceedings) said the employment tribunal was the appropriate forum to decide whether under EC law PTW Regs 2000 reg 13(2) should be disapplied.
9 PTW Regs 2000 reg 13.

House of Lords staff

The PTW Regs 2000 apply to those employed under a contract with the Corporate Officer of the House of Lords.[10]

House of Commons staff

The PTW Regs 2000 apply to those who have been appointed by the House of Commons Commission or who are members of the speaker's personal staff.[11]

Police service

The police are covered by the PTW Regs 2000 and this includes those holding the office of constable or an appointment as a police cadet.[12]

Holders of judicial offices

These are not covered where they are paid on a daily fee-paid basis.[13]

What is a part-time worker?

14.8   The distinction between a full-time and part-time worker depends on the 'custom and practice' of the employer in relation to workers employed by the employer under the same type of contract.[14] No hours limits are set out in the PTW Regs 2000 for either type of worker:

- a full-time worker is one who is paid by reference to the time s/he works and is 'identifiable as a full-time worker';
- a part-time worker is one who is paid by reference to the time s/he works and is not identifiable as a full-time worker.

14.9   This will be a question of fact in each case. Difficulties may arise in workforces with employees working different hours (eg, 20, 25, 30,

10   PTW Regs 2000 reg 14.
11   PTW Regs 2000 reg 15.
12   PTW Regs 2000 reg 16.
13   PTW Regs 2000 reg 17. But see *Shaikh v The Department for Constitutional Affairs and Others*, EAT/0234/05, 31 August 2005 (unreported) where it was noted no appeal was brought against the tribunal decision that EPA 1970 provisions excluding statutory office holders were disapplied by article 141.
14   PTW Regs 2000 reg 2(1), (2): see para 14.15 onwards for a discussion of similar contracts.

35, 40) where it could be difficult to determine who is a part-time worker. In *England v Turnford School*,[15] the 18-hour per week part-time claimant put forward as comparators two 35-hour per week term-time employees. She asserted that no one else in her department worked longer hours than they did and that the employer treated them as full-time workers. The EAT rejected these arguments as contractual weekly full-time hours were 37 and there was other compelling evidence that the employer regarded the comparators as part-time workers.

The relevant comparison

14.10   A part-time worker can only compare her/himself with an actual full-time[16] worker:

- with a similar contract;
- doing broadly similar work;
- who is employed by the same employer; and

is at the same establishment or, if there is no full-time worker with a similar contract doing similar work at the same establishment, at a different establishment.[17]

14.11   Under the EPA 1970 there must usually be an actual comparator of the opposite sex but, unlike the PTW Regs 2000, a comparison can be made with a man working for either the same or an associated employer. Thus, where a part-time worker wants to compare her/himself to a full-time worker (of the opposite sex) working for an associated employer, the claim must be brought under the EPA 1970.

14.12   Under the SDA 1975 the claimant may rely on an actual or hypoethical comparator (see paras 13.31 and 13.55).

14.13   Article 141 of the Treaty of Rome 1957 (which provides for equal pay) requires an actual comparator[18] except where legislation or a collective agreement can be shown to discriminate against women[19] and in pregnancy/maternity cases.[20] It allows a comparison with a

---

15   EAT/438/02, 6 February 2003 (unreported).

16   PTW Regs 2000 regs 2(4), 5; *England v Turnford School*, note 15.

17   PTW Regs 2000 reg 2(4).

18   *Macarthy's Ltd v Smith* [1980] IRLR 210, ECJ. But see charges to the definition of equal pay discrimination in the ETD as amended (ETAD, 2002/172/EC) which should allow hypothetical comparisons.

19   *Allonby v Accrington and Rossendale College* [2004] IRLR 224, ECJ.

20   *Alabaster v Barclays Bank plc (No 2)* [2005] IRLR 576, CA.

comparator who works in the same 'establishment or service',[21] but the pay difference must to be attributable to a single source.[22]

14.14   Hypothetical comparisons are unlikely to be possible under the PTW Regs 2000 as a comparison is required with an existing full-time worker.

Same type of contract

14.15   The comparison, for the purpose of determining whether there has been less favourable treatment, is between workers with the same type of contracts.[23]

14.16   The different contract categories are as follows:[24]

a) employees employed under a contract of employment (who are not apprentices);
b) employees who are employed under a contract of apprenticeship;
c) workers, who are not employees (see para 14.6);
d) any other description of worker that it is reasonable for the employer to treat differently from other workers on the ground that they have a different type of contract.

14.17   Permanent employees can compare themselves with those on fixed-term contracts, but not with workers who are genuinely self-employed as employees and workers are in different categories. Different provisons apply where a worker changes from being full-time to part-time (see paras 14.34–14.36).

14.18   In *Matthews and Others v Kent and Medway Towns and Fire Authority and others*,[25] the House of Lords considered whether part-time retained firefighters worked under the same type of contract as their full-time colleagues. They had similar duties, but there were very different hours arrangements. The part-timers worked largely on-call whereas the full-timers worked 42 hours per week on shifts with overtime. They also had differently structured pay packages. The part-timers argued that they were less favourably treated due to their

---

21 *Defrenne v Sabena* [1976] ICR 547, ECJ.
22 *Lawrence and Others v Regent Office Care Ltd* [2002] IRLR 822, ECJ; *Allonby v Accrington and Rosendale College* [2004] IRLR 224, ECJ; *Robertson and Others v Department for Environment, Food and Rural Affairs* [2005] IRLR, CA; *Armstrong v Newcastle upon Tyne NHS Hospital Trust* [2006] IRLR 124, CA; *South Ayrshire Council v Morton* [2002] IRLR 256, CS.
23 PTW Regs 2000 reg 2(4)(a)(i).
24 PTW Regs 2000 reg 2(3).
25 Note 3.

exclusion from the pension scheme, because their sick pay was calculated less favourably and because they received a lower hourly rate for additional duties.

14.19 The House of Lords decided that:

- the different working patterns, resulting in different pay arrangements, did not mean they were on different types of contract; despite the differences there were many similarities, such as ranking structure, disciplinary rules and aspects of the job description;
- the contract categories in PTW Regs 2000 reg 2(3) are mutually exclusive and paragraph 2(3)(d) refers to contract types other than those falling within the specific categories;
- each category is defined broadly and can encompass a wide variety of terms and conditions;
- the provision is only a threshold provision. If set too high it would prevent the required comparison being made and frustrate the purpose of the PTW Regs 2000 of securing equal treatment between full-timers and part-timers;
- regard must be had to the fact that part-time employment is inevitably different from full-time in a number of ways but the aim of the PTW Regs 2000 is to treat it equitably nevertheless.

14.20 In *Wippel*[26] the European Court of Justice (ECJ) considered what constituted a similar contract or employment relationship under the PTWD. Ms Wippel worked part-time when required by her employer and could refuse work. She claimed that her lack of fixed hours and pay was less favourable treatment than the full-time workers in the same establishment who had fixed hours of work which they could not refuse. The ECJ decided that the full-time workers had a different type of contract or employment relationship because of those differences, which meant that Ms Wippel had no full-time comparator. In *Matthews* the House of Lords distinguished *Wippel* because the claimants in *Matthews* were under a contractual obligation to their employers to work when required to do so. The House of Lords also commented that the PTW Regs 2000 may go further than the PTWD.

---

26 *Wippel v Peek and Cloppenburg GmbH & Co KG*, C313/02 [2005] IRLR 211, ECJ.

Broadly similar work

14.21   The full-time worker with whom the part-timer can compare her/
himself, must also be 'engaged in the same or broadly similar work
having regard, where relevant, to whether they have a similar level of
qualification, skills and experience'.[27]

14.22   Under the EPA 1970 the test for like work is:

- that the work is the same or of a broadly similar nature; and
- any differences are not of practical importance in relation to the
  terms and conditions of employment. Regard must be had to the
  frequency of such differences and their nature and extent.[28]

14.23   In *Matthews*,[29] the House of Lords said that despite the similarities
between the 'similar work' tests under the PTW Regs 2000 and the
EPA 1970, they are not the same. It provided guidance on how the
PTW Regs 2000 similar work test should be approached. This is
summarised below:

- under the EPA 1970, it is the central issue and examined more
  rigorously;
- regard must be had to the work actually done;[30]
  - particularly significant is the extent to which part-timers and
    full-timers do exactly the same work; if they do, the question is
    whether any differences are of such importance as to prevent
    their work being regarded overall as the same or broadly
    similar;
  - particular weight should be given to the extent of the import-
    ance of that same work to the enterprise as a whole. Dis-
    proportionate weight should not be given to the differences,
    for example, to full-timers' tasks additional to the core activ-
    ities, as there are bound to be differences;
- under the EPA 1970, more weight is given to identified
  differences;
- if a comparator has a higher level of qualification, skills and/or
  experience, this is only relevant where it affects the work done. It

---

27   PTW Regs 2000 reg 2(4)(a)(ii).
28   EPA 1970 s1(4).
29   Note 3.
30   Hale, LJ said that in a test case involving a large workforce the fact that a part-
timer under his contract must engage in the same range tasks as a full-timer,
even if in practice he is only rarely called upon to do so, is also of significance.

may also be irrelevant if it affects only additional (non-core) activities;[31]

- under the EPA 1970, these can be of practical importance (see para 14.25 onwards below).

14.24 The significance of the work actually done as between the claimant and her comparators was set out in *Birch v Leeds Metropolitan University*,[32] a claim by a part-time university lecturer. The tribunal also accepted that differences in work done by full-time and part-time workers particularly where such workers have the same skills and experience may of themselves indicate possible less favourable treatment. Where that might be the case, it attached less significance to those differences. Note that under the EPA 1970 the employer has a defence if it can show that the difference in pay or contractual terms is due to a non-discriminatory 'material factor difference'.[33] This applies, for example, where the comparator has superior skill, experience or qualifications.[34]

Similar work cases under the EPA 1970

14.25 Despite the differences between the tests under the PTW Regs 2000 and the EPA 1970, much of the EPA 1970 case law on like work is likely to be relevant in deciding whether the workers are doing similar work. The main principles under the EPA 1970 are as follows.

Broad approach to type of work and skills necessary to do it

14.26 A broad approach should be taken rather than too close an examination. In *Capper Pass Ltd v JB Lawton*[35] the woman cooked between 10 and 20 lunches for managers and worked a 40-hour week. The man cooked 350 meals a day and worked a 45-hour week. Their work was held to be broadly similar. In these circumstances the woman would have a claim under both the EPA 1970 and may have one under the PTW Regs 2000 if 45 hours was the full-time norm and 40 was considered part-time (see paras 14.8–14.9).[36]

31 See *Matthews*, note 3, at 18 and 45.
32 ET 1802230/03, see IDS Brief 800 (March 2006).
33 EPA 1970 s1(3).
34 For example, *Angestelltenbetriebsrat der Weiner Gebietskrankenkasse v Weiner Gebietskrankenkasse* [1999] IRLR 804, ECJ. These may also be relevant factors in deciding the 'similar work' issue under the EPA 1970, see paras 14.22 and 14.33.
35 [1976] IRLR 366, EAT.
36 See also *British Leyland Ltd v Powell* [1978] IRLR 57, EAT.

Trivial differences

14.27   These should be disregarded. In *British Leyland Ltd v Powell*,[37] the difference between a female driver in a catering department driving vans within the factory premises and a man driver in the transport section who drove vans on the public highway, was held not to be of practical importance.

Responsibility levels

14.28   The difference between an employee who has control of materials of small value and an employee controlling those of high value may be of practical importance, due to the difference in responsibility levels.[38]

Differing duties

14.29   Female warehouse workers did not do similar work to male warehouse workers who worked away from the warehouse two days per week.[39] A female clerk and a male trainee manager did the same work except that he deputised for a manager five weeks each year. This difference was of no practical importance.[40]

Time at which work is done is not relevant

14.30   The Employment Appeal Tribunal (EAT) has held that the time at which the work is done is not relevant.[41] Where the comparator does the same work but at night, unless there is added responsibility,[42] this should be classified as broadly similar work. Night workers can be compensated by a night shift premium rather than a difference in the basic hourly rate. Similar principles apply to other non-standard hours.[43]

---

37   [1978] IRLR 57, EAT.
38   *Eaton Ltd v Nuttall* [1977] IRLR 71, EAT.
39   *Dorothy Perkins Ltd v Dance* [1977] IRLR 226.
40   *Redland Roof Tiles Ltd v Harper* [1977] ICR 349.
41   *Dugdale and Others v Kraft Foods Ltd* [1976] IRLR 368, EAT, where women worked alternate shifts and their male comparators rotating ones.
42   *Thomas v National Coal Board* [1978] IRLR 451, EAT.
43   See *Electrolux Ltd v Hutchinson and Others* [1976] IRLR 410, EAT and *National Coal Board v Sherwin* [1978] IRLR 22, EAT.
44   In *Electrolux Ltd v Hutchinson and Others* [1976] IRLR 410, the EAT said that a flexibility clause not used in practice did not amount to a difference of practical importance.

It is the work done which is relevant

14.31 It is the work actually done which is relevant, not the contractual obligations.[44] The Court of Appeal has held that the comparison must be made between the tasks that the man and woman actually do and the frequency with which they are done, rather than between their respective contractual obligations.[45] However, significantly different tasks cannot be ignored when determining whether the work is broadly similar.[46]

Would the differences result in different grading?

14.32 The EAT has held that a practical guide is whether the differences are such as to put the two jobs into different categories or grades in an evaluation study.[47]

Skills, training and qualifications

14.33 These differences can be of practical importance if, for example, this affects their work methods or quality.[48]

Workers who change from full-time to part-time work

Workers who change to part-time work

14.34 Where a full-time worker changes to being a part-time worker, they should retain their previous pay and benefits, pro rata.[49] There is no need to identify another worker doing similar work employed on a similar contract. The comparison is effectively with their previous terms and conditions. This applies where:

- the worker was previously a full-time worker;
- the worker's contract is terminated or varied;

---

45 *E Coombes (Holdings) Ltd v Shields* [1978] IRLR 263, CA.
46 *Maidment v Cooper and Co (Birmingham) Ltd* [1978] IRLR 462, EAT. The type of disproportionate pay difference found here should now have a remedy under article 141.
47 *British Leyland v Powell* [1978] IRLR 57, EAT.
48 *Brodie and Another v Startrite Engineering Co Ltd* [1976] IRLR 101, EAT (skills); *Brunnhofer v Bank der Osterreichishouldschen Postsparkasse AG* [2001] IRLR 571, ECJ and *Angestelltenbetriebsrat*, note 34 (training, qualifications and working conditions).
49 PTW Regs 2000 reg 3.

- they continue to work under a new or varied contract, whether of the same type or not; and
- they are required to work fewer hours.

There is no requirement that the work done is the same or equivalent, so it could be a different job, though in most cases the change will only be to the hours of work.

Workers returning part-time after absence

14.35 Slightly different provisions apply where a worker changes from full-time to part-time work after an absence of less than 12 months.[50] In this situation too, the worker can simply compare his/her position before and after but the worker must return to the same or an equivalent job (unlike workers who have no such absence see above). Provided the following applies, the worker should retain the same pro rata pay and benefits as when they s/he was a full-time worker:

- the worker must have been a full-time worker immediately before the absence (whether the absence followed a termination of the worker's contract or not, ie even if the worker has not remained in the employment during the absence);
- the worker must return to work for the same employer within a period of less than 12 months from the start of the absence;
- the worker must return to the same job (see chapter 4) or to a job at the same level, whether under a different or varied contract, irrespective of whether it is the same type of contract;
- the worker must be required to work fewer weekly hours than they were doing immediately before the period of absence.

Thus, a woman returning from maternity leave of less than 12 months (or a woman or man from other leaves, eg, paternity, adoption, parental or sick leaves, a career break or a sabbatical) who reduces their hours but continues to do the same work or work at the same level, is entitled to retain the pro rata pay and benefits they had when they were working full-time. It does not matter if they have only reduced their hours by one or two per week, nor if they have changed their contract from, for example, being fixed-term to permanent or

---

50 PTW Regs 2000 reg 4. Note that the PTW Regs 2000 give no right to return to work part-time after maternity leave but the guidance encourages employers to consider this and a right to request such work now exists under Employment Rights Act 1996 ss80F–80I (see chapter 12) and an SDA claim for flexible work may also exist (see chapter 13).

vice versa. It may be worth returning a few days early from leave to benefit from this provision.

14.36   A requirement to do a lesser status job in order to work part-time, even on the same terms and conditions, could also amount to sex discrimination (see chapters 2 and 3).

What is less favourable treatment?

14.37   A part-time worker has the right not to be treated less favourably than a comparable full-time worker on the ground that s/he is a part-time worker, unless the employer can show the treatment is objectively justified. The right applies:

- in relation to the terms of the worker's contract; or
- where the worker is subjected to any other detriment by any act, or deliberate failure to act, of his/her employer.[51]

14.38   Less favourable treatment occurs where a part-time worker is not receiving pro rata pay and benefits unless pro rata treatment is inappropriate or is otherwise treated less favourably.[52]

14.39   Examples of less favourable treatment

- Dismissing (including selecting for redundancy) a part-time worker because she works part-time.
- In *Hendrickson European Ltd v Pipe*[53] the claimant, having reduced her hours to 28.5 by agreement, was pressurised to increase them so offered to do 32.5 hours, only five hours less than full-time colleagues. The employer insisted on her working full-time; she refused and was dismissed. The EAT upheld the tribunal's finding that she was treated less favourably because of her part-time status.
- Putting pressure on a worker to increase her or his hours.
- Requiring a part-time worker to do a disproportionate number of standby hours to that required of a full-time worker. In *Gibson v Scottish Ambulance Service*,[54] a part-time ambulance worker employed in one area of Scotland was required to keep 56 standby

---

51 PTW Regs 2000 reg 5(1).
52 PTW Regs 2000 reg 5(3).
53 EAT/0272/02 15 April 2003 (see IDS Brief 738, August 2003).
54 EAT/0052/04, 16 December 2004 (see IDS Brief 776, March 2005). The claimant lost his claim (see para 14.45).

to rostered hours which was held to be disproportionate to the 35
hours required of the full-time comparator employed in another
area.

• Appointing a part-time worker to a full-time position but only on a
temporary basis because of her previous part-time work, *Royal
Mail Group plc v Lynch.*[55]

14.40   The claimant must show not only that it is less favourable treatment
but that it was on the ground that the worker is part-time. Such
treatment can be justified.

Is the treatment on the ground that the worker is part time?

14.41   The right to equal treatment applies only if the unequal treatment is
on the ground that the worker is a part-time worker.[56] It is for the
employer to identify the ground.[57] Two main issues arise:

1. Is treatment 'on the ground' of being a part-time worker?

14.42   According to the EAT in *Gibson*, this involves looking at the subjective
reason (conscious or unconscious) why the employer treated the
claimant less favourably, ie, following the test set out by the House of
Lords in two Race Relations Act 1976 cases, *Nagarajan v London
Regional Transport*[58] and *Chief Constable of West Yorkshire Police v
Khan.*[59] This is a question of fact which may require the drawing of
inferences from the surrounding circumstances.

14.43   For example, in *Hendrickson*,[60] the EAT held that the employer's
motive was clear as the claimant had been told that if she wanted to
stay in her employment she would have to work full-time and her
refusal triggered her redundancy.

14.44   In *McMenemy*,[61] the claimant worked three days a week excluding
Mondays. He did not receive time off in lieu when public holidays fell
on Mondays. However, the business operated seven days a week so

---

55 EAT/0426/03, 2 September 2003 (unreported).
56 PTW Regs 2000 reg 5(2)(a).
57 PTW Regs 2000 reg 8(6).
58 [1999] IRLR 572.
59 [2001] IRLR 830.
60 *Hendrickson Europe v Pipe*, EAT, note 53.
61 *McMenemy v Capita Business Services Ltd*, UKEAT/0079/05, 8 March 2006 (see
    IDS Brief 806, June 2006).

both full-time and part-time workers worked patterns which meant they would not get the benefit of the Monday bank holiday. The EAT upheld the tribunal's decision that the claimant had been treated less favourably but that it was not because he worked part-time but because he did not work Mondays. The EAT also accepted that a hypothetical comparator could be constructed to determine the reason for the treatment. As the PTW Regs 2000 did not prohibit indirect discrimination, the fact that the policy disadvantaged more part-time workers than full-time workers was not relevant. However, a woman might have an indirect sex discrimination claim in such a situation (see chapter 13).

14.45 In *Gibson*,[62] the EAT said the employer's intention in imposing the less favourable treatment was to meet local demand for the ambulance service and not because the claimant worked part-time.[63]

2. Must part-time working be the only reason for the treatment?

14.46 In *Gibson* the EAT held that part-time status must be the only reason for the less favourable treatment. This was based on interpreting the PTW Regs to give effect to the Directive which states that part-timers must not be less favourably treated 'solely' because they work part-time.[64]

14.47 However, the EAT in *Coutts*[65] reached a different conclusion. This was a case under the FTE Regs 2002[66] where there is a similar discrepancy between the regulations and the relevant directive. The EAT said that the FTE Regs 2002 should be construed as they are and it would be sufficient that being a fixed-term employee was the predominant reason for the less favourable treatment. This approach is to be preferred as the directive provides that member states may 'maintain or *introduce* [our italics] more favourable provisions'.[67] The

---

62 *Gibson v Scottish Ambulance Service*, EAT, note 54.
63 The claimant therefore failed with his claim.
64 Cl 4, 97/81/EC.
65 *Coutts and Co plc and Another v Cure and Another*, EAT/0395/04, 17 September 2004 (see IDS Brief 769, November 2004) a case under the Fixed-term Employees (Prevention of Less Favourable Treatment) Regulations 2002 SI No 2034, where the treatment must also be 'on the ground' of the claimant's employment status.
66 Fixed-term Employees (Prevention of Less Favourable Treatment) Regulations (FTE Regs) 2002 SI No 2034.
67 Part-time Workers Directive Cl 6, 97/81/EC.

House of Lords in *Matthews*[68] made a similar point and is of higher authority than *Gibson*. It is also similar to the approach taken in SDA 1975 cases.[69]

The pro rata principle, term-by-term comparison and assessing less favourable treatment

14.48   The pro rata principle[70] applies 'unless it is inappropriate'.[71] Thus if a full-time worker is entitled to pay or any benefit a part-time worker should receive not less than the proportion of that benefit that his weekly hours bears to the hours of the full-time comparator. Thus, if a full-time worker doing 35 hours a week, five days a week, is entitled to 30 days' holiday a year, a worker doing 17.5 hours a week, 2.5 days a week, should get half this much. If a worker does a five-day week but only four hours per day, s/he will be entitled to 30 days' holiday, though each day is only four hours. Note that part-time as well as full-time workers are entitled to 20 days' (pro rata) holiday a year under the Working Time Regulations (WT Regs) 1998 (see para 1.36).[72]

14.49   'Weekly hours' means the number of hours a worker is required to work under their contract of employment in a week, ignoring any absences or overtime. If they work on a cycle, it is the average of such hours.[73]

14.50   In asessing whether treatment has been less favourable, consideration must be given to whether the principle:

- is appropriate.[74] If it is, the pro rata principle applies to a term which is more favourable in the full-timer's contract;

---

68   Note 3; see also *NTL Group Ltd v Difolco*, EAT/0120/05, 27 January 2006 (unreported), where the EAT implied that part-time status being a material cause was sufficient.

69   See *O'Donoghue v Redcar and Cleveland Borough Council* [2001] IRLR 615, CA: if there are mixed motives for doing the act complained of and the ET considers the unlawful motive(s) were of sufficient importance to be treated as a cause (not necessarily the sole cause) for the act, there will be unlawful discrimination.

70   PTW Regs 2000 reg 1(2) for definition.

71   PTW Regs 2000 reg 5(3). See *Matthews and Others v Kent and Medway Towns and Fire Authority and Others* [2003] IRLR 732, EAT, where the tribunal had decided that the pro rata principle was inappropriate which the parties accepted on appeal.

72   SI 1998 No 1833.

73   PTW Regs 2000 reg 1(3); applied in *James and Others v Great Northeastern Railways*, EAT/0496/04, 1 March 2005 (54–56) (see IDS Brief 780, March 2005).

74   See *James*, note 73.

- if it is inappropriate, the pro rata principle may not apply. This may be
  - because the benefit cannot be pro-rated (eg a company car). See paras 14.87–14.89 for an approach to such issues; or
  - for some other reason. In *Matthews* the House of Lords held that it was 'inappropriate' to look at whether more favourable terms may be offset against the less favourable ones, though this may happen in certain cases if one term was well balanced by a more favourable one. A term-by-term approach was to be preferred in this case even if the pro rata principle is not applied[75]

Overtime

14.51 Regulation 5(4) provides that part-time workers are entitled to premium overtime rates only once they have worked the same number of hours as would entitle a full-time worker to the premium. Thus if a full-time worker receives a premium when his/her hours exceed 35, the part-time worker would only receive a premium after working 35 hours.[76]

14.52 In *James v Great Northeastern Railways*[77] the full-time workers' weekly contractual rostered hours were 40, paid at a basic hourly rate for the first 35 with the next five ('additional hours') paid at 1.25 times basic pay. Overtime over 40 hours was paid at the same rate as the additional hours. The part-time claimants were contractually required to work 25 or 30 hours weekly and were paid the same basic rate as the full-time workers but not an additional hours rate unless they worked over 35 hours in any week. The EAT held that the additional hours allowance was not overtime but pay for normal working hours, thus the full-time workers received, on average, a higher hourly rate than the part-time workers based on their normal contractual hours. The case was remitted to the tribunal to decide whether this was justified.

14.53 See paras 14.67–14.71 for more detail on overtime.

---

75 In *Matthews and Others v Kent and Medway Towns and Fire Authority and Others*, HL, note 3, the House of Lords did not rule out the possibility of applying an overall assessment of less and more favourable terms in part-time equal treatment cases, to determine the less favourable treatment issue.

76 This is consistent with *Stadt Lengerich v Helmig* [1995] IRLR 216, ECJ, see para 14.69.

77 Note 73.

Objective justification under the PTW Regs 2000

14.54 The less favourable treatment may be justified on objective grounds.[78] The (non-binding) Guidance Notes at the end of the PTW Regs 2000 state that the employer must show that the less favourable treatment:

- is to achieve a legitimate objective, for example, a genuine business objective;
- is necessary to achieve that objective; and
- is an appropriate way to achieve the objective.

14.55 The test is similar to that for justifying indirect sex discrimination prior to October 2005 and many of the principles relevant to access to part-time work will apply (see chapter 13). In general, each aspect of less favourable treatment should be justified, though in *Matthews*, the House of Lords commented that it would not 'rule out the possibility that more favourable treatment on one point might supply justification for less favourable treatment on another'.[79]

14.56 The main question that is likely to arise is the cost involved in treating part-time workers the same as full-time workers. In *Hill*[80] the ECJ held that an employer had not justified a practice whereby job sharers' service should be treated as half that of a full-timer in a situation where a job sharer could acquire the same experience as a full-timer (see para 14.66 below). Generalised assertions and cost reasons were not sufficient to show justification.The ECJ said that the discrimination could not be justified *solely* (our emphasis) on the ground that avoiding it would involve increased costs.

14.57 Similarly in *Kutz-Bauer*,[81] the ECJ held that budgetary considerations cannot in themselves justify discrimination on grounds of sex. As the ECJ explained, if budgetary considerations could justify indirect discrimination, it would mean that the application of the principle of equal treatment might vary according to the state of the public finances of the particular member state. This should apply with even more force to private sector employers where there is not the same margin of appreciation which is accorded to member states (see further para 13.112 onwards for costs justification and indirect sex discrimination).

---

78 PTW Regs 2000 reg 5(2)(b).
79 Note 3 at 49.
80 *Hill v Revenue Commissioners* [1998] IRLR 466.
81 [2003] IRLR 368, ECJ; see also *Jorgensen v Foreningen af Speciallaeger and Sygesikringens Forhandlingsudvalg* [2000] IRLR 72, ECJ.

14.58   The need to apply a critical evaluation to the employer's justification as set out by the Court of Appeal in *Lax*[82] (see paras 13.95–13.96)
is another principle which should apply in assessing objective
justification.

Examples of less favourable treatment under the PTW Regs 2000 and comparable provisions of the EPA 1970 and SDA 1975

14.59   There are Guidance Notes at the end of the PTW Regs 2000 and
Compliance Guidance to the PTW Regs 2000 has also been published
by the government ('the Guidance').[83] The latter includes advice on
best practice. Although neither are legally binding, they give some
indication of how the PTW Regs 2000 should be interpreted and may
be useful to cite in tribunals. Where relevant they are set out below.

14.60   To avoid claims under the PTW Regs 2000 and comparable provisions of the EPA 1970 and SDA 1975, employers are advised to check
eligibility requirements for pay and other benefits, bearing in mind
the EOC Codes of Practice on discrimination and equal pay. Are there
restrictions which impact negatively on women? For example, are any
benefits limited to employees working over a minimum number of
hours? Can these requirements be justified objectively?[84]

Pay

Under the PTW Regs 2000

14.61   Part-timers must not receive a lower basic rate of pay than comparable full-timers unless the employer justifies this (see, for example
James[85] at para 14.52).

---

82   [2005] IRLR 726.
83   Published by the Department of Trade and Industry at: www.dti.gov.uk/
employment/employment-legislation/employment-guidance/page 19479.html.
84   The Equal Opportunities Commission (EOC) and the European Commission
have produced Codes of Practice on equal pay. The EOC Code is admissible in
evidence (SDA 1975 s56A(10)) and the EC Code (COM(96) 336) must be taken
into account when interpreting national or EC law. Both emphasise the
importance of systematically reviewing and monitoring pay systems for sex bias
including indirect discrimination against part-time workers. They provide
guidance on how this can be done.
85   See note 73.

Under the EPA 1970 and article 141

14.62   'Pay' under the EPA 1970 covers not only wages and salary but pensions, redundancy pay, and payments for time off for union duties. It must be interpreted consistently with article 141 of the Treaty of Rome which defines pay as 'the ordinary basic or minimum wage or salary or any consideration whether in cash or in kind which the worker receives, directly or indirectly, in respect of his employment from his employer' (see paras 1.21–1.23).

14.63   The general principle under the EPA 1970 and article 141, like the PTW Regs 2000, is that part-time workers should receive the same pro rata pay and benefits as full-timers.[86]

14.64   Further discussion of pay discrimination (including employer defences) can be found in the *Discrimination Law Handbook.*

Increments based on length of service[87]

Under the PTW Regs 2000

14.65   The PTW Regs 2000 do not specifically cover increments based on length of service but the pro rata principle should apply. The years of service of a part-time worker should be treated as equivalent to a full-timer unless it is objectively justified to do otherwise (see para 14.54 onwards).[88]

Under the EPA 1970 and article 141

14.66   In *Hill*[89] two women were told that two years' job sharing should be counted as one year's full-time service when they returned to full-time work. This meant they did not receive the same annual increments as full-timers with the same years of service. It was accepted that a job sharer could acquire over the same period the same experi-

---

86   See *Jenkins v Kingsgate (Clothing Productions) Ltd* [1981] IRLR 228, ECJ and *Jenkins v Kingsgate (Clothing Productions) Ltd (No 2)* [1981] IRLR 388, EAT where the EAT held that the employer must show that the difference in pay between full-time and part-time workers is reasonably necessary in order to obtain some result (other than cheap labour) which the employer wishes to achieve, for economic or other reasons.

87   The ECJ decision in *Cadman v Health and Safety Executive* which challenges using length of service increments under the EPA 1970 is pending.

88   Account should also be taken of the Employment Equality (Age) Regulations which came into force in October 2006. Regulation 32 deals with benefits based on length of service – though not specifically in relation to part-time workers.

89   See note 80; see also *Nimz v Freie und Hansestadt Hamburg* [1991] IRLR 222, ECJ.

ence as a full-time worker and the only difference was the time worked. The ECJ held that paying an increment based on actual hours of service worked (rather than years) had a disparate impact and the employers had to justify it as it applied to the particular job in question[90] (see para 14.51 onwards for justification).

Overtime

Under the PTW Regs 2000

14.67   A part-time employee is only entitled to receive overtime rates of pay where a comparable full-time worker would receive overtime rates (see also para 14.51 onwards).[91] Thus, where overtime rates are paid to full-time workers who exceed their normal hours of 35 per week, a part-timer working 21 hours weekly would not be entitled to such rates until s/he worked more than 35 hours during the week. The part-timer should then be paid the same rate as a full-time worker.[92]

14.68   A part-timer should receive pro rata benefits as well as pay for the extra hours worked below the overtime threshold, in the same way full-timers do (see also *Rees*,[93] para 14.70).

Under the EPA 1970 and article 141

14.69   The PTW Regs 2000 reflect the present position under UK and one strand of EU discrimination law. In *Stadt Lengerich v Helmig*[94] the ECJ held that it was lawful to provide for the payment of overtime premia for part-time workers only for hours worked in excess of the normal working hours for full-time employees, as in the example in para 14.67 above. This means that they receive the same overall pay as full-timers whatever number of weekly hours worked.

14.70   This principle was applied to the benefit of part-timers in *Rees*,[95] where a tribunal held part-timers' overtime was remunerated unequally. Their overtime was paid at standard rates until they had exceeded full-time hours. But the extra hours under the threshold

---

90   See also *Nimz*, note 89, and *Nikoloudi v Organismos Tilepikinonion Ellados* C196/02, 10 March 2005. The Court of Appeal in *Cadman v Health and Safety Executive* [2004] IRLR 971, analysed the ECJ cases on length of service increments.
91   PTW Regs 2000 reg 5(4).
92   See also *James v Great Northeastern Railways*, para 14.51, note 73.
93   *Rees v Natwest Bank plc*, ET 1200927/97.
94   [1995] IRLR 216, ECJ.
95   Note 93.

did not attract entitlement (pro rata) to contractual benefits such as holiday pay and leave, which full-timers obtained from each hour worked up to the threshold. This was unlawful as it could not be justified.

14.71   However, in *Elsner-Lakeberg v Land Nordrhein-Westfalen*,[96] a part-timer, like full-timers, was expected to work more than three additional hours in a month before receiving overtime. The ECJ decided that three additional hours is a proportionately greater burden for a part-timer and potentially indirectly discriminatory.[97] Employers would therefore be safer to base overtime rates on a percentage of contracted hours, for example where a worker does more than 10% over contracted hours. It is also safer to pay a part-time worker normal basic pay for any extra hours up to the full-time threshold.

Shift allowances and unsocial hours payments

Under the PTW Regs 2000

14.72   Where workers are entitled to anti-social hours payments, shift allowances and weekend payments, the Guidance points out that these should be paid on the same basis to part-time and full-time workers. For example, where a store has both full-time and part-time workers, working early, day and late shifts, if the early and late shifts attract time-and-a-half pay for full-time workers, comparable part-time workers should be treated in the same way.

Under the EPA 1970 and article 141

14.73   The position is the same under the EPA 1970. Employers should consider whether, if part-timers are excluded from such payments, this disadvantages women and, if so, whether this is justified.[98]

---

96 [2005] IRLR 209.
97 See also *Helmig*, note 94.
98 In *Montgomery v Lowfield Distribution Ltd*, EAT/932/95, 14 May 1996 (unreported), the mostly male full-timers were given particularly advantageous pay arrangements for bank holidays whereas the largely female part-timers were not. The EAT agreed this was justified by a GMF because the full-timers were contractually required to work variable work patterns whereas the part-timers had fixed hours (and received some extra payment only if they actually worked a bank holiday). A similar case might be decided differently under the PTW Regs 2000

Bonuses

Under the PTW Regs 2000

14.74 Part-time workers should be entitled to a pro rata bonus. The Guidance gives the example of a firm which awards its workers a Christmas bonus. It states that its part-time workers should receive a pro rata amount, depending on the number of hours they work. In *Coutts*,[99] non-payment of a non-contractual incentive bonus to a fixed-term employee was a detriment under the equivalent of PTW Regs 2000 reg 5(1)(b) in the FTE Regs.[100]

Under the EPA 1970 and article 141

14.75 In *Kruger*[101] the ECJ held that the exclusion of part-time workers from the scope of a collective agreement which provided for the grant of a special annual bonus was indirect discrimination under article 141 where it affected a considerably higher percentage of women than men. The employers argued that such workers did not pay social security contributions, but the ECJ said the exclusion was not justified. It distinguished two previous cases (*Nolte*[102] and *Megner*[103]) as they concerned state social insurance schemes that fell within the broad margin of discretion of member states.

Profit sharing, share options schemes

Under the PTW Regs 2000

14.76 The Guidance states that the benefits of profit sharing and share option schemes should be available on a pro rata basis to part-time workers. An employer may be able to justify excluding part-time workers where the value of the share options is so small that the potential benefit to the part-timer of the option was less than the cost of realising them. This is only likely to apply where a worker is doing very few hours per week (but see para 14.77).

---

99 Note 65.
100 FTE Regs 2002 reg 3(1)(b).
101 *Kruger v Kreiskrankenhaus Ebersberg* [1999] IRLR 808, ECJ.
102 *Nolte v Landesversicherungsanstalt Hannover* [1996] IRLR 225, ECJ.
103 *Megner and Scheffel v Innungskrankenkasse Vorderpfalz* C–444/93 [1996] IRLR 236, ECJ.

Under the EPA 1970, article 141 and the SDA 1975

14.77   The same principles should apply under the EPA 1970. In *Buckle v Abbey National plc*,[104] an employee working (just) less than eight hours per week succeeded in her SDA claim that she could not justifiably be excluded from the profit-related bonus and the share distribution schemes.

Contractual sick and maternity pay

Under the PTW Regs 2000

14.78   The Guidance states that the PTW Regs 2000 apply directly to contractual sick and maternity pay. A part-time worker should receive pro rata benefits unless the employer can justify not paying pro rata benefits, though it is difficult to anticipate when this might occur. The Guidance points out that the pro rata principle applies to:

• calculation of the rate of pay;
• any length of service requirement; and
• the length of time the payment is received.

It would not, for example, be lawful to require a part-timer to have longer length of service to qualify for payment unless it was objectively justified.

Under the EPA 1970 and article 141

14.79   In *Rinner-Kuhn*[105] the ECJ held it was a breach of article 141 to exclude employees working less than 10 hours a week from sick pay, where it affects a considerably greater number of women than men, unless it was justified.[106]

14.80   Statutory maternity pay is covered in chapter 6. Contractual maternity pay should be paid on a pro rata basis to part-timers. However, it may be difficult to enforce under the EPA 1970, because there would be no male comparator and a claim for equal pay cannot usually be made during maternity leave.

---

104   ET Case nos 13647/96 and 45501/96, 5 March 1998.
105   *Rinner-Kuhn v FWW Spezial-Gebaudereinigung GmbH* [1989] IRLR 493, ECJ.
106   See also the European Commission Code of Practice on equal pay, Comm (96) 336.

Occupational pensions

Under the PTW Regs 2000

14.81　The Guidance states that employers cannot deny access to both male and female part-time workers and they should not discriminate between full-time and part-time workers as to access, unless different treatment is justified on objective grounds.

14.82　The previous two-year limit on backdating pension claims, previously contained in the PTW Regs 2000 has been removed in order to comply with EU law.

Under the EPA 1970 and article 141

14.83　It is a breach of the EPA 1970 and article 141 to exclude part-timers from a pension scheme.[107] Equality of treatment between men and women doing equal work in relation to pensions is regulated by the Pensions Act 1995 and the Occupational Pension Schemes (Equal Treatment) Regulations 1995[108] (see para 2.100). Certain exceptions to the equal treatment principle are permitted. Imposing a different length of service requirement before a part-timer (as opposed to a full-timer) may join a scheme may indirectly discriminate against women. This may be justifiable if, for example, there is evidence that part-timers do not stay long and the setup costs of a pension are high. One solution which is sometimes adopted, is to allow access after a year of service and to backdate entitlement to the start of employment.

14.84　There are different methods of calculating the pension entitlement of part-time workers. Usually the part-time work is translated into the full-time equivalent. Thus, if a woman works 18 hours (as opposed to 36), after four years her pension will be based on two years' full-time service.

14.85　Until the ECJ decision in *Bilka*[109] in 1986 few, if any, realised that the exclusion of part-time workers from a pension scheme (and other benefits) was indirect sex discrimination and a breach of EU law. Now, reflecting ECJ case law, domestic legislation requires that women and men have equal access to scheme membership and once a member they should receive equal treatment (with certain

---

107　*Bilka Kaufhaus GmbH v Weber von Hartz* [1986] IRLR 317, ECJ; *Vroege v NCIV Instituut voor Volkshuisvesting BV* [1994] IRLR 651, ECJ

108　SI No 3183.

109　*Bilka*, note 107.

exceptions).[110] The House of Lords in *Preston*[111] has held that a claim could be made back to April 1976, the date of the *Defrenne*[112] decision. However backdating time limits will vary, depending upon the claimant's situation.

14.86   Pension provisions are complex and outside the scope of this book. Further discussion of them can be found in the *Discrimination Law Handbook*.[113]

Health insurance, subsidised mortgages, company cars and other benefits

Under the PTW Regs 2000 and the EPA 1970

14.87   These should be provided pro rata to part-time workers unless there is objective justification for a difference. The Guidance states that where a benefit, such as health insurance or a car, cannot be applied pro rata, this is not of itself an objective justification for denying it to part-time workers. Justification may include the disproportionate cost to the organisation of providing the benefit where the worker only works very short hours. Arguably, they should be given the option of a pro rata cash payment to contribute to a health insurance plan.

14.88   The Guidance states that a subsidised mortgage should be available at the same preferential interest rate and the same multiplier to determine the mortgage advance. It also suggests that where a part-timer would be entitled to a company car had they worked full-time, best practice would be for the employer to work out its financial value and provide an equivalent pro rata allowance to part-time workers or arrange for the part-timers to share the car. However, where a part-timer only works slightly fewer than full-time hours, it may arguably be hard to justify refusing a car where a full-timer would receive one.

14.89   The same principles should apply under the EPA 1970 and SDA 1975. In *Buckle v Abbey National plc*,[114] a tribunal held, under the SDA 1975, that the employer was justified in excluding an employee, employed for less than eight hours a week, from a staff subsidised mortgage (as she was earning too little to be a safe basis for such a

---

110   See Pensions Act 1995 s62 and related regulations in para 14.83. A comparator is needed, but see also paras 14.11 and 14.13.
111   *Preston v Wolverhampton NHS Trust* [2001] IRLR 237, HL.
112   *Defrenne v Sabena* (No 2) [1978] ECR 455.
113   2nd edn, 2006, forthcoming, Legal Action Group.
114   Note 104.

loan) and also from the private health insurance scheme (as being disproportionately expensive in view of her earnings).[115] A more favourable decision might be made under the PTW Regs 2000. Justification for such an exclusion will have to be provided on a case-by-case basis.

Holidays, other leave, career breaks

Under the PTW Regs 2000 and EPA 1970

14.90 The Guidance states that part-time workers, like their full-time colleagues, are entitled to a minimum of statutory annual leave, maternity leave and parental leave. Where enhanced by contractual conditions, part-time workers should receive pro rata holiday entitlement and other leave (including parental and maternity leave and career breaks) subject to objective justification.

14.91 The position with bank holidays is not clear.[116] Part-timers who do not work Mondays may lose out. The Guidance suggests that employers can compensate for the shortfall by applying the holiday entitlement to these workers pro rata. One option is for bank and public holidays to be added together and converted into hours. A part-time worker who works two days a week is entitled to two-fifths of these hours, regardless of the days they work. Arguably, job sharers should share the bank and public holidays so that the person who works at the end of the week does not lose out. However, in *McMenemy*[117] the claimant was unsuccessful (see para 14.44). The business was open seven days a week and full-timers also lost out if they did not work a Monday. A similar claim may be successful if the business was open five days a week so that only part-timers lost out.[118]

14.92 The same principles should apply under the EPA 1970.[119]

---

115 But see para 14.77 for the successful aspects of her claim.
116 The government is considering (at Summer 2006) adding eight days to the full-time statutory leave entitlement, the equivalent of bank holidays but not necessarily to be taken on those days. Part-timers are likely to have pro rata entitlements.
117 Note 61.
118 See also *Montgomery*, note 98.
119 See *Bowden, Chapman and Doyle v Tufnell Parcels Express Ltd*, C133/00, ECJ, a Working Time Directive case about part-time workers' right to holiday leave, where the court commented positively on the potential applicability of equal treatment principles.

Training: payment and access

Under the PTW Regs 2000

14.93 The Guidance says that employers should not exclude part-time staff from training simply because they work part-time; this will be less favourable treatment. The Notes to the PTW Regs 2000 say that training will need to be structured wherever possible to be at the most convenient times for the majority of staff including part-timers (though the latter may be able to change their working day). A part-time worker who works extra hours in order to do training should be paid for the extra time.

Under the EPA 1970 and article 141

14.94 Where a part-time worker has to attend a work-related training course, which exceeds her normal working hours, s/he should be paid for it. In *Botel*[120] a trades union official attended a training course as a member of the staff committee (which is similar to a trades union). German law provided that she was entitled to be released from work without a reduction in salary, but would not be paid for the full week as she only worked part-time. The ECJ held that part-timers were therefore treated less favourably than full-time members because they were not paid as the training took place outside their normal working hours although within the normal working hours of full-time workers.[121]

Under the SDA 1975

14.95 Refusal to allow a part-time worker to access training (pro rata) because they work part-time may breach the SDA 1975. The claimant would usually have to demonstrate indirect discrimination, ie, that access was subject to a PCP ('provision, criterion or practice' – see chapter 13) (eg, to be full-time) which particularly disadvantaged women and was to her disadvantage (eg, its hours or location or that it was available only to those working full-time). The employer would then have to justify the PCP.

---

120 *Arbeiterwohlfahrt der Stadt Berli eV v Botel* [1992] IRLR 423, ECJ.
121 A similar decision was reached in *Kuratorium fur Dialyse und Nierentransplantation eV v Lewark* [1996] IRLR 637, ECJ. It was followed in *Davies v Neath Port Talbot County BC* [1999] IRLR 769, EAT.

Promotion

Under the PTW Regs 2000

14.96   The Guidance points out that 'if individual companies and the economy as a whole are to reap the full benefit of the flexibility part-time work can offer, then more types of job and levels of management must be opened to part-time workers ... Part-time workers should also be given equal opportunity to seek promotion'. It continues: 'previous or current part-time status should not of itself constitute a barrier to promotion to a post, whether the post is full-time or part-time'. If, for example, promotion of a part-time worker is made subject to a condition which would not be applied to a full-time worker, this may amount to less favourable treatment.[122]

Under the SDA 1975 and Equal Treatment Directive (ETD)

14.97   Promotion is not a contractual benefit so any claim must be brought under the SDA 1975. In *Gerster*[123] the ECJ held that rules concerning access to career advancement did not fall within article 141, but the ETD, as they were only indirectly linked to pay.

14.98   In *Gold v Tower Hamlets LBC*[124] the tribunal found that a solicitor was not promoted because she was job sharing. The tribunal held that there were no good reasons for the council's failure to put her forward to the final appointment panel and she won her claim. In *Neary v Ladbrokes Casinos Ltd*[125] the tribunal found there was a culture within the casino 'which amounted to an unwritten, an unspoken policy and practice whereby to be considered for promotion the employee had to be full-time'. That policy, held the tribunal, amounted to a requirement which the employer did not seek to justify so it was indirect discrimination.

14.99   Where promotion is based on length of service and part-timers are deemed to accrue service at a slower rate, this may also be discriminatory. In *Gerster*[126] the applicant worked half time. The claimant's service was treated as less than an equivalent full-timer's and she was not promoted. The ECJ held that where part-time employees accrue

---

122   See *Royal Mail*, note 55, and para 14.39 where a successful part-time applicant for a full-time position had a condition imposed on her taking up the position which was less favourable than her full-time comparators.
123   *Gerster v Freistaat Bayern* [1997] IRLR 699, ECJ.
124   ET 05608/91/LN/C.
125   ET 5300122/2000, 28 July 2000.
126   See note 123.

length of service more slowly, and so take longer to achieve promotion, this was a breach of the ETD, unless the employer can justify it. The employer would need to show a link between length of service and acquisition of a certain level of knowledge or experience.[127]

Redundancy selection and pay and reorganising hours

Under the PTW Regs 2000

14.100 The Guidance states that the criteria used to select for redundancy should be objectively justified, and part-time workers must not be treated less favourably than comparable full-timers. Selecting part-timers for redundancy before full-timers or not considering them for alternative work, will be a breach of the PTW Regs 2000 unless objectively justified.[128]

14.101 It is not clear if the method of calculating statutory or contractual redundancy pay for employees who have changed from full-time to part-time work which is based on numbers of years of service (whether full or part-time) and salary only at time of redundancy would be a breach of the PTW Regs 2000. Arguably, the pro rata principle means that the part-timer should be credited with the full-time earnings on a proportionate basis (but see para 14.105).

14.102 In reorganising workloads, the Guidance states that part-time workers should not be treated less favourably than full-time ones, unless this treatment can be objectively justified.

Under the EPA 1970 and the SDA 1975

14.103 It is also unlawful discrimination under the SDA 1975 to select part-timers for redundancy before full-timers unless objectively justified.[129]

---

127 See also *Hill*, note 80 and para 14.66; *Nikoloudi*, note 90. The pending ECJ decision in *Cadman v Health and Safety Executive* which challenges using length of service increments under the EPA 1970 may be relevant to promotion.
128 See *Hendrickson Europe*, note 53.
129 *Clarke v Eley Kynock Ltd* [1982] IRLR 382. But see *Kachelmann v Bankhaus Hermann Lampe KG* [2001] IRLR 49 where the ECJ held that the German law, whereby full-time workers are not compared to part-time workers when an employer has to apply criteria to select an employee for dismissal when abolishing a job on economic grounds, was not a breach of the ETD even though it may create an indirect disadvantage for part-time workers. It accepted the law was objectively justified on social policy grounds, a justification which would not be available to employers applying non-statutory redundancy selection criteria.

14.104   The exclusion of part-timers from access to a severance payment on redundancy or termination of employment is likely to be discrimination unless justified.[130]

14.105   In relation to the calculation of redundancy pay the House of Lords, in *Barry v Midland Bank plc*,[131] held that the redundancy pay scheme (described in para 14.101), was not unlawful. The House of Lords acknowledged that part-time workers were disadvantaged by the calculation. However, the claimant had not shown that this was indirectly discriminatory in that it affected adversely considerably more women than men. The case also failed on objective justification. Arguably, the PTW Regs 2000 provide more scope for a challenge.

Other benefits and length of service

Under the PTW Regs 2000, EPA 1970 and SDA 1975

14.106   There is no specific mention of length of service in the PTW Regs 2000 but the principles are likely to be the same as established under the EPA 1970, the SDA 1975 and EU law. In *Nimz*[132] the ECJ held that a collective agreement whereby the length of service of full-time workers was fully taken into account for reclassification to a higher salary grade but only half the service of part-timers was taken into account, was a breach of article 141 where this had a disproportionate adverse effect on women and was not justifiable.

14.107   In *Kording*[133] German legislation provided that the total length of professional experience required for exemption from a qualifying examination was to be extended on a pro rata basis for part-time workers. The ECJ held that this would be indirect discrimination against women if substantially fewer men than women work part-time and must in principle be contrary to the ETD. It could be justified by objective factors unrelated to any discrimination. The employer would have to show that the extra hours worked made a significant difference to the competence of the worker. For example, in *Rinke*,[134] the ECJ held that requiring doctors training for general practice to do part of their training full time was justified. This

---

130   *Kowalska v Freie und Hansestadt Hamburg* [1990] IRLR 447, ECJ.
131   *Barry v Midland Bank plc* [1999] IRLR 581, HL.
132   See note 89.
133   *Kording v Senator fun Fionanzen* [1997] IRLR 710.
134   *Rinke v Arztekammer Hamburg*, Case C-25/02, 9 September 2003, ECJ.

enabled them to acquire sufficient experience in the various situations likely to arise in general practice.

14.108   Similar principles applied in *Gerster, Hill* and *Nikoloudi* (see paras 14.99 and 14.66).

Recruitment

Under the PTW Regs 2000, EPA 1970 and SDA 1975

14.109 External recruitment is not covered by the PTW Regs 2000. But if a job applicant states that they would wish to work part-time or flexibly in the position, an employer may be liable for indirect sex discrimination if it does not consider such an application seriously. Where the applicant is the best candidate, the employer should be able objectively to justify why the position cannot be done in the hours proposed (see chapter 13).

Denial of other benefits on the basis of part-time work

Under the PTW Regs 2000 and the SDA 1975

14.110 If a worker is allocated less interesting work or denied a non-contractual bonus or flexibility in work arrangements, on the basis that s/he is part-time, this may be both a breach of the PTW Regs and the SDA, if the employer cannot justify it. It should not be used to justify a difference in benefits.[135]

Right to written statement of reasons for less favourable treatment

14.111 Where part-time workers believe that they have been treated less favourably than a full-time worker:

- they can ask the employer in writing for a written statement giving particulars of the reasons for the treatment;
- the employer must provide a statement within 21 days of the request;[136]

---

135   See *Birch*, note 32.
136   PTW Regs 2000 reg 6(1).

- the statement is admissible as evidence in any proceedings under the PTW Regs 2000;
- where the employer deliberately, and without reasonable excuse, fails to provide a statement or provides one which is evasive or equivocal, the tribunal may draw any inference which it considers just and equitable to draw, including one that the employer has treated the claimant less favourably.[137]

These provisions are similar to the questionnaire procedure except that the only statement required is the reason for the less favourable treatment. There is no qualifying period.

14.112   Where a worker has been dismissed, s/he is entitled to a written statement of the reasons for dismissal not under the PTW Regs 2000, but under the different provisions of Employment Rights Act (ERA) 1996 s92.[138]

Unfair dismissal and the right not to be subjected to a detriment

14.113 A worker has a claim under the PTW Regs 2000 if the worker is subjected to any detriment (not amounting to dismissal) and, if an employee, a claim for automatic unfair dismissal including redundancy dismissal,[139] for the purposes of ERA 1996 Part X, where the reason or principal reason is that:

- the worker/employee has:
  - brought proceedings against the employer under the PTW Regs 2000;
  - requested a written statement of reasons for less favourable treatment;
  - given evidence or information in connection with such proceedings brought by any worker;
  - otherwise done anything under the PTW Regs 2000 in relation to the employer or any other person;
  - alleged that the employer has infringed the regulations,

---

137 PTW Regs 2000 reg 6(2), (3). Note this is the same as the questionnaire procedure.
138 PTW Regs 2000 reg 6(4).
139 PTW Regs 2000 reg 7; ERA 1996 s105(1) and (7E); workers who are not employees have no right to claim unfair dismissal.

provided the allegation is made in good faith, even if it is not true; or
- refused or proposed to refuse to forego a right under the regulations;
- the employer believes or suspects that the worker has done or intends to do any of the above and the worker is acting in good faith.[140]

There is no qualifying period[141] and the upper age limit does not apply.[142] Note that this is very similar to the victimisation provisions of the SDA 1975 (see para 2.89). The statutory disciplinary procedure applies to dismissals.

14.114   The statutory grievance procedure (see chapter 16) does not apply to a claim for detriment under PTW Regs 2000 reg 7. It does apply if a part-timer resigns and claims constructive dismissal for any reason (including being treated less favourably as a part-timer or being subjected to any detriment specified in regulation 7).[143]

Liability

14.115 As under the SDA 1975, any less favourable treatment by another worker is treated as having been carried out by the employer irrespective of whether the employer knew or approved of the action. The employer will not be liable if it took such steps as were reasonably practicable to prevent the worker from:

- doing that act; or
- doing, in the course of his/her employment, acts of that description.[144]

An employer is also liable for acts of an agent where done with the employer's authority.[145]

---

140 PTW Regs 2000 reg 7. See also ERA 1996 s104, dismissal for assertion of a statutory right.
141 ERA 1996 s108(3)(i).
142 ERA 1996 s109(2)(i).
143 It does apply if a claim under ERA 1996 s104 (dismissal for assertion of a statutory right) is brought.
144 PTW Regs 2000 reg 11(1), (3).
145 PTW Regs 2000 reg 11(2).

Burden of proof

14.116 The worker must establish that his/her case falls within the PTW Regs 2000, for example that the worker has identified an appropriate comparator and has suffered less favourable treatment. It is for the employer to identify the ground for the less favourable treatment or detriment.[146] If the ground is established as part-time work (see para 14.41 onwards), it is then for the employer objectively to justify the difference in treatment.

Procedure for bringing a claim

14.117 Under the PTW Regs 2000, a worker must bring a claim within three months of the date of the less favourable treatment or detriment. Where the act is part of a series of similar acts or failures, the time limit runs from the last act. The armed forces have six months in which to bring a claim.[147]

14.118 A claim may be brought out of time where it is just and equitable to do so.[148]

14.119 Where the complaint relates to a term of the contract, the less favourable treatment takes place each day the contract subsists, so is treated as continuing for as long as the contract continues.[149] This does not apply where the worker changes from being a full-time worker to a part-time worker, whether or not after a break. In this situation, the claim must be brought within three months from the first day on which the claimant worked under the new or varied contract or the first day on which the applicant returned to work.[150] Where a non-contractual detriment is complained of, time runs from the date of the detriment.[151]

14.120 A deliberate failure to act is treated as done on the day it was decided on.[152] In the absence of evidence to the contrary this will be when the person:

---

146 PTW Regs 2000 reg 8(6).
147 PTW Regs 2000 reg 8(2).
148 PTW Regs 2000 reg 8(3).
149 PTW Regs 2000 reg 8(4)(a).
150 PTW Regs 2000 reg 8(4)(b).
151 In *Coutts*, note 65, this was when eligibility for receipt of a non-contractual bonus was made sufficiently clear. It was neither the earlier provisional announcement nor the date of its subsequent non-payment to the claimants.
152 PTW Regs 2000 reg 8(4)(c).

- does an act inconsistent with doing the failed act; or
- when he would no longer be expected to do the failed act.[153]

14.121 For other time limits for equal pay, sex discrimination and unfair dismissal claims, see chapter 16.

Remedies

14.122 Where a complaint of less favourable treatmenr or detriment under PWT Regs 2000 reg 5 or reg 7(2) is upheld by a tribunal, it shall make such of the following orders as it considers 'just and equitable' (see also para 18.150):

- a declaration as to the rights of the employer and worker;
- an order the employer pay compensation;
- a recommendation that the employer take, within a specified period, reasonable action, in the circumstances of the case, to obviate or reduce the adverse effect on the worker of any less favourable treatment.[154]

Compensation

14.123 The amount is such as the tribunal considers 'just and equitable' in all the circumstances having regard to:

- the infringement to which the complaint relates;
- any loss attributable to the infringement, having regard to the pro rata principle except where inappropriate.[155]

14.124 Losses include:

- any expenses reasonably incurred by the complainant in consequence of the infringement; and
- loss of any benefit which s/he might reasonably be expected to have had but for the infringement.[156]

14.125 Compensation may be reduced where either:

- the complainant fails to mitigate her/his loss;

153 PTW Regs 2000 reg 8(5).
154 PTW Regs 2000 reg 8(7).
155 PTW Regs 2000 reg 8(9).
156 PTW Regs 2000 reg 8(10).

- the treatment by the employer was to an extent caused or contributed to by action of the complainant.[157]

14.126 If the employer fails, without reasonable justification, to comply with a recommendation made by a tribunal, the tribunal may, if it thinks it just and equitable to do so, increase the amount of compensation required to be paid or, if no compensation was ordered, make an order for compensation.[158]

14.127 No compensation is payable for injury to feelings.[159] This is explicitly excluded in the PTW Regs 2000, whereas it is not excluded from the other provisions relating to detrimental treatment of parents (see para 15.127 onwards).

14.128 See chapter 18 for remedies relating to dismissal.

---

157 PTW Regs 2000 reg 8(12), (13).
158 PTW Regs 2000 reg 8(14).
159 PTW Regs 2000 reg 8(11).

CHAPTER 15

Dismissal, redundancy and protection from detriment

Key points

- It is automatically unfair, irrespective of the employee's length of service, to dismiss (or make redundant) an employee where the reason or principal reason is related to:
  - pregnancy;
  - health and safety suspension;
  - childbirth;
  - maternity or adoption leave;
  - failing to return after maternity leave where the employer has failed to confirm her return date;
  - paternity, parental or dependants leave;
  - undertaking or refusing to undertake work during maternity or adoption leave;
  - requesting flexible working.
- Where a woman is made redundant while on ordinary maternity leave (OML) or additional maternity leave (AML) or adoption leave (OAL or AAL), she is entitled to any suitable alternative work with similar terms and conditions; failure to offer this will make the dismissal automatically unfair.
- Failure to consult a woman on maternity leave about redundancy is likely to be sex discrimination
- Dismissal for a reason related to pregnancy or maternity leave will also be direct sex discrimination; the employer must be aware of the pregnancy.
- Employees with one year's service may also claim ordinary unfair dismissal. There are five potentially fair reasons for dismissal.
- Dismissal includes actual dismissal by the employer, non-renewal of a limited-term contract, constructive dismissal.
- In dismissal cases (excluding constructive dismissal) the employer, and employee, must follow the statutory disciplinary and dismissal procedure (DDP). Where the employee has one year's service, the employer's failure to do so will make the dismissal automatically unfair.
- In constructive dismissal and detriment cases the employee must raise a written grievance before lodging a claim and the parties must follow the statutory procedure or risk an adjustment in compensation.
- An employee must not be subjected to a detriment for a reason

relating to her pregnancy, childbirth, suspension for health and safety reasons, or for taking adoption, paternity, parental or dependants leave.

Background and statutory framework

15.1 An employee who is dismissed or who resigns in response to a fundamental breach of contract by the employer, which includes discrimination, may have a claim for automatically unfair dismissal, discriminatory dismissal and, for employees with one year's service, ordinary unfair dismissal. It is important to consider all possible claims relating to dismissal, discrimination and detriment because the provisions relating to each differ. In addition, EC law should be taken into account. Both employer and employee should follow the statutory DDP or, in constructive dismissal and detriment cases, the grievance procedure (GP) (see chapter 16). Failure to follow the DDP will make the dismissal of an employee with one year's service automatically unfair. Where the grievance procedure applies, failure to raise a written grievance, in cases of constructive dismissal or detriment, will prevent the claimant pursuing a claim.

Employment Rights Act 1996

15.2 The Employment Rights Act (ERA) 1996, the Maternity and Parental Leave etc Regulations (MPL Regs) 1999 and the Paternity and Adoption Leave Regulations (PAL Regs) 2002 protect employees (not other workers) from the first day of employment by making it automatically unfair to dismiss or subject them to a detriment[1] where the reason or principal reason for the dismissal (including redundancy)[2] or the detriment (which may be an act or failure to act) relates to:

- the fact that the employee is *pregnant;*[3]
- the employee having *given birth;*[4] detriment and dismissal on the

---

1 'Detriment' is not defined but should be widely interpreted (see para 15.131); detriment is covered by MPL Regs 1999 reg 19, dismissal by reg 20.
2 ERA 1996 s99(3). See also MPL Regs 1999 reg 20(2) and PAL Regs 2002 reg 29(2).
3 MPL Regs 1999 reg 19(2)(a) and reg 20(3)(a).
4 MPL Regs 1999 reg 19(2)(b) and reg 20(3)(b).

grounds that the woman has given birth to a child is only covered when this occurs during OML or AML;[5]

- a relevant *health and safety requirement* or recommendation;[6]
- the fact that the employee took or sought to take *ordinary, compulsory or additional maternity leave* or availed herself of the benefits of OML;[7]
- the fact that the employee took or sought to take *ordinary or additional adoption leave* or where the employer believed the employee was likely to take OAL or AAL (see chapter 9);[8]
- undertaking, considering undertaking or refusing to undertake any work during maternity or adoption leave;[9]
- the fact that the employee took or sought to take *parental leave*, declined to sign a workforce agreement or performed activities as a representative (see chapter 10);[10]
- where an employee failed to return after OML, AML or AAL where the employer did not notify her/him of the date s/he was due to return or gave her/him less than 28 days' notice of that date and it was not reasonably practicable for her/him to return on that date;[11]
- the fact that s/he took or sought to take *paternity leave* (see chapter 8);[12]

---

5 MPL Regs 1999 reg 19(5), reg 20(4)(b).
6 This applies where the employee is the subject of a relevant requirement, or a relevant recommendation, defined by ERA 1996 s66(2), MPL Regs 1999 reg 19(2)(c), reg 20(3)(c).
7 MPL Regs 1999 reg 19(2)(d)(e), reg 20(3)(d)(e) refer to the fact that the employee took, sought to take or availed herself of the benefits of, ordinary maternity leave, or took or sought to take AML. It also covers parental leave and time off for dependants.
8 Paternity and Adoption Leave Regulations 2002 SI No 2788 reg 28(1)(a)(b), reg 29(3)(a)(b).
9 The Maternity and Parental Leave etc and the Paternity and Adoption Leave (Amendment) Regulations 2006 SI No 2014 amended the MPL Regs to insert reg 19(2)(eee) and reg 20(3)(eee) and the PAL regs to insert 28(3)(bb) and reg 29(3)(bb).
10 This relates not only to taking, and seeking to take, parental leave (MPL Regs 1999 reg 19(2)(e)(ii), reg 20(3)(e)(ii)), but declining to sign a workforce agreement performing any functions or activities as a representative of the workforce or candidate for election as a representative (reg 19(2)(f), (g), reg 20(3)(f), (g)).
11 MPL Regs 1999 reg 19(2)(ee), reg 20(3)(ee); PAL Regs 2002 reg 28(1)(c), reg 29(3)(c).
12 PAL Regs 2002 reg 28(1)(a), (b), reg 29(3)(a), (b).

- the fact that s/he took or sought to take *time off for dependants* (see chapter 11);[13]
- *flexible working applications* (see para 12.87 onwards);
- a dismissal for *redundancy* during maternity or adoption leave where the employee has not been offered suitable alternative work.[14]

15.3   Apart from protection for automatically unfair dismissal (see also para 15.58) and discriminatory dismissal, employees with one year's service may have a claim for ordinary unfair dismissal. There are five potentially fair reasons for dismissal (capabability, conduct, redundancy, contravention of a statutory duty and, some other substantial reason justifying dismissal). In addition the tribunal must decide whether it was fair to dismiss the employee for that reason (see para 15.70). Where the employer does not follow the statutory dismissal procedure in relation to employees with one year's service, the dismissal will be automatically unfair and compensation may be increased.

15.4   An employee may have further claims if dismissed without proper notice (wrongful dismissal), in health and safety cases or for asserting a statutory right (see paras 15.116–15.126).

Sex Discrimination Act 1975

15.5   Discrimination claims can be made by workers as well as employees and protection applies, as it does for automatically unfair dismissal, from the first day of employment.[15] A dismissal will be automatically directly discriminatory if it is related to the woman's pregnancy or maternity leave (para 2.34 onwards).[16] It may be indirect discrimination if the reason for dismissal is that the woman is working part-time or other flexible hours (see chapter 13) or if related to taking

---

13 ERA 1996 s99 (dismissal), s47C (detriment) and MPL Regs 1999 reg 19(2)(e)(iii) and reg 20(3)(e)(iii).

14 MPL Regs 1999 reg 20(1)(b). PAL Regs 2002 reg 23, 29(1)(b). Note that making an employee redundant for one of these reasons will also be automatically unfair.

15 The distinction between an employee and worker is not clear and increasingly the courts are finding that those categorised as 'workers' are in fact employees, particularly where there is a long term relationship, there is a mutual obligation to supply and perform work, control of the work by the employer and method of payment. The details are outside the scope of this book.

16 The definition of discrimination on the ground of pregnancy or maternity leave is in SDA 1975 s3A.

other leave, such as parental leave, adoption leave or time off for dependants (see para 15.54 onwards). A woman or man dismissed for taking adoption, parental or paternity leave may have a claim for direct or (indirect) discrimination, though not for automatic sex discrimination (see para 15.54). For a detailed discussion of discrimination law see chapter 2.

EC law

15.6   In all cases UK legislation must be interpreted in line with EC law. The EC directives are directly enforceable against emanations of the state (see para 1.22). Even then, the employee must link the claim with a UK statute (see para 17.13). In relation to pregnancy and maternity leave, the aim of the Equal Treatment Directive (ETD) and Pregnant Workers Directive (PWD) is to protect pregnant women, and women who have recently given birth, from dismissal because of the harmful effects the dismissal may have on their physical and mental state. The PWD requires member states to take:

> . . . the necessary measures to prohibit the dismissal of workers . . . during the period from the beginning of their pregnancy to the end of the maternity leave save in exceptional cases not connected with their condition which are permitted under national legislation.

See also paras 1.21–1.23. Note also that the Recast Directive 2006/54/EC will replace the ETD from August 2008.

Knowledge of pregnancy necessary in pregnancy cases

15.7   In order to show that the dismissal was for a pregnancy-related reason (and therefore unfair and discriminatory), the employer must be aware that the woman is pregnant. For example, the provision of a sick note that refers to the woman's pregnancy (even in Latin) should be sufficient (see *Day v Pickles*[17]). However, in *Del Monte Foods Ltd v Mundon*[18] the woman was dismissed because of continued absence caused by gastro-enteritis. The day after the dismissal the company discovered she was pregnant. The Employment Appeal Tribunal (EAT) held that the dismissal was not automatically unfair because the employers were unaware that the absence was connected to her pregnancy.

17 [1999] IRLR 217, EAT.
18 [1980] IRLR 224, EAT.

15.8   In *Eildon Ltd v Sharkey*[19] the EAT said that the company was not to be fixed with knowledge of the employee's pregnancy just because one of its managers knows that the claimant is pregnant. The EAT said the critical questions are:

- Who, on behalf of the company, dismissed the claimant?
- Did that person at the time know she was pregnant?
- If so, did that person dismiss her for a reason that relates to her pregnancy?

If there was no knowledge in the mind of the relevant decision-maker, the dismissal cannot relate to the pregnancy.

15.9   In *Ramdoolar v Bycity Ltd*[20] the EAT followed *Mundon* but added one 'possible qualification':

> It is conceivable that circumstances will arise in which an employer, detecting the symptoms of pregnancy and fearing the consequences, if the employee is in fact pregnant, but neither knowing nor believing that she is, simply suspecting that she might, dismisses her before his suspicion can be proved right. In such circumstances it may well be that a dismissal would be automatically unfair. If such circumstances arise they should be judged as and when they do.

15.10   It is usually advisable for the woman to inform her employer that she is pregnant so that she obtains health and safety protection and the protection from dismissal. There is a danger that the employer will become aware that the woman is pregnant through office gossip. Knowledge may be denied and the employee could be 'fairly' dismissed for ordinary sickness absence.

15.11   Disclosure of pregnancy at an early stage may not be appropriate in some cases, for example, if the woman is in her probationary period and fears it will not be confirmed and she cannot afford to be without a job. Although, if she is dismissed because of her pregnancy she can make a claim, this may be of little consolation if she is without income in the meantime and has a mortgage to pay.

Exclusions from protection

15.12   Some categories of workers are excluded from protection under the ERA 1996 (see para 1.31) and the SDA 1975 (see para 2.22). The table on page 523 summarises the position.

19 [2004] UKEAT 0109/03 28 July 2004. See paras 20 and 21.
20 UKEAT/0236/04/DM 30 July 2004.

Type of claim	Worker or employee?	Service	Compensation	Exceptions
Automatically unfair dismissal ERA 1996 ss99 and 104C	Employee	None	Capped at £58,400 to 1 February 2007 plus basic award	Police, share fishers, armed forces See ERA ss191–199 Illegal contracts
Ordinary unfair dismissal including unfair redundancy ERA 1996 s98	Employee	One year	As above	Employees with less than one year's service, those working abroad and some seafarers, the police, illegal contracts, upper age limits[21]
Redundancy payment ERA 1996 Part XI	Employee	Two years for redundancy payment	As above	Employees with less than two years' service, those above normal retirement age
Discrimination Sex Discrimination Act 1975	Worker, ie employees, self-employed, contract and agency workers, partners, trainees	None	No cap, includes injury to feelings	See chapter 2
Wrongful dismissal	Employee	None	No limits, but usually limited to the notice period Maximum £25,000 in employment tribunal (ET)	
Assertion of statutory rights ERA 1996 s104	Employee	None	Capped at £58,400 to 1 February 2007 plus basic award	As for unfair dismissal
Dismissal in health and safety cases ERA 1996 s100	Employee	None	No limits, a minimum basic award, ERA 1996 ss120	As for unfair dismissal
Detriment ERA 1996 ss47C and 47E	Employee	None	No cap	As under ERA 1996

21 The details are outside the scope of this book (see T Lewis *Employment Law Handbook* LAG, 2006). The upper age limit is subject to the Employment Equality (Age) Regulations 2006 SI No 1031, which are outside the scope of this book. The rule by which service under the age of 18 is disregarded for the purposes of calculating a statutory redundancy payment is to be abolished.

What is a dismissal?

15.13 An employee can only be dismissed if s/he has a written or verbal contract of employment.

15.14 A dismissal of an employee occurs in the following circumstances:

- where the employer terminates the contract with or without notice including in a redundancy situation;[22]
- where a limited-term contract terminates because of the limiting event without being renewed under the same contract;[23]
- constructive dismissal (see para 15.23 onwards).[24]

15.15 Dismissal would, for example, take place in a situation where:

- the employer dismisses the employee;
- the employee is made redundant and is not given suitable alternative work;
- the employer tells the employee she cannot take maternity leave so she leaves (this would be constructive dismissal);
- the employer does not allow a woman to return to her job after maternity leave (or, in some circumstances, to an equivalent job after AML, AAL or parental leave) (see paras 4.65 onwards, 9.49 onwards and 10.30 onwards). This may be an actual or constructive dismissal depending on the circumstances.

What if the employee is given a different job on return from leave?

15.16 There may still be a dismissal even if the employee returns to work but is not given her job or an equivalent one. A dismissal takes place

---

22 ERA 1996 s95(1)(a); if there is a dispute about whether the employee has been dismissed, for example if ambiguous words are used, the onus is on the employee to show that there was a dismissal.
23 ERA 1996 s95(1)(b); this was substituted by the Fixed-term Employees (Prevention of Less Favourable Treatment) Regulations 2002 SI 2034 reg 11, Sch 2 para 3(1), (7); details of the fixed term regulations are outside this book. Note however that any fixed-term contract renewed after 10 July 2006 could automatically become permanent if the employee has 4 years' continuous service, unless the employer can show there was objective justification for it or the rules have been modified by a collective or workforce agreement (regulation 8).
24 ERA 1996 s95(1)(c).

if the contract under which the employee is employed is terminated by the employer.[25]

15.17   In addition, where employees retain their job title and terms and conditions but are not given their duties and responsibilities, this may constitute a fundamental breach of contract entitling the employee to resign and claim constructive dismissal (see para 15.23 onwards). It will be a question of fact whether the contract has been terminated or varied.[26] For example, if a woman returns from maternity leave to find that the work she is allocated no longer includes responsibility and the reason for this is her absence on maternity leave, this could be a fundamental breach of contract entitling her to resign and claim unfair and discriminatory dismissal, it is likely to be direct sex discrimination. On the other hand, if the variation is only minimal, since no job ever remains exactly the same it might not be a dismissal. The question is whether her job has been changed to her disadvantage, she has suffered a detriment and the reason is related to her absence on maternity leave. If so, it is likely to be a breach of contract and discrimination.

15.18   For example, in *Matthews v (1) J D Williams and Company Ltd (2) House of Stirling (Direct Mail) Ltd*[27] a tribunal found that the failure to give back to the claimant her 'round' on her return from maternity leave was a breach of contract entitling her to resign and claim constructive dismissal, which was automatically unfair and discriminatory. The claimant's duties included selling (by face-to-face contact in the customer's home), developing new customers and collecting payments. She was paid a basic salary plus commission. The repondent reserved the right to require her to work on any other round if necessary but this rarely happened. After her maternity leave she was allocated another round, which she concluded would take eight to nine months to reach the same level of business that she had before her leave. She was told she could not have her old round back as the person who had taken her round had been doing it for too long (which was in fact only six weeks). The respondent then said that the old round was possibly going to be closed but the claimant was not

---

25   ERA 1996 s95(1)(a) which states that an employee is dismissed by his employer if the contract under which he is employed is terminated by the employer. See, for example *Alcan Extrusions v Yates* [1996] IRLR 327, EAT.

26   It is usually advisable to argue both. Note that if the employer has terminated the contract the DDP will apply but if it has been varied and the employee resigns claiming constructive dismissal the GP applies (see chapter 16).

27   22 February 2005; case no 2510599/04 ET; EOR No 147, November 2005.

told so as not to worry her or other team members. It was then closed and redistributed. Ms Matthews resigned. The tribunal concluded that if the true reason was the original one (ie someone else had taken the round) this was less favourable treatment linked to her maternity leave return. If the subsequent reason was correct the respondent had lied to Ms Matthews which was a breach of the implied term of trust and confidence. The breach arose upon Ms Matthews' return from maternity leave and was pregnancy-related, so that the whole catalogue of events would not have occurred but for the maternity leave. The tribunal held that the breach that constituted unfair constructive dismissal was also sex discrimination and automatically unfair dismissal as it was related to her maternity leave.

15.19   Similar principles would apply to a return after adoption or parental leave except that as this leave is available to men and women it will not be automatic direct discrimination but may be indirect discrimination (as more women than men are likely to take such leave) or automatically unfair dismissal (see paras 15.2 and 15.54). Alternatively, an employee could claim that s/he had been subjected to detriment (see para 15.127 onwards).

Limited-term contracts

15.20   Failure to renew a limited-term contract (on the same terms) is also a dismissal.[28] Thus, the employer will be liable for dismissal in the same way as if it had dismissed the employee. A 'limited-term contract' is one that is not intended to be permanent and there is provision for it to be terminated by a limiting event. A limiting event is the expiry of a fixed term, the performance of the specific task envisaged by the contract and where the contract provides for termination on the occurrence of an event, the occurrence of that event.[29]

15.21   If the reason for the non-renewal of a limited-term contract is related to pregnancy or family leave, it will be automatically unfair and, possibly, sex discrimination (see *Caruana v Manchester Airport plc*[30]). If the dismissal is due to redundancy, an employee on maternity or adoption leave is entitled to be consulted and offered suitable available work in the same way as an employee on a permanent

---

28   ERA 1996 s95(1)(b).
29   ERA 1996 s235(2A), (2B). Note that fixed-term contracts renewed after 10 July 2006, where the employee has been employed for 4 years continuously, could automatically become permanent (see note 23).
30   [1996] IRLR 378, EAT.

contract (see paras 15.92 and 15.100). In other circumstances it may be an ordinary unfair dismissal, although dismissal at the end of a limited-term contract when a limiting event occurs may be fair if it is for 'some other substantial reason' (see para 15.77 onwards).

15.22　　Although there is some protection for fixed-term contract employees under the Fixed-term Employees (Prevention of Less Favourable Treatment) Regulations (FTE Regs) 2002[31] in relation to the terms of the contract or by being subjected to any other detriment, the Court of Appeal has held that it is not a breach of these regulations to dismiss an employee just before the end of one year's service where a permanent employee would not be dismissed in these circumstances.[32] This is arguably a breach of the European directive on fixed-term work[33] which states that in respect of employment conditions fixed-term workers shall not be treated in a less favourable manner than comparable permanent workers solely because they have a fixed-term contract unless such treatment is justified on objective grounds.[34] 'Employment conditions' must surely cover dismissal. The directive further states that employers shall inform fixed-term workers about vacancies which become available in the establishment to ensure that they have the same opportunity to secure permanent positions as other workers. This should apply generally but will be particularly relevant in redundancy situations.

Constructive dismissal

15.23　Constructive dismissal is where the employee terminates the contract (with or without notice) in circumstances in which s/he is entitled to terminate it without notice by reason of the employer's conduct. This is where:

- s/he is entitled to terminate it without notice because the employer has committed a fundamental breach of contract which has gone to the heart of the employment relationship. This could be a breach of an express term or implied term such as the right to mutual trust and confidence between employer and employee;

31　SI No 2034; the regulations give fixed-term employees the right not to be treated less favourably than the employer treats a comparable permanent employee by reason of their contract status unless such treatment is objectively justified. The DTI have produced guidance (PL 512) which is available on the DTI website (www.dti.gov.uk).
32　*DWP v Webley* [2005] IRLR 288, CA.
33　99/70 of 28 June 1999.
34　Clause 4 of the Directive.

- the employee resigned as a result of the breach; and
- the employee did not delay in accepting the employer's breach as an action terminating the contract. If s/he does delay s/he might be taken to have affirmed the contract.[35]

15.24 There is no separate definition of constructive discriminatory dismissal in the SDA 1975 but s82(1)(A) provides that a dismissal under SDA 1975 includes constructive dismissal.

15.25 It is often difficult to judge whether there has been a fundamental breach of contract entitling the employee to resign and advice should be sought. The claimant must identify the term of the contract that has been broken and this may be an express or implied term, a written or oral term. Implied terms include that of trust and confidence, the obligation to take reasonable care for the employee's health and safety and, arguably, not to discriminate. Some examples where the courts have held there has been a breach are as follows:

- failure to notify a woman on maternity leave of a job vacancy for which she would have applied had she been aware of it. This was a breach of the implied term of trust and confidence entitling her to resign and claim constructive dismissal;[36]
- refusing to allow a woman to return to the same job after maternity leave and offering her a significantly diminished job where the reason is related to her absence;[37]
- refusal to allow a woman to work part-time or job-share where this is found to be indirect discrimination.[38]

---

35 In *Western Excavating (EEC) Ltd v Sharp* [1978] IRLR 27, CA the Court of Appeal said 'an employee is entitled to treat himself as constructively dismissed if the employer is guilty of conduct which is a significant breach going to the root of the contract of employment; or which shows that the employer no longer intends to be bound by one or more of the essential terms of the contract. The employee in those circumstances is entitled to leave without notice or to give notice, but the conduct in either case must be sufficiently serious to entitle him to leave at once'.

36 *Visa International Service Association v Paul* [2004] IRLR 42, EAT.

37 In *Nelson v Kinston Cables Distributors Ltd* EAT 662/99 the claimant's employers told her that the job she used to perform had significantly diminished and on her return she would be required to join a different team. The EAT held that if an employer gave a clear indication that her job would not be available to her on her return this could be an anticipatory breach of contract entitling her to resign.

38 In *Craddock v Cornwall Country Council & The Governing Body of Indian Queens CP School & Nursery* [2005] UKEAT 0367 1 September 2005 the EAT said that the two matters of sex discrimination and constructive dismissal are inherently connected. The EAT remitted the case to a different tribunal to decide if the refusal to allow a teacher to work part-time was indirect sex discrimination.

15.26   It is likely that any discrimination will be a fundamental breach of contract of itself. It certainly will be if it amounts to a breach of trust and confidence. In *Morrow v Safeway Stores plc*[39] the EAT held that:

> The question is whether, objectively speaking, the employer has conducted itself in a manner likely to destroy or seriously damage the relationship of confidence and trust between the employer and employee.

> If the employer is found to have been guilty of such conduct, that is something which goes to the root of the contract and amounts to a repudiatory breach, entitling the employee to resign and claim constructive dismissal.

When to resign

15.27   If there is a fundamental breach of (see para 15.23) contract this entitles an employee to resign with or without notice. It is important that the employee does not resign too soon, ie before the employer has indicated that it intends to breach the contract. On the other hand, once there has been a breach, there must not be too long a delay otherwise the tribunal may find that the employee has accepted the breach. The employee must make up her/his mind soon after the conduct of which s/he complains. It is advisable to object in writing to the breach so that it is clear that the employee considers it to be a breach and does not accept it. Any letter of resignation should explain that the resignation is in response to the breach. It should be the employee's decision whether and when to resign. Although the employee may be advised by a lawyer or other adviser that there has been a breach entitling her/him to resign the resignation should be in response to the employer's breach, not the advice received, particularly as the adviser may not be fully aware of the situation.

In *Quigley v University of St Andrews* UKEATS/0025/05 RN, 9 August 2006, the EAT held that the delay in resigning was not justified by the time the claimant took to take advice from a solicitor. He has also threatened to resign six months earlier. The EAT summarised the case law.

15.28   If the employee cannot afford to resign until s/he has found another job, it will depend on the circumstances as to whether a tribunal will find that the employee has accept the breach by delaying.

---

39 [2002] IRLR 9 at para 23: see also *BG plc v Mr P O'Brien* [2001] IRLR 496 and *Woods v WM Car Services (Peterborough Ltd)* [1981] IRLR 347 EAT.

Arguably, this is a good reason for delaying provided the delay is not too long.

15.29   Where delay is caused by absence on maternity leave, arguably, such absence should not prejudice an employee. To do so would, in itself, be discrimination as maternity leave only affects women.

15.30   The effect of the statutory grievance procedure on the timing of the resignation is unclear. Arguably, an employee can, and, depending on the circumstances, should, go through the whole of the procedure before resigning as the point of the GP is for the parties to try and resolve the situation internally. However, there is no legal obligation to put in a grievance before resigning, only before lodging a claim (see chapter 16). Therefore, if the employee finds the situation unbearable and, for example, is suffering stress as a result, s/he may want resign before completing the procedure but should explain when resigning why she is doing so.

15.31   Once the grievance has been finally decided, it is risky to delay further unless, possibly, the employee is off sick as a result of the employer's breach. The position is not clear and depends on a detailed analysis of the facts in each case.

15.32   If the constructive dismissal claim is not upheld, the employer may claim that the employee is in breach of contract for failing to work her notice period, though any damages would be limited to the actual loss suffered (if any). However, in most cases, where an employee resigns, claiming constructive dismissal, the employer will not want an employee to serve their notice and will agree to waive the notice period. If an employee resigns and gives notice, it will not be fatal to her constructive dismissal claim although she will need to explain why she felt she could continue to work on in the face of a fundamental breach. Reasons may include that she is on maternity, adoption or parental leave, on sick leave, or not at work for some other reason, or cannot afford to leave.

Dismissal during family leave ends the contract and leave

15.33   The contract continues during OML, AML, OAL, AAL, parental leave and paternity leave, even though the terms are not all maintained (see chapters 5, 9 and 10). However, if the employee is dismissed and the termination date falls during the leave, then the contract will also terminate and any rights, apart from statutory pay, will cease. This would include the right to accrue holiday and to any contractual pay which exceeds statutory pay. The leave ends at the same time and the employee is not entitled to return to work at the end of it.[40] The employee can claim loss of statutory and contractual pay as part of compensation if s/he brings a claim for unfair and/or discriminatory dismissal (see para 18.51 onwards).

Notice pay

15.34   Where either the employer or employee gives notice to terminate the contract at a time when the employee is absent from work because of pregnancy, childbirth, adoption leave, parental leave or paternity leave, s/he is entitled to the minimum remuneration during the statutory notice period, provided s/he has been employed for at least one month.[41] This does not apply where the contract requires the employer to give a period of notice which is at least one week longer than the statutory minimum (see para 5.20).[42] If maternity, adoption, paternity, sick pay or holiday pay is paid for the period, this can be offset against the notice pay.[43]

Written reasons for dismissal

15.35   If an employee is dismissed while she is pregnant or where her maternity or adoption leave ends by dismissal, the employer must give written reasons for her dismissal.[44] This applies irrespective of the employee's length of service and regardless of whether s/he requests such a statement. The statement is admissible in evidence.[45] This does not apply to paternity, parental or dependants leave where the employee will only be entitled to written reasons for dismissal

---

40   MPL Regs 1999 reg 7(5); PAL Regs 2002 reg 24.
41   ERA 1996 ss86, 87, 88(1)(c) and 89(3)(b). Minimum remuneration is set out in s86, ie one week if employed less than two years, one week's notice for each year's service between 2 and 12 years for the employer's liability under these provisions to apply.
42   ERA 1996 s86 lays down minimum periods of notice (eg, one week's notice where the employee has less than two years' service and one week's notice for each year from two up to 12 years). Sections 87–89 lay down the rights of the employee in the period of notice. The details are beyond the scope of this book, but note that where the employee gives notice, she must actually leave to take advantage of her rights (section ERA 1996 s88(3) s89(5)).
43   ERA 1996 ss88(2), 89(4).
44   ERA 1996 s92(4), (4A).
45   ERA 1996 s92(5).

if s/he has been employed for one year and requests written reasons.[46]

15.36   Where the employer unreasonably fails to provide an employee with written reasons or if the reasons are inadequate or untrue, the employee may complain to a tribunal. If the complaint is upheld, the tribunal may make a declaration stating the reasons for the dismissal and must order the employer to make a payment to the employee of two weeks' pay.[47]

Statutory grievance and disciplinary procedures

15.37   Where an employer dismisses or contemplates dismissing an employee with more than one year's service, it must follow the requirements of the statutory DDP unless one of the exceptions apply (see para 16.43 onwards). Failure to do so will make the dismissal automatically unfair and lead to an increase in compensation (see para 16.2). The employee must also follow the procedure, which includes pursuing an appeal, or compensation will be reduced (see para 18.14 onwards). Even where the employee has less than one year's service and cannot bring an 'ordinary' unfair dismissal claim, where s/he can claim discriminatory dismissal, the employer and employee should also follow the procedure or risk an increase in compensation (where the employer is in breach) or reduction (where the employee is in breach).[48] The statutory GP applies to constructive dismissal (see para 16.13).

15.38   Sometimes it is not clear whether there has been an actual or a constructive dismissal. If there is any doubt the employee should put in a grievance and wait 28 days before making a claim as failure to do so in a claim for constructive dismissal means the claim may be barred (see para 16.39). Time for lodging a claim is then extended by three months from the normal time limit. The claimant should make it clear that the primary claim is for actual dismissal in which case the DDP applies and not the grievance procedure. Where the DDP applies a claim must be made within three months of actual dismissal unless there is an ongoing DDP at the expiry of the three-month time limit (see para 16.104 onwards). It may be necessary to

---

46   ERA 1996 s92(1)–(3).
47   ERA 1996 s93.
48   Though the dismissal will not be automatically unfair.

lodge alternative claims to comply with both the GP and the time limit for an actual dismissal.

15.39   Similarly, if an employer is not clear whether there has been an actual or constructive dismissal, it is safer to go through the DDP to avoid a finding of automatically unfair dismissal, but at the same time maintaining that there was no actual dismissal. There is no easy answer. The requirements of the procedure and consequences of failure to comply are set out in chapters 16 and 18.

Sex discrimination – discriminatory dismissal

15.40   The first type of dismissal claim to consider is sex discrimination. A pregnancy or maternity-related dismissal will be automatic direct discrimination under the SDA 1975 and EC law. A dismissal connected to parental, adoption or dependants leave may be directly or indirectly discriminatory.

Advantages of discrimination claim

15.41   The advantages of a discrimination claim are that:

- a sex discrimination claim can be brought by an employee, a self-employed person, independent contractor or contract worker irrespective of length of service, whereas an unfair dismissal claim can only be brought by an employee with one year's service;
- a claim for automatically unfair dismissal may fail in circumstances where a discrimination claim might succeed. This is because in discrimination claims the claimant only needs to show that the reason for dismissal (such as pregnancy) is a substantial one rather than the principal reason;
- the questionnaire procedure can be used in discrimination cases;
- in discrimination cases once the claimant has shown facts which indicate that there may be less favourable treatment on grounds of sex, the burden of proof shifts to the employer to show that there has been no discrimination whatsoever (see para 17.124 onwards);
- in discrimination cases, unlike unfair dismissal ones, the question is not whether the employer followed a correct procedure and acted 'fairly' or 'reasonably', but whether there was less favourable treatment on grounds of pregnancy/maternity leave. 'Fairness' is not relevant;

- there is no cap on compensation payable in discrimination claims;
- in discrimination claims an amount can be awarded for injury to feelings;
- the rules in an unfair dismissal case for reducing compensation do not apply in the same way in cases of discriminatory dismissal;[49] though see para 18.43 onwards for what can be taken into account;
- only in limited circumstances can the tribunal reduce compensation because of contributory fault.[50]

Duration of automatic protection from discrimination in maternity cases

15.42 The SDA 1975 provides that the protection from automatic sex discrimination for employees (ie without the need to show that a man has been or would be treated more favourably) on the ground of pregnancy or maternity leave lasts from the beginning of the woman's pregnancy until the end of her maternity leave (see para 2.34 onwards).[51] Where, during the protected period, a female worker is treated less favourably on the ground of her pregnancy than she would have been treated if not pregnant, this will be discrimination (SDA 1975 s3A(1)(a) (see para 2.40)).

15.43   Similarly where an employee is treated less favourably on the ground that she is exercising or seeking to exercise, or has exercised or sought to exercise a statutory right to maternity leave, this will be unlawful discrimination (SDA 1975 s3A(1)(b)).[52] Where a discriminatory decision is taken after the end of maternity leave but is related to the employee's absence on maternity leave this is covered by SDA 1975 s3A(1)(b) so will be unlawful discrimination (see para 2.40). For example, if an employee returns to work to find that her work has been changed to her disadvantage and this is related to her absence on leave, this would be discrimination. The principles governing sex discrimination are covered in chapter 2.

---

49 *Polkey v A E Dayton Services* [1988] ICR 142, HL.
50 There is no equivalent in the SDA 1975 to ERA 1996 s123.
51 SDA 1975 s3A which came into force on 1 October 2005.
52 Note that under the amended SDA 1975, protection during maternity leave (apart from two weeks after the birth) only applies to women who are entitled to OML/AML, ie, only employees.

They must be read in conjunction with EU law (also set out in chapter 2).[53]

15.44   In *Brown v Rentokil*[54] the ECJ held that dismissal for a reason resulting from pregnancy is automatically sex discrimination and it does not matter whether the employer's decision is based on pregnancy or the consequences of pregnancy. It is not relevant how a man would be treated in similar circumstances. Thus, dismissal of a woman for a reason relating to her absence with pregnancy-related illness (which lasted from the beginning of her pregnancy until the start of her maternity leave) was direct sex discrimination (see para 2.65). Protection lasts throughout pregnancy and maternity leave. After maternity leave pregnancy and maternity leave related matters must not be taken into account in a decision to dismiss. However, dismissal for pregnancy-related absence arising after the end of maternity leave will not be automatic sex discrimination (see para 2.64).

Automatic discrimination and fixed-term contracts

15.45   Although the House of Lords, in *Webb*, expressed doubt about whether the same principles would apply to fixed-term contracts as to permanent contracts, the ECJ have now made it clear that there is no difference. In *Tele Danmark A/S v Handels-og Kontorfunktionaerernes Forbund i Danmark (HK) acting on behalf of Brandt-Neilsen*[55] the claimant was employed in July 1995 for a six-month period with training during the first two months. In August she told her employers that she was pregnant and due to give birth in early November. She was dismissed with effect from 30 September on the ground that she had not informed her employer of her pregnancy when she was recruited. The ECJ held that article 5 of the ETD and article 10 of the PWD precluded a worker from being dismissed on the ground of

---

53   The ECJ has held that the automatic protection from discrimination in pregnancy and maternity cases lasts from the beginning of the woman's pregnancy until the end of her maternity leave, but not afterwards (see *Webb, Hertz* and other ECJ cases at para 2.61 onwards).

54   [1998] IRLR 445 see also *Habermann-Beltermann v Arbeiterwohlfahrt* [1994] IRLR 364 ECJ where the ECJ held that it 'is clear that the termination of an employment contract on account of the employee's pregnancy . . . concerns women alone and constitutes, therefore, direct discrimination on grounds of sex'. See also *Mahlburg v Land Mecklenburg-Vorpommern* [2000] IRLR 276, ECJ.

55   [2001] IRLR 853, ECJ.

pregnancy, notwithstanding that she was recruited for a fixed period, failed to inform the employer that she was pregnant and because of her pregnancy was unable to work during a substantial part of the contract. The ECJ said:

> It was also in view of the risk that a possible dismissal may pose for the physical and mental state of pregnant workers, workers who have recently given birth or those who are breastfeeding, including the particularly serious risk that they may be encouraged to have abortions, that the Community legislature, in Article 10 of Directive 92/85, laid down special protection for those workers by prohibiting dismissal during the period from the start of pregnancy to the end of maternity leave.
>
> During that period, Article 10 of Directive 92/85 does not provide for any exception to, or derogation from, the prohibition of dismissing pregnant workers, save in exceptional cases not connected with their condition where the employer justified the dismissal in writing.[56]

15.46　A similar decision was reached by the ECJ in *Jimenez Melgar v Ayuntamiento de Los Barrios* where the ECJ held that the non-renewal of a fixed-term employment contract for reasons connected with the pregnancy is direct sex discrimination and amounts to a refusal to engage a pregnant woman.[57] The ECJ held that the PWD:

> . . . makes no distinction, as regards the scope of the prohibition of dismissal of pregnant workers, workers who have recently given birth or workers who are breastfeeding, according to the duration of the employment relationship in question. If the Community legislature had intended to exclude fixed-term contracts, which represent a significant proportion of employment relationships, from the scope of that Directive, it would have made express provision to that effect.[58]

15.47　Thus, the PWD does not distinguish according to the duration of the employment relationship so, for the purposes of discriminatory dis-

56　Paras 26 and 27.
57　[2001] IRLR 848, ECJ; although the ECJ held that there was no breach of article 10 of the PWD as there had been no dismissal because the fixed term contract had come to an end, in practice, there is little difference between non-renewal of a fixed-term contract and a dismissal as the principles of non discrimination are the same.
58　Para 43.

missals, fixed-term contracts should be treated the same as indefinite contracts.[59]

15.48   In *Busch* an employee asked to return early from parental leave in order to get maternity pay for her second pregnancy, but did not inform the employer of her reason, and the employer withdrew consent. The ECJ held in *Busch*[60] (and *Tele Danmark*) that the loss suffered by the employer, the short-term nature of the contract or its uncertainty, the inability of the woman to perform her contract and the failure by the employee to inform her employer of her pregnancy are all irrelevant. Thus, the employer's withdrawal of consent to her early return was discrimination. Arguably, the reference to 'exceptional cases' in the PWD (see para 15.6) means that a restrictive interpretation should be given to the potentially fair reasons for dismissal where the employee is pregnant and/or on maternity leave. The ECJ has said that member states do not need to specify the exceptions, see *Jiménez Melgar* above, paras 37 and 38.

15.49   Pregnancy or maternity leave need not be the only reason for the dismissal but it must be an effective or substantial cause (see paras 2.74–2.78).[61]

Examples of discriminatory dismissals

15.50   The following are examples of when it is likely to be discriminatory to dismiss, or fail to appoint, a woman:

- withdrawal of an offer of employment to a woman because she became pregnant (see *Mahlburg*[62]); the fact that the employer would suffer a financial loss was no justification for refusing to employ a woman on account of her pregnancy;
- where a woman is offered a job but it is withdrawn once the

---

59   In *Caruana v Manchester Airport plc* [1996] IRLR 378 EAT the claimant had been employed (as an independent sub-contractor) on a series of fixed-term contracts. Soon after she told her employers that she was pregnant, she was informed that her current 12-month contract would not be renewed. The tribunal found that the reason was because she would not be available for work (because of her maternity leave) at the beginning of the renewed contract. Following *Webb*, the EAT held that the failure to renew the fixed-term contract was because of the applicant's pregnancy and was therefore discriminatory.

60   *Busch v Klinikum Neustadt GmbH and Co Betriebs-KG* [2003] IRLR 625, ECJ.

61   See in particular *O'Neill v Governors of St Thomas More RCVA Upper School* [1997] ICR 33.

62   *Mahlburg v Land Mecklenburg-Vorpommem* [2000] IRLR 276, ECJ. See para 3.88.

employer finds out she is pregnant (see *Fitzgerald v Staffordshire CC*);[63]

- where a woman's probationary period is terminated early on acount of a woman's pregnancy;

- where a woman is dismissed because she is pregnant and/or for any reason related to her pregnancy, such as the need to have time off for antenatal appointments (see para 3.113);[64]

- where a woman is dismissed because she has a pregnancy-related sickness, irrespective of how long this lasts (*Brown v Rentokil Ltd*[65] at para 3.119). This would also apply if her pregnancy-related sickness absence or maternity leave was later taken into account when, for example, determining who should be made redundant;

- where the employer fails to carry out a health and safety assessment and the employee resigns (see *Day v T Pickles Farms Ltd*[66] and *Hardman v Mallon* at paras 3.22–3.23);

- where a woman is dismissed because she is unable to carry out her work because of a health and safety risk (see *Habermann-Beltermann*[67] at para 3.92);

- where an employee is dismissed because there was no prospect of her returning to work in the near future since she could not have neurological tests until after her pregnancy;[68]

- where a woman is dismissed after she is unable to attend a disciplinary hearing because of pregnancy-related absence (see *Abbey National plc v Formoso*[69]);

- where a temporary worker is replaced by a permanent worker because of her absence on maternity leave (*Patefield*[70] and *Gillick* at para 2.11);

- where a woman is made redundant for any reason related to her pregnancy (*Brown*[71] at para 15.59);

- where an employer fails to consult a woman about redundancy (or a reorganisation) and so she is not considered for alternative

63 [1997] DCLD 33, p7.
64 See, for example, *Dixon v Motorcise (Torbay) Ltd* 21 October 2004; Case no 1702438/03 EOR No 147, November 2005.
65 [1998] ICR 790; [1998] IRLR 445, ECJ.
66 [1999] IRLR 217, EAT.
67 [1994] IRLR 364, ECJ.
68 *Hyde v H M Prison Service Agency Ltd*, 4 February 2005; Case no 1500901/04 EOR 147, November 2005.
69 [1999] IRLR 222, EAT.
70 *Patefield v Belfast City Council NICA* [2000] IRLR 664; *BP Chemicals Ltd v Gillick* [1995] IRLR 128, EAT.
71 *Brown v Stockton on Tees BC* [1988] IRLR 263, HL.

employment; this would include the situation where she was not offered suitable alternative employment because she was on maternity leave (*McGuigan v TG Baynes* at para 15.94);

- where a decision to eliminate the post of a pregnant woman, as opposed to another employee, is influenced by the claimant's pregnancy and impending maternity leave;[72]

- where the employer prefers the maternity locum. In *Rees v Apollo Watch Repairs plc* the claimant was dismissed while on maternity leave because the employers found that her replacement was more efficient. The EAT held that the claimant would not have been dismissed had she not been on maternity leave. Following *Webb*, that meant the dismissal was discriminatory. The EAT said that the protection afforded to women on maternity leave would be drastically curtailed if an employer was able to defeat a complaint of direct discrimination by saying that it preferred her replacement, a state of affairs which had arisen solely as a result of her pregnancy and therefore because of her sex;[73]

- where a woman facing disciplinary proceedings would have had the chance to improve her performance 'but for' her maternity leave. In *Indans v Merit Ice Bream Ltd*[74] a woman was dismissed two days after she returned from maternity leave on the basis of poor performance. The tribunal found that she had been dismissed for poor performance. However, 'but for' her absence on leave, her employers would have addressed the problem when it arose. She won her claim for sex discrimination, as she had not been given an opportunity to improve. It would also have been automatically unfair;

- where a man is dismissed in part because of his lack of flexibility due to chilcare commitments where a woman would have been treated more favourably.[75]

72 *Dial-a-Phone & Brown v Butt* [2004] UKEAT 0286, 30 January 2004.
73 *Rees v Apollo Watch Repairs* [1996] ICR 466, EAT. See also *Matthews v (1) J D Williams and Company Ltd (2) House of Stirling (Direct Mail) Ltd*, 22 February 2005; Case no 1520566/04 EOR No 147, November 2005; this was an automatic unfair constructive dismissal and sex discrimination.
74 ET 2305027/98.
75 *Obu v The Salvation Army UK Territory*, 7 February 2006; Case no 2302868/05; EOR No 153, June 2006. The ET inferred from the evidence regarding the respondent's attitude to women with childcare responsibilities that the respondent would have enquired about a woman's childcare responsibilities but they did not explore with Mr Obu whether there was a way of accommodating his responsibilities.

Abortion to avoid dismissal

15.51   In *Brown v Rentokil Ltd* (see para 3.119) and *Tele Danmark* (see para 14.45) the ECJ specifically referred to the serious risk that women may decide to have an abortion in order to avoid dismissal.

Fertility treatment

15.52   In *Joyce v Northern Microwave Distributors Ltd*[76] the ET held that a woman who was dismissed because she was on a course of fertility treatment had suffered discrimination. The ET said that the assumptions, which were made about the fertility treatment and the possible pregnancy, were totally stereotyped. They were evidence of a discriminatory attitude and a man would not have been treated in the same way. The employer admitted that the claimant had been dismissed because she would be away having fertility treatment *and* she might get pregnant.

Direct and indirect discrimination claims and adoption leave, paternity, parental leave or time off for dependants

15.53   Since parental leave, adoption leave and time off for dependants can be taken by both male and female employees, it will not be direct sex discrimination to dismiss a woman (or a man) for taking such leave where a man (or a woman) would be treated in the same way, but only if a man (or a woman) was treated differently in similar circumstances. For example, a man might be dismissed for taking adoption leave because his employer would not accept that his family came first whereas a woman in similar circumstances would not be dismissed because it was regarded as only natural for her to take time off. This would be discrimination.

Indirect discrimination claims and adoption leave, paternity, parental leave or time off for dependants

15.54   It may, however, be indirect discrimination to dismiss a woman for taking family leave (not maternity leave) because more women than men are likely to take adoption leave, parental leave and time off for dependants.[77]

---

76   ET 5564/93, 22 September 1993, Leeds ET.
77   See, for example, *Lewen v Denda* [2000] IRLR 67, ECJ.

15.55   In *Lewen v Denda*[78] the ECJ held that if a bonus, awarded for work performed in the course of a year, was denied to women on parental leave because their contracts were in suspension, this would be indirect (not direct) discrimination under article 141. This was because they had been put at a disadvantage compared to those whose contract was not in suspension and since female workers were more likely to be on parental leave, when the bonus was awarded, than men, this had a disproportionate adverse impact on women (see para 10.27). Similar principles would arguably apply to dismissals relating to adoption, parental and dependants leave. The dismissal may be indirectly discriminatory because the requirement (not to be on such leave) would affect women disproportionately. It is unlikely to be justified. The legal principles relating to indirect sex discrimination in these cases are similar to claims for flexible working hours (see chapter 13).

15.56   In 2000 the DTI estimated that in the UK 35% of women but only 2% of men were taking parental leave so a dismissal for taking parental leave is likely to be indirect sex discrimination as it particularly disadvantages women.

Claims by men dismissed for wanting the equivalent parental rights to women

15.57   Although the SDA 1975 provides that a man cannot claim less favourable treatment than a woman because he does not receive the special treatment afforded to women in connection with pregnancy or childbirth (see SDA 1975 s2(2) at para 2.22), this does not apply to parental and other types of leave nor rights relating to flexible working. Thus, if a man is treated less favourably or is dismissed for taking parental leave or time off for dependants this will be sex discrimination if a woman would not be treated less favourably or dismissed for taking such leave in similar circumstances. It will not be automatic sex discrimination so the ordinary principles of discrimination will apply (see para 2.28).

---

78 [2000] ICR 648 ECJ.

Automatically unfair dismissal under ERA 1996

15.58 The ERA 1996 (s99), MPL Regs 1999 and PAL Regs 2002[79] provide that it is automatically unfair dismissal to dismiss an employee where the reason or principal reason is connected with:

- The pregnancy of the employee[80] (eg, pregnancy-related sickness, obligation to pay SMP, miscarriage, abortion). Note that as with discrimination claims the employer must know or believe that the woman is pregnant (see para 15.7). This is not specifically limited in time (unlike the SDA 1975 s3A(1)(a)) and could arguably apply, for example, to dismissal for a pregnancy-related illness which occurs after the woman has returned to work (see para 2.38 onwards).
- The fact that the employee has given birth to a child.[81] This only applies where the dismissal takes place during the employee's OML or AML and brings to an end the leave.[82] Thus, if a woman suffers post-natal depression that is related to the birth, she is only protected during her leave, not after her return. However, the restriction does not apply if the post-natal depression is, despite its common name, not specifically birth-related.
- The application of a health and safety requirement or recommendation (as defined by ERA 1996 s66(2)) (see para 3.59).[83]
- The fact that the employee took or tried to take the benefits of OML.[84] This applies, for example, where an employee takes the benefit of or asserts her rights to her contractual terms and conditions during OML.[85]
- The fact that the employee:
  - took or sought to take AML;
  - took or sought to take parental leave;
  - took or sought to take time off to look after a dependant;[86] or
  - took or sought to take paternity or adoption leave or the employer believed that the employee was likely to take OAL or

---

79 PAL Regs 2002.
80 MPL Regs 1999 reg 19(2)(a), reg 20(3)(a).
81 MPL Regs 1999 reg 20(3)(a).
82 MPL Regs 1999 reg 20(4).
83 MPL Regs 1999 reg 20(3).
84 MPL Regs 1999 reg 20(3)(d).
85 MPL Regs 1999 reg 19(3) and 20(5).
86 MPL Regs 1999 reg 20(3)(e).

AAL.[87] This would include dismissal to avoid paying statutory adoption or paternity pay.

- The fact that an employee failed to return after OML, AML or AAL where the employer did not notify her (or him in the case of a man taking AAL) of the date her leave would end and she reasonably believed that that period had not ended or the employer gave her less than 28 days' notice of the end of her leave and it was not reasonably practicable for her to return on that date (see para 4.62).[88]

- The employee declined to sign a workforce agreement for the purposes of Schedule 1 to the MPL Regs 1999 (see chapter 10).[89]

- The employee, being either a representative of the workforce or a candidate in an election, carried out any activities as such for the purposes of Schedule 1 to the MPL Regs 1999.[90]

- The reason or principal reason for the dismissal is that
  a) the employee is made redundant; and
  b) the circumstances constituting the redundancy applied equally to other employees who held similar positions, but were not made redundant; and
  c) the reason or principal reason why the employee was selected for dismissal was her pregnancy, childbirth, maternity or other family leave, ie the reasons set out in MPL Regs 1999 reg 20(3) and PAL Regs 2002 reg 29(3) which relate to pregnancy and taking or seeking to take family leave.[91]

- Where the redundancy occurs during maternity or adoption leave,[92] the reason or principal reason for the dismissal is the employee is redundant and s/he has not been offered suitable alternative employment.[93] A redundancy is also a dismissal and that may be automatically unfair for any of the above reasons in any event (see para 15.83 onwards).

- The reason or principal reason for the dismissal is that the employee:

---

87 PAL Regs 2002 reg 29(3)(b).
88 MPL Regs 1999 reg 20(3)(ee); PAL Regs 2002 reg 29(3)(c).
89 MPL Regs 1999 reg 20(3)(f).
90 MPL Regs 1999 reg 20(3)(g).
91 MPL Regs 1999 reg 20(2)(3); PAL Regs 2002 reg 29(2)(3). There is an exception for small employers where the dismissal is before 1 April 2007, see MPL Regs 1999 reg 20(6), (7), PAL Regs 2002 reg 29(4); see also para 15.66.
92 MPL Regs 1999 reg 20(1)(b), (4); PAL Regs 2002 reg 23, ie here the dismissal ends the employee's OML, AML, OAL or AAL.
93 MPL Regs 1999 reg 20(1)(b). PAL Regs 2002 reg 29(1)(b).

a) made or proposed to make and application for flexible working; or
b) exercised or proposed to exercise a right in the flexible working regulations; or
c) brought proceedings for breach of the flexible working procedure; or
d) alleged the existence of any circumstance which would be a ground for bringing such proceedings (see para 12.87 onwards).[94]

- Where the reason or principal reason for the dismissal is that the employee is undertaking, is considering undertaking or has refused to undertake any work during maternity or adoption leave (see para 4.48).[95]

15.59 In *Brown v Stockton-on-Tees BC*,[96] the House of Lords said that:

An employer faced with deciding which of several employees to make redundant must disregard the inconvenience that inevitably will result from the fact that one of them is pregnant and will require maternity leave. If he does not do so and makes that absence the factor that determines the pregnant woman's dismissal, that dismissal will be deemed unfair.[97] [ERA s99 and regulation 20] must be seen as a part of social legislation passed for the specific protection of women and to put them on an equal footing with men. Although it is often a considerable inconvenience to an employer to have to make the necessary arrangements to keep a woman's job open for her whilst she is absent from work in order to have a baby, *that is a price that has to be paid as a part of the social and legal recognition of the equal status of women in the work place.*[98]

What is the effective cause of dismissal?

15.60 The question in automatically unfair dismissal cases is whether the sole or principal reason for the dismissal is any of the above

---

94 ERA 1996 s104C; originally this claim could only be made if the employee had a year's service but the service threshold was removed by Employment Relations Act 2004. See also para 12.88.
95 MPL Regs 1999 reg 20(3)(eee) inserted and PAL Regs reg 29(3)(bb) as amended by the Maternity and Parental Leave etc and the Paternity and Adoption Leave (Amendment) Regulations 2006 SI No 2014 in force on 1 October 2006.
96 [1988] IRLR 263, HL at 264.
97 Under Employment Protection (Consolidation) Act 1978 s60, now ERA 1996 s99 and MPL Regs 1999 reg 20.
98 Emphasis added.

grounds.[99] This contrasts with ordinary unfair dismissal cases where the reason for dismissal is the set of facts or beliefs held by the employer which cause him/her to dismiss the employee. In pregnancy dismissal cases, as in discrimination cases, it is usually necessary to look beneath the purported reason to what the claimant believes to be the real reason.

15.61   Most successful claims for automatically unfair dismissal on grounds of pregnancy or maternity leave will also be sex discrimination. It is generally easier to prove discrimination as it is not necessary to show that pregnancy or maternity leave is the principal reason for the dismissal (see para 2.72 onwards).

15.62   If a claimant has only argued ordinary unfair dismissal in her claim, but the facts make it clear that she believes the reason was her pregnancy or maternity leave, the tribunal should consider claims for automatically unfair dismissal and sex discrimination, though this may depend on any prejudice to the respondent (see para 17.84).[100] However, it is advisable to include all claims in the form so there can be no argument.

15.63   In *O'Neill*[101] the EAT said that the critical question was whether the dismissal was on the ground of the claimant's pregnancy or on some other ground (see para 2.73). In *Clayton v Vigers*[102] the dismissal of a woman on maternity leave was automatically unfair where the reason was the employer's inability to find a temporary replacement for her. The EAT held that the regulation prohibiting dismissal under ERA 1996 s99 (ie MPL Regs reg 20(3)) had to be interpreted widely and it covers dismissal associated with the 'after-effects' of pregnancy.

---

99   *O'Neill v Governors of St Thomas More Roman Catholic Voluntary Aided Upper School* [1997] ICR 33.
100 See *Corcoran v Harrison Ingram and Shore* [2003] UKEAT 0840, 24 March 2003 where the EAT allowed an amendment to include automatically unfair dismissal but not sex discrimination because the claimant, having taken advice from two sources, should have made the claim earlier and the respondent would be prejudiced. If, however, the application had been made earlier it may have been allowed. However, in *Brannan v Wilkinson Hardware Stores Ltd* EAT/712/98, 25 May 2006 the EAT criticised the ET for failing to consider ERA 1996 s99 and sex discrimination where the claim related to unfair dismissal related to pregnancy.
101 *O'Neill v Governors of St Thomas More Roman Catholic Voluntarily Aided Upper School & another* [1997] ICR 33.
102 [1989] ICR 713.

> EXAMPLE: Where a woman is dismissed shortly after she announces she is pregnant, the reason for her dismissal will be scrutinised by the tribunal and is likely to shift the burden to the respondent to show there was no discrimination. In *Pirie v Loughton Photographic Ltd*[103] the dismissal of an employee a few days after announcing her pregnancy and after pregnancy-related absence was held to be automatically unfair and sex discrimination. Similarly in *Walker v The Beeches Nursing Home*[104] the claimant was dismissed three days after she announced her pregnancy. She was told it was because she did not intend to continue with her NVQ course and she had said she was no longer interested in caring for elderly people. The tribunal did not believe this and held it was a cold and calculated decision to dismiss her because of her pregnancy.

Dismissals after maternity leave has ended

15.64 There are some situations where a claim for automatically unfair dismissal can only be made where the dismissal takes place during maternity leave. This applies where the reason or main reason for the dismissal is that the employee has given birth or the employee has been made redundant and has not been offered available suitable alternative work.[105]

15.65 A woman who is dismissed after she returns to work for any other of the other reasons set out above may be able to claim automatically unfair dismissal. For example, if a woman is dismissed for pregnancy-related sickness which continued after her leave, and she was dismissed as a result, she may be able to claim that the principal reason for the dismissal was connected with her pregnancy but the position is not clear.[106] If the dismissal occurs after return from maternity leave but is related to the leave, or pregnancy-related absence before the leave, it is likely to be automatically unfair under reg 20(3)(a) and (e).

---

103   28 September 2004; Case no 3300622/04; EOR No 147, November 2005.
104   ET 2503457/98.
105   MPL Regs 1999 reg 20(4).
106   *Caledonia Bureau Investment & Property v Caffrey* [1998] IRLR 110, though this decision should be treated with caution as it was decided before the implementation of MPL Regs 1999 and is inconsistent with the decision in *Hertz* (see para 2.64).

Exceptions to protection from automatically unfair dismissal after AML

15.66 Although the right is to return to the same job after AML, AAL or parental leave[107] and this must be considered first (see para 4.68 onwards), there are two exceptions to the protection from automatically unfair dismissal:

1) *Small employers* where the woman is returning from AML[108] or AAL.[109] This applies:
   - where the number of employees (including those employed by an associated employer) is five or less. The time at which the number must be counted is immediately before the end of the AML (or AAL) or, if earlier, immediately before the dismissal; and
   - it is not reasonably practicable for the employer (or a successor) either to allow her to return to her job or to an alternative job which is both suitable for her and appropriate for her to do in the circumstances or for an associated employer to offer her a job of that kind.

   The small employer exception will no longer apply in relation to dismissals after 1 April 2007.[110]

2) Where a woman is returning from AML, AAL[111] or from parental leave of more than four weeks[112] and:
   - it is not reasonably practicable for a reason other than redundancy for the employer (or successor) to allow the woman either to return to the same job or to a suitable job which is appropriate in the circumstances;
   - an associated employer offers her a suitable appropriate job; and
   - she accepts or unreasonably refuses that offer.

---

107 Under MPL Regs 1999 reg 18 and PAL Regs 2002 reg 18.
108 MPL Regs 1999 reg 20(6).
109 PAL Regs 2002 reg 29(4).
110 Maternity and Parental Leave etc and the Paternity and Adoption Leave (Amendment) Regulations 2006 SI No 2014 reg 11(6)(c) which repeals reg 20(6).
111 MPL Regs 1999 reg 20(7). PAL Regs 2002 reg 29(5).
112 MPL Regs 2002 reg 18(2) provides that, if it is not practicable for the employee to return to the same job, an employee taking AML or parental leave for more than four weeks may be given another job which is both suitable and appropriate.

15.67   This applies if it is not feasible for her/him to exercise her/his right to return under the regulations. The dismissal will not be automatically unfair in these two limited situations.[113]

15.68   The onus is on the employer to show that one of these exceptions applies.[114] There have been very few cases where these exceptions have been tested.

Exceptions may be discriminatory and 'ordinary' unfair dismissal

15.69   In either case, where an employee can show that, 'but for' a woman's pregnancy or absence on maternity leave (OML or AML), she would have been able to return to the same (or even similar) job, she will have a claim for automatic sex discrimination. She needs to show that her pregnancy and/or maternity leave was a substantial and effective cause, a substantial reason, or an important factor.[115] Where, for example, a small employer decided to recruit a permanent replacement to cover the absence of a woman on maternity leave and keeps the replacement rather than allowing the woman to return, this is likely to be discrimination. The SDA 1975 does not allow the employer the opportunity to justify such treatment. The woman would have an ordinary unfair dismissal claim as well, as employees of small employers are not excluded from making a claim under ERA 1996 s98.

Ordinary unfair dismissal

15.70   An employee may also have a claim for ordinary unfair dismissal as well as automatically unfair dismissal and discrimination. This is limited to employees who have worked for the employer for one year.[116] A discriminatory dismissal will generally also be an unfair one but the only extra orders that the tribunal can make are the basic award, loss of statutory rights and reinstatement or re-engagement.[117] Otherwise compensation is not payable twice (see para 18.25). This

---

113   MPL Regs 1999 reg 18(2), PAL Regs 2002 reg 26(2).
114   MPL Regs 1999 reg 20(8); PAL Regs 2002 reg 29(6).
115   *Nagarajan v London Regional Transport* [1999] IRLR 572, HL at 576.
116   ERA 1996 s108.
117   *Clarke v Eley (IMI) Kynock Ltd* [1982] IRLR 482. In *Ursell v Manor Bakeries Ltd* there was no dispute that if sex discrimination were found in respect of the dismissal, there would also be a finding of unfair dismissal (UKEAT/0759/04/ TM 21 February 2005).

section deals only very briefly with ordinary unfair dismissal. For further detail see *Employment law handbook* by Tamara Lewis.[118]

15.71   The burden of proof is on the employer to show that the reason (or principal reason) for dismissal (including constructive dismissal) is a potentially fair one (see below) and the tribunal must then decide whether the employer acted fairly in dismissing the employee (see para 15.82). Where the employer has not followed the statutory disciplinary and dismissal procedure the dismissal will be automatically unfair.

Potentially fair reasons for dismissal

15.72   There are five potentially fair reasons for dismissing a worker.[119]

Reasons relating to (1) the capability or qualifications or (2) the conduct of the employee

15.73   These two categories may include lateness, sickness, absence or performance, which are common reasons for dismissing pregnant employees. Where the employer dismisses an employee because of pregnancy-related sickness it will be automatically unfair and discriminatory. Similarly, if an employee is dismissed for poor performance and that is caused by pregnancy-related illness, that is likely to be discriminatory. However, if this is not proved (for example, because the employer was not aware that the employee was pregnant), the dismissal may nevertheless be ordinarily unfair.[120] When considering whether to dismiss an employee because of sickness absence, the employer should take account of the length and frequency of absences, the likelihood of future absences, and the effect of the absences on the employee's work. The employer should consult the employee to get the relevant information and take account of the employee's comments.

15.74   Account should be taken of ACAS guidance.[121] In relation to absence from work. The ACAS Code recommends in relation to

118   LAG, 2006.
119   ERA 1996 s98.
120   It is usually advisable for a woman to tell her employer that she is pregnant as this gives her protection from less favourable treatment, though does not stop the employer dismissing her in which case her remedy is to bring a claim for discrimination.
121   ACAS Code of Practice: Disciplinary and grievance procedures 2004.

genuine illness (which would relate to capability) that the employer consider:

- how soon the employee's health and attendance will improve;
- whether alternative work is available;
- the effect of the absence on the organisation;
- how similar situations have been handled in the past; and
- whether the illness is a result of disability.[122]

15.75 If a father takes time off to be at the birth of his child without going through the correct paternity leave procedure and is dismissed for unauthorised absence, he may be able to show that the dismissal was unfair under ERA 1996 s98(4). For example, he may have long service, have never been absent without leave before and account should be taken of the fact that his employer did know that he was going to be away from work, so was not caught by surprise. As the ACAS guide says, there may be some very limited cases where summary dismissal will be fair but these are exceptional cases and an employer is rarely entitled to dismiss for a single occasion of absenteeism. It may be different if the employer has told the employee that he cannot take the leave and he disobeys.

(3) Redundancy

This is covered at para 15.83.

(4) The employee could not continue working without contravening a statutory duty or restriction

15.76 Despite this being a potentially fair reason for dismissal, if an employer dismisses a pregnant woman because her presence at work, while pregnant, contravenes the health and safety regulations, this would be an automatically unfair and discriminatory dismissal as well as an ordinary unfair one. ERA 1996 ss64–70 and the Management of Health and Safety at Work Regulations (MHSW Regs) 1999[123] impose a duty on the employer to suspend an employee on full pay where there is an unavoidable risk to a pregnant or breastfeeding woman or new mother. Thus, this potentially fair reason would not make the dismissal fair where there is a breach of the positive obligations towards pregnant women, new mothers and breastfeeding

---

122 ACAS Guide at paras 37 and 38.
123 SI No 3242.

women. The provisions relating to health and safety are set out at para 3.5 onwards.

(5) Some other substantial reason (SOSR)

15.77 The most common SOSR dismissals relate to a business reorganisation where the employer has a 'substantial reason' for dismissing the employee. It is sometimes difficult to distinguish this from a redundancy situation. The employer may claim there is a reorganisation in order to avoid making a redundancy payment. SOSR may arise where an employer has a substantial business reason for a reorganisation, as a result of which it terminates the employees' contracts and offers reasonable new ones. An employee who refuses the new agreements may be fairly dismissed. If the employee cannot be employed elsewhere, this may also be 'some other substantial reason' justifying the dismissal. A SOSR may also arise on a transfer of an undertaking where there is an economic, technical or organisational reason entailing changes in the workforce.

15.78 Where an employer has employed a temporary replacement to cover for an employee on maternity or adoption leave (or an employee who has been suspended on health and safety grounds), s/he will have no protection if s/he has been employed for less than a year – unless she is dismissed for a reason which makes the dismissal automatically unfair and discriminatory, such as pregnancy. S/he would be entitled to her contractual or statutory notice.

15.79 Even if the employee has one year's service, ERA 1996 s106 gives the employer a potentially fair reason to dismiss the replacement on the basis that there is 'some other substantial reason' provided:

a) the employer has informed the employee in writing that her/his employment will end when the woman for whom s/he is covering returns to work after maternity leave (or suspension); and

b) the employer dismisses the replacement in order to give the work back to the returning woman.[124]

15.80 The tribunal will still have to consider whether the dismissal was in fact fair if the locum has been employed for a year – see para 15.82.[125] Even if the employer does not comply with ERA 1996 s106 (for example, gives verbal instead of written notice) the dismissal of the replacement might not be unfair if the locum knew that their status

---

124 ERA 1996 s106(2)(b) and (3)(b).
125 ERA 1996 s106(4) states that the provisions do not affect ERA 1996 s98(4).

was temporary. It will depend on the circumstances, but an employer does not have carte blanche to dismiss a locum for 'some other substantial reason' without following the correct procedure. Where the temporary replacement becomes pregnant, it will still be automatically unfair and discriminatory if she is dismissed for a reason relating to her pregnancy (see paras 15.5 and 15.58).

15.81   Note that:

- In relation to the above five grounds for dismissal, the employee must have a year's service to bring a claim.
- A tribunal does not have to accept the employer's reason for dismissal – it may find that the given reason is not the true reason.
- The dismissal may be automatically unfair (and discriminatory) even if part of the reason constitutes a fair dismissal, provided the main, effective or substantial (for discrimination cases) reason is due to pregnancy or family leave.
- Whilst a woman is on maternity or adoption leave, the employer should apply the same disciplinary procedures as for other employees. If it does not, the dismissal will be an ordinary unfair one and may be automatically unfair and discriminatory.[126]

Was it fair to dismiss for that reason?

15.82   If the employer has a potentially fair reason for dismissal, when deciding whether the dismissal was fair in the circumstances, the tribunal must decide whether the employer 'acted reasonably or unreasonably in treating it as a sufficient reason for dismissing the employee' and it is to be determined 'in accordance with equity and the substantial merits of the case'. Relevant circumstances include the employer's size and administrative resources, the merits of the case and procedural fairness.[127] The employer must follow, at a minimum, the statutory disciplinary and dismissal procedure otherwise the dismissal will be automatically unfair.[128] However, even if the minimum procedure is followed, this will not necessarily mean that the dismissal is fair. Once the reason for dismissal has been determined, the first question for the tribunal is whether the employer's decision comes within the band of reasonable responses open to a reasonable employer. The tribunal must not substitute its decision as to what is

---

126 MPL Regs 1999 regs 9 and 17(a)(iii); PAL Regs 2002 regs 19 and 21(a)(iii).
127 ERA 1996 s98(4).
128 ERA 1996 s98A.

the right course to adopt for the employer.[129] The second question for the tribunal to decide is whether the procedure followed was procedurally fair *in addition to* following the statutory procedure. Account should be taken of the ACAS Code of Practice.[130]

Redundancy

15.83 Redundancy is a very common reason for dismissal and it is not uncommon for employees on maternity leave to be made redundant without a proper procedure having been followed. This is likely to make the dismissal unfair and possibly discriminatory.

What is redundancy?

15.84 An employer who dismisses an employee on the grounds of redundancy must first show that there is a redundancy situation, ie, either:

- that the business is to close, either completely or where the employee works; or
- that the requirements of the business for employees to carry out work of a particular kind (or of a particular kind in the place where s/he works) have ceased or diminished or are expected to cease or diminish.[131]

'Business' includes the business of associated employers.

15.85 The second question is whether the employee's dismissal was attributable wholly or mainly to the redundancy situation. Although it is difficult to challenge the existence of a redundancy situation in that a tribunal will not usually investigate the economic reasons which led to a closure or reduction in work, it can investigate whether the

---

129 *Post Office v Foley* [2000] IRLR 827, CA.
130 ACAS Code of Practice: Disciplinary and grievance procedures 2004, which says that even if the statutory procedure is followed the dismissal may be unfair 'if the employer has not acted reasonably in all the circumstances' (see para 6).
131 ERA 1996 s139(1) that the employer has ceased or intends to cease:
- to carry on that business for which the employee was employed or
- to carry on that business in the place where the employee was so employed, or
(2) that the requirements of that business:
- for employees to carry out work of a particular kind, or
- for employees to carry out work of a particular kind in the place where the employee was employed by the employer, have ceased or diminished or are expected to cease or diminish.

redundancy is genuine. The employer must show that the dismissal was genuinely because of a redundancy.

15.86　Where an employee has been made redundant while pregnant or when on OML, AML, OAL, AAL, paternity, parental, or dependants leave, s/he will need to consider whether there really is a redundancy situation or whether it is a pretext to dismiss her/him on these grounds. If the reason, or main reason, for the employee's redundancy is pregnancy or maternity leave, this will be automatically unfair[132] and automatic discrimination. If it is on grounds of other family leave (see para 15.58) it will be automatically unfair and may be discrimination (see para 15.53). This is a question for the tribunal to decide. If, for example, a woman is made redundant soon after her pregnancy at a time when there is no apparent redundancy situation (for example, no other employees are redundant) or if the redundancy is brought forward because she was absent with pregnancy-related sickness, this may give rise to an inference that the dismissal is automatically unfair and discriminatory.

A fair procedure must be followed

15.87　The employer must follow, at a minimum, the statutory disciplinary and dismissal procedure, as well as any contractual procedure.

15.88　The EAT, in *Alexander v Bridgen Enterprises Ltd*[133] said that Step 2 of the statutory DDP requires an explanation to be given as to why the employer is contemplating dismissing that particular employee. This will involve providing information both as to why the employer considers that there is a redundancy situation and also why the employee is being selected. Thus, before the step 2 meeting, the employer should notify the employee of the selection criteria which have been used and also the assessment of the employee according to those criteria. This will give the employee an opportunity to make representations not only about whether the criteria are justified and appropriate but also, more importantly, whether the marking given to the employee in respect of any particular criterion is arguably unjust, and why. Failure to provide this information will make the dismissal automatically unfair.

15.89　Under the statutory DDP it is not necessary to provide the

---

132　But only where the dismissal ends the employee's OML, AML, OAL or AAL, see MPL Regs 1999 reg 20(4), PAL Regs 2002 reg 23(1).

133　[2006] IRLR 422.

assessments of other employees, although the EAT said that failure to provide such information may, in certain circumstances, render the dismissal unfair under general unfair dismissal law.

15.90   If there is a genuine reason for the redundancy, which is more likely to be the case if there are several redundancies, the employee should consider:

- whether there has been proper consultation at an early stage in order to consider if there are any alternatives to redundancy and the possibility of redeployment;
- whether the selection process was fair; and
- whether there was any suitable alternative work which that should have been offered.

15.91   In *Polkey v AE Dayton Services Ltd*[134] Lord Bridge said that in all circumstances 'the employer will normally not act reasonably unless he warns and consults any employees affected or their representative, adopts a fair basis on which to select for redundancy and takes such steps as may be reasonable to avoid or minimise redundancy by redeployment within his own organisation'.

Consultation

15.92   As part of a fair procedure employers must consult their employees and give as much warning as possible of impending redundancies.[135] This includes those on fixed-term contracts (see para 15.22). The aim of the consultation, which must include consultation about redeployment, must be to avoid redundancies if possible and to mitigate the effect of any which are unavoidable. Where the employer is planning to dismiss as redundant 20 or more employees within 90 days, the employer has a specific legal duty to consult employee representatives at the earliest opportunity, and also employees who are not trade union members.[136]

15.93   Failure to carry out consultation with an employee who is on some form of family leave may make the redundancy unfair. In particular, failure to consult a woman on maternity leave is likely to be discrimination.

15.94   In *McGuigan v TG Baynes*[137] the claimant was made redundant

---

134   [1987] IRLR 503, HL.
135   *Williams v Compare Maxam Ltd* [1982] IRLR 83.
136   Trade Union and Labour Relations (Consolidation) Act 1992 s188.
137   EAT 1114/97, 24 November 1998.

while on maternity leave. She was not consulted. The EAT held that the failure to consult was on the ground, among others, of her being absent on maternity leave. This was a maternity-related reason and so was discrimination. It was not necessary to show that other employees, not on maternity leave, had been consulted as less favourable treatment on grounds related to pregnancy does not require a comparison. Nor, said the EAT, was it relevant that the claimant would have been selected for redundancy as opposed to the other two men in the pool. The failure to consult was, nevertheless, and of itself, detrimental treatment.

15.95   In *John Menzies GB Ltd v Porter*[138] the EAT held that the tribunal was entitled to take the view that the failure to consult was particularly blatant because the employee's absence was due to pregnancy. The EAT upheld the tribunal finding that the employers had not given any real consideration to the possibility of offering the claimant alternative employment. That meant the dismissal was automatically unfair. If there is no suitable alternative vacancy it will be up to the employer to show this. In *Porter* the EAT upheld the tribunal finding of unfair dismissal even though the tribunal did not find that there had been a suitable vacancy.

15.96   Where there is a failure to consult an employee on adoption or parental leave it will not be automatic discrimination but may be indirect sex discrimination if it can be shown that it is disproportionately women who take such leave so are particularly disadvantaged (see para 15.53). It may, however, make the dismissal automatically unfair if the main reason for the dismissal was absence on such leave. It is likely to make the dismissal an ordinary unfair dismissal.

Selection process

15.97   The employer must follow a fair selection procedure to avoid the dismissal being unfair. If the reason or main reason for the selection is that the employee has taken some form of family leave or for one of the reasons set out in ERA 1996 s99 and MPL Regs 1999 reg 20 and PAL Regs 2002 reg 29 (see para 15.58) it will be automatically unfair. If related to pregnancy or maternity leave it will, in addition, be automatic direct discrimination. If related to other types of leave available to men and women, it may be indirect discrimination.

15.98   In *Dial-a-phone & Brown v Butt*[139] the claimant was told, six weeks

---

138   EAT 644/91, 19 February 1992.
139   [2004] UKEAT 0286, 30 January 2004.

after the announcement of her pregnancy, that her post could not be afforded and would have to go. Prior to her pregnancy the company's managing director (Mr Brown) had clearly been satisfied with her performance. After the announcement his attitude to her changed in that he spoke sharply to her, excluded her from a meeting, asked other managers to report to him about issues with which she usually dealt and failed to copy to her important information. The company did not consider making another employee (Mr Kemp), her junior manager redundant nor did it consider other alternative positions including those on a lower salary.

15.99   The tribunal concluded that there should have been a selection process between Mrs Butt and Mr Kemp and rejected as unreasonable the company's claim that this was unnecessary saying they did not believe there was a genuine and non-discriminatory reason for the dismissal. The tribunal found that it was very surprising that the company did not consider Mrs Butt for Mr Kemp's post and making him redundant instead simply because Mrs Butt had never said that she wished to be considered for his post. The tribunal inferred that it was Mrs Butt's pregnancy and the fact that she was to go on maternity leave shortly which made the company decide that it was she rather than Mr Kemp who had to be made redundant. The EAT upheld this decision saying that it was open to the tribunal to draw that inference, especially in the light of its findings about Mr Brown's initial reaction to her pregnancy and his significant change in attitude towards her. This was despite some evidence about the company's positive attitude to gender issues and maternity leave.

The absolute right to alternative work for those on maternity and adoption leave

15.100   An employee who is made redundant while on OML, AML, OAL or AAL is entitled to be offered suitable alternative work, in preference to other employees, and if s/he is not it will be automatically unfair dismissal (see para 15.58).[140] This is an absolute right; s/he should be given priority over other redundant employees (who must also be considered for suitable alternative work under ordinary redundancy principles). Note that this applies even where the employee does not have the two years' qualifying service necessary for redundancy pay. The right to be offered a job ceases after the end of the leave period or,

---

140   MPL Regs 1999 regs 10 and 20(1)(b); PAL Regs 2002 regs 23 and 29(1)(b).

if earlier, when the employee's contract has come to an end. This happens once the redundancy dismissal has taken effect.

15.101 This entitlement does not apply to pregnant women before or after their maternity leave nor to employees on parental leave or dependants leave. It does not apply after a woman has returned to work after leave. If two employees are entitled to this absolute right, because they are both made redundant while on maternity/adoption leave, and there is only one role the employer must make a fair choice between them. The regulations do not require the special creation of a role.

15.102 In *Community Task Force v Rimmer*,[141] Mrs Rimmer was made redundant while she was on AML. The employers did not redeploy Mrs Rimmer into a new job because this would result in a funding cut for the charity. The EAT upheld the ET finding that failure to offer the post to Mrs Rimmer made her dismissal automatically unfair. The EAT held that if a suitable vacancy was available, the economic (or other) consequences of the employer giving the job to the redundant employee were not relevant.

15.103 In other circumstances, an employee must still be considered for suitable alternative work. There is no automatic right to be given suitable available work unless the employee is on maternity or adoption leave (see para 15.58), but if work is available and not offered to the employee, it may make the dismissal unfair. If an employee refuses suitable alternative work the dismissal will be fair and the employee will lose the right to a redundancy payment.[142] Employees are encouraged to try out potential new roles, even if they differ from the previous role, by a statutory provision which keeps open their right to take redundancy if they change their mind during a trial period of four weeks.[143] If there is no alternative work she will be redundant (see para 15.115).

What is suitable alternative work?

15.104 The new employment[144] must take effect immediately on the ending of the existing employment and the new contract must be such that:
(a) the work which is 'both suitable in relation to the employee and appropriate for her to do in the circumstances'; and

141 [1986] IRLR 203, EAT.
142 ERA 1996 s141.
143 ERA 1996 s138.
144 Which may be with a successor or associated employer.

(b) the provisions as to the capacity and place in which she is to be employed, and as to other terms and conditions of her employment, are not substantially less favourable to her than if she had continued to be employed under the previous contract'.[145]

15.105   If the alternative work is of lower status, it may be unsuitable even if the grade and salary is the same. In *Brown-Williams v Microgen Ltd*[146] Ms Brown-Williams was one of two regional production managers. During her maternity leave a single national production manager replaced the two managers. She was not offered this job but only jobs as 'client services representative' and 'inquiry service manager' which were of lower status. The ET held that the two jobs were not suitable and failure to offer the applicant the suitable available vacancy (the national production manager) made the dismissal automatically unfair.

15.106   The job must be appropriate for the employee. If, for example, it involves an increase in travelling time and/or additional childcare costs, the job may not be appropriate.[147]

Refusal of suitable alternative work

15.107   The MPL Regs 1999 and the PAL Regs 2002 do not specify what will happen if the employee unreasonably refuses an offer. The ERA 1996 states that if suitable work is unreasonably refused, initially or after a trial period, the dismissal will be fair and the employee will not be entitled to compensation for unfair dismissal nor to a redundancy payment.[148] However, even if it is a suitable job the employee may reasonably refuse for good personal reasons, for example travelling time (a requirement to take on a role requiring excessive travelling time to work might be indirectly discriminatory), or medical reasons. Thus, it may be reasonable for one employee to refuse a job but not another. If the refusal is reasonable, the employee will still be entitled to a redundancy payment. The employee should be consulted on what is suitable alternative work. The employee may, for example,

---

145 MPL Regs 1999 reg 10(3), PAL Regs 2002 reg 23(3). Note that these regulations allows the terms and conditions to be less favourable (but not substantially less favourable). The right to return under MPL Regs reg 18A and PAL Regs reg 27 provide that the right to return is on no less favourable terms and conditions with preserved seniority, pension and other similar rights though AML and AAL is not counted as service for contractual rights.
146 COIT 1415/176.
147 *Hill v Supasnaps Ltd* COIT 1930/200.
148 ERA 1996 s141.

wish to be redeployed into another job that s/he considers is more suitable.

15.108   In addition, if an employee is not offered a suitable job because s/he is, for example, unable to take up the job immediately, because s/he is on adoption leave, the dismissal will be automatically unfair. If it is maternity-related it will also be direct discrimination (see para 15.58).

Redundancy related to pregnancy and maternity leave

15.109 Where a redundancy dismissal is related to pregnancy or maternity leave it is likely to be discriminatory as well as automatically unfair.

15.110   In *Brown v Stockton-on-Tees BC*[149] the House of Lords said that it cannot have been intended that an employer should be able to take advantage of a redundancy situation to weed out its pregnant employees (see para 15.59). The same principles as set out in *Brown* apply if a woman is made redundant for reasons connected with her pregnancy or childbirth while on maternity leave.

Redundancy during and after leave

15.111 If a woman is selected for redundancy while on maternity leave, the dismissal will also be automatically unfair and discriminatory if related to her pregnancy or the fact that she has taken maternity leave. This was confirmed by the EAT in *Rees v Apollo Watch Repairs plc.*[150]

15.112   In *Intelligent Applications Ltd v Wilson*[151] the tribunal found that the claimant's duties were re-allocated simply because she went on maternity leave. Her employment was terminated because the re-allocation became permanent. The ET held that her duties had been re-allocated only because she had taken maternity leave, which was inextricably linked to her pregnancy and therefore automatically unfair dismissal. The EAT upheld the decision but on other grounds, ie, because another employee might have been made redundant rather than Mrs Wilson, had she not been on maternity leave.

15.113   If a woman returns to work to find that she is redundant and the reason is related to her pregnancy and/or maternity leave, this is

149   [1988] IRLR 263, HL.
150   [1996] ICR 466, EAT.
151   EAT 412/92 Edinburgh.

likely to be discriminatory and may be automatically unfair. SDA 1975 s3A makes it clear that protection from unfavourable treatment applies where the employee *has* taken maternity leave. There are no appeal level cases on this point.

15.114   If an employee is made redundant after the end of their leave this will only be automatically unfair (and in the case of maternity leave discriminatory) if the period of leave, or pregnancy-related absence, has been taken into account when deciding on the redundancy. Otherwise normal principles relating to unfair dismissal apply but there is no special protection.

Entitlement to redundancy payment

15.115 If there is no suitable available work (or the employee reasonably refuses it), the employee will be entitled to a redundancy payment if s/he has been employed for at least two years.[152] The payment is based on a specified number of weeks' pay for each year of service. For the purposes of calculating a week's pay for those on family leave, the relevant date is the last day s/he worked immediately before the leave period began.[153] A claim for redundancy pay must be brought within six months. S/he should also receive notice pay (see para 5.126). There is no rule that s/he does not have to work the notice period although many employers will pay notice pay in a lump sum. A claim for notice pay should be brought within three months.

Automatic unfair dismissal for reasons other than family leave

Dismissal in health and safety cases (ERA 1996 s100)

15.116 Employees are protected from dismissal (or detriment) if they complain about, or refuse to work in, unsafe conditions and this is the reason or principal reason for their dismissal. This protection starts from day one of employment.

15.117   It is automatically unfair to dismiss an employee in various situ-

---

152 The qualifying period for a redundancy payment is still two years' continuous employment (ERA 1996 s155).
153 MPL Regs 1999 reg 22; PAL Regs 2002 reg 33.

ations relating to health and safety. In the family context, it is most likely to arise in maternity cases where:

a) there is a danger which the woman reasonably believes is serious and imminent and which she could not reasonably have been expected to avoid where she either:

- left work (or proposed to leave); or
- (while the danger persisted) refused to return to work;[154] or

b) in dangerous circumstances she took or proposed to take appropriate steps to protect herself.[155]

15.118 Thus where there are dangerous circumstances and an employee leaves work because of the employer's refusal to carry out a risk assessment or to take appropriate steps to deal with serious health and safety risks, and is dismissed as a result, this will be automatically unfair under ERA 1996 s100. The employee would probably also be entitled to resign and claim constructive dismissal if she could show that there had been a breach of the health and safety provisions, which had forced her to resign but advice should be taken (see chapter 3).

15.119   Alternatively, a woman in such a situation could claim that the underlying reason for her dismissal was her pregnancy and obligation to comply with health and safety requirements and so claim automatically unfair dismissal and discrimination.[156]

15.120   There cannot be two principal reasons for dismissal. Section 100 could be argued in the alternative to, for example, ERA 1996 s99, but the tribunal must decide in favour of one or the other, not both.

15.121   In addition, female employees who are dismissed because of the application of a maternity health and safety requirement to suspend on full pay have protection from automatically unfair dismissal[157] (see paras 3.59 and 15.58).

Dismissal for assertion of statutory right

15.122 It is automatically unfair to dismiss where the reason (or, if more than one, the principal reason) is that the employee has brought proceedings to enforce a statutory right or alleged that the employer

---

154   ERA 1996 s100(1)(d).
155   ERA 1996 s100(1)(e).
156   Under ERA 1996 s99, MPL Regs 1999 reg 20 and the SDA 1975.
157   Under ERA 1996 s99 and MPL Regs 1999 reg 20.

has infringed a particular statutory right (ERA 1996 s104). It is irrelevant if the right has in fact been breached, provided the claim is made in good faith. Relevant statutory rights are those specified in section 104(4) and include, for example:

- paid time off for antenatal care (ERA 1996 ss55 and 56);
- the right to parental leave (ERA 1996 s76);
- the right to time off for dependants leave (ERA 1996 s57A);
- right to paid remuneration on maternity suspension and alternative work (ERA 1996 ss67 and 68);
- protection from detriment in relation to family leave and flexible working (ERA 1996 s47C);[158]
- right to receive a written statement of reasons for dismissal (ERA 1996 s92);
- right not to be unfairly dismissed (ERA 1996 s94);
- right to a redundancy payment (ERA 1996 s135);
- the right to have an application for flexible working properly considered (ERA 1996 ss80G and 80H).

Note that protection starts from day one of employment.

15.123   The employee must make it reasonably clear what the right claimed to have been infringed was, but does not need to cite the statutory provisions.

15.124   Such a claim can be added in the alternative to a claim for automatically unfair dismissal on other grounds but the tribunal must decide in favour of one or the other, not both.

Dismissal on transfer of the business

15.125 The Transfer of Undertaking (Protection of Employment) Regulations 2006[159] apply to transfers that take place after April 2006. In brief, where the reason for the dismissal is the transfer or a reason connected to it, which is not an economic, technical or organisational reason, the dismissal is automatically unfair. A dismissal which is connected with the tranfer and for an ETO (economic, technical or organisational) reason is not automatically unfair but the test of reasonableness will apply. If the transferor dismisses the employee for an unfair reason the transferee should be joined as a respondent. The details are outside the scope of this book.

---

158 Chapter 12 covers flexible working and dismissal.
159 SI No 246.

Wrongful dismissal

15.126 Where an employee has been dismissed without notice and that was in breach of contract s/he would have a claim of wrongful dismissal in respect of the notice period. The contract may contain notice provisions or alternatively they are set out in ERA 1996 Part IX. It may be possible to increase the total compensation payable by arguing for compensation for wrongful dismissal to be added on to the top of any compensation for unfair dismissal which is restricted by the statutory cap.

Protection from detriment

15.127 ERA 1996 s47C, the MPL Regs 1999 and the PAL Regs 2002 introduced protection from disadvantage for employees exercising their rights to maternity, adoption, paternity, parental and dependants' leave.

15.128 An employee is entitled not to be subjected to any detriment by any act, or any deliberate failure to act (not being a dismissal), by her employer for the following main reasons:

- she is pregnant;[160]
- she has given birth (where the act or omission took place during OML or AML);[161]
- she has been suspended from work for health and safety reasons being the subject of a relevant requirement or recommendation (see chapter 3);[162]
- she has taken or has sought to take OML or the benefits during OML;[163]
- s/he has taken or has sought to take:
  - AML;
  - parental leave;
  - time off for dependants under s57A;[164]
- s/he took or sought to take paternity or adoption leave or the employer believed that the employee was likely to take OAL or AAL;[165]

160   MPL Regs 1999 reg 19(2)(a).
161   MPL Regs 1999 reg 19(2)(b), (5).
162   ERA 1996 s66(2); MPL Regs 1999 reg 19(2)(c).
163   MPL Regs 1999 reg 19(2)(d), (3).
164   MPL Regs 1999 reg 19(2)(e).
165   PAL Regs 2002 reg 28.

- she declined to sign a workforce agreement;[166]
- as a representative of the workforce or candidate in an election s/he performed any functions as a representative or candidate;[167]
- the fact that s/he failed to return after OML or AML or AAL where the employer did not notify her (or him) of the date leave would end and s/he reasonably believed that that period had not ended or the employer gave her/him less than 28 days' notice of the end of leave and it was not reasonably practicable for her/him to return on that date;[168]
- where the employee is undertaking, considering undertaking or refusing to undertake any work during maternity or adoption leave (see para 4.49).[168a]
- where the employee takes specified action such as exercising a right or bringing proceedings under the flexible working procedure (see para 12.92 onwards).

15.129   The right not to suffer detrimental treatment at work starts as soon as the employer is aware that the woman is pregnant and lasts up to the end of her OML or AML. The provisions are very similar to those providing protection from dismissal (see para 15.58). There is also protection from detriment under ERA 1996 s44 for taking action in health and safety cases, which is similar to the protection from dismissal (see para 15.116 onwards).

Exception

15.130   The provisions do not apply where there has been a dismissal as this falls under MPL Regs 1999 reg 20 or PAL Regs 2002 reg 29.

What is a detriment?

15.131   The Department of Trade and Industry (DTI) describes a detriment as 'unfair treatment at work'. 'Detriment' has been described in a number of cases under the SDA 1975 and the Race Relations Act 1976. For example, in *Ministry of Defence v Jeremiah*[169] it was held to

---

166   MPL Regs 2002 reg 19(2)(f).
167   MPL Regs 2002 reg 19(2)(g).
168   MPL Regs 1999 reg 19(2)(ee); PAL Regs 2002 reg 28(1)(c).
168a MPL Regs reg 19(2)(eee), PAL Regs reg 28(1)(bb) as amended from 1 October 2006 which effect from April 2007.
169   [1980] QB 87, CA.

mean 'putting at a disadvantage'. The detriment must be more than trivial but need not necessarily be substantial. In *McGuigan v TG Baynes*[170] the EAT held that marking a woman down in a redundancy exercise because she had criticised her employer's attitude to women was a detriment even though it made no difference to the decision to select her for redundancy. The EAT held that the expression 'subjecting to any other detriment' in SDA 1975 s6(2)(b) is to be given its 'broad, ordinary meaning and it is plain that almost any discriminatory conduct by an employer against an employee in relation to his or her employment will be rendered unlawful by s6(2)(b)'. There is no appeal level authoriy suggesting that a 'detriment' under the ERA 1996 should be defined differently and there is no reason why this interpretation should not be applied to 'detriment' under the ERA 1996.

15.132   There does not need to be a deliberate act. In *George v Burns (Jewellers) Ltd*[171] an administrative error which led to the employee receiving her maternity pay one month late was a detriment, particularly as the employee was unpaid at a time when she was unwell and about to give birth.

15.133   There is also likely to be a substantial overlap between a detriment under the ERA 1996 and discrimination where the detriment is related to pregnancy and maternity leave. A woman should claim both. A claim of detriment may be more useful to a man than to a woman as a discrimination claim is less likely, particularly as there is scope for claiming the equivalent of injury to feelings as part of a detriment claim (see para 18.139), though not, oddly, as part of a dismissal claim.

Examples of detriments

15.134 It is difficult to predict the situations that may give rise to a claim under these provisions. Examples might be:

- asking a woman, in response to her question about plans for her future, 'That really depends on what your long-term plans are . . . Are you planning on having any more children?';[172]
- denial of training to a man who is about to go on parental leave;

---

170   EAT 1114/97, 24 November 1998.
171   ET 2303442/98.
172   *Herbert Smith Solicitors & George Kalorkoti v Langton* [2005] UKEAT/0242 10 October 2005.

- allocation of less work or less interesting work;[173]
- denial of the right to return to the same job;[174]
- comments and assumptions that the woman will no longer be committed to her work;
- excluding a pregnant worker from foreign business trips;
- pressurising a woman to change her original contractual hours.[175]

Remedies are covered in chapter 18.

173 See, for example, *Walton v The Nottingham Gateway Hotel Ltd*, 29 September 2004; Case no 2600273/04 where a room maid was not allocated work after she informed her employer that she was pregnant. This was a detriment and the reason for the treatment was because she was pregnant.
174 This may also give rise to actual or constructive dismissal or may fall short of a fundamental breach of contract entitling the woman to resign in response.
175 *Herbert Smith*, see note 173.

CHAPTER 16

Statutory dispute resolution and time limits

Key points

- Where the statutory disciplinary procedure (DDP) applies, failure by the employer to follow it will make the dismissal automatically unfair; where either party fails to follow the DDP to the end, compensation will be increased or reduced depending on who is at fault.
- Where the statutory grievance procedure (GP) applies an employee must put in a written grievance and wait 28 days before lodging a claim with the tribunal. Time is then extended by three months. Failure by either party to follow the GP will lead to an increase or reduction in compensation depending on who is at fault.
- The DDP applies where:
  - the employer dismisses or is contemplating dismissing the employee;
  - the employer takes relevant disciplinary action (which is on grounds of conduct or capability but excluding warnings and paid suspension).
- The GP applies where:
  - an employee complains of discrimination, constructive dismissal, detriment and other claims specified in Employment Act (EA) 2002 Schs 3 and 4.
  - the employer has not dismissed and is not contemplating dismissing the employee, and
  - none of the exceptions apply.
- There may be an overlap where, for example, the employee alleges that relevant disciplinary action is discriminatory, in which case a grievance should be raised.
- Where it is not clear which procedure applies, eg, whether the dismissal is actual or constructive, the employee should put in a claim within the normal time limit but also raise a grievance and follow the GP.
- The standard procedures involve three steps:
  - raising a written grievance under the GP or setting out in writing the alleged conduct or characteristics which may lead to disciplinary action or dismissal under the DDP;
  - a meeting to discuss the allegations, followed by the employer informing the employee of its decision and right to appeal;
  - an appeal, followed by the decision on appeal.

- There is a modified procedure under the DDP where the dismissal is for gross misconduct.
- There is a modified procedure under the GP for ex-employees where certain conditions apply and the parties agree in writing. This avoids the need for a meeting.
- The employee is entitled to be accompanied by another worker or trade union representative.
- There are exceptions to both the DDP and GP when either the procedures do not apply or they are treated as having been complied with.
- The time limit for bringing a claim is usually three months less one day, unless the grievance procedure applies in which case it is extended by three months.
- In dismissal cases, the time limit is only extended if there is an ongoing procedure at the expiry of the three months.
- If there is continuing discrimination over a period, time starts to run at the end of the period.
- In discrimination cases, time can be extended where it is just and equitable to do so; this does not apply to equal pay claims.
- With other claims, time may be extended if it was not reasonably practicable to lodge the claim in time and it was lodged within such further time as was reasonably practicable.

Background and statutory framework

16.1   This chapter sets out the statutory disciplinary and grievance procedures, the circumstances in which they apply and the relationship between the procedures and time limits for bringing a claim in the tribunal. There are standard and modified procedures in both cases.

Overview of main points

16.2   The statutory grievance and disciplinary procedures came into effect on 1 October 2004, the main aim being to ensure that the parties try to resolve disputes internally before resorting to an employment tribunal. The law is set out in the EA 2002 and the Dispute Resolution Regulations (DR Regs) 2004.[1] It is very important for employees and

---

1   SI No 752. All references in this chapter are to the DR regs 2004 unless otherwise stated.

employers to follow the correct procedure under the statutory GP and DDP where they apply (and there are some exceptions). The procedures only apply to employees, not other workers. The employee and employer must usually comply with all the requirements of the GP and DDP to avoid compensation being reduced/increased by between 10% and 50%. Below is a summary of the main points.

Disciplinary and dismisssal procedures (DDP)

- Where an employer dismisses or contemplates dismissing (apart from constructive dismissal) an employee with more than one year's service, it must follow all the requirements of the DDP or risk a finding of automatically unfair dismissal and/or increased compensation.
- Where the employee, even with less than one year's service, is successful in a discrimination and other specified claims, compensation will be increased if the employer has not been through the DDP; it may be decreased if the employee has not complied with the DDP.
- The time limit for lodging a claim for actual dismissal is extended by three months, but only if the employee lodges a claim after the expiry of three months and has reasonable grounds for believing, when the time limit expired, that a dismissal or disciplinary procedure was being followed (see paras 16.104–16.105).[2]
- The procedures are only a minimum legal standard, not best practice. Thus, a dismissal may still be unfair if the employer does not act reasonably, even though it followed the DDP.

Grievance procedures (GP)

- In most discrimination, equal pay, constructive unfair dismissal and some other cases, except where the employer actually dismisses the employee or is contemplating dismissal (which does not include constructive dismissal), the employee must raise a written grievance against the employer *within* three months (and *must* do so with four months) of the discrimination (or other complaint) unless it is just and equitable to extend time.[3] In

2   Reg 15(2).
3   See *Spillett v Tesco, BUPA Care Homes (BNH) Ltd v Cann* [2006] IRLR 248, EAT
    see paras 16.78–16.79; although this was a disability discrimination case it must
    be assumed that the same principles apply to other claims where the 'not
    reasonably practicable' test applies.

equal pay cases a grievance should be raised within six months (maximum seven months) of the end of the contract of employment. The employee must then wait 28 days before lodging a claim with the tribunal. Failure to comply with the procedure may lead to the claim being barred.

- Where the GP applies, provided a grievance is raised or a claim is lodged within the normal time limit, the time limit without having raised a grievance for submitting a claim to the tribunal is extended by three months, ie, to within six months from the date of discrimination or within nine months of the end of the contract of employment in equal pay cases. This is to allow a grievance to be raised and the claim resubmitted. If the GP does not apply, time is not extended.

- If the claim is lodged within the normal time limit but the employee has not first put in a grievance and/or waited the required 28 days, the tribunal will return the claim but the time limit for resubmitting a valid claim will be extended by three months (ie, to within six months from the discrimination, but see note 105).

- Where the employee has not raised a grievance or lodged the claim within the appropriate time limit (three months for discrimination claims) the employee must rely on the provisions which allow the tribunal to extend time (see para 16.139).

- Failure to raise a grievance within four months may lead to the employee being barred from making a claim to the tribunal if it is not just and equitable to extend time (see para 16.75 onwards).

- If the employee starts tribunal proceedings after waiting 28 days but before the statutory procedures are completed, s/he risks having any compensation reduced if the non-completion was due to her/him.[4]

- 'Grievance' means a complaint by an employee about action which the employer has taken or is contemplating taking. It must be written but otherwise there is no specified format. Raise a grievance means make a complaint.

- The best advice for employees, unsure if the GP applies, is to raise a grievance within two months and lodge a claim within three months so there is no danger of being out of time, although if the GP has not been completed at the date of lodging the claim, it may

---

4   EA 2002 s31(2) and (3).

lead to a reduction in compensation if the employee is at fault (see above).

- The best advice for employers is to treat all complaints as a grievance – or at least ask the employee if it should be treated as such, because failure to do so and to follow the procedure may lead to an increase in compensation.

The procedures: when they apply

16.3   The DDP and GP are meant to be mainly mutually exclusive. The DDP applies where the employer is contemplating dismissal or dismisses; the GP applies where the employee has a grievance about a claim in EA 2002 Sch 4. However, it is not always clear which procedure applies and the DDP and GP sometimes overlap (see para 16.37). There are also exceptions as well as situations where the procedures are treated as having been completed (see paras 16.54 and 16.60). There is a standard and modified procedure under both the DDP and GP.

DDP: when it applies

16.4   Subject to the exceptions, which are set out in para 16.43 onwards, the DDP applies in the following situations:

16.5   *Where the employer has dismissed or is contemplating dismissing an employee* (but not constructive dismissal).[5] It applies to all dismissals including the non renewal of a fixed-term contract, redundancies and dismissal for some other substantial reason (but not where there would be a contravention of a legal duty or restriction). There is no definition of 'contemplating dismissal', though if the employer has told the employee that the procedure may end in dismissal, this is likely to be sufficient. In *Madhewoo v NHS Direct*[6] the Employment Appeal Tribunal (EAT) held that the test of whether the employer contemplated dismissal was a subjective one, though of course this must be tested by the evidence. This is very common, as many employers warn their employees at the start of disciplinary proceedings that they could end in a dismissal.

5   DR Regs 2004 reg 3(1); see also regulation 2(1) which defines dismissal by reference to ERA 1996 s95(1)(a) and (b), not constructive dismissal in section 95(1)(c).
6   UKEAT/0030/06.

16.6   *Where the employer contemplates taking or takes relevant disciplinary action on grounds of conduct or capability.*[7] Relevant disciplinary action is defined as 'action, short of dismissal, which the employer asserts to be based wholly or mainly on the employee's conduct or capability, other than suspension on full pay or the issuing of warnings'.[8] It could include monitoring the employee's performance, demotion and will include suspension without pay. Employers should follow the DDP where, in conduct and capability cases, it is anticipated that such action is possible. The regulations say that the employer does not have to follow the DDP in relation to any other action short of dismissal (such as warnings and paid suspension). However, in practice the employer should follow the DDP in all conduct and capability cases as dismissal may be the end result. If it does not, it will have to start the procedure again before dismissing the employee. See para 16.14 where an employee resigns during the disciplinary process.

DDP: standard procedure

16.7   The standard procedure applies in the vast majority of cases. The modified procedure applies only where there is very obvious gross misconduct (see para 16.10). There is a three-step standard procedure:[9]

a)   *Step 1:* The employer must send a written statement to the employee setting out the employee's alleged conduct or characteristics or other circumstances which lead it to contemplate dismissing or taking disciplinary action against the employee. In *Silman v ICTS (UK) Ltd*[10] the EAT held that if the allegations change during the course of the procedure, provided they are 'closely related to the original alleged misconduct' so as to be only a variation the employer will not have to start Step 1 again. However, if there is a quite distinct act of misconduct which has emerged it would be necessary to send a fresh statement in writing so the employee knows in advance precisely what s/he has to meet. The employer must invite the employee to discuss the matter.

b)   *Step 2:* The meeting must take place before action is taken except in the case where the disciplinary action consists of warnings or

---

7   Reg 3(1).
8   Reg 2.
9   EA 2002 Sch 2 Chapter 1.
10 UKEAT/0630/05/LA.

suspensions.¹¹ Before the meeting takes place the employer must provide the basis for the allegations, which should include, for example, the evidence gathered during the investigation, and allow the employee a reasonable opportunity to consider her/his response. The employee must take all reasonable steps to attend the meeting. Following the meeting the employer must give the employee its decision and notify her/him of the right of appeal.

c) *Step 3:* If the employee does wish to appeal, s/he must inform the employer. The employer must invite the employee to an appeal meeting which the employee must take all reasonable steps to attend. The appeal meeting need not take place before the dismissal or disciplinary action takes effect. The employer must then give its decision on the appeal.

16.8 The only step that must be in writing is the initial Step 1 written statement. The employer need not give its decision in writing, though it is advisable to do so. None of the other steps need to be in writing, though it is generally advisable for them to be in writing to avoid any misunderstandings.

16.9 The EAT held in *Alexander and Hatherley v Bridgen Enterprises Ltd*¹² that in a redundancy case the employer should provide information as to both why the employer considers there is a redundancy situation and also why the employee is being selected. This should include the selection criteria including the employee's own assessment (see para 15.88).

DDP: Modified procedure

16.10 The modified (shorter) procedure applies where there is gross misconduct in circumstances where it would be futile to carry out any further investigation. The tightly defined circumstances are where:

a) there is a dismissal without notice on the ground of conduct;

b) the employer is entitled to dismiss the employee without notice (or pay in lieu) because of the conduct;

c) the dismissal takes place when the employer becomes aware of the conduct or immediately afterwards, and

---

11 Although the regulations do not limit this to paid suspension, as suspension on less than full pay is relevant disciplinary action (and the DDP applies) an employer would be advised to hold a Step 2 meeting before suspension on less than full pay.

12 [2006] IRLR 422, EAT.

d) it is reasonable for the employer to dismiss the employee before enquiring further into the circumstances.[13]

16.11 The ACAS Code states that a tribunal will only, very exceptionally, find a dismissal to be fair where there has been gross misconduct and the standard DDP has not been followed. Similarly the Department of Trade and Industry (DTI) guidance says that 'It is almost always unfair to dismiss an employee instantly, without first going through some form of procedure or carrying out some form of investigation, even in a case of apparently obvious gross misconduct'.[14]

16.12 The modified procedure involves only two steps:

a) *Step 1:* The employer must set out in writing the employee's alleged misconduct which led to the dismissal and what the basis was for thinking at the time of the dismissal that the employee was guilty of the alleged misconduct. This is a more detailed statement than under the standard procedure as it must contain the 'basis' for the allegations of misconduct. The employer must notify the employee of the right to appeal.

b) *Step 2:* if the employee wants to appeal and so notifies the employer, the employer must hold an appeal meeting, which the employee must take all reasonable steps to attend. After the meeting the employer must inform the employee of its final decision.

Summary of differences between DDP standard and modified procedure

Standard procedure: three steps	Modified procedure: two steps
Step 1. Employer must set out in writing the employee's alleged conduct or characteristics, which led to the employer contemplating dismissing or taking disciplinary action. The employer must send the statement to the employee and invite her/him to a meeting to discuss the matter.	**Step 1.** The employer must set out in writing and send to the employee details of a) the employee's alleged misconduct which led to the dismissal, b) the basis for thinking that the employee was guilty of the misconduct, c) the employee's right to appeal against dismissal.

13 DR Regs 2004 reg 3(2).
14 ACAS Code para 36, DTI para 15.

Standard procedure: three steps	Modified procedure: two steps
Step 2. The meeting must take place before a claim is taken (except where the disciplinary action consists of suspension). Prior to the meeting the employer must inform the employee of the grounds for the action and the employee must have a reasonable opportunity to consider his/her response. The employee must take all reasonable steps to attend the meeting. After the meeting the employer must inform the employee of its decision and notify the employee of the right to appeal.	**Step 2.** The employee must inform the employer if s/he wants to appeal The employer must then invite the employee to attend a meeting The employee must take all reasonable steps to attend the meeting. After the meeting the employer must inform the employee of its decision.
Step 3 If the employee wishes to appeal s/he must inform the employer and the employer must arrange another meeting.[15] The employee must take all reasonable steps to attend the meeting. The appeal meeting need not take place before the dismissal or disciplinary action takes effect. After the appeal meeting, the employer must inform the employee of his final decision.	

GP: when it applies

16.13   The GP applies where the employee has a complaint about action (which includes omissions)[16] which the employer has taken or is contemplating taking, which could form a complaint specified in

---

15   Although the employee is not obliged to appeal, compensation may be reduced if s/he does not.
16   DR Regs 2004 reg 2(1).

Schedule 3 or 4 to the EA 2002,[17] apart from actual or contemplated dismissal.[18] It covers constructive dismissal, detriment (except under the Part-time Workers Regulations), and all discrimination claims by employees including equal pay and some associated claims (see para 16.42). It applies whether the employee is still employed or has resigned and where disciplinary action is alleged to be discriminatory. The employee does not need to remain in employment whilst the procedure is followed. The exceptions are set out at para 16.43 onwards. Special provisions apply to whistleblowing and its relationship with the grievance procedure[19] but these are outside the scope of this book.

16.14   An employment tribunal (ET) has held that the GP did not apply where the employee resigned when facing dismissal for misconduct. Since the employer was contemplating dismissal, the DDP applied instead, even though the claim was for constructive dismissal.[20]

16.15   Although the EAT has held that where a grievance has already been raised it is not necessary to raise another grievance in relation to a constructive dismissal claim *after resigning*, it may be advisable to do so as the statutory provisions could be interpreted as requiring a grievance to be raised *after* the act complained of, ie the constructive dismissal. The wide interpretation given to the rules by the EAT may not necessarily be followed by the Court of Appeal.[21] It is not necessary for the employee to wait for the grievance to be resolved before resigning; it is only necessary to wait (28 days) from raising a grievance to lodging a claim (see para 15.27 onwards).

16.16   Where an employee is victimised following a grievance, a further grievance should be raised before putting in a tribunal claim for victimisation. If the employee complains that the way the grievance was dealt with was discriminatory, this may lead to another grievance.[22]

---

17 Schedule 3 covers adjustments in compensation.
18 DR Regs 2004 reg 6; EA 2002 Sch 3 or 4.
19 See ERA 1996 ss43A–43L; EA 2002 Sch 2 para 15.
20 *Cooke v Secure Move Property Services* ET IDS Employment Law Brief 788 September 2005 p11.
21 See, for example, *Galaxy Showers Ltd v Wilson* [2006] IRLR 83 and *Shergold v Fieldway Medical Centre* [2006] IRLR 76 where the EAT held that provided a grievance was raised before a resignation, it was not necessary to raise another one subsequent to the resignation.
22 In *Mudchute Association v Mr D Petherbridge* [2005] UKEAT 0569/05, 21 December 2005 (unreported), the EAT noted that the definition of grievance is 'capable of including action by the employer on an earlier grievance raised by the employee . . . failure to deal with a grievance properly may itself amount to a breach of the implied term of trust and confidence, giving rise of itself to a claim of constructive unfair dismissal'.

If the parties agree that the procedures have been exhausted, for example there was a full grievance procedure before the employee resigned, the claimant may be able to rely on that though it is not necessarily safe to do so as the ET may decide otherwise. However if the position is unclear, this may lead to a succession of grievances and claims but this is the only 'safe' way of avoiding a finding that there has been no timely and relevant grievance prior to the claim.

16.17   An employee should bring a grievance before making a tribunal claim in respect of, for example:

a) constructive dismissal;
b) failure to give an appropriate pay rise or bonus because of pregnancy or maternity leave, which may be direct sex discrimination;
c) being treated less favourably as a result of applying to work flexibly – which may be a 'detriment' or discrimination;
d) indirect sex discrimination where a female employee's application for flexible working is refused;
e) direct sex discrimination where a male employee is refused flexible working because of his sex;
f) refusal to allow an employee to return to the same job after maternity or other leave, where such refusal is related to the absence;
g) an equal pay claim.

16.18   The grievance procedure does not apply where the claim is against a fellow employee, only against the employer. Thus for claims against employees (for discrimination) the GP does not apply and the time limits are not extended.[23]

GP: standard procedure

Step 1

16.19   The first step is for the employee to send a *written* grievance to the employer (Step 1). DR Regs reg 2 defines a grievance as 'a complaint by an employee about action which his employer has taken or is contemplating taking in relation to him'.[24] It covers not only an act but a failure to act.[25] There is a distinction between what is required

23 *Bisset v (1) Ms Martins and (2) Castlehill Housing Association* UKEATS/0022/06/RN and UKEATS/0023/06/RN, 18 August 2006.
24 DR Regs 2004 reg 2(1).
25 *Galaxy Showers Ltd v Wilson* [2006] IRLR 83. See para 16.20.

for the standard and modified procedure. The modified procedure states that the employee must set out the *basis* for the grievance whereas the standard GP only refers to 'the grievance', though the basis for the grievance must be provided before the first meeting (see para 16.31).

16.20   According to the EAT, the requirements for the Step 1 grievance are minimal. It need not say it is a grievance, as it is no more than a 'written complaint'.[26] It need not be in any particular form or style nor need it be signed.[27] The grievance may refer to earlier communications if they are part of the context.[28] The employer only needs to be put on notice, in writing, that the employee is complaining about its actual or apprehended conduct. As Langstaff J said in *Galaxy Showers v Wilson*:[29]

> The definition of grievance does not upon the face of it contain any requirements that the complaint should go any further than being a complaint about what the employer has or has not done. There is no particular formality required by the statutory wording.[30]

16.21   However, in practice, if possible, it is advisable for the Step 1 grievance letter to say that it is a grievance to avoid any argument by the employer that there was a failure to comply with the GP.[31] It is also better to set out all complaints and incidents in some detail so that the grievance is clear and in any event this is required before the meeting.

16.22   Subject to complying with the time limits for raising a grievance and lodging a claim, there is no maximum time limit prior to the lodging of the claim to the tribunal in which the grievance must have been raised. It does not matter that the grievance was raised a long

---

26   DR Regs 2004 reg 2 defines 'grievance'; see *Shergold v Fieldway Medical Centre* [2006] IRLR 76 at para 33 and *Canary Wharf Management Ltd v Edebi* [2006] IRLR 416. *Thorpe v Soleil Investments Ltd* UKEAT/0503/05, 18 October 2005, where the EAT held that the ET were entitled to find that a letter setting out complaints was a grievance even if it did not comply with a contractual grievance procedure.

27   *Arnold Clark Automobiles Ltd v Steward and Barnetts Motor Group Ltd*, 20 December 2005 EATS/0052/05RN.

28   *Canary Wharf*; as the EAT said in certain circumstances one can only fairly understand the content of a later letter by reference to earlier correspondence.

29   [2006] IRLR 83 at para 10.

30   See also *Canary Wharf*, note 26, where Elias J said that 'the objective of the statute can be fairly met if the employers, on a fair reading of the statement and having regard to the particular context in which it is made, can be expected to appreciate that the relevant complaint is being raised' (para 25).

31   The response to a tribunal claim (ET3) asks the employer if the employee has raised the complaint 'in writing under a grievance procedure'.

time previously provided the claim is lodged in time. The grievance must be ongoing. If dealt with or not pursued in circumstances where it may be inferred that the employee no longer wishes to have it determined, then a further grievance must be raised.[32]

16.23   It does not matter whether the written communication deals with any other matters.[33] Thus, a letter could cover a range of matters in addition to the 'complaint' and still constitute a 'grievance'. In *Cooke* (see 16.14) the tribunal held that an employee's letter expressing his concern that a conclusion had already been reached that he had committed fraud and that the disciplinary investigation was tainted by an element of bias so he would not get a fair hearing; this letter was held to be a grievance.

16.24   In *Shergold v Fieldway Medical Centre*[34] the EAT held that a letter of resignation is a grievance. The grievance could be raised after a dismissal has taken effect and may be raised by a solicitor. The claimant does not need to be actively invoking the grievance procedure, statutory or contractual.[35]

16.25   The EAT has held that a solicitor's letter before action amounted to the raising of a grievance for the purposes of the statutory grievance procedures even if 'without prejudice'.[36]

16.26   In *Commotion Ltd v Rutty*[37] the EAT held that a request for flexible working will be a grievance if the employee has previously requested this on an informal basis and been refused. Similarly, it is likely that where there has been no request prior to the formal application, an appeal under the procedure will count as a grievance. Note that a grievance is only necessary for discrimination claims so that if the claim only relates to a breach of the procedure there is no need to raise a grievance as the GP does not apply. In practice most claims will be for indirect discrimination if the request is refused as breach of the procedure only gives rise to a small amount of compensation.

---

32 *Canary Wharf* at para 19.
33 DR Regs 2004 reg 2(2); see also *Shergold*.
34 [2006] IRLR 76; see also *Martin v Class Security Installations Ltd*, 16 March 2006 UKEAT/0188/06 where it was held that a solicitor's letter referring to constructive dismissal but also saying that the details of the complaint would be provided in the future, was a grievance.
35 This was followed in *Canary Wharf*. See paras 20–25 for full discussion about the requirements for a grievance.
36 *Mark Warner Ltd v Aspland* [2006] IRLR 87 *Arnold Clark Automobiles v Stewart & or* UKEATS/0052/05/RN where Lady Smith said that the use of 'without prejudice' did not prevent the letter being a grievance.
37 [2006] IRLR 171, EAT.

16.27   The questions in a questionnaire do not constitute a grievance, nor does the background information that is required.[38]

16.28   There is no need to refer to the relevant legal provisions, though the claim should reflect what is included in the grievance. As Burton J said in *Shergold*:[39]

> . . . the grievance in question must relate to the subsequent claim, and the claim must related to the earlier grievance, if the relevant statutory provision is to be complied with. It is clearly no compliance with the requirement that there must be a grievance in writing before proceedings if the grievance in writing relates, for example, to unpaid holiday pay and the proceedings, which are then sought to be issued, are based upon race discrimination or sex discrimination with no relevant to any question of holiday pay. In those circumstances, it is likely that it will be found that the proceedings were issued in breach of the statutory procedure because no grievance in writing had been set out beforehand . . . But that does not begin to mean that the wording of the simple grievance in writing required under paragraph 6, and the likely much fuller exposition of the case set out in proceedings, must be anywhere near identical . . . provided that the general nature of the grievance in writing was substantially the same as the matter which then forms the subject matter of the claim, its different description or a difference by way of precise ingredients or particular does not affect the statutory compliance.

16.29   It is important to include all complaints in the GP such as failure to pay a bonus, or pay rise, as it may not be possible to amend the claim at a later stage to include matters not raised in the grievance. In *Canary Wharf* the EAT held that the claimant's reference to his health problems could not be said to have 'fairly raised, even in a non-technical and unsophisticated way, an issue which the employers could reasonably understand had arisen under the Disability Discrimination Act'. He had not identified any failures to make adjustments nor alleged less favourable treatment than other employees in the same situation. It was only a generalised complaint about the adverse consequences to health but not an issue about disability discrimination. This part of the claim was not allowed.[40]

16.30   It is advisable for employers to treat all complaints as a grievance. If the tribunal finds that it is a grievance but the employer did not treat it as one (and so did not go through the grievance procedure) then if the employee's claim is successful, compensation is likely to

---

38   DR Regs 2004 reg 14; see *Holc-Gale v Makers UK Ltd* [2006] IRLR 178.
39   At paras 35–37, note 26.
40   See para 41, note 26.

be increased. The other option is for the employer to ask the employee if s/he wants the complaint to be treated as a grievance, though a denial will not necessarily be conclusive as it is for the tribunal to decide whether or not it is a grievance.

Standard procedure Step 2 – the grievance meeting

16.31 Once the employee has sent in the written grievance, the employer must invite the employee to attend a meeting to discuss the grievance. Before the meeting, the employee must inform the employer of the basis for the grievance, though providing more information will not be necessary if the Step 1 grievance has sufficient detail. The employer must have a reasonable opportunity to consider its response. The employee must take all reasonable steps to attend the meeting and is entitled to be accompanied (see para 16.70 onwards).

16.32 After the meeting the employer must inform the employee of its decision and notify the employee of their right to appeal. Although there is no obligation for this to be in writing it is advisable to put it in writing so there is no misunderstanding about the grounds for the decision.

Standard procedure Step 3: appeal

16.33 An employee who wants to appeal must inform the employer and the employer must arrange an appeal meeting which the employee must take all reasonable steps to attend. Although there is no obligation on the employee to appeal, failure to do so means that the procedure has not been completed so compensation is likely to be reduced (see para 18.15 onwards). After the appeal meeting the employer must inform the employee of its final decision.

GP: modified procedure

16.34 The modified procedure applies to ex-employees where:

a) the employer was unaware of the grievance before the employment ceases or was aware but the GP has not been commenced or completed before the last day of the employee's employment;

b) the employee has left the employer's employment; and

c) there is written agreement between the parties after the employer became aware of the grievance that (the modified procedure) should apply.[41]

---

41 DR Regs 2004 reg 6(3)(a). See also the exceptions in reg 6(4)–(7).

16.35　If the modified procedure applies, the employee must set out in writing the grievance and the basis for it and send a copy to the employer. The employer must set out its response in writing and send the statement to the employee. There is no meeting or appeal.

Summary of differences between GP standard and modified procedure[42]

Standard procedure: three steps	Modified procedure: two steps
Step 1. Employee must set out grievance in writing and send it to the employer.	**Step 1.** The employee must: a) set out in writing the grievance and basis for it; and b) send a copy to the employer.
Step 2. The employer must invite the employee to a meeting to discuss the grievance. This must not take place unless: a. the employee has told the employer the basis for the grievance; and b. the employer has had a reasonable opportunity to consider its response. The employee must take all reasonable steps to attend the meeting.	Note that there are no meetings.
After the meeting the employer must inform the employee of its response to the grievance and notify him/her of the right to appeal.	**Step 2.** The employer must set out its response in writing and send the statement to the employee.
Step 3. If the employee wishes to appeal s/he must inform the employer and the employer must arrange another meeting.[42] The employee must take all reasonable steps to attend the meeting.	
After the appeal meeting, the employer must inform the employee of its final decision.	

42　Although the employee is not obliged to appeal, compensation may be reduced if s/he does not.

Where both DDP and GP procedures apply

16.36   There are situations where both the DDP and GP are running at the same time, eg where the employee alleges that disciplinary action is discriminatory (see para 16.55). In such a situation, the employer may disentangle them, but this is not necessary under the statutory procedures. The letters and meetings under the procedures can be multi-purpose but this should be made clear prior to the meeting. Thus, a meeting could cover the issues raised under both the DDP and the GP and the employer's decision in relation to both may be set out in one letter. Note, however, that the ACAS Code suggests that the employer should consider suspending the disciplinary procedure for a short period while the grievance is deal with.[43]

Where it is unclear which, if any, procedure applies

16.37   There are a number of situations where it is unclear which, if any, procedure applies. This may not be resolved until the tribunal hears the case, by which time it will be too late to correct the position by, for example, raising a grievance within the time limit, where this has not previously been done, or going through the DDP. In such cases it may be advisable for the claimant to lodge separate claims, one assuming the grievance procedure applies and one assuming it does not. This may also apply where there are a number of claims only some of which are covered by the grievance procedure and time limit constraints not allow them to be argued in the alternative in the same claim. Two examples are set out below.

Employee or worker?

16.38   It is sometimes not clear if the claimant is an employee or worker. A *worker* must put in a claim within the normal time limit (three months for discrimination or six months for equal pay) whereas an *employee* covered by the GP must raise a grievance and will then have a further three months (see para 16.102). If in doubt, the employee/worker should try both to complete the GP and lodge a claim within three months, thus covering both possibilities. If this is not possible, it may be necessary to lodge two claims in the alternative, one within three months and another, having started the grievance procedure, within the further time limit. The claims should then be combined.

43   ACAS Code of Practice 1 para 33.

Actual or constructive dismissal?

16.39 It may not be clear if a dismissal is actual or constructive, for example, if the employer says 'if you don't like it here you know what you can do', or suggests that the employee resign rather than be dismissed.[44] An employer may argue that there was no dismissal but if wrong and it fails to follow the DDP, then the dismissal will be automatically unfair (if the employee has been employed for one year) and compensation is likely to be increased. If the employee argues it was an actual dismissal but it is a constructive dismissal and s/he has failed to raise a grievance, she may be barred from bringing a claim. The alternative, for a claimant, is either to:

- raise a grievance, wait 28 days and lodge the claim within the three-month period,[45] but if there is no time to do this;
- put in a claim within three months assuming the GP does not apply; and
- put in a further claim, after raising a grievance and waiting 28 days on the assumption that the GP does apply.

16.40 If the GP does apply but a grievance has not been raised and the employer does not raise the issue in the response, as required by the rules, the requirements of Employment Act (EA) 2002 s32(2)–(4) have not been met by the employer. In *Holc-Gale v Makers UK Ltd* the EAT held that the question as to whether the claimant complied with the requirements of EA 2002 s32 goes to the tribunal's jurisdiction, holding that 'subject to any prejudice to the Claimant it was then open to the respondent to apply for leave to amend the response'.[46] Arguably, however, an amendment to the response should not be allowed if it does prejudice the claimant because it is by then too late to raise a grievance, particularly as the tribunal rules require the employer to include its full defence on the prescribed form (the ET3).

16.41 In *Shergold* it notable that the EAT said:

> It is not, in our judgment, the intention of the legislation either that employees should be barred or that employers should unwittingly find themselves liable for automatic unfair dismissal.

---

44 In which case it may be an enforced resignation.
45 Thus, the statutory GP has been complied with *and* if the GP does not apply the claim is still in time.
46 [2006] IRLR 178. The EAT also said that they did not believe any question of estoppel would arise.

16.42　There are situations where the procedure need not be followed as one of the exceptions apply (see para 16.43 onwards). In addition, in some situations the parties may be treated as having complied with the procedures (see para 16.60). The position where the procedures overlap is covered in para 16.36.

Summary of claims relevant to this book where GP or DP applies

The claim	Which statutory procedure applies?
Any dispute where the claimant is a worker not an employee	Neither procedure applies
Claimant is a job applicant	Neither procedure applies
Dismissal, including a discriminatory dismissal (employee is sacked or made redundant) or the employer is contemplating dismissal.	DDP
Constructive dismissal (employee resigns) under ERA 1996 or SDA 1975	GP
Where the employee is warned (orally or in writing) or suspended on full pay and believes this to be discriminatory	GP. These actions are not defined as 'relevant disciplinary action' so the DDP does not apply unless the employer is contemplating dismissal. BUT if dismissal is contemplated, the GP will not apply
'Relevant' disciplinary action (ie, action short of dismissal, for example demotion or suspension on no pay) taken against the employee for conduct or capability, which employee believes is discriminatory	Where employee suspects action is discrimination (or a pretext), both DDP and GP apply. Otherwise only DDP applies
Employee is discriminated against but not disciplined or dismissed, eg, s/he is not promoted or is victimised	GP

Detriment claims under ERA 1996 s48, relating to pregnancy, maternity, childbirth and leave for family and domestic reasons (maternity, adoption, parental, paternity, dependants' leave)	GP
Detriment claims relating to flexible working under ERA 1996 s47E and Procedural Regs 2002 reg 16[47]	GP[48]
Breach of right to request flexible working procedure	Neither
Breach of PTW Regs[49]	Neither unless there has been a dismissal–see 'dismissal' and 'constructive dismissal' above
Breach of FTW Regs[50]	Neither
Refusal of time off for antenatal care	Neither
Refusal of time off for dependants	Neither
Failure to pay employee during maternity suspension	Neither
Postponement/ refusal of parental leave	Neither
Unlawful deduction of wages, breach of contract	GP

Exceptions

Circumstances where the GP and DDP need not be started/completed (DR Regs reg 11)

16.43   There are some circumstances where the statutory procedures will not apply, so it is not necessary to start them or, where started, they

47   Flexible Working (Procedural Requirements) Regulations 2002.
48   This was amended by the Employment Relations Act 2004 s41(3) as from 6 May 2005.
49   Part-time Workers (Prevention of Less Favourable Treatment) Regulations 2000 SI No 1551.
50   Fixed-term Employees (Prevention of Less Favourable Treatment) Regulations 2002 SI No 2034.

will be treated as having been completed. If the procedure has not been commenced in these circumstances time will not be extended. Where the procedure has been commenced (but not completed) time limits are still extended and the statutory admissibility conditions for grievances[51] must be met, but it will not be necessary to go through the remaining stages of the procedures.

16.44   It is unwise to rely on these exceptions unless it is necessary to do so, as it will be the tribunal which determines whether they apply. If the tribunal decides that the exception does not apply, the claim may be out of time and so barred as the time limit may have expired for raising a grievance (see para 16.75). It may be possible to rely on the 'just and equitable' extension of time following the EAT decision in *BUPA Care Homes v Cann* (see para 16.78).

16.45   These exceptions, which apply to both the GP and DDP, are set out below.

Threat to person or property

16.46   Where either party has reasonable grounds for believing that commencing the procedure or complying with it would result in a significant threat to themselves or property, any other person or the property of any other person.[52] This is intended to cover both violence and threats of violence.

Harassment

16.47   Where there has been harassment and either party has reasonable grounds to believe that commencing the procedure or complying with the remainder of it would result in being subjected to further harassment.[53] 'Harassment' is defined as creating an intimidating, hostile, degrading, humiliating environment (see para 2.88). Stress or anxiety on the part of one of the parties is unlikely to come within this exception.[54]

16.48   In both the above cases the party responsible for the threat may be subject to an adverse adjustment of any award (ie, increase or decrease of between 10% and 50%).

---

51 Ie, the requirement to grieve within a maximum of a month after the expiry of the normal time limit and wait 28 days before lodging a claim: EA 2002 s32.
52 DR Regs 2004 reg 11(3)(a).
53 DR Regs 2004 reg 11(3)(b).
54 See DTI guidance paras 96–98.

Not practicable to comply

16.49 It is not practicable for the party to commence the procedure or comply with a requirement of it within a reasonable period.[55] The scope of this is unclear. The DTI guidance refers to factors beyond the control of either party such as illness, incapacity, cessation of the employer's business (paras 93, 99, 100). It could be because, for example, a woman is on maternity leave, particularly if either mother or child are ill. Arguably, this exception might apply where the tribunal has registered the claim, believing the GP does not apply, and where it later transpires that the GP did apply, but it is too late to raise a grievance. This exception is likely to apply mainly to the GP.

16.50 For example, if an employee is on maternity leave, and so is unaware of a promotion opportunity she may not be able to raise a grievance within four months, though time may be extended in these circumstances (see para 16.78). These are questions that will have to be resolved by the courts in due course.

16.51 Where it is not practicable to start or complete the procedures within a reasonable period, neither party will be held at fault so no adjustment to the award will apply.

Where DDP procedure does not apply

16.52 These are covered by DR Regs reg 4 and mainly cover situations in which the individual characteristics of the employee are not significant in the decision to dismiss, for example collective dismissals or where there is industrial action (which are outside the scope of this book). The normal unfair dismissal rules will still apply to such cases.

16.53 The DDP does not apply, so time limits are not extended and compensation is not affected in the following circumstances:

- where the employer's business suddenly ceases to function because of an event unforeseen by the employer so that it is impractical to employ any employees. However, in most redundancy situations the DDP will apply;[56]
- where the reason or principal reason for dismissal is that the employee could not continue to work in the position without contravention of a duty or restriction imposed by or under any enactment.[57] It might be argued that this would apply where a pregnant

55 DR Regs 2004 reg 11(3)(c).
56 DR Regs 2004 reg 4(1)(e).
57 ERA 1996 s98(2)(d); DR Regs 2004 reg 4(1)(f).

woman cannot work because of a health and safety prohibition related to her pregnancy. However, less favourable treatment or dismissal in these circumstances is likely to be sex discrimination and a breach of the employer's obligation to vary her conditions of employment or find suitable alternative work or suspend her on full pay so it is likely that such a dismissal would be unfair. Any failure to follow the DDP would be unfair (see chapter 3);

- where employees have been offered re-engagement, there are collective redundancies, there has been industrial action or dismissal procedures agreements apply.[58] These are all beyond the scope of this book;
- where DR Regs reg 11 applies (see para 16.43 onwards).

Circumstances where parties are treated as complying with DDP

16.54   The parties are treated as complying with the DDP where Step 1 of the DDP has been complied with and the employee presents an application for interim relief, or where there is a collective agreement relating to appeal rights and the employee has appealed under that procedure.[59] This is outside the scope of this book. In addition, para 16.43 onwards sets out the circumstances where the DDP and GP are treated as having been completed.

Exceptions to the GP

16.55   The GP does not apply, so time limits are not extended, the admissibility requirements do not apply and compensation is not affected, in the following situations:

- where the claimant is an ex-employee, neither grievance procedure has been commenced, and since the end of employment it has ceased to be reasonably practicable for the employee to put in a grievance;[60]
- where the employer has dismissed or is contemplating dismissing an employee.[61] The definition of 'dismissal' does not include

---

58 DR Regs 2004 reg 4(1)(a)–(g).
59 DR Regs 2004 reg 5; see ERA 1996 s128, this may apply where there has been a dismissal arising out of the right to be accompanied.
60 DR Regs 2004 reg 6(4).
61 DR Regs 2004 reg 6(5).

constructive dismissal, when the GP does apply (see para 16.13 onwards);

- where the employer has taken or is contemplating taking relevant disciplinary action[62] (defined as action on the basis of conduct or capability excluding warnings and suspension on full pay) unless it is alleged that the disciplinary action is discriminatory or a pretext (ie, in reality not being taken on conduct or capability grounds), in which case the GP does apply.[63] In such a case the employer should follow the DDP and the employee should put in a grievance about the action. The problem is that it may not be clear whether, when the employer is taking relevant disciplinary action, the employer is also contemplating dismissal, in which case the GP does not apply at all (see para 16.63).

16.56 Unless the employer is contemplating dismissal,[64] the GP would also apply if the employer had suspended the employee on full pay or given a warning as these actions do not fall within the definition of relevant disciplinary action so are outside of the provisions of the above paragraph.[65] So where the employer takes any action short of dismissal which is thought to be discrimination or unfair, the employee should raise a grievance in case the GP applies. However, the employee should not rely on doing this to extend the time limits, as if the employer is contemplating dismissal, the GP does not apply and time will not be extended for lodging a discrimination or unfair dismissal.

16.57 In *Cooke v Secure Move Property Service*,[66] C was suspended while his employer investigated alleged gross misconduct. A disciplinary meeting was arranged for 5 November 2004, but C resigned the day before saying that his position was untenable and he did not accept the allegations against him. The meeting went ahead and C was summarily dismissed for gross misconduct. C brought claims for unfair and constructive dismissal. The employer argued that C's constructive dismissal claim was inadmissible because he had failed to submit a grievance.[67]

16.58 The tribunal held that the exceptions set out above (para 16.55 onwards) applied so he had not been required to raise a grievance.

---

62 DR Regs 2004 reg 6(6).
63 DR Regs 2004 reg 6(5).
64 So comes within the exception in para 6(5).
65 See also DTI guidance para 8.
66 EDS Employment Law Brief 788 September 2005, p11.
67 Under EA 2002 s32.

Even though the exception from the requirement to raise a greivance due to actual or contemplated dismissal does not include constructive dismissals, the claimant's case was about the fact that his employer was contemplating dismissing him or taking other relevant disciplinary action.[68]

16.59　Note the exception where DR Regs reg 11 applies (see para 16.43).[69]

Parties are treated as complying with the GP having started but not finished it

16.60　DR Regs regs 7–10 set out the circumstances where the parties are treated as complying with the grievance procedures. Time limits are extended, the admissibility conditions apply, but compensation will not be affected as the procedure is treated as having been completed, even where it has not been. These are set out below.

Discriminatory disciplinary action

16.61　The parties are treated as having complied with the GP where:

- the employer has taken or is contemplating taking relevant discriplinary action (on grounds of conduct or capability) against the employee (apart from a warning or suspension on full pay);
- the grievance is that the action is discriminatory or a pretext (ie the reason is not a genuine one);[70] and
- the employee sends a grievance to the employer before the appeal meeting under the DDP or before complaining to the tribunal, where there is no ongoing procedure.[71]

16.62　Once this has been done, no further steps need to be taken in relation to the grievance.

16.63　There is a potential conflict between the requirement to put in a grievance[72] if the employee believes that disciplinary action is dis-

68　There was no claim that the disciplinary action was discrimination.
69　DR Regs 2004 reg 6(7) and reg 11(1).
70　DR Regs 2004 reg 6(6).
71　DR Regs 2004 reg 7(1)–(3). If a grievance is raised about disciplinary action and the employee raises the grievance before the appeal stage of the DDP where the statutory DDP is being followed, or, in other cases before a claim is lodged, the parties will be treated as having complied with the statutory GP. Where the DDP is being followed the grievance can be dealt with at the appeal. If the grievance is raised during the appeal stage or before the employer give its final decision, the parties must comply with the GP in full.
72　Under DR Regs 2004 reg 7(1).

criminatory and the exception whereby the GP does not apply if the employer is contemplating dismissal as the employer may be contemplating dismissal when taking disciplinary action. If in doubt, the safest option for the employee is to put in a grievance and, if possible, put the discrimination claim in within three months. However, if there is eventually a dismissal the obligation is on the employer to follow the DDP and failure to do so will make the dismissal automatically unfair (if the employee has one year's service). The GP does not apply to dismissals. Thus, the reality of the situation is that, unless the employee wants to pursue a claim irrespective of whether there is a dismissal, it is not necessary to put in a grievance about discriminatory disciplinary action. Once dismissed, a claim can be made for discriminatory (and unfair) dismissal within either three months or a further three months if there is an ongoing DDP at the expiry of the normal time limit.

16.64   If, in the *Cooke* case above, the claimant was complaining that the *relevant disciplinary action* was discriminatory then if, as is likely, the employer was, at the same time contemplating dismissal the exception in DR Regs 2004 reg 6(5) will apply and there is no need for the employee to put in a grievance. If, however, the employer was not contemplating dismissal, and there is *relevant disciplinary action*, which is discriminatory, a grievance should be lodged (but see para 16.63).

16.65   If action taken by the employer is not on grounds of conduct or capability, the GP, not DDP, applies. Thus, if the employee is not consulted about redundancy because she is on maternity leave, she should put in a grievance. (but see also para xx). However, if she is made redundant this is a dismissal and the GP will not apply so time will not be extended.

Ex-employees

16.66   The parties are also treated as having complied with the GP where the standard GP applies, the employee has put in a written grievance, is no longer employed and since then it has ceased to be reasonably practicable for the parties to comply with the requirement to have a Step 2 meeting or appeal.[73]

16.67   If there has been a Step 2 meeting the employer must inform the employee of the result or will be in breach.

73 DR Regs 2004 reg 8.

Situations where employee representatives are dealing with the grievance[74]

16.68   Where this applies, the parties may be treated as having complied with the GP. This is outside the scope of this book.

General requirements under the disciplinary and grievance procedures

Timetable

16.69   All steps and actions under the procedures must be taken without unreasonable delay.[75] What is reasonable or unreasonable is not defined, but steps should be taken without delay. Twenty-eight days is the period envisaged by the government to complete the procedure.

Meetings

16.70   The timing and location of meetings must be reasonable and the employee must take reasonable steps to attend. The employee is entitled to be accompanied by a union representative or work colleague of choice.[76] If the employee or companion is unable to attend the meeting for an unforeseeable reason the employer must reschedule the meeting within five days (unless the parties agree otherwise) but need only do so once.[77]

16.71   Meetings must be conducted so that both employer and employee can explain their case. It is anticipated that they will be face to face meetings, not telephone discussions. Meetings can be multipurpose, ie cover disciplinary and grievance matters (see para 16.36).

16.72   In relation to appeal meetings, which are not the first meeting, the employer should, so far as is reasonably practicable, be represented by a more senior manager than attended the first meeting.[78]

16.73   The GP is treated as having been completed where the employer has invited the employee to attend two meetings and the employer or employee has not been able to attend for a reason which was not

---

74   DR Regs 2004 reg 9.
75   EA 2002 Sch 3 Part 3 para 11–13.
76   EA 2002; Employment Relations Act 1999 s10; a GP meeting is a hearing under Employment Relations Act 1999 s13(4), (5).
77   DR Regs 2004 reg 13.
78   EA 2002 Sch 2.

foreseeable when the meeting was arranged, ie a meeting has twice been abandoned for an unforeseeable reason.[79]

Effect of failure to comply with DDP or GP

16.74 Where one party is in breach of a DDP or GP the other party is not under any obligation to take any further steps under it. The non-completion, which may lead to an increase or reduction in compensation, will be attributable to the party in breach. However, it is for the tribunal to decide if there has been a breach so it is risky for either party to assume a breach and take no further steps under the procedure unless the position was very clear.

Time limits for sending a grievance to the employer and the statutory 'bar'

16.75 EA 2002 s32(2)–(3) provides that where the GP applies, a claimant shall not present a claim to the tribunal unless:

- s/he has put in a Step 1 grievance within the original time limit, ie within three months of the act complained of (or six months in equal pay cases); and
- waited 28 days following the grievance.

Time is extended by three months, so the claim must be lodged within a further three months of the original time limit.[80]

16.76 If the claim is rejected by the tribunal, due to a breach of the procedure or failure to provide the required information, the tribunal must return the form, notifying the claimant of the reasons, the time limit which applies to the claim and the consequences of not complying with section 32.[81] The aim of this is to enable the employee to go back to square one, ie lodge a written grievance, wait 28 days (to see if it can be resolved) and then re-submit the claim, confirming this has

---

79 DR Regs 2004 reg 13.
80 DR Regs 2004 reg 15(3). However, if there is any doubt about whether the GP applies (and thus whether time limits are extended), it is advisable to put in a Step 1 grievance within two months and lodge the claim within a further month (ie within a total of three months, or six months for equal pay) thus protecting the position whether or not the GP applies.
81 Employment Tribunal (Constitution and Rules etc) Regs 2004 (ET Rules) Sch 1 r3(6).

been done. Note that a decision to accept or not to accept a claim does not bind any future tribunal.[82]

16.77   Section 32(4) provides that an employee shall not present a complaint to a tribunal if Step 1 was complied with more than one month after the end of the 'original time limit' for making the complaint, which is usually four months (and seven months in equal pay cases). Section 32(4) imposes what has been called 'the statutory bar'.

Original time limit is subject to just and equitable extension

16.78   However, this 'bar' is less absolute than at first appeared as the EAT have held that in a discrimination case the 'original time limit' under EA 2002 s32(4) is the time limit provided for in the relevant legislation thus in a discrimination case it includes the power of the ET to allow an extension of time where it is just and equitable to do so.[83] Thus, the grievance is not out of time if the just and equitable extension applies, thereby extending the original time limit. In other words, the grievance must be raised not with four months but within a month of any just and equitable extension.

16.79   Further, the provisions in the Sex Discrimination Act (SDA) 1975 allowing the just and equitable extension, have not been amended by EA 2002 s32(4), so the ability to extend time on this basis would be undermined if there was no parallel power allowing an extension of time for raising a grievance (see para 16.139 onwards). As the EAT said in *BUPA Care Homes v Cann*, if 'Parliament wished to restrict that discretion to extend time it would have said so in the principal Act'. This is consistent with the DTI guidance which said that 'the existing discretion of the tribunal to extend a time limit where . . . it is just and equitable to extend it . . . is unaffected by these changes'.

16.80   If, at a hearing, it transpires that no grievance has been raised, the claimant could request an adjournment to give her/him time to raise a grievance (relying if necessary on the power to extend time), wait 28 days and lodge a further claim. This would be very cumbersome but may be the only way, in some circumstances, of allowing a claim to proceed.

---

82   ET Rules 2004 Sch 1 r3(9).
83   *Spillett v Tesco; BUPA Care Homes v Cann* [2006] 1RLR 248, EAT: The EAT held that 'original time limit' referred to in section 34 and which is not defined is different from 'normal time limit' in regulation 15 which is explicitly defined 'as being the period within which a complaint must be presented ignoring any discretion to extend it'.

16.81   There is no just and equitable power in relation to grievances raised under the Equal Pay Act (EPA) 1970 and under the Employment Rights Act (ERA) 1996 the test would be whether it was reasonably practicable (see para 16.40).

Circumstances where a tribunal may have jurisdiction when the 'bar' applies

16.82   The theory is that the claim will not be accepted if the employee has not followed the full procedure, and it will be returned by the tribunal. However, some claims will be wrongly accepted (or rejected) by the tribunal. The difficulty arises where the employee is unaware of (or has failed to comply with) the requirements of the statutory grievance procedure,[84] and this is only discovered at the hearing by which time it is too late to comply and the section 32(4) bar applies.

16.83   Arguably the tribunal is only barred from considering a complaint in limited circumstances. Section 32(6) provides that:

> . . . an employment tribunal shall be prevented from considering a complaint presented in breach of s32(2)–(4) *but only if:*[85]
> a) the breach is apparent to the tribunal from the information supplied to it by the employee in connection with the bringing of the proceedings, or
> b) the tribunal is satisfied of the breach as a result of the employer raising the issue of compliance with those provisions in accordance with . . . employment tribunal procedure regulations.

16.84   In order for the ET3 to be completed 'in accordance with . . . employment tribunal procedure regulations' the respondent must provide the grounds for defending the claim including any defence based on the claimant's failure to raise a grievance.[86] Respondents must use a prescribed form which asks if the grievance procedure has been complied with.[87] The tribunal must not accept the response if it does not include all the required information.[88] Arguably, if the ET3 is not properly completed the respondent should not then be allowed later to raise a failure to comply with the grievance, particu-

---

84 Whether it be the obligation to put in a grievance within a maximum of four months and/or wait 28 days before lodging the claim.
85 Our emphasis.
86 Employment Tribunals (Constitution and Rules etc) Regulations 2004 Sch 1 r4(3)(d).
87 ET Regs 2004 Sch 1 rule 4. Schedule sets out the main rules.
88 ET Regs 2004 Sch 1 r6(2).

larly if by then the claimant is out of time for raising a grievance so the claim would be struck out.[89]

ERA 2002 s32(2)–(4) is about gatekeeping, not barring claims

16.85   The purpose of the dispute resolution legislation is that the parties should try to resolve the issues before litigating. Rule 1(8) of the ET rules states that the tribunal shall not consider the substance of the claim *until there has been compliance*. If the gatekeeper (ie tribunal) lets in the claim, albeit wrongly, and the respondent does not raise the failure to put in a grievance in its response (when it is obliged to do so by the rules),[90] arguably that should be the end of the matter and the claim should proceed without any further arguments as to whether there has been compliance with the GP.

16.86   This interpretation is supported by the EAT President's judgment in *Richardson v U Mole Ltd*.[91] In *Mole* the tribunal rejected a claim for unfair dismissal for non-compliance with Rule 1(4)(f) (requiring the claimant to state where he was an employee). The EAT said in *Mole*:

> If, however, the result of the imposition of the gateway is not simply to point out gaps which ought to be corrected, but to drive away a claimant so that, as, for example, in this case, it means that by the time the completely immaterial defect is corrected the claimant is out of time, then injustice is inevitably going to be done. I have no doubt that that is not, and if it were it should not be, the purpose of the Rules, and . . . there ought to be, and is, an overriding objective of encouraging dealing with cases justly and fairly, such that the tribunals ought to be in the business of ensuring that this is the case, rather than driving possibly meritorious claimants or indeed respondents from the judgment seat.

16.87   Although *Mole* concerned the failure by the claimant to state whether he was an employee the President compared it, in his judgment, to a

---

89   Note that ERA 1996 s111 has not been amended to deal with the time limits relating to the procedures in EA 2002. Again this may indicate that the intention of EA 2002 s34 is not to act as an absolute bar, unlike section 111 which states that the tribunal shall not consider a complaint if presented out of time so that a tribunal has no jurisdiction when it is aware of the breach of a time limit. This is not qualified as is section 32(6), which states that the ET shall *only* be prevented from considering a complaint where the breach is apparent from the claim or raised in the response.

90   Which provide that the respondent must provide its grounds for resistance in the response (ET Rules Sch 1 r4(2)).

91   [2005] 1RLR 668 EAT.

similar appeal where the claim had been rejected by the tribunal because the claimant did not state in the claim (as required by the tribunal rules) that he had complied with the grievance procedure (when in fact he had).[92] *Mole* was cited with approval in *Canary Wharf Management v Edebi* (see para 16.20) and the EAT has generally interpreted the regulations widely to prevent a claimant being barred (but see *Holc-Gale* at para 16.40).

16.88   Even if, in the parallel case, there *had* been a failure to comply with the procedure, the tribunal's obligation is to return the claim with advice about what to do next and an extension of time to enable the failure to be rectified.[93] If the tribunal fails to do so and the claim is subsequently dismissed by the tribunal as being time barred, the claimant will be prevented from proceeding with the claim because of the tribunal's failure. Arguably, this cannot have been the intention of the rules. In *Excel Management Ltd v Lumb* UKEAT 0121/06/2807, 28 July 2006, there were three claims but in two of them the claimant had not waited 28 days before lodging the claim. The ET heard evidence for all claims though the claimant relodged the others to comply with the requirement to wait 28 days. The EAT held that the ET should have adjourned the hearing to allow 28 days to run so all three claims could be decided together. It was wrong to refuse to allow the respondent to present further evidence because it had been heard at the first hearing for one of the claims.

Breach of Human Rights Act 1998

16.89   If there is a bar, this could be a breach of the Human Rights Act (HRA) 1998 which provides a right to a fair hearing under article 6.

16.90   In *Grimmer v KLM Cityhopper UK*[94] Judge Prophet in the EAT was forthright in his criticism of the tribunal's refusal to accept an application because it did not contain sufficient details saying:

> It is a very serious step to deny a claimant or for that matter a respondent the opportunity of having an employment rights issue resolved by an independent judicial body, ie an employment tribunal. Most chairmen would not wish to feel forced to do so without there being a very good reason . . .

---

92   ET Rules Sch 1 1(4)(h) which requires information about whether the claimant has raised the subject matter of the claim in a grievance 28 days before lodging the claim.
93   ET Rules Sch 1 r3(6), 1(8).
94   [2005] IRLR 596, EAT.

16.91   Judge Prophet questioned the purpose of insisting through Rules that a failure to provide all the required information can lead to a claim not being accepted suggesting that it took no account of:

- the overriding object of dealing with a case justly;
- the fact that claimants are often not represented;
- the effect on time limits for presenting a claim;
- the principles of prejudice to the claimant and respondent; or
- the fact that a rigid application of the rules might result in a breach of the safeguards enshrined in article 6 of the European Convention on Human Rights.[95]

16.92   The EAT also said that the Rules of Procedure 'cannot cut down on an employment tribunal's jurisdiction to entertain a complaint which the primary legislation providing an employment right empowers it to determine'. What might be regarded as mandatory should not be taken to the point of denying a claimant access to the employment tribunal. If there is a conflict, the Rules must give way.

16.93   Employees may, in addition, be able to rely on the various exceptions, for example whereby it is not practicable for the employee to commence the procedure (see para 16.49).[96]

Time limits for lodging a claim with the tribunal

16.94   All tribunal claims must be brought within a prescribed time limit unless this is extended by the tribunal. The parties cannot agree between themselves to waive the time limits or extend them, whether this relates to raising a grievance or lodging a claim.

16.95   This section needs to be read with the sections on the dispute resolution regulations which extend the normal time limit by three months where the GP applies. Thus, any reference to a three-month time limit may be extended under the DR Regs 2004. The earlier legislation such as the SDA and ERA has not been amended to reflect the DR Regs 2004 or EA 2002.

16.96   Claims for unfair dismissal must be made 'before the end of the period of three months beginning with the effective date of termination' (EDT).[97] This is three calendar months less one day,

95 Which provides for the right to a fair trial (see also paras 1.24 and 17.9).
96 DR Regs 2004 regs 11(3)(c), 6 and 8.
97 ERA 1996 ss97 and 111.

eg, 31 January to 29 April. An employee can lodge an unfair dismissal claim after notice has been given but before the expiry of the notice, ie, the effective date of termination.[98] This also applies where the employee resigns, giving notice, and then claims constructive dismissal,[99] but does not apply where the dismisal arises on the expiry of a fixed-term contract.[100] In discrimination cases, a claim for discriminatory dismissal cannot be brought before the EDT as there are no parallel provisions in the SDA. Loss of earnings may, however, flow from any discrimination occurring during employment (see paras 18.47–18.48).

16.97   Most claims, including discrimination claims, except for equal pay and a redundancy payment,[101] must also be made within three months, though this period is likely to be extended to six months as the grievance procedure will normally apply.

16.98   An equal pay claim must be brought within six months of the end of the employment to which the claim relates – or nine months if the statutory dispute procedures apply.[102] This time limit cannot be extended. Where a woman works under a series of fixed term contracts in a stable employment relationship, time will usually run from the end of the last one.[103]

16.99   The period is generally six months for members of the armed forces because they must first use the internal redress procedure before bringing a claim. (See SDA 1975 s85(9A)–(10)).

Effect of DR Regs 2004

16.100 The DR Regs 2004 provide that normal time limits are extended by three months if the statutory GP (or, in some circumstances, the DDP) applies. This is intended to give the parties a chance to resolve any dispute before resorting to litigation.

16.101   However, an employee needs to be careful about making an assumption that time limits will automatically be extended in all cases. First, many claims are not covered by the procedures at all.

---

98   ERA 1996 s111(3).
99   ERA 1996 s97(4); *Presley v Llanelli BC* [1979] IRLR 381 EAT.
100 Unless notice is given to expire before the end of the fixed term contract.
101 ERA 1996 s145. The details are outside the scope of this book.
102 Time can be extended in limited circumstances, such as where the employer deliberately concealed information or where the claimant has a disability. EPA 1970 ss2(4), 2ZA.
103 *Preston v Wolverhampton Healthcare NHS Trust (No 2)* [2001] IRLR 237, HL.

Second, where there is an exception in the regulations, so that they do not apply, time will not be extended. Third, it may not be clear which, if either, procedure applies.

Time limit for claims where the GP applies

16.102 Where the grievance procedure applies, in order to give the parties time to try to resolve a grievance, DR Regs 2004 reg 15 extends the normal time limit[104] for lodging a claim by three months.[105] This applies where either a grievance has been raised or an inadmissible claim lodged within the original time limit, ie in the following situations:

a) the employee lodges a claim within the normal time limit (ie, three months, or six months in equal pay cases)[106] but it is inadmissible as s/he has not sent a Step 1 grievance. The tribunal will return the claim. The employee must re-submit the claim once s/he has sent the Step 1 grievance to the employer (which must be within one month from the expiry of the normal time limit) and wait 28 days;

b) where the employee has sent the Step 1 letter within the normal time limit but not waited 28 days. The tribunal will return the claim for the employee to wait 28 days and resubmit the claim;

c) where the employee sends the Step 1 grievance within the normal time limit and submits a claim within three months of the normal time limit.

16.103 The tribunal will still have discretion to extend time beyond the extra three months where it is just and equitable (in discrimination cases) or where, in other cases, it was not reasonably practicable to lodge the claim in time (see para 16.131 onwards).

---

104 'Normal time limit' under regulation 15 does not include the tribunal's power to extend on a just and equitable or reasonably practicable basis – see regulation 15(5).

105 In *J Singh t/a Rainbow International v Taylor* UKEAT/0183/06MAA, 27 June 2006, the EAT held that the extension of time under reg 15 means three months not three months less a day. Thus, where a claimant served a combined resignation and grievance on 30 June 2005 and lodged a claim on 20 December 2005 the claims was in time.

106 'Normal time limit' is defined as the time limit ignoring any discretion to extend it (eg just and equitable extension in discrimination cases).

Time limits for claims where DDP applies

16.104 In unfair dismissal cases, the time limit is extended by three months where:

a) the DDP applies, ie, in all dismissal cases (except constructive dismissal) unless an exception applies;

b) the employee presents a claim to the tribunal after the expiry of the three months from the effective date of termination EDT;

c) the employee had reasonable grounds for believing, when that time limit expired, that a dismissal or disciplinary procedure, whether statutory or otherwise (ie contractual), was being followed in respect of matters that consisted of or were included in the substance of the tribunal complaint.[107]

16.105 Thus, if the disciplinary procedure had been completed by the end of the three-month time limit for bringing an unfair dismissal claim, time is not extended. Where it is not clear whether the procedure will be complete at that time, the employee should be prepared to lodge the claim within three months. For example, if the EDT is on 4 March 2006, the normal time limit expires on 3 June 2006. If the DDP appeal is on 25 May 2006, the employer may or may not inform the employee of the outcome by the deadline of 3 June 2006. If it is known by then, there will be no extension of time as the procedure will have been completed by the expiry of the time limit.

Time limits for bringing a claim: where the dispute resolution procedures do not apply

16.106 Where the statutory dispute resolution regulations do not apply, so that time is not extended under regulation 15, the time limit for bringing a claim is three months less one day from the act complained of, though time may be extended in certain circumstances (see para 16.139 onwards). It is important to check whether the claim is included in Schedule 4 to the EA 2002, as this provides a definitive list of claims covered by the procedures. For example, the following 'parental rights' complaints are not included in Schedules 3 or 4 so time is not extended under the DR Regs 2004:

---

107 DR Regs 2004 reg 15(1)(a), (2).

a) refusal of paid time off for ante natal care (ERA 1996 ss55–57);
b) refusal of time off for dependants (ERA 1996 ss57A and 57B);
c) failure to pay an employee who is suspended from work on maternity grounds (ERA 1996 ss66–70);
d) postponement or refusal of parental leave (ERA 1996 ss76, 77, 80);
e) breach of flexible working procedure (ERA 1996 ss80F–80I); note, however, that if there is a claim for indirect sex discrimination the grievance procedure does apply;
f) breach of part-time workers regulations;
g) breach of fixed-term workers regulations;
h) equal treatment of pensions rule (Penions Act 1995 ss62–66).

16.107   By contrast, where the procedures are *treated* as having been complied with under various regulations[108] (see para 16.43 onwards) the procedures do apply and the statutory time limits may be extended. This would apply, for example, where the employee put in a grievance about disciplinary action being discriminatory (see para 16.55 onwards).[109]

When does time start to run

Dismissal claims

16.108   Where the employer dismisses a worker, time runs from the date the notice of dismissal expires and the employment ceases. The EAT held, in *British Gas Services Ltd v McCaull*,[110] that in discriminatory dismissal cases, individuals suffer a detriment as a result of discrimination when they find themselves out of work.[111]

16.109   In constructive dismissal cases the same principles apply as for an actual dismissal. Note that the SDA 1975 definition of 'dismissal' includes constructive dismissal.[112] In *Derby Specialist Fabrication Ltd v Burton*[113] the EAT held that a number of discriminatory acts amounted to a continuing act of discrimination and that the time limit ran from the date the employee accepted the employer's repu-

---

108   DR Regs 2004 regs 5, 7, 8, 9, 10 or 11.
109   DR Regs 2004 reg 7; note that failure to put in the grievance within these time limits means that the procedures are not treated as having been complied with.
110   [2001] IRLR 60, Keene J at para 25.
111   See also *Lupetti v Wrens Old House Ltd* [1984] IRLR 348.
112   SDA 1975 s81(1A).
113   [2001] IRLR 69.

diatory breach of contract and was dismissed. If there is a notice period it is unclear whether in discrimination cases the time limit runs from the resignation or the end of the employment. This is because unlike the ERA 1996, there is no provision in the SDA 1975 for a claim to be lodged during the notice period (see para 16.96).[114]

16.110   A common scenario is where a woman returns to work and finds that her job responsibilities have been taken away from her and she resigns some weeks or months later, the problems not having been resolved. It is safer to lodge the complaint for discrimination within three months of her return to work (or 6 months if the GP applies), even if she is still at work because arguably the discrimination, and indeed a dismissal, has taken place on her return to work. If she then resigns and works her notice period, she will need to lodge a further claim for dismissal after the contract has terminated and ask for the claims to be consolidated. She should put in a grievance at both times. In *Gledhill v Employment Service*[114] the employer's postponement of the woman's return after maternity leave was a continuing act which ended only when she returned to work.

16.111   If the employee does not put in a fresh claim, it is arguable that a claim for discriminatory refusal to allow the woman to return to the same job gives rise, in itself, to a claim for loss of earnings suffered *after* she resigns – without the need to put in a further claim – as this loss follows directly from the discrimination suffered (see para 18.47 onwards). However, the safest course is to put in a further claim, albeit one which is very similar to the previous one.

16.112   In many cases an employee will not feel able to litigate before s/he resigns so must take the small risk of being out of time. S/he will have a good argument for asking for an extension to the time limit (see para 16.131 onwards) even if s/he is considered out of time. S/he will also have to take the risk of facing a statutory bar in relation to the grievance procedure – unless s/he can show there is continuing discrimination.

Other discrimination claims

16.113 In discrimination cases, the critical date is the occurrence of the act, not the date the claimant was aware of it. In *Mensah v Royal College of Midwives*[115] the EAT said that 'An act occurs when it is done, not when

---

114   ET 2546/94.
115   17 November 1995, EAT (unreported).

you acquire knowledge of the means of proving that the act done was discriminatory'. However, knowledge is a factor relevant to the discretion to extend time (see below). For equal pay claims see para 16.98.

Continuing discrimination

16.114　If discrimination is continuing, time runs from the last act of discrimination. 'Any act extending over a period shall be treated as done at the end of that period.'[116] Similarly, a discriminatory contractual term is treated as extending throughout the duration of the contract so time does not start to run until it is removed or the contract comes to an end.

16.115　It is often not clear whether the discrimination is continuing or whether there is one act with continuing consequences. In *Owusu v London Fire and Civil Defence Authority*[117] the EAT held that an act extends over a period of time 'if it takes the form of some policy, rule or practice, in accordance with which decisions are taken from time to time'. Thus, a repeated failure to upgrade the claimant or allow him to act up at a higher grade was a continuing act, but a failure to promote on one occasion was not. A similar decision was reached by the Court of Appeal in *Rovenska v General Medical Council.*[118]

16.116　In *Hendricks v Commissioner of Police for the Metropolis*[119] the Court of Appeal gave a liberal interpretation to 'continuing discrimination', saying that the focus of the inquiry should be on whether there is 'an act extending over a period' as distinct from 'a succession of unconnected or isolated specific acts, for which time would begin to run from the date when each specific act was committed'. Thus the claimant must show an 'ongoing situation' or 'continuing state of affairs' in which incidents of discrimination were linked to one another. This is a wider test than showing a policy, rule, practice, scheme or regime, which the Court of Appeal said in *Hendricks* were only examples of when an act extends over a period and should not be treated as a complete and constricting statement of the indicators of an act extending over a period'.[120]

16.117　In *Cast v Croydon College*[121] Mrs Cast asked, on several occasions,

---

116　SDA 1975 s76(6)(b).
117　[1995] IRLR 574.
118　[1997] IRLR 367, CA.
119　[2003] IRLR 96, CA.
120　Mummery, para 52.
121　[1997] IRLR 318, CA.

to work part-time and was refused each time. The Court of Appeal held that the employer's refusal gave rise to a 'policy' and a discriminatory policy or regime pursuant to which decisions may be taken from time to time is an act extending over a period. It could be a policy even though not formal or in writing and even when confined to a particular post or role. The Court of Appeal further held that time started to run again from the date each of her requests was refused, having been reconsidered on each occasion by her employer. Thus, time does not start to run until the end of the period where:

a) there is an act extending over a time; or
b) there are repeated requests, which are considered again on each occasion and refused, the last refusal being the critical date; or
c) there is a 'policy' which continues beyond the last refusal.

16.118 Where the claimant complains of indirect sex discrimination after a refusal of flexible working having followed the procedure, time should run from the dismissal of the appeal (see para 12.55). If there was no appeal, time should run from the date of the refusal. Note that the grievance procedure does not apply where the claim is for breach of the flexible working procedure but it does apply where the claim is for discrimination arising out of the refusal including where the discrimination leads to a resignation which will be a constructive discriminatory dismissal.

16.119 It is for the claimant to prove that the incidents of discrimination are linked to each other and were evidence of a continuing discriminatory state of affairs covered by the concept of 'an act extending over a period'.

16.120 However, if there is any doubt about the time limit, it is always advisable for the claimant to lodge the claim as early as possible following the act complained of (ie, within three months), bearing in mind the obligation to comply with the grievance procedure if it applies, in which case the time limit is extended to six months.

Refusal of a job

16.121 It will be very difficult to argue that there is a continuing act where a job applicant complains that the refusal of a job offer is discriminatory. In *Tyagi v BBC World Service*[122] the CA drew a distinction between a job applicant and someone already in employment who

---

122 [2001] IRLR 465, CA.

had been denied access to promotion opportunities. A job applicant is not complaining about employment generally but the particular employment that is being offered whereas an employee may be complaining about a continuing failure to promote.

Omissions

16.122 A deliberate discriminatory omission is treated as done when the person decided on it.[123] In the absence of evidence to the contrary, an employer shall be taken to decide on a failure to act when:

a) it does an act inconsistent with doing the omitted act or;
b) if it has done no such inconsistent act, when the period expires within which it might reasonably have expected to do the omitted act if it was to be done.

16.123 Thus, the decision not to confer a benefit on a worker is treated as being done when the employer decided not to confer the benefit.[124] In the absence of evidence to the contrary, there is an assumption that a person decides on the discriminatory omission when they do an act inconsistent with the omitted act. The provisions are very similar to those relating to detriment (see para 6.126).

Example

16.124 For example, if there is a training programme running over a period of a year and an employee is not offered any training because she wants to take additional maternity leave (AML) and parental leave, the time limit would probably run from the end of the year, when it was clear that she was not going to be offered any training. On the other hand, if a woman is not promoted because she is on AML, time will run from the date that the employer decided not to promote her and promoted another employee instead.

Pre-review hearing

16.125 It is generally not appropriate for there to be a pre hearing review to determine if there is continuing discrimination or to consider points on time limits as this will involve considering all the alleged acts of discrimination and generally involve hearing substantial evidence, which will be duplicated at the main hearing.

---

123   SDA 1975 s76(6).
124   See *Swithland Motors plc v Clarke and others* [1994] ICR 231.

Detriment claims

16.126 Where a claim is made under ERA 1996 s47C or s47E, which is where an employee is subjected to a detriment for a reason relating to her pregnancy, childbirth, maternity, time off for maternity, other family leave or flexible working, they may make a complaint to an ET within three months (or six months where the grievance procedure applies):

- beginning with the date of the act or failure to act to which the complainant relates; or
- where that act or failure is part of a series of similar acts or failures, the date of the last of them; or
- within such further period as the ET considers reasonable in a case where it is satisfied that it was not reasonably practicable for the complainant to be presented before the end of the three months (or six months where the GP applies).[125]

Claim for breach of flexible working procedure

16.127 A complaint, which can only be brought on limited grounds (see para 12.70 onwards) must be brought within three months of:

a) the date on which the employee is notified of the employer's decision on the appeal; or
b) where there has been a breach of the requirements of the regulation, the date of the breach;[126] or
c) from the date of the failure or threat in relation to the right to be accompanied;[127] or
d) from the failure to permit a companion to take time off or pay them for it.[128]

16.128 The tribunal may extend time in the normal way, where it was not reasonably practicable for the complaint to have been brought within the three-month period.[129]

---

125 ERA 1996 s48(3).
126 ERA 1996 s80H(5).
127 Flexible Working Procedural Regs 2002 reg 15(2)(a).
128 FW Procedural Regs reg 14(7) applying TULRCA 1992 s171.
129 ERA 1996 s80H(5)(b). FW Procedural Regs 2002 reg 15(2)(b).

Claim for unlawful deduction of wages

16.129   This claim under the ERA 1996[130] must be made within three months of the last deduction of wages or six months if the GP applies.[131]

Breach of contract

16.130   Proceedings may be brought in an ET where there is a claim outstanding which arises at the end of the woman's employment, but the time limit for bringing a claim in the ET is only three months from the effective date of termination.[132] No claim for breach of contract can be made in the ET where the contract is continuing. There is a six-year time limit for bringing a claim for breach of contract in the county court.

Out of time claims

16.131   An application may be made to lodge a claim outside the time limit. The test is different under the ERA 1996 and SDA 1975.

16.132   Under the ERA 1996 (and TULRCA 1992) the tribunal can extend time: 'within such further period as the tribunal considers reasonable in a case where it is satisfied that it was not reasonably practicable for a complaint to be presented before the end of the period of three months'.

16.133   There is a different test for discrimination and part-timer or fixed-term contract discrimination claims where the test for extending time is whether 'in all the circumstances of the case, it [the tribunal] considers that it is just and equitable to do so'.[133]

Under the ERA 1996

16.134   Where the DDP procedures apply time will be extended for an unfair dismissal claim (including a discriminatory dismissal) by three months where the employee had reasonable grounds for believing,

---

130   ERA 1996 s13.
131   ERA 1996 s23 sets out the time limits for making a claim; where there is a series of deduction time runs from the last one (section 23(3)).
132   Employment Tribunals (Extension of Jurisdiction) (England and Wales) Order 1994 SI No 1623 reg 7.
133   SDA 1975 s76(5); Part-time Workers (Prevention of Less Favourable Treatment) Regulations (PTW Regs) 2000 SI No 1551 reg 8(3). Fixed-Term Employees (Prevention of Less Favourable Treatment) Regulations (FTW Regs) 2002 SI No 2034 reg 7(3).

when the normal time limit expired, that there is an ongoing disciplinary procedure (contractual or under the statutory scheme). Time will also be extended by three months where the grievance procedure applies (see paras 16.102–16.103).[134]

16.135   In addition, under the ERA 1996,[135] the ET has power to extend time to such further period as it considers reasonable in a case where it is satisfied that it was not reasonably practicable for a complaint to be presented within the three months (and where the claim is presented as soon as practically possible). The Court of Appeal have said that the question is whether it was 'reasonably feasible to present the complaint to the tribunal' in time.[136]

16.136   Examples where time has been extended include those where:

a) the claimant has a physical or mental illness, particularly where this occurs towards the end of the time limit;[137]
b) there are postal delays;[138]
c) the claimant was not aware of the right to complain and time limits;[139]
d) the claimant has been wrongly or inadequately advised;[140]
e) ignorance of a relevant fact, for example where the claimant has been made redundant and then discovers that someone else has been appointed to do the same job;[141]
f) where the employer has misrepresented any relevant matter.

16.137   Ignorance of rights or mistaken belief as to essential matters may be sufficient but not in every case. A young pregnant woman was allowed to claim out of time after a citizens advice bureau wrongly advised her. In *Marks & Spencer plc v Williams-Ryan*[142] a Citizens Advice Bureau had advised the claimant that she should exhaust the employers' internal procedure and did not refer to her right to complain to a tribunal nor about the time limits. By the time she received the result of her appeal, the time limit had expired. Other relevant circumstances included the fact that the employer's procedure

134   DR Regs 2004 reg 15.
135   ERA 1996 s111(2).
136   *Palmer and Saunders v Southend-on-Sea Borough Council* [1984] IRLR 119, CA.
137   *Schultz v Esso Petroleum Ltd* [1999] IRLR 488, CA.
138   *Consignia plc v Sealy* [2002] IRLR 624, CA.
139   *Walls Meat Co Ltd v Khan* [1978] IRLR 499, CA.
140   *Marks & Spencer plc v Williams-Ryan* [2005] IRLR 562.
141   See *Machine Tool Industry Research Association v Simpson* [1988] IRLR 212, CA.
142   [2005] IRLR 562.

referred to the right to go to a tribunal but did not refer to any time limits. The Court of Appeal said that the discretion to extend time under the ERA 1996 (s111(2)) should be given a 'liberal interpretation in favour of the employee'. Regard should be had to what, if anything, the employee knew about the right to complain to the tribunal and of the time limit for making such a complaint. Ignorance did not necessarily render it not reasonably practicable to bring a complaint in time. It was necessary to consider what the employee knew and what knowledge the employee should have had if they had acted reasonably in all the circumstances.[143]

16.138   Once the ET has found that it was not reasonably practicable for the complaint to be presented in time, it must then decide whether the claim was brought within a further reasonable period. There are no time limits on what is a further reasonable period[144] but the longer the delay, the less likely is it than an application for an extension will be granted. It is largely a question of fact for the tribunal to decide whether time should be extended.[145]

Under the SDA 1975

16.139   A court or tribunal may consider any complaint that is out of time if 'in all the circumstances of the case, it considers that it is just and equitable to do so'.[146] This gives the tribunal more flexibility to allow an out of time claim than under ERA 1996. Factors that will be taken into account include those set out above and, in addition:

- any prejudice that might be caused to the respondent if the claim is allowed to proceed (excluding the prejudice involved in having to defend them);
- the conduct of the respondent and claimant between the act of discrimination and the date of the claim;
- the health of the claimant (this might include for example, a difficult birth or subsequent post-natal illness);
- the length of time the claim is out of time;
- whether advice was sought and if so what advice was given;
- misunderstanding of the law;

---

143 Phillips at para 21 in which he approved the judgment in *Wall's Meat Co Ltd v Khan* [1978] IRLR 499 at p503.
144 *Marley (UK) Ltd and another v Anderson* [1994] IRLR 152, EAT.
145 *Palmer v Southend-on-Sea Borough Council* [1984] IRLR 119, CA.
146 SDA 1975 s76(5).

- the merits of the case;[147]
- any other relevant circumstance.[148]

16.140 In *Robertson v Bexley Community Centre*,[149] CA, the court held that the tribunal has a very wide discretion in determining whether or not it is just and equitable to extend time. It is entitled to consider anything that it considers relevant. However, the Court of Appeal added that time limits are exercised strictly in employment cases and there is no presumption that they should extend the time limit. The claimant must convince the tribunal that it is just and equitable to extend time. Finally, the Court of Appeal said that the exercise of discretion is the exception rather than the rule. Thus, claimants should argue such extension carefully and thoroughly, providing relevant evidence. Similarly, respondents arguing that they will be prejudiced by the delay because of lack of evidence or non availability of relevant witnesses should provide evidence of this to the tribunal.

16.141   In *Berry v Ravensbourne National Health Service Trust*,[150] it was held that relevant matters were:

- the date on which the claimant became aware of the event giving rise to the claim;
- the lapse of time between this date and presentation of the complaint; and
- the reasons for the delay.

16.142 In *London Borough of Southwark v Afolabi*[151] the claimant did not discover material which led to his claim until he inspected his file in connection with another discrimination complaint. The Court of Appeal held that the tribunal was not wrong to find that it was just and equitable to extend time even though the complaint was presented nearly nine years after the expiry of the time limit. However, the court said that the decision was heavily influenced by the fact that the employer provided no evidence of prejudice it would suffer in not being able to provide relevant documents or call witnesses able to give evidence about events that happened so long ago.[152] The Court of

---

147 *Hutchinson v Westwood Television Ltd* [1977] IRLR 69, EAT.
148 Ibid.
149 [2003] IRLR 434, CA.
150 [1993] ICR 871, EAT.
151 [2003] IRLR 220.
152 Gibson LJ said, 'it can only be in a wholly exceptional case that the ET could properly conclude that despite a delay of a magnitude anywhere approaching nine years it was just and equitable to extend time'.

Appeal also held that the tribunal was not wrong in failing to consider the matters listed in Limitation Act 1980 s33(3) provided that no significant factor had been ignored by the tribunal in exercising its discretion.

16.143   In *Chohan v Derby Law Centre*[153] a trainee solicitor received a letter from the Law Society on 23 April 2002 informing her that they received notification from her employers dated 22 March that her training contract had been terminated. There was no dispute that the time limit ran from 22 March (when the decision was made) though a solicitor advised her that it ran from the date she became aware of the letter of 23 April, ie 2 May and so she did not lodge her claim until 9 July 2002. The EAT held that the tribunal were wrong to find that it was not just and equitable to extend time. They held that wrong advice, or the existence of a claim against negligent solicitors, ought not to defeat a claim. Thus, time was extended. The EAT also held that failure to consider a significant factor, using the checklist under the Limitation Act, is an error of law. Thus, tribunals are advised to consider the check list though failure to do so will not be an error of law unless a singificant factor is omitted.

16.144   An extension of three years was allowed in *Mills and another v Marshall*.[154] The claimant presented a claim for discrimination three years after the European Court of Justice's (ECJ) decision in *P v S*[155] in which the ECJ held that discrimination against transsexuals was unlawful. The EAT held that the words 'just and equitable . . . could not be wider or more general', saying that the ET had to balance all the factors including, importantly and perhaps crucially, whether it was possible to have a fair trial. The discretion to extend time, said the EAT, is unfettered and may include a consideration of the date from which the complainant could reasonably have become aware of their right to present a worthwhile claim. The claim was therefore allowed.

16.145   In *BCC v Keeble*[156] the EAT held that it was 'just and equitable' to extend the time limit because the reason for the delay was the claimant's 'wholly understandable' mistaken understanding of the law. The EAT pointed out that the discretion under the SDA 1975 was very much wider than under the ERA 1996.[157]

153   [2004] IRLR 685, EAT.
154   [1998] IRLR 494, EAT.
155   *P v S and Cornwall County Council* [1998] IRLR 347, ECJ.
156   [1997] IRLR 336, EAT.
157   See also *Hawkins v Ball and Barclays Bank plc* [1996] IRLR 258.

16.146   In *Faulkner v Fuller Foods International plc*[158] the ET allowed an out of time claim because of the stress the applicant suffered after a miscarriage.

Late discovery of facts giving rise to new claim

16.147 In *Ali v Office of National Statistics*[159] during the discovery process or during the hearing the claimant discovered facts which gave rise to an indirect discrimination claim – in addition to his claims for direct discrimination and victimisation. The Court of Appeal (Waller LJ) said that:

> . . . where the appellant only discovered the facts on which he relies for bringing his indirect discrimination claim during the process of disclosure or during the hearing, it is inconceivable that an application to amend to add that claim as soon as it was discovered would have been refused. The fact that technically it was being brought out of time could not have been an answer, having regard to the appellant's ignorance.

16.148 It is always advisable to put in a claim in time to avoid any argument that it is out of time. However there is little to lose by lodging a claim out of time if there is good reason for the delay.

158 ET 64704/94, 1 March 1995 Leeds.
159 [2005] IRLR 201.

Employment tribunal procedure

Key points

- Early resolution of a dispute is advisable and should be considered by both parties.
- The procedure in tribunals is meant to be informal and accessible to litigants in person; unfortunately this is not always the case.
- Account should be taken of European law where this provides more favourable rights.
- Financial help may be available from a variety of sources (such as advice agencies, the Equal Opportunities Commission (EOC)) and parties should check if they have legal expenses insurance which generally covers legal costs in employment cases.
- An employer must provide written reasons for dismissal where this occurs during a woman's pregnancy or maternity leave.
- Claimants in discrimination and equal pay cases cases should serve on their employer a questionnaire asking questions about why they were treated unfavourably. Unreasonable delay or failure to reply may lead to the tribunal drawing an adverse inference.
- In dismissal cases claimants must mitigate their loss by seeking alternative work otherwise compensation is likely to be reduced.
- Except where there has been a dismissal, or the employer was contemplating dismissal, where the statutory grievance procedure applies, an employee must raise a written grievance and wait 28 days before lodging a claim.
- Employers must follow the statutory dismissal procedure when contemplating dismissal and before dismissing an employee.
- The claim and response *must* be on the prescribed forms and set out prescribed information. This includes the details of the claim including whether the discrimination is direct, indirect, harassment or victimisation.
- The respondent must lodge its response within 28 days of receiving the claim, unless before the deadline expires, it has the tribunal's permission to extend the time. Failure to do this may lead to a default judgment, in which case it cannot take part in the proceedings.
- Stages before the hearing include the power to ask for further

information, disclosure of documents, preparation of a bundle
for the hearing, exchange of witness statements and other
appropriate steps.

- The tribunal may hold a Case Management Conference in discrimination (and other) cases in order to agree the issues and
procedure.
- In discrimination claims the initial burden of proof is on the
claimant to show that it is more likely than not that there has
been discrimination, ie, show a prima facie case. The burden
then moves to the respondent to show that there has been no
discrimination at all.
- A claim can be withdrawn at any time by notifying the tribunal.
It cannot then be revived.
- Where a party has behaved vexatiously, abusively, disruptively
or otherwise unreasonably, or the bringing or conducting of
proceedings has been misconceived, the tribunal can order
costs against that party.
- There is a right to appeal, on a point of law, to the Employment
Appeal Tribunal (EAT).

Introduction

17.1   This chapter covers steps to be taken before lodging a claim with
the employment tribunal (ET) (such as the questionnaire procedure)
and the procedure in tribunals from lodging a claim through to
judgment with particular emphasis on claims covered in this book.
References to rules are to the Employment Tribunals (Constitution
and Rules of Procedure) Regulations (ETR Regs) 2004[1] Sch 1 (the
rules) unless otherwise stated. The statutory dispute resolution procedures[2] and time limits for bringing a claim are covered in chapter
16 though they are closely linked with the tribunal procedure so
should be considered together.

17.2   Most employment claims are started in the ET, with an appeal on a
point of law to the EAT, then the Court of Appeal (Court of Session in
Scotland) and finally the House of Lords. Any tribunal or court can

---

1   SI 2004 No 1861 which came into force on 1 October 2004. Similar changes were
made in Northern Ireland (Industrial Tribunal (Constitution and Rules of
Procedure) Regulations NI 2005 SI No 150.
2   Employment Act 2002 (Dispute Resolution) Regulations 2004 SI 2004 No 752.

refer a question of law to the European Court of Justice (ECJ).[3] This chapter is mainly concerned with employment tribunal procedure.

Early resolution of the dispute

17.3   Before deciding which is the appropriate right or claim and whether to proceed, workers should consider what they want to achieve and how far they are prepared to take any action, including legal proceedings. For example, employees whose priority is to keep their job and a good working relationship with the employer should think very carefully before taking proceedings or instructing a lawyer to act on their behalf. Inevitably, legal action or, in some cases, even taking out a grievance, is likely to lead to a deterioration in the employment relationship. Although the law protects workers from victimisation, compensation is often inadequate for the possible loss of a job, particularly as the complainant may not be able to get another suitable job on a comparable salary.

17.4   It is also important to consider what tribunal proceedings can achieve. For example, a priority for many employees is a good reference. The tribunal cannot order the employer to write the employee a reference in terms that are acceptable to the employee. This will only be achieved by negotiation and is often linked to a compromise agreement.[4]

17.5   In many situations the best outcome for both employer and employee is a speedy settlement as this achieves finality and avoids the uncertainty inherent in litigation, stress, legal costs and time-consuming preparation of the case. Thus, both employers and employee would be well advised to consider the strengths and weaknesses of a claim at an early stage and try and reach agreement if possible.

17.6   For example, a woman who has been offered a different job on her return from maternity leave should try to negotiate to get her old job back, unless the employment relationship has already been destroyed and she feels she cannot return (see para 15.23). Similarly, an employee wanting to work child-friendly hours should generally try to negotiate these with the employer and/or should put in an applica-

---

3   See rule 58.
4   However, it should be noted that increasingly employers are increasingly refusing to provide more than a standard reference giving start and finish dates and details of the job carried out.

tion under the flexible working procedure. An employer should seriously consider any application under the flexible working procedure as an unjustified refusal of flexible working may be indirect sex (or marital) discrimination (see chapter 13).

17.7   See chapter 16 for time limits. A table setting out the remedies for each claim is at para 18.12.

Employment tribunals

17.8   Employment tribunals have no powers other than those given to them by statute, eg, the Employment Rights Act (ERA) 1996, the Equal Pay Act (EPA) 1970, the Sex Discrimination Act (SDA) 1975 and the European Communities Act 1972 (see chapter 1). Tribunal decisions are persuasive but not binding on other tribunals. Appellate court decisions (EAT, CA, HL, ECJ) are binding.

17.9   The overriding objective of tribunals is to deal with cases justly which includes, so far as practicable, ensuring that the parties are on an equal footing, dealing with cases in ways proportionate to the complexity or importance of the issues, ensuring that a case is dealt with expeditiously and fairly and saving expense.[5] The parties must assist the tribunal in achieving these objectives. In addition, article 6 of the European Convention of Human Rights provides that there is a right to a 'fair and public hearing within a reasonable time by an independent and impartial tribunal established by law' (see para 16.91).[6]

17.10   The procedure in tribunals is meant to be informal and accessible to litigants in person. There are no strict rules of evidence and the ET has a wide power to regulate its own procedure.[7] Despite the intended informality, ET procedure is often technical, particularly where the parties are represented. Some tribunals are interventionist, in that they will explain the law and procedure and ask a lot of questions; others are not and expect the parties to present their case unaided. Where an unrepresented party or inexperienced representative is unsure of the procedure, or even the legal issues, it is worth seeking an explanation from the chairman.

---

5   ETR Regs 2004 reg 3.
6   For a summary of the effect of the ECHR and HRA in tribunals, see IDS Employment Law Brief 779, April 2005, p14.
7   Sch 1 rule 60; see rule 10 for the wide variety of orders the ET can make.

17.11   For those who have not previously been involved in tribunal proceedings it is advisable to go to the tribunal due to hear the case to watch another ET case to get an idea of what it is like and what to expect. Members of the public can attend most hearings.

European law and the Human Rights Act 1998

17.12   Tribunals must interpret UK law, where possible, in accordance with EU law. In some cases, where EU law is directly effective (eg, article 141 and claims under directives where the employer is an emanation of the state) it prevails over any inconsistent UK law (see para 1.23). In all cases, UK law should be interpreted, where possible, so as to be consistent with EU Law. Thus, if it appears that there is less favourable treatment on grounds of gender but no clear remedy under UK law, a worker should consider whether there is a claim under EU law. Where it appears that there is an inconsistency between EU and UK law or the meaning of EU law is not clear, a tribunal or court can refer a point of law to the ECJ to interpret it.

17.13   There is no freestanding right to make a claim under European law.[8] Any claim, if specifically relied on, should generally be included in the claim form, and it must be brought relying on the most appropriate UK law (referred to as the 'way in'). The 'way in' for a discrimination claim is through the SDA 1975 and for equal pay under the EPA 1970.[9] Any breach of the European Pregnant Workers Directive (PWD) should also probably be brought in conjunction with the ERA 1996. If in doubt, it is advisable to make claims in the alternative.

17.14   Tribunals must take into account the Human Rights Act (HRA) 1998 and any judgment of the European Court of Human Rights (ECHR).[10] Thus in *R v Secretary of State for the Home Department, ex p Simms*[11] Lord Hoffmann said:

> In the absence of express language or necessary implication to the contrary, the courts therefore presume that even the most general words were intended to be subject to the basic rights of the individual.

---

8   *Biggs v Somerset County Council* [1996] IRLR 203, CA.
9   *Alabaster v Barclays Bank plc (No 2)* [2005] IRLR 576, CA.
10 HRA 1998 s3 states that the obligation is to 'read and give effect' to convention rights.
11 [2000] 2 AC 115, at 131, HL.

17.15   Neither tribunals nor the EAT can make a declaration that any legislation is incompatible with the European Convention on Human Rights.[12]

Financial help and legal advice for individuals

17.16   Legal Services Commission (LSC) funding is not generally available for representation in ETs, though it may be in exceptionally complex cases. Legal help (the old 'green form' scheme) may cover the preparation of the case for those on a very low family income with little capital. LSC funding is available (for those whose income is within the income and capital limits) for an appeal to the EAT or to the higher courts, provided that the case has sufficient merit.

17.17   Unions often provide legal help for complainants, either through local branch officers or stewards or national officers and legal departments.

17.18   Law centres, Citizens Advice Bureaux or other advice agencies in the area may offer legal advice and/or representation (see appendix E).

17.19   CLS (Community Legal Service) Regional Directories provide information on legal advice and information services across the coutnry. Directories can be found in public libraries or advice centres, on the website www.clsdirect.org.uk and from the CLS Advice Line 0845 345 4345.

17.20   Working Families offers free legal advice on maternity rights and benefits to employees and employers, but is not able to provide legal representation. Some advisers and solicitors give free initial advice or will take a case on a 'no-win, no-fee' basis.

EOC/CEHR

17.21   The EOC, which is due to be replaced by the Commission for Equality and Human Rights (CEHR) in October 2007,[13] gives advice and will occasionally represent a claimant or provide financial assistance for a solicitor to assist with claims under the SDA 1975 or the EPA 1970.[14] It has no power to grant assistance for claims made solely under the

---

12   HRA 1998 s4, which gives some courts power to make a declaration of incompatibility, does not apply to employment tribunals nor the EAT.

13   The CEHR will combine the EOC, Disability Rights Commission (DRC) and eventually Commission for Racial Equality (CRE) as well as covering human rights.

14   SDA 1975 s75 to be repealed by the Equality Act 2006 from day to be appointed.

ERA 1996. However, most maternity-related ERA 1996 claims will also include a discrimination claim under the SDA 1975. Assistance may include giving advice (for example, on the merits, on drafting an ET1 or questionnaire), negotiating a settlement, and arranging for assistance or representation. A formal application for funding should be made where representation is sought. The EOC provide advice about legal rights and remedies on their website (see EOC website www.eoc-law.org.uk).

Legal expenses insurance

17.22 It is quite common for a mortgage, contents insurance or car insurance to include cover for legal expenses which covers the legal costs of bringing or defending proceedings. Any person considering litigation should check their mortgage and insurance policies to see if they have such cover.

17.23 Some insurance companies argue that tribunal claims are not 'proceedings'. This is wrong and should be challenged.[15] However, cover will often not be provided to advise in relation to the grievance procedure, but only when proceedings are about to be lodged.

17.24 An insured person has, by law, the right to choose his/her own solicitor though many insurance companies refuse to acknowledge this. The right to choose your own solicitor should be expressly acknowledged in the policy and it is an offence to deny the insured this right.[16]

Choosing a representative

17.25 Working Families, the EOC/CEHR, Citizens Advice Bureaux, Law Centres and other advice agencies may be able to help with names of local advisers or solicitors who specialise in maternity and parental rights. It is worth travelling to find someone with expertise, as

---

15 See *Quaza v Quaza* [1974] ER 424 where Lord Justice Ormrod said that 'the phrase "judicial proceedings" implies some form of adjudication and some kind of order or accord or some other personal body acting in a judicial capacity'. Tribunal proceedings clearly fall into this category and so are covered by insurance.

16 Insurance Companies (Legal Expenses Insurance) Regulations 1990 SI No 1159 reg 6 provides that 'where, under a legal expenses insurance contract, recourse is had to a lawyer . . . to defend represent or serve the interests of the insured in any enquiry or proceedings, the insured shall be free to choose that lawyer'. Infringement amounts to an offence under the Insurance Companies Act 1992.

maternity and parental rights are not an easy area of law and many advisers and solicitors are not familiar with it.

Written statement of reasons for dismissal

17.26   An employer is obliged to provide a written statement about reasons for dismissal where an employee is dismissed either during her pregnancy or where the employee's maternity or adoption leave ends with dismissal.[17] Employees dismissed in other circumstances, who have been employed for a year, can request such a statement.[18] A complaint that written reasons were either not given or were inadequate or untrue can only be considered by the ET if it is made at the same time as an unfair dismissal complaint.[19] A written statement is admissible in proceedings.[20]

Written statement of reason for differential treatment of part-time workers

17.27   Where a part-time worker is not given pro rata rights with a comparable full-time worker, s/he can ask for a written statement of reasons. The employer must reply within 21 days and the statement is admissible in proceedings (see para 14.111).[21] Where the employer deliberately and without reasonable excuse fails to provide a statement or the statement is evasive or equivocal, the tribunal may draw any inference it considers just and equitable including one that the employer has infringed the regulations.[22]

Questionnaire procedure

17.28   Questionnaires, which can be served only in discrimination and equal pay claims, are usually very important. In cases under SDA 1975 s74 and EPA 1970 s7B (but not under the ERA 1996) the employee can ask the employer any question relevant to the alleged discrimination or pay inequality, which may include matters of

---

17   ERA 1996 s92(4), (4A).
18   ERA 1996 s92(1)(2),(3).
19   ERA 1996 s93. Where an ET upholds the complaint it may make a declaration and still make an award of two weeks' pay.
20   ERA 1996 s92(5).
21   Part-time Workers (Prevention of Less Favourable Treatment) Regulations (PTW Regs) 2000 SI No 1551 reg 6.
22   PTW Regs 2000 reg 6(2),(3).

evidence. There are standard forms which can be filled in with appropriate questions, though it is not essential to use the standard form.[23] The purpose of this procedure is to help workers decide if they should start proceedings, and, if so, to help them present their claim in the most effective way. If the questionnaire is served before a claim is lodged, the information required in paragraph 1 and 2 should be the same as that contained in the claim. If the claim has been lodged it is sufficient to refer to the claim.

17.29　The questionnaire must be served by delivering or posting it to the respondent or its solicitor (or appropriate representative). There is apparently no provision for faxing or emailing the questionnaire and some employers object to such service.

17.30　The questions and replies are admissible as evidence provided the questions were served on the employer at any time up to three months from the act of discrimination under the SDA 1975 or within any extension of the normal time limit provided for by regulation 15 of the Dispute Resolution Regulations (DR Regs) 2004. Thus, if the time limit for lodging a claim is extended by three months under the regulations, the time limit for serving a questionnaire will also be extended in the same way. The time limit under the EPA is any time after 6 April 2003 and ending on the day before a complaint is presented to an ET.[24]

17.31　If the questionnaire is sent after proceedings have been commenced whether under the SDA or EPA, it must be served within 21 days of their commencement, otherwise the permission of the ET is required. An application to the tribunal should be made as soon as possible, giving reasons for it, and attaching a copy of the draft questionnaire. There is also a procedure which allows either party to request further information from the other (see para 17.92).

17.32　If there is time, before the expiry of the time limit for bringing a claim, it is worth serving a questionnaire before bringing a claim. This is particularly useful when the grounds for the discrimination or equal pay claim are not clear.

17.33　It is possible, with leave of the ET, to serve another questionnaire if, after receiving a reply to the first, further questions need to be

---

23　Sex Discrimination (Questions and Replies) Order 1975 SI No 2048. Equal Pay (Questions and Replies) Order 2003 SI No 722.
24　DR Regs reg 17 amended para (a) of article 5 of the Sex Discrimination (Questions and Replies) Order. Equal Pay (Questions and Replies) Order 2003 art 3.

asked. The EAT has approved this, saying it is a 'sensible and necessary part of the procedure'.[25]

17.34   If the employer deliberately or without reasonable excuse fails to reply to the questions within eight weeks[26] or is evasive or equivocal, the ET can draw any inference it thinks appropriate, including that the employer has discriminated unlawfully.[27] *Igen Ltd v Wong*[28] the Court of Appeal pointed out that inferences could be drawn from an evasive or equivocal reply to a questionnaire or any other questions that fall within SDA 1975 s74(2). Failure by the tribunal to consider the questionnaire and replies is a breach of the guidelines laid down by the Court of Appeal in *Igen*, which are now commonly adopted by tribunals and higher courts.

17.35   If the employer refuses to reply to a question in the questionnaire, it may be possible to ask questions again in a request for further information (see para 17.33). Although some tribunals say this is not appropriate, this is arguably wrong. In particular, if there is no reply to the questionnaire there may be no other way of acquiring the statistics that may be necessary to prove an indirect discrimination claim (see chapter 13).

17.36   Any relevant questions can be asked. However, if too many questions or irrelevant questions are asked, the respondent may not reply saying that the questions are oppressive. If the ET accepts this it may refuse to draw an inference The questions depend on the nature of the case, but in a pregnancy maternity claim, for example, it would be useful to ask about:

- the reasons why the woman was dismissed, who made the decision and when;
- details of other employees dismissed in similar circumstances;
- what procedure should have been followed and whether it was;
- how the work of the claimant is now being done, by whom and the qualifications and experience of the replacement employee;
- pay and terms and conditions of other workers doing like or equal work.

17.37   The tribunal should take account of any inconsistencies in the questionnaire. In *Hinks v Riva Systems and another*[29] the EAT criticised the

25   *Carrington v Helix Lighting Ltd* [1990] IRLR 6 EAT.
26   SDA 1975 s74(2), (2A). Equal Pay (Quesstions and Replies) Order 2003 art 4.
27   SDA 1975 s74(2)(b). EPA 1970 s7B(4).
28   [2005] IRLR 258, CA.
29   EAT 501/96.

ET for failing to take account of inconsistencies. A sample question-naire can be found in appendix B.

Contemporaneous notes

17.38 Employees and employers should make contemporaneous notes of all relevant events and discussions as they happen, including meet-ings and conversations, and keep the original documents. These can be used in the tribunal to support the claim or response. A copy will have to be sent to the other party as part of the disclosure process so legal advice should not be included in these notes as this is privileged.

Letter before lodging a claim

17.39 Before issuing proceedings, it is usually advisable to write a letter to the employer setting out the broad nature of the claim. It is important that the information contained in the letter is accurate and com-prehensive in every respect, as it may be used at the hearing to high-light inconsistencies in the claim. An employer should reply in some detail dealing with the allegations also making sure that the informa-tion is accurate and comprehensive.

17.40 If re-employment or reinstatement is sought in an unfair dis-missal claim, the employer should be informed as soon as possible so as to try and avoid the respondent employing a replacement (see para 18.26 onwards). It should also be included in the ET1.

Duty to mitigate

17.41 In recruitment and dismissal cases, the claimant should take reason-able steps to find alternative employment otherwise the compensa-tion will generally be reduced (see para 18.106). Evidence of such steps will be required, so it is important to keep a record of job applications, interviews, visits to the job centre and any other meas-ures taken to find work. The costs of taking such steps are recoverable (provided that evidence is available) (see para 18.36).

Initial steps in bringing a claim

17.42 The sequence is usually as follows:

- Where the statutory grievance procedure (GP) applies (see chapter

16), lodge Step 1 grievance within three months of the act complained of (or at most four months – unless it is an equal pay claim when it is seven months).

- Employee serves questionnaire (which may be served before or after the claim) – see para 17.28 onwards.
- Employer replies to questionnaire within eight weeks.
- Lodge claim within three or six months (six or nine months for equal pay claims) depending on whether statutory dispute procedures apply.
- Response to claim to be lodged by employer within 28 days of receipt of claim.
- Request by either party for further information (or further and better particulars) of the claim or response.
- Disclosure of documents.
- Preparation and agreement of the tribunal bundle.
- Exchange of all witness statements.

How to apply: claim form (ET1)

17.43　All claims referred to in this book (except breach of contract claims while the employee is still employed[30] and some claims in respect of maternity pay) must be lodged with:

- the employment tribunal office specified on the ET1 form for the postal district concerned; or
- the Office of Industrial and Fair Employment Tribunal in Northern Ireland.

17.44　Since 1 October 2005 both claimant and respondent *must* use the forms prescribed by the tribunal, otherwise the claim or response will be returned by the ET with an explanation why it has been rejected and with a prescribed form.[31]

17.45　The claim form can be obtained from a tribunal office or from the

---

30　Breach of contract claims must be brought in the county court during the course of employment and can be brought there, as well as the tribunal, after the end of the employment. Tribunals can only award a maximum of £25,000.

31　Rule 3(1). In *(1) Butlins Skyline Ltd (2) Mr Smith v Miss Beynon* UKEAT/0042–0045/06/DA the tribunal rejected the employer's response as it was not in the correct form. A second attempt was rejected because it could not be scanned and the respondents were barred from taking part in proceedings. The EAT held that the tribunal's refusal of a review (on the basis that there was no decision involved) was wrong and the response was allowed to proceed. The rejection of the response was reviewable and appealable.

website. It must be lodged by post, fax, email (or completed online at www.employmenttribunals.gov.uk) with the ET local to the employee's place of work. The claim must arrive at the ET by the expiry of the time limit (see chapter 16). The onus is on the claimant to check if it has arrived though email often generates an automatic reply showing that it has been received. If the claimant does not receive a response within a week, or earlier if the time limit is about to expire, s/he should check it has been received.

What the claim must contain

17.46 The ET1 must contain the following information:

- the claimant's name and address (rule 1(4)(a)(b));
- the respondent's name and address (rule 1(4)(c)(d));
- details of the claim (rule 1(4)(e));
- whether or not the claimant is or was an employee of the respondent (rule 1(4)(f));
- if the claimant is an employee, whether or not the claim includes a complaint that the respondent has dismissed the claimant or has contemplated doing so (rule 1(4)(g));
- if the claimant is an employee, where the statutory grievance procedure applies (so not where the claim is *only* that the respondent dismissed or contemplated dismissal), whether or not the claimant has raised the subject matter of the claim with the respondent in writing at least 28 days prior to presenting the claim to an ET office, and if not, why not (rule 1(4)(h)(i)).[32]

17.47 It is important that the prescribed forms are used and that the relevant boxes are completed. Rule 3(2)(a) provides that where a form is incomplete or incorrectly completed, the tribunal may reject it. However, the EAT have adopted a very lenient approach to avoid what they see as technicalities and have overturned a number of restrictive tribunal decisions rejecting claims for being incomplete.

17.48 For example, in *Grimmer v KLM Cityhopper UK*[33] the tribunal chair refused to admit a claim which was described as being for 'flexible working'. The EAT said:

> The test for 'details of the claim' emerges as being whether it can be discerned from the claim as presented that the claimant is

---

32 Rule 1(4)–(6).
33 [2005] IRLR 596, para 15.

complaining of an alleged breach of an employment right which falls within the jurisdiction of the Employment Tribunal. It follows that if that test is met there is no scope for either the Secretary or a Chairman interpreting 'details of the claim' as being 'sufficient particulars of the claim'. It was not for the Secretary or the Chairman to 'determine that it was appropriate to deny Mrs Grimmer access to the Employment Tribunal by refusing to accept her claim on the basis that she had not provided "required information" in the form of "details of the claim" '.

17.49   The EAT was very critical of the rules stressing the importance of the overriding objective of dealing with a case justly and ensuring the parties are on an equal footing.[34] Judge Prophet also questioned whether a rigid application of the rules might result in a breach of article 6 of the European Convention on Human Rights.

17.50   Similarly, in *Richardson v U Mole*[35] the EAT overruled the tribunal's rejection of a claim because the claimant had not expressly stated that he had been an employee, though he had given his dates of employment. The EAT said again that rules were not intended to drive away a claimant so that by the time the completely immaterial defect was corrected the claimant was out of time. The EAT approved comments made in *Grimmer* saying that 'there ought to be, and is, an overriding objective of encouraging dealing with cases justly and fairly, such that the tribunals ought to be in the business of ensuring that that is the case, rather than driving possibly meritorious claimants or indeed respondents from the judgment seat'.[36]

17.51   Similar rules have been applied to respondents where the response has been late or the form incorrectly completed and the respondent has applied for a review or appealed the tribunal's decision.[37]

---

34 Reg 3.
35 [2005] IRLR 668; [2005] ICR 1664.
36 See also *Mark Warner Ltd v Aspland* [2006] IRLR 87 where the EAT held that a claim could proceed even though the claimant did not state that she had raised a grievance 28 days before lodging the claim. Reference to a letter of grievance in the details of claim was sufficient as it satisfied the requirements of rule 1(4)(h). (See para 17.46).
37 See, for example, *NSM Music Ltd v Mr J H Leefe* UKEAT/0663/05/CK where the EAT held that where a respondent has been debarred from taking part in proceedings it may request reasons for the purpose of an application for review. Other decisions include *Butlins Skyline Ltd* (see note 31), *British School of Motoring v Fowler* UKEAT/0059/06ZT, *Maroak v Cromie* [2005] IRLR 535, where the response was lodged 44 minutes late so rejected, but a review was allowed on appeal.

17.52   References to dismissal in the rules (see above para 17.46) do not include constructive dismissal as the GP, not DDP (disciplinary and dismissal procedures), applies to constructive dismissal. Thus, where the claim is only for constructive dismissal employees must state whether they have raised a grievance.

17.53   Where the grievance procedure applies to any part of the claim, the tribunal cannot register the claim if it considers that either:

- no Step 1 grievance has been raised;
- that the employee has not waited 28 days after raising the grievance and before lodging a claim; or
- the grievance was not raised within one month after the end of the orginal time limit or such further time as is just and equitable in discrimination cases (see paras 16.78–16.79).[38]

17.54   The claim will be sent back to the claimant with reasons for its rejection, and where there has been a breach of the statutory GP, giving details of the time limit that applies and the consquences of failing to comply. If the employee has failed to raise a grievance and wait 28 days, provided the ET is aware of this it will allow a further three months to complete these steps (see para 16.75 onwards). If there is more than one claim and a failure to wait 28 days in respect of some claims, the ET will not hear these claims and the claimant will have to re-submit the claims. This entitles the parties to a further hearing. See *Excel Management Ltd v Lumb* ET 0121/06/2807, 28 July 2006.

Name of claimant(s) and respondent(s)

17.55   The first two sections require information about the name and address of the parties. Two or more claimants may present their claims in the same documents if the facts are the same.[39] More than one party may be named as a respondent.

17.56   An **employer** may be directly liable or alternatively will be vicariously liable for discrimination carried out by a worker (whether an employee or self-employed) in the course of his/her employment, irrespective of whether the discrimination was done with the

---

38   Rule 1(8) ie there has been a breach of s32(2)–(4) (see para 16.85).
39   Rule 1(7).

employer's knowledge or approval.[40] 'In the course of employment' is to be interpreted very broadly.[41] The employer has a defence if it has not itself carried out the act of discrimination and it can prove that it took such steps as were reasonably practicable to prevent the discrimination.[42] The employer should always be named. If there is any doubt about the identity of the employer, it is advisable to name all the alternatives and seek clarification about the identity of the correct respondent (see paras 2.15–2.20 for liability of others apart from the employer).

Liability of employees

17.57   An **individual** who aids an unlawful act will be personally liable under the SDA 1975 and an employee or agent who is responsible for the discrimination 'in the course of his employment' will be deemed to aid the discrimination and will be liable even where the employer has a defence.[43] Thus, a claim can be brought against both employer and employee. Compensation may be awarded against an individual as well as the employer.[44]

Liability of principals

17.58   Principals are liable for the discriminatory acts of their agents. The relationship between principal and agent arises where one person (the principal) consents to another person (the agent) acting on his/her behalf. Where an agent has authority (express or implied) and whether given before or after the event) to act for the principal, both the principal and the agent will be liable for the discriminatory acts of the agent (see para 2.16).[45]

17.59   It is important to complete the third section accurately (see sample below).

---

40   SDA 1975 s41.
41   See *Jones v Tower Boot Co Ltd* [1997] IRLR 168, CA.
42   SDA 1975 s41(3).
43   SDA 1975 s42.
44   See *Gilbank v Miles* where the manager was held to be personally liable for colleagues' bullying and ordered to pay £25,000 for injury to feelings [2006] IRLR 538, CA (see para 2.18).
45   SDA 1975 s41(2).

Sample form (box 3)

3.1*	Are you, or were you, an employee of the respondent? If 'Yes' please now go straight to section 3.3. *This must be completed as the GP and DDP applies to employees.*	Yes [**x**] No [ ]
3.2	Are you, or were you, a worker providing services to the respondent? If 'Yes' please now go straight to section 4. If 'No' please now go straight to section 6. *The GP and DDP do not apply to workers claiming discrimination, unlawful deduction of wages etc.*	Yes [ ] No [ ]
3.3*	Is your claim, or part of it, about a dismissal by the respondent? If 'No' please go straight to section 3.5. *If the claim is not about dismissal, then the GP will apply to employees, so they must show they have followed the GP.*	Yes [**x**] No [ ]
3.4*	Is your claim about anything else, in addition to the dismissal? If 'No' please now go straight to section 4. If 'Yes' please answer questions 3.5 to 3.7 about the non-dismissal aspects of your claim *If the claim is only about dismissal, the GP does not apply but if there are other claims employees must show they have followed the GP*	Yes [**x**] No [ ]
3.5*	Have you put your complaint in writing to the Respondent?[46] Yes [**x**] Please give the date you put it to them in writing No [ ] *Unless the claim is only about dismissal the employee must show s/he has raised a grievance and waited 28 days before lodging a claim.*	**4 / 6 / 06**

46 Where there are a number of claims made, the claimant should list each of the claims and how the grievance procedure has been followed or not, as the case may be, on the form, for example using the box at section 3.7. The form is badly designed but claimants are advised to provide this information even though space is not provided on the printed form.

If 'No' please now go straight to section 3.7

3.6*	Did you allow at least 28 days between the date you put your complaint to the respondent and the date you sent us the claim?	Yes [x] No [ ]

If 'Yes' please now go straight to section 4

3.7*	Please explain why you did not put your complaint in writing to the respondent or, if you did, why you did not allow at least 28 days before sending us your claim. (In most cases, it is a legal requirement to take these procedural steps. Your claim will not be accepted unless you give a valid reason why you did not have to meet the requirement in your case. If you are not sure, you may want to get legal advice). *The employee will need to show that one of the exceptions applies, for example where it was not practicable for them to commence the procedure or where there has been harassment and it may result in further harassment.*	

* = information must be provided

17.60   Box 4, which is not mandatory, requires information about the dates of employment, details of job, pay and if notice pay has been paid.

17.61   Box 5 requires details of whether there is a claim for unfair dismissal or constructive dismissal. It requests details of whether the claimant has got another job, when it started and the employee's pay.

17.62   Box 6 requires details of any claim for discrimination. If the claim is for ordinary unfair, automatically unfair and discriminatory dismissal, it is advisable to set out the details in one box and cross refer to the other box, so it is clear that the claim is for both unfair and discriminatory dismissal.

17.63   Boxes 7, 8 and 9 require information as to whether there are other complaints, including redundancy payments, other payments (such as unpaid wages, holiday, notice pay).

17.64   The main incidents on which the claimant will rely should be set out, including discrimination even if it occurred outside the time limit, as it may be taken into account (see para 17.134). In maternity cases it is often advisable to make a claim under UK law (ERA 1996,

SDA 1975 and possibly EPA 1970 (if it concerns a contractual matter)), under EU law if it appears that this may provide more extensive protection (eg, ETD, PWD, PLD, PTWD and article 141) and for breach of contract (see page 671). A sample ET1 can be found in appendix B.

17.65   It is important to set out on the form all the relevant facts, including background material relevant to the claim, and the nature of the claims (including those under EU law and the HRA 1998) but it is not necessary to quote from the statute.

17.66   In a discrimination claim, the claimant should make it clear whether the claim is for direct discrimination, indirect discrimination, harassment and/or victimisation and set out supporting facts. Referring only to 'discrimination' may not be sufficient unless the facts make it clear what type of discrimination is claimed.[47]

17.67   In *Housing Corporation v Bryant*[48] the Court of Appeal held that the claimant's failure to refer, in her unfair dismissal claim, to victimisation prevented her from amending the claim to pursue the victimisation claim (see also para 17.84). However, where the facts make it clear that the claimant had been dismissed because of her pregnancy, the tribunal should treat the claim as one for unfair dismissal (provided the employee had been employed for one year), automatically unfair dismissal and sex discrimination because all these claims arise from the same facts.

17.68   If an amendment to add a further claim is later required it is more likely to be allowed if the facts set out in the ET1 support it (see para 17.84 on amendments).

17.69   Sometimes the strength of a claim will only become apparent after documents have been disclosed or the replies to the questionnaire received and it may be necessary to elucidate or apply to amend the claim. A claim can also be withdrawn if it becomes clear that it has no chance of success, although there is a risk that costs will be awarded if the withdrawal is late and the tribunal find that the claimant has behaved unreasonably (see para 17.138 onwards). However, a claim should not be made unless it is genuine. A very weak claim is likely to undermine the strength of the stronger claims.

17.70   Despite the prescriptive nature of the requirements under the rules for set information, the EAT has, in two cases, made it very clear that a tribunal (or chairman) should consider it a very serious step to

---

47 *Ali v Office for National Statistics* [2005] IRLR 201 (see para 17.89).
48 [1999] IRLR 123, CA.

deny a claimant or respondent the opportunity of having their employment rights issues resolved by the tribunal (see para 17.48 onwards).[49] The clear message from the EAT is that tribunals should interpret the rules in accordance with the overall interests of justice to enable claims to be heard.

17.71   Where a claim or response is rejected, the affected party can apply for a review of the decision under rule 34 on the basis that the decision was wrongly made as a result of an administrative error or the interests of justice require it (see *Richardson* para 17.50).

The employer's response: the ET3

17.72   The ET will send a copy of the ET1 to the employer. The employer has 28 days from receipt to submit its response (the ET3) to the tribunal;[50] if it is not on the prescribed form it will be returned.[51] The employer can apply for an extension of time but this must be done within the 28 days and the application must explain the grounds.[52] Despite this, in one case the EAT ordered that a response lodged 44 minutes late because of a computer failure should be accepted even though there had been no application to extend time within the 28 days.[53] The tribunal shall only extend the time limit if satisfied that it is just and equitable to do so.[54]

17.73   The response should set out:

- the respondent's full name and address;
- whether or not the respondent intends to resist the application; and
- the grounds on which the respondent intends to resist the claim.[55]

17.74   It should contain details of why the claim is contested, making sure that all facts are correct. In particular, it should make it clear whether there has been any breach of the grievance procedure.

---

49 *Grimmer v KLM Cityhopper UK* [2005] IRLR 596 and *Richardson v U Mole* note 35.
50 Rule 4(1).
51 Rule 6(1) with an explanation and with a prescribed response form.
52 Rule 4(4) where a party is legally represented, the representative must provide prescribed information to the claimant (see rule 11, which is set out in para 17.80).
53 See *Moroak t/a Blacke Envelopes v Cromie* [2005] IRLR 535 which sets out the test to be applied.
54 Rule 4(4).
55 Rule 4(3).

17.75   If the response does not contain all the relevant information or is outside the time limit, it will be referred to a chairman to decide whether it should be accepted.[56] If it is rejected, the parties will be informed with reasons. The respondent can request that the rejection be reviewed.

17.76   Where the time limit for responding has passed, the tribunal may then issue a default judgment.[57] This means that the respondent will generally not be able to take any part in the proceedings except to request a review of the judgment, be called as a witness and other limited matters. It is therefore very important that the response is lodged in time and contains the required information. Despite this rule the EAT have held that a respondent can participate in a remedies hearing even though it did not submit a response and a default judgment was issued (see *(1) D & H Travel and (2) Henderson v Foster* UKEAT 0226/06/MAA, 2 August 2006. The details relating to default judgments are outside the scope of this book.[58]

17.77   The respondent's response will then be sent to the claimant.

ACAS

17.78   All claims are sent to ACAS (Advisory Conciliation and Arbitration Service), who have a duty to conciliate and should contact the parties as a matter of course. Since 1 October 2004 there are different conciliation periods according to the type of claim. During this period a hearing will not be fixed, though there may be pre-hearing reviews and case management discussions. The periods are as follows:

a)   a short conciliation period of seven weeks; this applies, for example, to right to time off and renumeration for antenatal care, failure to pay remuneration while suspended on maternity grounds;

b)   a standard conciliation period of 13 weeks; this applies, for example, to unfair dismissal claim and all claims not covered by the claims covered by a) and c));

c)   no fixed conciliation period; this applies to all discrimination and

---

56   Rule 6(3).
57   See rules 8 and 9; a default judgment may determine liability and remedies or liability only (rule 8(3)).
58   See EAT decisions *Moroak t/a Blakes Envelopes v Cromie* [2005] IRLR 535, *Pendragon t/a CD Bramall Bradford v Copus* [2005] ICR 1671; *Pestle and Mortar v Turner* EAT 0652/05; *Sodexho Ltd v Gibbons* [2005] IRLR 836.

equal pay claims.[59] If there is no fixed period for one of the claims on the ET1 there will be no fixed period for them all.

17.79   The details of these provisions are outside the scope of this book (but see the ACAS website: www.acas.org.uk).

Stages before the hearing

Procedure for applying for any orders: rule 11

17.80   At any stage of the proceedings a party may apply for an order to be issued, varied or revoked (such as one that the other party disclose documents) or request a case management discussion (CMD) or pre-hearing review (PHR) (see para 17.114). The following requirements apply:[60]

1) the application must be made at least ten days before the hearing at which it is to be considered unless it is not reasonably practicable to do so or the tribunal considers it in the interests of justice that there be shorter notice;[61]

2) the application must be in writing to the tribunal and include the case number and the reasons for request. If the request is for a CMD or PHR it must identify any orders sought;

3) an application for an order must explain how the order would assist the tribunal;

4) where a party is legally represented (apart from requests for witness orders) it must, when applying to the tribunal, provide all other parties with the following information in writing and confirm to the tribunal that it has been provided:

   a) details of the application and reasons why it is sought;

   b) notification that any objection by that other party must be sent to the tribunal within seven days of receiving the application or before the date of the hearing (whichever is earlier);

   c) notification that any objection must be copied to the tribunal and all other parties.

17.81   Where a party is not legally represented, the tribunal will provide the above information.

---

59   Rule 22.
60   Rule 11.
61   Rule 11(2).

17.82   The chairman may also make orders without consultation with the parties though must give them the opportunity of challenging the order.[62]

Consequences of failing to comply with an order

17.83   Where a party fails to comply with an order the tribunal may make a costs order or (at a PHR or full hearing) strike out the whole or part of the claim or response.[63] Any order may provide that unless there is compliance with the order the claim or response may be struck out on the date of non-compliance without further consideration or the need to give notice or hold a PHR or full heairng. Thus, it is important for both parties to comply with tribunal orders within the timescale given. If it is difficult to do so within the time given application should be made to the tribunal to extend time – complying with rule 11. In practice it is unusual for a tribunal to strike out a claim.

Amendment

17.84   Where the substance of the claim can be found in the claim, albeit not in the right place, it is arguable that an amendment is not required as all the tribunal needs to do is attach the right label to the facts to identify the cause of action. If in doubt it is, however, advisable to apply for an amendment, particularly if the time limit has not expired, in order to be sure that all claims are included. Alternatively, a claimant could write to the tribunal with a list of claims which s/he asserts are set out in the ET1 and request confirmation that this is correct. Ultimately it is for the tribunal hearing the case to decide if a particular claim has been included.

17.85   Either before or at the hearing, the ET can allow amendments, which may either change the basis of the claim, from say unfair dismissal to discrimination, or add discrimination as a new claim. It is likely to be allowed only if the facts set out in the claim would also give rise to the further claim so that it is primarily a 'labelling' exercise. A tribunal is more likely to allow an amendment if the claim is not out of time. However, if the time limit is about to expire it may be simpler to lodge a further claim and ask for the claims to be combined. If the complaint concerns facts that arose after the previous claim, a further claim should be made in any event.

62   Rule 12.
63   Rule 13.

17.86　Since the implementation of the statutory Dispute Resolution Regs 2004, claimants are unlikely to be able to amend claims unless they have raised a grievance within three months (maximum four months; six months, maximum seven, for equal pay claims) of the act complained of, subject to the just and equitable power to extend time (see para 16.102).

17.87　The relevant guidelines relating to amendments are set out in *Cocking v Sandhurst (Stationers) Ltd*,[64] and *Selkent Bus Co Ltd v Moore*,[65] where the EAT held that the discretion should be exercised consistently with the requirements of 'relevance, reason, justice and fairness' and the tribunal should 'balance the injustice and hardship of allowing the amendment against the injustice and hardship of refusing it'. The following issues are relevant:

- did the original claim comply with the rules for presenting claims and was it presented in time?[66] If not, there is no power to amend and a new claim must be presented;
- the tribunal is likely to amend the name of a respondent if the claimant has made a genuine mistake or the position is unclear;
- whether hardship or injustice would be caused to either party by granting or withholding permission to amend;
- if the facts in the original claim are sufficient for the amended claim so the respondent will not be taken by surprise an amendment is more likely to be allowed. This could cover a situation where a claim is for unfair dismissal but it is clear from the facts that it is also a discrimination claim as it relates to pregnancy.[67]

17.88　In discrimination claims, claimants who have not made clear whether they are claiming direct or indirect discrimination and/or victimisation may not be allowed to amend the claim unless the amendment is supported by the facts set out in the original claim.

64　[1974] ICR 650 NIRC.
65　[1996] ICR 836.
66　However, whether it is in time is not determinative. See, for example, *Lehman Brothers Ltd v Smith* EAT 0486/05.
67　See *Capek v Lincolnshire CC* [2000] IRLR 590, CA where a claim for breach of contract was made prematurely and the Court of Appeal said that the tribunal should have considered whether the breach of contract involved unauthorised deductions from wages which it could consider, it ordered that the matter be remitted to the ET to consider an unlawful deduction claim. See also *Brannon v Wilkinson Hardware Stores Ltd* EAT/712/98, 25 May 2000 where an unrepresented claimant claimed unfair dismissal due to pregnancy related sickness. The EAT said that the ET should have also considered ERA 1996 s99 and sex discrimination.

17.89 In *Ali v Office of National Statistics*[68] the Court of Appeal held that the tribunal erred in holding that the claimant did not need permission to amend his claim of race discrimination to add a claim of indirect discrimination where the claim was that he had been discriminated against on racial grounds. The court held that whether the ET1 contains a particular claim has to be judged by reference to the whole document and in this case there was no assertion of indirect discrimination. It was clear in *Ali* that, despite the fact that the ET1 appeared to contain full particulars, a claim of indirect discrimination was not apparent from those particulars.[69] This was because the claimant only discovered the facts on which he relied (for his indirect discrimination claim) during the process of disclosure or during the hearing. The correct test, in these circumstances, is whether is is 'just and equitable' to allow the amendment as time would need to be extended under the SDA 1975 (see also para 16.139).[70]

17.90 Similar principles apply to amending the response, though it is important that the original ET3 raises any issues about non-compliance with the statutory dispute resolution regulations (see para 17.72). If not, an amendment may be refused on the grounds that the claimant would be prejudiced if by the time of the amendment they would be out of time for raising a grievance (see also para 16.82 onwards).

Tribunal's power to manage proceedings (rule 10)

17.91 Chairmen may, at any time, either by considering the papers in the absence of the parties, or at a hearing, either on the application of a party or on their own initiative, make an order in relation to any matter which appears to be appropriate. Common orders are listed in

---

68 [2005] IRLR 201.
69 Ironically, it may be that where there is a less full claim, this would lead to the respondent or tribunal seeking further details which may then make the nature of the claims clear, thus avoiding any need for amendment.
70 See also *Ennever v Metropolitan Police* UKEAT/0051/06SM 24 February 2006 where the EAT said that 'where a new claim arose out of facts which had already been alleged in the . . . claim form, the proposed amendment was considered under the general principles applicable to amendments. Only new claims which arose out of new facts would be subject to scrutiny in respect of time limits . . . Since the protected disclosure claim simply applied a new label to the facts which had already been set out in para 6.2 of the claim form, the application for leave to amend should have been decided in accordance with the general principles applicable to amendments'. Thus the EAT allowed the claim to be amended to cover victimisation and protected disclosure (see paras, 11, 15, 16).

rule 10 but this is not an exclusive list. There are 20 examples given, but the most important types of orders are summarised below.

Requirement for a party to provide additional information of the ET1 and ET3 (rule 10(2)(b))

17.92 Either party can ask for further details of the grounds on which the other party relies and of any facts and contentions that are relevant. If legally represented the party must comply with rule 11 (see para 17.80). The tribunal itself can require the provision of additional information and may do so in response to a request from a party. This may be useful, for example, where the claimant has not served a questionnaire so does not have a breakdown of employees by, say, gender, part-time/full-time status where this is necessary to show disparate impact in an indirect sex discrimination claim.

Giving leave to amend a claim or response (rule 10(2)(q))

17.93 The tribunal can give leave to amend a claim or response (see para 17.84).

Discovery: disclosure of relevant documents (rule 10(2)(d))

17.94 Documents can be crucial to maternity, pregnancy and discrimination cases because they are often proved by inferences of discrimination rather than by direct evidence. The tribunal can require any person in Great Britain to disclose documents or information to a party to allow a party to inspect such material as might be orderd by a county court. The usual order is that each party discloses documents which it relies on or which support the other party's case. The party must make a reasonable search for documents.[71] It is subject to the principle of proportionality so that a party will not be required to disclose documents which would be disproportionate in the circumstances.

17.95 An order may be made against a person who is not a party to the proceedings but in relation to non-parties an order will only be made where the disclosure is necessary to dispose fairly of the claim or to save expense.[72] That party can be ordered to attend the tribunal to give evidence or to produce documents or information (see para 17.106).

---

71 CPR Part 31; 31.7 deals with the duty to make a reasonable search.
72 Rule 10(5).

17.96 Discovery involves each party listing all relevant documents and either giving copies to the other side or allowing them to inspect the documents.

17.97 If claimants are aware that the employer has particular documents, they should make a specific request for these, as well as a request for all other relevant documents including computer generated material such as emails, relevant notebooks or diaries. There is no duty on the parties to disclose documents unless the ET has made an order for discovery.

17.98 If a party refuses to disclose all relevant documents an application should be made to the ET for an order. The test to be applied in deciding whether disclosure or production of the documents should be ordered is whether they are material and relevant to the issues in the proceedings. The ET will not allow a fishing expedition, which is where a claimant is looking for documents to back up a claim that has not otherwise been substantiated.

17.99 The Court of Appeal has set out important criteria for deciding on what orders for discovery should be made in discrimination cases in *West Midlands Passenger Transport Executive v Singh*.[73] These are:

- the evidence need not decisively prove that the respondent had discriminated – the question is whether it may tend to prove the case;
- statistical evidence may show a discernible pattern of less favourable treatment and may give rise to an inference of discrimination;
- evidence is often accepted from employers that they have a policy of non-discrimination; for example if statistics show imbalances or disparities they may indicate areas of discrimination;
- suitability of candidates can rarely be measured objectively. A high failure of members of a particular group may indicate a discriminatory attitude involving stereotyped assumptions.

17.100 In *EB v BA*[74] the claimant argued that, on the grounds of her gender reassignment, she was discriminated against in allocation of work, which adversely affected her billing which then led to her redundancy. The ET refused to make an order for discovery of the projects which she could have been given and the claimant had to rely on the limited documents she had and guess the work she could have been

---

73 [1988] IRLR 186, CA.
74 [2006] IRLR 471, CA.

given. Thus, the onus was put on the claimant. The Court of Appeal said that the ET overlooked the fact that the burden of proof was on the respondent, it being clear that the claimant had been given much less work, following her gender reassignment. The Court of Appeal said that the tribunal allowed its attention to be diverted to that which was produced by the claimant wheras it ought to have grappled with the consequences for the respondent. 'Once the burden of proof had shifted those consequences could only be adverse to the respondent'.[75] The Court of Appeal did not accept that it would have been disporportionate for the respondent to have listed all the projects.

17.101   In response to the respondent's submission that if they were not asked about a particular project they were not required to prove it, the Court of Appeal said:

> That demonstrates the respondent's approach to this litigation and renders section 63A all but meaningless. If an employer takes the stance adopted by the respondent, namely 'You prove it' – then claimants, particularly those with limited or no means, who challenge large corporations in cases of this kind would be at a great disadvantage. Such an approach may well render the reverse burden of proof provision of little or no use to a claimant. The stance taken by the respondent . . . is not suitable for a difficult discrimination case . . . Employers should not be permitted to escape the provisions of section 63A by leaving it to the empoyee to prove her case.

17.102   As the Court of Appeal said, the respondent could only discharge the burden of proof by providing a detailed analysis. Without such analysis it was very difficult to see how the respondent could justify the fact that the appellant was only allocated to some three projects over such a long period.

17.103   This decision is likely to be very useful where work is taken away or not given to a pregnant woman (or to a woman following her maternity leave) and she believes this is related to her pregnancy (or maternity leave). Based on the principles set out in *EB v BA*, it is for the employer to show that the difference in treatment is not due to her pregnancy, and failure to disclose relevant documents means that it may not be able to discharge the burden.

17.104   Where the document is confidential, the ET could inspect the

---

75   [2006] IRLR 471, CA, para 51. Para 17.124 onwards explains the burden of proof set out in SDA 1975 s63A.

document to decide whether disclosure is necessary.[76] Names and addresses can be blanked out or redacted.

17.105   It is usually preferable to ask for a list of all relevant documents as well as the actual copies, as this will avoid any dispute over whether a particular document has been disclosed.

Witness orders (rule 10(2)(c))

17.106 The tribunal can require the attendance of any person in Great Britain to give evidence or produce documents or information. The tribunal will want information about what relevant evidence the witness can give and confirmation that they will not attend voluntarily. Note that it is not advisable to call a witness in support of a party unless the witness is willing to give evidence. Hostile witnesses are likely to be damaging to the party calling them.

Witness statements (rule 10(2)(s))

17.107 The tribunal can order that witness statements are prepared or exchanged. This is now very common and some tribunals will only hear evidence set out in the statements so it is important that they are comprehensive. Four copies must be provided for the tribunal.

17.108   Any medical evidence on which party intends to rely should also be prepared and exchanged.

Experts or interpreters (rule 10(2)(t))

17.109 The tribunal can make orders on the use of experts or interpreters in the proceedings. Usually tribunals have a list of interpreters who will be asked to interpret if a party has any problems understanding English. The tribunal will usually pay for the interpreter.

Agreed bundle of documents and chronology

17.110 Usually there is an agreed bundle of documents for the hearing. ETs prefer to have one bundle with a contents page and page numbers. A chronology is useful, as is a 'who's who' (with job titles) if there are a lot of individuals involved.

---

76 *Science Research Council v Nasse; Vyas v Leyland Cars* [1979] IRLR 465 HL; see also *National Probation Service (Teeside) v Devon* EAT 0419/05 (which was not a discrimination claim) where the EAT held that the tribunal should weigh up the conflicting interests of the parties and decide whether disclosure is necessary for a fair trial.

17.111   Although it is usually the claimant's responsibility to prepare the bundle, the respondent may do so and the tribunal can order the respondent to do so particularly if they have most of the documents. In addition to the copies for the parties four copies are required (one for each panel member and one for the witness). These should be paginated with the tribunal documents (such as ET1, ET3, SD74, further and better particulars) at the beginning, followed by documents in chronological order.

Power to strike out Rule 13, 18

17.112 The ET has power to strike out the whole or part of the ET1 or ET3 if a party does not comply with a tribunal order; or if a claim has not been actively pursued, or where a claim is scandalous, unreasonable or vexatious. This may be done at a Pre-hearing review. In practice this is not often done. There is a power to review a strike out.[77]

Power to order a deposit of up to £500

17.113 If the tribunal (usually a chairman) decides that either party has little reasonable prospect of success, it can order that party to pay a deposit of up to £500 as a condition of being allowed to continue. A different tribunal must conduct the main hearing. If the party wins, the deposit will usually be refunded.[78]

Hearings

17.114 There are three types of hearings:

a)   Case management discussions (CMDs), which deal with procedural matters and management of proceedings (such as orders under rule 10).[79] In *EB v BA* (see para 17.100) the Court of Appeal recommended that in difficult discrimination cases there be a pre-hearing case management conference during which the consequences of the burden of proof moving to the respondent (if it was later found that it did move) were worked out.

b)   Pre-hearing reviews (PHRs), where the tribunal may determine

---

77   See *Sodexho Ltd v Gibbons* [2005] ICR 1647, EAT.
78   Rules 20 and 47; see also *Sodexho Ltd* above.
79   Rule 17.

any interim or preliminary matter, such as whether the claim has been lodged in time, whether a claim or response should be struck out or whether the claim or whether a party should be required to pay a deposit in order to continue to take part in the proceedings (on the basis that they have little prospect of success).[80]

c)   The full hearing, where the merits of the claim and remedy are decided.[81]

Adjournments, extension of time

17.115   The ET has power to grant an extension of time or to adjourn a hearing. An adjournment may be granted if the claimant is ill, about to give birth or has recently given birth, where a witness is ill, or where there are proceedings pending in the High Court or county court.[82]

Equal value cases

17.116   There are special rules for equal value cases. The detail is outside the scope of this book.[83] There is a set procedure, ie:

1.   A Stage 1 equal value hearing at which a full tribunal:
   - must decide whether to strike out the claim on the ground that the claimant's work has been rated lower than her comparator's under the employer's job evaluation scheme;
   - must decide whether to appoint an independent expert (IE) or decide the question of equal value itself. The tribunal may require the parties to copy to the IE specified information. If an IE is appointed, there will be a Stage 2 hearing but if not a full hearing date will be fixed;
   - will give standard orders for the conduct of the case, including dates for the parties to agree job descriptions of the claimant and her comparator(s) and other facts relevant to whether the work is of equal value. The tribunal will, unless inappropriate, order that the claimant disclose to the respondent the name of

80   Rule 18.
81   Rule 26.
82   Rule 10(2)(m); see *Eastwood v Winckworth Sherwood EAT* 0174/05 for relevant factors.
83   Employment Tribunals (Equal Value) Rules of Procedure (Schedule 6 to the Employment Tribunals (Constitution and Rules of Procedure) Regulations 2004 (Equal Value Rules 2004).

any comparator and identify the period when equal work was being carried out;

- may, on the application of a party, hear evidence on whether the material factor defence applies before deciding whether to appoint an IE.

2. Where an IE has been appointed the tribunal will hold a Stage 2 hearing, where it must:

- decide the facts on which the IE will base his/her report; and
- set a deadline for the report.

17.117 Where an IE has been appointed, the parties may put written questions to the expert to clarify factual issues. There is an indicative timetable which envisages 25 weeks between lodging the claim and final hearing where there is no IE, and 37 weeks in cases involving an IE.

The hearing

17.118 This will be in public. At least 14 days' notice of the hearing date must be given. Some ETs will split the remedies hearing from the main hearing of the case but parties should be prepared to give evidence of loss, injury to feelings, etc, on the day of the main hearing as most ETs will expect to deal with both issues in the allocated time.

17.119   The ET has a very wide discretion as to how the proceedings are conducted. There is a duty on ETs to 'make such enquiries of persons appearing before it and of witnesses as it considers appropriate and shall otherwise conduct the hearing in such manner as he or it considers most appropriate for the clarification of the issues and generally for the just handling of the proceedings (see Rule 14(3))'.

Burden of proof

17.120 The ET will decide the facts in a case on a balance of probabilities, having read documents to which it has been referred and heard evidence from witnesses. The burden of proof is important for the order of proceedings. The party who has to prove any particular issue will usually start.

17.121   Employees with one year's service can claim ordinary unfair dismissal. First, they must prove that there has been a dismissal, but this is normally not in dispute except that in constructive dismissal cases where the employer claims that the employee resigned.

17.122   Once it has been established that there has been a dismissal, the employer must then show that it genuinely and reasonably believed there is a reason that is prescribed as a potentially 'fair' reason. If the employer cannot show a potentially fair reason for the dismissal it will be unfair (see para 15.72 onwards). If the dismissal was for a potentially fair reason, the ET must then decide if the dismissal was fair and reasonable in the circumstances (see para 15.82). The burden of proof does not rest on either party.

17.123   Employees who are claiming automatic unfair dismissal must establish that the reason or principal reason for the dismissal is an automatically unfair one (see para 15.58 onwards). The principles are similar to those for establishing discrimination except that with automatically unfair dismissal the burden is on the employee and the reason (eg, pregnancy) must be the 'principal' or only reason for dismissal. With direct discrimination cases the discrimination may only be a significant or substantial reason, this being an easier test to satisfy (see para 2.72 onwards). If this is established, the employer has no defence so cannot justify the dismissal on any grounds.

Burden of proof in discrimination cases

17.124   In discrimination cases the burden is on the claimant to show facts from which discrimination may be inferred so that the claimant will usually go first. Where the claim is for both an unfair dismissal and discrimination the claimant will usually open but there are no clear rules and the ET will decide.[84]

17.125   Section 63A of the SDA 1975 provides that:

> Where, on the hearing of the complaint, the claimant proves facts from which the tribunal could, apart from this section, conclude in the absence of an adequate explanation that the respondent–
>
> (a) has committed an act of discrimination or harassment against the claimant which is unlawful by virtue of Part 2 [the employment field], or section 35A or 35B] or
> (b) is by virtue of s41 or s42 [liability of employers and aiding unlawful acts, see para 2.15] to be treated as having committed such an act of discrimination or harassment against the complainant,
>
> the tribunal shall uphold the complaint unless the respondent proves

---

84 See, in particular, the decision in *EB v BA* for a useful summary of how the failure to provide proper disclosure of documents may defeat the purpose of the shift in the burden of proof.

that he did not commit, or, as the case may be, is not to be treated as having committed, that act.

17.126   Where the claimant proves facts from which the tribunal could conclude 'in the absence of an adequate explanation' that the respondent has committed an unlawful act of discrimination, the burden will shift to the employer to prove a non-discriminatory reason. It follows that an ET must uphold a complaint of sex discrimination where the employer cannot prove that it did not discriminate. In pregnancy claims, it should be sufficient for the burden of proof to shift if the claimant shows that there was a difference of treatment before and after she announced her pregnancy and that the employer was aware of her pregnancy.

17.127   The change in the burden of proof in October 2003 has made a significant difference to the way a claimant proves discrimination.[85]

17.128   There are two separate stages involved. The rationale for this was explained in *Igen*, ie that it is for the claimant to know how s/he has been treated by the respondent whereas the respondent can be expected to explain why the claimant has been so treated. In *Laing v Manchester City Council* the EAT held that the ET should have regard to all the facts at the first stage to see what inferences can be drawn to decide if there is a prima facie case.[86] The guidance given in *Igen* is as follows:

(1)   Pursuant to SDA 1975 s63A, it is for the claimant who complains of sex discrimination to prove on the balance of probabilities facts from which the tribunal could conclude, in the absence of an adequate explanation, that the respondents have committed an act of discrimination against the claimant which is unlawful by virtue of Part II or which by virtue of SDA 1975 s41 or s42 is to be treated as having been committed against the claimant. These are referred to below as 'such facts'.

(2)   If the claimant does not prove such facts, s/he will fail.

(3)   It is important to bear in mind in deciding whether the claimant has proved such facts that it is unusual to find direct evidence of sex discrimination. Few employers would be prepared to admit

---

85   See *Igen Ltd v Wong* [2005] IRLR 258, CA (para 18) and *Dresdner Kleinwort Wasserstein Ltd v Adebayo* [2005] IRLR 514 where LJ Cox said that 'while the meaning of direct discrimination remains unchanged, the manner in which it will henceforth fall to be proved has altered significantly'. In *Igen* the Court of Appeal said that the comment to the contrary in *Nelson v Carillion Service Ltd* [2003] IRLR 428, CA was wrong.

86   *Igen* para 31; *Laing* [2006] UKEAT/0128/06, 28 July 2006.

such discrimination, even to themselves. In some cases the discrimination will not be an intention but merely based on the assumption that 'he or she would not have fitted in'.

(4) In deciding whether the claimant has proved such facts, it is important to remember that the outcome at this stage of the analysis by the tribunal will therefore usually depend on what inferences it is proper to draw from the primary facts found by the tribunal.

(5) It is important to note the word is 'could'. At this stage the tribunal does not have to reach a definitive determination that such facts would lead it to the conclusion that there was an act of unlawful discrimination. At this stage a tribunal is looking at the primary facts proved by the claimant to see what inferences of secondary fact could be drawn from them.

(6) These inferences can include, in appropriate cases, any inferences that it is just and equitable to draw in accordance with SDA 1975 s74(2)(b) from an evasive or equivocal reply to a questionnaire or any other questions that fall within SDA 1975 s74(2); see *Hinks v Riva Systems*.[87]

(7) Likewise, the tribunal must decide whether any provision of any relevant code of practice is relevant and if so, take it into account in determining such facts pursuant to SDA 1975 s56A(10). This means that inferences may also be drawn from any failure to comply with any relevant code of practice.

(8) Where the claimant has proved facts from which inferences could be drawn that the respondents have treated the claimant less favourably on the grounds of sex (or pregnancy or maternity leave), then the burden of proof moves to the respondent.

(9) It is then for the respondent to prove that it did not commit, or as the case may be, is not to be treated as having committed, that act.

(10) To discharge that burden it is necessary for the respondent to prove, on the balance of probabilities, that the treatment was in no sense whatsoever on the grounds of sex, since 'no discrimination whatsoever' is compatible with the EU Burden of Proof Directive.

(11) That requires a tribunal to assess not merely whether the respondent has proved an explanation for the facts from which such inferences can be drawn, but further that it is adequate to

discharge the burden of proof on the balance of probabilities that sex (pregnancy or maternity leave) was not any part of the reasons for the treatment in question.

(12) Since the facts necessary to prove an explanation would normally be in the possession of the respondent, a tribunal would normally expect cogent evidence to examine carefully explanations for failure to deal with the questionnaire procedure and/or code of practice.

17.129   In *Dresdner Kleinwort Wasserstein Ltd v Adebayo*[88] the EAT held the claimant's circumstances must be similar to those of the comparator. However, in pregnancy cases there is no need for a comparator, so that if the less favourable treatment was related to the woman's pregnancy or absence on maternity leave, this will be sex discrimination in itself. Pregnancy and unfavourable treatment should be enough to move the burden of prove to the respondent to show that there was no discrimination.

17.130   As the EAT said in *Dresdner*:

> . . . discriminatory assumptions will frequently underpin the stated reason, even where the reason is given in good faith and genuinely believed, and the discriminator is unaware that such assumptions are operating . . . Employment tribunals cannot look inside the mind of an alleged discriminator and expose stereotypical assumptions . . . The solution, at least in part, to such problems in deciding cases is . . .. the requirement now placed upon employers, where a prima facia case has been shown, to adduce evidence and prove on the balance of probabilities that they have not discriminated.[89]

17.131   It is important for employers, in all areas, to have transparent and fair procedures, objectively and consistently applied, to show that the process (whether recruitment, promotion, training, dismissal etc) was not tainted by discrimination. See, eg, *Aziz v Crown Prosecution*

---

88   [2005] IRLR 514, EAT. Note that although this was decided just after *Igen*, there was no reference to *Igen* and it was clearly not taken into account The difficulty with the analysis is the 'like for like' test and the employer's 'adequate explanation' are often different sides of the same coin; the employer's explanation as to why there is no discrimination is often that the woman was in a different situation to her comparator (eg the successful candidate was better qualified).

89   EAT para 76; the EAT also said at para 77 that it is not incumbent on a tribunal to analyse the states of mind of individuals involved in events which are found to have involved unlawful discrimination, particularly when many were not called making such analysis impossible and when the respondents' response to the allegations was little more than a bare denial of discrimination.

Service [2006] EWCA Civ 1136, 31 July 2006, where the CA agreed that an adverse inference could be drawn from the Respondent's breach of its own code where it could not give a satisfactory explanation for the breach. It will now be more difficult for employers to rely on incompetence or unreasonableness as the burden is on them to show that the incompetence is nothing to do with sex and proving a negative is less easy.

17.132   If the tribunal finds that the employer has not proved that the treatment was not tainted by discrimination, it must uphold the claim of discrimination.

Evidence

17.133 The main evidence is often given through the witnesses reading out their statements.

17.134   Hearsay evidence is often allowed in ETs, though it is not as valuable as first hand evidence. In discrimination cases, events which took place both before and after the discrimination may be used in evidence 'if logically probative of a relevant fact'.[90]

17.135   If a witness cannot come to the ET but submits a written statement, the ET will decide how much importance to give it, taking into account the fact that the witness cannot be cross-examined. Such statements are much less valuable than live evidence.

17.136   The detail of the hearing is beyond the scope of this book. Usually, however, the order is as follows:

- The party who opens is unlikely to be allowed to make an opening statement unless the case is particularly complex and the issues have not been clarified previously. Usually, they will be expected to call the first witness who will read their statement. Some tribunals read the statements themselves. In discrimination cases it is usually the claimant who opens.
- Each witness will be questioned (cross-examined) by the other side and the ET will ask questions if it wants.
- There may then be re-examination, which consists of further questions which have arisen out of the cross-examination.
- The same procedure applies to each witness.
- When all the opening party's witnesses have given evidence, the same process applies to the other side.

90 *Chattopadhyay v Headmaster of Holloway School* [1981] IRLR 487, EAT.

- Finally, both parties have a right to make a closing speech. Normally, the party who started addresses the ET last, but the ET will decide this.
- If either party intends to refer to cases, these should be copied for the other side and the ET or, at the least, the names and references should be provided.

Expenses of claimant and witnesses

17.137 The claimant and witnesses can make a claim for some of the costs of travel, meals and loss of earnings. The ET clerk will provide a form and advise about a claim.

Costs

17.138 Generally, costs are not awarded against the unsuccessful party. However, there are an increasing number of situations where costs are awarded and the number of awards has increased dramatically over the past few years. A brief summary of the main provisions is set out below.

Costs against legally represented parties

17.139 Costs against a party may or must be awarded in the following situations:

a) where a claimant has told the respondent that they want reinstatement or re-engagement and a hearing has been postponed because of the respondent's failure, without good reason, to provide reasonable evidence of the availability of the claimant's job or an alternative. In this situation the tribunal must order the respondent to pay the claimant's costs;[91]
b) where a hearing or PHR has been postponed a costs order may be made against the party responsible for the postponement;[92]
c) the tribunal must consider making a costs order where it considers it appropriate:

Where the paying party has in bringing the proceedings or he or his representative has in conducting the proceedings, acted vexatiously,

91   Rule 39.
92   Rule 40(1).

abusively, disruptively or otherwise unreasonably, or the bringing or conducting of the proceedings by the paying party has been misconceived.[93]

d) a tribunal may make a costs order against a party who has not complied with a order or practice direction.[94]

17.140 The tribunal may specify the sum to be paid, but this cannot exceed £10,000. Alternatively, the parties can agree a sum or the tribunal may order that costs be assessed in accordance with the Civil Procedure Rules 1998, in which case costs can exceed £10,000.[95]

17.141 The tribunal may have regard to the paying party's ability to pay costs when considering whether or not to award costs.

17.142 It is quite common for respondents to threaten costs when faced with a claim or threat of a claim. Such a threat should only be used where the case is clearly misconceived. If not, the claimant may seek to claim aggravated damages for making an inappropriate threat (see para 18.83 onwards).

Costs in favour of parties not legally represented

17.143 Costs may now also be awarded to parties who are not legally represented. These are called 'preparation time orders' and the hourly rate is £26 (which is increased every April by £1). The details are outside the scope of this book.[96]

Costs against representatives: Wasted costs orders

17.144 Costs may now be awarded against a party's representative (legal or other) where costs have been incurred:

a)   as a result of any improper, unreasonable or negligent act or omission on the part of any representative; or

b)   which, in the light of any such act or omission occurring after they were incurred, the tribunal considers it unreasonable to expect that party to pay.[97]

This is outside the scope of the book.

---

93 Rule 40(2)(3).
94 Rule 40(4).
95 Rule 41.
96 See rules 42–46.
97 Rule 48.

Withdrawal and dismissal of a claim

17.145 Rule 25 provides that a claimant may withdraw all or part of his claim at any time, either in writing or orally at a hearing, by informing the tribunal as to which claim (or parts) are to be withdrawn. Withdrawal takes effect on the date the Employment Tribunal Office receives notice of it. It does not require the tribunal to do anything except to inform the respondent. The withdrawal brings the proceedings (or that part) to an end. The respondent may subsequently apply for the proceedings to be dismissed and/or for an order for costs against the claimant. A withdrawal means that the claimant cannot continue with the proceedings in the tribunal. A dismissal means that any second claim on the same facts will generally be barred (by action estoppel) in any forum.[98]

17.146   In *Dr Khan v Heywood & Middleton Primary Care Trust*[99] the claimant's solicitor wrote to the tribunal stating that he sought to withdraw his claim and asking that it be moved from the listings. The tribunal confirmed this in writing to both parties. The claimant then sought advice and applied to set aside the withdrawal notice and this was refused. The EAT held that a tribunal does not have power to set aside a notice of withdrawal as withdrawn proceedings cannot be reactivated. Thus, the tribunal was correct to decide that it did not have the power to set aside the claimant's notice of withdrawal. The EAT said that the sense of the rule:

> . . . is to convey that the consequence of the dismissal of a previously withdrawn claim will be to prevent the claimant from starting a further claim based on the same cause of action, whereas (by inference) a mere withdrawal of the claim will not . . . if a withdrawn claim is also dismissed, the claimant cannot start a fresh claim based on the same cause of action as that on which the dismissed claim was based.[100]

17.147 One reason why the claimant may wish to resist the application to dismiss is that they want to resurrect the claim in fresh proceedings.

---

98   See *Ako v Rothschild Asset Management Ltd* [2002] IRLR 348.
99   [2006] IRLR 345, EAT. This has been upheld by the CA which held that an ET cannot set aside the claimants notice of withdrawal. The claimant can issue new proceedings unless the claim has been dismissed in which case s/he is estopped from starting a second claim based on the same facts: *Khan v Heywood and Middleton Primary Care Trust* [2006] EWCA 1087, 27 July 2006.
100 Para 24.

For example, an employee may wish to make a claim in the High Court or a county court for personal injury instead of pursuing it in the tribunal as part of a sex discrimination claim. In *Verdin v Harrods Ltd*[101] the claimant sought to withdraw part of her claim for breach of contract so she could pursue it in the High Court. The EAT held that usually a claim will be dismissed but there are circumstances in which there will be good reason for withdrawing and bringing a claim in a different way. The tribunal should ask whether the claimant intends to bring the claim elsewhere and, if so, would that be an abuse of process. In *Verdin*, the EAT held that tribunal should have permitted the claim to be withdrawn without dismissing it.[102] However, the position is not clear and the Court of Appeal has held that a claimant cannot bring a claim for notice monies in the tribunal and High Court just because the tribunal limit is £25,000. Once the tribunal has decided the breach of contract the claimant cannot then apply to the High Court for the balance.[103]

The decision

17.148 The decision can be a majority one. It may be given at the end of a hearing or at a later date. Tribunals must either give the decision (ie, judgment) orally at the end of the hearing, explaining the reasons at the same time, or if no decision has been reached, the decision will be reserved and given in writing at a later date, in which case full written reasons must be provided. If the reasons are given orally at the end of the hearing, either party can ask for written reasons but these must be requested either at the hearing or within 14 days of the date the written judgment is sent to the parties (though this time limit can be extended by the chairman).[104]

101 [2006] IRLR 339.
102 See also *Tamborrino v Keypers* EAT 0483/05 where a letter of withdrawal was not complete when it stated that the employee's written instructions had not been received and a representative would attend to inform the tribunal of the withdrawal.
103 *Fraser v HLMAD Ltd* [2006] EWCA Civ 738, 15 June 2006.
104 Employment Tribunals (Constitution and Rules of Procedure) Regulations 2004 SI No 1861 Sch 1 rr28–30.

Review of decisions

17.149 An ET has power to review its decision on specified grounds. A review must be requested within 14 days of the decision being sent to the parties, the tribunal has the power to extend the time limit.[105]

Enforcement

17.150 Enforcement of compensation orders is in the county court. The Employment Tribunals (Interest) Order 1990[106] provides that interest is payable on any sums unpaid after 42 days. The current rate is 6% (see paras 18.91–18.92 for interest on discrimination awards).

Appeals

17.151 An appeal to the EAT must be lodged within 42 days of the date the written reasons or written record of the judgment are sent to the parties.[107] The EAT has the power to order the tribunal to provide written reasons.[108] The EAT will decide, at a preliminary hearing, whether the appeal has any prospects of success. If not, it will not be allowed to proceed. An appeal to the EAT can be made at the same time as a review. The detail of reviews and appeals is outside the scope of this book.

17.152   EAT decisions are binding on ETs and county courts. There is a further appeal to the Court of Appeal and the House of Lords. A tribunal or court can refer a question about the interpretation of European Union law to the ECJ (see para 1.23).

---

105   ET Regs 2004 Sch 1 rr33–37.
106   SI No 479.
107   EAT Rules 1993 SI No 2854.
108   EAT Practice Direction 2004 para 2.3.

CHAPTER 18

Remedies and compensation

18.128   Average awards in discrimination cases

18.131   Remedies for refusal of family time off and flexible working

Refusal of paid time off for antenatal care. • *Breach of flexible working procedure* • *Denial or unreasonable postponement of parental leave* • *Refusal of time off for dependants* • *Failure to pay remuneration while suspended on maternity health and safety grounds* • *Equal pay* • *Breach of Part-time Workers (Prevention of Less Favourable Treatment) Regs 2000* • *Detriment claims* • *Failure to give written reasons (or inadequate ones) for dismissal* • *Unlawful deduction from wages and breach of contract* • *Refusal of SMP* • *Wrongful dismissal* • *Dismissal for assertion of a statutory right and in health and safety cases* • *Enforcement* • *EOC powers*

18.167   Future developments: general public sector duty

Key points

- Settlement should be considered early, either through ACAS (Advisory, Conciliation and Arbitration Service), a mediator or representatives.
- The parties cannot contract out of statutory employment rights except where there is an ACAS negotiated agreement (COT3) or a compromise agreement which satisfies minimum requirements.
- Claimants should consider all claims, which include:
  - breach of the particular statutory right, eg, to time off;
  - automatically and ordinary unfair dismissal;
  - detriment claims;
  - sex discrimination;
  - dismissal for assertion of a statutory right;
  - personal injury.
- An award may be increased or decreased where a party has not complied with either the relevant disciplinary and dismissal procedure (DDP) or the grievance procedure (GP) before proceedings are issued.
- Remedies for unfair dismissal are:
  - reinstatement or re-engagement
  - compensation (including basic award) subject to a cap of £58,400 (up to end January 2007).
- Remedies for discrimination are:
  - declaration;
  - recommendation;
  - compensation for loss of earnings and benefits, injury to feelings, aggravated damages, personal injury and interest; there is no cap.
- Pension loss can be substantial and regard should be had to the tribunal chairman's guidance booklet.
- Injury to feelings can be awarded in some detriment cases.
- In discrimination cases the complainant must be put into the position she would have been in but for the unlawful conduct of the discriminator.
- Deductions may be made from the compensation; this includes:
  - payments made by the employer;

> - failure by the claimant to mitigate loss, by taking reasonable steps to find alternative work;
> - breach of the statutory procedures;
> - contributory fault – at least in unfair dismissal cases.
> - The tribunal may, in some cases, reduce compensation on the basis of a percentage chance that the claimant would not have returned to work after maternity leave.
> - Compensation may be awarded against both employer and an individual who has discriminated.
> - The Equal Opportunities Commission (EOC) (or Commission for Equality and Human Rights (CEIIR)) may give advice and assistance to claimants which can include paying legal costs.
> - The parties should check whether they have legal expenses insurance to cover legal costs.

Overview

18.1   This chapter looks at settlement and remedies including the effect of a failure by either party to follow the dispute resolution regulations on compensation awards.

18.2   The main remedies available are as shown in the table on pp 671–672.

Settlement

18.3   In 2003/04 69% of claims were settled by the parties or withdrawn by the claimant. Early settlement is advisable for both parties. However, the parties cannot contract out of statutory employment rights except where there is either:

- an ACAS negotiated agreement, through a COT3 (see para 18.6–18.7);
- a compromise agreement which complies with minimum requirements (see para 18.8 onwards);[1]
- a settlement incorporated into a tribunal judgment.

---

1   Thus if there is no such agreement, the employee is free to bring a claim against the employer even if there is an agreement.

18.4 If it has not been possible to resolve internally a dispute between the employer and employee the parties should consider the following options:

a) *Mediation* through an independent mediator; mediation is available through various agencies (see appendix E). Although not always cheap, if successful, costs are likely to be much less than litigation. Mediation is an option at any stage and more often takes place after proceedings have been lodged.

b) *Conciliation* through ACAS. Although ACAS becomes involved as a matter of course when a tribunal claim is lodged (see para 17.78); they may be prepared to conciliate before a claim is lodged if requested to do so by the parties.

c) In addition, where the claim is for unfair dismissal or flexible working, there is an *ACAS statutory scheme* which is an alternative to tribunal proceedings.[2] An independent arbitrator will resolve the dispute. The arbitrator's decision is binding and will prevent a claimant making a claim to the tribunal. It does not apply where there is also a claim for sex discrimination.

d) *Resolution through lawyers.* Once the strengths and weaknesses of the case have been assessed, the parties should consider early settlement. In some cases, ACAS are prepared to aid this conciliation process and host a conciliation meeting at their offices.

e) *Tribunal proceedings.* The tribunal can award compensation and in a discrimination case make a recommendation and in unfair dismissal cases make an order for reinstatement or re-engagement. This chapter covers the orders that can be made by tribunals.

Advisory, conciliation and arbitration service (ACAS)

18.5 Where a complaint is presented to an employment tribunal under the Employment Rights Act (ERA) 1996, the Sex Discrimination Act (SDA) 1975, the Equal Pay Act (EPA) 1970 or other employment legislation, a copy is sent to an ACAS conciliation officer. In some cases there will be a short or standard conciliation period (see para 17.78),[3] although this does not apply to any discrimination and equal

---

2 ACAS Arbitration Scheme (GB) Order 2004 SI No 753 in force from 6 April 2004 and a ACAS (Flexible Working) Arbitration Scheme (GB) Order 2004 SI No 2333 in force from 1 October 2004.

3 Employment Tribunals (Constitution & Rules etc) Regulations 2004, rules 22–24.

pay claims. Usually, an ACAS officer will contact the parties (or their representatives) to find out if there is any prospect of settlement.[4] ACAS will not get involved before a claim is lodged unless specifically asked to do so.

18.6   Any settlement reached through ACAS, which is usually recorded on a COT3 form, is binding on the parties. The agreement can settle all claims but will not settle future claims unless the agreement makes it 'absolutely clear' that this is intended. It is arguable that as a matter of legal principle a party cannot settle claims relating to matters which have not yet arisen.[5]

18.7   Discussion and correspondence with ACAS is confidential to the parties and will not be disclosed to the tribunal unless and until the COT3 is agreed, when the ACAS officer will normally tell the tribunal that the matter has been settled. In practice, the COT3 will usually settle any claim arising out of the employee's employment.

Compromise agreements

18.8   If the parties agree a settlement without ACAS, the agreement will only be valid if:

- the agreement is in writing;
- the agreement relates to the specific complaint or proceedings;
- the employee has received independent legal advice from a qualified lawyer or certified independent adviser who is insured to give such advice;[6]
- the agreement identifies the adviser; and
- the agreement states that the conditions regulating compromise agreements are satisfied.[7]

---

4   Employment Tribunals Act 1996 s18 sets out conciliation officer's statutory duties.
5   See *Royal National Orthopaedic Hospital Trust v Howard* [2002] IRLR 849 where the EAT held that the claimant was not prevented from bringing a victimisation claim against her previous employer for refusing to employ her due to her previous discrimination claim. The COT3 referred to compromising claims the claimant 'has or may have' and the EAT said this could cover existing claims whether or not they were known to the employee, but not possible future claims.
6   The adviser must be a qualified lawyer or a union official, employee or member certified as competent and authorised to give advice or an employee or volunteer at an advice centre, certified as competent and authorised to give advice or a legal executive employed by a firm of solicitors. It is common for the employer to contribute to the costs of any legal adviser.
7   ERA 1996 s203, SDA 1975 s77 (as amended), Part-time Workers (Prevention of Less Favourable Treatment) Regulations (PTW Regs) 2000 reg 9.

18.9   A failure to comply with any of the above requirements will render the agreement invalid. All claims to be compromised should be specifically included in the agreement so it is clear what is being compromised.[8]

18.10   Breach of a compromise agreement is enforced in the county court or High Court, not the tribunal.[9]

Affect of agreement on recoupment of benefits

18.11   The recoupment provisions apply where there is a judgment awarding compensation. This means that any compensation to the claimant will be reduced by any job seekers' allowance received.[10] Where there is a COT3, compromise agreement or tribunal order with a schedule setting out the terms (as opposed to being included in the order) then if the claimant has been claiming job seekers' allowance, the benefit claimed will not be recouped from the compensation. In sex discrimination/equal pay cases benefits are not recoupable in any case. However, any welfare benefits received will usually be taken into account as income when determining loss.

Remedies: Overview

18.12   Details of the remedies available are set out below. NB There are no specific remedies for refusal of maternity leave, adoption or paternity leave. General remedies for discrimination, dismissal or detriment can be sought instead. Tribunals now commonly require claimants to prepare a schedule of loss setting out details of all losses, including benefits, up to the date of the hearing. Credit must be given for earnings, any other income and any ex gratia payment made by the employer.

18.13   In many cases, as well as seeking a remedy for a specific breach

---

8   See *Hinton v University of East London* [2005] IRLR 552, CA, where the agreement did not refer to a claim for protected disclosure, so the claimant was not prohibited from bringing such a claim.

9   See Philip Tsamados (ed) *Enforcing ET awards and settlements*, 2 March 2006, available from the Central London Law Centre as a photocopy (tel: 020 7839 2998).

10 See Employment Protection (Recoupment) of Jobseeker's Allowance and Income Support Regulations 1996 SI No 2349.

The right	Statutory reference	Financial compensation	Injury to feelings	Other remedy	GP or DDP applies
Sex discrimination	SDA 1975 ss65 and 66	Yes plus interest and aggravated damages – no cap applies	Yes – plus personal injury	Declaration and/or recommendation	DDP – dismissal; GP – with constructive dismissal or other claims
Equal pay	EPA 1970 ss2, 2ZA, 2ZB and 2ZC	Back pay plus interest	No	Equality clause implied into the contract	GP
Automatically unfair dismissal, failure to follow DDP, ERA 1996 s98A	ERA 1996 ss112–126	Basic award, minimum four weeks' pay plus compensatory award of up to £58,400*	No	Reinstatement or re-engagement	DDP – or GP with constructive dismissal
Automatically unfair dismissal ERA s99/s100/s104	ERA 1996 ss112–126	Basic award plus compensatory award of up to £58,400*	No	Reinstatement or re-engagement	DDP – or GP with constructive dismissal
'Ordinary' unfair dismissal	Ditto	Ditto	Ditto	Ditto	Ditto
Protection from detriment	ERA 1996 s 49	Yes	Yes	Declaration	GP
Paid time off for antenatal care	ERA 1996 s57(4) and (5)	Pay attributable to the time off	No	Declaration	No
Failure to offer alternative job prior to H&S suspension	ERA 1996 s70(6) and (7)	Yes	Yes	No	No

* Up to 31 January 2007

The right	Statutory reference	Financial compensation	Injury to feelings	Other remedy	GP or DDP applies
Failure to pay full pay during a H&S suspension	ERA 1996 s70(3)	Yes	No	No	No
Unlawful deduction for wages: Failure to pay SMP, SAP, SPP	ERA 1996 s24	Yes	No	Declaration	GP
Refusal to pay SMP (enforcement outside the ET)		HMRC will pay if the employer refuses		Criminal prosecution	
Refusal or postponement of parental leave	ERA 1996 s80(3) and (4)	Yes	Yes	Declaration	No
Refusal of ToD	ERA 1996 s57B(3) and (4)	Yes	Yes	Declaration	No
Breach of Right to ask for flexible working procedure	ERA 1996 s80I	Yes, up to eight weeks' pay (at £290 pw) *	No	Declaration/ order that the employer reconsider	No
Breach of the Part time work regulations	PTW Regs 2000 reg 8	Yes	No	Declaration/ recommendation	No
Failure to provide written reasons for dismissal	ERA 1996 s93	Yes, two weeks' pay (at £290 pw) *	No	Declaration of the reasons for dismissing the employee	No

* Up to 31 January 2007

(such as refusal of parental or dependants' leave or paid time off for antenatal care), an employee will have other claims such as:

- *Ordinary or automatically unfair dismissal* (where the employee has been dismissed for taking time off or other reason related to pregnancy, maternity or family leave). This would include constructive dismissal. The provisions are set out in chapter 15 the remedies in para 18.26.
- *Unlawful detriment* (where the employee is treated less favourably for a reason related to pregnancy, maternity or family leave). The provisions are set out in para 15.127, the remedies in para 18.152.
- *Sex discrimination*; the provisions are set out in chapter 2, the remedies in para 18.41.
- *Asserting a statutory right*. The provisions are set out in chapter 15, the remedies in para 18.41.
- *Personal injury*. This could either be part of injury to feelings in a tribunal discrimination claim or a separate personal injury claim in the county court or High Court (see also para 18.80 on estoppel).

Reduction or increase of award where breach of dispute resolution regulations

18.14 Compensation for any claim covered by the DDP or GP will be affected by any failure of either party to comply with the requirements of the DDP or GP. For details of when the DDP and GP apply see chapter 16. The main principles relating to how the procedures affect compensation are set out below.

The general rule: EA 2002 s31

18.15 Compensation will be affected, under EA 2002 s31, where:

a) 'the claim to which the proceedings relate concerns a matter to which one of the statutory procedures applies' ie a claim listed in Schedule 3 (ie where the GP or DDP applies), which includes unfair dismissal, detriment and discrimination; the procedures would not apply where there is an exception;

b) 'the statutory procedure was not completed before the proceedings were begun'; and

c) 'the non-completion of the statutory procedure was wholly or mainly attributable to failure by the employee–

- to comply with a requirement of the procedure, or
- to exercise a right of appeal under it'.[11]

18.16 The same provisions apply where the employer has failed to comply with a requirement of the procedure.[12] Where the above conditions apply, the tribunal must reduce the total compensatory award which it makes to the employee by 10%, and may, if it considers it just and equitable in all the circumstances to do so, reduce it by a further amount, but not so as to make a total reduction of more than 50%. The same applies to employers who fail to follow the DDP or GP; the total compensatory award[13] can be similarly increased by between 10% and 50%. Where there are exceptional circumstances, which would make an adjustment unjust and inequitable, the tribunal may make no, or a lower, adjustment.[14]

18.17 At first reading, EA 2002 s31 appears to apply only where the statutory procedure was not completed *before* (our emphasis) the proceedings were begun, rather than where they are not complete even after the issue of procceedings. If this is correct it means that the claimant should wait until the procedures have been completed before lodging a claim with the tribunal or risk a reduction in compensation; this may mean waiting for more than the required 28 days (after raising the grievance) before lodging (see para 16.102). Until the position has been clarified by the courts it may be safest to wait (in order to avoid any reduction in compensation), provided the claim is lodged within the extended time period (ie, within six months of the discrimination, where time is extended though time is not normally extended where there has been an actual dismissal).

18.18 However, it is arguable that section 31 means only that, even when proceedings have been lodged, the employee must still comply with any requirements of the procedure including an appeal, not that the procedure must be completed *before* lodging a claim. This is the interpretation given in the DTI guidance which states that 's31 requires employment tribunals to increase or decrease compensation . . . where the statutory procedures have not been completed and that failure is attributable to one of the parties'[15]. In any event, the tribunal

---

11 EA 2002 s31(2).
12 EA 2002 s31(3).
13 While the percentage increase applies to the compensatory award, the basic award is increased to four weeks where the dismissal was automatically unfair.
14 EA 2002 s31(4).
15 Para 129.

may not think that it is just and equitable to make any adjustment in these circumstances.

18.19   A parallel provision applies to employers so that they too would be penalised if the statutory procedure was not completed before the proceedings were begun and the non-completion was due to failure by the employer to comply with a requirement. In *Giles v Geach and Jones*, the ET made an uplift of 40 percent following the employer's failure to comply with the statutory grievance procedure after a successful indirect sex discrimination claim. The total award was £29,294.19.[16]

18.20   Thus, section 31 penalises the party who is at fault. Regulation 12[17] provides that if either party fails to comply with a requirement of a procedure then, unless that party is treated as so complying under one of the rules (see below), the non-completion will be attributable to that party. The difficult question is knowing whether a party is at fault, for example by delaying a meeting, and ultimately it is for the tribunal to decide.

Exception where parties treated as having completed the procedures

18.21   In some circumstances the parties are treated as having complied with the procedures (see para 16.43 onwards)[18] and in these cases, time limits are extended but there will be no adjustment of the award. For example, where it is not reasonably practicable for either party to attend a meeting for a reason not foreseeable when the meeting was arranged, that party is not treated as having failed to comply with the procedure. The employer must invite the employee to another meeting and if it is not reasonably practicable for a party or companion to attend a second scheduled meeting due to unforeseen circumstances, the parties are treated as having complied with the procedure.[19] However, if it was reasonably practicable for the party to attend and s/he does not, then that party will be in breach of the procedure.

18.22   Where the DDP or GP applies, there may be arguments about whether the requirements of the procedures have been completed or are treated as completed, particularly as many questions revolve around 'reasonableness' for example:

16   EA 2002 s31(3). *Giles v Geach*, ET 3100720/05, 8 August 2005, EOR 150.
17   Dispute Resolution Regulations (DR Regs) 2004 SI No 752.
18   Eg, if the employee alleges that disciplinary action is discriminatory, and raises a grievance before the appeal under the DPP (or if there is no procedure, before putting in a claim). See para 16.61 onwards.
19   DR Regs reg 13.

a) whether it is was reasonably practicable for a party to comply with a requirement within a reasonable period, for example, where the employee (or child) is ill;
b) whether the employer has delayed a part of the procedure, such as holding a meeting;
c) whether the employer has insisted on a meeting being held at an inconvenient time;
d) whether the employee has failed to put in an appeal in reasonable time.

18.23   It will be for the tribunal to decide whether there has been a breach and the extent of any increase or reduction in compensation.

Compensation for failure to provide a written statement of employment particulars

18.24   Where there is a successful claim (eg, for discrimination, equal pay, detriment in employment, unfair dismissal, unlawful deduction of wages or breach of contract)[20] and, at the date proceedings were commenced, the employer had failed to provide written particulars of employment the tribunal must award compensation of a minimum of two weeks pay and may award up to four weeks' pay.[21] A week's pay is limited to the statutory maximum (£290 up to 31 January 2007). This is in addition to any other award but may be made even if there is no other award. In exceptional circumstances the tribunal may not make an award. However, there is no freestanding right to bring a claim only for failure to provide a written statement and no compensation will be awarded if the claim is not successful even if there is a breach of this right.

Remedies for unfair dismissal and discrimination: overview

18.25   The claims which attract substantial compensation are for unfair and discriminatory dismissal. A discriminatory dismissal will usually also be an unfair one,[22] but the remedies are different. Compensation will not be awarded twice for the two claims.[23] Employees will be better off

---

20 Claims set out in EA 2002 Sch 5 – which are the same as Sch 3.
21 ERA 1996 s1 which sets out the details that must be provided and EA 2002 s38.
22 See, for example, *Clarke v Eley Kynock Ltd* [1982] IRLR 482.
23 ERA 1996 s126.

with the compensatory award being for discrimination as there is no cap, interest is payable and the recoupment provisions do not apply. They would in addition receive the basic award for unfair dismissal if the employee has a year's service (see para 18.26).

Remedies for unfair dismissal (automatic and ordinary dismissal)

18.26 Where the tribunal makes a finding that the claimant has been unfairly dismissed, it must make a declaration to that effect and may make the following orders:

- reinstatement or re-engagement,
- compensation which consists of:
  - a basic award, calculated according to age and length of service (for those with service of a year or more);
  - a compensatory award (see below).

Reinstatement and re-engagement

18.27 Reinstatement is an order that the employee returns to the same job on the same terms and conditions as if there had been no dismissal.[24] Re-engagement is where the tribunal orders that the claimant be employed by the employer (or a successor or associated employer) in other suitable employment.[25] Such orders cannot be made in discrimination claims.

18.28 The tribunal must inform claimants that an order may be made for reinstatement or re-engagement and ask if they wish the tribunal to make such an order.[26] Where the dismissal is automatically unfair because of a breach of the DDP, the tribunal must, where reinstatement or re-engagement is ordered, also order the employer to pay the employee an award of four weeks' pay unless this would cause injustice to the employer.[27]

18.29 The ET1 form asks if the claimant wishes to be reinstated or re-engaged and this section should be completed if an order for re-engagement or reinstatement is sought. An application for

---

24 ERA 1996 s114.
25 ERA 1996 s115.
26 ERA 1996 s112(2).
27 ERA 1996 s112(5)(6) inserted by EA 2002 s34(2).

reinstatement or re-engagement may be made later in the proceedings but if the employer has already employed a permanent
replacement, having taken into account that their former employee
seeks compensation only, the tribunal may refuse to make an order.[28]

18.30   Reinstatement and re-engagement are rare where discrimination
is claimed as well as unfair dismissal as the relationship has usually
broken down. The details are outside the scope of this book.[29]

Compensation

18.31   This is made up of a basic and a compensatory award. Broadly similar
principles apply to the assessment of the compensatory award
whether the claim is for unfair or discriminatory dismissal – apart
from the statutory cap in unfair dismissal cases and the lack of any
provision for contributory fault in discrimination cases.

Basic award for unfair dismissal (not discriminatory dismissal)

18.32   This is calculated in broadly the same way as a redundancy payment.
It consists of:

- half a week's gross pay for each year worked while under the age
  of 22;
- one week's gross pay for the years in which the worker was
  between the ages of 22 and 40; and
- one-and-a-half week's gross pay for each year of employment
  when the employee was 41 years old or more, until s/he reaches
  65 years.

18.33   Length of service is calculated up to the effective date of termination.[30]
Employees with less than one year's service are not entitled to a basic
award even in automatic unfair dismissal case (where there is no
service requirement for bringing the claim). The week's pay used to
calculate the basic award is subject to a maximum limit. In 2006–
2007 the maximum was £290 gross per week[31] based on a maximum
of 20 years' calculable continuous service.[32]

---

28   ERA 1996 s116(5), (6).
29   See ERA 1996 ss114–117.
30   ERA 1996 s97.
31   It increases every February.
32   ERA 1996 s227.

18.34   The award may be reduced:[33]

- if the employee unreasonably refuses an offer of reinstatement;
- on the ground of the employee's conduct before the dismissal except in most redundancy cases;
- if the employee received a redundancy payment (statutory or otherwise),
- if the employee received a payment under a designated dismissal procedure agreement.[34]

Increase in basic award for breach of DDP

18.35   Where the employer is in breach of the DDP making the dismissal automatically unfair under ERA 1996 s98A(1) and a compensatory award has been made under ERA 1996 s112(4), the minimum basic award is four weeks' pay. This minimum can be waived where it would cause injustice to the employer. This applies before any reduction is made for sums already awarded or paid in respect of redundancy.[35] Otherwise the basic award is not subject to the percentage increase or deduction as a result of failure to comply with the dispute resolution procedures.

Compensatory award

18.36   This is an amount which the tribunal considers 'just and equitable in all the circumstances having regard to the loss sustained by the complainant in consequence of the dismissal in so far as that loss is attributable to action taken by the employer'.[36] It includes:

- loss of earnings (past and future) after deduction of tax and national insurance, so it is the net loss that is relevant;
- loss of pension and other benefits (such as car allowance, health insurance);
- expenses incurred in consequence of the dismissal such as in looking for work (this could include travel expenses and the cost of some re-training);
- loss of statutory protection in respect of unfair dismissal – usually in the region of £300.

33   ERA 1996 s122.
34   ERA 1996 s122(3A).
35   ERA 1996 s120(1A), (1B) as amended by EA 2002 s43(6).
36   ERA 1996 s123(1).

18.37   The compensatory award may be reduced if:

- the employer has made an ex gratia payment, for example, in respect of redundancy; the basic award will be reduced by any redundancy payment;[37]
- the employee has failed to take reasonable steps to mitigate his/her loss[38] (see para 18.106);
- the dismissal is unfair on procedural grounds, but the employee would have been dismissed in any event[39] (see para xx);
- the employee has contributed to the dismissal;[40] the extent to which contributory fault applies in discriminatory dismissal cases has yet to be decided[41] (see para 18.93);
- the employee has not complied with the DDP (see para 18.15); it will be increased if the employer has not complied with the DDP (see para 18.16).

The order of deductions is set out at para 18.93 onwards.

Maximum compensatory award

18.38   The maximum amount that can be awarded for unfair dismissal to 31 January 2007 is £58,400.[42] This applies *after* any adjustments have been made.

Loss of benefits

18.39   In assessing compensation account will be taken of past and future loss of such benefits (see para 18.52).

---

37   ERA 1996 s123(7).
38   ERA 1996 s123(4).
39   ERA 1996 s98A(2) which provides that subject to compliance with the statutory procedure, the dismissal will be unfair even if the employer failed to follow a fair procedure provided this would have made no difference, ie the employee would have been dismissed in any event. This is the *Polkey* reduction *Polkey v AE Dayton Services Ltd*; [1988] ICR 142; [1987] IRLR 503, HL; see also *Alexander v Bridgen Enterprises Ltd* [2006] IRLR 422 where the EAT held that ERA 1996 s98A(2) meant that an employer could escape liability in respect of failure to follow *any* procedure – provided it has followed the statutory procedure – if the employee would have been dismissed in any event. A different approach was taken by the EAT in *Mason v Governing Body of Ward End Primary School* [2006] IRLR 432 where the EAT held that ERA 1996 s98A(2) only applies to the employer's procedure. The details are outside the scope of this book.
40   ERA 1996 s123(6).
41   *Way v Crouch* [2005] IRLR 604. See note 118.
42   ERA 1996 s124(1)(b); this is increased annually on 1 February.

Recoupment

18.40 Claimants who have received job seekers' allowance will have the total jobseeker's allowance (JSA) recouped from the award by the Department of Social Security (DSS).[43] This does not apply to discrimination claims nor if the case is settled and no compensation order is made by the tribunal (see para 18.11).

Remedies under the SDA 1975 including discriminatory dismissal

18.41 Where a complaint is upheld the tribunal shall make such of the following orders as it considers just and equitable:

- an order declaring the rights of the parties;
- compensation for damages as could be ordered by a county court for tort (see para 18.43(e)), including aggravated damages, injury to feelings, personal injury and interest and exemplary damages in exceptional cases; and
- recommendation for action. See para 18.94.[44]

Declaration

18.42 This is a statement declaring the rights of the complainant and respondent. It is not enforceable, so if the employer chooses not to comply with it, nothing can be done.

Compensation for discrimination: the principles

18.43 Account should be taken of EC law when assessing compensation. The ETD (as amended) provides that there must be real and effective compensation or reparation for the loss and damage sustained as a result of the discrimination in a way which is dissuasive and proportionate to the damage suffered. In discrimination cases (apart from slightly different rules for indirect discrimination, see para 18.49 onwards), the main principles tribunals should follow are:

a) A tribunal can award what it considers 'just and equitable'. An appellate court will not usually interfere with the amount

---

43 Employment Tribunals Act 1996 ss16–17.
44 SDA 1975 s65.

awarded unless the tribunal has acted on a wrong principle of law or misunderstood the facts or where there was a wholly erroneous estimate of the damage suffered.[45]

b) There is no cap on the amount of compensation that can be awarded in discrimination claims.[46] The claimant should be compensated fully for all loss suffered as a result of the discrimination.[47]

c) A claimant cannot recover twice for the same loss. Thus, where there has been a successful claim for unfair dismissal and discriminatory dismissal, loss of earnings will be assessed once but the statutory cap will not apply to any compensation for discrimination.[48] Tribunals should order compensation under the discrimination legislation to give full compensation free from the unfair dismissal cap. Failure to do so is likely to be a breach of the EC principles set out in *Marshall*.[49] Interest will only be awarded on compensation for discrimination.

d) The financial consequences of being deprived of the opportunity of promotion should be compensated for under damages for loss of employment; there is no separate head of damage for loss of career prospects.[50] This loss would be assessed on the difference in earnings between the present job and the promotion based on the percentage chance of the claimant getting the promotion.

e) Compensation is assessed on the basis that claimants must be put in the position they would have been in if the discrimination had not been committed (ie, in the same way as in an action in tort). In *MOD v Cannock*[51] the CA said that:

> . . . as best as money can do it, the [complainant] must be put into the position she would have been in but for the unlawful conduct of [the discriminator].

---

45 *Coleman v Skyrail Oceanic Ltd* [1981] IRLR 398, CA.
46 Section 65(2), which set a limit on compensation, was repealed by the Sex Discrimination and Equal Pay (Remedies) Regulations 1993 SI No 2798.
47 This is reinforced by the ECJ decision in *Marshall v Southampton Area Health Authority (No 2)* [1993] IRLR 445 where the ECJ held that compensation must enable the loss actually suffered as a result of the discrimination to be made good in full.
48 See note 46.
49 *Marshall v Southampton Area Health Authority (No 2)* [1993] IRLR 445.
50 *MOD v Cannock* [1994] IRLR 509, EAT.
51 *MOD v Cannock* [1994] IRLR 509 at 517 Morrison; see also *MOD v Wheeler* [1998] IRLR 23, CA.

Cannock was followed by the Court of Appeal in *Brash-Hall v Getty Images Ltd*[52] where the tribunal had found that the claimant would have returned to her previous job at her previous rate of pay at the end of maternity leave had there not been discrimination (in the form of a bogus restructuring). However, it found that there was a genuine restructuring three months later when she would have been offered suitable alternative work but she would have refused it. The *Cannock* test was, 'what would have happened if the Appellant, absent any sex discrimination, had returned to her old job and had then rejected a suitable alternative post with the same employer?' (see also below at para 18.57).

Predicting the future

f)   When assessing compensation for future loss, the tribunal will consider how long the claimant is likely to have remained with the same employer but for the dismissal.[53] Thus, there would need to be good evidence to find that the claimant would definitely have remained with the respondent for, say, a further 20 years. In *Vento (No 2)* where the Court of Appeal upheld the tribunal decision that the claimant would have remained with the police for 21 years as serving in the police had been a long-held ambition of hers. Statistics about past patterns in women's employment should not be relevant with the introduction of family friendly employment practices and the increasing number of women returning to work after leave (see para 1.1 onwards).

g)   In pregnancy dismissal cases, the Court of Appeal has held that the tribunal must assess what the woman would have earned had she remained in the job, deduct from that monies earned and then discount the net loss by a percentage to reflect the chance that she might not have returned from maternity leave in any event (see para 18.100 onwards).[54]

h)   In *Abbey National v Formoso*[55] a woman was dismissed for a reason other than pregnancy following a disciplinary hearing which she could not attend because of a pregnancy-related reason. The EAT said that when awarding compensation, the question was,

---

52   [2006] EWCA Civ 531 9 May 2006.
53   *Vento v Chief Constable of West Yorkshire Police (No 2)* [2003] IRLR 102, CA.
54   *Ministry of Defence v Wheeler* [1998] IRLR 23, CA.
55   *Abbey National plc v Formoso* [1999] IRLR 222, EAT.

'what were the chances, in percentage terms, that the employer would have dismissed the claimant had she not been pregnant and had a fair procedure been followed?'. The EAT said that the correct approach in awarding compensation for discrimination was more akin to the question posed in *Polkey*[56] following a finding of procedurally unfair dismissal: 'what were the chances that the compainant would have been dismissed had a fair procedure been followed? The loss of a chance of retaining employment is to be expressed in percentage terms.'[57] In practice, this principle is most likely to apply in cases where the dismissal is not related to pregnancy but where a fair procedure is undermined by pregnancy or maternity leave. This is because once a dismissal (or other act) is tainted by discrimination, it is very difficult to envisage that a dismissal which follows shortly afterwards will be uncontaminated by that discrimination.

Causation

i) The claimant can claim for any pecuniary loss properly attributable to the unlawful discrimination, which could include interest on a bank overdraft if directly attributable to the dismissal.[58] Compensation is to compensate for loss suffered, subject to the duty on the claimant to mitigate the loss. It is not for the purpose of punishing the respondent, except in situations where aggravated or exemplary damages are awarded (see para 18.83 onwards).

j) The loss must have been caused by the act of discrimination. If there were other causes, such as personal difficulties (unconnected with the discrimination) that contributed to a claimant's future inability to seek work, the tribunal will need to assess the extent of loss attributable to the discrimination, by applying a percentage. In stress cases, the EAT has held that the ET should assess the chance that the fact that the claimant was unable to work (because of her underlying illness) was not caused by the respondent (see *Seafield Holdings v Drewett* [2006] UKEAT 0199/06/2706, 27 June 2006).

k) The loss does not have to be reasonably foreseeable, at least in cases of direct discrimination. In *Essa v Laing Ltd* one judge (LJ

---

56 *Polkey v A E Dayton Services Ltd* [1987] IRLR 503 (see note 39).
57 *Abbey National plc v Formoso* at para 40.
58 *Coleman v Skyrail Oceanic Ltd* [1981] IRLR 398, CA.

Clarke) held that compensation should be calculated on a test of causation,[59] so that foreseeability was not necessary. Pill LJ said that where there is direct discrimination by racial abuse the need to establish foreseeability does not apply, that racial abuse was akin to the tort of assault and battery and the victim should be compensated for the loss which arises naturally and directly from the wrong. However, he said it was possible that where discrimination takes other forms different considerations will apply.[60] An example might be indirect discrimination where the employer was unaware of the impact of a practice on the claimant. The Court of Appeal held that even if foreseeability did apply, the employer will be liable unless the damage differs *in kind* (rather than in extent) from what was foreseeable. As injury to feelings and psychiatric injury are similar in kind, if one is foreseeable so should the other be.[61]

l) The chain of causation is not broken by the employer's second wrong, for example where discrimination is followed by unfair dismissal. This does not terminate liability for the earlier wrong of discrimination thereby leading to further losses having to be assessed under the unfair dismissal regime with its statutory cap on compensation (see para 18.47 onwards).[62]

m) In determining the claimants' losses, the discriminator must take the claimants as it finds them, thus if the victim is particularly sensitive then provided the loss is caused by the discrimination, the discriminator will be liable for the loss.[63]

Reductions and percentage adjustments

n) A claimant must give credit for any savings made as a result of the discrimination. Thus, if an employee is dismissed and so saves the costs of childcare, which she needed in order to work, these will be deducted from the compensation. The EAT held, in *MOD v Cannock*,[63a] that childcare costs which notionally would

---

59 Ie, was the damage caused by the discrimination, applying the 'but for' test.
60 *Essa v Laing Ltd* [2004] IRLR 313; this was a case of gross racial abuse; see *Clarke* at para 44 and *Pill* at paras 37–39. The third judge dissented.
61 Thus, if it is foreseeable that the claimant will suffer injury to feelings, it is foreseeable that s/he will also suffer psychiatric injury; see paras 19–20.
62 See *HM Prison Service v Beart (No 2)* [2005] IRLR 568.
63 This is often referred to as the 'eggshell skull principle'.
63a See note 50.

have had to be incurred to enable a claimant to return to work should be set off in full against her damages for loss of earnings. At that time (1994) the EAT held that the fact that the claimant's husband might have borne half the burden should be ignored. That, in itself, is arguably a discriminatory assumption. Increasingly, the reality is that parents expect to share the cost of childcare and if this reflects the position of the claimant (and her partner) only 50% of childcare costs should be deducted. However, a failure by the tribunal to consider childcare costs may lead to an appeal.[64]

o)   In some circumstances, compensation will be reduced if the claimant failed to follow a requirement of the statutory GP or DDP and increased if the employer failed to comply with a requirement of either (see para 18.14 onwards).

p)   As with unfair dismissal claims, a claimant is under an obligation to take reasonable steps mitigate the loss (see para 18.106 onwards).

q)   A percentage reduction may be made on the basis that the claimant may not have remained with the employer (see para 18.56) or would not have obtained the job for which she applied (see para 18.54) or would have been dismissed in any event (see para 18.43(h)).

r)   Conduct has not normally been relevant in discrimination cases so that the compensation should not be reduced because of the claimant's behaviour. However, the position is not entirely clear. In *Way v Crouch*[65] the EAT held that the test for contributory fault in discriminaton cases, came under the Law Reform (Contributory Negligence) Act 1945 so that there may be a reduction where the claimant's conduct amounts to negligence or breach of a legal duty and it contributed to the damage.[66]

Joint liability

18.44   Compensation can be awarded against the employer and an employee (who is liable for the discrimination) but the tribunal must

---

64   *Wallington v S & B Car Hire* EAT/0240/03/MAA where the EAT remitted the case to the ET for consideration of childcare costs and other matters.

65   [2005] IRLR 605.

66   *Way and another v Crouch* [2005] IRLR 603; the relevance of contributory conduct was raised in *Taylor v OCS Group Ltd* but was not decided [2006] EWCA Civ 702.

make clear its reason for doing so and consider the extent of the individual's responsibility and their culpability, compared to that of the employer. It will be rare for 100% of the award to be made against each party jointly and severally.[67] In *Way and another v Crouch*,[68] the managing director dismissed the claimant when she broke off their relationship and the tribunal found both he and the company liable for the dismissal. The EAT upheld the tribunal's award of compensation for the dismissal on a joint and several basis against the respondent company and its managing director (so both were liable for the whole award if one party is insolvent). However, the EAT said the tribunal should have apportioned liability between the company and its employee, having regard to the relative responsibility of each wrongdoer, not financial resources. The EAT stressed that such awards would be unusual and set out guidelines.[69] It said that the tribunal must have regard to the Civil Liability (Contribution) Act 1978 which applies in tort cases, such as discrimination.

18.45   In *Gilbank v Miles*,[70] a case where the company was dissolved just before the tribunal hearing, the tribunal found the behaviour of the second respondent, Ms Miles, to a pregnant employee was 'downright vicious', being an inhumane and sustained campaign of bullying and discrimination' that was 'targeted, deliberate, repeated and consciously inflicted'. The EAT upheld the tribunal's award of £25,000 for injury to feelings to be awarded jointly and severally against Ms Miles (a director of the first respondent and main shareholder). As the EAT said that 'we have no doubt that in 'lifting the veil', the person who made this company tick was Ms Miles. If the claimant was not paid, undoubtedly the tribunal can draw an inference that it was at Ms Miles's behest'. The EAT's decision was upheld by the Court of Appeal which analysed in some detail the liability of a

---

67   *Way v Crouch* [2005] IRLR 603; the EAT held that the tribunal must have regard to the Civil Liability (Contribution) Act 1978 which applies in tort cases, such as discrimination.

68   [2005] IRLR 603; an individual may be personally liable for an act of dismissal under section 42(2) read with section 41(1) (see para 2.15 on vicarious liability).

69   See para 23; this mainly relates to allocating responsibility and not the ability to pay.

70   *Gilbank v Miles* [2006] IRLR 538, CA.

worker which is particularly important where the employing organ-isation no longer exists (see paras 2.17–2.20).[71]

Tax and grossing up

18.46   Where the award, or part of it, is taxable (eg, more than £30,000), that part should be grossed up so that the claimant receives the full net compensation, after deduction of tax. Otherwise the claimant will be taxed twice, by having tax deducted from the award and then paying tax on any compensation over £30,000 (see para 18.125).

Discrimination followed by unfair dismissal: effect on compensation

18.47   In *HM Prison Service v Beart (No 2)* the claimant requested an adjustment in her hours so that she could collect her children. This was not only refused but treated by her line manager as a resignation from her job. She was offered an alternative job in the afternoon on a lower pay, which would not help with her childcare. She then went off sick, suffering from depresssion (which was a disability) and never returned to work. She was subsequently dismissed (unfairly as the tribunal found) for undertaking work in a shop while claiming sick pay from the Prison Service. She asked twice to find out why the doctor's recommendation that she be relocated had not been imple-mented. She claimed disability discrimination and unfair dismissal.

18.48   The Court of Appeal gave short shrift to the respondent's argu-ment that the dismissal broke the chain of causation thereby termin-ating the liability for the earlier wrong of disability discrimination so that all further losses had to be assessed under the unfair dismissal regime with its statutory cap on compensation. The Court of Appeal held that all that happened was that the employer committed two discrete wrongs in respect of which the statute has provided a cap for one but not the other.[72] Even if the dismissal had been fair the claim-

---

71   [2006] IRLR 538, CA.
72   [2005] IRLR 568, CA; [2005] IRLR 171. Rix LJ paras 30–34 where he said that it was puzzling that the respondent's own act of unfair dismissal could break the chain of causation, saying: 'This is the language of new intervening act, but I do not understand how it is said that the unfair dismissal is an 'intervening' act, when it is the act of the tortfeasor itself . . . Nor do I understand why the mere act of dismissal, even if it were justified which of course it was not, could do more to wash away the long-lasting effects of the prior discriminatory act than merely to prevent the damages for loss of earnings being measured by a comparison with earnings under the old employment' (see para 30).

ant would still have been entitled to damages in respect of losses incurred as a result of the employer's previous discriminatory act; this had contributed to her psychiatric injury which prevented her working in the future. Thus, compensation was awarded for loss suffered as a result of the discrimination. This was future loss of earnings (to be assessed by an actuary), injury to feelings (£10,000), personal injury (£22,000), aggravated damages (£5,000) in respect of the discrimination claim and £3,300 basic award for the unfair dismissal claim.

Unintentional indirect discrimination

18.49 The SDA 1975 used to provide that no compensation could be awarded for unintentional indirect discrimination. The present position under SDA 1975 s65(1B) is that no compensation will be awarded if the employer proves that the provision, criterion or practice was not applied with the intention of treating the claimant unfavourably on the ground of her sex or marital status unless:

a) the tribunal makes a declaration or recommendation as though it had no power to order compensation; and
b) it considers it just and equitable to make an order for compensation in addition.

18.50 Thus, if the application of the PCP (provision, criterion or practice, see Chapter 13) is treated as intentional it is not necessary to prove a) and b). The EAT, in *London Underground v Edwards*[73] held that where the employer was aware of the effect of a PCP on the claimant as a member of a particular disadvantaged group, that was sufficient to establish intentionality. Similarly, in *Walker Ltd v Hussain*[74] (a race discrimination case) Mummery J said that the tribunal may infer that a person wants to produce certain consequences from the fact that he acted knowing what those consequences would be. In most cases, particularly as the employee must have raised a grievance, the employer will be aware of the consequences of, for example, a provision requiring full-time work or overtime. Further, even if there is no 'intention' it will be rare that a declaration or recommendation will be a sufficient remedy. In most cases it is not possible to make a recommendation and it will be 'just and equitable' to order compensation. In practice tribunals do award

73 [1995] IRLR 355.
74 [1996] IRLR 1.

compensation in indirect discrimination cases, which is often sub-stantial. The highest tribunal award in a sex discrimination case in 2004 was in an indirect sex discrimination case when £175,000 was awarded.[75]

Types of compensation

18.51   Compensation is broken down into different categories:

- *actual past losses* which can be quantified, such as loss of earnings and benefits up to the date of the hearing, less any earnings received (or which should have been earned had there been appropriate mitigation);
- *future losses*, including loss of earnings, pension and other benefits;
  - *injury to feelings*;
  - *personal injury*;
  - *aggravated damages*;
  - *exemplary damages*;
  - *interest*.

18.52   Loss of benefits includes:

- pension rights (see para 18.116 onwards);
- company car and car allowance;
- medical and other insurance;
- profit-related pay and bonuses;
- subsidised mortgage and/or loans;
- subsidised accommodation;
- subsidised childcare;
- maternity pay.

18.53   The calculation is the same as for unfair dismissal, ie add the net loss suffered as a result of the dismissal (subject to the need to gross up to avoid double taxation), including benefits, plus expenses in looking for other work, then subtract wages and benefits received and, where appropriate childcare costs (or a proportion of them) if no longer incurred (because of the dismissal).

18.54   Where there is uncertainty about whether, for example, the claim-ant would have been dismissed in any event or, but for the discrimin-

---

75 *Griffin v West Midlands Policy Authority* Case no 5208776/00. See EOR 144 August 2005.

ation, been appointed to the job or promotion, the tribunal will have to assess the compensation on the basis of a percentage chance. Thus, if the claimant had a 75% chance of being appointed or promoted, the award will be 75% of that element of the total loss. If the chance of the claimant being dismissed for a reason other than her pregnancy was 40%, the compensation will be reduced by 40% (see para 18.43).

Future loss

18.55 This is the most difficult area of loss to calculate as it is by definition uncertain. In determining losses up to the date of the hearing the ET must decide what would have occurred on the balance of probabilities, so can rely on the 'but for' test. However, for future damages the ET must estimate the chances that a particular event would have happened. (See *Seafield Holdings Ltd v Drewett* [2006] UKEAT 0199/06/2706, 27 June 2006.) The tribunal will have to assess, in respect of the claimant:

- the likelihood that s/he would have remained with the same employer and for how long;
- if s/he has no job, length of unemployment;
- likelihood of getting another job and the probability of the alternative job having the same or similar terms and conditions;
- future prospects;
- loss of benefits, including pension or a lower benefits package.

18.56 In *Vento*[76] the Court of Appeal upheld a tribunal finding that there was a 75% chance that the claimant would have remained in the police force all her working life. The court said that the question of how long an employee would have remained employed has to be answered on the basis of the best assessment that can be made on the relevant material available, which includes statistical material showing the percentage of women who have in the past continued to serve in the police force until the age of retirement. At the time this was 9%. However, the court recognised that recent and continuing social changes affecting women in the workplace were reflected in adjustments to working conditions in the police force, such as family friendly policies aimed at retaining women. Thus, although 75% was high it was not perverse so could not be overruled. As acknowledged, the assessment is not an exact science.

---

76 *Vento v Chief Constable of West Yorkshire Police (No 2)* [2003] IRLR 102, CA.

18.57   A claimant may not receive as much compensation if, following a discriminatory dismissal, she would have been made redundant some months later in any event. In *Brash-Hall* (see para 18.43) the tribunal found that there had been an unfair and discriminatory constructive dismissal at the end of her maternity leave in August 2003 but that three months after this happened (in November 2003) there was a genuine reorganisation during which she would have been offered a suitable job, but she would have refused. Thus her 'hypothetical refusal of a suitable alternative job' would have been unreasonable so she would not have received a redundancy payment. The tribunal only awarded compensation up to November 2003 finding that she would have left in November in any event. However, if she had turned down the alternative job because she had been discriminated against then the hypothetical refusal should not have reduced compensation.

18.58   The Court of Appeal held that the claimant must be put in the position she would have been in had there been no unlawful constructive dismissal. She would have been entitled to three months' notice at the time of the redundancy but there was insufficient evidence to show that she would have received the enhanced contractual severance package as it was unclear if she would have been willing to sign a compromise agreement.[77]

18.59   This judgment is specific to the facts found by the tribunal and the fact that in the Court of Appeal the claimant based her appeal on the ET's findings that she would have been offered a job in the second restructuring and she would have refused it. In many cases it will not be possible to predict that an employee, who has suffered discrimination during her maternity leave, would have refused a suitable alternative job during a genuine restructing some months later. It is almost impossible for a tribunal to say with any degree of certainty what would have happened had the claimant not suffered the previous act(s) of discrimination leading to her resignation and successful constructive dismissal claim.

18.60   The tribunal will take into account at the hearing:

a) in relation to the chance of the employee remaining in the same job;
    • the employee's commitment to her or his career;

---

77 In the tribunal she was claiming over £200,000 which the Court of Appeal thought was excessive. She was awarded loss of benefits and pay for her 3-month notice period.

- statistical evidence as to length of time employees (male or female) tended to spend in that same job;
- other factors such as whether or not she would have been made redundant in any event in the foreseeable future.

b) in relation to future work;
  - attempts the claimant has made to find work;
  - the job market for the particular type of job;
  - any particular disadvantage suffered by the claimant and this could include any disability suffered or the fact that s/he wants to work part-time;
  - the claimant's age;
  - length of time the claimant has been unemployed. It is usually easier to get a job when in work;

18.61 If the claimant is looking for part-time work, in most jobs, it will take longer to find alternative employment. Although an increasing number of employers are in practice prepared to allow their own employees to work part-time (or otherwise flexibly) this rarely applies to external applicants, even though this may be indirect discrimination.

18.62 Where there is likely to be substantial loss, it is worth considering whether to instruct an employment expert who will consider the claimant's job history, experience, qualifications, time out of the job market, age and other relevant factors and prepare a report advising on what type of job the claimant may be expected to get, when, career progression and long-term future loss.[78] This would enable a detailed schedule of loss to be prepared.

18.63 The usual way to calculate compensation for long-term future losses is to calculate net losses for the number of years the claimant is likely to be unemployed or earning less and discounting this to take into account factors such as age. This calculation can be done by using the Ogden tables which are used by personal injury lawyers to calculate future loss taking into account contingencies such as death. The tables refer to the total years of future loss as the 'multiplicand.' and the adjusted figure taking into account the appropriate discount as the 'multiplier'.[79] The steps are as follows:

---

78 It may be possible to get details of experts through Google on the internet, searching under 'forensic employment experts'.
79 Tables with an explanation are produced by Sweet & Maxwell, *Facts and Figures: Tables for the Calculation of Damages*. They are updated regularly.

a) Assess the period during which the claimant is likely to be without work and/or is likely to be on a lower income, say five years – this will depend on individual circumstances.

b) Calculate what the claimant would have received by way of net earnings and benefits from the respondent during this period, including any pay rises or promotions.[80]

c) Calculate the net earnings the claimant is likely to receive during this period from alternative employment. This will also be based on an assessment of likely earnings and benefits. If the claimant sets up in business this would be the profit after deducting expenses.

d) Deduct, if appropriate, any childcare costs not incurred due to unemployment.

e) The resulting figure, which is the total future net loss is the multiplicand.

f) Apply to the multiplicand the mutliplier; this is determined by reference to the number of years of future loss. It reduces the multiplicand to take account of contingencies, such as death, and the fact that the claimant receives a lump sum up front (ie, accelerated receipt). Thus, it is used to assess the present capital value of future annual loss calculated on the basis of various assumptions. There are different tables for men and women.

Injury to feelings

18.64 The tribunal should normally award a sum for injury to feelings suffered as a result of the discrimination or harassment.[81] This includes stress, anger, embarrassment, anxiety, mental distress, humiliation, depression, interference with family life, frustration at having a chosen career brought to an end, loss of congenial employment,[82] damage to reputation.[83] An award can include consideration of those matters that arise out of the discrimination and are consequential upon it, such as an employee having to undergo an unjustified disciplinary investigation, a lengthy grievance procedure and stress coping with the aftermath of the discrimination.[84] Awards

---

80 The chance of promotion may need to be calculated on a percentage basis, ie, there is a 60% chance of promotion.

81 SDA 1975 s66(4).

82 Loss of congenial employment is not a separate head from injury to feelings but is part of it.

83 *Vento v Chief Constable of West Yorkshire Police (No 2)* [2003] IRLR 102, CA.

84 See *British Telecommunications plc v Reid* [2004] IRLR 327, CA.

for injury to feelings are increasing. In 2004 the average award for a sex discrimination claim was £4,601, up from £3,685 in 2003.[85]

18.65   In *Vento* the Court of Appeal adopted the principles set out in *HM Prison Service v Johnson* stating:[86]

- awards for injury to feelings should compensate fully without punishing;
- awards should not be too low as to diminish respect for the policy of the anti-discrimination legislation, but should not be excessive in that they could be seen as 'untaxed riches';
- awards should bear some broad general similarity to the range of awards in personal injury cases In *Vento* the court looked at the Judicial Studies Board Guidelines;
- tribunals should consider the value in everyday life of the sum;
- there must be public respect for the level of awards.

18.66   The claimant must provide evidence of injury to feelings. In *Cannock*[87] the EAT said that, although an award was not automatic, no tribunal will take much persuasion that the anger, distress and affront caused by the act of discrimination has injured the claimant's feelings. In *Murray v Powertech (Scotland) Ltd*[88] the EAT said that a claim for hurt feelings is so fundamental to a sex discrimination case that it is almost inevitable. The hurt feelings should be set out in a statement or the claimant should give evidence about the effect of the discrimination. It is very important to provide evidence of any injury to feelings. This may be brought out through the claimant's evidence and witnesses, including, if possible, a doctor or psychotherapist's report.

18.67   The Court of Appeal has given guidance on the assessment of injury to feelings, which must be followed by tribunals.[89] There are three bands but it is important to note that these should be adjusted to take into account inflation.[90]

---

85 Equal Opportunities Review publishes an annual review of compensation in discrimination cases.
86 *Armitage, Marsden and HM Prison Service v Johnson* [1997] IRLR 162 EAT; £21,000 was awarded for injury to feelings and £7,500 for aggravated damages in a case involving a campaign of racial harassment.
87 *MOD v Cannock and Others* [1994] IRLR 509, EAT.
88 [1994] IRLR 509, EAT.
89 *Vento v Chief Constable of West Yorkshire Police (No 2)* [2003] IRLR 102, CA.
90 In *Miles v Gilbank* the EAT pointed out that *Vento* was then three years old and whilst there is not raging inflation there is quiet inflation which devalues monetary values. The award was upheld by the Court of Appeal (see para 18.74).

18.68   The top band is normally between £15,000 and £25,000. This is for the most serious cases, such as where there has been a lengthy campaign of discriminatory harassment on the ground of sex or race. Only in the most exceptional case should an award of compensation exceed £25,000.

18.69   The middle band is between £5,000 and £15,000. This is for serious cases, which are not in the top band.

18.70   The lowest band is between £500 and £5,000 and this is appropriate for less serious cases, such as where the act of discrimination is an isolated or one off occurrence. In general awards of less than £500 should be avoided altogether as they risk being regarded as so low as not to be a proper recognition of injury to feelings.

18.71   Within each band there is 'considerable flexibility, allowing tribunals to fix what is considered to be fair, reasonable and just compensation in the particular circumstances of the case'.[91] Generally, the appellate courts will not interfere unless there is a clear error. However, in *Zaiwalla & Co v Walia*[92] the EAT overturned a tribunal's award of £15,000 for injury to feelings and substituted £10,000 saying that the injury was not, as the tribunal found, in the bracket of mid-range, moderately severe post-traumatic stress disorder, and the personal injury comparison was overemphasised as a criterion.

18.72   In *Vento* the court said that regard should be had to the overall magnitude of the sum total of awards of compensation for non-pecuniary loss made for injury to feelings, psychiatric damage and aggravated damage. Double recovery should be avoided by taking appropriate account of the overlap between the individual heads of damage. Thus, in *Vento* the court commented on the overlap between injury to feelings and psychiatric injury.

18.73   The award should be the going rate for compensation at the time of the hearing, even if it is more in real terms than it would have been at the date of the injury complained of. The amounts awarded have varied enormously.[93]

18.74   In *Miles v Gilbank*[94] the EAT in 2005 upheld a tribunal award of £25,000 for injury to feelings and £500 for personal injury in a case where the tribunal found that there was 'an inhumane and sustained campaign of bullying and discrimination' which was 'targeted, delib-

---

91 *Vento* para 66.
92 [2002] IRLR 697.
93 Equal Opportunities Review publishes an annual summary of the year's awards.
94 [2005] UKEAT 0396 05 1409, 14 September 2005, EAT upheld by the CA: *Gilbank v Miles* [2006] IRLR 538, CA.

erate, repeated and consciously inflicted' against the claimant following the announcement of her pregnancy. The award was made jointly and severally against the company and the director and majority shareholder. The EAT pointed out that the tribunal found that the claimant was put through the anxiety and distress of being prevented from doing things needed to protect the child, saying:

> A woman will suffer a great deal of anguish if she is denied doing that, without good cause, which she knows is in the child's best interests and has been advised as such. We do not believe that we, sitting here remote from the claimant's evidence, should have the arrogant imperialist view that we know better than the tribunal which included two women and a man . . . who said 'it not only demonstrated to the claimant a total lack of concern for the welfare of the claimant itself but a callous disregard or concern for the life of an unborn child'.

18.75   The Court of Appeal upheld the EAT's decision. Arden LJ said that the guidance laid down by the Court of Appeal in *Vento was* not intended to be applied like rules of law, emphasising that

> . . . it involved the well being of Ms Gilbank's unborn child. That gives this case added seriousness and must have imposed an additional level of stress on Ms Gilbank as an expectant mother.[95]

18.76   In *McGuigan v TG Baynes*[96] the tribunal awarded £5,000 for injury to feelings, saying that the actions of the respondents, in making the claimant redundant while on maternity leave,

> . . . were an affront to the Applicant's desire to pursue her career as a committed professional lawyer, and, at the same time, to fulfill her responsibilities as a mother of three children, including a young baby. We also think it relevant to take into account that the actions of the Respondents must have diminished the pleasure of childbirth, in that the baby which ought to have been an unmixed joy for the Applicant must inevitably have been seen as the cause of the loss of her job.

Compensation for personal injury

18.77   In *Sheriff v Klyne Tugs (Lowestoft) Ltd*[97] the Court of Appeal held that a tribunal can award compensation for personal injury, which will generally be psychiatric injury. Thus, if the discrimination has led to a personal injury, such as identifiable damage to health (physical or

95   Para 42.
96   ET 1100249/96/SS, 1 February 1999 Ashford.
97   [1999] IRLR 481, CA.

mental), compensation can include an element for personal injury. This is in addition to injury to feelings.

18.78   Difficult questions arise where the claimant has a history of depression. In *HM Prison Service v Salmon* the EAT pointed out that conventionally a claimant is entitled to recover damages on a 100% basis where the discrimination has made a material contribution to the injury even though there may have been other (or even more) material contributory causes.[98] However, the EAT said that a tribunal may conclude that, because of the vulnerability, the injury might have occurred in any event, in which case this would be reflected, often by a percentage, in the calculation of damages. That may produce a similar result to what would have been achieved by an apportionment of causation, but the reasoning is different and it will certainly not always so do.

18.79   Claims for personal injury will require medical evidence. Where psychiatric injury is claimed usually a report will be required from a consultant psychiatrist, who will usually be required to attend the tribunal unless the report is agreed.

PI claims: Tribunal or county/High Court

18.80   It is not clear whether, if an employee has made a sex discrimination claim in the tribunal s/he can subsequently bring a personal injury claim in the county court or High Court. *Klyne Tugs* suggests not on public policy grounds, as 'claims that have been or could have been litigated in one tribunal, should not be allowed to be litigated in another'. This is a difficult area on which advice should be sought. If there is a serious personal injury, a worker should consider whether it is better to bring the claim in the tribunal or alternatively in a court, where there is a three-year time limit and there is no need to prove discrimination. On the other hand, in the tribunal, there is no need to prove a breach of the employer's duty of care nor foreseeability in respect of the harm suffered (see *Waters v Commissioner of Police of the Metropolis*).[99]

18.81   For discussion about withdrawal and dismissal of a claim and its effect on the claimant's ability to bring a similar claim elsewhere, see para 17.145 onwards.

98 [2001] IRLR 425, EAT at para 20.
99 [2000] IRLR 720, HL.

18.82 Where a claimant has suffered psychiatric injury s/he may be disabled and within the protection of the Disability Discrimination Act 1995.

Aggravated damages

18.83 Compensation may include aggravated damages where the respondent has behaved in a high-handed, malicious, insulting or oppressive manner in committing the act of discrimination.[100] This is separate from injury to feelings and should not be treated as part of them.[101] Examples of behaviour that might lead to aggravated damages include failing to take a complaint seriously,[102] poor handling of a grievance, promotion of the perpetrator during the investigation[103] unsatisfactory answers to a questionnaire,[104] unjustified criticisims of the claimant, the conduct of proceedings.[105]

18.84 In *Ministry of Defence v Meredith*[106] the EAT held that there must be a causal connection between the exceptional or contumelious conduct or motive in committing the wrong and the intangible loss, such as injury to feelings. The claimant must have had some knowledge or suspicion of the conduct or motive that caused it. The claimant in this case was not aware that the employer's conduct was unlawful when she was dismissed. Therefore, any injury to feelings she suffered as a result of her dismissal could not have been aggravated by any improper conduct or motive on the part of the employer of which she was wholly unaware.

18.85 A tribunal can take account of all matters up to and including the hearing, so would include the way a complaint was handled including the comparative treatment of the claimant and perpetrator, a character attack on the worker. In *Zailwalla & Co*[107] the EAT held that although cases would be few and far between there was no reason why misconduct in the defence of proceedings should

---

100 See *Alexander v The Home Office* [1988] IRLR 190, CA and *Armitage, Marsden and HM Prison Service v Johnson* where the EAT held that the torts of discrimination may be sufficiently intentional as to enable the claimant to rely upon malice or the respondent's manner of committing the tort or other conduct as aggravating the injury to feelings.
101 *Scott v Commissioners of Inland Revenue* [2004] IRLR 713, CA.
102 *HM Prison v Salmon* [2001] IRLR 425 EAT.
103 *British Telecommunications plc v Reid* [2004] IRLR 327, CA.
104 *City of Bradford Metropolitan Council v Arora* [1989] IRLR 442, EAT.
105 *Zaiwalla & Co v Walia* [2002] IRLR 697, EAT.
106 [1995] IRLR 539, EAT.
107 [2002] IRLR 697.

not attract aggravated damages; in particular, the EAT said that this may be a more sensible way of dealing with what may amount to victimisation as it would avoid further proceedings. Arguably, an unjustified threat of costs, which are sometimes made as a matter of course by solicitors, could lead to an award for aggravated damages.

18.86   In *HM Prison Service v Salmon*[108] the tribunal made an award of £20,000 for injury to feelings which included £5,000 for aggravated damages. This was based on the fact that the Prison Service perceived the discrimination as trivial and communicated that perception to the claimant. In particular, no disciplinary action was taken against the perpetrator until after the conclusion of the proceedings, which the tribunal found added to the injury to Mrs Salmon's feelings.[109] She was also awarded £11,250 for psychiatric injury. These awards were upheld by the EAT who said it was necessary to stand back and consider the non-pecuniary award as a whole and that a total of £31,250 could not be described as wholly excessive bearing in mind all the unlawful acts and the prolonged depressive illness which followed.

18.87   In *Scott v Commissioners of Inland Revenue*[110] the Court of Appeal said that aggravated damages were intended to deal with cases where the injury was inflicted by conduct which was high-handed, malicious, insulting or oppressive. They should not therefore be treated as part of injury to feelings. In *Virgo Fidelis Senior School v Boyle* the EAT awarded a separate amount for aggravated damages, ie, £10,000, in addition to £25,000 for injury to feelings. Thus, the bands set out in *Vento* do not include an amount for aggravated damages.[111]

Exemplary damages

18.88   Exemplary damages are intended to punish the perpetrator rather than compensate the victim. Although there is no statutory right to exemplary damages for sex discrimination under either UK or EC law, the House of Lords have held, in *Kuddus*, that exemplary dam-

---

108 [2001] IRLR 425.
109 See also *British Telecommunications plc v Reid* [2003] EWCA 1675 where the EAT upheld an award for aggravated damages of £2,000 the tribunal having taken into account the fact that the transgressor was not punished and was promoted even though the charges against hi had not bee determined.
110 [2004] IRLR 713, CA.
111 See para 63 where the EAT said that 'we do not accept that such an award [for aggravated damages] is now subsumed into the *Vento* guidelines'.

ages are not restricted to particular types of cases and are available in any case where the criteria for awarding them are met.[112]

18.89 The criteria are that:

- the conduct constitutes oppressive, arbitrary or unconstitutional actions by public sector employers; or
- the respondent's conduct is calculated to make a profit for himself that may exceed the compensation payable to the claimant; and
- the compensation is inadequate to punish the wrongdoer.

18.90 There are no reported cases where exemplary damages have been awarded in discrimination claims in the tribunal.[113] However, in *Virgo Fidelis* the EAT said that the decision in *Kuddus* opened up the possibility of exemplary damages being awarded provided the criteria were satisfied.[114]

Interest in discrimination claims

18.91 In discrimination cases the tribunal has power to award interest up until the hearing.[115] In relation to injury to feelings interest is for the period beginning on the date of the discrimination and ending on the day of calculation (ie, the remedies hearing). Arguably, in cases of continuing discrimination this could be from the first act of discrimination depending on its severity compared to other acts in the continuing course. In relation to all other sums of damages or compensation interest is awarded from the mid-point date between the act of discrimination and the date of the tribunal hearing. However, the tribunal may award interest over a different period in exceptional circumstances. In *Cannock*[116] the EAT said payment over a longer period may be appropriate where the whole of the loss was incurred many years previously – as in the Ministry of Defence pregnancy cases (see para 18.98 onwards).

112 *Kuddus (AP) v Chief Constable of Leicestershire Constabulary* [2001] UKHL 29.
113 In *Thompson & Hsu v Commissioner of Police for the Metropolis* [1998] QB 498 (a civil action against the police for false imprisonment) the Court of Appeal indicated that where appropriate exemplary damages were likely to be between £5,000 and £50,000.
114 *Virgo Fidelis Senior School v Boyle* [2004] IRLR 268 at para 78 the EAT said that 'we see no reason why in principle exemplary damages could not be awarded, provided that the other conditions are made out'.
115 Employment Tribunals (Interest on awards in discrimination cases) Regulations 1996 SI 1996 No 2803.
116 *MOD v Cannock* [1994] IRLR 509; see also *Derby Specialist Fabrication Ltd v Burton* [2001] IRLR 69.

18.92   Interest is payable only on losses incurred up to the date of the tribunal hearing at which compensation is determined.[117] The current rate of interest is 6%, but it changes periodically.

Order of deductions

18.93 The order of deductions in relation to the compensatory award for unfair dismissal/discrimination is as follows:

a)   calculate the loss suffered as a result of the discrimination, dismissal, detriment or other act; this includes earnings and benefits s/he would have received less those she has received from other employment (see para 18.113 for calculation of percentage chance that a woman would not have returned from maternity leave);

b)   deduct any payments made by the employer as compensation for the dismissal other than an enhanced redundancy payment;

c)   if there has been a failure by the claimant to mitigate his/her loss, deduct any amount that should have been earned (see para 18.106);

d)   in unfair dismissal cases make a percentage reduction to reflect the fact, if relevant, that the claimant would have been dismissed in any event, even if a fair procedure had been followed (*Polkey*); this may apply to some discrimination cases too though the test is slightly different (see para 18.43(h));

e)   increase or reduce an award by 10–50% for failure to comply with a statutory dispute resolution procedure (see para 18.114 onwards);

f)   make any reduction for contributuory fault, in unfair dismissal claims. Note that in *Way v Crouch*[118] the EAT held that there may be a reduction in compensation in discrimination claims where the claimant's conduct itself amounts to negligence or breach of a legal duty and contributed to the damage; these cases are likely to be very rare and no deduction was made in this case;

g)   deduct any enhanced redundancy payment to the extent that it exceeds the basic award.

117 SI No 2803 reg 5 precludes interest in respect of a sum awarded for a loss or matter which will occur after the day of calculation.

118 [2005] IRLR 604; and *Fife Council v McPhee* EAT 750/00 EAT. The Law Reform (Contributory Negligence) Act 1945 allows for reduction in compensation in tortious claims, which includes discrimination claims.

Recommendation

18.94 The tribunal can make 'a recommendation that the respondent take within a specified period action appearing to the tribunal to be practicable for the purpose of obviating or reducing the adverse effect on the claimant of any act of discrimination to which the complaint relates'.[119] A recommendation must have a time limit. Possible recommendations could include:

- that the claimant be allowed to work part-time (see chapter 13);
- that the employer provides the worker with an apology;
- that details of the case be posted in the workplace.

18.95 In *Noone v North West Thames Regional Health Authority (No 2)*[120] the Court of Appeal rescinded a recommendation made by the tribunal that a woman be offered the next available post as a consultant microbiologist. The court thought it wrong that the health authority would have had to seek the secretary of state's authority to dispense with its statutory obligation to advertise the post. It is not clear whether the statutory provisions influenced the court and whether, without them, it would have upheld the recommendation.[121] In *Scottish Agricultural College v O'Mara*[122] the EAT held there was no power to make a recommendation that the claimant be appointed to the first suitable post as this was positive discrimination. A recommendation could say that s/he should be considered for such a position. Arguably, the failure to include reinstatement and re-engagement remedies for sex discrimination is a breach of the Equal Treatment Directive (ETD) (see para 18.43).

18.96 It is not clear if a recommendation can be made if the claimant has left the job as it will not affect the claimant personally. The tribunal could recommend that the employer provide a suitable reference, though it will not stipulate the contents.

---

119 SDA 1975 s65.
120 [1988] IRLR 530, CA.
121 See also *British Gas v Sharma* [1991] IRLR 101 where the EAT held that the tribunal had not power to recommend that the employers promote the complainant to the next suitable vacancy as the Act did not allow positive action.
122 [1991] DCLD 12 EAT.

Increase in compensation for non-compliance with recommendation

18.97   If an employer fails to comply with a recommendation, the tribunal may order that compensation be paid or increased.[123]

Principles in assessing compensation in pregnancy dismissal cases – unfair dismissal and sex discrimination

18.98   The courts have considered principles relating to assessment of compensation in pregnancy dismissal cases against the Ministry of Defence (MOD). The MOD conceded that its policy of dismissing women because they were pregnant was a breach of the ETD. As a result about 5,000 women issued sex discrimination claims for compensation.

18.99   Guidelines were laid down by the EAT in *MOD v Cannock*[124] and *MOD v Hunt*,[125] and then by the Court of Appeal in *MOD v Wheeler*.[126] Although these were cases decided on their facts, the guidelines will be relevant for all pregnancy dismissals and other sex discrimination cases. However, account should be taken of the fact that they are old cases and there have been substantial differences in the working patterns of women since 1994 that make it necessary to review some of the assumptions made by the EAT and CA.

Assessment of chance of woman returning and for how long

18.100 The Court of Appeal and the EAT held that tribunals should assess the chances of a woman returning to work rather than make findings of fact.

18.101   The first question is 'what are the chances that, had she been given maternity leave and an opportunity to return to work, the claimant would have returned?'. In *Cannock* Morrison J said this is 'entering the realm of conjecture and speculation. . . . The question is

---

123   SDA 1975 s65(3).
124   [1994] IRLR 139, EAT.
125   [1996] IRLR 140, see also *MOD v Mutton* [1996] ICR 590, EAT.
126   [1998] IRLR 23, CA.

to be answered on the basis of the best assessment that the Industrial Tribunal can make having regard to all the available material'. The EAT also said that account may be taken of statistics (which showed that less than 50% of servicewomen who had been given the choice since 1990 had elected not to return). However, in *Hunt* the EAT stressed that the tribunal must base its assessment on the individual's evidence and said that 'statistics contain severe limitations'. In *Hunt* the EAT said the tribunal was entitled to assess the chance of a woman's return as 100%.

18.102 Since the introduction of longer maternity leave and the right to apply for flexible working, an increasing number of women are returning to work. National statistics indicate a return rate of more than 70% and it may be that some of the remaining 30% do not return because discrimination, for example they are not offered the same job or refused flexible working (see chapter 1).

18.103 According to EOC research nearly 50% of pregnant women and women on maternity leave suffer from discrimination. Thus, the figures do not reflect accurately what women are likely to do absent any discrimination. This makes relying on statistics about women returners even more unreliable. In addition, employers with generous maternity leave and good maternity policies have much higher rates of return than the national average. Despite the uncertainty of statistics, failure by a tribunal to consider the chances of a woman returning to work after maternity leave may lead to appeal.[127]

18.104 The tribunal should take into account the claimant's individual circumstances. If, for example, a woman returns after her first child but resigns because she cannot work part-time, the chances are that she would have remained in employment but on a part-time basis. Where there is evidence that the woman would definitely have returned to work, there should be no percentage deduction (see also para 18.101).

Cumulative deduction

18.105 In some cases, the tribunal may assess the chances of the woman returning as being 100% – ie, she would certainly return. The tribunal may then look at different points in her career, such as the birth of further children, and assess the likelihood of the woman

---

127 *Wallington v S & B Car Hire* EAT/0240/03/MAA, 28 March 2003. The EAT remitted the case to the ET for reconsideration.

returning at each point. For example, in *Wheeler*, the tribunal assessed one claimant's chance of returning after her first baby as 90%, after her second as 50% and after her third as 25%. The Court of Appeal, in *Wheeler*, held that the percentage chances must be applied cumulatively on the basis of a percentage on a percentage. Thus, if the loss between the first and second baby is £10,000, the claimant would recover 90%, ie, £9,000. If the loss between the second and third baby is £10,000, the loss is 50% of the 90%, ie, £4,500.

Mitigation: duty to look for alternative work

18.106 There is a duty on claimants to take reasonable steps to mitigate their losses by seeking alternative employment. Failure to do so will mean the tribunal will reduce the compensation payable. It should be assumed that a woman on maternity leave, or an employee on adoption leave, is entitled to take the full leave of up to a year before the duty to start seeking alternative employment begins. However, if it is clear that she planned to return to work earlier she should start looking for work earlier.

18.107   After the end of maternity leave, an employee would be expected to be in the job market actively looking for work and applying for jobs, including applying for job seeker's allowance and if she is not, then however understandable her behaviour may be, she risks not being about to recover damages for loss of employment thereafter and would have to have a good reason, such as illness, for not doing so. Unless active steps are taken to find alternative work, the tribunal may find that the claimant would have not returned to work at all. One particular difficulty for women with children is finding affordable childcare to look for work. Without an income to pay for childcare this can become a vicious circle. The tribunal should consider what steps the worker should have taken, the date the steps should have been taken and the likely consequence. For employees not on maternity leave they should start looking for work as soon as they are dismissed.

18.108   The burden of proving a failure to mitigate is on the employer, who must provide evidence. A vague submission of failure to mitigate unsupported by any evidence is unlikely to succeed. For example, in *Orthet Ltd v Vince-Cain*[128] the EAT held that the claimant

128 [2004] IRLR 857.

had not failed to mitigate her loss when she changed careers, so attended a course (thereby abstaining from the labour market). The employers could not show that there was suitable work which she could and should have taken and the tribunal found that if such work had become available she would have given up her course.

18.109   In *MOD v Hunt* (see para 18.99) the EAT held that the tribunal was entitled to find that there was a disadvantage in the labour market in being a woman with a young child or children. This acknowledges the difficulty women may have in finding employment and applies 'collective common sense to historical circumstance'.

18.110   In *ICTS (UK) Ltd v Tchoula*,[128a] a race case in which similar principles apply, the EAT held that a tribunal was entitled to find that Mr Tchoula had not failed to mitigate his loss even though this meant that he was awarded compensation for being out of work for two years. The tribunal had accepted his evidence that he could not obtain work in the security sector where he worked originally because he did not have an employment record. This meant that it was reasonably foreseeable that he would have to retrain before he could get work.

18.111   In *AON Training Ltd and another v Dore*[129] the Court of Appeal held that the tribunal was wrong to award compensation amounting only to the employee's borrowing on his business loan as this failed to take account of the remuneration that he lost as a result of his employer's actions. The Court of Appeal inferred that the claimant's steps to migitate his loss (ie, setting up his business) were reasonable, given the difficulty he was likely to have finding an appropriate job. The Court of Appeal held that the correct way of assessing compensation was:

a)   calculate the sum representing lost remuneration from the respondent;

b)   add the costs reasonably incurred by the employee in mitigating that loss, which would include the expenses in setting up the business;

c)   deduct from that sum the earnings from the new business.

128a [2000] IRLR 643 EAT.
129   [2005] IRLR 891, CA.

Loss of earnings should include an amount for loss of promotion

18.112 In *MOD v Hunt* the tribunal found there was a 100% chance the claimant have continued in the army for a 16-year term and a 100% chance she would have obtained significant promotions during that time. This was upheld by the EAT (see para 18.101).

How the calculation should be done

18.113 The correct order is as follows:

- Calculate the sum the claimant would have earned if she had remained in her job (X) – say this is £10,000.
- Deduct the amount she had earned or should have earned elsewhere (Y) – say this is £2,500. Note that even if the woman has not earned anything, an amount for potential earnings may be deducted if the tribunal finds that she failed to mitigate her loss (see para 18.106).
- Apply the percentage discount to reflect the chance that she would not have remained in the same employment after maternity leave (Z) – say this is 50%.

Thus, the calculation is (X – Y) × Z%, which leaves a loss of £3,750.[130]

18.114 For example, a woman earns £500 per week before her dismissal. She then earns (or could earn, acting reasonably to mitigate her loss) £250 per week. The tribunal assesses her chances of remaining in the army after maternity leave as 40%. The loss is calculated by:

- subtracting £250 from £500, leaving £250;
- taking 40% of £250, ie, £100.

Her loss is £100 per week.

18.115   It was wrong to take 40% of £500 (£200) and then to subtract actual earnings (£250) making a weekly loss of £50. The EAT in *Hunt* thought such a result (which was argued by the MOD) could lead to injustice and was not in line with the ECJ decision in *Marshall v Southampton and South-West Hampshire Area Health Authority (Teaching) (No 2)* (see note 47). See also para 18.193 for other factors

---

130   Not, as argued by the MOD, (X × Z%) – Y which would lead to a loss of £2,500.

taken into account when assessing compensation and the order of deductions.

Pension loss

18.116 Pension loss may be a substantial element of the loss, particularly as fewer employers are offering a final salary scheme to new employees and many employers offer no pension at all. A committee of Chairmen of Employment Tribunals and the Government Actuary have produced guidance on compensation for loss of pension rights in employment tribunals. This distinguishes the 'normal run of tribunal cases, where the amount of compensation is limited and the pension element is, therefore, comparatively small and those few cases, many of them discrimination cases, where the sums involved are considerable. Thus, a 'simplified approach' is recommended for the former and the 'substantial loss approach' where the tribunal is considering 'career loss' of a particular employment.[131] In some cases, where there is likely to be substantial loss, the parties may want to instruct an actuary.

18.117 Where pension loss is likely to be small because the employee has obtained alternative pensionable employment or is likely to do so quickly, the tribunal is more likely to make an award based on the employer's contribution.[132]

18.118 Where the period of loss is likely to be more than two years, the correct method of calculating future pension loss is the substantial loss approach.[133]

18.119 In *Greenhoff v Barnsley Metropolitan Borough Council*[134] the EAT gave procedural guidance for tribunals to follow when calculating compensation for the loss of pension rights in cases of unfair dismissal, though this is also likely to apply in discrimination cases. The EAT said tribunals should approach cases in the following logical sequence:

131 *Compensation for loss of pension rights*, 3rd edn, 2003 (Introduction); it is available from The Stationery Office. However, in *Network Rail Infrastructure Ltd v Booth* [2006] UKEAT 0071/06/2206, 22 June 2006 the EAT said that a tribunal should not slavishly follow the guidance where this would lead to injustice. In this case failure to give credit for benefits in the claimant's new employment would give her a windfall so was wrong.
132 Ogden Tables paras 6–12.
133 *Orthet Ltd v Vince-Cain* [2004] IRLR 857, EAT.
134 [2006] IRLR 98.

- identify all the benefits the employee could obtain under the scheme;
- set out the terms of the pension scheme relevant to each benefit;
- for each benefit consider the advantages and disadvantages of applying:
  - the simplified approach;
  - the substantial loss approach; or
  - any other approach the tribunal or parties consider appropriate,
- explain why a particular approach has been taken and others rejected;
- set out their conclusions and explain the amount of compensation for each head.

18.120   In *Greenhoff*, where the claimant was a member of the council's final salary pension scheme,[135] the EAT said that the tribunal was wrong to award the claimant an amount equivalent to the employer's contributions over a period of seven years on the basis that it represented roughly half the period of time until Mr Greenhoff reached 60. The tribunal should have used his estimated pay at age 60 for his pensionable pay, compensated him for the loss of a lump sum on retirement and taken into account the benefit of his own contributions.

18.121   In *MOD v Mutton*[136] the EAT upheld the assessment of pension loss based on specific expert evidence rather than the usual guidance set out in the booklet and the claimant was awarded £60,635, which was the value of the benefits lost. The EAT in *Cannock* rejected the MOD's argument that loss could not be recovered for a period before 1990 (the date of the ECJ's decision in *Barber v Guardian Royal Exchange Assurance Group Ltd*[137]).

18.122   Where the pension is based on final salary, it can be calculated by estimating the appropriate salary and applying the appropriate multiplier provided by the pension scheme and then multiplying the annual pension payment by the number of years an individual is likely to be in receipt of their pension before they die. If it is a money purchase scheme the loss may be based on the employer's contribu-

---

135   Which was based on accruing 1/80th of his salary for each year of service and had a retirement age of 60. The council contributed 15.2% of Mr Greenhoff's pensionable pay to the scheme, with Mr Greenhoff contributing 6%. The tribunal found that he had an 85% chance of staying in his job until his retirement.
136   [1996] ICR 590, EAT.
137   [1990] IRLR 240, ECJ.

tions. However, specialist advice should be taken where the loss is likely to be significant.

Other losses

18.123 In a sexual harassment case[138] the tribunal awarded an amount for psychotherapist's fees incurred. Costs incurred in looking for other work (such as travel and phone calls) and possibly removal costs,[139] can be claimed, though evidence must be available.

Overlap with unfair dismissal compensation

18.124 There can be no double recovery of compensation under the SDA 1975 and the ERA 1996 for the same loss.[140] It is more advantageous to get the compensatory award under the SDA 1975 (rather than the ERA 1996), as there is no upper limit, interest is awarded and the recoupment provisions do not apply.

Tax position

18.125 The position is complex and beyond the scope of this book, but is usually as follows:

- £30,000 for loss of employment is tax-free;[141]
- the basic award and redundancy payment is tax-free;
- injury to feelings is probably not taxable, though the position is by no means clear;[142]
- personal injury is not taxable;
- legal fees, where payable directly to a solicitor, are not taxable;
- generally, payments directly into a pension fund are not taxable;
- the employer is liable to account to the Inland Revenue for tax on any amount awarded in respect of wages and holiday pay; there is no exemption.

---

138 *Longmore v Lee* [1989] DCLD 4, No 21745/88.
139 *Griffin v West Midlands Police Authority*; ET decision reported in EOR 137.
140 ERA 1996 s126.
141 Income Tax (Earnings and Pensions) Act 2003 (see brief 768).
142 *Orthet Ltd v Vince-Cain* [2004] IRLR 857.

18.126 In *Wilson (HM Inspector of Taxes) v Clayton*[143] the Court of Appeal held that a payment received by an employee from his employer, following a negotiated settlement of his unfair dismissal complaint, was tax exempt up to £30,000.[144]

18.127   In *Orthet Ltd v Vince-Cain* (see note 133) the EAT held that the tribunal was correct to make an award of compensation for injury to feelings for sex discrimination without regard to the tax implications, and therefore in not grossing-up the award.

Average awards in discrimination cases

18.128 In 2004, 49% of sex discrimination cases featured pregnancy and childcare issues.[145]

18.129   The average compensatory award in sex discrimination cases in 2004 was £11,898, up from £7,960 in 2003. The highest award in 2004 was £175,000, though previous awards have exceeded £1 million.

18.130   In *Griffin v West Midlands Police Authority*,[146] the claimant was forced to resign because of the introduction of new shift-working arrangements which she could not comply with due to childcare. She found alternative employment at a reduced salary and the tribunal assessed that there was a 10% chance she would get comparative alternative employment between February 2004 and February 2009.

Remedies for refusal of family time off and flexible working

18.131 Some, but not all, rights to family time off have a specific right to compensation attached. Where they do not, for example, the refusal of maternity, adoption or paterntiy leave, general rights to protection from unfair dismissal, discrimination and detriment will apply.

---

143 [2003] EWCA Civ 1657, CA IDS Brief 773 Jan 2005.
144 It appears that notice pay is taxable even if there is no payment in lieu of notice (PILON) clause see *SCA Packaging Ltd v Revenue & Customs SCA Packaging Ltd v Revenue & Customs* [2006] UKSPC SPC00541 (23 May 2006).
145 EOR No 144, August 2005. This refers only to cases where tribunals have made awards.
146 Case no 5208776/00, 3 June 2004 (EOR 137 and 144).

Refusal of paid time off for antenatal care.

18.132 Where the complaint is upheld that the employer unreasonably refused to allow the employee to take time off or to pay her for time off (see para 3.113 onwards), the tribunal:

- must make a declaration; and
- if either the employer refused time off or refused to pay for the time off, shall award compensation equal to the amount the employee would have received for the time off.[147]

18.133 The GP does not apply so any compensation is unaffected. The short conciliation period applies.

Breach of flexible working procedure

18.134 Compensation, of up to eight weeks' pay (limited to the statutory week's pay) can be awarded where the employer is in breach of the flexible working procedure (see para 12.83 onwards).[148] The tribunal can also make an order for reconsideration of the application.[149] Such a claim is not covered by the GP so compensation is unaffected. However, an employee claiming indirect sex discrimination must first put in a grievance (unless s/he is actually dismissed by the employer) and any subsequent failure to comply with the GP will affect compensation (see para 18.14 onwards).

Denial or unreasonable postponement of parental leave

18.135 Where the complaint is upheld that the employer has unreasonably postponed parental leave or prevented or attempted to prevent the employee from taking parental leave, the tribunal:

- must make a declaration to that effect; and
- may award compensation.[150]

18.136 The compensation must be such amount as the tribunal considers to be just and equitable having regard to 'the employer's behaviour' and any loss sustained by the employee as a result of the refusal to take

---

147   ERA 1996 s57(3)–(5).
148   ERA 1996 s80I; reg 7, Flexible Working (Eligibility, Complaints and Remedies) Regs 2002 SI No 3236.
149   ERA 1996 s80I.
150   ERA 1996 s80(3).

time off.[151] The employer's behaviour is not relevant in unfair dismissal cases where the House of Lords have held that compensation for injury to feelings is not payable.

18.137 However, there is a parallel in Trade Union and Labour Relations (Consolidation) Act (TULRCA) 1992 s149 (remedies for detriment on grounds related to union membership) and ERA s49 (other detriment case). ERA s49 provides that, in detriment claims, the tribunal must have regard to 'the infringement to which the complaint relates'. Thus, compensation in detriment claims may include non-financial loss such as injury to feelings. Where a 'just and equitable' award has been made in cases where trade unionists have suffered detriment from action that falls short of dismissal compensation has included compensation for injury to feelings.

18.138 In *Cleveland Ambulance NHS Trust v Blane* the EAT held that

> Section 149(2) adds the words: 'having regard to the infringement complained of' and . . . it seems to us that those words grant the industrial tribunal a power to award compensation over and above the pure pecuniary loss suffered by the applicant . . . what do the words add to the normal formulation of aviable pecuniary loss claims for unfair dismissal, if not to include an award for non-pecuniary loss including injury to feelings?[152]

18.139 In *Virgo Fidelis Senior School v Boyle*[153] the EAT held that injury to feelings could be awarded in whistleblowing cases under ERA s47B which also obliges the tribunal to have regard to the infringement to which the complaint relates. As the EAT said, adopting the principles set out by Smith J in *Armitage Marsden and HM Prison Service v Johnson*, 'We see no reason for detriment under section 47B to be treated differently; it is another form of discrimination'. This would apply to detriment claims under ERA 1996 s47C and flexible working claims under s47E. The same principles apply as to discrimination claims.[154]

18.140 The GP does not apply so compensation is unaffected. The standard conciliation period applies to such proceedings.[155]

---

151 ERA 1996 s80(4); note that it is unusual to refer to the employer's behaviour except in injury to feelings awards.
152 See *Cleveland Ambulance NHS Trust v Blane* [1997] IRLR 332, EAT and *London Borough of Hackney v Adams* [2003] IRLR 402.
153 [2004] IRLR 268, EAT.
154 See principles set out in *Vento*.
155 ET Rules rules 22(1), (6).

Refusal of time off for dependants

18.141 Where the complaint, that the employer unreasonably refused to allow an employee to take time off, is upheld the tribunal:

- must make a declaration; and
- may make an award of compensation.[156]

18.142 The compensation must be of such an amount as the tribunal considers to be just and equitable having regard to the employer's default and any loss sustained by the employee as a result of the refusal to take time off.[157] This could include injury to feelings (on the same basis as for parental leave) and cover the cost of arranging for care of the dependant (see also chapter 11).

18.143   The GP does not apply except for detriment claims under ERA 1996 s47C. The standard conciliation period applies.

Failure to pay remuneration while suspended on maternity health and safety grounds

18.144 Where there is a successful complaint that the employer has failed to pay an employee while suspended from work on maternity grounds, the tribunal must order the employer to pay the employee the amount of remuneration due.[158]

18.145   Where the tribunal finds that the employer failed to offer the employee suitable alternative work (to which she is entitled before being suspended)[159] the tribunal shall award such compensation as it considers just and equitable having regard to the infringement of the employee's right and any loss sustained as a result.

18.146   The GP does not apply. The short conciliation period applies.[160]

Equal pay

18.147 If the claim is upheld, the tribunal will award the claimant arrears of pay or damages for breach of the equality clause (plus interest) for up to six years preceding the date of the claim (five years in Scotland).[161]

---

156 ERA 1996 s57B.
157 ERA 1996 s57B(3), (4).
158 ERA 1996 s70(3).
159 ERA 1996 s67, 70(4), (6) and (7).
160 ET Rules 22(5).
161 Equal Pay Act (EPA) 1970 ss2(5), 2ZB, 2ZC. For further details see Palmer et al, *Discrimination Law Handbook* (2nd edn, forthcoming, 2006, Legal Action Group).

Time may be extended where the claimant has a disability or the employer has concealed facts. The tribunal does not have power to make an award for injury to feelings or aggravated damages.[162]

18.148   In addition, once there is a finding of equal pay, an equality clause is automatically inserted into the woman's contract giving her the same pay and other contractual terms as her male comparator.

18.149   The GP applies so that any failure to follow it will affect the compensation awarded. There is no fixed conciliation period.

Breach of Part-time Workers (Prevention of Less Favourable Treatment) Regs 2000

18.150   Where a complaint is upheld the tribunal can make the following orders as it considers just and equitable:

a)   a declaration as to the rights of the claimant and employer;

b)   order the employer to pay compensation to the claimant having regard to the infringement and any loss attributable to the infringement. This can include expenses incurred as a result of the infringement and the loss of any benefit, but not injury to feelings; compensation may be reduced if the claimant was at fault. There is also a duty to mitigate;

c)   recommend that the employer take, within a specified time, action to obviate or reduce the adverse effect on the claimant of any matter to which the complaint relates. Failure to comply with the recommendation may lead to increased compensation (see also para 14.122 onwards).[163]

18.151 The GP does not apply. The standard conciliation period applies.

Detriment claims

18.152 Where there is a successful complaint that the employee has suffered a detriment for taking leave for family and domestic reasons[164] or for

---

162   *Council of the City of Newcastle upon Tyne v Allan and Degnan v Redcar and Cleveland Borough Council* [2005] IRLR 504 where the EAT held that a claim under the EPA 1970 is a claim in contract, not tort.

163   Part-time Workers (Prevention of Less Favourable Treatment) Regulations (PTW Regs) 2000 reg 8.

164   Related to pregnancy, childbirth, maternity or adoption leave, parental leave, paternity leave or time off for dependants.

requesting or exercising a flexible working right (see para 12.83 onwards),[165] the tribunal:

- must make a declaration to this effect;[166] and
- may award compensation which is 'just and equitable' in all the circumstances having regard to the infringement to which the complaint relates and any loss caused by the employer's act or failure to act.[167] The loss includes:
  - any expenses reasonably incurred by the claimant as a result of the detriment; and
  - loss of any benefit which the employee might reasonably be expected to have had but for that act or failure to act.[168]

18.153 Compensation may include injury to feelings and it should be awarded on the same basis as in discrimination cases. In *Virgo Fidelis* (see above) the EAT held that 'detriment suffered by trade union members was clearly accepted in the *Hackney* case as another species of discrimination and it is therefore important as far as possible there is consistency in awards throughout all areas of discrimination'.[169] The EAT reduced the tribunal award from £45,000 to £25,000, ie, the top of the *Vento* band.

18.154 Compensation may be reduced if the claimant was at fault.[170] There is also the duty to mitigate (see para 18.106).[171]

18.155 The GP does apply so compensation may be adjusted if there has been a failure to comply with the procedure (see para 18.14 onwards). The standard conciliation period applies.

Failure to give written reasons (or inadequate ones) for dismissal

18.156 Where a complaint for unfair dismissal is upheld the tribunal:

- must make a declaration; and
- shall order the employer to pay a sum equivalent to two weeks' pay.[172]

---

165 This includes victimisation as a result of bringing proceedings or alleging a breach of the regulations.
166 ERA 1996 s49(1)(a).
167 ERA 1996 s49(2).
168 ERA 1996 s49(3).
169 See para 44.
170 ERA 1996 s49(5).
171 ERA 1996 s49(4).
172 ERA 1996 s93.

The GP and/or DDP do not apply, except to the unfair dismissal claim. The standard conciliation period applies.

Unlawful deduction from wages and breach of contract

18.157   Where the complaint of unlawful deduction is upheld, the tribunal:

- must make a declaration; and
- shall order the employer to pay what is due (or repay what has been unlawfully deducted from the worker's wages).[173]

18.158   The GP applies. The short conciliation period applies.

18.159   A worker can pursue a claim for wages that are due both under statute such as statutory maternity pay (SMP) and under their contract of employment. An employee is entitled to make a claim for breach of contract in the tribunal (under the Employment Tribunal Extension of Jurisdiction Order 1994) if it arises on termination of employment (subject to a limit of £25,000) or otherwise in the county court. The remedy would be the sum due under the contract. An employee might, however, prefer to make a claim for unlawful deduction since a claim for breach of contract opens the way for the employer to counterclaim in respect of any breach by the employee.

Refusal of SMP

18.160   Although SMP is defined as 'wages' and so can be awarded by a tribunal, there are two other routes that an employee can take to enforce payment. The first is that the employee may apply to HMRC officer at her/his local Jobcentre Plus who will make a decision on whether the employer is liable to pay. An employer who fails to pay SMP may also incur a civil penalty in the form of a fine. See chapter 6 for more information.

Wrongful dismissal

18.161   A tribunal will award the claimant contractual notice pay if wrongfully dismissed subject to a cap of £25,000. Any excess cannot be recovered in the civil courts (see *Fraser v HLMAD Ltd* [2006] EWCA Civ 738, 15 June 2006. This includes compensation for the time it would take, for example, to follow the contractual disciplinary

---

173   ERA 1996 ss24, 25.

procedure rather than dismissing on the spot. In practice, where the claimant has also been unfairly dismissed, the compensatory award will include any loss in respect of the notice period but it is only the unfair dismissal claim which is subject to a cap (£58,400) and there is a separate cap for breach of contract, so arguably the total payable for unfair dismissal and breach of contract is up to £58,400 and £25,000. The claimant generally has a duty to mitigate the loss and make efforts to obtain new employment during the notice period.[174]

Dismissal for assertion of a statutory right and in health and safety cases

18.162 A dismissal under ERA 1996 s104 is an unfair dismissal as is a dismissal for raising a health and safety concern under ERA 1996 s100. The remedy is the same as for unfair dismissal cases.

Enforcement

18.163 It is the county court, not the tribunal, which enforces compensation awards.[175]

EOC/CEHR powers

18.164 The EOC/CEHR has a number of powers[176] but the most important for individuals is the power to advise and assist individuals with discrimination claims where:

- the case raises a question of principle; or
- it is unreasonable, having regard to the complexity of the case or the applicant's position in relation to the respondent or another person involved or anyother matter, to expect the applicant to deal with the case unaided.

---

174 See *Langley and another v Burlo* [2006] IRLR 460 where the EAT held that damages for notice pay is subject to the duty to mitigate. The claimant was not entitled to full notice pay as she was incapable of working during her notice period. She was not entitled to a bonus over and above the loss flowing from the dismissal.

175 See Philip Tsamados (ed) *Enforcing ET awards and settlements*, 2 March 2006, available from the Central London Law Centre (tel: 020 7839 2998).

176 For example, to produce Codes of Practice, conduct formal investigations, take action in respect of discriminatory advertisements. The details are outside the scope of this book.

18.165 Assistance may include:

- giving advice;
- attempting to settle a dispute;
- arranging for advice or assistance by a solicitor or counsel;
- arranging representation;
- any other form of assistance it considers appropriate.[177]

18.166 The EOC will become part of the Commission for Equality and Human Rights (CEHR). It is anticipated that the main provisions will come into force in October 2007. The CEHR will have the power to:

- assist an individual who is or may become party to legal proceedings, provided the proceedings related (wholly or partly) to the equality legislation;[178]
- carry out inquiries and investigations;[179]
- issue Codes of Practice;[180]
- carry out research, provide eduction or training, give advice or guidance.[181]

Future developments: general public sector duty

18.167 SDA s76A provides that a public authority shall, in carrying out its functions, have due regard to the need:

- to eliminate unlawful discrimination and harassment; and
- to promote equality of opportunity between men and women.

18.168 These duties may be similar to those under the Race Relations Act 1976 which require, in particular, public bodies to prepare and publish a race equality scheme showing how they will meet their duty and to monitor specified employment procedures and practices by racial group. These duties only apply to the public sector but are good practice for all employers.

---

177 SDA 1975 s75. Note that if an individual wants assistance s/he should specifically apply for section 75 assistance as the commission then has to consider the application.
178 Equality Act (EA) 2006 s28.
179 EA 2006 ss16, 20.
180 EA 2006 s14
181 EA 2006 s13.

18.169   The CEHR may assess the extent to which, or the manner in which, a person has complied with a generally statutory duty. If it believes that a person has failed to comply with such a duty, it may give the person a notice requiring him/her to comply with the duty and also to the CEHR written information of steps taken, or proposed, for the purpose of complying with the duty.[182]

182 EA 2006 ss31, 32.

APPENDICES

Checklist for maternity/paternity rights claim

1 What does the worker want?

The first and most important question is 'what does the worker want'? This will determine the action taken by the worker/adviser. Options include:

- A satisfactory internal resolution of the complaint;
- to keep her job;
- to return to work, either in the same or equivalent job;
- to work part-time;
- compensation;
- a good reference.

2 The costs

The second most important question is whether it is cost effective to bring a claim taking into account how the claim is to be funded. Workers and advisers should consider:

- advice and representation from a law centre or other voluntary organisation;
- legal expenses insurance (check all policies, eg contents and building insurance and mortgage);
- funding from the Equal Opportunities Commission (or CEHR – see appendix E);
- a no-win, no-fee agreement if a solicitor is prepared to act on this basis;
- free representation from the Bar Pro Bono Unit or Free Representation Unit may do free representation;
- costs of a solicitor; if paying privately, what will the solicitor charge? (the Equal Opportunities Commission keep a list of solicitors who specialise in maternity cases);
- that if the employee gets another job quickly loss of earnings will be low, though in a discrimination claim compensation is payable for injury to feelings.

Legal Services Commission funding is not available for ET proceedings although it may be for initial advice and for appeals for people on very low incomes.

3 Chronology of events and summary of facts, including dates[1]

It is very useful for the worker and the adviser to prepare a chronology and many ETs request this for the hearing. An adviser will want to ask about:

- Commencement of employment;
- any promotion during employment and details;
- the date that the act complained of occurred;
- if the worker has been dismissed, when did this happen? Did the employer and employee comply fully with the statutory disciplinary and dismissal procedure with them[2]; if not, what were the breaches?
- If the worker has resigned, when did this happen? Has the worker raised a written grievance and if so, when? Has there been full compliance with the statutory grievance procedure?[3] If not, what were the breaches?
- approximate date of start of pregnancy;
- when the employer was told about pregnancy/placement of child for adoption, and who else was told and when;
- employer's reaction when told of pregnancy/placement of child and subsequently;
- any sickness during pregnancy, absences and causes of sickness;
- any problem with time off for antenatal care;
- any health and safety issue;
- expected date of childbirth/placement;
- actual date of childbirth/placement;
- date notice given of start of maternity/adoption leave;
- start of maternity/adoption leave and pay;
- how much maternity/adoption pay has been paid;
- length of maternity/adoption leave;
- who was appointed, if anyone, to cover maternity/adoption leave;
- if no-one appointed who carried out the employee's work;
- any discussions with employer during maternity/adoption leave;
- were all benefits paid during OML/OAL, eg, pension, bonus, accrued holiday, company car, insurance;
- any parental leave at end of maternity/adoption/paternity leave;
- any problems taking parental or dependants leave;
- whether and when notice was given of early return from maternity/adoption leave (no notice needed otherwise);
- date of return from maternity/adoption leave;
- job on return from maternity/adoption leave and whether it is the same;
- whether other employees' jobs have changed during the maternity/adoption period;
- if redundancy situation, when was the employee made redundant, was she/he consulted (if so, when), was she/he offered suitable alternative work (if so, when), was anyone else made redundant, was she/he unfairly selected;

---

1 It is very important to get dates because, in a discrimination claims, the time limit runs from the date of each act of discrimination but see chapter 16.
2 See chapter 16.
3 See chapter 16.

- if dismissed was she/he given notice pay;
- if dismissed was she/he given the reasons for dismissal;
- has the employer complied with all the relevant procedures for dismissal;
- how other employees in similar position were treated;
- has the employee applied for flexible working under the statutory procedure. If so, what type of working. Was the procedure properly followed. If refused has the employee appealed.

4 Relevant documents to get from employee and employer
- contract of employment;
- letter of appointment;
- terms and conditions of employment, eg, in staff handbook, redundancy procedure, maternity procedure, equal opportunities policy;
- any letters, emails between employee and employer concerning the dispute;
- payslips, P45 and P60;

any contemporaneous notes. If these have not been made, the worker should be encouraged to start making a note of any contact with employer and what was said;
- notes of meetings;
- records of written grievance;
- records of disciplinary and dismissal procedures;
- letter of dismissal;
- appraisals;
- if reorganisation or redundancy, all documents relating to the reorganisation: these should be requested on discovery;
- a personnel file should be requested on discovery;

During the discovery process it is important to ask the employer for all relevant documents not just those on which it is intended to rely.

5 Discrimination cases: what is the less favourable treatment?
Depending on the facts, it could cover:
- refusal to appoint;
- failure to confirm probationary period;
- dismissal or redundancy;
- demotion;
- failure to promote;
- failure to carry out appraisal;
- failure to give pay rise, or lower than usual pay rise;
- failure to pay benefits during pregnancy or (apart from pay) contractual benefits during ordinary maternity/adoption leave;
- failure to pay bonus or commission or lower than the usual payments relating to pregnancy;
- detriment, eg, less interesting work;
- refusal of parental leave;
- refusal of dependants leave;
- refusal to allow part-time or other flexible working.

6 Why did the dismissal/detriment/less favourable treatment take place?

Was it related to:

- pregnancy or matters relating to pregnancy;
- pregnancy related absence;
- request for health and safety risk assessment or obligation to carry out steps to protect a woman's health and safety;
- absence on maternity/adoption/paternity leave;
- responsibility for young children;
- taking or seeking to take parental or dependants leave;
- absence on any type of family leave;
- request to work part-time or flexible hours;
- part-time status;
- application for flexible working,
- enforcement of rights (eg, time off for antenatal care).

7 Main claims

- ordinary unfair dismissal (including redundancy);
- automatically unfair dismissal;
- sex and marital discrimination (direct and indirect) including discriminatory dismissal;
- equal pay claim where less favourable contractual term, eg, failure to provide benefit;
- unlawful deduction of wages including failure to pay SMP;
- breach of antenatal provisions;
- breach of health and safety provisions;
- wrongful dismissal – notice monies;
- failure to provide written statement of reasons for dismissal;
- detriment on one of prescribed grounds;
- refusal of dependants leave;
- refusal of parental leave;
- less favourable treatment of part-time worker;
- breach of statutory flexible working procedure;

NB: Time limits – three months less on day subject to extension of time if statutory grievance procedure applies or, in dismissal cases, where there is an ongoing procedure at the expiry of the three months (see chapter 16).

8 Procedure for making claim

(a) Apart from dismissal cases (except constructive dismissal) where the GP applies has there been a written grievance about the matter which is the subject of the complaint;

(b) request for written reasons for dismissal; note this should be provided automatically if the dismissal occurs during pregnancy or maternity leave;

(c) Sex Discrimination Act 1975 and Equal Pay Act questionnaire (within three months of discrimination – subject to extension of time if statutory grievance procedure applies);

(d) letter before action (if time);

(e) lodge ET1 with ET;
(f) Sex Discrimination Act 1975 or Equal Pay Act questionnaire within 21 days of ET1 if not already served or request an extension of time from ET;
(g) receive ET3 from ET;
(h) request for further and better particulars of ET3;
(i) request for answers to written questions;
(j) discovery and inspection;
(k) agree pre-hearing arrangements, eg, outstanding discovery, documents for tribunal, witness statements;
(l) directions or interlocutory hearings (sometimes);
(m) agree bundle of documents for ET and prepare six copies;
(n) apply to ET for witness order, if necessary;
(o) exchange witness statements;
(p) hearing.

The above are the main steps but there are other steps which may be necessary (see chapter 17).

Precedents

ET1: Details of Complaint[1] (pregnancy dismissal)

(1) In October 2006 I became pregnant.

(2) I started work as a part-time shelf stacker with the respondent, which runs a supermarket, on 17 November 2006. I had a three-month probation period. Two weeks after I started work my line manager told me that she was pleased with my work.

(3) On 17 December 2006 I told my line manager in writing that I was pregnant. From this time my line manager became hostile towards me and started ignoring me.

(4) On 4 January 2007 I asked for time off to attend an antenatal appointment. I was told that I should take time off when I was not due to work.

(5) On 12 January 2006 I told my line manager that I could no longer carry heavy boxes because of my pregnancy. I was told that I should ask someone else to do this or carry the contents separately if there was no-one else available.

(6) On 1 February 2007 I was called to see the managing director and told that my performance was not good enough, that I was often late for work and that I had not passed my probationary period.

(7) I was given no warning about my performance. The respondent failed to follow any procedure.

(8) I was dismissed because of my pregnancy and/or my impending maternity leave, and/or because I requested time off for an antenatal appointment and/or because I could not carry heavy boxes.

(9) The dismissal was automatically unfair and discriminatory.

(10) Further, I was not given written reasons for my dismissal.

(11) Further, I was not given notice pay.

(12) I claim:
   (a) compensation for automatically unfair dismissal as the principal reason(s) for my dismissal was related to my pregnancy;
   (b) compensation for sex discrimination including injury to feelings and interest. Compensation should be increased by 50 per cent as the respondent failed to go through the statutory dismissal procedure;
   (c) a declaration that I suffered discrimination;
   (d) compensation for failure to give me paid time off for ante-natal care;
   (e) notice monies;
   (f) two weeks' pay for failure to give written reasons for dismissal.

---

1 To be included in appropriate part of claim form. Note that it is mandatory to use the prescribed form and to complete all the required details.

Sex Discrimination Act questionnaire (Part 6; questions)

(1) Do you accept that, on 17 December 2006 I told my line manager in writing that I was pregnant? If not, when were you first aware that I was pregnant?

(2) Do you accept that I was told I could not attend my ante-natal appointment? Please state why I was told this.

(3) Has any other employee not attended the team meeting over the last year? Please give the name of the employee and reasons why s/he has not attended and any action taken for failure to attend.

(4) My line manager praised my performance on 1 December 2006. Why was it subsequently decided that it was not satisfactory?

(5) Do you accept I was told to ask someone else to carry heavy boxes? Who did you expect would carry the heavy boxes? How heavy were the boxes, has there been a risk assessment under the manual handling regulations?

(6) Did you carry out a health and safety risk assessment a) in respect of women of child bearing age in the workplace; and b) when I told you in writing I was pregnant? If so, please state when and what steps were taken as a result. If not, please state why not.

(7) Please state all criticisms of my performance, when they occurred, who made them, and if it is alleged they were raised with me, when and by whom, what was my response?

(8) Who took the decision to dismiss me? Please state:
   (a) why I failed my probationary period;
   (b) how long the probationary period lasted;
   (c) when the decision to dismiss me was taken;
   (d) who was consulted and their views;
   (e) all reasons for my dismissal.

(9) Have any other employees been late to work over the last year? If so, please state:
   (a) the time they arrived;
   (b) reason for lateness;
   (c) action taken against the employee.

(10) Have any other employees failed to pass their probation period? Please state:
   (a) name of employee;
   (b) sex of employee and whether she was pregnant;
   (c) reasons s/he failed to pass the probation period;
   (d) date of dismissal.

(11) How many employees have been dismissed (or made redundant) in the last five years? Please state:
   (a) sex of employee;
   (b) whether the employee was pregnant, on maternity leave or had taken maternity or parental leave in the six months prior to dismissal;

    (c) reasons for dismissal;

    (d) date of dismissal;

    (e) if made redundant, whether the employee was offered and accepted alternative work;

    (f) whether in each case the respondent followed the statutory dismissal procedure.

(12) Of employees who have been pregnant and/or on maternity leave in the past three years, please state:

    (a) the total number;

    (b) how many returned to their original posts;

    (c) how many were offered alternative posts and how many accepted;

    (d) how many were dismissed or made redundant;

    (e) reason for dismissal;

    (f) how many resigned and at what stage of their pregnancy or maternity leave.

(13) Please provide a breakdown of your workforce by sex and grade of employee.

(14) Please provide a copy of your equal opportunities and/or maternity policy and probationary policy.

(15) Please provide details of any training carried out in respect of equal opportunities, when it was carried out and who attended.

ET3 Notice of Appearance[2]

(1) The respondents deny that they refused the claimant time off for antenatal care. The claimant's line manager only asked whether the claimant could try to re-arrange the appointment to avoid it clashing with a meeting, but stated if this was not possible then of course she should attend.

(2) The respondents deny that they required the claimant to carry heavy boxes. The claimant works alongside a male employee and he was told that he should carry the heavy boxes.

(3) The respondents deny that the claimant was dismissed for the reasons set out in the Claim. The claimant's probationary period was not extended because she was frequently late to work and her performance was not satisfactory. This was not related to her pregnancy.

(5) The respondents deny that the dismissal was either automatically unfair or discriminatory or that there was failure to follow the statutory dismissal procedure.

(6) The respondents were unaware that they were obliged to provide written reasons for dismissal and these have now been sent to the claimant.

---

2   To be included in the appropriate part of the form. Note that it is mandatory to use the prescribed form and to complete all the required details.

(7)   The claimant is entitled to one week's notice pay and this has been paid.

Request for Further and Better Particulars of the Notice of Appearance

Under paragraph 1
Of 'the claimant's line manager only asked whether the claimant could try to re-arrange the appointment to avoid it clashing with a meeting, but stated if this was not possible then of course she should attend'
Please state:
(a) when the claimant's line manager stated the above;
(b) whether anyone else was present at the time of the conversation;
(c) why it was felt necessary for the claimant to attend the meeting (giving the nature of the meeting and providing the names of attendees).

Under paragraph 2
Of 'the claimant works alongside a male employee and he was told that he should carry the heavy boxes'
Please state:
(a) the name of the male employee;
(b) when and by whom he was told he should carry the heavy boxes.

Under paragraph 3
Of 'the claimant's probationary period was not extended because she was frequently late to work and her performance was not satisfactory'
Please state:
(a) the dates when the claimant was late to work and the time she arrived;
(b) whether it is alleged that this was raised with the claimant and, if so, when, by whom and what was said (if the lateness was not raised, please state why not; were the reasons for any lateness recorded?);
(c) all facts and matters relied on in support of the allegation that the claimant's performance was not satisfactory;
(d) whether it is alleged that the claimant's unsatisfactory performance was raised with her and, if so, when, by whom and what was said. If her performance was not raised, please state why not. Was this a breach of the probationary policy?

Request for discovery[3]

Please provide all documents relevant to the claim including, but not limited to, copies of the following documents:

---

3   The claimant or her representative should write to the respondents requesting the documents and giving 14 days to provide the documents. If they are not forthcoming the claimant can ask the ET for an order.

- the claimant's contract of employment and letter of appointment;
- the claimant's letter of appointment;
- the claimant's personnel file;
- the Staff Handbook and/or disciplinary procedure and probationary procedure;
- any equal opportunities and maternity policies;
- any notes of meetings relating to the claimant;
- any correspondents, notes, e-mails relating to the claimant;
- any other documents relevant to the claimant's claim.

Witness statement of claimant

(1) I, Freda S, of . . . address . . . will say as follows:

Education and previous employment history[4]
(2) My education and previous employment history is as follows . . .
(3) I have worked for the respondents as a shelf stacker since 17 November 2006.
(4) My job involves . ... [set out day to day requirements of the job]. . .[5]

Announcement of pregnancy
(5) On 17 December 2006 I told my line manager in writing that I was pregnant. I said that I would need maternity leave but would be returning after leave.

Refusal of time off for ante-natal appointment
(6) On 4 January 2007 I asked my line manager, for time off to attend an ante-natal appointment on ...... He said that this was a very inconvenient time because it clashed with the team meeting and it was important that all employees in his team were present. I was not asked if I could re-arrange the appointment nor was I told that if it was not possible, I could attend.

Failure to carry out health and safety assessment
(7) Part of my job involves carrying boxes of tins that are very heavy. I told my line manager that because of my pregnancy I would not be able to carry these. He became very impatient with me, and asked what could he do about it. He suggested that I ask someone else to carry the boxes and if no one was available I should just carry what I could. I felt under pressure to continue carrying the boxes but felt very anxious about the effect this would have on my pregnancy.
(8) I do not believe that the respondents carried a health and safety

---

4 It is always helpful to put in headings particularly if the statement is long. The statement should usually start with relevant background such as the employee's education and employment history and then set out the facts in chronological order.
5 The job should be described in some detail, especially where relevant to the claim. In practice the statement will usually be a great deal longer than this precedent.

assessment. My working conditions were not changed as a result of my inability to carry heavy boxes and I was not offered any alternative work.

Dismissal and reasons given for dismissal

(9)   On 1 February 2007, I was called to see the managing director, [name], and told that my performance was not good enough and I had not passed my probationary period. When I started to ask what the problems were with my performance, he was not interested and said he had an urgent appointment and he would speak to me later. I was never given the reasons why my performance was considered bad.

(10) It has been suggested that I was often late to work. I was late on three occasions. The first time was on . . . . because of a delay with the trains. The other two occasions were because I was feeling very sick and faint because of my pregnancy. I telephoned my line manager to explain and said I would come in at 10 am when I was better, which I did. I made up the time at the end of the day.

(11) I know that other employees are sometimes late because of train delays. In addition, one employee,[name] regularly comes in an hour late because he twisted his ankle playing football and finds it easier to travel outside the rush hour.

(12) I was never given any warning about my lateness.

(13) I was not given any warning about my alleged poor performance and do not understand why it is suggested that my performance was poor.[6] As far as I was aware my performance was good. Before I announced my pregnancy my line manager said to me that I was settling in well and seemed to have a good grasp of the job.

Conclusion

(14) I do not believe I would have been dismissed if I had not been pregnant and this is both unfair and discriminatory.

(15) I felt very anxious about my job after I told the respondents about my pregnancy. It ruined what should have been a very happy time for me.[7] [set out details for claim for injury to feelings, for example any sleeplessness, anxiety etc].

(16) I have not been able to get another job as my pregnancy really shows. I was very upset by being dismissed. No one has ever criticised my work before.

Compromise Agreement

THIS AGREEMENT dated the day of . . . . is made between:

(1)   Name of employer . . . (the employer) of . . . . . . and

---

6   If the reply to the request for further particulars gives details of poor performance, all the allegations should be dealt with in the statement.

7   Set out details of how the dismissal affected the employee, including any medical symptoms. It is always advisable to see a doctor if the employee is suffering from stress.

(2) Name of employee . . . (the employee) of . . . . . .
     WHEREAS it is agreed as follows:

(3) The employee's employment terminated on . . . .

(4) The employer shall, within 21 days of the date of this agreement, pay to the employee the gross sum of £30,000 for loss of employment, such payment to be made in full and without deductions.

(5) The employee agrees to accept the payment in full and final settlement of any claim arising out of the employee's employment, and in particular her claim before the Tribunal no: 0000000, whether under the Employment Rights Act 1996, the Sex Discrimination Act 1975 or otherwise (with the exception of the employee's accrued pension rights and any claim for damages for personal injury, which is not the subject of the present claim no: 0000000).

(6) The employer agrees to provide a reference, in the terms attached in appendix 1, and where a prospective employer requests further oral or written information, to provide such information in a manner, which is consistent and no less favourable than the reference in appendix 1.

(7) The employee agrees to withdraw her claim no: 0000000 from the Tribunal forthwith upon the conclusion of this agreement.

(8) The employee acknowledged that, before entering into this agreement, she received independent legal advice from a qualified lawyer (or authorised adviser), [name] of [solicitor's firm or details of certified adviser] who carries a policy of insurance, as to the terms and effect of this agreement and in particular as to its effect in relation to her rights to bring a claim of discrimination, unfair dismissal, breach of contract in respect of her employment in the employment tribunal. A certificate signed by the adviser is attached at appendix 2.

(9) The conditions regulating compromise agreements under the Employment Rights Act 1996 and the Sex Discrimination Act 1975 are satisfied in relation to this agreement.

ET1: Details of complaint (Redundancy after maternity leave)

(1) The respondents are . . . . . . They employ about 500 employees in the UK.

(2) On 4 November 2004, the respondents employed the claimant as Personnel Officer. She was promoted to Personnel Manager in . . . . .

(3) In December 2005 the claimant told the respondents that she was pregnant, would start her maternity leave on 1 July 2006 and intended to return to work after her leave. As a result Jane Woods was appointed to cover the claimant's maternity leave.

(4) The claimant met with her manager in March 2006 to discuss her return to work. She asked if she could work part-time. The respondents agreed to the claimant working part-time but only for three months.

The respondents failed to follow the flexible working procedure and the refusal to allow the claimant to work part-time for longer than three months was indirect sex discrimination.

(5) The claimant returned to work on June 2007.

(6) Immediately on her return the claimant had a meeting with her manager. She was told that Jane Woods had been appointed as director of personnel and her position was redundant. The respondent failed to follow the statutory dismissal procedure thus making her dismissal automatically unfair.

(7) But for the claimant's absence on maternity leave and/or her working part-time on a temporary basis, she would have remained in the same job with the same responsibilities she held prior to her maternity leave.

(8) The respondents' failure to allow the claimant to return to the same job after maternity leave, failure to consult her about her redundancy and failure to offer her suitable alternative employment under regulation 10 of the Maternity and Parental Leave Regulations 1999 made the dismissal:

(a) automatically unfair under Employment Rights Act 1996 s99 and the Maternity and Parental Leave etc Regulations 1999;

(b) ordinarily unfair under Employment Rights Act 1996 ss94 and 98;

(c) direct and indirect sex and marital discrimination under the Sex Discrimination Act 1975; and

(d) a breach of the Part-time Workers (Prevention of Less Favourable Treatment) Regulations 2000.

(9) Further, the failure to consult the claimant about the new structure while she was on maternity leave was sex discrimination.

(10) Further and in the alternative the claimant was discriminated against because she was denied the opportunity of being considered for promotion, either because she was on maternity leave and/or because she was working part-time. This was sex and marital discrimination and a breach of the Part-time Workers Regulations.

(11) The claimant claims:

(a) compensation for automatically unfair dismissal, the respondent having failed to follow the statutory dismissal procedure. The claimant claims an uplift of compensation of 50%;

(b) compensation for automatically unfair dismissal, the principal reason for dismissal being the claimant's absence on maternity leave and/or the failure to offer her suitable alternative work when she was on maternity leave;

(c) compensation for ordinary unfair dismissal;

(d) compensation for direct and indirect sex and marital discrimination including injury to feelings, interest;

(e) compensation for failure to follow the Flexible Working Procedure;

(f) compensation for personal injury;

(g) a declaration that the claimant suffered sex and marital discrimination;

(h) compensation for breach of the Part-time Workers Regulations.

Sex Discrimination Act questionnaire (Part 6) (Redundancy after maternity leave)

(1) What is the respondents' redundancy procedure? Please provide a copy or, if none, give details of the procedure adopted in a redundancy situation.

(2) Why was it necessary to make the claimant redundant? What were the selection criteria, when were these drawn up and by whom?

(3) Is it accepted that the Complainant was not consulted about the redundancy? If so, please state why she was not consulted.

(4) When was the position of Director of Personnel created? Please state:
    (a) all reasons why it was created;
    (b) who decided to create the job and when;
    (c) who was consulted about the position;
    (d) whether it was advertised and, if so, when and where;
    (e) whether anyone else was considered for the position and, if so, please provide details.

(5) Why was the Complainant not considered for the position of Director of Personnel? Please give all reasons.

(6) When was the decision taken to offer Jane Woods the position of Director of Personnel?

(7) When was Jane Woods offered the position of Director of Personnel?

(8) Why was Jane Woods more qualified then the Complainant? Please state all reasons.

(9) Were any other employees made redundant from January 2006 to the present? If so, please state:
    (a) who was made redundant, including job title and grade;
    (b) whether s/he was offered alternative employment (if so, please state what alternative employment was offered);
    (c) whether a redundancy or other payment was made and, if so, how much;
    (d) why it was necessary to make redundancies.

(10) Have any employees, whether permanent or temporary, been appointed since January 2006, and/or are there any proposals to make such an appointment. Please state:
    (a) details of the appointment, including job title and grade;
    (b) when the appointment was made and commencement date;
    (c) termination date, if any, and reason for termination;
    (d) whether male or female;
    (e) whether married or unmarried.

(11) Please state the number of staff who have become pregnant over the last three years, stating:
    (a) their job title and grade;
    (b) whether the employee returned from maternity leave;
    (c) if not, the reasons why not;
    (d) termination date.

(12) Please state the number of staff working on a part-time, reduced hours or job-share basis in the three years prior to the date of this questionnaire. In each case please state:
  (a) job title, grade and location;
  (b) hours worked;
  (c) whether male or female;
  (d) whether married or single.
(13) Do you have an equal opportunities policy, maternity policy or job-share policy? If so, please provide a copy.

ET1: Details of complaint (Dismissal/detriment from taking parental and dependants leave)

(1) The respondents, a large international company with approximately 500 employees, employed the claimant as a telephone operator on 8 June 2006. She was required to work rotating shifts and some weekends.
(2) In about September 2007 before her return from maternity leave, the claimant asked the respondents if she could work part-time, job-share or do fixed shifts. The respondents refused saying that this would set an undesirable precedent.
(3) The claimant returned to work on 4 October 2007. On 20 October her husband, who cared for her son when she was working evening shifts, left the claimant unexpectedly. As a result the claimant asked for time off. The respondents said she had to work the evening shift as they were short staffed. As a result the claimant had to pay for childcare for that night.
(4) On 23 October 2007 the claimant requested one week's parental leave from 13 November because her son had to have an operation. The respondents agreed but said that the claimant would not be able to take any more time off until after Christmas. This meant that the claimant would have to cancel part of her holiday she had booked.
(5) On 15 November 2007 the claimant was ill and was told by her doctor that this was partly stress-related and she should reduce her working hours. She had to take a week off work.
(6) On 15 December the respondents told the claimant that they had to reduce the number of telephone operators and her job would be made redundant. The claimant was not consulted nor was she offered alternative employment.
(7) The claimant was entitled to be permitted to take a reasonable amount of time off in order to take action necessary because of the unexpected disruption or termination of arrangements for the care of a dependant. The respondents refused to allow the claimant to take time off which was a breach of Employment Rights Act 1996 s57A and indirect sex discrimination.
(8) The claimant was subjected to a detriment, as a result of requesting and/or taking parental leave, by being refused further time off until

after Christmas, and this was a breach of Employment Rights Act 1996 s47C and the Maternity and Parental Leave etc Regulations 1999 and indirect sex discrimination.

(9) But for the fact that the claimant requested time off to care for a dependant and requested and took parental leave, she would not have been made redundant.

(10) The dismissal was automatically and/or ordinarily unfair and/or discriminatory[8] in that the claimant was dismissed because she attempted to take dependant's leave and/or took parental leave and/or had sole responsibility for the care of young children.

(11) Further, if, which is not accepted, the reason for dismissal was that the claimant was redundant:

(a) the claimant was not consulted about the redundancy;

(b) the claimant was selected for redundancy because she requested dependants leave and requested and took parental leave;

(c) further the claimant was unfairly selected for redundancy and in breach of the respondent's procedure;

(d) the respondent failed to offer the claimant suitable alternative employment.

(12) The refusal to allow the claimant to work either part-time, or job-share or fixed shifts was indirect sex and marital discrimination.

(13) The claimant claims

(a) compensation for unfair dismissal;

(b) compensation for sex and marital discrimination including injury to feelings, personal injury and interest;

(c) compensation in respect of the detriment suffered as a result of the claimant taking parental leave;

(d) compensation in respect of the refusal to allow the claimant to take dependants leave;

(e) a declaration that the claimant has suffered discrimination.

---

8 Dismissal for taking parental or dependants leave may be directly discriminatory, if a man would be treated more favourably, or indirectly discriminatory if there is a disproportionate impact.

Statutory maternity and paternity pay tables

Table showing important dates for SMP and SPP and maternity/parental leave.

Baby due between 29 October 2006 and 26 May 2007							
Week baby due			Start of 15th week before the week baby due			Latest start date for employment with you	Start of 11th week before the week baby due	Start of 4th week before the week baby due
Sunday		Saturday	Sunday		Saturday	Saturday	Sunday	Sunday
29/10/06	to	04/11/06	16/07/06	to	22/07/06	28/01/06	13/08/06	01/10/06
05/11/06	to	11/11/06	23/07/06	to	29/07/06	04/02/06	20/08/06	08/10/06
12/11/06	to	18/11/06	30/07/06	to	05/08/06	11/02/06	27/08/06	15/10/06
19/11/06	to	25/11/06	06/08/06	to	12/08/06	18/02/06	03/09/06	22/10/06
26/11/06	to	02/12/06	13/08/06	to	19/08/06	25/02/06	10/09/06	29/10/06
03/12/06	to	09/12/06	20/08/06	to	26/08/06	04/03/06	17/09/06	05/11/06
10/12/06	to	16/12/06	27/08/06	to	02/09/06	11/03/06	24/09/06	12/11/06
17/12/06	to	23/12/06	03/09/06	to	09/09/06	18/03/06	01/10/06	19/11/06
24/12/06	to	30/12/06	10/09/06	to	16/09/06	25/03/06	08/10/06	26/11/06
31/12/06	to	06/01/07	17/09/06	to	23/09/06	01/04/06	15/10/06	03/12/06
07/01/07	to	13/01/07	24/09/06	to	30/09/06	08/04/06	22/10/06	10/12/06
14/01/07	to	20/01/07	01/10/06	to	07/10/06	15/04/06	29/10/06	17/12/06
21/01/07	to	27/01/07	08/10/06	to	14/10/06	22/04/06	05/11/06	24/12/06
28/01/07	to	03/02/07	15/10/06	to	21/10/06	29/04/06	12/11/06	31/12/06
04/02/07	to	10/02/07	22/10/06	to	28/10/06	06/05/06	19/11/06	07/01/07
11/02/07	to	17/02/07	29/10/06	to	04/11/06	13/05/06	26/11/06	14/01/07
18/02/07	to	24/02/07	05/11/06	to	11/11/06	20/05/06	03/12/06	21/01/07
25/02/07	to	03/03/07	12/11/06	to	18/11/06	27/05/06	10/12/06	28/01/07
04/03/07	to	10/03/07	19/11/06	to	25/11/06	03/06/06	17/12/06	04/02/07
11/03/07	to	17/03/07	26/11/06	to	02/12/06	10/06/06	24/12/06	11/02/07
18/03/07	to	24/03/07	03/12/06	to	09/12/06	17/06/06	31/12/06	18/02/07
25/03/07	to	31/03/07	10/12/06	to	16/12/06	24/06/06	07/01/07	25/02/07
01/04/07	to	07/04/07	17/12/06	to	23/12/06	01/07/06	14/01/07	04/03/07
08/04/07	to	14/04/07	24/12/06	to	30/12/06	08/07/06	21/01/07	11/03/07
15/04/07	to	21/04/07	31/12/06	to	06/01/07	15/07/06	28/01/07	18/03/07
22/04/07	to	28/04/07	07/01/07	to	13/01/07	22/07/06	04/02/07	25/03/07
29/04/07	to	05/05/07	14/01/07	to	20/01/07	29/07/06	11/02/07	01/04/07
06/05/07	to	12/05/07	21/01/07	to	27/01/07	05/08/06	18/02/07	08/04/07
13/05/07	to	19/05/07	28/01/07	to	03/02/07	12/08/06	25/02/07	15/04/07
20/05/07	to	26/05/07	04/02/07	to	10/02/07	19/08/06	04/03/07	22/04/07

Health and Safety Guidance (Council Directive 92/85/EEC)[1]

European Commission Guidelines on the assessment of the chemical, physical and biological agents and industrial processes considered hazardous for the safety or health of pregnant workers and workers who have recently given birth or are breastfeeding (Council Directive 92/85/EEC)

Summary

Article 3(1) of Council Directive 92/85/EEC of 19 October 1992 (OJ L 348 of 28 November 1992, p1) on the implementation of measures to encourage improvements in the safety and health at work of pregnant workers and workers who have recently given birth or are breastfeeding (tenth individual Directive within the meaning of Article 16(1) of Directive 89/391/EEC) provides that:

'In consultation with the Member States and assisted by the Advisory Committee on Safety, Hygiene and Health Protection at Work, the Commission shall draw up guidelines on the assessment of the chemical, physical and biological agents and industrial processes considered hazardous for the safety or health of workers within the meaning of Article 2.
The guidelines referred to in the first subparagraph shall also cover movements and postures, mental and physical fatigue and other types of physical and mental stress connected with the work done by workers within the meaning of Article 2.'

Pursuant to Article 3(2), the purpose of the guidelines is to serve as a basis for the assessments referred to in Article 4(1), which in turn provides that 'For all activities liable to involve a specific risk of exposure to the agents, processes or working conditions of which a non-exhaustive list is given in Annex I, the employer shall assess the nature, degree and duration of exposure, in the undertaking and/or establishment concerned, of workers within the meaning of Article 2, either directly or by way of the protective and preventive services referred to in Article 7 of Directive 89/391/EEC, in order to:
- assess any risks to the safety or health and any possible effect on the pregnancy or breastfeeding of workers within the meaning of Article 2,
- decide what measures should be taken'.

[1] Only European Community legislation printed in the paper edition of the *Official Journal of the European Union* is deemed authentic.

The Commission, in consultation with the Member States and assisted by the Advisory Committee on Safety, Hygiene and Health Protection at Work, has prepared the Guidelines set out below.

The Commission attaches the greatest importance to all measures designed to protect the health and safety of workers, and notably certain groups of particularly vulnerable workers such as is clearly the case of pregnant workers and workers who have recently given birth or are breastfeeding – all the more so because the risks to which they may be exposed are liable to damage not only their own health but also that of their unborn or newborn children, given that there is a very close physiological and indeed emotional link between mother and child.

Hence the Commission considers that this Communication constitutes an effective and eminently practical tool which can serve as guidance in assessing the risks to the health and safety of pregnant workers and workers who have recently given birth or are breastfeeding. On the basis of this assessment it will be possible to take more effective measures.

For these reasons the Commission will see to it that these guidelines are disseminated as widely as possible by the bodies and persons responsible for health and safety at work.

Introduction

Pregnancy should be regarded not as an illness but as part of everyday life. Protection of health and safety in respect of pregnant women can often be achieved by applying existing rules and procedures in the relevant areas. Many women work while they are pregnant, and many return to work while they are still breastfeeding. However, some hazards in the workplace may affect the health and safety of new and expectant mothers and of their children. A pregnancy entails great physiological and psychological changes. The hormonal balance is very sensitive and exposures capable of disrupting it can lead to complication, possibly resulting, for example, in miscarriage.

Conditions which may be considered acceptable in normal situations may no longer be so during pregnancy.

The approach to risk assessment

Risk assessment is a systematic examination of all aspects of work in order to identify the probable causes of injuries or damage and to establish how these causes can be contained in order to eliminate or reduce risks.

In accordance with the requirements of Directive 92/85/EEC, assessment must comprise at least three phases:

(1)   identification of hazards (physical, chemical and biological agents; industrial processes; movements and postures; mental and physical fatigue; other physical and mental burdens);

(2)   identification of worker categories (exposed pregnant workers, workers who have recently given birth or workers who are breastfeeding);

(3)   risk assessment in both qualitative and quantitative terms.

Hazard: the intrinsic property or ability of something (e.g. work materials, equipment, methods and practices) with the potential to cause harm;

Risk: the likelihood that the potential for harm will be attained under the conditions of use and/or exposure, and the possible extent of the harm.

As regards point 1 (identification of hazards), extensive data are already available in respect of physical agents (including ionising radiation) and chemical and biological agents.

With specific reference to chemical agents, Council Directive 67/548/EEC, as most recently amended by Commission Directive 2000/33/EC on the approximation of the laws, regulations and administrative provisions relating to the classification, packaging and labelling of dangerous substances makes provision for the following risk phrases for substances and preparations:

–   possible risks of irreversible effects (R40);
–   may cause cancer (R45);
–   may cause heritable genetic damage (R46);
–   may cause cancer by inhalation (R49);
–   may cause harm to the unborn child (R61);
–   possible risk of harm to the unborn child (R63);
–   may cause harm to breastfed babies (R64).

In connection with the assessment of existing substances and with the work of the SCOEL (Scientific Committee for Occupational Exposure Limits), the Commission has also produced a series of documents partly concerned with the subject.

Point 2 (identification of exposed worker category). Whereas there is no difficulty targeting workers who have recently given birth or are breastfeeding, this does not apply in the case of pregnant workers. There is a period of between 30 and 45 days during which a worker may not be aware that she is pregnant and is therefore unable or reluctant to inform her employer. However, some agents do exist, especially physical and chemical agents, which may cause harm to the unborn child during the period immediately following conception, which means that appropriate preventive measures are essential. The problem is not easy to solve, in that it requires special care to be taken in respect of all workers by reducing their exposure to these harmful agents.

Point 3 (qualitative and quantitative risk assessment) represents the most delicate phase in the process, in that the person carrying out the assessment must be competent and take due account of relevant information, including information from the pregnant woman herself or her advisors, in applying appropriate methods in order to be able to conclude whether or not the hazard identified entails a risk situation for workers.

Legal background

Article 3(1) of Council Directive 92/85/EEC of 19 October 1992 (OJ No L 348 of 28 November 1992, p. 1) on the introduction of measures to encourage improvements in the safety and health at work of pregnant workers and workers who have recently given birth or are breastfeeding (10th individual Directive within the meaning of Article 16(1) of Directive 89/391/EEC) requires the Commission to draw up risk assessment guidelines in consultation with the Member States and assisted by the Advisory Committee on Safety, Hygiene and Health Protection at Work.

These guidelines will serve as a basis for the assessment referred to in Article 4(1) of the same Directive, which is an integral part of the assessment of the risks referred to in Article 9 of the 'framework' Council Directive 89/391/EEC on the introduction of measures to encourage improvement in the safety and health at workers at work, which states that:

> 'For all activities liable to involve a specific risk of exposure to the agents, processes or working conditions of which a non-exhaustive list in given in Annex I, the employer shall assess the nature, degree and duration of exposure, in the undertaking and/or establishment concerned, of workers within the meaning of Article 2, either directly or by way of the protective and preventive services referred to in Article 7 of 'framework' Council Directive 89/391/EEC, in order to:
> - assess any risks to the safety or health and any possible effect on the pregnancy or breastfeeding of workers within the meaning of Article 2,
> - decide what measures should be taken.'

It should be noted that:
- the employer is obliged to carry out a risk assessment for all female workers who fulfil the criteria laid down in Article 2 of the Directive (see definitions on page 7). This includes those in the armed forces, the police, and certain specific activities in the civil protection services;
- the risk assessment for pregnant workers is an additional risk assessment which is to be carried out in accordance with the provisions of the framework Directive.

This risk assessment must take into account the preventive aspects of the framework Directive and should also at least refer to the potential risks to pregnant workers, in so far as such risks are known (eg, risks related to certain chemicals, etc).

Previous measures connected with the present action

In 1993–94 the Commission produced a document entitled 'Guidance on risk assessment at work' [ISBN 97–727–4278–9]. This document is intended for the Member States, to be used or adapted for the purposes of providing guidelines for employers, workers, and any other parties who may be confronted with the practical aspects of rules on risk assessment laid down in Council 'framework' Directive 89/391/EEC on the introduction of measures to encourage improvements in the safety and health of workers at work, particularly Articles 6(3)(a) and 9(1)(a).

This document, which was published in 1996, constitutes an ideal basis for the preparation of the guidelines referred to in Article 3(1) of Directive 92/85/EEC.

Specific points to be stressed

- In order to take the framework Directive's principle of prevention into account, if the work is reorganised the risk assessment should be revisited and workers adequately trained in the new organisation.
- It is clear that the risk assessment referred to in this Directive is of a special nature, as it is designed for a continually changing state which varies according to each individual. In addition, it does not only affect the woman herself, but also the unborn child and the breast-feeding baby. In branches where hazards for reproduction and for pregnancy can be expected it is necessary to inform all workers of the potential risks.
- A one-off assessment may not be enough, as pregnancy is a dynamic process and not a static condition. Furthermore, not only during the various stages of a pregnancy but also after delivery, different risks can affect a woman and her unborn or new-born child to a varying extent. The same also applies where there is a change in working conditions, equipment or machines.
- Medical advice, reports and certificates should take working conditions into consideration. This is of particular relevance to an individual's conditions (eg, morning sickness, heightened sensitivity or smells such as tobacco smoke, etc.), which must be dealt with in strict confidentiality. The confidentiality concerning a woman's 'condition' must also ensure that an employer cannot make it known that a woman is pregnant if she does not wish it to be known or if she does not consent to it. Otherwise, for instance, it could lead to a considerable psychological strain for a woman who has already had one or more miscarriages.
- In certain circumstances it may be necessary to take steps (including limited disclosure) to protect the woman's health, safety and welfare, but this should be done with the woman's agreement following consultation.

Risk assessments should take due account of medical advice and the concerns of the individual woman.

- In respect of chemical hazards, it should be noted that occupational exposure limits are set for adult workers, and women working with hazardous substances should therefore be made aware of the additional risks that these substances might pose to a unborn or breastfed child.
- The directive allows for some flexibility for both the Member States and the women themselves concerning maternity leave after birth (it grants compulsory maternity leave of only two weeks but a total of at

least 14 weeks (divided between the time before and after giving birth) are granted). The various risks which could arise for pregnant women or women who have just given birth should be recorded and assessed.

– Since the first trimester of pregnancy is the most vulnerable period in terms of causing permanent damage to the unborn child, all necessary protection to the mother and the unborn child should be started as soon as possible.

General Duties for Employers Concerning Risk Assessment

The Directives require employers to assess risks to all workers, including new and expectant mothers, and to avoid or control those risks. In carrying out the risk assessment the employer should take into account existing occupational exposure limits. Exposure limits for hazardous substances and other agents are normally set at levels which should not put a pregnant or breastfeeding worker or her child at risk. In some cases, there are lower exposure levels for pregnant workers than for other workers.

The PWD specifically requires employers to take particular account of risks to new, breastfeeding and expectant mothers when assessing risks in the work activity. If the risk cannot be avoided by other means, there will be a need to change the working conditions or hours, or offer suitable alternative work. If that is not possible the worker should be exempted from normal duties for as long as necessary to protect her health or safety or that of her child.

What must an employer do?

In addition to carrying out the general risk assessment required by the Framework Directive and Directive 92/85/EEC, on receiving notification that an employee is pregnant an employer must assess the specific risks to that employee and take action to ensure that she is not exposed to anything which will damage either her health or that of her developing child.

The employer must:

– assess the risk;

this means that he must determine:

(a) the risks to which the pregnant woman or new mother who has recently given birth or is breastfeeding is exposed;

(b) the nature, intensity and duration of the exposure.

[Appendix 1 contains references to some aspects of pregnancy which may require adjustments to the work or the organisation thereof]

– **remove the hazard and avoid or reduce the risk;**

– **act to ensure there is no damage to health.**

Damage to health means for this purpose any disease or damage to a person's physical or mental condition, or any possible effect on the pregnancy or the unborn or new-born infant, or to women who have recently given birth.

If the assessment reveals that there is a risk, the employer must inform the woman about the risk and explain the measures to be taken to ensure that the health and safety of the woman or the developing child is not adversely affected.

Definitions

For the purposes of the PW Directive:

(a) *pregnant worker* shall mean a pregnant worker who informs her employer of her condition, in accordance with national legislation and/or national practice;

(b) *worker who has recently given birth* shall mean a worker who has recently given birth within the meaning of national legislation and/or national practice and who informs her employer of her condition, in accordance with that legislation and/or practice;

(c) *worker who is breastfeeding* shall mean a worker who is breastfeeding within the meaning of national legislation and/or national practice and who informs her employer of her condition, in accordance with that legislation and/or practice.

Identifying the hazards

Physical, biological and chemical agents, processes and working conditions which may affect the health and safety of new or expectant mothers are set out in the chapter on specific hazards (see below). They include possible hazards listed in the Annexes to the Directive on the health and safety of pregnant workers.

Many of the hazards included in the table are already covered by specific European health and safety legislation, for example Council Directive 90/394 EEC (and its amendments) on carcinogens, Council Directive 90/679/EEC (and its amendments) on biological agents, Council Directive 80/1107/EEC on chemical, physical and biological agents, which will be repealed upon transposal by the Member States of Directive 98/24/EC (before 5 May 2001), Council Directive 82/605/EEC on lead, Council Directive 97/43/EURATOM on ionising radiation, Directive 90/269/EEC on the manual handling of loads and Directive 90/270/EEC on display screen equipment. If any of these hazards are present in the workplace, the employers should refer to the relevant legislation for information on what they should do. Hazards may be multifactorial in their effects.

Deciding who might be harmed, and how

The risk assessment may show that there is a substance, agent or work process in the workplace that could damage the health or safety of new or expectant mothers or their children. There is a need to bear in mind that there could be different risks depending on whether workers are pregnant, have recently given birth or are breastfeeding. The definition of workers includes, for example, maintenance and cleaning staff and there may need to be cooperation between employers where employees of one are working, e.g. as contractors, on the premises of another.

Informing employees of the risk

If the risk assessment does reveal a risk, the employers should inform all employees concerned of the potential risks. They should also explain what they intend to do to make sure that new and expectant mothers are not exposed to risks that could cause them harm. The information should be given also to employees' representatives.

If there is a risk, employers should inform employees of the importance of early detection of pregnancy.

Avoiding the risk

If a significant risk to the health or safety of a new or expectant mother is identified, the action to be taken to reduce this should be decided upon.

Keeping the risks under review

The employer will review the risk assessments for new or expectant mothers if he is aware of any change. Although any hazards are likely to remain constant, the possibility of damage to the unborn child as a result of a hazard will vary at different stages of pregnancy. Furthermore, there are different risks to consider for workers who have recently given birth or are breastfeeding.

Employers need to ensure that workers who are breastfeeding are not exposed to risks that could damage health or safety for as long as they continue to breastfeed. The Directive concerning the minimum safety and health requirements for the workplace (89/654/EEC) requires appropriate conditions to be provided for pregnant women and nursing mothers to rest. Where workers continue to breastfeed for many months after birth, employers will need to review the risks regularly. Where they identify risks, there is a need to continue to follow the three steps to avoid exposure to the risks, ie, adjustment of working hours/conditions, alternative work or exemption from normal duties, for as long as it threatens the health and safety of a breastfeeding worker or her child. The main concern is exposure to substances such as lead, organic solvents, pesticides and antimitotics, as some of the substances are excreted through the milk, and the child is assumed to be particularly sensitive. The most important aspect is 'to avoid' – or to reduce – exposure. Professional advice from occupational health specialists may be required in special cases.

RISK ASSESSMENT OF GENERIC HAZARDS AND ASSOCIATED SITUATIONS

Generic hazards and associated situations which are likely to be met by most pregnant women, new/or breastfeeding mothers are listed below:

List of generic hazards and situations	What is the risk?	How to deal with the risk Examples of preventive measures*	European legislation other than Directive 92/85/EEC
Mental and physical fatigue and working hours	Long working hours, shift work and night work can have a significant effect on the health of new and expectant mothers, and on breastfeeding. Not all women are affected in the same way, and the associated risks vary with the type of work undertaken, working conditions and the individual concerned. This applies especially to health care. Generally, however, both mental and physical fatigue increases during pregnancy and in the postnatal period due to the various physiological and other changes taking place. Because they suffer from increasing tiredness, some pregnant and breastfeeding women may not be able to work irregular or late shifts or night work, or overtime. Working time arrangements (including provisions for rest breaks, and their frequency and timing) may *continued*	It may be necessary to adjust working hours temporarily, as well as other working conditions, including the timing and frequency of rest breaks, and to change shift patterns and duration to avoid risks. With regard to night work, alternative day work should be organised for pregnant women.	

* The examples in this column are for guidance only. Other preventive measures exist for all the risks listed. It is up to individual employers to select the measures most appropriate to their situation, while complying with applicable Community and national legislation.

List of generic hazards and situations	What is the risk?	How to deal with the risk Examples of preventive measures*	European legislation other than Directive 92/85/EEC
	affect the health of the pregnant woman and her unborn child, her recovery after childbirth, or her ability to breastfeed, and may increase the risks of stress and stress related ill health. Because of changes in blood pressure which may occur during and after pregnancy and childbirth, normal patterns of breaks from work may not be adequate for new or expectant mothers.		
Postural problems connected with the activity of new or expectant mothers	Fatigue from standing and other physical work has long been associated with miscarriage, premature birth and low birth weight.\n\nIt is hazardous working in tightly fitting workspaces or with workstations which do not adjust sufficiently to take account of increased abdominal size, particularly during the later stages of pregnancy. This may lead to strain or sprain injuries. Dexterity, agility, co-ordination, speed of movement, reach and balance may also be impaired, and an increased risk of accidents may need to be considered.	Ensure that the hours, volume and pacing of work are not excessive and that, where possible, the employees themselves have some control over how work is organised.\n\nEnsure that seating is available where appropriate.\n\nFatigue can be avoided or reduced by making it possible to take longer and more frequent breaks during the work session.\n\nAdjusting workstations or work procedures may help remove postural problems and the risk of accidents.	
Work at heights	It is hazardous for pregnant workers working at heights, for example ladders, platforms.	The employer must ensure that pregnant workers are not exposed to work at heights.	

Working alone	Pregnant women are more exposed to risk than others when working alone, particularly if they fall or if urgent medical attention is required.	Depending or their medical condition, access to communications with others and levels of (remote) supervision involved, may need to be reviewed and revised to ensure that help and support is available when required, and that emergency procedures (if needed) take into account the needs of new and expectant mothers.
Occupational stress	New and expectant mothers can be particularly affected by occupational stresses, for various reasons: – hormonal, physiological and psychological changes occur and sometimes change rapidly during and after pregnancy, sometimes affecting susceptibility to stress, or to anxiety or depression in individuals; – financial, emotional and job insecurity may be affected by the changes in economic circumstances brought about by pregnancy, especially if this is reflected in workplace culture; – it may be difficult to combine work and private life, especially with long, unpredictable or unsociable working hours or where other family responsibilities are involved; – possible exposure to situations involving violence at the workplace.	In laying down measures, employers will need to take account of known stress factors (such as shift patterns, job insecurity, workloads, etc) and the particular medical and psychosocial factors affecting the individual woman.

continued

List of generic hazards and situations	What is the risk?	How to deal with the risk Examples of preventive measures*	European legislation other than Directive 92/85/EEC
	If a woman is exposed to the risk of violence at work during pregnancy, when she has recently given birth or while she is breastfeeding this may be harmful. It can lead to detachment of the placenta, miscarriage, premature delivery, underweight birth and it may affect the ability to breastfeed.		
	This risk particularly affects workers in direct contact with customers and clients.		
	Additional work-related stress may occur if a woman's anxiety about her pregnancy, or about its outcome (eg, where there is a past history of miscarriage, stillbirth or other abnormality) is heightened as a result of peer group or other pressure in the workplace.	Protective measures may include adjustments to working conditions or working hours, and ensuring that the necessary understanding, support and recognition is there when the woman returns to work, whilst her privacy is also respected.	Framework Directive 89/391/EEC is applicable.
	Stress is associated in some studies with increased incidence of miscarriage and pregnancy loss, and also with impaired ability to breastfeed.		
	Women who have recently suffered loss through stillbirth, miscarriage, adoption at birth or neonatal death, will be especially vulnerable to stress, as will women who have experienced serious illness or trauma		

			Directive 89/654/EEC (health and safety requirements for the workplace)	
	(including Caesarean section) associated with pregnancy or childbirth. However, in certain circumstances, returning to work after such events may help to alleviate stress, assuming a sympathetic and supportive work environment.			
Standing activities	Physiological changes during pregnancy (increased blood and systolic volume, general dilatation of blood vessels and possible compression of abdominal or pelvic veins) promote peripheral congestion while standing. Venous compression may reduce the venous return from the pelvis which leads to compensatory increases in the maternal heart rate and to contractions of the uterus. If the compensation is insufficient, this may lead to dizziness and faintness. Continuous standing (and/or walking) for long periods during the working day also contributes to an increased risk of premature childbirth.	Ensure that seating is available where appropriate. Constant sitting or constant standing are both inadvisable. It is better to alternate between the two. If this is not possible, provision should be made for breaks.		
Sitting activities	Pregnancy-specific changes in the coagulation factors and mechanical compression of the pelvic veins by the uterus pose a relatively high risk of thrombosis or embolism for pregnant women. When sitting still during pregnancy, the venous filling in the legs increases significantly and may cause aching and *continued*			

List of generic hazards and situations	What is the risk?	How to deal with the risk Examples of preventive measures*	European legislation other than Directive 92/85/EEC
	oedema in the legs. The increase in lumbar lordosis caused by the increase in abdominal circumference can lead to muscular pain in the lumbar region of the spine, which may be intensified by remaining in a specific position for an excessively long period of time.		
Lack of rest and other welfare facilities	Rest is important for new and expectant mothers. Tiredness increases during and after pregnancy and may be exacerbated by work-related factors. The need for rest is both physical and mental. Cigarette smoke is mutagenic and carcinogenic and is a known risk to pregnancy where the mother smokes. The effects of passive smoking are less clear but are known to affect the heart and lungs, and to pose a risk to infant health. Cigarette smoke is also a respiratory sensitiser, and is known to be associated with asthma, the onset of which is associated in some cases with pregnancy.	The need for physical rest may require suitable facilities for the woman concerned to have access to somewhere where she can sit or lie down comfortably in privacy, and without disturbance, at appropriate intervals. Expectant mothers must be warned of the dangers of smoking, including passive smoking. Where there is no official ban on smoking in communal areas such as rest rooms and canteens, the employer must take account of the potential danger to pregnant women of exposure to cigarette smoke; adopting, if necessary, preventive and protection measures.	Council Directive 89/654/EEC (health and safety requirements for the workplace)

		Council Directive 89/654/EEC (health and safety requirements for the workplace)
Risk of infection or kidney disease as a result of inadequate hygiene facilities	Without easy access to toilets (and associated hygiene facilities) at work, due to distance, work processes or systems, etc, there may be increased risks to health and safety, including significant risks of infection and kidney disease. Because of pressure on the bladder and other changes associated with pregnancy, pregnant women often have to go to the toilet more frequently and more urgently than others. Breastfeeding women may also need to do so because of increased fluid intake to promote breast milk production.	Protective measures include adaptation of rules governing working practices, for example in continuous processing and teamworking situations, and appropriate measures to enable expectant and nursing mothers to leave their workstation/activity at short notice more frequently than normal, or otherwise (if this is not possible) making temporary adjustments to working conditions as specified in Directive 92/85/EC.
Hazards as a result of inappropriate nutrition	Adequate and appropriate nutrition and liquid refreshment (especially clean drinking water) at regular intervals is essential to the health of the new or expectant mother and her child(ren). Appetite and digestion are affected by the timing, frequency and duration of meal breaks and other opportunities for intake of food and drink, and this also affects the health of the unborn child. This is affected during and after pregnancy by hormonal and physiological changes, including those resulting in or affecting morning sickness (usually in early pregnancy), the position of the unborn child in the womb, the nutritional needs of the individual mother and her unborn or breastfeeding child(ren), etc	New and expectant mothers' particular needs concerning rest, meal and refreshment breaks may be established in consultation with the individuals concerned. These needs may change as the pregnancy progresses. Protective measures must be taken to deal with these constraints, particularly with regard to the need for rest, meal and refreshment breaks, and to maintain appropriate hygiene standards.

continued

List of generic hazards and situations	What is the risk?	How to deal with the risk Examples of preventive measures*	European legislation other than Directive 92/85/EEC
Hazards as a result of inappropriate nutrition _continued_	Pregnant women may need more frequent meal breaks and more frequent access to drinking water or other light refreshments, and may also only be able to tolerate food 'little and often' rather than in larger quantities at 'normal' mealtimes. Their eating patterns and preferences may change, especially in early stages of pregnancy, not only in response to morning sickness but also due to discomfort or other problems in the later stages of pregnancy.		
Hazard due to unsuitable or absent facilities	Access to appropriate facilities for expressing and safely storing breast milk for breastfeeding mothers, or to enable infants to be breastfed at or near the workplace, may facilitate breastfeeding by working women, and may significantly protect the health of both mother and infant. Evidence shows that breastfeeding can help to protect the mother against cancer and helps protect the child from certain diseases in infancy. Obstacles to breastfeeding in the workplace may significantly affect the health of both mother and child.	Protective measures include: – access to a private room in which to breastfeed or express breast milk; – use of secure, clean refrigerators for storing expressed breast milk whilst at work, and facilities for washing, sterilising and storing receptacles; – time off (without loss of pay or benefits, and without fear of penalty) to express milk or breastfeed.	

RISK ASSESSMENT: SPECIFIC HAZARDS (AND WAYS OF AVOIDING RISKS*) (INCLUDING PHYSICAL, CHEMICAL AND BIOLOGICAL AGENTS AND WORKING CONDITIONS LISTED IN ANNEX 1 AND 2 TO THE DIRECTIVE 92/85/EEC)

Working conditions can have important effects on the health, safety and welfare of new and expectant mothers. Sometimes it will be the relationship between the different factors involved which determines the type of risk, rather than one factor on its own.

Since pregnancy is a dynamic state involving continuous changes and developments, the same working conditions may raise different health and safety issues for different women at different stages of pregnancy, and again on returning to work after childbirth or whilst breastfeeding. Some of these issues are predictable and apply generally (such as those listed below). Others will depend on individual circumstances and personal medical history.

List of agents/ working conditions	What is the risk?	How to deal with the risk Examples of preventive measures*	Other European legislation
PHYSICAL AGENTS – where these are regarded as agents causing foetal lesions and/or likely to disrupt placental attachment, and in particular:			
Shocks, vibration or movement	Regular exposure to shocks, ie, sudden severe blow to the body or low frequency vibration, for example driving or riding in off-road vehicles, or excessive movement, may increase the risk of a miscarriage. Long-term exposure to whole body vibration may increase the risk of premature birth or low birth weight. Breastfeeding workers are at no greater risk than other workers.	Work shall be organised in such a way that pregnant workers and those who have recently given birth are not exposed to work entailing risk arising from unpleasant vibration of the entire body, particularly at low frequencies, microtraumas, shaking, shocks or where jolts or blows are delivered to the lower body.	None specific Framework Directive 89/391/EEC is applicable

* The examples in this column are for guidance only. Other preventive measures exist for all the risks listed. It is up to individual employers to select the measures most appropriate to their situation, while complying with applicable Community and national legislation.

List of agents/ working conditions	What is the risk?	How to deal with the risk? Examples of preventive measures*	Other European legislation
Noise	Prolonged exposure to loud noise may lead to increased blood pressure and tiredness. Experimental evidence suggests that prolonged exposure of the unborn child to loud noise during pregnancy may have an effect on later hearing and that low frequencies have a greater potential for causing harm. There are no particular problems for women who have recently given birth or who are breastfeeding.	National provisions applying Council Directive 86/188/EEC must be respected. The employer must ensure that workers who are pregnant, who have recently given birth or who are breastfeeding are not exposed to noise levels exceeding national exposure limit values based on Directive 86/188/EEC. It should be recognised that use of personal protective equipment by the mother will not protect the unborn child from the physical hazard.	Council Directive 86/188/EEC (exposure to noise at work)
Ionising radiation	Exposure to ionising radiation involves risks to the unborn child; there are therefore particular provisions to limit the exposure of the expectant mother and the unborn child. If a nursing mother works with radioactive liquids or dusts, the child may be exposed, particularly through contamination of the mother's skin. Also, there may be a risk from radioactive contamination breathed in or ingested by the mother and transferred to the milk or via the placenta to the unborn child.	As soon as a pregnant woman informs the undertaking of her condition, the protection of the child to be born must be comparable with that provided for members of the public. The conditions for the pregnant woman in the context of her employment are therefore such that the equivalent dose to the unborn child will be as low as reasonably achievable and that it will be unlikely that this dose will exceed 1 mSv during at least the remainder of the pregnancy.	Council Directive 96/29/EURATOM (protection of health against dangers from ionising radiation)

			Council Directive 97/43/EURATOM (dangers of ionising radiation in medical exposure)
		Average exposure over 5 years for any worker may not exceed 20 mSv per year (and may not exceed 50 mSv in any one year).	
		The employer must inform female workers exposed to ionising radiation of the need to declare the pregnancy as soon as possible, having regard to the risks of exposure for the unborn child and of contamination of the breastfed child in the event of bodily radioactive contamination.	
		Work procedures should be designed to prevent pregnant women from being exposed to ionising radiation.	
		Special attention should be paid to the possibility of nursing mothers receiving radioactive contamination and they should not be employed in work where the risk of such contamination is high.	
Radiation protection policy for all workers, including pregnant women and nursing mothers, has recently been reviewed in the light of revised recommendations from the International Commission on Radiological Protection, and dose limits are changed.			
Non-ionising electromagnetic radiation	*The possibility cannot be excluded that electromagnetic or magnetic fields, including those associated with short-wave therapy, the welding of plastics and the curing of adhesives, may involve an increased risk for the unborn child.*	It is advised to minimise exposure by means of health and safety measures.	Framework Directive 89/391/EEC is applicable.

List of agents/ working conditions	What is the risk?	How to deal with the risk Examples of preventive measures*	Other European legislation
Extremes of cold or heat	Pregnant women tolerate heat less well and may more readily faint or be more liable to heat stress. The risk is likely to be reduced after birth but it is not certain how quickly an improvement comes about. Exposure to heat may lead to adverse pregnancy outcomes. Breastfeeding may be impaired by heat dehydration. Working in extreme cold may be a hazard for pregnant women and their unborn child. Warm clothing should be provided. The risks are increased particularly in the event of sudden changes in temperature.	Pregnant workers should not be exposed to prolonged excessive heat or cold at work.	
Work in hyperbaric atmosphere, for example pressurised enclosures and underwater diving	Compressed air: People working under high pressure are at risk of developing the bends. This is due to free bubbles of gas in the circulation. It is not clear whether pregnant women are more at risk of the bends but the unborn child could potentially be seriously harmed by such gas bubbles. For those who have recently given birth there is a small increase in the risk of the bends.	Pregnant workers should not work in a high-pressure atmosphere.	Framework Directive 89/391/EEC

There is no physiological reason why a breastfeeding mother should not work under high pressure (although there would be obvious practical difficulties).

Diving: Pregnant workers are advised not to dive at all during pregnancy due to the possible effects of exposure to a hyperbaric environment on the unborn child.

There is no evidence to suggest that breastfeeding and diving are incompatible.

Pregnant workers may not be required to dive

The employer must ensure that workers who are pregnant are aware that pregnancy can constitute a medical reason not to dive; and such workers should inform the employer if there is any medical reason why they should not dive, so that the employer can take appropriate action.

BIOLOGICAL AGENTS
Directive 90/679/EEC (biological agents at work) and its amendments:
1. Group 1 biological agent means one that is unlikely to cause human disease;
2. Group 2 biological agent means one that can cause human disease and might be a hazard to workers: it is unlikely to spread to the community; there is usually effective prophylaxis or treatment available;
3. Group 3 biological agents means one that can cause severe human disease and present a serious hazards to workers; it may present a risk of spreading to the community, but there is usually effective prophylaxis or treatment available;
4. Group 4 biological agent means one that cause severe human disease and is a serious hazard to workers; it may present a high risk of spreading to the community; there is usually no effective prophylaxis or treatment available.

| Any biological agent in groups 2, 3 and 4 (see above) | Many biological agents within the three risk groups can affect the unborn child if the mother is infected during pregnancy. These may be transmitted through the placenta while the child is in the womb, or during or after *continued* | Depends on the risk assessment, which will take account firstly of the nature of the biological agent, how infection is spread, how likely contact is, and what control measures there are. These include physical containment *continued* | See above |

continued

List of agents/ working conditions	What is the risk?	How to deal with the risk Examples of preventive measures*	Other European legislation
Any biological agent in groups 2, 3 and 4 *continued*	birth, for example through breastfeeding or through close physical contact between mother and child. Examples of agents where the child might be infected in one of these ways are hepatitis B, hepatitis C, HIV (the AIDS virus), herpes, TB, syphilis, chickenpox and typhoid. For most workers, the risk of infection is not higher at work than from living in the community; but in certain occupations, exposure to infections is more likely.	and the usual hygiene measures. The use of available vaccines is to be recommended, with due regard for any contra-indications for administering certain of them to women in the early stages of pregnancy. If there is a known high risk of exposure to a highly infectious agent, then it will be appropriate for the pregnant worker to avoid exposure altogether. The employer must ensure immunity testing (chickenpox, toxoplasmosis, parvovirus) for risk occupations, and job transfer or temporary leave during epidemics, if seronegative.	
Biological agents known to cause abortion of the unborn child, or physical and neurological damage. These agents are included in groups 2, 3 and 4	Rubella (German measles) and toxoplasmosis can harm the unborn child, as can some other biological agents, for example cytomegalovirus (an infection common in the community) and chlamydia in sheep.	See above. Exposure to these, biological agents should be avoided, except if the pregnant women is protected by her state of immunity.	See above

CHEMICAL AGENTS – Chemical agents may enter the human body through different pathways: inhalation, ingestion, percutaneous penetration, dermal absorption. The following chemical agents in so far as it is known that they endanger the health of pregnant women and the unborn child:

| Substances labelled R40, R45, R46, R49, R61, R63 and R64 | The substances are listed in Annex 1 of Directive 67/548/EEC and are labelled with the risk phrases:

R40: possible risk of irreversible effects;
R45: may cause cancer;
R46: may cause heritable genetic damage;
R49: may cause cancer by inhalation;
R61: may cause harm to the unborn child;
R63: possible risk of harm to the unborn child;
R64: may cause harm to breastfed babies.

The actual risk to health of these substances can only be determined following a risk assessment of a particular substance at the place of work – ie, although the substances listed may have the potential to endanger health or safety, there may be no risk in practice, for example if exposure is below a level which might cause harm.

continued | For work with hazardous substances, which include chemicals which may cause heritable genetic damage, employers are required to assess the health risks to workers arising from such work, and where appropriate prevent or control the risks. In carrying out assessments, employers should have regard for women who are pregnant, or who have recently given birth. Prevention of exposure must be the first priority. Where it is not appropriate to prevent the risk, control of exposure may be by a combination of technical measures, along with good work planning and housekeeping, and the use of Personal Protective Equipment (PPE). PPE should only be used for control purposes if all other methods have failed. It may also be used as secondary protection in combination with other methods.

Substitution of harmful agents should be made, if possible. | Council Directive 98/24/EC (risks related to chemical agents at work)

Council Directive 90/394/EEC (carcinogens at work)

Council Directive 67/548/EEC (classification, packaging and labelling of dangerous substances) and its amendments

Council Directive 98/24/EC (risks related to chemical agents at work)

continued |

List of agents/ working conditions	What is the risk?	How to deal with the risk Examples of preventive measures*	Other European legislation
Substances labelled R40, R45, R46, R49, R61, R63 and R64	Industries which use chemicals are referred to the 'Guidance on the health protection of pregnant women at work' issued by CEFIC 1. It gives particular attention to chemical hazards and guidance on risk assessment.		Council Directive 90/394/EEC (carcinogens at work) Council Directive 67/548/EEC (classification, packaging and labelling of dangerous substances) and its amendments Directive 91/155/EEC as amended by Directive 93/112/EEC establishing a system of safety data sheets
Preparations labelled on the basis of Directive 83/379/EEC or 1999/45/EC	A preparation containing more than specified concentrations of a substance bearing one of the risk phases R40, R45, R46, R49, R61, R63 and R64 would be expected to present similar hazards. The prudent employer would apply the assessment principles appropriate for substances to similarly labelled preparation, should these occur on the workplace.	Hazardous preparations should be assessed and risk management action undertaken in the same way as for similar hazardous substances.	Directive 88/379/EEC or 1999/45/EC (classification, packaging and labelling of dangerous preparation) as amended or adapted.

Mercury and mercury derivatives	Organic mercury compounds could have adverse effects on the unborn child. Animal studies and human observations have demonstrated that exposure to these forms of mercury during pregnancy can slow the growth of the unborn baby, disrupt the nervous system, and cause the mother to be poisoned. Organic mercury is transferred from blood to milk. That may pose a risk to offspring, if a woman is highly exposed before and during pregnancy.	Prevention of exposure must be the first priority. Where it is not appropriate to prevent the risk, control of exposure may be by a combination of technical measures, along with good work planning and housekeeping, and the use of Personal Protective Equipment (PPE). PPE should only be used for control purposes if all other methods have failed. It may also be used as secondary protection in combination with other methods.	Council Directive 80/1107/EEC (chemical, physical and biological agents at work) which will be repealed upon transposal by the Member States of Directive 98/24/EC (before 5 May 2001).
Antimitotic (cytotoxic) drugs	In the long-term these drugs cause damage to genetic information in sperm and eggs. Some can cause cancer. Absorption is by inhalation or through the skin. Assessment of the risk should look particularly at preparation of the drug for use (pharmacists, nurses), administration of the drug and disposal of waste (chemical and human).	There is no known threshold limit and exposure must be avoided or reduced. Those trying to conceive a child or who are pregnant or breastfeeding should be fully informed of the reproductive hazard. When preparing the drug solutions, exposure should be minimised by the use of protective garments (gloves, gowns and mask), equipment (flow hood), and good working practices. A pregnant worker preparing antineoplastic drug solutions should be transferred to another job.	Council Directive 90/394/EEC (carcinogens at work)

List of agents/ working conditions	What is the risk?	How to deal with the risk Examples of preventive measures*	Other European legislation
Chemical agents of known and dangerous percutaneous absorption (ie, that may be absorbed through the skin). This includes some pesticides.	Some chemical agents can also penetrate intact skin and become absorbed into the body, causing harmful effects. These substances are specifically marked in the lists contained in the relevant Directives. As with all substances, the risks will depend on the way the substance is being used as well as on its hazardous properties. Absorption through the skin can result from localised contamination, for example from a splash on the skin or clothing, or in certain cases, from exposure to high atmospheric concentrations of vapour.	Prevention of exposure must be the first priority. Special precautions should be taken to prevent skin contact. Where possible, technical measures to control exposure should be used in preference to personal protective equipment, such as gloves, overalls or face shields. For example, enclose the process or redesign it so that vaporisation is reduced. Where an employee is obliged to use personal protective equipment (either alone or in combination with technical measures), its suitability should be ensured.	Commission Directives 91/322/EEC and 96/94/EC (indicative limit values for chemical agents at work)
Agents of percutaneous absorption	In the case of agricultural workers, the risk assessment should consider whether there is a residual risk of contamination from, eg, pesticides used at an earlier stage.		
Carbon monoxide	Carbon monoxide is produced by using petrol, diesel and liquefied petroleum gas (LPG) as a source of power in engines and in domestic appliances. Risks arise when engines or appliances are operated in enclosed areas. Pregnant women may have heightened susceptibility to the effects of exposure to carbon monoxide.	The best preventive measure is to eliminate the hazard by changing processes or equipment. Where prevention is not appropriate, technical measures should be considered, in combination with good working practices and personal protective equipment. Chronic exposure of female workers should be avoided. Even occasional exposure to CO could potentially be harmful.	

	Pregnant workers should be informed about the dangers of exposure to carbon monoxide during smoking.
Carbon monoxide readily crosses the placenta and can result in the unborn child being starved of oxygen. Data on the effects of exposure to carbon monoxide on pregnant women are limited, but there is evidence of adverse effects on the unborn child. Both the level and duration of maternal exposure are important factors in the effect on the unborn child.	
There is no indication that breastfed babies suffer adverse effects from their mother's exposure to carbon monoxide, nor that the mother is significantly more sensitive to carbon monoxide after giving birth.	
Given the extreme risk of exposure to high levels of CO, risk assessment and prevention of high exposure are identical for all workers.	
Risk assessment may be complicated by active or passive smoking and/or ambient air pollution. If those sources lead to a higher COHb than occupational exposure would, the level of risk is determined by those outside sources, as the effect on COHb is not cumulative.	
However, careful documentation of such 'outside' sources may be required to avoid liability and litigation.	

List of agents/ working conditions	What is the risk?	How to deal with the risk Examples of preventive measures*	Other European legislation
Lead and lead derivatives – in so far as these agents are capable of being absorbed by the human organism	Historically, exposure of pregnant women to lead is associated with abortions and miscarriages, but there is no indication that this is still relevant at current accepted standards for exposure. There are strong indications that exposure to lead, both intra-uterine and post-partum, leads to developmental problems, especially of the nervous system and the blood-forming organs. Women, new-born and young children are more sensitive to lead than male adults. Lead is transferred from blood to milk. This may pose a risk to offspring if a woman is highly exposed before and during pregnancy. **Indications of safe levels** Exposure to lead cannot safely be measured in terms of airborne exposure levels, because of the different uptake routes. Biological monitoring of blood lead levels (PbB) and biological effects monitoring (eg, tests for zinc proto porphyrin and levels of amino laevulinic acid in blood or urine) are the best exposure indicators.	Women with reproductive capacity must be subject to a lower blood-lead suspension level than other workers, to protect any developing unborn child. Once their pregnancy is confirmed, women who are subject to medical surveillance under the lead Directive will normally be suspended from work which exposes them significantly to lead. European limit values are in the process of being reviewed. Because the elimination of lead from the body is a very slow process, fertile women should be informed of this. The employer must ensure that exposure to lead is reduced and that women have the option of placement elsewhere until this has been done.	Council Directive 82/605/EEC (exposure to metallic lead at work) which will be repealed upon transposal by the Member States of Directive 98/24/EC (by 5 May 2001).

			Council Directive 90/394/EEC (carcinogens at work)
	Risk assessment A risk of exposure of pregnant and breastfeeding women to lead is specifically prohibited under Article 6 of the Directive if the exposure might jeopardise safety or health. The risk assessment should be based upon both the individual's and the work group's historical record of blood lead levels or similar parameters, not on ambient air monitoring. Where these are within the range of unexposed people, it could be concluded that the health is not in jeopardy. However, PbB levels and other biological indicators of exposure may change over time without apparent relation to (airborne) exposure. There is therefore a possibility that a change in the monitoring indicator might occur without an increase in exposure. This could be interpreted as indicating that health had been jeopardised.	In view of this, banning pregnant and breastfeeding women from all lead-containing areas may be the only acceptable option. This is particularly advisable if there is exposure to organic lead compounds.	
Chemical agents and industrial processes in Annex 1 to Directive 90/394/EEC	Those industrial processes listed in Annex 1 of Directive 90/394/EEC and referred to in Annex 1B of Directive 92/85/EEC may give rise to carcinogenic risk. If there are carcinogens, this should be clearly stated.	Directive 90/394/EEC requires a detailed risk assessment to be carried out. Avoid exposure. If risks cannot be assessed and controlled by collective measures, appropriate steps should be taken to inform and train workers.	

WORKING CONDITIONS

List of agents/ working conditions	What is the risk?	How to deal with the risk Examples of preventive measures*	European legislation other than Directive 92/85/EEC
Manual handling of loads	Manual handling of heavy loads is considered to pose a risk to pregnancy, such as risk of foetal injury and premature birth. The risk depends on strain, ie, the weight of the load, how you lift and how often it occurs during work time. As the pregnancy progresses, a pregnant worker is at greater risk from manual handling injury. This is due to hormonal relaxation of the ligaments and the postural problems of advancing pregnancy. There can also be risks for those who have recently given birth, for example after a Caesarean section there is likely to be a temporary limitation on lifting and handling capability. Breastfeeding mothers may experience discomfort due to increased breast size and sensitivity.	The changes an employer should make will depend on the risks identified in the assessment and the circumstances of the business. For example, it may be possible to alter the nature of the task so that risks from manual handling are reduced for all workers, including new or expectant mothers. Or it may be necessary to address the specific needs of the worker and reduce the amount of physical work, or provide aids for her in future to reduce the risks she faces. Where there is a risk particularly of back injury to workers, Directive 90/269/EEC requires employers to: – avoid the need for hazardous manual handling; – assess the risks from those operations that cannot be avoided; and – take steps to reduce these risks to the lowest level.	Directive 90/269/EEC on health and safety requirements for the manual handling of loads

* The examples in this column are for guidance only. Other preventive measures exist for all the risks listed. It is up to individual employers to select the measures most appropriate to their situation, while complying with applicable Community and national legislation.

| Movements and postures | Postural problems can arise at different stages of pregnancy, and on returning to work, depending on the individual and her working conditions. These problems may increase as the pregnancy progresses, especially if the work involves awkward movements or long periods of standing or sitting in one position where the body is exposed to risks of prolonged static load or impaired circulation. These may contribute to the development of varicose veins and haemorrhoids as well as backache.

Backache in pregnancy may be associated with prolonged work and poor working posture, as well as excessive movement. A pregnant woman may need more workspace, or may need to adapt the way she works (or the way she interacts with the work of others or with her work equipment) as pregnancy changes both her size and the ways in which she can move, stand or sit still for a long time in comfort and safety.

There may also be additional risks if a woman is returning to work after a childbirth with medical complications such as a Caesarean birth or deep vein thrombosis. | The employer must ensure that workers who are pregnant, have recently given birth or are breastfeeding are not exposed to:
– manual handling involving risk of injury;
– awkward movements and postures, especially in confined spaces;
– work at heights;
– where appropriate, work equipment and lifting gear should be introduced or adapted, storage arrangements altered, or workstations or job content redesigned;
– long periods spent handling loads, or standing or sitting without regular exercise or movement to maintain healthy circulation should be avoided. |

List of agents/ working conditions	What is the risk?	How to deal with the risk Examples of preventive measures*	Other European legislation
Travelling either inside or outside the establishment	Travelling in the course of work, and to and from the workplace, can be problematic for pregnant women, involving risks including fatigue, vibration, stress, static posture, discomfort and accidents. These risks can have a significant effect on the health of new and expectant mothers.		
Underground extractive industries	Mines often have difficult physical conditions and many of the physical agents described in this guidance are a regular part of the mining environment.	Employers are responsible for assessing risks and should take action in line with Directive 92/104/EEC.	Directive 92/104/EEC (protection of workers in mineral-extracting industries)
Work with display screen equipment (VDUs)	Although not specifically listed in Directive 92/85/EEC, the Advisory Committee and the Commission are aware that anxiety about radiation emissions from display screen equipment and possible effects on pregnant women has been widespread. However, there is substantial evidence that these concerns are unfounded. The advice below summarises scientific understanding.		

The levels of electromagnetic radiation which are likely to be generated by display screen equipment are well below those set out in international recommendations for limiting risk to human health created by such emissions, and the Radiological Protection Board does not consider such levels to pose a significant risk to health. No special protective measures are therefore needed to protect the health of people from this radiation.	In the light of the scientific evidence, pregnant women do not need to stop working with VDUs. However, to avoid problems caused by stress and anxiety, women who are pregnant and are worried about working with VDUs should be given the opportunity to discuss their concerns with someone adequately informed of current authoritative scientific information and advice.	Council Directive 90/270/EEC on display screen equipment
There has been considerable public concern about reports of higher levels of miscarriage and birth defects among some groups of visual display unit (VDU) workers, in particular due to electromagnetic radiation. Many scientific studies have been carried out, but taken as a whole their results do not show any link between miscarriages or birth defects and working with VDUs. Research and reviews of the scientific evidence will continue to be undertaken. There may also be ergonomic risks from work with VDUs – see above.		

List of agents/ working conditions	What is the risk?	How to deal with the risk Examples of preventive measures*	Other European legislation
Work equipment and personal protective equipment (including clothing)	Work equipment and personal protective equipment is not generally designed for use by pregnant women. Pregnancy (and breastfeeding) involves physiological changes which may make some existing work and protective equipment not only uncomfortable but also unsafe for use in some cases – for example, where equipment does not fit properly or comfortably, or where the operational mobility, dexterity or co-ordination of the woman concerned is temporarily impeded by her pregnancy or recent childbirth.	The employer must carry out a risk assessment which takes account of changes in risks as pregnancy progresses. Wherever possible, the risk should be avoided by adaptations or substitution, eg, of suitable alternative equipment to allow the work to be conducted safely and without risk to health. Where this is not possible, the provisions of Directive 92/85/EC (Article 5) come into effect. Unsafe working must not be allowed.	Directive 89/655/EEC (safety and health requirements for the use of work equipment by workers at work) Directive 89/656/EEC (safety and health requirements for the use by workers of personal protective equipment at the workplace)

ANNEX

Aspects of pregnancy which may require adjustments to work organisation

Apart from the hazards listed in the table, there are other aspects of pregnancy that may affect work. The impact will vary during the course of the pregnancy and their effect should be kept under review; for example, the posture of expectant mothers changes to cope with increasing size.

Aspects of pregnancy	Factors in work
Morning sickness	Early shift work Exposure to strong or nauseating smells/poor ventilation Travel/transport
Backache	Standing/manual handling/posture
Varicose veins/other circulatory problems/haemorrhoids	Prolonged standing/sitting
Rest and welfare Frequent/urgent visits to toilet Comfort	Regular nutrition Proximity/availability of rest/washing/eating/drinking facilities Hygiene Difficulty in leaving job/work site
Increasing size Dexterity, agility, co-ordination, speed of movement, reach may be impaired because of increasing size	Use of protective clothing/work equipment Work in confined areas/at heights Postural demands, eg, bending over, reaching Manual handling Problems of working in restricted spaces
Fatigue/stress	Overtime Evening/night work Lack of rest breaks Excessive hours Pace/intensity of work
Balance (also relevant for breastfeeding mothers)	Problems of working on slippery, wet surfaces

Source: Health and Safety Executive website www.hse.gov.uk
Link: europa.eu.int/eur-lex/en/com/cnc/2000/com2000_0466en02.pdf

Useful names and address

Advisory, Conciliation and Arbitration Service (ACAS)
Website: www.acas.org.uk

Citizens Advice Bureau – local bureaux will be listed in telephone directory and Community Legal Service directory found in libraries, community centres, doctors' surgeries etc.
Websites:
www.citizensadvice.org.uk/
www.adviceguide.org.uk

Community Legal Service
To find a solicitor with a CLS quality mark, phone: 0845 608 1122
For Legal help:
Website:
www.clsdirect.org.uk
Tel: 0845 345 4345

Bar Pro Bono Unit – offers legal advice and representation in some cases where public funding is not available or the claimant is unable to afford legal assistance.
Website:
www.barprobono.org.uk
289-293 High Holborn
London WC1V 7HZ
Tel: 020 7611 9500

Website: www.cehr.org.uk/
Commission for Equality and Human Rights – a newly created commission which aims to eliminate inequality, discrimination and promote human rights. Their powers to provide assistance by way of advice and representation will come into force in October 2007.

Discrimination Law Association – a not for profit membership organisation which aims to promote and improve the giving of advice, support and representation to individuals complaining of discrimination. They can provide a list of specialist discrimination lawyers.
Website: www.discrimination-law.org.uk
E-mail: info@discrimination-law.org.uk

DTI Employment Guidance
Website:
www.dti.gov.uk/employment/
employment-legislation/
employment-guidance/
The website provides fairly
detailed guidance on all areas of
family rights.

Employment Tribunals Service:
Website:
www.employmenttribunals.gov.uk
Enquiry line:
Tel: 0845 795 9775

The Fawcett Society -
campaigns for equality between
women and men in the UK on
pay, pensions, poverty, justice
and politics. They may have
relevant research papers.
Website:
www.fawcettsociety.org.uk

**Employers For Work-Life
Balance** - aims to help all UK
organisations implement and
continuously improve
sustainable work-life strategies
which meet customer needs,
corporate goals and enhance
the quality of life for
individuals. The website
provides a practical guide for
employers in relation to work-
life balance policies.
Website:
www.employersforwork-
lifebalance.org.uk
Tel: 0870 165 6700

**Equal Opportunities
Commission** – the EOC works
towards eliminating sex
discrimination. This will be
replaced by the CEHR in 2007.
There are factsheets available on
their website about the different
forms of discrimination and
what to do if you think you are
being discriminated against.
The EOC also runs a helpline
which provides legal advice to
those who believe they have
been discriminated against,
which is open Monday – Friday,
9am to 5pm. They provide legal
assistance by way of advice and
representation but a formal
application for assistance must
be made.
Website: www.eoc.org.uk
Helpline: 0845 601 5901

**Free Representation Unit
(FRU)**
They provide free representation at Employment Tribunals
to those who cannot otherwise
afford it.
49–51 Bedford Row
London WC1R 4LR
Tel: 020 7831 0692

Health and Safety Executive (HSE)
Website: www.hse.gov.uk
Information line: 08701 545500

Law Works
A charity (formerly known as the Solicitors' Pro Bono Group) which aims to promote access to free legal help. The website has contact details for its projects.
Website:
www.lawworks.org.uk

TIGER (Tailored Interactive Guidance on Employment Rights) – now part of Directgov – provides general and specific information sheets about employment rights, including maternity and parental rights:
Website: www.direct.gov.uk/
Employment/Employees/fs/en

Working Families – this organisation provides factsheets about maternity and parental rights, in-depth information and guidance on its website, and a free legal helpline offering advice and support to working parents and coaching around flexible work requests

Website: www.workingfamilies.org.uk
1–3 Berry Street
London
EC1V 0AA
Tel: 020 7253 7243
Helpline for low income families: 0800 013 0313

Law Centres Federation
There are law centres around the country who provide advice and representation for low income workers living in their area.
Website:
www.lawcentres.org.uk
Tel: 020 7387 8570

Rights of Women – an organisation which aims to empower women to access their legal rights. Rights of Women runs a legal advice service on Tuesdays, Wednesdays and Thursdays from 2pm–4pm and 7pm–9pm and on Fridays from 12pm–2pm.
Website:
www.rightsofwomen.org.uk/
Advice Line: 020 7251 6577

Women Returner's Network (WRN) – a research and lobbying organisation which aims to encourage and support women wanting to return to work
Website:
www.women-returners.co.uk/
cms/

Index